*my*Perspectives®

BRITISH AND WORLD LITERATURE

SAVVAS
LEARNING COMPANY

ISBN-13: 978-1-41-837115-9
ISBN-10:   1-41-837115-7

6 2022

Welcome!

myPerspectives™ English Language Arts is a student-centered learning environment where you will analyze text, cite evidence, and respond critically about your learning. You will take ownership of your learning through goal-setting, reflection, independent text selection, and activities that allow you to collaborate with your peers.

Each unit of study includes selections of different genres—including multimedia—all related to a relevant and meaningful Essential Question. As you read, you will engage in activities that inspire thoughtful discussion and debate with your peers allowing you to formulate, and defend, your own perspectives.

myPerspectives ELA offers a variety of ways to interact directly with the text. You can annotate by writing in your print consumable, or you can annotate in your digital Student Edition. In addition, exciting technology allows you to access multimedia directly from your mobile device and communicate using an online discussion board!

We hope you enjoy using *myPerspectives ELA* as you develop the skills required to be successful throughout college and career.

Authors' Perspectives

myPerspectives is informed by a team of respected experts whose experiences working with students and study of instructional best practices have positively impacted education. From the evolving role of the teacher to how students learn in a digital age, our authors bring new ideas, innovations, and strategies that transform teaching and learning in today's competitive and interconnected world.

66 The teaching of English needs to focus on engaging a new generation of learners. How do we get them excited about reading and writing? How do we help them to envision themselves as readers and writers? And, how can we make the teaching of English more culturally, socially, and technologically relevant? Throughout the curriculum, we've created spaces that enhance youth voice and participation and that connect the teaching of literature and writing to technological transformations of the digital age."

Ernest Morrell, Ph.D.

is the Macy professor of English Education at Teachers College, Columbia University, a class of 2014 Fellow of the American Educational Research Association, and the Past-President of the National Council of Teachers of English (NCTE). He is also the Director of Teachers College's Institute for Urban and Minority Education (IUME). He is an award-winning author and in his spare time he coaches youth sports and writes poems and plays. Dr. Morrell has influenced the development of *my*Perspectives in Assessment, Writing & Research, Student Engagement, and Collaborative Learning.

Elfrieda Hiebert, Ph.D.

is President and CEO of TextProject, a nonprofit that provides resources to support higher reading levels. She is also a research associate at the University of California, Santa Cruz. Dr. Hiebert has worked in the field of early reading acquisition for 45 years, first as a teacher's aide and teacher of primary-level students in California and, subsequently, as a teacher and researcher. Her research addresses how fluency, vocabulary, and knowledge can be fostered through appropriate texts. Dr. Hiebert has influenced the development of *my*Perspectives in Vocabulary, Text Complexity, and Assessment.

> The signature of complex text is challenging vocabulary. In the systems of vocabulary, it's important to provide ways to show how concepts can be made more transparent to students. We provide lessons and activities that develop a strong vocabulary and concept foundation—a foundation that permits students to comprehend increasingly more complex text."

Kelly Gallagher, M.Ed.

teaches at Magnolia High School in Anaheim, California, where he is in his thirty-first year. He is the former co-director of the South Basin Writing Project at California State University, Long Beach. Mr. Gallagher has influenced the development of *my*Perspectives in Writing, Close Reading, and the Role of Teachers.

> The *my*Perspectives classroom is dynamic. The teacher inspires, models, instructs, facilitates, and advises students as they evolve and grow. When teachers guide students through meaningful learning tasks and then pass them ownership of their own learning, students become engaged and work harder. This is how we make a difference in student achievement—by putting students at the center of their learning and giving them the opportunities to choose, explore, collaborate, and work independently."

> It's critical to give students the opportunity to read a wide range of highly engaging texts and to immerse themselves in exploring powerful ideas and how these ideas are expressed. In *my*Perspectives, we focus on building up students' awareness of how academic language works, which is especially important for English language learners."

Jim Cummins, Ph.D.

is a Professor Emeritus in the Department of Curriculum, Teaching and Learning of the University of Toronto. His research focuses on literacy development in multilingual school contexts as well as on the potential roles of technology in promoting language and literacy development. In recent years, he has been working actively with teachers to identify ways of increasing the literacy engagement of learners in multilingual school contexts. Dr. Cummins has influenced the development of *my*Perspectives in English Language Learner and English Language Development support.

UNIT **1** Forging a Hero
Warriors and Leaders

INDEPENDENT LEARNING

These selections can be accessed via the Interactive Student Edition.

 PERFORMANCE-BASED ASSESSMENT PREP

PERFORMANCE-BASED ASSESSMENT

UNIT REFLECTION

DIGITAL PERSPECTIVES

- Unit Introduction Videos
- Media Selections/Media Enrichment
- Modeling Videos
- Selection Audio Recordings

Additional digital resources can be found in:

- Interactive Student Edition
- *my*Perspectives+

UNIT **2** Reflecting on Society

Argument, Satire, and Reform

 INDEPENDENT LEARNING

These selections can be accessed via the Interactive Student Edition.

 PERFORMANCE-BASED ASSESSMENT PREP

 PERFORMANCE-BASED ASSESSMENT

UNIT REFLECTION

DIGITAL ⌖ PERSPECTIVES

- Unit Introduction Videos
- Media Selections/Media Enrichments
- Modeling Videos
- Selection Audio Recordings

Additional digital resources can be found in:

- Interactive Student Edition
- *my*Perspectives+

UNIT (3) Facing the Future, Confronting the Past

Shakespeare Extended Study

INDEPENDENT LEARNING

These selections can be accessed via the Interactive Student Edition.

PERFORMANCE-BASED ASSESSMENT PREP

PERFORMANCE-BASED ASSESSMENT

UNIT REFLECTION

DIGITAL PERSPECTIVES

- Unit Introduction Videos
- Media Selections/Media Enrichment
- Modeling Videos
- Selection Audio Recordings

Additional digital resources can be found in:

- Interactive Student Edition
- *my*Perspectives+

UNIT **4** Seeing Things New

Visionaries and Skeptics

(icon) INDEPENDENT LEARNING

These selections can be accessed via the Interactive Student Edition.

(icon) PERFORMANCE-BASED ASSESSMENT PREP

(icon) PERFORMANCE-BASED ASSESSMENT

UNIT REFLECTION

DIGITAL (cursor icon) PERSPECTIVES

- Unit Introduction Videos
- Media Selections/Media Enrichment
- Modeling Videos
- Selection Audio Recordings

Additional digital resources can be found in:

- Interactive Student Edition
- *my*Perspectives+

UNIT (5) Discovering the Self

Individual, Nature, and Society

INDEPENDENT LEARNING

These selections can be accessed via the Interactive Student Edition.

PERFORMANCE-BASED ASSESSMENT PREP

PERFORMANCE-BASED ASSESSMENT

UNIT REFLECTION

DIGITAL
PERSPECTIVES

- Unit Introduction Videos
- Media Selections/Media Enrichment
- Modeling Videos
- Selection Audio Recordings

Additional digital resources can be found in:
- Interactive Student Edition
- *my*Perspectives+

UNIT 6 Finding a Home

Nation, Exile, and Dominion

 INDEPENDENT LEARNING

These selections can be accessed via the Interactive Student Edition.

 PERFORMANCE-BASED
ASSESSMENT PREP

 PERFORMANCE-BASED
ASSESSMENT

UNIT REFLECTION

DIGITAL
PERSPECTIVES

- Unit Introduction Videos
- Media Selections/Media Enrichment
- Modeling Videos
- Selection Audio Recordings

Additional digital resources can be found in:
- Interactive Student Edition
- *my*Perspectives+

Standards Overview

The following **English Language Arts** standards will prepare you to succeed in college and your future career. The College and Career Readiness Anchor Standards define what you need to achieve by the end of high school, and the grade-specific Standards define what you need to know by the end of your current grade level.

The following provides an overview of the Standards.

Standards for Reading

College and Career Readiness Anchor Standards for Reading

Key Ideas and Details

1. Read closely to determine what the text says explicitly and to make logical inferences from it; cite specific textual evidence when writing or speaking to support conclusions drawn from the text.

2. Determine central ideas or themes of a text and analyze their development; summarize the key supporting details and ideas.

3. Analyze how and why individuals, events, and ideas develop and interact over the course of a text.

Craft and Structure

4. Interpret words and phrases as they are used in a text, including determining technical, connotative, and figurative meanings, and analyze how specific word choices shape meaning or tone.

5. Analyze the structure of texts, including how specific sentences, paragraphs, and larger portions of the text (e.g., a section, chapter, scene, or stanza) relate to each other and the whole.

6. Assess how point of view or purpose shapes the content and style of a text.

Integration of Knowledge and Ideas

7. Integrate and evaluate content presented in diverse formats and media, including visually and quantitatively, as well as in words.

8. Delineate and evaluate the argument and specific claims in a text, including the validity of the reasoning as well as the relevance and sufficiency of the evidence.

9. Analyze how two or more texts address similar themes or topics in order to build knowledge or to compare the approaches the authors take.

Range of Reading and Level of Text Complexity

10. Read and comprehend complex literary and informational texts independently and proficiently.

Grade 12 Reading Standards for Literature

Standard

Key Ideas and Details

Cite strong and thorough textual evidence to support analysis of what the text says explicitly as well as inferences drawn from the text, including determining where the text leaves matters uncertain.

Determine two or more themes or central ideas of a text and analyze their development over the course of the text, including how they interact and build on one another to produce a complex account; provide an objective summary of the text.

Analyze the impact of the author's choices regarding how to develop and relate elements of a story or drama (e.g., where a story is set, how the action is ordered, how the characters are introduced and developed).

Craft and Structure

Determine the meaning of words and phrases as they are used in the text, including figurative and connotative meanings; analyze the impact of specific word choices on meaning and tone, including words with multiple meanings or language that is particularly fresh, engaging, or beautiful. (Include Shakespeare as well as other authors.)

Analyze how an author's choices concerning how to structure specific parts of a text (e.g., the choice of where to begin or end a story, the choice to provide a comedic or tragic resolution) contribute to its overall structure and meaning as well as its aesthetic impact.

Analyze a case in which grasping a point of view requires distinguishing what is directly stated in a text from what is really meant (e.g., satire, sarcasm, irony, or understatement).

Integration of Knowledge and Ideas

Analyze multiple interpretations of a story, drama, or poem (e.g., recorded or live production of a play or recorded novel or poetry), evaluating how each version interprets the source text. (Include at least one play by Shakespeare and one play by an American dramatist.)

Demonstrate knowledge of eighteenth-, nineteenth- and early-twentieth-century foundational works of American literature, including how two or more texts from the same period treat similar themes or topics.

Range of Reading and Level of Text Complexity

By the end of grade 12, read and comprehend literature, including stories, dramas, and poems, at the high end of the grades 11–CCR text complexity band independently and proficiently.

Standards Overview

Grade 12 Reading Standards for Informational Text

Standard

Key Ideas and Details

Cite strong and thorough textual evidence to support analysis of what the text says explicitly as well as inferences drawn from the text, including determining where the text leaves matters uncertain.

Determine two or more central ideas of a text and analyze their development over the course of the text, including how they interact and build on one another to provide a complex analysis; provide an objective summary of the text.

Analyze a complex set of ideas or sequence of events and explain how specific individuals, ideas, or events interact and develop over the course of the text.

Craft and Structure

Determine the meaning of words and phrases as they are used in a text, including figurative, connotative, and technical meanings; analyze how an author uses and refines the meaning of a key term or terms over the course of a text (e.g., how Madison defines *faction* in *Federalist* No. 10).

Analyze and evaluate the effectiveness of the structure an author uses in his or her exposition or argument, including whether the structure makes points clear, convincing, and engaging.

Determine an author's point of view or purpose in a text in which the rhetoric is particularly effective, analyzing how style and content contribute to the power, persuasiveness or beauty of the text.

Integration of Knowledge and Ideas

Integrate and evaluate multiple sources of information presented in different media or formats (e.g., visually, quantitatively) as well as in words in order to address a question or solve a problem.

Delineate and evaluate the reasoning in seminal U.S. texts, including the application of constitutional principles and use of legal reasoning (e.g., in U.S. Supreme Court majority opinions and dissents) and the premises, purposes, and arguments in works of public advocacy (e.g., *The Federalist*, presidential addresses).

Analyze seventeenth-, eighteenth-, and nineteenth-century foundational U.S. documents of historical and literary significance (including The Declaration of Independence, the Preamble to the Constitution, the Bill of Rights, and Lincoln's Second Inaugural Address) for their themes, purposes, and rhetorical features.

Range of Reading and Level of Text Complexity

By the end of grade 12, read and comprehend literary nonfiction at the high end of the grades 11-CCR text complexity band independently and proficiently.

Standards for Writing

College and Career Readiness Anchor Standards for Writing

Key Ideas and Details

1. Write arguments to support claims in an analysis of substantive topics or texts, using valid reasoning and relevant and sufficient evidence.

2. Write informative/explanatory texts to examine and convey complex ideas and information clearly and accurately through the effective selection, organization, and analysis of content.

3. Write narratives to develop real or imagined experiences or events using effective technique, well-chosen details, and well-structured event sequences.

Production and Distribution of Writing

4. Produce clear and coherent writing in which the development, organization, and style are appropriate to task, purpose, and audience.

5. Develop and strengthen writing as needed by planning, revising, editing, rewriting, or trying a new approach.

6. Use technology, including the Internet, to produce and publish writing and to interact and collaborate with others.

Research to Build and Present Knowledge

7. Conduct short as well as more sustained research projects based on focused questions, demonstrating understanding of the subject under investigation.

8. Gather relevant information from multiple print and digital sources, assess the credibility and accuracy of each source, and integrate the information while avoiding plagiarism.

9. Draw evidence from literary or informational texts to support analysis, reflection, and research.

Range of Writing

10. Write routinely over extended time frames (time for research, reflection, and revision) and shorter time frames (a single sitting or a day or two) for a range of tasks, purposes, and audiences.

Grade 12 Writing Standards

Standard

Text Types and Purposes

Write arguments to support claims in an analysis of substantive topics or texts, using valid reasoning and relevant and sufficient evidence.

Introduce precise, knowledgeable claim(s), establish the significance of the claim(s), distinguish the claim(s) from alternate or opposing claims, and create an organization that logically sequences claim(s), counterclaims, reasons, and evidence.

Standards Overview

Grade 12 Writing Standards
Standard
Text Types and Purposes (continued)
Develop claim(s) and counterclaims fairly and thoroughly, supplying the most relevant evidence for each while pointing out the strengths and limitations of both in a manner that anticipates the audience's knowledge level, concerns, values, and possible biases.
Use words, phrases, and clauses as well as varied syntax to link the major sections of the text, create cohesion, and clarify the relationships between claim(s) and reasons, between reasons and evidence, and between claim(s) and counterclaims.
Establish and maintain a formal style and objective tone while attending to the norms and conventions of the discipline in which they are writing.
Provide a concluding statement or section that follows from and supports the argument presented.
Write informative/explanatory texts to examine and convey complex ideas, concepts, and information clearly and accurately through the effective selection, organization, and analysis of content.
Introduce a topic; organize complex ideas, concepts, and information so that each new element builds on that which precedes it to create a unified whole; include formatting (e.g., headings), graphics (e.g., figures, tables), and multimedia when useful to aiding comprehension.
Develop the topic thoroughly by selecting the most significant and relevant facts, extended definitions, concrete details, quotations, or other information and examples appropriate to the audience's knowledge of the topic.
Use appropriate and varied transitions and syntax to link the major sections of the text, create cohesion, and clarify the relationships among complex ideas and concepts.
Use precise language, domain-specific vocabulary, and techniques such as metaphor, simile, and analogy to manage the complexity of the topic.
Establish and maintain a formal style and objective tone while attending to the norms and conventions of the discipline in which they are writing.
Provide a concluding statement or section that follows from and supports the information or explanation presented (e.g., articulating implications or the significance of the topic).
Write narratives to develop real or imagined experiences or events using effective technique, well-chosen details, and well-structured event sequences.
Engage and orient the reader by setting out a problem, situation, or observation and its significance, establishing one or multiple point(s) of view, and introducing a narrator and/or characters; create a smooth progression of experiences or events.
Use narrative techniques, such as dialogue, pacing, description, reflection, and multiple plot lines, to develop experiences, events, and/or characters.

Grade 12 Writing Standards

Standard

Text Types and Purposes (continued)

Use a variety of techniques to sequence events so that they build on one another to create a coherent whole and build toward a particular tone and outcome (e.g., a sense of mystery, suspense, growth, or resolution).

Use precise words and phrases, telling details, and sensory language to convey a vivid picture of the experiences, events, setting, and/or characters.

Provide a conclusion that follows from and reflects on what is experienced, observed, or resolved over the course of the narrative.

Production and Distribution of Writing

Produce clear and coherent writing in which the development, organization, and style are appropriate to task, purpose, and audience. (Grade-specific expectations for writing types are defined in standards 1–3 above.)

Develop and strengthen writing as needed by planning, revising, editing, rewriting, or trying a new approach, focusing on addressing what is most significant for a specific purpose and audience. (Editing for conventions should demonstrate command of Language standards 1–3 up to and including grades 11–12)

Use technology, including the Internet, to produce, publish, and update individual or shared writing products in response to ongoing feedback, including new arguments or information.

Research to Build and Present Knowledge

Conduct short as well as more sustained research projects to answer a question (including a self-generated question) or solve a problem; narrow or broaden the inquiry when appropriate; synthesize multiple sources on the subject, demonstrating understanding of the subject under investigation.

Gather relevant information from multiple authoritative print and digital sources, using advanced searches effectively; assess the strengths and limitations of each source in terms of the task, purpose, and audience; integrate information into the text selectively to maintain the flow of ideas, avoiding plagiarism and overreliance on any one source and following a standard format for citation.

Draw evidence from literary or informational texts to support analysis, reflection, and research.

Apply grades 11–12 Reading standards to literature (e.g., "Demonstrate knowledge of eighteenth-, nineteenth- and early-twentieth-century foundational works of American literature, including how two or more texts from the same period treat similar themes or topics").

Apply grades 11–12 Reading standards to literary nonfiction (e.g., "Delineate and evaluate the reasoning in seminal U.S. texts, including the application of constitutional principles and use of legal reasoning [e.g., in U.S. Supreme Court Case majority opinions and dissents] and the premises, purposes, and arguments in works of public advocacy [e.g., The Federalist, presidential addresses]").

Range of Writing

Write routinely over extended time frames (time for research, reflection, and revision) and shorter time frames (a single sitting or a day or two) for a range of tasks, purposes, and audiences.

Standards Overview

Standards for Speaking and Listening

Comprehension and Collaboration

1. Prepare for and participate effectively in a range of conversations and collaborations with diverse partners, building on others' ideas and expressing their own clearly and persuasively.

2. Integrate and evaluate information presented in diverse media and formats, including visually, quantitatively, and orally.

3. Evaluate a speaker's point of view, reasoning, and use of evidence and rhetoric.

Presentation of Knowledge and Ideas

4. Present information, findings, and supporting evidence such that listeners can follow the line of reasoning and the organization, development, and style are appropriate to task, purpose, and audience.

5. Make strategic use of digital media and visual displays of data to express information and enhance understanding of presentations.

6. Adapt speech to a variety of contexts and communicative tasks, demonstrating command of formal English when indicated or appropriate.

Grade 12 Standards for Speaking and Listening

Standard

Comprehension and Collaboration

Initiate and participate effectively in a range of collaborative discussions (one-on-one, in groups, and teacher-led) with diverse partners on *grades 11–12 topics, texts, and issues*, building on others' ideas and expressing their own clearly and persuasively.

Come to discussions prepared, having read and researched material under study; explicitly draw on that preparation by referring to evidence from texts and other research on the topic or issue to stimulate a thoughtful, well-reasoned exchange of ideas.

Work with peers to promote civil, democratic discussions and decision-making, set clear goals and deadlines, and establish individual roles as needed.

Propel conversations by posing and responding to questions that probe reasoning and evidence; ensure a hearing for a full range of positions on a topic or issue; clarify, verify, or challenge ideas and conclusions; and promote divergent and creative perspectives.

Respond thoughtfully to diverse perspectives; synthesize comments, claims, and evidence made on all sides of an issue; resolve contradictions when possible; and determine what additional information or research is required to deepen the investigation or complete the task.

Integrate multiple sources of information presented in diverse formats and media (e.g., visually, quantitatively, orally) in order to make informed decisions and solve problems, evaluating the credibility and accuracy of each source and noting any discrepancies among the data.

Evaluate a speaker's point of view, reasoning, and use of evidence and rhetoric, assessing the stance, premises, links among ideas, word choice, points of emphasis, and tone used.

Presentation of Knowledge and Ideas

Present information, findings, and supporting evidence, conveying a clear and distinct perspective, such that listeners can follow the line of reasoning, alternative or opposing perspectives are addressed, and the organization, development, substance, and style are appropriate to purpose, audience, and a range of formal and informal tasks.

Make strategic use of digital media (e.g., textual, graphical, audio, visual, and interactive elements) in presentations to enhance understanding of findings, reasoning, and evidence and to add interest.

Adapt speech to a variety of contexts and tasks, demonstrating a command of formal English when indicated or appropriate. (See grades 11–12 Language standards 1 and 3 for specific expectations.)

Standards Overview

Standards for Language

College and Career Readiness Anchor Standards for Language
Conventions of Standard English
1. Demonstrate command of the conventions of standard English grammar and usage when writing or speaking.
2. Demonstrate command of the conventions of standard English capitalization, punctuation, and spelling when writing.
Knowledge of Language
3. Apply knowledge of language to understand how language functions in different contexts, to make effective choices for meaning or style, and to comprehend more fully when reading or listening.
Vocabulary Acquisition and Use
4. Determine or clarify the meaning of unknown and multiple-meaning words and phrases by using context clues, analyzing meaningful word parts, and consulting general and specialized reference materials, as appropriate.
5. Demonstrate understanding of figurative language, word relationships, and nuances in word meanings.
6. Acquire and use accurately a range of general academic and domain-specific words and phrases sufficient for reading, writing, speaking, and listening at the college and career readiness level; demonstrate independence in gathering vocabulary knowledge when considering a word or phrase important to comprehension or expression.

Grade 12 Standards for Language
Standard
Conventions of Standard English
Demonstrate command of the conventions of standard English grammar and usage when writing or speaking.
Apply the understanding that usage is a matter of convention, can change over time, and is sometimes contested.
Resolve issues of complex or contested usage, consulting references (e.g., *Merriam-Webster's Dictionary of English Usage, Garner's Modern American Usage*) as needed.
Demonstrate command of the conventions of standard English capitalization, punctuation, and spelling when writing.
Observe hyphenation conventions.
Spell correctly.

Grade 12 Standards for Language

Standard

Knowledge of Language

Apply knowledge of language to understand how language functions in different contexts, to make effective choices for meaning or style, and to comprehend more fully when reading or listening.

Vary syntax for effect, consulting references (e.g., Tufte's *Artful Sentences*) for guidance as needed; apply an understanding of syntax to the study of complex texts when reading.

Vocabulary Acquisition and Use

Determine or clarify the meaning of unknown and multiple-meaning words and phrases based on *grades 11–12 reading and content*, choosing flexibly from a range of strategies.

Use context (e.g., the overall meaning of a sentence, paragraph, or text; a word's position or function in a sentence) as a clue to the meaning of a word or phrase.

Identify and correctly use patterns of word changes that indicate different meanings or parts of speech (e.g., *conceive, conception, conceivable*).

Consult general and specialized reference materials (e.g., dictionaries, glossaries, thesauruses), both print and digital, to find the pronunciation of a word or determine or clarify its precise meaning, its part of speech, its etymology, or its standard usage.

Verify the preliminary determination of the meaning of a word or phrase (e.g., by checking the inferred meaning in context or in a dictionary).

Demonstrate understanding of figurative language, word relationships, and nuances in word meanings.

Interpret figures of speech (e.g., hyperbole, paradox) in context and analyze their role in the text.

Analyze nuances in the meaning of words with similar denotations.

Acquire and use accurately general academic and domain-specific words and phrases, sufficient for reading, writing, speaking, and listening at the college and career readiness level; demonstrate independence in gathering vocabulary knowledge when considering a word or phrase important to comprehension or expression.

Forging a Hero

Warriors and Leaders

Before the Battle

② Discuss It Around the world and throughout time, leaders have sent warriors into battle. What inspires warriors to make such personal sacrifices?

Write your response before sharing your ideas.

UNIT INTRODUCTION

ESSENTIAL QUESTION:

What makes a hero?

LAUNCH TEXT
ARGUMENT MODEL
A World of Heroes

WHOLE-CLASS LEARNING

HISTORICAL PERSPECTIVES

Focus Period: 750–1066
Ancient Warriors

COMPARE

ANCHOR TEXT: EPIC POETRY

from **Beowulf**
translated by
Burton Raffel

MEDIA: GRAPHIC NOVEL

from **Beowulf**
Gareth Hinds

SMALL-GROUP LEARNING

POETRY COLLECTION 1

To Lucasta, on Going to the Wars
Richard Lovelace

The Charge of the Light Brigade
Alfred, Lord Tennyson

COMPARE

POETRY COLLECTION 2

The Song of the Mud
Mary Borden

Dulce et Decorum Est
Wilfred Owen

MEDIA: INTERACTIVE WEBSITE

How Did Harry Patch Become an Unlikely WWI Hero?
BBC iWonder

INDEPENDENT LEARNING

ESSAY

Accidental Hero
Zadie Smith

SCIENCE ARTICLE

The New Psychology of Leadership
Stephen D. Reicher, Michael J. Platow, and S. Alexander Haslam

SPEECH

Speech Before Her Troops
Queen Elizabeth I

POETRY

The Battle of Maldon
translated by Burton Raffel

SPEECH

Defending Nonviolent Resistance
Mohandas K. Gandhi

SPEECH

Pericles' Funeral Oration
Thucydides, translated by Rex Warner

PERFORMANCE TASK

WRITING FOCUS:
Write an Argument

PERFORMANCE TASK

SPEAKING AND LISTENING FOCUS:
Present an Argument

PERFORMANCE-BASED ASSESSMENT PREP

Review Evidence for an Argument

PERFORMANCE-BASED ASSESSMENT

Argument: Essay and Speech

PROMPT: **Which contributes more to heroism—sacrifice or success?**

Unit Goals

Throughout this unit, you will deepen your perspective on the nature of heroism by reading, writing, speaking, listening, and presenting. These goals will help you succeed on the Unit Performance-Based Assessment.

Rate how well you meet these goals right now. You will revisit your ratings later when you reflect on your growth during this unit.

SCALE	1	2	3	4	5
	NOT AT ALL WELL	NOT VERY WELL	SOMEWHAT WELL	VERY WELL	EXTREMELY WELL

READING GOALS

	1	2	3	4	5
• Read a variety of texts to gain the knowledge and insight needed to write about heroism.	○	○	○	○	○
• Expand your knowledge and use of academic and concept vocabulary.	○	○	○	○	○

WRITING AND RESEARCH GOALS

	1	2	3	4	5
• Write an argument that has a clear structure and that draws evidence from texts and background knowledge to support a claim.	○	○	○	○	○
• Conduct research projects of various lengths to explore a topic and clarify meaning.	○	○	○	○	○

LANGUAGE GOAL

	1	2	3	4	5
• Use rhetorical devices effectively to strengthen arguments and add interest to writing and presentations.	○	○	○	○	○

SPEAKING AND LISTENING GOALS

	1	2	3	4	5
• Collaborate with your team to build on the ideas of others, develop consensus, and communicate.	○	○	○	○	○
• Integrate audio, visuals, and text to present information.	○	○	○	○	○

☰ STANDARDS

Language
Acquire and use accurately general academic and domain-specific words and phrases, sufficient for reading, writing, speaking, and listening at the college and career readiness level; demonstrate independence in gathering vocabulary knowledge when considering a word or phrase important to comprehension or expression.

Academic Vocabulary: Argument

Understanding and using academic terms can help you read, write, and speak with precision and clarity. Here are five academic words that will be useful to you in this unit as you analyze and write arguments.

Complete the chart.

1. Review each word, its root, and the mentor sentences.

2. Use the information and your own knowledge to predict the meaning of each word.

3. For each word, list at least two related words.

4. Refer to a dictionary or other resources if needed.

TIP

FOLLOW THROUGH
Study the words in this chart, and highlight them or their forms wherever they appear in the unit.

WORD	MENTOR SENTENCES	PREDICT MEANING	RELATED WORDS
purport ROOT: **-port-** "to carry"	**1.** This is a work of fiction and does not *purport* to tell the true story. **2.** You never read the article but you *purport* to know all about it.		purportedly; purported
credible ROOT: **-cred-** "to believe"	**1.** His alibi was not *credible*, so the officers questioned him further. **2.** The movie's plot was imaginative but not at all *credible*.		
assertion ROOT: **-ser-** "to connect"	**1.** Is it your *assertion* that Pluto should be renamed a planet? **2.** California's drought supports our *assertion* about the crisis of water shortages.		
presume ROOT: **-sum-** "to take"	**1.** I *presume* you want to go since you've packed your suitcase. **2.** Check the facts, and do not *presume* that what you read was true.		
contradictory ROOT: **-dic-** "to speak"	**1.** The senator's various *contradictory* positions on issues confused many voters. **2.** My boss and I have *contradictory* opinions about raising the minimum wage.		

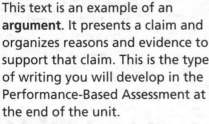

This text is an example of an **argument**. It presents a claim and organizes reasons and evidence to support that claim. This is the type of writing you will develop in the Performance-Based Assessment at the end of the unit.

As you read, try to understand why the author has included certain facts and details. Mark the details that provide strong evidence to reinforce the author's claim.

A World of Heroes

NOTES

1   Literature is rife with heroes. It has been so since the beginning. Homer's *Odyssey*, an epic poem from ancient Greece, is about a hero, Odysseus, and his quest to return home after a ten-year war between the Greeks and the people of Troy. Every step of Odysseus' journey is larger than life and filled with danger. One moment, he's escaping from a Cyclops (a one-eyed giant); the next, he is speaking directly to the gods. Many modern fictional heroes are just as outsized. They sail through popular culture on movie screens, in comic books, and on smartphones, each moment of their lives filled with drama and weight. However, these unrealistic fictional characters are heroes only in great, entertaining stories. Today, in the twenty-first century, I believe that true heroes are most often ordinary people who in a brief moment behave heroically.

2   Modern heroes have to deal with the same reality as the rest of us. They fill out forms, sweat in the heat, and stand in supermarket lines. If the life of a modern hero has any drama, it is in that single moment in which he or she performs one extraordinary act, garnering a brief bit of attention and earning the title of "hero."

3   Consider, for example, the case of Chesley Sullenberger. Prior to January 15, 2009, he had led a life of quiet successes. He had attended the United States Air Force Academy, piloted fighter planes, and become a pilot for US Airways. Then, on the morning of January 15, 2009, as he was piloting a passenger jet that had taken off from New York City's LaGuardia Airport, his plane hit a flock of geese, causing the jet's engines to fail. As the jet began a rapid dive over New York

City, Sullenberger remained calm, kept the plane steady, and landed it on the Hudson River. All of the passengers and crew survived. The media hailed him as a hero. For weeks, he was interviewed on television. Gradually, though, he faded from public life and quietly retired.

4   Another display of everyday heroism was the monumental response of volunteers immediately following the terrorist attacks on September 11, 2001. The captains and crews of hundreds of ferries, tug boats, and private vessels selflessly sailed directly into the heart of the attack to rescue nearly 500,000 New Yorkers from the piers and seawalls of Lower Manhattan. These were ordinary citizens who risked their own safety to help those in need.

5   Some may argue that there are true larger-than-life heroes who leave a permanent shadow, not by virtue of a single act, but through a lifetime of heroic deeds. What about the life of someone such as the American aviator Amelia Earhart? Earhart's life was filled with heroism—her 1932 solo flight across the Atlantic Ocean was just one example. Even after that journey had made her a celebrity, she continued to seek new challenges. Most notably, in 1937, she took on the greatest challenge of her life—a flight around the world. Unfortunately, she never completed the journey, vanishing somewhere in the Pacific Ocean.

6   Despite her legendary reputation, a fair share of Earhart's life was devoted to everyday concerns. She spent long, grueling hours performing routine maintenance on her airplane. Moreover, she endured weeks of monotonous train travel during her lecture tours. What is larger-than-life about that!

7   In the twenty-first century, we understand that time is humbling. No one fully escapes everyday annoyances or tasks. We understand, too, that it is possible for someone not very different from ourselves to step forward at a critical moment and act with extraordinary courage and selflessness. Our heroes may fade from the news and go back to their ordinary lives, but they are heroes nonetheless. ❧

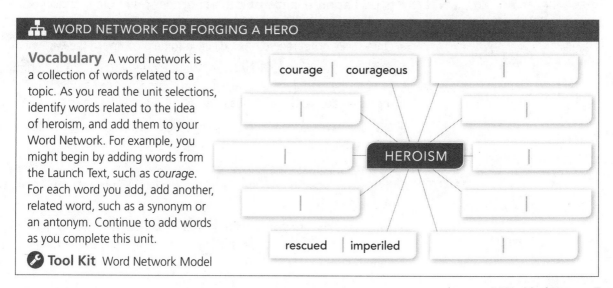

WORD NETWORK FOR FORGING A HERO

Vocabulary A word network is a collection of words related to a topic. As you read the unit selections, identify words related to the idea of heroism, and add them to your Word Network. For example, you might begin by adding words from the Launch Text, such as *courage*. For each word you add, add another, related word, such as a synonym or an antonym. Continue to add words as you complete this unit.

courage | courageous

HEROISM

rescued | imperiled

🔧 **Tool Kit** Word Network Model

Summary

Write a summary of "A World of Heroes." Remember that a **summary** is a concise, complete, and accurate overview of a text. It should not include a statement of your opinion or an analysis.

Launch Activity

Draft a Focus Statement Consider this question: **Which character traits do I admire in my personal heroes?** Complete this focus statement: A hero should be _____, _____, and _____.

- On a sticky note, record one adjective to help complete the statement.

- As a class, review the sticky notes. Work together to reduce the number of notes by identifying and eliminating those that are synonyms or represent the same basic ideas.

- On your own, decide which three adjectives you think best complete the focus statement.

- As a class, vote on the words. After you have voted, discuss whether the three words that receive the most votes create a strong statement. If not, vote again.

- Once your class has selected three words, discuss an order for the words in the focus statement. Choose the best order, and complete the statement.

QuickWrite

Consider class discussions, presentations, the video, and the Launch Text as you think about the prompt. Record your first thoughts here.

PROMPT: **Which contributes more to heroism—sacrifice or success?**

 EVIDENCE LOG FOR FORGING A HERO

Review your QuickWrite, and summarize your initial position in one sentence to record in your Evidence Log. Then, record evidence from "A World of Heroes" that supports your initial position.

Prepare for the Performance-Based Assessment at the end of the unit by completing the Evidence Log after each selection.

Tool Kit
Evidence Log Model

Title of Text: _____ Date: _____

CONNECTION TO PROMPT	TEXT EVIDENCE/DETAILS	ADDITIONAL NOTES/IDEAS

How does this text change or add to my thinking? Date: _____

ESSENTIAL QUESTION:

What makes a hero?

As you read these selections, work with your whole class to explore how heroes are made.

From Text to Topic Beowulf's defeat of the brutal Grendel and his vengeful mother is an epic contest between good and evil. The reasons that Beowulf is considered a hero are obvious. However, there are many forms of heroism that do not involve fighting monsters. As you read, consider the characteristics that make people heroes.

Whole-Class Learning Strategies

These learning strategies are key to success in school and will continue to be important in college and in your career.

Look at these strategies and the actions you can take to practice them. Add ideas of your own for each step. Get ready to use these strategies during Whole-Class Learning.

STRATEGY	ACTION PLAN
Listen actively	• Eliminate distractions. For example, put your cellphone away. • Jot down brief notes on main ideas and points of confusion. •
Clarify by asking questions	• If you're confused, other people probably are, too. Ask a question to help your whole class. • Ask follow-up questions as needed; for example, if you do not understand the clarification or if you want to make an additional connection. •
Monitor understanding	• Notice what information you already know, and be ready to build on it. • Ask for help if you are struggling. •
Interact and share ideas	• Share your ideas, and answer questions, even if you are unsure of them. • Build on the ideas of others by adding details or making a connection. •

CONTENTS

Ancient Warriors

Voices of the Period

"It seems to me that the life of man on earth is like the swift flight of a single sparrow through the banqueting hall where you are sitting at dinner on a winter's day with your captains and counselors. In the midst there is a comforting fire to warm the hall. Outside, the storms of winter rain and snow are raging. This sparrow flies swiftly in through one window of the hall and out through another. While he is inside, the bird is safe from winter storms, but after a few moments of comfort, he vanishes from sight into the wintry world from which he came. So man appears on earth for a little while—but of what went before this life, or what follows, we know nothing."

—Bede, author of *A History of the English Church and People*

"A.D. 878. This year about mid-winter, after twelfth-night, the Danish army stole out to Chippenham, and rode over the land of the West-Saxons; where they settled, and drove many of the people over sea; and of the rest the greatest part they rode down, and subdued to their will; —ALL BUT ALFRED THE KING."

—from the *Anglo-Saxon Chronicle*

"I have taken England with both my hands."

—William the Conqueror, setting foot on English soil in 1066

History of the Period

In the Beginning From the Roman invasion of Britain in 55 B.C. to the Norman Conquest 1,100 years later, the Britons were beset—and the eventual nation was shaped—by invaders. They came to conquer and stayed to build. In the first century A.D., the Romans drove the original inhabitants of Britain into the north (Scotland) and west (Wales) of the island. The Romans brought with them their well-ordered civilization of roads and schools, of towns and trade. Dividing Britain into two provinces, they established a capital at London and another at what would become York. With a population of about 2 million people, Roman Britain thrived until the fifth century.

The Anglo-Saxon Arrival Then, in A.D. 449, after the last Roman troops had been summoned home to defend Rome against the barbarian invaders, a group of Germanic tribes—the Angles, the Saxons, and the Jutes—crossed the North Sea and occupied the island the Romans had called Albion. Britons were pushed to the west as Anglo-Saxons established kingdoms along the coasts and in the river valleys. Albion became "Angle Land," which became England. By the beginning of the eighth century, people would think of themselves as "the nation of the English."

Each successive wave of invaders brought its distinctive culture, including its language. As the different groups fought and eventually united

TIMELINE

c. 750: Surviving version of *Beowulf* is composed.

750

768: Europe Charlemagne, crowned king of the Franks, becomes ruler of what would be called the Holy Roman Empire.

787: First papal legation to England conducts first coronation.

793: Vikings attack Lindisfarne.

Integration of Knowledge and Ideas

Notebook Modern English evolved from the languages of successive waves of invaders. What does each of the words in blue tell you about the culture from which it came?

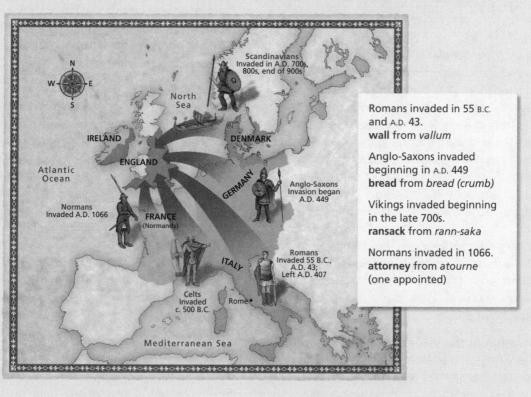

Romans invaded in 55 B.C. and A.D. 43.
wall from *vallum*

Anglo-Saxons invaded beginning in A.D. 449
bread from *bread (crumb)*

Vikings invaded beginning in the late 700s.
ransack from *rann-saka*

Normans invaded in 1066.
attorney from *atourne* (one appointed)

to form a single nation, their languages, too, conflicted and—eventually—combined.

A Peaceful Invasion The period between the fall of the Roman Empire, at the end of the fifth century, and the year 1000 is sometimes called the Dark Ages, a time of great social, political, and economic turmoil in Europe. It was a period when the strongest surviving institution was the Roman Catholic Church. In A.D. 597, the Roman cleric Augustine arrived in Anglo-Saxon Britain, intent on converting the pagan English to Christianity. Along with Celtic missionaries from Ireland, the Christian clergy spread their faith in England, founding monasteries as centers of

842: Vikings sack London in 842 and 851.

878: King Alfred defeats Vikings at Wessex.

890: King Alfred orders compilation of the *Anglo-Saxon Chronicle*, which continues into the twelfth century.

900

861: North Atlantic Vikings discover Iceland.

886: King Alfred, now called "the Great," captures London and is accepted as ruler of all the English.

c. 900: Western Europe Feudalism develops.

religious life. By the end of the seventh century, England was a leader of scholarship in Europe.

The Venerable Bede In Northumbria especially, scholars such as Bede wrote histories and other scholarly works. (It was in this atmosphere that works such as *Beowulf* were written.) Bede, a learned monk, wrote *A History of the English Church and People,* marking an important stage in England's developing sense of itself as an island-nation. With his knowledge of Latin and history, Bede was not interested in merely telling the story of a single clan's mead-hall. The reader can sense how "the island in the ocean" that he describes is on its way to becoming a nation, a place that is as much a product of its history as of its geography. Bede's history is included in the *Anglo-Saxon Chronicle,* seven documents that are a major source of information on early English history. Created between the ninth and twelfth centuries and recorded by monks in different monasteries, the *Chronicle* gives an account of events year by year, beginning with Caesar's invasion of Britain.

Invasion of the Vikings In the eighth century, the Vikings arrived from what is now Denmark. For about a hundred years, they raided and looted the towns and monasteries of the northeast, but eventually they settled that area. In 871, when the Vikings tried to overrun the rest of the island, they were stopped by Alfred the Great, now considered the first King of England.

William the Conqueror The last successful invasion of England occurred in 1066, when France's William, Duke of Normandy, claimed and won the throne. Known as William the Conqueror, he was crowned king of England on December 25, 1066. William brought his court and his language to the country he seized. For some time, England was a bilingual country of conquerors and conquered. The Normans brought more than their language to the island. They also solidified a form of government, social order, and land tenure we call *feudalism.*

A Feudal World In the centuries between the Germanic invasions and the dawn of the modern world, England changed from a place of warrior bands and invading tribes to a country ruled by a king, nobles, and bishops. By the year 1000, English kings controlled the entire island, with the rulers of Wales and Scotland paying them homage. In the feudal system, the king reigned from the top of a pyramid of power, in which he granted land to nobles, who in exchange owed him loyalty and military service. The nobles in turn granted land to knights on the same terms. At the base of the pyramid were the peasants—called villeins or serfs—who worked the land controlled by the knights.

The Rise of Towns At the same time, towns such as Jorvik (today's York) were becoming thriving centers of international trade, with several thousand households. Merchants, traders, and artisans or crafts workers formed a new middle class, ranked between nobles and peasants. This class gained power in medieval towns, with merchants and artisans forming associations called guilds. Over time, the rise of towns and expansion of trade would change feudalism.

TIMELINE

c. 975: Saxon monks copy Old English poems into the *Exeter Book.*

991: English are defeated by Danes at Battle of Maldon.

975

c. 985: Eric the Red establishes first Viking colony in Greenland.

1000: Year cited by historians as end of Dark Ages.

Literature Selections

Literature of the Focus Period Two of the selections in this unit were written during the Focus Period and reflect the hopes and fears of the people of the time. The selections also reflect society's loyalty to valiant warriors and its desire for an almost superhuman hero.

from *Beowulf*, translated by Burton Raffel

"The Battle of Maldon," translated by Burton Raffel

Connections Across Time Society's need for and interest in heroism and leadership have in no way diminished since the Focus Period. These ideas have continued to influence writers, speakers, and commentators throughout the centuries.

from *Beowulf*, Gareth Hinds

"To Lucasta, on Going to the Wars," Richard Lovelace

"The Charge of the Light Brigade," Alfred, Lord Tennyson

"The Song of the Mud," Mary Borden

"Dulce et Decorum Est," Wilfred Owen

"How Did Harry Patch Become an Unlikely WWI Hero?" BBC iWonder

"Accidental Hero," Zadie Smith

"The New Psychology of Leadership," Stephen D. Reicher, Michael J. Burton, and S. Alexander Haslam

Speech Before Her Troops, Queen Elizabeth I

"Defending Nonviolent Resistance," Mohandas K. Gandhi

"Pericles' Funeral Oration," Thucydides, translated by Rex Warner

ADDITIONAL LITERATURE OF THE FOCUS PERIOD

Student Edition

UNIT 3
from *Oedipus Rex,* Sophocles, translated by David Grene

UNIT 4
from *The Pillow Book,* Sei Shonagon

UNIT 6
"The Seafarer," translated by Burton Raffel

from *A History of the English Church and People,* Bede, translated by Leo Sherley-Price

1013: English accept Sweyn, king of Denmark, as ruler.

c. 1020: North America Viking Leif Ericson explores Canadian coast.

1040: Historical Macbeth becomes king of Scotland after killing King Duncan.

1066

1066: Normans defeat Saxons at Hastings; William the Conqueror becomes king of England.

About the Translator

Burton Raffel
(1928–2015) attended high school and college in Brooklyn, New York. After learning a law degree from Yale University, he practiced as an attorney for two years. He went on to work as an editor, an English professor, a freelance writer, and a television and radio broadcaster. What Raffel is best known for, however, is his work as a translator. In addition to *Beowulf,* he has translated a broad range of classics from world literature, including *The Canterbury Tales, Gargantua and Pantagruel,* and *Don Quixote.* His translations have won numerous awards.

🔧 **Tool Kit**
First-Read Guide and Model Annotation

from Beowulf

Concept Vocabulary

You will encounter the following words as you read this excerpt from *Beowulf.* Before reading, note how familiar you are with each word. Then, rank the words in order from most familiar (1) to least familiar (6).

WORD	YOUR RANKING
lair	
stalked	
gorge	
gruesome	
writhing	
loathsome	

After completing the first read, come back to the concept vocabulary and review your rankings. Mark changes to your original rankings as needed.

First Read EPIC POETRY

Apply these strategies as you conduct your first read. You will have an opportunity to complete the close-read notes after your first read.

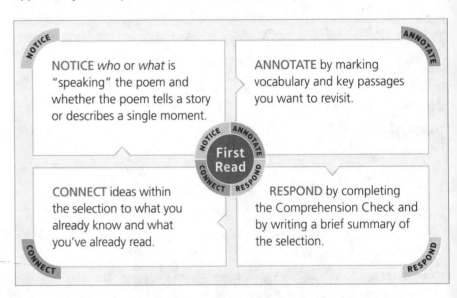

NOTICE *who* or *what* is "speaking" the poem and whether the poem tells a story or describes a single moment.

ANNOTATE by marking vocabulary and key passages you want to revisit.

CONNECT ideas within the selection to what you already know and what you've already read.

RESPOND by completing the Comprehension Check and by writing a brief summary of the selection.

First Read

BACKGROUND

The Anglo-Saxon Scribes The author of *Beowulf* is unknown, but it seems likely that he was an Anglo-Saxon descendant of people who migrated from northern Germany to settle in England starting in the fifth century. Recent archaeological discoveries include burial sites in Anglian settlements that include items that are both similar to those mentioned in *Beowulf* and closely linked to Beowulf's homeland in southern Sweden. Although there is no evidence that Beowulf himself ever existed, people and events in the poem are, indeed, historical. Higlac, for example, truly was king of the Geats. Hrothgar, likewise, was likely a true historical character. The interweaving of characters and legends from the 500s and 600s argues for *Beowulf's* composition's having taken place in the 600s or 700s, when audiences would have still been familiar with these events due to their exposure to the oral tradition.

Translating Old-English Texts *Beowulf* was written in Old English, the language used by Anglo-Saxons up until about A.D. 1150. Although Old English is the earliest historical form of modern English, it is very different from modern English—so different, in fact, that it often requires a translation in order for modern speakers of English to understand it.

Consider this passage from *Beowulf* in Old English. These are the opening lines of the section that appears in text you are about to read under the title "The Wrath of Grendel":

> *ða se ellengæst earfoðlice*
> *þrage geþolode, se þe in þystrum bad,*
> *þæt he dogora gehwam dream gehyrde*
> *hludne in healle; þær wæs hearpan sweg,*
> *swutol sang scopes.*

Here is another version of these lines, translated by Francis Gummere in the early twentieth century:

> *With envy and anger an evil spirit*
> *endured the dole in his dark abode,*
> *that he heard each day the din of revel*
> *high in the hall: there harps rang out,*
> *clear song of the singer.*

Look closely at the Old English, and try to pick out familiar modern words. For example, you may spot *healle* ("hall"), *hearpan* ("harps") and *sang* ("song"). Furthermore, once you learn that the character þ (called a *thorn*) represents the *th* sound in *thin* and the character ð (called an *edh*) represents the <u>th</u> sound in *the*, you may recognize even more familiar words—for example, *þæt* ("that") and *þær* ("there").

Still, Old English will likely seem like a foreign language to most speakers of English today. Because of this, translators try both to be true to the original poem and to capture its qualities in a way modern readers can appreciate. Translation, then, is a form of interpretation.

The Hero Beowulf In the epic poem you are about to read, Beowulf, a Geat from a region that is today southern Sweden, sets sail to aid the Danish king Hrothgar in his fight against the monster Grendel, a terrifying swampland creature whose eyes burn with "gruesome light." Grendel has been terrorizing Hrothgar's great banquet hall, Herot, for twelve years. The battle between Beowulf, a young warrior of great strength and courage, and Grendel, his bloodthirsty foe, is the first of three mortal battles that are fought in this long epic poem.

Forging an Epic The tales in *Beowulf* originated from a time when stories and poems were passed along by word of mouth. This process is known as *oral tradition*, and it included many different literary forms, such as riddles and proverbs, in addition to epic poems.

In Anglo-Saxon England, traveling minstrels called *scops* captivated audiences with long narrative poems. These poems changed and grew as they were passed from one scop to another. *Beowulf* was told and retold in this fashion throughout England for hundreds of years. In the eleventh century, the epic was finally written down. Today, it survives in a single manuscript, which is in the collection of the British Museum in London.

Beowulf grew out of other, earlier traditions. The monsters and dragons of the tale, the brave warriors steadfastly loyal to their heroic chief, the descent into the eerie regions below the earth—these were familiar elements of Scandinavian and Celtic folk tales. Even a detail as specific as Beowulf's seizure of Grendel's arm can be traced to earlier tales.

Poetry in Performance From the clues provided in *Beowulf* itself, we gain a general idea of how the epic may have sounded in performance. Anglo-Saxon poetry was sung or chanted to musical accompaniment, with the scop playing a primitive harp as he performed the narrative. Each rhythmic verse had four stressed syllables and an indefinite number of unstressed ones, with two or three of the stressed syllables tied together by *alliteration*, the repetition of initial consonant sounds. Each line of verse was divided in half by a slight pause called a *caesura*.

A Guide to Life By forging different traditions into one unified tale, and by incorporating the later influence of Christianity, the Anglo-Saxon scops created a central reference point for their culture. Listening to *Beowulf*, an Anglo-Saxon could learn of bravery and loyalty to one's fellows, of the monsters that spite and hatred could breed, and of the heroism needed to conquer such monsters.

Besides its relationship to Anglo-Saxon culture, *Beowulf* displays archetypal literary elements. *Archetypes* are patterns in literature found around the world. Beowulf himself is an archetypal hero: extraordinarily strong and unshakably loyal. His struggle against the monsters and the dragon is an archetypal conflict of good versus evil.

from
Beowulf
translated by Burton Raffel

The Wrath of Grendel

     A powerful monster, living down
In the darkness, growled in pain, impatient
As day after day the music rang
Loud in that hall,[1] the harp's rejoicing
5 Call and the poet's clear songs, sung
Of the ancient beginnings of us all, recalling
The Almighty making the earth, shaping
These beautiful plains marked off by oceans,
Then proudly setting the sun and moon
10 To glow across the land and light it;
The corners of the earth were made lovely with trees
And leaves, made quick with life, with each
Of the nations who now move on its face. And then
As now warriors sang of their pleasure:
15 So Hrothgar's men lived happy in his hall

---

1. **hall** Herot.

Till the monster stirred, that demon, that fiend,
Grendel, who haunted the moors, the wild
Marshes, and made his home in a hell
Not hell but earth. He was spawned in that slime,
20 Conceived by a pair of those monsters born
Of Cain,[2] murderous creatures banished
By God, punished forever for the crime
Of Abel's death. The Almighty drove
Those demons out, and their exile was bitter,
25 Shut away from men; they split
Into a thousand forms of evil—spirits
And fiends, goblins, monsters, giants,
A brood forever opposing the Lord's
Will, and again and again defeated.
30   Then, when darkness had dropped, Grendel
Went up to Herot, wondering what the warriors
Would do in that hall when their drinking was done.
He found them sprawled in sleep, suspecting
Nothing, their dreams undisturbed. The monster's
35 Thoughts were as quick as his greed or his claws:
He slipped through the door and there in the silence
Snatched up thirty men, smashed them

---

2. **Cain** oldest son of Adam and Eve, who murdered his brother, Abel.

Unknowing in their beds and ran out with their bodies
The blood dripping behind him, back
40 To his lair, delighted with his night's slaughter.
        At daybreak, with the sun's first light, they saw
How well he had worked, and in that gray morning
Broke their long feast with tears and laments
For the dead. Hrothgar, their lord, sat joyless
45 In Herot, a mighty prince mourning
The fate of his lost friends and companions,
Knowing by its tracks that some demon had torn
His followers apart. He wept, fearing
The beginning might not be the end. And that night
50 Grendel came again, so set
On murder that no crime could ever be enough,
No savage assault quench his lust
For evil. Then each warrior tried
To escape him, searched for rest in different
55 Beds, as far from Herot as they could find,
Seeing how Grendel hunted when they slept.
Distance was safety; the only survivors
Were those who fled him. Hate had triumphed.
        So Grendel ruled, fought with the righteous,
60 One against many, and won; so Herot

CLOSE READ

ANNOTATE: Mark the repeated word in lines 67–73.

QUESTION: Why might an author choose to repeat a word in such rapid succession?

CONCLUDE: What does the repetition here reveal about Grendel?

stalked (stawkt) *v.* pursued stealthily; hunted

Stood empty, and stayed deserted for years,
Twelve winters of grief for Hrothgar, king
Of the Danes, sorrow heaped at his door
By hell-forged hands. His misery leaped
65 The seas, was told and sung in all
Men's ears: how Grendel's hatred began,
How the monster relished his savage war
On the Danes, keeping the bloody feud
Alive, seeking no peace, offering
70 No truce, accepting no settlement, no price
In gold or land, and paying the living
For one crime only with another. No one
Waited for reparation from his plundering claws:
That shadow of death hunted in the darkness,
75 **Stalked** Hrothgar's warriors, old
And young, lying in waiting, hidden
In mist, invisibly following them from the edge
Of the marsh, always there, unseen.
        So mankind's enemy continued his crimes,
80 Killing as often as he could, coming
Alone, bloodthirsty and horrible. Though he lived
In Herot, when the night hid him, he never
Dared to touch King Hrothgar's glorious
Throne, protected by God—God,
85 Whose love Grendel could not know. But Hrothgar's
Heart was bent. The best and most noble
Of his council debated remedies, sat
In secret sessions, talking of terror
And wondering what the bravest of warriors could do.
90 And sometimes they sacrificed to the old stone gods,
Made heathen vows, hoping for Hell's
Support, the Devil's guidance in driving
Their affliction off. That was their way,
And the heathen's only hope, Hell
95 Always in their hearts, knowing neither God
Nor His passing as He walks through our world, the Lord
Of Heaven and earth; their ears could not hear
His praise nor know His glory. Let them
Beware, those who are thrust into danger,
100 Clutched at by trouble, yet can carry no solace
In their hearts, cannot hope to be better! Hail
To those who will rise to God, drop off
Their dead bodies and seek our Father's peace!

The Coming of Beowulf

So the living sorrow of Healfdane's son[3]
105 Simmered, bitter and fresh, and no wisdom
Or strength could break it; that agony hung
On king and people alike, harsh
And unending, violent and cruel, and evil.
In his far-off home Beowulf, Higlac's[4]
110 Follower and the strongest of the Geats—greater
And stronger than anyone anywhere in this world—
Heard how Grendel filled nights with horror
And quickly commanded a boat fitted out,
Proclaiming that he'd go to that famous king,
115 Would sail across the sea to Hrothgar,
Now when help was needed. None
Of the wise ones regretted his going, much
As he was loved by the Geats: the omens were good,
And they urged the adventure on. So Beowulf
120 Chose the mightiest men he could find,
The bravest and best of the Geats, fourteen
In all, and led them down to their boat;
He knew the sea, would point the prow
Straight to that distant Danish shore.
125 Then they sailed, set their ship
Out on the waves, under the cliffs,
Ready for what came they wound through the currents,
The seas beating at the sand, and were borne
In the lap of their shining ship, lined
130 With gleaming armor, going safely
In that oak-hard boat to where their hearts took them.
The wind hurried them over the waves,
The ship foamed through the sea like a bird
Until, in the time they had known it would take,
135 Standing in the round-curled prow they could see
Sparkling hills, high and green
Jutting up over the shore, and rejoicing
In those rock-steep cliffs they quietly ended
Their voyage. Jumping to the ground, the Geats
140 Pushed their boat to the sand and tied it
In place, mail shirts[5] and armor rattling
As they swiftly moored their ship. And then
They gave thanks to God for their easy crossing.
High on a wall a Danish watcher
145 Patrolling along the cliffs saw

---

3. **Healfdane's** (HAY alf deh nuhz) **son** Hrothgar.
4. **Higlac's** (HIHG laks) Higlac was the king of the Geats (GAY ots) and Beowulf's feudal lord and uncle.
5. **mail shirts** flexible body armor made of metal.

ANNOTATE: Mark two
details in lines 151–171
that show what the
watchman finds unusual
about the arrival of
Beowulf and his men.

QUESTION: What do these
details suggest about the
threats the Danes face and
the personal qualities they
value?

CONCLUDE: What is
the effect of describing
Beowulf's arrival from
the point of view of the
watchman?

The travelers crossing to the shore, their shields
Raised and shining: he came riding down,
Hrothgar's lieutenant, spurring his horse,
Needing to know why they'd landed, these men

150 In armor. Shaking his heavy spear
In their faces he spoke:
                 "Whose soldiers are you,
You who've been carried in your deep-keeled ship
Across the sea-road to this country of mine?
Listen! I've stood on these cliffs longer

155 Than you know, keeping our coast free
Of pirates, raiders sneaking ashore
From their ships, seeking our lives and our gold.
None have ever come more openly—
And yet you've offered no password, no sign

160 From my prince, no permission from my people for your landing
Here. Nor have I ever seen,
Out of all the men on earth, one greater
Than has come with you; no commoner carries
Such weapons, unless his appearance, and his beauty,

165 Are both lies. You! Tell me your name,
And your father's; no spies go further onto Danish
Soil than you've come already. Strangers,
From wherever it was you sailed, tell it,
And tell it quickly, the quicker the better,

170 I say, for us all. Speak, say
Exactly who you are, and from where, and why."
      Their leader answered him, Beowulf unlocking
Words from deep in his breast:
                 "We are Geats,
Men who follow Higlac. My father

175 Was a famous soldier, known far and wide
As a leader of men. His name was Edgetho.
His life lasted many winters;
Wise men all over the earth surely
Remember him still. And we have come seeking

180 Your prince, Healfdane's son, protector
Of this people, only in friendship: instruct us,
Watchman, help us with your words! Our errand
Is a great one, our business with the glorious king
Of the Danes no secret; there's nothing dark

185 Or hidden in our coming. You know (if we've heard
The truth, and been told honestly) that your country
Is cursed with some strange, vicious creature
That hunts only at night and that no one
Has seen. It's said, watchman, that he has slaughtered

190 Your people, brought terror to the darkness. Perhaps
Hrothgar can hunt, here in my heart,

For some way to drive this devil out—
If anything will ever end the evils
Afflicting your wise and famous lord.
195 Here he can cool his burning sorrow.
Or else he may see his suffering go on
Forever, for as long as Herot towers
High on your hills."

               The mounted officer
Answered him bluntly, the brave watchman:
200   "A soldier should know the difference between words
And deeds, and keep that knowledge clear
In his brain. I believe your words, I trust in
Your friendship. Go forward, weapons and armor
And all, on into Denmark. I'll guide you
205 Myself—and my men will guard your ship.
Keep it safe here on our shores,
Your fresh-tarred boat, watch it well,
Until that curving prow carries
Across the sea to Geatland a chosen
210 Warrior who does battle with the creature
Haunting our people, who survives that horror
Unhurt, and goes home bearing our love."

        Then they moved on. Their boat lay moored,
Tied tight to its anchor. Glittering at the top
215 Of their golden helmets wild boar heads gleamed,
Shining decorations, swinging as they marched,
Erect like guards, like sentinels, as though ready
To fight. They marched, Beowulf and his men
And their guide, until they could see the gables
220 Of Herot, covered with hammered gold
And glowing in the sun—that most famous of all dwellings,
Towering majestic, its glittering roofs
Visible far across the land.
Their guide reined in his horse, pointing
225 To that hall, built by Hrothgar for the best
And bravest of his men; the path was plain,
They could see their way. . . .

Beowulf and his men arrive at Herot and are called to see the King.

           Beowulf arose, with his men
Around him, ordering a few to remain
With their weapons, leading the others quietly
230 Along under Herot's steep roof into Hrothgar's
Presence. Standing on that prince's own hearth.
Helmeted, the silvery metal of his mail shirt
Gleaming with smith's high art, he greeted
The Danes' great lord:

ANNOTATE: Mark details in lines 235–253 that show the specific heroic deeds Beowulf recounts to Hrothgar.

QUESTION: What can you infer about Beowulf from the details he shares with Hrothgar?

CONCLUDE: What do these details reveal about the world in which this story is set?

"Hail, Hrothgar!

235   Higlac is my cousin[6] and my king; the days
        Of my youth have been filled with glory. Now Grendel's
        Name has echoed in our land: sailors
        Have brought us stories of Herot, the best
        Of all mead-halls,[7] deserted and useless when the moon

240   Hangs in skies the sun had lit,
        Light and life fleeing together.
        My people have said, the wisest, most knowing
        And best of them, that my duty was to go to the Danes'
        Great king. They have seen my strength for themselves,

245   Have watched me rise from the darkness of war,
        Dripping with my enemies' blood. I drove
        Five great giants into chains, chased
        All of that race from the earth. I swam
        In the blackness of night, hunting monsters

250   Out of the ocean, and killing them one
        By one; death was my errand and the fate
        They had earned. Now Grendel and I are called

---

6. **cousin** here, used as a general term for a relative.
7. **mead-halls** To reward his retainers, the king in heroic literature would often build a hall where mead (a drink made of fermented honey) was served.

Together, and I've come. Grant me, then,
Lord and protector of this noble place,
255 A single request! I have come so far,
O shelterer of warriors and your people's loved friend,
That this one favor you should not refuse me—
That I, alone and with the help of my men,
May purge all evil from this hall. I have heard,
260 Too, that the monster's scorn of men
is so great that he needs no weapons and fears none.
Nor will I. My lord Higlac
Might think less of me if I let my sword
Go where my feet were afraid to, if I hid
265 Behind some broad linden[8] shield: my hands
Alone shall fight for me, struggle for life
Against the monster. God must decide
Who will be given to death's cold grip.
Grendel's plan, I think, will be
270 What it has been before, to invade this hall
And gorge his belly with our bodies. If he can,
If he can. And I think, if my time will have come,
There'll be nothing to mourn over, no corpse to prepare
For its grave: Grendel will carry our bloody
275 Flesh to the moors, crunch on our bones
And smear torn scraps of our skin on the walls
Of his den. No, I expect no Danes
Will fret about sewing our shrouds, if he wins.
And if death does take me, send the hammered
280 Mail of my armor to Higlac, return
The inheritance I had from Hrethel, and he
From Wayland.[9] Fate will unwind as it must!"

*That night, Beowulf and his men stay inside Herot. While his men sleep,
Beowulf lies awake, eager to meet with Grendel.*

The Battle With Grendel

Out from the marsh, from the foot of misty
Hills and bogs, bearing God's hatred
285 Grendel came, hoping to kill
Anyone he could trap on this trip to high Herot.
He moved quickly through the cloudy night,
Up from his swampland, sliding silently
Toward that gold-shining hall. He had visited Hrothgar's
290 Home before, knew the way—
But never, before nor after that night,

gorge (gawrj) *v.* to fill by eating greedily

---

8. **linden** (LIHN duhn) very sturdy type of wood.
9. **Wayland** blacksmith from Germanic folklore.

gruesome (GROO suhm) *adj.*
horrible; ghastly

Found Herot defended so firmly, his reception
So harsh. He journeyed, forever joyless,
Straight to the door, then snapped it open,
295 Tore its iron fasteners with a touch
And rushed angrily over the threshold.
He strode quickly across the inlaid
Floor, snarling and fierce: his eyes
Gleamed in the darkness, burned with a **gruesome**
300 Light. Then he stopped, seeing the hall
Crowded with sleeping warriors, stuffed
With rows of young soldiers resting together.
And his heart laughed, he relished the sight,
Intended to tear the life from those bodies
305 By morning; the monster's mind was hot
With the thought of food and the feasting his belly
Would soon know. But fate, that night, intended
Grendel to gnaw the broken bones
Of his last human supper. Human
310 Eyes were watching his evil steps,
Waiting to see his swift hard claws.
Grendel snatched at the first Geat
He came to, ripped him apart, cut
His body to bits with powerful jaws,
315 Drank the blood from his veins and bolted
Him down, hands and feet; death
And Grendel's great teeth came together,
Snapping life shut. Then he stepped to another
Still body, clutched at Beowulf with his claws,
320 Grasped at a strong-hearted wakeful sleeper—
And was instantly seized himself, claws
Bent back as Beowulf leaned up on one arm.
        That shepherd of evil, guardian of crime,
Knew at once that nowhere on earth
325 Had he met a man whose hands were harder;
His mind was flooded with fear—but nothing
Could take his talons and himself from that tight
Hard grip. Grendel's one thought was to run
From Beowulf, flee back to his marsh and hide there:
330 This was a different Herot from the hall he had emptied.
But Higlac's follower remembered his final
Boast and, standing erect, stopped
The monster's flight, fastened those claws
In his fists till they cracked, clutched Grendel
335 Closer. The infamous killer fought
For his freedom, wanting no flesh but retreat,
Desiring nothing but escape; his claws
Had been caught, he was trapped. That trip to Herot
Was a miserable journey for the **writhing** monster!

CLOSE READ

ANNOTATE: In English syntax, **apposition** may be used to rename or explain a person or thing. Mark the two identifying, appositive phrases used to rename Grendel in line 323.

QUESTION: How do the renamings of Grendel in this line emphasize the significance of the battle that is about to begin?

CONCLUDE: What is the effect of using two or more appositives in a row?

writhing (RY thihng) *adj.*
making twisting or turning motions

340   The high hall rang, its roof boards swayed,
       And Danes shook with terror. Down
       The aisles the battle swept, angry
       And wild. Herot trembled, wonderfully
       Built to withstand the blows, the struggling
345 Great bodies beating at its beautiful walls;
       Shaped and fastened with iron, inside
       And out, artfully worked, the building
       Stood firm. Its benches rattled, fell
       To the floor, gold-covered boards grating
350 As Grendel and Beowulf battled across them.
       Hrothgar's wise men had fashioned Herot
       To stand forever; only fire,
       They had planned, could shatter what such skill had put
       Together, swallow in hot flames such splendor
355 Of ivory and iron and wood. Suddenly
       The sounds changed, the Danes started
       In new terror, cowering in their beds as the terrible
       Screams of the Almighty's enemy sang
       In the darkness, the horrible shrieks of pain
360 And defeat, the tears torn out of Grendel's
       Taut throat, hell's captive caught in the arms
       Of him who of all the men on earth
       Was the strongest.
                              That mighty protector of men
       Meant to hold the monster till its life
365 Leaped out, knowing the fiend was no use
       To anyone in Denmark. All of Beowulf's
       Band had jumped from their beds, ancestral
       Swords raised and ready, determined
       To protect their prince if they could. Their courage
370 Was great but all wasted: they could hack at Grendel
       From every side, trying to open
       A path for his evil soul, but their points
       Could not hurt him, the sharpest and hardest iron
       Could not scratch at his skin, for that sin-stained demon
375 Had bewitched all men's weapons, laid spells
       That blunted every mortal man's blade.
       And yet his time had come, his days
       Were over, his death near; down
       To hell he would go, swept groaning and helpless
380 To the waiting hands of still worse fiends.
       Now he discovered—once the afflictor
       Of men, tormentor of their days—what it meant
       To feud with Almighty God: Grendel
       Saw that his strength was deserting him, his claws
385 Bound fast, Higlac's brave follower tearing at
       His hands. The monster's hatred rose higher,

NOTES

from Beowulf **29**

But his power had gone. He twisted in pain,
And the bleeding sinews deep in his shoulder
Snapped, muscle and bone split
390 And broke. The battle was over, Beowulf
Had been granted new glory: Grendel escaped,
But wounded as he was could flee to his den,
His miserable hole at the bottom of the marsh,
Only to die, to wait for the end
395 Of all his days. And after that bloody
Combat the Danes laughed with delight.
He who had come to them from across the sea,
Bold and strong-minded had driven affliction
Off, purged Herot clean. He was happy,
400 Now, with that night's fierce work; the Danes
Had been served as he'd boasted he'd serve them: Beowulf,
A prince of the Geats, had killed Grendel,
Ended the grief, the sorrow, the suffering
Forced on Hrothgar's helpless people
405 By a bloodthirsty fiend. No Dane doubted
The victory, for the proof, hanging high
From the rafters where Beowulf had hung it, was the monster's
Arm, claw and shoulder and all.

The Danes celebrate Beowulf's victory. That night, though, Grendel's mother kills Hrothgar's closest friend and carries off her child's claw. The next day, the horrified king tells Beowulf about the two monsters and their underwater lair.

The Monsters' Lair

"I've heard that my people, peasants working
410 In the fields, have seen a pair of such fiends
Wandering in the moors and marshes, giant
Monsters living in those desert lands.
And they've said to my wise men that, as well as they could see,
One of the devils was a female creature.
415 The other, they say, walked through the wilderness
Like a man—but mightier than any man.
They were frightened, and they fled, hoping to find help
In Herot. They named the huge one Grendel:
If he had a father no one knew him,
420 Or whether there'd been others before these two,
Hidden evil before hidden evil.
They live in secret places, windy
Cliffs, wolf-dens where water pours
From the rocks, then runs underground, where mist

425   Steams like black clouds, and the groves of trees
       Growing out over their lake are all covered
       With frozen spray, and wind down snakelike
       Roots that reach as far as the water
       And help keep it dark. At night that lake
430   Burns like a torch. No one knows its bottom,
       No wisdom reaches such depths. A deer,
       Hunted through the woods by packs of hounds,
       A stag with great horns, though driven through the forest
       From faraway places, prefers to die
435   On those shores, refuses to save its life
       In that water. It isn't far, nor is it
       A pleasant spot! When the winds stirs
       And storms, waves splash toward the sky,
       As dark as the air, as black as the rain
440   That the heavens weep. Our only help,
       Again, lies with you. Grendel's mother
       Is hidden in her terrible home, in a place
       You've not seen. Seek it, if you dare! Save us,
       Once more, and again twisted gold,
445   Heaped-up ancient treasure will reward you
       For the battle you win!"

Beowulf resolves to kill Grendel's monstrous mother. He travels to the lake in which she lives.

The Battle With Grendel's Mother

       Then Edgetho's brave son[10] spoke:
                     "Remember,
       Hrothgar, O knowing king, now
       When my danger is near, the warm words we uttered,
450   And if your enemy should end my life
       Then be, O generous prince, forever
       The father and protector of all whom I leave
       Behind me, here in your hands, my beloved
       Comrades left with no leader, their leader
455   Dead. And the precious gifts you gave me,
       My friend, send them to Higlac. May he see
       In their golden brightness, the Geats' great lord
       Gazing at your treasure, that here in Denmark
       I found a noble protector, a giver
460   Of rings whose rewards I won and briefly
       Relished. And you, Unferth,[11] let

---

10. **Edgetho's brave son** Beowulf. Elsewhere he is identified by such phrases as "the Geats' proud prince" and "the Geats' brave prince."
11. **Unferth** Danish warrior who had questioned Beowulf's bravery before the battle with Grendel.

My famous old sword stay in your hands:
I shall shape glory with Hrunting, or death
Will hurry me from this earth!"

                              As his words ended
465 He leaped into the lake, would not wait for anyone's
Answer; the heaving water covered him
Over. For hours he sank through the waves;
At last he saw the mud of the bottom.
And all at once the greedy she-wolf
470 Who'd ruled those waters for half a hundred
Years discovered him, saw that a creature
From above had come to explore the bottom
Of her wet world. She welcomed him in her claws,
Clutched at him savagely but could not harm him,
475 Tried to work her fingers through the tight
Ring-woven mail on his breast, but tore
And scratched in vain. Then she carried him, armor
And sword and all, to her home; he struggled
To free his weapon, and failed. The fight
480 Brought other monsters swimming to see
Her catch, a host of sea beasts who beat at
His mail shirt, stabbing with tusks and teeth
As they followed along. Then he realized, suddenly,
That she'd brought him into someone's battle-hall,
485 And there the water's heat could not hurt him.
Nor anything in the lake attack him through
The building's high-arching roof. A brilliant
Light burned all around him, the lake
Itself like a fiery flame.
                              Then he saw
490 The mighty water witch and swung his sword,
His ring-marked blade, straight at her head;
The iron sang its fierce song,
Sang Beowulf's strength. But her guest
Discovered that no sword could slice her evil
495 Skin, that Hrunting could not hurt her, was useless
Now when he needed it. They wrestled, she ripped
And tore and clawed at him, bit holes in his helmet,
And that too failed him; for the first time in years
Of being worn to war it would earn no glory;
500 It was the last time anyone would wear it. But Beowulf
Longed only for fame, leaped back
Into battle. He tossed his sword aside,
Angry; the steel-edged blade lay where
He'd dropped it. If weapons were useless he'd use
505 His hands, the strength in his fingers. So fame
Comes to the men who mean to win it
And care about nothing else! He raised

CLOSE READ

ANNOTATE: Mark words
and phrases in lines
477–489 that contain
sound devices and parallel
structures.

QUESTION: What effect
might these word choices
have had on listeners?

CONCLUDE: In what
way does the language
of the story help make
it memorable for both
the storyteller and the
audience?

His arms and seized her by the shoulder; anger
Doubled his strength, he threw her to the floor.
510 She fell, Grendel's fierce mother, and the Geats'
Proud prince was ready to leap on her. But she rose
At once and repaid him with her clutching claws,
Wildly tearing at him. He was weary, that best
And strongest of soldiers; his feet stumbled
515 And in an instant she had him down, held helpless.
Squatting with her weight on his stomach, she drew
A dagger, brown with dried blood, and prepared
To avenge her only son. But he was stretched
On his back, and her stabbing blade was blunted
520 By the woven mail shirt he wore on his chest.
The hammered links held; the point
Could not touch him. He'd have traveled to the bottom of the earth,
Edgetho's son, and died there, if that shining
Woven metal had not helped—and Holy
525 God, who sent him victory, gave judgment
For truth and right, Ruler of the Heavens,
Once Beowulf was back on his feet and fighting.
      Then he saw, hanging on the wall, a heavy
Sword, hammered by giants, strong
530 And blessed with their magic, the best of all weapons
But so massive that no ordinary man could lift
Its carved and decorated length. He drew it
From its scabbard, broke the chain on its hilt
And then, savage, now, angry
535 And desperate, lifted it high over his head
And struck with all the strength he had left,
Caught her in the neck and cut it through.
Broke bones and all. Her body fell
To the floor, lifeless, the sword was wet
540 With her blood, and Beowulf rejoiced at the sight.
      The brilliant light shone, suddenly,
As though burning in that hall, and as bright as Heaven's
Own candle, lit in the sky. He looked
At her home, then following along the wall
545 Went walking, his hands tight on the sword,
His heart still angry. He was hunting another
Dead monster, and took his weapon with him
For final revenge against Grendel's vicious
Attacks, his nighttime raids, over
550 And over, coming to Herot when Hrothgar's
Men slept, killing them in their beds,
Eating some on the spot, fifteen
Or more, and running to his loathsome moor
With another such sickening meal waiting
555 In his pouch. But Beowulf repaid him for those visits,

loathsome (LOHTH suhm) *adj.*
disgusting; detestable

Found him lying dead in his corner,
Armless, exactly as that fierce fighter
Had sent him out from Herot, then struck off
His head with a single swift blow. The body
560 jerked for the last time, then lay still.
      The wise old warriors who surrounded Hrothgar,
Like him staring into the monsters' lake,
Saw the waves surging and blood
Spurting through. They spoke about Beowulf,
565 All the graybeards, whispered together
And said that hope was gone, that the hero
Had lost fame and his life at once, and would never
Return to the living, come back as triumphant
As he had left; almost all agreed that Grendel's
570 Mighty mother, the she-wolf, had killed him.
The sun slid over past noon, went further
Down. The Danes gave up, left
The lake and went home, Hrothgar with them.
The Geats stayed, sat sadly, watching,

575 Imagining they saw their lord but not believing
They would ever see him again.
                                        —Then the sword
Melted, blood-soaked, dripping down
Like water, disappearing like ice when the world's
Eternal Lord loosens invisible
580 Fetters and unwinds icicles and frost
As only He can. He who rules
Time and seasons, He who is truly
God. The monsters' hall was full of
Rich treasures, but all that Beowulf took
585 Was Grendel's head and the hilt of the giants'
Jeweled sword; the rest of that ring-marked
Blade had dissolved in Grendel's steaming
Blood, boiling even after his death.
And then the battle's only survivor
590 Swam up and away from those silent corpses;
The water was calm and clean, the whole
Huge lake peaceful once the demons who'd lived in it
Were dead.
          Then that noble protector of all seamen
Swam to land, rejoicing in the heavy
595 Burdens he was bringing with him. He
And all his glorious band of Geats
Thanked God that their leader had come back unharmed;
They left the lake together. The Geats
Carried Beowulf's helmet, and his mail shirt.
600 Behind them the water slowly thickened
As the monsters' blood came seeping up.
They walked quickly, happily, across
Roads all of them remember, left
The lake and the cliffs alongside it, brave men
605 Staggering under the weight of Grendel's skull,
Too heavy for fewer than four of them to handle—
Two on each side of the spear jammed through it—
Yet proud of their ugly load and determined
That the Danes, seated in Herot, should see it.
610 Soon, fourteen Geats arrived
At the hall, bold and warlike, and with Beowulf,
Their lord and leader, they walked on the mead-hall
Green. Then the Geats' brave prince entered
Herot, covered with glory for the daring
615 Battles he had fought; he sought Hrothgar
To salute him and show Grendel's head.
He carried that terrible trophy by the hair,
Brought it straight to where the Danes sat,
Drinking, the queen among them. It was a weird
620 And wonderful sight, and the warriors stared.

After being honored by Hrothgar, Beowulf and his fellow Geats return home,
where he eventually becomes the king. Beowulf rules Geatland for fifty years.
When a dragon menaces his kingdom, Beowulf, now an old man, determines
to slay the beast. Before going into battle, he tells his men about the royal
house and his exploits in its service.

The Last Battle

And Beowulf uttered his final boast:
"I've never known fear, as a youth I fought
In endless battles. I am old, now,
But I will fight again, seek fame still,
625 If the dragon hiding in his tower dares
To face me."
        Then he said farewell to his followers,
Each in his turn, for the last time:
        "I'd use no sword, no weapon, if this beast
Could be killed without it, crushed to death
630 Like Grendel, gripped in my hands and torn
Limb from limb. But his breath will be burning
Hot, poison will pour from his tongue.
I feel no shame, with shield and sword
And armor, against this monster: when he comes to me
635 I mean to stand, not run from his shooting
Flames, stand till fate decides
Which of us wins. My heart is firm,
My hands calm: I need no hot
Words. Wait for me close by, my friends.
640 We shall see, soon, who will survive
This bloody battle, stand when the fighting
Is done. No one else could do
What I mean to, here, no man but me
Could hope to defeat this monster. No one
645 Could try. And this dragon's treasure, his gold
And everything hidden in that tower, will be mine
Or war will sweep me to a bitter death!"
        Then Beowulf rose, still brave, still strong,
And with his shield at his side, and a mail shirt on his breast,
650 Strode calmly, confidently, toward the tower, under
The rocky cliffs: no coward could have walked there!
And then he who'd endured dozens of desperate
Battles, who'd stand boldly while swords and shields
Clashed, the best of kings, saw
655 Huge stone arches and felt the heat
Of the dragon's breath, flooding down
Through the hidden entrance, too hot for anyone
To stand, a streaming current of fire

And smoke that blocked all passage. And the Geats'
660 Lord and leader, angry, lowered
His sword and roared out a battle cry,
A call so loud and clear that it reached through
The hoary rock, hung in the dragon's
Ear. The beast rose, angry,
665 Knowing a man had come—and then nothing
But war could have followed. Its breath came first.
A steaming cloud pouring from the stone,
Then the earth itself shook. Beowulf
Swung his shield into place, held it
670 In front of him, facing the entrance. The dragon
Coiled and uncoiled, its heart urging it
Into battle. Beowulf's ancient sword
Was waiting, unsheathed, his sharp and gleaming
Blade. The beast came closer; both of them
675 Were ready, each set on slaughter. The Geats'
Great prince stood firm, unmoving, prepared
Behind his high shield, waiting in his shining
Armor. The monster came quickly toward him,
Pouring out fire and smoke, hurrying
680 To its fate. Flames beat at the iron
Shield, and for a time it held, protected
Beowulf as he'd planned; then it began to melt,
And for the first time in his life that famous prince
Fought with fate against him, with glory
685 Denied him. He knew it, but he raised his sword
And struck at the dragon's scaly hide.
The ancient blade broke, bit into
The monster's skin, drew blood, but cracked
And failed him before it went deep enough, helped him
690 Less than he needed. The dragon leaped
With pain, thrashed, and beat at him, spouting
Murderous flames, spreading them everywhere.
And the Geats' ring-giver did not boast of glorious
Victories in other wars: his weapon
695 Had failed him, deserted him, now when he needed it
Most, that excellent sword. Edgetho's
Famous son stared at death.
Unwilling to leave this world, to exchange it
For a dwelling in some distant place—a journey
700 Into darkness that all men must make, as death
Ends their few brief hours on earth.
        Quickly, the dragon came at him, encouraged
As Beowulf fell back; its breath flared,
And he suffered, wrapped around in swirling
705 Flames—a king, before, but now
A beaten warrior. None of his comrades

Came to him, helped him, his brave and noble
Followers; they ran for their lives, fled
Deep in a wood. And only one of them
710 Remained, stood there, miserable, remembering
As a good man must, what kinship should mean.

His name was Wiglaf, he was Wexstan's son
And a good soldier; his family had been Swedish,
Once. Watching Beowulf, he could see
715 How his king was suffering, burning. Remembering
Everything his lord and cousin had given him,
Armor and gold and the great estates
Wexstan's family enjoyed, Wiglaf's
Mind was made up; he raised his yellow
720 Shield and drew his sword—an ancient
Weapon that had once belonged to Onela's
Nephew, and that Wexstan had won, killing
The prince when he fled from Sweden, sought safety
With Herdred, and found death.[12] And Wiglaf's father
725 Had carried the dead man's armor, and his sword,
To Onela, and the king had said nothing, only
Given him the armor and sword and all,
Everything his rebel nephew had owned
And lost when he left this life. And Wexstan
730 Had kept those shining gifts, held them
For years, waiting for his son to use them,
Wear them as honorably and well as once
His father had done; then Wexstan died
And Wiglaf was his heir, inherited treasures
735 And weapons and land. He'd never worn
That armor, fought with that sword, until Beowulf
Called him to his side, led him into war.
But his soul did not melt, his sword was strong;
The dragon discovered his courage, and his weapon,
740 When the rush of battle brought them together.
And Wiglaf, his heart heavy, uttered
The kind of words his comrades deserved:
"I remember how we sat in the mead-hall, drinking
And boasting of how brave we'd be when Beowulf
745 Needed us, he who gave us these swords
And armor: all of us swore to repay him.
When the time came, kindness for kindness—
With our lives, if he needed them. He allowed us to join him,
Chose us from all his great army, thinking
750 Our boasting words had some weight, believing

---

12. **Onela's / Nephew . . . found death** When Onela seized the throne of Sweden, his two
nephews sought shelter with the king of Geatland, Herdred. Wiglaf's father, Wexstan,
killed the older nephew for Onela.

Our promises, trusting our swords. He took us
For soldiers, for men. He meant to kill
This monster himself, our mighty king,
Fight this battle alone and unaided,
755 As in the days when his strength and daring dazzled
Men's eyes. But those days are over and gone
And now our lord must lean on younger
Arms. And we must go to him, while angry
Flames burn at his flesh, help
760 Our glorious king! By almighty God,
I'd rather burn myself than see
Flames swirling around my lord.
And who are we to carry home
Our shields before we've slain his enemy
765 And ours, to run back to our homes with Beowulf
So hard-pressed here? I swear that nothing
He ever did deserved an end
Like this, dying miserably and alone
Butchered by this savage beast: we swore
770 That these swords and armor were each for us all!"
        Then he ran to his king, crying encouragement
As he dove through the dragon's deadly fumes.

*Wiglaf and Beowulf kill the dragon, but the old king is mortally wounded.
As he dies, Beowulf asks Wiglaf to bring him the treasure that the dragon
was guarding.*

The Spoils

        Then Wexstan's son went in, as quickly
As he could, did as the dying Beowulf
775 Asked, entered the inner darkness
Of the tower, went with his mail shirt and his sword.
Flushed with victory he groped his way,
A brave young warrior, and suddenly saw
Piles of gleaming gold, precious
780 Gems, scattered on the floor, cups
And bracelets, rusty old helmets, beautifully
Made but rotting with no hands to rub
And polish them. They lay where the dragon left them;
It had flown in the darkness, once, before fighting
785 Its final battle. (So gold can easily
Triumph, defeat the strongest of men,
No matter how deep it is hidden!) And he saw,
Hanging high above, a golden
Banner, woven by the best of weavers
790 And beautiful. And over everything he saw

CLOSE READ
ANNOTATE: Mark details in lines 743–770 that show what Beowulf's men were like in the beginning and how they changed.

QUESTION: How have Beowulf's men, with the exception of Wiglaf, changed?

CONCLUDE: How do these contrasting details help the reader better understand Beowulf's dilemma?

A strange light, shining everywhere,
On walls and floor and treasure. Nothing
Moved, no other monsters appeared;
He took what he wanted, all the treasures
795 That pleased his eye, heavy plates
And golden cups and the glorious banner,
Loaded his arms with all they could hold.
Beowulf's dagger, his iron blade,
Had finished the fire-spitting terror
800 That once protected tower and treasures
Alike; the gray-bearded lord of the Geats
Had ended those flying, burning raids
Forever.
              Then Wiglaf went back, anxious
To return while Beowulf was alive, to bring him
805 Treasure they'd won together. He ran,

Hoping his wounded king, weak
And dying, had not left the world too soon.
Then he brought their treasure to Beowulf, and found
His famous king bloody, gasping
810 For breath. But Wiglaf sprinkled water
Over his lord, until the words
Deep in his breast broke through and were heard.
Beholding the treasure he spoke, haltingly:
    "For this, this gold, these jewels, I thank
815 Our Father in Heaven, Ruler of the Earth—
For all of this, that His grace has given me,
Allowed me to bring to my people while breath
Still came to my lips. I sold my life
For this treasure, and I sold it well. Take
820 What I leave, Wiglaf, lead my people,
Help them; my time is gone. Have
The brave Geats build me a tomb.
When the funeral flames have burned me, and build it
Here, at the water's edge, high
825 On this spit of land, so sailors can see
This tower, and remember my name, and call it
Beowulf's tower, and boats in the darkness
And mist, crossing the sea, will know it."
    Then that brave king gave the golden
830 Necklace from around his throat to Wiglaf,
Gave him his gold-covered helmet, and his rings,
And his mail shirt, and ordered him to use them well:
    "You're the last of all our far-flung family.
Fate has swept our race away,
835 Taken warriors in their strength and led them
To the death that was waiting. And now I follow them."
    The old man's mouth was silent, spoke
No more, had said as much as it could;
He would sleep in the fire, soon. His soul
840 Left his flesh, flew to glory.

Wiglaf denounces the warriors who deserted Beowulf. The Geats burn their king's body on a funeral pyre and bitterly lament his death.

The Farewell

    Then the Geats built the tower, as Beowulf
Had asked, strong and tall, so sailors
Could find it from far and wide; working
For ten long days they made his monument,
845 Sealed his ashes in walls as straight

CLOSE READ
ANNOTATE: Mark details in lines 814–828 that show how Beowulf wants to be buried and remembered.

QUESTION: What do Beowulf's dying wishes tell you about him?

CONCLUDE: What can you conclude about the character of Beowulf, based on his last words?

And high as wise and willing hands
Could raise them. And the riches he and Wiglaf
Had won from the dragon, rings, necklaces,
Ancient, hammered armor—all
850 The treasures they'd taken were left there, too,
Silver and jewels buried in the sandy
Ground, back in the earth, again
And forever hidden and useless to men.
And then twelve of the bravest Geats
855 Rode their horses around the tower,
Telling their sorrow, telling stories
Of their dead king and his greatness, his glory,
Praising him for heroic deeds, for a life
As noble as his name. So should all men
860 Raise up words for their lords, warm
With love, when their shield and protector leaves
His body behind, sends his soul
On high. And so Beowulf's followers
Rode, mourning their beloved leader,
865 Crying that no better king had ever
Lived, no prince so mild, no man
So open to his people, so deserving of praise.

Comprehension Check

Complete the following items after you finish your first read.

1. Who is Hrothgar, and who is Grendel?

2. Where does Beowulf come from, and why does he travel to Herot?

3. After the first battle, what trophy does Beowulf hang from the rafters of the hall?

4. Where does the battle with Grendel's mother take place, and what is the outcome?

5. What is the result of Beowulf's battle with the dragon?

6. 🖥 **Notebook** Write a summary of the excerpt from *Beowulf* to confirm your understanding of the epic.

RESEARCH

Research to Clarify Choose at least one unfamiliar detail from the text. Briefly research that detail. In what way does the information you learned shed light on an aspect of the epic?

Research to Explore Choose something that interested you from the text, and formulate a research question about it. Write your question here.

Close Read the Text

1. This model, from lines 23–29 of the epic, shows two sample annotations, along with questions and conclusions. Close read the passage, and find another detail to annotate. Then, write a question and your conclusion.

Close Read

ANNOTATE QUESTION CONCLUDE

ANNOTATE: These words emphasize how plentiful and diverse these evil forces are.

QUESTION: Is there anything they have in common? If so, what does this suggest?

CONCLUDE: They all sprang from the same source. Perhaps all evil is essentially the same, despite its many forms.

ANNOTATE: These verbs and participles all show conflict.

QUESTION: Who or what are in conflict? What does this suggest?

CONCLUDE: God and men are opposing demons. This suggests a struggle between good and evil.

. . . The Almighty drove / Those demons out, and their exile was bitter. / Shut away from men; they split / Into a thousand forms of evil—spirits / And fiends, goblins, monsters, giants. / A brood forever opposing the Lord's Will, and again and again defeated.

2. For more practice, go back into the text, and complete the close-read notes.

3. Closely reread a section of the text you found important during your first read. **Annotate** what you notice. Ask yourself **questions** such as "Why did the author make this choice?" What can you **conclude**?

 Tool Kit

Close-Read Guide and Model Annotation

Analyze the Text

CITE TEXTUAL EVIDENCE to support your answers.

Notebook Respond to these questions.

1. (a) Why does Beowulf travel to Herot? (b) **Infer** What do his motives for the trip suggest about his character?

2. **Analyze** How does the contrast between Grendel and Beowulf turn their conflict into a clash between good and evil?

3. **Compare and Contrast** How is Beowulf's fight with the dragon similar to his two previous battles? How is it different?

4. (a) What details show the importance of Christian beliefs? (b) What details reveal pagan values, such as a belief in fate, a pride in loyalty, and a desire for fame? (c) **Draw Conclusions** What can you conclude about this mix of Christian and pagan details?

5. **Historical Perspectives** Explain how the poem, by keeping Beowulf's memory alive, also keeps a culture's values alive.

6. **Essential Question:** What makes a hero? What have you learned about heroism and leadership from reading this epic poem?

STANDARDS

Reading Literature
• Cite strong and thorough textual evidence to support analysis of what the text says explicitly as well as inferences drawn from the text, including determining where the text leaves matters uncertain.

• Analyze the impact of the author's choices regarding how to develop and relate elements of a story or drama.

• Analyze how an author's choices concerning how to structure specific parts of a text contribute to its overall structure and meaning as well as its aesthetic impact.

Analyze Craft and Structure

Author's Choices: Structure An **epic** is a long narrative poem, sometimes developed orally, that celebrates heroic deeds and legendary events. Epics, like Homer's *Iliad* from ancient Greece, are among the earliest forms of literature. As such, they reveal the values of the people who created them. Common features of epics include the following:

- a story that is told in a serious manner, with elevated language
- a hero battling forces that threaten the world order
- a hero that possesses extraordinary strength
- a story that is told in episodes, with various settings

Most epics celebrate the exploits of an **epic hero**, a legendary, larger-than-life character. Often, epics follow **archetypal patterns**—that is, patterns of plot and theme that recur in the literature of different cultures all over the world. In *Beowulf*, two such archetypes are the quest and the struggle of good against evil.

Practice

CITE TEXTUAL EVIDENCE to support your answers.

🗐 **Notebook** Respond to these questions and prompts.

1. (a) List two characteristics that make Beowulf an epic hero. (b) Identify a passage that shows the hero's more human side. Explain your choice.
2. Is Beowulf a believable character, or is he "too heroic"? Explain.
3. Frustrated pride may lead to spite, just as loyalty may lead to vengeance, and eagerness for glory may lead to greed. Explain how each creature Beowulf battles represents an extreme and dangerous form of moral values and behavior.
4. A storyteller's choices regarding how to develop and relate story elements (such as plot, setting, character development, and archetypal patterns) affect audiences' reactions to the story. Complete the partially filled-in chart, noting specific story elements, the storyteller's choices regarding these elements, and the effects of these choices on the audience.

STORY ELEMENT	STORYTELLER'S CHOICE	EFFECT
Character development: Beowulf	the arrival of Beowulf: gleaming armor, the watchman's stunned, amazed reaction	creates the sense of a larger-than-life, almost godlike figure
Plot		
Settings		
Archetypal Pattern		

from BEOWULF

Concept Vocabulary

lair	gorge	writhing
stalked	gruesome	loathsome

Why These Words? These concept vocabulary words show to various degrees the vile, monstrous, predatory nature of the monsters Beowulf faces. For example, a *gruesome* sight is something that is hideous and repulsive. The sight of a *writhing* creature, on the other hand, would probably be unpleasant but not provoke quite as strong a reaction.

1. How does the concept vocabulary sharpen the reader's understanding of the foes and challenges Beowulf faces?

2. What other words in the selection connect to this concept?

Practice

Notebook Respond to these questions.

1. What sort of person or creature would you expect to find in a *lair*?

2. How would you describe the behavior of a person or creature that tends to *gorge* when eating?

3. Why might a creature have *stalked* another creature?

4. Would you want to witness a *gruesome* sight? Why, or why not?

5. What story characters do you consider *loathsome*? *Why*?

6. What might you do if you saw an animal *writhing*? What might cause such movement?

Word Study

Anglo-Saxon Suffix: -*some* The Anglo-Saxon suffix -*some* means "causing," "tending to," or "to a considerable degree" and forms adjectives from nouns, verbs, and other adjectives. The concept word *gruesome* was formed from the Scottish noun *grue,* meaning "shudder." The concept word *loathsome* was formed from the English adjective *loath,* which in the past meant "hated" or "repulsive."

1. Write definitions of *gruesome* and *loathsome* that demonstrate how the suffix -*some* contributes to their meanings.

2. Using a college-level dictionary, identify the word origins and write the meanings of these words featuring the suffix -*some*: *burdensome, cumbersome, meddlesome, noisome*.

⊹ WORD NETWORK

Add interesting words related to heroism from the text to your Word Network.

▤ STANDARDS

Language
• Vary syntax for effect, consulting references for guidance as needed; apply an understanding of syntax to the study of complex texts when reading.
• Identify and correctly use patterns of word changes that indicate different meanings or parts of speech.
• Consult general and specialized reference materials, both print and digital, to find the pronunciation of a word or determine or clarify its precise meaning, its part of speech, its etymology, or its standard usage.

Conventions and Style

Using Syntax for Elaboration The **syntax** of a sentence is its structure, or the arrangement of and relationships among its words. Writers may use various syntactic devices to build up and extend accounts of action and descriptions of characters. Two of those devices are apposition and diazeugma.

Apposition is the placement of two elements, typically nouns or noun phrases, side by side so that the second identifies, clarifies, or elaborates on the first. **Diazeugma** is the linkage of a single subject with two or more verbs, either to add dimension to the first verb or to establish a clear sequence of actions or events.

The chart shows examples from *Beowulf* of apposition and diazeugma.

DEVICE	EXAMPLE	EFFECT
apposition	. . . **Hrothgar,** *their lord,* sat joyless / In Herot. . . . (lines 44–45)	identifies
	. . . so Herot *Stood empty,* and stayed deserted for **years,** *Twelve winters of grief for Hrothgar.* . . . (lines 60–62)	elaborates
diazeugma	That **shadow** of death *hunted* in the darkness, *Stalked* Hrothgar's warriors. . . . (lines 74–76)	adds dimension
	He *slipped* through the door and there in the silence *Snatched up* thirty men, *smashed* them Unknowing in their beds and *ran* out with their bodies (lines 36–38)	establishes a clear sequence

Read It

1. Mark and label each instance of apposition or diazeugma in the sentences.
   a. Grendel, that most heartless of creatures, continued his onslaught.
   b. Beowulf engaged the beast, fought valiantly, and emerged victorious.
   c. Rejoicing rang out in Herot, the banquet hall of King Hrothgar.

2. **Connect to Style** Reread lines 208–212 of *Beowulf*. Mark and label the syntactic device that is employed. Explain the effect of the use of apposition or diazeugma in those lines.

Write It

📓 **Notebook** Expand these sentences so that each contains an instance of both apposition and diazeugma. Label each device in parentheses.

> Example
>
> Beowulf led his men to Herot.
> Beowulf, Edgetho's son *(apposition),* led his men to Herot and greeted the king *(diazeugma).*

1. Grendel's mother emerged from her lair.
2. Just before his death, Beowulf removed his golden necklace.

from BEOWULF

Writing to Sources

The ability to convince your audience is the key to a successful argument. Effective persuasion requires you to convey ideas in a clear manner. To clarify ideas that may be unfamiliar to your audience, you may choose to point out similarities or differences between your ideas and other, more familiar, concepts.

Assignment

Write a **comparison-and-contrast essay** in which you compare and contrast the character of Beowulf with that of a modern hero in a television show, video game, or other medium. In your comparison, consider the type of monster or threat each hero faces, as well as each hero's characteristics. Based on your comparison, draw a conclusion about differences between Anglo-Saxon and modern-day values. Include these elements in your essay:

- quotations from Beowulf that support your statements
- relevant examples from your other source
- transitional words and phrases that clarify comparisons and contrasts

You may wish to use point-by-point organization, in which you move between your subjects as you discuss points of comparison and contrast. Alternatively, you may wish to use subject-by-subject organization, in which you compare and contrast your subjects as complete units.

Vocabulary and Conventions Connection In your comparison-and-contrast essay, consider including several of the concept vocabulary words. Also, consider using apposition to clarify your ideas.

lair	gorge	writhing
stalked	gruesome	loathsome

Reflect on Your Writing

Once you have finished drafting your comparison-and-contrast essay, answer the following questions.

1. What details have you used to present your thesis and provide support?

2. Which details provide clarification and elaboration of your ideas?

3. **Why These Words?** The words you choose make a difference in your writing. Which transitional words and phrases did you choose to clarify comparisons? Which did you choose to clarify contrasts?

STANDARDS

Writing
• Write informative/explanatory texts to examine and convey complex ideas, concepts, and information clearly and accurately through the effective selection, organization, and analysis of content.

• Use appropriate and varied transitions and syntax to link the major sections of the text, create cohesion, and clarify the relationships among complex ideas and concepts.

• Use technology, including the Internet, to produce, publish, and update individual or shared writing products in response to ongoing feedback, including new arguments or information.

Speaking and Listening
• Integrate multiple sources of information presented in diverse formats and media in order to make informed decisions and solve problems, evaluating the credibility and accuracy of each source and noting any discrepancies among the data.

• Make strategic use of digital media in presentations to enhance understanding of findings, reasoning, and evidence and to add interest.

Speaking and Listening

Assignment

With a partner, prepare a **research presentation** focusing on one aspect of the culture that told and retold the story of Beowulf—the Anglo-Saxons of the eighth to eleventh centuries. Enrich your presentation with digital media that you find online. Deliver your presentation to the class.

1. **Choose Your Topic** With your partner, choose one aspect of Anglo-Saxon culture to research. You may select a topic of your own, or you may research one of the following:

   - the life of a seafaring warrior
   - the construction of a mead-hall
   - the concept of fate
   - the design of Beowulf's ship

2. **Conduct Research** With a partner, choose text and digital media. Then, evaluate the credibility and accuracy of each source, using this checklist:

   - [ ] yes [ ] no Is the source reputable? Is it known to provide solid information?
   - [ ] yes [ ] no Is the source transparent, or open, about its information-gathering practices?
   - [ ] yes [ ] no Does the source avoid bias or a political agenda?
   - [ ] yes [ ] no Is the content thorough and well-written?
   - [ ] yes [ ] no Does the source accurately cite other sources?

3. **Prepare and Deliver Your Presentation** With a partner, decide how best to incorporate text and other resources, and practice delivering your presentation.

4. **Evaluate Presentations** As your classmates deliver their presentations, listen attentively. Use a presentation guide like the one shown to analyze their presentations.

PRESENTATION EVALUATION GUIDE

Rate each statement on a scale of 1 (not demonstrated) to 5 (demonstrated).

- [ ] The speaker held my attention by communicating clearly.
- [ ] The speaker used body language effectively.
- [ ] The information was presented in a logical order.
- [ ] The digital material was informative and well explained.
- [ ] The speaker's presentation showed a firm grasp of the subject matter.

✎ EVIDENCE LOG

Before moving on to a new selection, go to your Evidence Log and record what you learned from *Beowulf*.

from BEOWULF

Comparing Text to Media

The text and images on the following pages tell another version of the story of Beowulf. After reading and viewing this selection, you will analyze similarities and differences between the epic poem and the graphic.

from BEOWULF
(graphic novel)

About the Author

Gareth Hinds (b. 1971) was always drawing as a child. "But," he says, "I had a lot of really good training and encouragement along the way. And I'm a very strong believer in the power of good art instruction." He earned two Bachelors of Fine Art degrees, one from Rochester Institute of Technology and the second from Parsons School of Design in New York City. In addition to this graphic novel of *Beowulf*, Hinds has published graphic novels of other classics, including Shakespeare's *Macbeth*.

from Beowulf

Media Vocabulary

The following terms will be useful to you as you analyze, discuss, and write about graphic novels.

palette: range of colors and shades used by an illustrator	**panel:** individual scene in graphic novel, often framed by a border
composition: arrangement of the parts of an image, whether drawn or recorded in some other visual format	**angle:** measurement of how much space, horizontal and vertical, is included in a single visual
perspective: point of view of an image, which may be *close up*, *middle distance*, or *long distance*	**lighting/color:** use of light and dark shades; dark and high-contrast images draw the eye more than light and low-contrast images

First Review MEDIA: GRAPHIC NOVEL

Apply these strategies as you conduct your first review. You will have an opportunity to complete a close review after your first review.

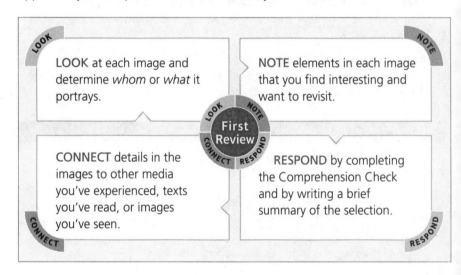

LOOK at each image and determine *whom* or *what* it portrays.

NOTE elements in each image that you find interesting and want to revisit.

CONNECT details in the images to other media you've experienced, texts you've read, or images you've seen.

RESPOND by completing the Comprehension Check and by writing a brief summary of the selection.

BACKGROUND

After Beowulf defeats Grendel and Grendel's mother, he returns to his homeland. He eventually becomes king of the Geats, ruling for fifty years of prosperity. Despite his age, however, he must return to battle one last time after one of his subjects accidentally wakes a dragon by stealing from its hoard.

Then Beowulf ordered his smiths to forge a great iron war-shield to protect him from the dragon's breath, and taking eleven comrades, he went to seek the dragon.

MANY A FIGHT, my friends, have I fought since my youth, always first in the ranks to meet the enemy. Such deeds have I done in times past, and yet one more will I do, if only the destroyer will come out of his dwelling to meet me in battle.

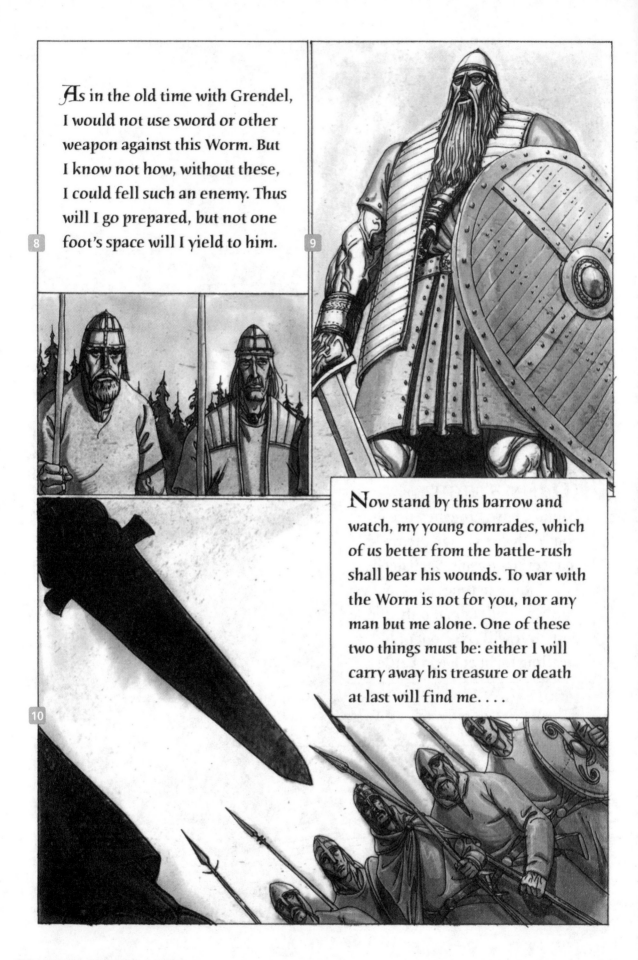

As in the old time with Grendel, I would not use sword or other weapon against this Worm. But I know not how, without these, I could fell such an enemy. Thus will I go prepared, but not one foot's space will I yield to him.

Now stand by this barrow and watch, my young comrades, which of us better from the battle-rush shall bear his wounds. To war with the Worm is not for you, nor any man but me alone. One of these two things must be: either I will carry away his treasure or death at last will find me. . . .

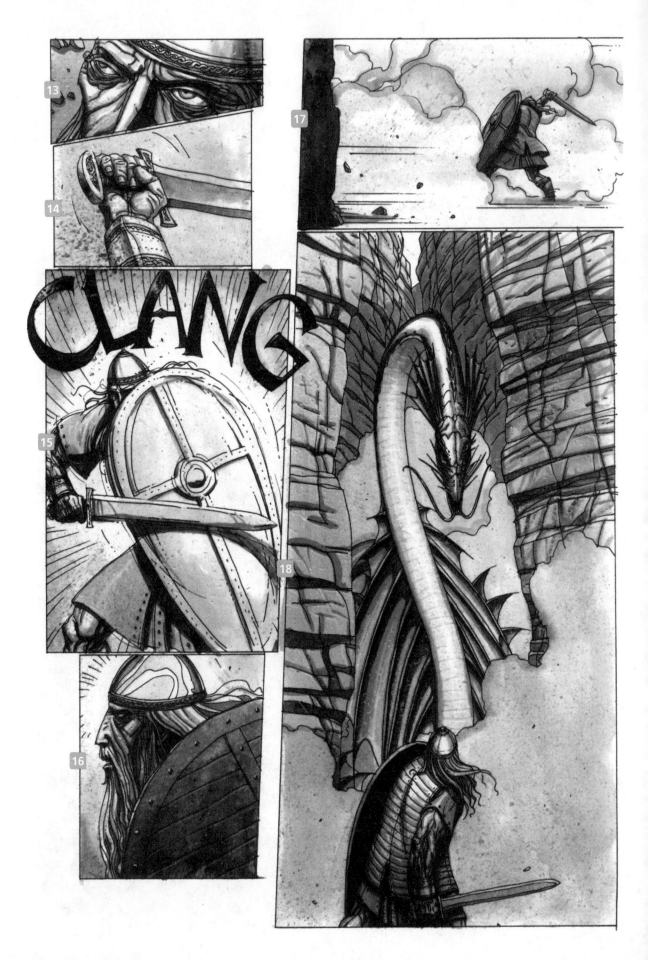

Comprehension Check

Complete the following after you finish your first review.

1. What does Beowulf order his smiths to do at the beginning of the excerpt?

2. How does Beowulf's physical stature compare to that of his men?

3. By what other word or name does Beowulf refer to the dragon?

4. According to Beowulf, what are the only two possible outcomes of his encounter with the dragon?

5. How does the excerpt end?

6. 🗐 **Notebook** Write a brief summary to confirm your understanding of this excerpt from the graphic novel.

- -

RESEARCH

Research to Explore Choose something that interested you from the graphic novel, and formulate a research question about it. Write your question here.

Close Review

Revisit the excerpt from the graphic novel and your first-review notes. Write down any new observations that seem important. What **questions** do you have? What can you **conclude**?

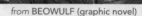

from BEOWULF (graphic novel)

Analyze the Media

> **CITE TEXTUAL EVIDENCE**
> to support your answers.

📓 **Notebook** Respond to these questions.

1. **Respond** In this excerpt from the graphic novel, Hinds depicts the lead-up to the battle with the dragon. Does the way in which Hinds portrays characters and scenes agree with the way that you pictured them when you were reading the epic poem? Why or why not?

2. **(a) Analyze** In what visual ways does Hinds build suspense for the battle with the dragon? **(b) Connect** How do the words within the text boxes work with the images to create suspense?

3. **Historical Perspectives** Do you think it surprising that a very new form, the graphic novel, draws its subject matter from a very old form, an ancient epic? Why or why not?

4. **Essential Question:** *What makes a hero?* What have you learned about heroism and leadership from reading this text?

Media Vocabulary

palette	perspective	angle
composition	panel	lighting/color

Use these vocabulary words in your responses to the following:

1. Identify a scene from the graphic novel in which, in your opinion, the composition is particularly effective. What aspects of the composition make it effective?

2. In which panel does the dragon make its first appearance? Describe the panel in one or two sentences.

3. **(a)** Where does Hinds use close-up, middle-distance, and long-distance perspectives in telling the story? **(b)** Do you think he effectively combines these different perspectives? Explain.

STANDARDS

Language
Acquire and use accurately general academic and domain-specific words and phrases, sufficient for reading, writing, speaking, and listening at the college and career readiness level; demonstrate independence in gathering vocabulary knowledge when considering a word or phrase important to comprehension or expression.

from BEOWULF

from BEOWULF (graphic novel)

Writing to Compare

You have read the story of Beowulf's last battle in two forms—as part of an epic poem, and as part of a graphic novel. Now, deepen your understanding by comparing and writing about the two works.

Assignment

Critical writing is a type of argumentation. The writer makes a claim about the effectiveness of a text and supports the claim with reasons and evidence. Critical writing also anticipates **counterclaims**—differing points of view—and responds to them fairly. Write a **critical evaluation** of the excerpt from the graphic novel *Beowulf*. In your essay, make a claim about the graphic novel as a storytelling medium. As you craft your claim, consider these questions:

- How effective is the graphic novel excerpt as an adaptation of "The Last Battle"?

- What are the strengths and weaknesses of the graphic novel medium?

To support your claim, cite evidence from both the graphic novel and the epic poem. Include at least one counterclaim and present an argument in response to it.

Planning and Prewriting

Compare the Graphic Novel and the Text Identify segments of the epic poem and the graphic novel that correspond with each other. Decide how the segments are similar and different. Take notes in a chart like this one.

PANELS FROM THE GRAPHIC NOVEL	LINES FROM THE EPIC POEM	SIMILARITIES AND DIFFERENCES

📓 **Notebook** Respond to these questions.

1. What tools or techniques are used to bring a detail to life in the epic poem? In the graphic novel?

2. What moods are created in each segment? How?

3. What is the effect of each segment on the reader?

≣ STANDARDS

Reading Literature
Analyze multiple interpretations of a story, drama, or poem, evaluating how each version interprets the source text.

Writing
• Write arguments to support claims in an analysis of substantive topics or texts, using valid reasoning and relevant and sufficient evidence.

• Introduce precise, knowledgeable claims(s), establish the significance of the claim(s), distinguish the claim(s) from alternate or opposing claims, and create an organization that logically sequences claim(s), counterclaims, reasons, and evidence.

• Develop claim(s) and counterclaims fairly and thoroughly, supplying the most relevant evidence for each while pointing out the strengths and limitations of both in a manner that anticipates the audience's knowledge level, concerns, values, and possible biases.

• Apply *grades 11–12 Reading standards* to literature.

Drafting

Determine your central claim and reasons. Review your Prewriting notes. Use them to draw some conclusions about the effectiveness of the graphic novel excerpt. Then, write your claim and supporting reasons.

Central Claim: _____

_____

Reason 1: _____

_____

Reason 2: _____

_____

Support each reason with examples. To convince readers your evaluation is valid, support your ideas with specific references to both the epic poem and the graphic novel.

> ## Example
>
> **Claim:** The graphic novel tells the story of "the last battle" more effectively than the poem does.
> **Reason:** Visual imagery is better able to convey epic proportions.
> **Supporting Example:** Near the beginning of "The Last Battle," the aging Beowulf is said to be "still brave, still strong" (l. 650). The first panel of the graphic novel expresses the same idea. Beowulf's head soars among the sky and clouds, while his followers hunker toward the earth. This visual contrast conveys Beowulf's stature much more powerfully than the descriptive phrases of the poem.

Acknowledge and respond to counterclaims. What different claim about the graphic novel might another reader make? What reasons could be used to support it? Give this point of view a hearing. State it fairly, acknowledge its strengths, and then argue against it, supporting your own ideas with textual evidence.

Strengthen your argument with a rhetorical flourish. To strengthen the persuasive power of your argument, use at least one rhetorical device.

- You might offer an **analogy**, or comparison, to describe the power of the imagery in either the epic poem or the graphic novel.

- You might end your essay with a **rhetorical question**—a question that strikes an emotional note or focuses readers' thoughts.

Review, Revise, and Edit

Review and revise your draft, making sure your claim, reasons, and evidence are as precise as possible. Decide which ideas you want to reaffirm, and restate them in your conclusion. Finally, edit your work carefully. Correct any errors in grammar, spelling, or punctuation that you discover.

EVIDENCE LOG

Before moving on to a new selection, go to your Evidence Log and record what you've learned from both the epic poem *Beowulf* and its retelling as a graphic novel.

WRITING TO SOURCES

• *from* BEOWULF

• *from* BEOWULF
  (graphic novel)

🔧 **Tool Kit**
Student Model of an
Argument

**ACADEMIC
VOCABULARY**

As you craft your
argument, consider using
some of the academic
vocabulary you learned
in the beginning of the
unit.

purport
credible
assertion
presume
contradictory

Write an Argument

You have just read two variations on an ancient epic. In "The Coming of Beowulf," the hero muses to Hrothgar on his reasons for standing up to Grendel, saying, "Fate will unwind as it must!" He does not know whether his mission will succeed or fail, but he is willing to try.

Assignment

Write a brief argumentative essay in which you address this question:

Which counts more—taking a stand or winning?

In your essay, take a clear position on the question. Incorporate your analysis of the Beowulf texts to support your ideas. You may also cite incidents from history or from your own experience or observations to support your claim.

Elements of an Argument

An **argument** is a logical way of presenting a viewpoint, belief, or stand on an issue. A well-written argument may convince the reader, change the reader's mind, or motivate the reader to take a certain action.

An effective argument contains these elements:

- a precise claim
- consideration of counterclaims, or opposing positions, and a discussion of their strengths and weaknesses
- logical organization that makes clear connections among claims, counterclaims, reasons, and evidence
- valid reasoning and evidence
- use of specific rhetorical devices to support claims and counterclaims
- a concluding statement or section that logically completes the argument
- formal and objective language and tone
- error-free grammar, including accurate use of transitions

Analyze the Writing Model

Argument Model For a model of a well-crafted argument, see the Launch Text, "A World of Heroes." Review the Launch Text for examples of the elements described above. You will look more closely at these elements as you prepare to write your own argument.

📋 STANDARDS

Writing
• Write arguments to support claims in an analysis of substantive topics or texts, using valid reasoning and relevant and sufficient evidence.
• Write routinely over extended time frames and shorter time frames for a range of tasks, purposes, and audiences.

Prewriting / Planning

Write a Claim Reread the question in the prompt, and think about the texts you have read. Anticipate your audience's knowledge level, concerns, values, and possible biases. Write a sentence in which you state your **claim**, or position on the question posed in this assignment. As you write, you may revise your claim if necessary. For now, establishing a clear claim will help you choose reasons and supporting evidence.

_____

_____.

Consider Possible Counterclaims A strong argument anticipates **counterclaims**, or opposing positions. No matter which side of the argument you chose, you should consider what opposing writers might say. Complete these sentences to address a counterclaim.

Another reader might claim that _____.

He or she might offer these reasons: _____.

However, my position is stronger because _____.

Gather Evidence In addition to your insights about the Beowulf texts, the assignment invites you to use an incident from history or an anecdote from your own experience or observations as evidence for your claim. You might consider these specific types of evidence as you write.

- **facts:** relevant statements that can be proven true

- **statistics:** facts presented in the form of numbers

- **definitions:** explanations of key terms that may be unfamiliar to readers

- **quotations:** statements from authoritative sources (such as historical documents)

- **examples:** events or situations that support a general idea

Always confirm your evidence using more than one source.

Connect Across Texts The prompt asks you to connect your ideas to the two Beowulf texts you read. You may **paraphrase**, or use your own words to restate an idea. You may also use **direct quotations**, picking up exact language from the text, but be sure to clearly indicate quoted material.

📝 **EVIDENCE LOG**

Review your Evidence Log and identify key details you may want to cite in your argument.

📋 **STANDARDS**

Writing
- Introduce precise, knowledgeable claim(s), establish the significance of the claim(s), distinguish the claim(s) from alternate or opposing claims, and create an organization that logically sequences claim(s), counterclaims, reasons, and evidence.
- Develop claim(s) and counterclaims fairly and thoroughly, supplying the most relevant evidence for each while pointing out the strengths and limitations of both in a manner that anticipates the audience's knowledge level, concerns, values, and possible biases.

Drafting

Organize Your Argument Every argument includes three parts:

- the **introduction,** in which you state your claim
- the **body,** in which you provide analysis, supporting reasons, evidence, counterclaims, and counterarguments
- the **conclusion,** in which you summarize or restate your claim

Review your notes. Rank your reasons from most to least convincing. Choose an organization that will highlight your strongest reasons and evidence. The chart shows two structures you might follow to shape your writing.

INTRODUCTION	
Include a strong claim that identifies the issue and clearly states your position.	
BODY ORGANIZATION A	**BODY ORGANIZATION B**
• Begin with your second strongest reason and evidence. • Present the reasons and evidence in descending order of strength. • Present and refute opposing claims. • End with your strongest reasons and evidence.	• Begin with your strongest reason and evidence. • State and refute the strongest opposing claims or counterclaims. • Present other reasons and evidence in increasing order of strength. • End with your second strongest reason and evidence.
CONCLUSION	
End with a memorable paragraph that restates your claim and sums up your strongest supporting evidence.	

Include sufficient, relevant supporting evidence. For each major idea, provide adequate examples and reasons that support the claim.

Maintain a formal style and tone. A calm, formal tone, or attitude, is more persuasive than a reactive, emotional tone.

Integrating Elaboration

Integrate reasons and examples smoothly and in a way that assures a varied and interesting sentence structure. Look at the examples below.

TYPE OF ELABORATION	AWKWARDLY INTEGRATED	SMOOTHLY INTEGRATED
Quotation	Dr. Hennigan spoke to the school committee. He said, "The biological clocks of teenagers actually program them to sleep late."	As Dr. Hennigan said in his speech before the school committee, "The biological clocks of teenagers actually program them to sleep late."
Example	Students are often late for class. This is because they just can't wake up in the morning.	Many students, for example, are late for class simply because they cannot wake up in the morning.

STANDARDS

Writing
• Introduce precise, knowledgeable claim(s), establish the significance of the claim(s), distinguish the claim(s) from alternate or opposing claims, and create an organization that logically sequences claim(s), counterclaims, reasons, and evidence.
• Establish and maintain a formal style and objective tone while attending to the norms and conventions of the discipline in which they are writing.
• Provide a concluding statement or section that follows from and supports the argument presented.

LANGUAGE DEVELOPMENT: CONVENTIONS

Create Cohesion and Clarity: Transitions

Transitions are words and phrases that connect and show relationships among ideas. Transitions perform an essential function in an argument because they help guide a reader through the writer's line of reasoning.

Look at the following examples from the Launch Text.

POSITION OF TRANSITION	PUNCTUATION	EXAMPLES
start of the sentence	comma after the transitional expression	_However_, these unrealistic fictional characters are heroes only in . . . stories. _Moreover_, she endured weeks of monotonous train travel during her lecture tours.
middle of the sentence	commas before and after the transitional expression	Consider, _for example_, the case of Chesley Sullenberger. Gradually, _though_, he faded from public life and quietly retired.

Read It

Each of these sentences contains a transition. Mark the transitional word or phrase, and add the correct punctuation.

a. As a result the plane landed safely.

b. Similarly the heroes who manned the volunteer armada of boats on September 11, 2001, fearlessly risked their own safety to help others.

c. Amelia Earhart on the other hand led a life filled with heroic deeds.

Write It

As you draft your argument, choose transitions that accurately show how your ideas relate to one another. Transitions may help you connect sentences, or they may help you connect one paragraph to the next.

If you want to . . .	consider using one of these transitions:
illustrate	_for example, for instance, specifically_
compare	_in the same way, similarly, likewise_
contrast	_though, conversely, however, on the other hand_
show effect	_therefore, as a result, consequently_

STANDARDS

Writing
Use words, phrases, and clauses as well as varied syntax to link the major sections of the text, create cohesion, and clarify the relationship between claim(s) and reasons, between reasons and evidence, and between claim(s) and counterclaims.

MAKING WRITING SOPHISTICATED

Using Rhetorical Devices Writers often use **rhetorical devices,** or special persuasive techniques, to make their arguments more convincing. Using rhetorical devices in your writing can help you add emphasis, point out important ideas, draw audiences into the conversation, and to highlight important concepts through rhythm and repetition. Two examples of rhetorical devices are parallelism and rhetorical questions.

- **Parallelism** occurs when similar ideas are stated in a similar grammatical form.

- A **rhetorical question** is a question asked for effect, for emphasis or for the purpose of drawing readers into the conversation. Authors do not expect answers to rhetorical questions, because the answers are obvious.

Read It These examples, both taken from the Launch Text, show how using parallelism and rhetorical questions add power and sophistication to writing by subtly emphasizing important ideas.

LAUNCH TEXT EXCERPTS

> ... Many modern fictional heroes are just as outsized. They sail through popular culture on movie screens, in comic books, and on smartphones, each moment of their lives filled with drama and weight. However, these unrealistic fictional characters are heroes only in great, entertaining stories. Today, in the twenty-first century, I believe that true heroes are most often ordinary people who in a brief moment behave heroically.
>
> Modern heroes have to deal with the same reality as the rest of us. They fill out forms, sweat in the heat, and stand in supermarket lines. If the life of a modern hero has any drama, it is in that single moment in which he or she performs one extraordinary act, garnering a brief bit of attention and earning the title of "hero." ...
>
> Some may argue that there are true larger-than-life heroes who leave a permanent shadow, not by virtue of a single act, but through a lifetime of heroic deeds. What about the life of someone such as the American aviator Amelia Earhart? Earhart's life was filled with heroism— her 1932 solo flight across the Atlantic Ocean was just one example. ...

The writer's use of parallelism emphasizes how ubiquitous fictional heroes are, in a grammatically logical way.

The writer's use of parallelism establishes a rhythm and emphasizes the various ways in which modern heroes are just like us.

The writer's use of a rhetorical question draws readers into the conversation, as well as encouraging them to think about an alternate idea.

STANDARDS

Writing
Use specific rhetorical devices to support assertions.

 College and Career Readiness

Write It

As you prepare to revise your argument, think about places where you might strengthen your writing by adding parallelism or rhetorical questions. Ask yourself the following questions:

- Are there places where I have two or more similar ideas that might be rewritten in parallel structure?

- Are there places where using parallel structure would vary my sentence structure and add emphasis to important ideas?

- Is there a place where asking a rhetorical question might be an effective way of drawing the audience into the conversation or emphasizing an important idea?

Read over your draft, and consider ways in which you might strengthen your argument either by using parallelism or by posing rhetorical questions. In the chart, record your ideas for strengthening your argument with the use of rhetorical devices.

PARAGRAPH	CHANGES RECOMMENDED	NEW WORDING

Revising
Evaluating Your Draft

Use the following checklist to evaluate the effectiveness of your first draft. Then, use your evaluation and the instruction on this page to guide your revision.

FOCUS AND ORGANIZATION	EVIDENCE AND ELABORATION	CONVENTIONS
☐ Provides an introduction that establishes a precise claim and focus.	☐ Develops the claim using relevant facts and details that provide evidence and reasons.	☐ Attends to the norms and conventions of the discipline, especially the correct use and punctuation of transitions.
☐ Distinguishes the claim from opposing claims.	☐ Provides adequate examples for each major idea.	
☐ Establishes a logical organization and develops a progression throughout the argument.	☐ Uses words, phrases, and clauses to clarify relationships among ideas.	
☐ Provides a conclusion that follows from the argument.	☐ Establishes and maintains a formal style and an objective tone.	

Revising for Purpose and Organization

Response to the Prompt Before completing your final draft, reread the prompt. Have you responded directly to the question that was asked? Have you included what was required of you? You will need to respond to prompts for college entry applications and certain standardized and professional tests. It is important to make sure that your response connects clearly to the prompt.

Revising for Conventions

Coordinating Conjunctions Combine short, choppy sentences by using coordinating conjunctions to join them. A coordinating conjunction connects words or groups of words that have equal importance in a sentence.

Choppy Sentence: Beowulf fought hard against the monster. He didn't win his last battle.

Revised Sentence: Beowulf fought hard against the monster, *but* he didn't win his last battle.

Transitional Expressions Vary your sentences and create clarity among ideas by using transitional expressions. For example, conjunctive adverbs make a transition between two independent clauses and show the relationship between the ideas in the clauses.

Unclear Relationship: The men knew that Beowulf depended on their help. They gave into their fear and abandoned their leader.

Revised Sentence: The men knew that Beowulf depended on their help; *however,* they gave into their fear and abandoned their leader.

PEER REVIEW

Exchange papers with a classmate. Use the checklist to evaluate your classmate's argument and provide supportive feedback.

1. Is the claim clear?

☐ yes ☐ no   If no, explain what confused you.

2. Did you find the argument convincing?

☐ yes ☐ no   If no, tell what you think might be missing.

3. Does the essay conclude in a logical way?

☐ yes ☐ no   If no, suggest what you might change.

4. What is the strongest part of your classmate's argument? Why?

_____

_____

_____

Editing and Proofreading

Edit for Conventions Reread your draft for accuracy and consistency. Correct errors in grammar and word usage. If you are unsure of a difficult word's precise meaning, check a dictionary before using it.

Proofread for Accuracy Read your draft carefully, looking for errors in spelling and punctuation. Correct any errors that you find.

Publishing and Presenting

Create a final version of your argument. Add it to a classroom booklet that allows you and your classmates to read and comment on each other's work. Remember to use a respectful, positive tone when commenting—your goal should be to improve your classmates' writing, not to discourage them.

Reflecting

Reflect on what you learned from writing your argument. Was the specific example you used sufficient to support your claim? Think about what you will do differently the next time you write an argument.

▤ STANDARDS

Writing
Develop and strengthen writing as needed by planning, revising, editing, rewriting, or trying a new approach, focusing on addressing what is most significant for a specific purpose and audience.

ESSENTIAL QUESTION:

What makes a hero?

As you read these selections, work with your group to explore the factors that make people heroes.

From Text to Topic In earliest British literature, the qualities a hero had to possess were obvious: tremendous physical strength, courage, and a sense of honor. However, heroism takes many forms. As you read the texts in this section, consider how they demonstrate a change in the way heroes are created and perceived.

Small-Group Learning Strategies

Throughout your life, in school, in your community, and in your career, you will continue to develop strategies when you work in teams. Use these strategies during Small-Group Learning. Add ideas of your own for each step.

STRATEGY	ACTION PLAN
Prepare	• Complete your assignment so you are prepared for group work. • Take notes on your reading so you can contribute to your group's discussions. •
Participate fully	• Make eye contact to signal that you are listening and taking in what is being said. • Use text evidence when making a point. •
Support others	• Build off ideas from others in your group. • State the relationship of your points to the points of others—whether you are supporting someone's point, refuting it, or taking the conversation in a new direction. •
Clarify	• Paraphrase the ideas of others to ensure that your understanding is correct. • Ask follow-up questions. •

CONTENTS

PERFORMANCE TASK

SPEAKING AND LISTENING FOCUS
Present an Argument

The Small-Group readings are by authors who explore how ordinary people facing extraordinary situations may—or may not—become heroes. After reading, your group will present a slide show exploring the character traits of traditional war heroes.

Working as a Team

1. **Take a Position** In your group, discuss the following question:

   Is one heroic act enough to make someone a "hero"?

   As you take turns sharing your positions, be sure to provide reasons for your choice. After all group members have shared, discuss what types of heroic acts make the most lasting impression on other people.

2. **List Your Rules** As a group, decide on the rules that you will follow as you work together. Two samples are provided. Add two more of your own. As you work together, you may add or revise rules based on your experience.

   • Group members should share responsibilities for the tasks equally.

   • Group members should stay on task.

   • _____

   _____

   • _____

   _____

3. **Apply the Rules** Share what you have learned about what makes someone a hero. Make sure each person in the group contributes. Take notes and be prepared to share with the class one thing that you heard from another member of your group.

4. **Name Your Group** Choose a name that reflects the unit topic.

   Our group's name: _____

5. **Create a Communication Plan** Decide how you want to communicate with one another. For example, you might use online collaboration tools, email, or instant messaging.

   Our group's decision: _____

   _____

Making a Schedule

First, find out the due dates for the Small-Group activities. Then, preview the texts and activities with your group, and make a schedule for completing the tasks.

SELECTION	ACTIVITIES	DUE DATE
To Lucasta, on Going to the Wars The Charge of the Light Brigade		
The Song of the Mud Dulce et Decorum Est		
How Did Harry Patch Become an Unlikely WWI Hero?		

Working on Group Projects

As your group works together, you'll find it more effective if each person has a specific role. Different projects require different roles. Before beginning a project, discuss the necessary roles, and choose one for each group member. Some possible roles are listed here. Add your ideas to the list.

Project Manager: monitors the schedule and keeps everyone on task

Researcher: organizes research activities

Recorder: takes notes during group meetings

_____

_____

_____

_____

_____

_____

_____

POETRY COLLECTION 1

Comparing Texts

In this lesson, you will compare the poems "To Lucasta, on Going to the Wars" and "The Charge of the Light Brigade" with two other poems, "The Song of the Mud" and "Dulce et Decorum Est." First, complete the first-read and close-read activities for the first two poems. The work you do with your group on these titles will prepare you for your final comparison.

POETRY COLLECTION 2

POETRY COLLECTION 1

To Lucasta, on Going to the Wars
The Charge of the Light Brigade

Concept Vocabulary

As you perform your first read of "To Lucasta, on Going to the Wars" and "The Charge of the Light Brigade," you will encounter these words.

> embrace   adore   honor

Context Clues When you read a word you don't know, you can often determine its meaning by using **context clues**—the surrounding words and phrases. The example sentence has context clues to the meaning of *idyllic*.

> **Example:** They wanted an **idyllic** setting—something <u>peaceful</u> and <u>beautiful</u>.

Apply your knowledge of context clues and other vocabulary strategies to determine the meanings of unfamiliar words you encounter during your first read.

First Read POETRY

Apply these strategies as you conduct your first read. You will have an opportunity to complete a close read after your first read.

≡ STANDARDS

Reading Literature
By the end of grade 12, read and comprehend literature, including stories, dramas, and poems, at the high end of the grades 11–CCR text complexity band independently and proficiently.

Language
• Determine or clarify the meaning of unknown and multiple-meaning words and phrases based on *grades 11–12 reading and content*, choosing flexibly from a range of strategies.

• Use context as a clue to the meaning of a word or phrase.

NOTICE *who* or *what* is "speaking" the poem and whether the poem tells a story or describes a single moment.

ANNOTATE by marking vocabulary and key passages you want to revisit.

First Read

CONNECT ideas within the selection to what you already know and what you've already read.

RESPOND by completing the Comprehension Check.

About the Poets

Richard Lovelace (1617–1657), the son of a wealthy family, publicly supported Charles I of England as the kingdom was about to plunge into civil war—resulting in Lovelace's imprisonment. During this time, he wrote "To Althea, From Prison," one of his most famous poems. He was released from prison, but when the war ended with the defeat and execution of the king, the poet was imprisoned again, for another year. Upon his final release, he returned to his home in Kent, where he continued to write. He died at the age of 39.

Alfred, Lord Tennyson (1809–1892), was the fourth of twelve children. As a teenager, Alfred was sent to Cambridge University. There he met Arthur Henry Hallam, who became his closest friend. Hallam, who intended to marry Alfred's sister, died suddenly. Grief-stricken, Tennyson wrote a series of poems as an elegy to his friend, published under the title *In Memoriam, A.H.H.* The collection so impressed Prince Albert that he encouraged Queen Victoria to name Tennyson Poet Laureate of Great Britain and Ireland.

Backgrounds

To Lucasta, on Going to the Wars

Tensions between the Church of England and the Puritans who wished to reform it had risen to a dangerous level. Foreign wars had led to a money shortage. Charles I made the situation worse by mishandling the legislature. In 1642, England's Parliament went to war against England's king. Lovelace, as a loyal supporter of Charles, wrote "To Lucasta, on Going to the Wars" as a statement of the principle that honor and loyalty to one's king must come before other considerations.

The Charge of the Light Brigade

The Battle of Balaclava, which is the subject of "The Charge of the Light Brigade," occurred during the Crimean War (1853–1856). The charge resulted in the deaths of approximately forty percent of the brigade. The war was not popular with the British middle class, and when the news came that so many had been killed and injured as the result of mistaken orders by those in command, the public was outraged. The poem, which dramatically re-creates the experience of the battle, celebrates the courage of the cavalry and the nobility of their sacrifice.

To Lucasta,
on Going to the Wars

Richard Lovelace

Tell me not, Sweet, I am unkind,
    That from the nunnery
Of thy chaste breast, and quiet mind,
    To war and arms I fly.

5 True, a new mistress now I chase,
    The first foe in the field;
And with a stronger faith **embrace**
    A sword, a horse, a shield.

10 Yet this inconstancy is such,
    As thou too shalt **adore**;
I could not love thee, Dear, so much,
    Loved I not honor more.

NOTES

Mark context clues or indicate
another strategy you used that
helped you determine meaning.

embrace (ehm BRAYS) *v.*

MEANING:

adore (uh DAWR) *v.*

MEANING:

The Charge of the Light Brigade

Alfred, Lord Tennyson

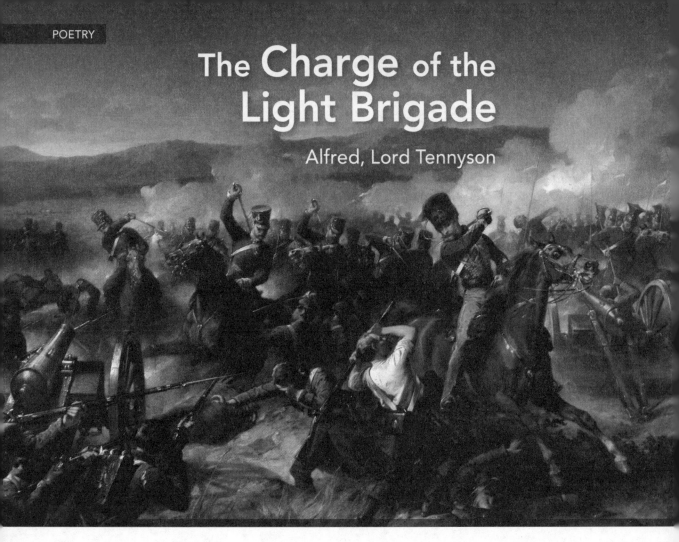

NOTES

I

Half a league,[1] half a league,
Half a league onward,
All in the valley of Death
   Rode the six hundred.
5 "Forward, the Light Brigade!
Charge for the guns!" he said.
Into the valley of Death
   Rode the six hundred.

II

"Forward, the Light Brigade!"
10 Was there a man dismayed?
Not though the soldier knew
   Someone had blundered.
Theirs not to make reply,
Theirs not to reason why,
15 Theirs but to do and die.
Into the valley of Death
   Rode the six hundred.

---

1. **half a league** about a mile and a half.

III

Cannon to right of them,
Cannon to left of them,
20 Cannon in front of them
    Volleyed and thundered;
Stormed at with shot and shell,
Boldly they rode and well,
Into the jaws of Death,
25 Into the mouth of hell
    Rode the six hundred.

IV

Flashed all their sabers bare,
Flashed as they turned in air
Sab'ring the gunners there,
30 Charging an army, while
    All the world wondered.
Plunged in the battery smoke
Right through the line they broke;
Cossack[2] and Russian
35 Reeled from the saber stroke
    Shattered and sundered.
Then they rode back, but not,
    Not the six hundred.

V

Cannon to right of them,
40 Cannon to left of them,
Cannon behind them
    Volleyed and thundered;
Stormed at with shot and shell,
While horse and hero fell,
45 They that had fought so well
Came through the jaws of Death,
Back from the mouth of hell,
All that was left of them,
    Left of six hundred.

VI

50 When can their glory fade?
O the wild charge they made!
    All the world wondered.
Honor the charge they made!
Honor the Light Brigade,
55   Noble six hundred!

NOTES

Mark context clues or indicate another strategy you used that helped you determine meaning.

honor (ON uhr) *v.*

MEANING:

---

2. **Cossack** The Cossacks were people with a tradition of independence who received privileges from the Russian government in exchange for military service.

Comprehension Check

Complete the following items after you finish your first read. Review and clarify details with your group.

TO LUCASTA, ON GOING TO THE WARS

1. Why might Lucasta think the speaker in the poem is being unkind?

2. What is the "inconstancy" that the speaker wants Lucasta to understand?

3. What is the one thing the speaker loves more than Lucasta?

THE CHARGE OF THE LIGHT BRIGADE

1. How many soldiers rode into battle?

2. What name does the speaker give the valley into which the six hundred ride?

3. What does the speaker urge readers to do at the end of the poem?

RESEARCH

Research to Clarify Choose at least one unfamiliar detail from one of the poems. Briefly research that detail. In what way does the information you learned shed light on an aspect of the poem?

Research to Explore Briefly research the English Civil War of 1642–1651, to which Lovelace refers in his poem, or the Battle of Balaclava in the Crimean War, which is the subject of Tennyson's poem. Share what you discover with your group.

Close Read the Text

With your group, revisit sections of the text you marked during your first read. **Annotate** details that you notice. What **questions** do you have? What can you **conclude**?

Analyze the Text

> **CITE TEXTUAL EVIDENCE**
> to support your answers.

📓 **Notebook** Complete the activities.

1. **Review and Clarify** With your group, discuss how lines 11–12 of "To Lucasta, on Going to the Wars" and lines 50–55 of "The Charge of the Light Brigade" reveal each poet's attitude toward war.

2. **Present and Discuss** Now, work with your group to share the passages from the two poems that you found especially important. Take turns presenting your passages. Discuss what details you noticed, what questions you asked, and what conclusions you reached.

3. **Essential Question:** *What makes a hero?* What have these two poems taught you about heroism and leadership? Discuss with your group.

> 🔵 **TIP**
>
> **GROUP DISCUSSION**
> Listen carefully as each of your group members speaks. Do not frame your questions while a person is still speaking. Often, your questions will be answered as the speaker continues.

LANGUAGE DEVELOPMENT

Concept Vocabulary

embrace	adore	honor

Why These Words? The three concept vocabulary words from the text are related. With your group, determine what the words have in common. Write your ideas, and add another word that fits the category.

> ⬛ **WORD NETWORK**
>
> Add interesting words related to heroism from the text to your Word Network.

Practice

📓 **Notebook** Confirm your understanding of the concept vocabulary words by using them in sentences. Be sure to use a synonym, an antonym, a definition, or another context clue to suggest each word's meaning.

Word Study

📓 **Notebook Latin Prefix:** *ad-* In the last stanza of "To Lucasta, on Going to the Wars," the speaker tells Lucasta, "Yet this inconstancy is such / As thou too shalt adore." The word *adore* begins with the Latin prefix *ad-*, which means "to" or "toward."

Use a dictionary to look up these words from mathematics and science: *addition, adapt, adhesive, adsorption.* Write their definitions, and explain how the prefix *ad-* contributes to their meanings.

> 📊 **STANDARDS**
>
> **Language**
> • Identify and correctly use patterns of word changes that indicate different meanings or parts of speech.
> • Consult general and specialized reference materials, both print and digital, to find the pronunciation of a word or determine or clarify its precise meaning, its part of speech, its etymology, or its standard usage.

POETRY COLLECTION 1

Analyze Craft and Structure

Word Choice and Theme A writer's **diction,** or word choice, is an important element of his or her style. It helps convey the **tone** of a work, or the writer's attitude toward his or her subject or audience. Together, word choice and tone may provide significant clues to the **theme** of a work, or the central idea or insight about life the writer wishes to convey. A single work can often have two or more themes.

In "The Charge of the Light Brigade," Tennyson uses exciting and vivid diction to set a dramatic tone in lines 44–47: "While horse and hero fell, / They that had fought so well / Came through the jaws of Death, / Back from the mouth of hell." Tennyson's word choice and tone in these lines help develop one of his themes: Soldiers are courageous and worthy of admiration.

Practice

CITE TEXTUAL EVIDENCE to support your answers.

As a group, review the Lovelace and Tennyson poems to pick out strong examples of diction. Then, complete the tone and theme columns individually, and answer the questions that follow. Compare your responses with the rest of the group once you are finished.

LITERARY WORK	DICTION	TONE	THEME(S)
The Charge of The Light Brigade			
To Lucasta, on Going to the Wars			

📧 Notebook

1. (a) In "The Charge of the Light Brigade," Tennyson frequently repeats words and phrases. What language does he repeat? (b) What is the effect of this repetition? (c) What do the repeated words and phrases suggest?

2. (a) What words reveal how the speaker in "To Lucasta, on Going to the Wars" feels about Lucasta? (b) What tone is revealed by these words? (c) What theme do these words suggest?

☰ STANDARDS

Reading Literature
• Determine two or more themes or central ideas of a text and analyze their development over the course of the text, including how they interact and build on one another to produce a complex account; provide an objective summary of the text.
• Determine the meaning of words and phrases as they are used in the text, including figurative and connotative meanings; analyze the impact of specific word choices on meaning and tone, including words with multiple meanings or language that is particularly fresh, engaging, or beautiful.

Conventions and Style

Coordinating Conjunctions A **coordinating conjunction** connects words, phrases, or clauses that have equal importance in a sentence. The seven coordinating conjunctions are *and, but, yet, or, nor, for,* and *so.*

Writers use coordinating conjunctions to establish logical relationships among ideas. Different coordinating conjunctions show different relationships. *And* shows addition or similarity. *But* and *yet* indicate contrast. *Or* and *nor* indicate a choice. *For* and *so* show a cause or a result.

For example, Lovelace uses conjunctions to show addition and contrast.

> To war *and* arms I fly. (addition)

> *Yet* this inconstancy is such (contrast)

Writers also use coordinating conjunctions to vary sentence structure. For example, Tennyson uses them to create simple pairs of words, such as "volleyed and thundered" and "shot and shell." However, he chooses not to use them to link phrases and clauses. This omission creates a compressed, energetic rhythm. Notice the effect of these famous lines with and without a coordinating conjunction:

With Conjunctions: Cannon to right of them, / Cannon to left of them, / *and* Cannon in front of them

Without Conjunctions: Cannon to right of them, / Cannon to left of them, / Cannon in front of them

Read It

In each example from the poems, identify the coordinating conjunction and the words that it connects.

1. True, a new mistress now I chase, / The first foe in the field; / And with a stronger faith embrace / A sword, a horse, a shield

2. Theirs … to do and die.

3. **Connect to Style** Reread lines 35–38 of "The Charge of the Light Brigade." Identify any coordinating conjunctions, and explain how they help increase the dramatic impact of the poem.

Write It

 Notebook Use a coordinating conjunction to create a sentence that logically links each pair of clauses. Then, rewrite the sentence to make it concise. Explain the relationship created by the conjunction.

1. The speaker tells his side of the story. He does not reveal how Lucasta feels.

2. The men rode into the jaws of hell. The men were extremely courageous.

TIP

PUNCTUATION
- When a coordinating conjunction joins two words, phrases, or subordinate clauses, no comma is needed.
- When a coordinating conjunction joins three or more elements, insert a comma between each element.
- When a coordinating conjunction joins two independent clauses, use a comma before the conjunction.

STANDARDS

Language
- Demonstrate command of the conventions of standard English grammar and usage when writing or speaking.
- Demonstrate command of the conventions of standard English capitalization, punctuation, and spelling when writing.
- Apply knowledge of language to understand how language functions in different contexts, to make effective choices for meaning or style, and to comprehend more fully when reading or listening.

POETRY COLLECTION 1

Comparing Texts

You will now read two more poems, "The Song of the Mud" and "Dulce et Decorum Est." First, complete the first-read and close-read activities. Then, compare the literary elements in "To Lucasta, on Going to the Wars" and "The Charge of the Light Brigade" with the elements in these poems.

POETRY COLLECTION 2

POETRY COLLECTION 2

The Song of the Mud
Dulce et Decorum Est

Concept Vocabulary

As you perform your first read of "The Song of the Mud" and "Dulce et Decorum Est," you will encounter these words.

impertinent	putrid	vile

Context Clues When you come upon a word in a text that you don't know, you can often determine its meaning by using **context clues**—the surrounding words and phrases. These clues may include synonyms, antonyms, definitions, or elaborating details.

> **Example/Antonyms:** His honesty made him an ideal candidate, in contrast to the **duplicity** of his opponent.

Apply your knowledge of context clues and other vocabulary strategies to determine the meanings of unfamiliar words you encounter during your first read.

First Read POETRY

Apply these strategies as you conduct your first read. You will have an opportunity to complete a close read after your first read.

STANDARDS

Reading Literature
By the end of grade 12, read and comprehend literature, including stories, dramas, and poems, at the high end of the grades 11–CCR text complexity band independently and proficiently.

Language
• Determine or clarify the meaning of unknown and multiple-meaning words and phrases *based on grades 11–12 reading and content*, choosing flexibly from a range of strategies.
• Use context as a clue to the meaning of a word or phrase.

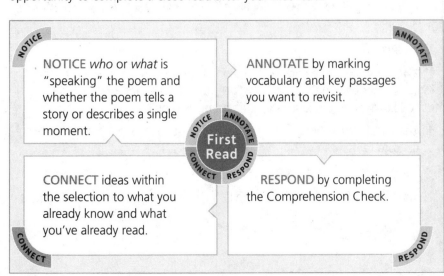

NOTICE *who* or *what* is "speaking" the poem and whether the poem tells a story or describes a single moment.

ANNOTATE by marking vocabulary and key passages you want to revisit.

CONNECT ideas within the selection to what you already know and what you've already read.

RESPOND by completing the Comprehension Check.

First Read

About the Poets

Mary Borden (1886–1968) was born in Chicago to a wealthy family. When World War I broke out, she worked as a nurse in a field hospital that she had equipped with her own money. During this time, she wrote "The Song of the Mud." She continued to write after the war and published *The Forbidden Zone*, a book of short stories, in 1929. During World War II, she helped set up an ambulance unit that supported the exiled French government's forces in the Middle East, Africa, and Europe.

Wilfred Owen (1893–1918) was one of the most memorable poets of World War I. He had always wanted to be a poet, and his experiences as a soldier gave him his voice. He was a teacher when he enlisted in the British army in 1915. He experienced shell shock and was sent back to England. While in the hospital there, he met a fellow poet, Siegfried Sassoon, who encouraged him to explore his war experiences in poetry. Owen returned to the Front, eventually earning the Military Cross for his courage. He was killed in battle in 1918.

Backgrounds

The Song of the Mud

The trenches of World War I were constantly being eroded by weather. Rains turned battlefields to mud, and trenches were filled with water. Rats abounded, and they ate the men's food and chewed on the corpses. Trench foot, a fungal disease, was common because of the muddy environment. In extreme cases, the soldier's foot would have to be amputated. Lice caused trench fever, another illness that thrived in the unhealthy mud at the Front.

Dulce et Decorum Est

Great Britain had no propaganda machine at the beginning of World War I, but British schoolboys had long been exposed to the idea that it was a noble thing to die for one's country. They studied the Latin poet Horace, who had written that death for one's country is "sweet and honorable." British war heroes were venerated. The reality of war, however, contradicted the subtle propaganda of the schoolroom. The sheer misery of life in the trenches and the unconscionable loss of a generation of young men revealed the underlying reality.

The Song of the Mud

Mary Borden

This is the song of the mud,
The pale yellow glistening mud that covers the hills like satin;
The gray gleaming silvery mud that is spread like enamel over the
    valleys;
The frothing, squirting, spurting, liquid mud that gurgles along the
    road beds;
5 The thick elastic mud that is kneaded and pounded and squeezed
    under the hoofs of the horses;
The invincible, inexhaustible mud of the war zone.
This is the song of the mud, the uniform of the poilu.[1]
His coat is of mud, his great dragging flapping coat, that is too big for
    him and too heavy;
His coat that once was blue and now is gray and stiff with the mud
    that cakes to it.
10 This is the mud that clothes him. His trousers and boots are of mud,
And his skin is of mud;
And there is mud in his beard.

---

1. **poilu** (pwah LOO) *n.* French for "hairy one;" a slang term for French soldiers during
    World War I.

His head is crowned with a helmet of mud.
He wears it well.

15 He wears it as a king wears the ermine[2] that bores him.
He has set a new style in clothing;
He has introduced the chic of mud.
This is the song of the mud that wriggles its way into battle.
The **impertinent**, the intrusive, the ubiquitous, the unwelcome,

20 The slimy inveterate nuisance,
That fills the trenches,
That mixes in with the food of the soldiers,
That spoils the working of motors and crawls into their secret parts,
That spreads itself over the guns,

25 That sucks the guns down and holds them fast in its slimy
        voluminous lips,
That has no respect for destruction and muzzles the bursting shells;
And slowly, softly, easily,
Soaks up the fire, the noise; soaks up the energy and the courage;
Soaks up the power of armies;

30 Soaks up the battle.
Just soaks it up and thus stops it.
This is the hymn of mud—the obscene, the filthy, the **putrid**,
The vast liquid grave of our armies. It has drowned our men.
Its monstrous distended belly reeks with the undigested dead.

35 Our men have gone into it, sinking slowly, and struggling and
        slowly disappearing.
Our fine men, our brave, strong, young men;
Our glowing red, shouting, brawny men.
Slowly, inch by inch, they have gone down into it,
Into its darkness, its thickness, its silence.

40 Slowly, irresistibly, it drew them down, sucked them down,
And they were drowned in thick, bitter, heaving mud.
Now it hides them, Oh, so many of them!
Under its smooth glistening surface it is hiding them blandly.
There is not a trace of them.

45 There is no mark where they went down.
The mute enormous mouth of the mud has closed over them.
This is the song of the mud,
The beautiful glistening golden mud that covers the hills like satin;
The mysterious gleaming silvery mud that is spread like enamel over
        the valleys.

50 Mud, the disguise of the war zone;
Mud, the mantle of battles;
Mud, the smooth fluid grave of our soldiers:
This is the song of the mud.

NOTES

Mark context clues or indicate another strategy you used that helped you determine meaning.

impertinent (ihm PURT uhn uhnt) *adj.*

MEANING:

Mark context clues or indicate another strategy you used that helped you determine meaning.

putrid (PYOO trihd) *adj.*

MEANING:

2. **ermine** (UR mihn) *n.* soft white fur from a type of weasel, historically used to trim royal robes in Europe.

Dulce et Decorum Est

Wilfred Owen

Bent double, like old beggars under sacks,
Knock-kneed, coughing like hags, we cursed through sludge,
Till on the haunting flares we turned our backs
And towards our distant rest began to trudge.
5 Men marched asleep. Many had lost their boots
But limped on, blood-shod. All went lame; all blind;
Drunk with fatigue; deaf even to the hoots
Of tired, outstripped Five-Nines[1] that dropped behind.

Gas! GAS! Quick, boys!—An ecstasy of fumbling,
10 Fitting the clumsy helmets just in time;
But someone still was yelling out and stumbling
And flound'ring like a man in fire or lime . . .
Dim, through the misty panes and thick green light,
As under a green sea, I saw him drowning.

15 In all my dreams, before my helpless sight,
He plunges at me, guttering, choking, drowning.

If in some smothering dreams you too could pace
Behind the wagon that we flung him in,
And watch the white eyes writhing in his face,
20 His hanging face, like a devil's sick of sin;
If you could hear, at every jolt, the blood
Come gargling from the froth-corrupted lungs,
Obscene as cancer, bitter as the cud
Of vile, incurable sores on innocent tongues,—
25 My friend, you would not tell with such high zest
To children ardent for some desperate glory,
The old Lie: *Dulce et Decorum est*
Pro patria mori.[2]

NOTES

Mark context clues or indicate another strategy you used that helped you determine meaning.

vile (vyl) adj.

MEANING:

---

1. **Five-Nines** 5.9-inch artillery shells.
2. ***Dulce et Decorum est / Pro patria mori*** Latin for "it is sweet and honorable to die for one's country," a line from the Roman poet Horace's *Odes.*

Comprehension Check

Complete the following items after you finish your first read. Review and clarify details with your group.

THE SONG OF THE MUD

1. What specific mud is the speaker describing in this poem?

2. According to the speaker, for what does the mud have no respect?

3. According to the speaker, with what does the "belly" of the mud reek?

DULCE ET DECORUM EST

1. Describe the soldiers' physical state at the beginning of the poem.

2. What causes one of the soldiers to "drown" in the second stanza?

3. What is the source of the poem's title?

- -

RESEARCH

Research to Clarify Choose at least one unfamiliar detail from one of the poems. Briefly research that detail. In what way does the information you learned shed light on an aspect of the poem?

Research to Explore Briefly research the conditions of trench warfare in World War I. Share what you discover with your group.

Close Read the Text

With your group, revisit sections of the text you marked during your first read. **Annotate** details that you notice. What **questions** do you have? What can you **conclude**?

POETRY COLLECTION 2

Analyze the Text

CITE TEXTUAL EVIDENCE
to support your answers.

Complete the activities.

1. **Review and Clarify** With your group, discuss how lines 40–46 of "The Song of the Mud" and lines 21–28 of "Dulce et Decorum Est" reveal each poet's attitude toward war.

2. **Present and Discuss** Now, work with your group to share the passages from the two selections that you found especially important. Take turns presenting your passages. Discuss what details you noticed, what questions you asked, and what conclusions you reached.

3. **Essential Question:** *What makes a hero?* What have these two poems taught you about heroism and leadership? Discuss with your group.

TIP

GROUP DISCUSSION
Encourage speakers by paying close attention to them. Make eye contact and lean forward when they make key points. Nod to show that you understand something the speaker is saying. Doing so helps the speaker express his or her ideas more easily.

LANGUAGE DEVELOPMENT

Concept Vocabulary

| impertinent | putrid | vile |

Why These Words? The three concept vocabulary words from the text are related. With your group, determine what the words have in common. Write your ideas, and add another word that fits the category.

Practice

📓 **Notebook** Confirm your understanding of the concept vocabulary words by using them in sentences. Be sure to include context clues that suggest each word's meaning.

Word Study

📓 **Notebook** **Denotation and Connotation** *Impertinent, rude,* and *bold* have the same denotation (dictionary meaning) but different connotations (emotional overtones). *Impertinent,* which suggests that someone is being intrusive or presumptuous, has a less negative connotation than *rude,* which suggests an insolent or vulgar lack of respect. *Bold* has the same denotation as *impertinent* and *rude* but a more positive connotation, as it suggests that someone is courageously breaking the rules for good reason. Look up the words *putrid* and *vile* in a thesaurus and in a college-level dictionary. Find three synonyms for each word, and write a sentence for each synonym. Use the sentences to show how the connotations of the synonyms differ.

WORD NETWORK

Add interesting words related to heroism from the text to your Word Network.

STANDARDS

Language
• Consult general and specialized reference materials, both print and digital, to find the pronunciation of a word or determine or clarify its precise meaning, its part of speech, its etymology, or its standard usage.
• Demonstrate understanding of figurative language, word relationships, and nuances in word meanings.
• Analyze nuances in the meaning of words with similar denotations.

POETRY COLLECTION 2

Analyze Craft and Structure

Word Choice and Theme A writer's **diction**, or word choice, is an important part of his or her style. Diction helps to convey the writer's **tone,** or attitude toward his or her subject or audience. Many writers also use **irony**—words used to suggest the opposite of their usual meaning—to convey tone and meaning. Together, word choice, tone, and the use of irony may provide significant clues to the **theme** of a work, or the central idea or insight about life the writer wishes to convey.

The title of "The Song of the Mud" suggests a cheerful message, but the poem is anything but cheerful. This use of irony, as well as word choice throughout the poem, helps to convey one of the poem's themes: War, like mud, is indifferent to human suffering.

Practice

CITE TEXTUAL EVIDENCE
to support your answers.

As a group, review the Borden and Owen poems to identify powerful words and phrases. Then, complete the tone, irony, and theme columns individually, and answer the questions that follow. Compare your responses with the rest of the group once you are finished.

LITERARY WORK	DICTION	TONE	IRONY	THEME(S)
The Song of the Mud				
Dulce et Decorum Est				

📓 **Notebook** Respond to the following questions, and share your responses with the group.

1. **(a)** In lines 16–17 of "The Song of the Mud," the speaker describes the soldiers covered in mud as setting "a new style in clothing" and introducing "the chic of mud." Explain how these descriptions are examples of irony. **(b)** How does word choice, tone, and the use of irony in these lines reveal the theme that war does not care about human suffering?

2. **(a)** In the opening lines of "Dulce et Decorum Est," the speaker compares the soldiers to "old beggars under sacks, / Knock-kneed, coughing like hags. . . ." What tone does Owens's word choice convey? **(b)** What larger message about warfare do the word choice and tone of the poem reveal?

3. What additional themes related to war and people's responsibility in it are revealed in these poems?

TIP

CLARIFICATION

Literary works often have more than one theme, and the themes may even appear to be contradictory. That is because writers often convey layers of meaning, especially in poems.

STANDARDS

Reading Literature
• Determine two or more themes or central ideas of a text and analyze their development over the course of the text, including how they interact and build on one another to produce a complex account; provide an objective summary of the text.
• Determine the meaning of words and phrases as they are used in the text, including figurative and connotative meanings; analyze the impact of specific word choices on meaning and tone, including words with multiple meanings or language that is particularly fresh, engaging, or beautiful.
• Analyze a case in which grasping point of view requires distinguishing what is directly stated in a text from what is really meant.

Conventions and Style

Types of Phrases A **preposition** shows the relationship between a noun or pronoun and another word in a sentence. A **prepositional phrase** consists of a preposition and a noun or pronoun, known as the **object of the preposition**, as well as any modifiers it may have. Writers use prepositional phrases to add detail to sentences.

A prepositional phrase acts as either an adjective or an adverb within a sentence. It acts as an adjective if it modifies a noun or pronoun by telling *what kind* or *which one*. It acts as an adverb if it modifies a verb, an adjective, or an adverb by telling *where, why, when, in what way,* or *to what extent.*

In this chart, the prepositional phrases are underlined, and the words they modify are in boldface.

EXAMPLE	FUNCTION	TELLS
Eliza appreciates the **beauty** of a well-crafted poem.	adjective	*what kind*
She finds Owen's **poem** about the gas attack moving.	adjective	*which one*
She **reads** all of his poems with great pleasure.	adverb	*in what way*
Their imagery **lingers** in her mind long afterward.	adverb	*where*

Read It

1. Mark the prepositional phrase in each line from "The Song of the Mud." Then, indicate whether it is acting as an adjective or as an adverb.

    a. The invincible, inexhaustible mud of the war zone.

    b. Slowly, inch by inch, they have gone down into it.

    c. Under its smooth glistening surface it is holding them blandly.

2. **Connect to Style** Reread the last stanza of "Dulce et Decorum Est." Mark two prepositional phrases used as adverbs. Indicate which word each phrase is modifying. Then, explain how the use of that phrase conveys something about the gas attack in a unique way.

Write It

📓 **Notebook** Expand these sentences by adding prepositional phrases. You may use multiple phrases in a sentence.

> **Example:** The mud spoils the motors.
> The mud spoils the motors and crawls into their secret parts.

1. The soldiers move.
2. The mud spread.

STANDARDS

Language
• Demonstrate command of the conventions of standard English grammar and usage when writing or speaking.
• Apply knowledge of language to understand how language functions in different contexts, to make effective choices for meaning or style, and to comprehend more fully when reading or listening.

POETRY COLLECTION 1

POETRY COLLECTION 2

Writing to Compare

You have read two sets of poems about war: "To Lucasta, on Going to the Wars" and "The Charge of the Light Brigade," written in the seventeenth and nineteenth centuries; and "The Song of the Mud" and "Dulce et Decorum Est," written in the twentieth century. Now, deepen your understanding of both sets of poems by comparing the poets' use of **diction,** their word choices and arrangement of words and phrases. Note that diction helps convey a writer's **tone,** or attitude toward a subject. Together, diction and tone give significant clues to the **theme**, or central idea, of a work.

Assignment

The two sets of poems share a topic, but they are very different in diction and tone. Write a **compare-and-contrast essay** in which you analyze the diction and tone of Lovelace's and Tennyson's poems and the diction and tone of Borden's and Owen's poems. Draw conclusions about how the poets use these elements to develop one or more themes.

Planning and Prewriting

Analyze the Texts With your group, identify words and phrases in each set of poems that have strong connotations or are used in surprising or effective ways. Discuss the specific effects that the diction of each passage has on the reader. Use the chart to record your ideas.

POEM	WORDS / PHRASES	EFFECT OF DICTION
To Lucasta, on Going to the Wars		
The Charge of the Light Brigade		
The Song of the Mud		
Dulce et Decorum Est		

Notebook Respond to these questions.

1. In what ways are the poets' attitudes toward war similar and different?

2. What theme(s) do the diction and tone of each set of poems suggest?

Drafting

Write a Working Thesis Work independently. First, review your Prewriting notes. Then, write one or two sentences stating the central idea, or thesis, you will develop. Your thesis should clearly state how the diction in each set of poems creates particular tones and suggests certain themes.

Choose Evidence Identify passages you will use to illustrate and support your ideas. Share your choices with the group. After sharing, change your choices, if you wish.

Passage: _____

Idea it Supports: _____

Passage: _____

Idea it Supports: _____

Passage: _____

Idea it Supports: _____

Passage: _____

Idea it Supports: _____

Organize Ideas Consider using one of the following two structures. With your group, discuss the pros and cons of each.

Block Organization

I. Poetry Collection 1 ("To Lucasta . . ."; "The Charge of the Light Brigade")
   A. how diction helps create tone
   B. how diction and tone suggest certain themes

II. Poetry Collection 2 ("The Song of the Mud"; "Dulce et Decorum Est")
   A. how diction helps create tone
   B. how diction and tone suggest certain themes

Point-by-Point Organization

I. How diction contributes to the tones of the poems
   A. "To Lucasta . . ." and "The Charge of the Light Brigade"
   B. "The Song of the Mud" and "Dulce et Decorum Est"

II. How diction and tone suggest certain themes
   A. "To Lucasta . . ." and "The Charge of the Light Brigade"
   B. "The Song of the Mud" and "Dulce et Decorum Est"

Review, Revise, and Edit

Share your completed draft with your group. Ask for feedback about the clarity of your thesis, the integrity of your organization, the strength of your evidence, and the effectiveness of your conclusion. Use your group members' feedback to refine your draft.

EVIDENCE LOG

Before moving on to a new selection, go to your Evidence Log and record what you have learned from Poetry Collection 1 and Poetry Collection 2.

STANDARDS

Writing
• Write informative/explanatory texts to examine and convey complex ideas, concepts, and information clearly and accurately through the effective selection, organization, and analysis of content.
• Introduce a topic; organize complex ideas, concepts, and information to make important connections and distinctions; including formatting, graphics, and multimedia when useful to aiding comprehension.
• Apply *grades 11–12 Reading standards* to literature.

Speaking and Listening
• Initiate and participate effectively in a range of collaborative discussions with diverse partners on *grades 11–12 topics, texts, and issues,* building on others' ideas and expressing their own clearly and persuasively.
• Come to discussions prepared, having read and researched material under study; explicitly draw on that preparation by referring to evidence from texts and other research on the topic or issue to stimulate a thoughtful, well-reasoned exchange of ideas.

About the Source

BBC iWonder The British Broadcasting Corporation (BBC) has used its new digital learning program, iWonder, to create interactive guides on a series of thought-provoking subjects. Using archival footage, interviews, and original material, iWonder created this interactive guide to the heroes of World War I.

How Did Harry Patch Become an Unlikely WWI Hero?

Media Vocabulary

The following words will be helpful to you as you analyze, discuss, and write about interactive websites.

navigation: moving from place to place on a website or on the Internet to find information	• Navigation within a website often involves using a navigation bar at the top or side of the screen. • Navigation may involve following links to other websites.
embedded video: video that has been placed within the HTML (HyperText Markup Language) code of a Web page	• *Embedding* is the act of putting a video or other piece of media on a website. • Many websites contain embedded videos that provide additional information on a subject.
slide show: presentation based on or supplemented by a series of still images	• Slide shows can be simple or complex, depending on the number of images and whether there are links to related images or text. • Slide shows are often useful when giving presentations.

First Review MEDIA: INTERACTIVE WEBSITE

Apply these strategies as you conduct your first review. You will have an opportunity to complete a close review after your first review.

EXPLORE the interactive media to learn about the ideas it presents.

NOTE elements that you find interesting and want to revisit.

First Review

CONNECT ideas in the interactive media to other media you've experienced, texts you've read, or images you've seen.

RESPOND by completing the Comprehension Check.

STANDARDS

Reading Informational Text
By the end of grade 12, read and comprehend literary nonfiction at the high end of the grades 11–CCR text complexity band independently and proficiently.

Language
Acquire and use accurately general academic and domain-specific words and phrases, sufficient for reading, writing, speaking, and listening at the college and career readiness level; demonstrate independence in gathering vocabulary knowledge when considering a word or phrase important to comprehension or expression.

How Did Harry Patch Become an Unlikely WWI Hero?

BBC iWonder

BACKGROUND

The soldiers of World War I were fighting a new kind of war with far more potent weapons than those of the previous century. After the Allied victory at the Battle of the Marne, both sides dug in for a conflict that was more costly in lives and equipment than either side had anticipated. They dug in literally; trenches snaked their way across Europe from northern Belgium to the French border with Switzerland. The two armies lived in and fought from the trenches. The soldiers existed in abysmal conditions and constant danger. It was appropriate that the world eventually came to recognize the heroism of the common soldier.

NOTES

Comprehension Check

Complete the following items after you finish your first review. Review and clarify details with your group.

1. For what is Harry Patch most well-known?

2. The website depicts heroic women in what profession?

3. What is the difference between the two World War I medals that Harry Patch received?

4. Identify a hero or group of heroes that one of the commentators mentions on the final page of the website.

MEDIA VOCABULARY

Use these words as you discuss, analyze, and write about the selection.

navigation
embedded video
slide show

🔀 WORD NETWORK

Add interesting words related to heroism from the website to your Word Network.

Close Review

With your group, revisit the interactive website and your first-review notes. Record any new observations that seem important. What **questions** do you have? What can you **conclude**?

Analyze the Media

CITE TEXTUAL EVIDENCE to support your answers.

Complete the activities.

1. **Review and Clarify** With your group, review material about Harry Patch's role in World War I. Discuss how Harry Patch became a hero.

2. **Present and Discuss** Now, work with your group to share parts of the interactive website you found especially important. Take turns presenting what you found. Discuss what details you noticed, what questions you asked, and what conclusions you reached.

3. **Essential Question:** *What makes a hero?* What has this selection revealed about the relationship between heroism and leadership? Discuss with your group.

Writing to Sources

Assignment

Write a brief **critical analysis** of the website in one to three paragraphs.

- Summarize the main point the site makes about heroism.
- Discuss the way the site draws on visuals and audio to support its point.
- Conclude your analysis by listing one aspect of the site you found effective and one you think might be improved.

HOW DID HARRY PATCH BECOME AN UNLIKELY WWI HERO?

Research

Assignment

With your group, find out more about how World War I differed from previous wars and helped change people's attitudes toward war. Use print and online sources and summarize what you have learned in a **research overview**, listing three to five main conclusions with supporting references. Assess the strengths and limitations of each source you chose. Choose from the following topics.

☐ the roles of a variety of participants in World War I, including such figures as generals, infantry soldiers, cavalrymen, nurses, ambulance drivers, stretcher-bearers, and fighter pilots.

☐ technology in World War I, including the importance of railroads, motorized vehicles, and horses.

☐ trench warfare, including the digging, arrangement, and size of the trenches as well as the conditions, hazards, and physical misery of the trench environment.

As you research online, use advanced search techniques to locate targeted information.

Quotation Marks: Quotation marks indicate that you want information that includes a specific phrase. For example: if you search for "Battle of Passchendaele," your results will be limited to only those sites containing that exact phrase.

"Or" Search: If you use several keywords in your search, your results will include sites that contain both words—this is called an "AND" search. If you want results that contain either of the terms, use "OR."
Example: "Harry Patch" OR "Battle of Passchendaele"

Asterisk Search: If you're not exactly sure of a term or its spelling, use an asterisk.
Example: "Battle of *"

📝 **EVIDENCE LOG**

Before moving on to a new selection, go to your log and record what you learned from "How Did Harry Patch Become an Unlikely WWI Hero?"

STANDARDS
Writing
• Write informative/explanatory texts to examine and convey complex ideas, concepts, and information clearly and accurately through the effective selection, organization, and analysis of content.

• Conduct short as well as more sustained research projects to answer a question or solve a problem; narrow or broaden the inquiry when appropriate; synthesize multiple sources on the subject, demonstrating understanding of the subject under investigation.

• Gather relevant information from multiple authoritative print and digital sources, using advanced searches effectively; assess the strengths and limitations of each source in terms of the task, purpose, and audience; integrate information into the text selectively to maintain the flow of ideas, avoiding plagiarism and overreliance on any one source and following a standard format for citation.

Present an Argument

Assignment

You have just finished reading an assortment of poems and a Web page that deal with the heroes of wartime. Work with your group to develop a scripted **slide show** that addresses this question:

> What heroic traits does the traditional war hero exhibit?

Plan With Your Group

Analyze the Text With your group, discuss the personality traits that apply to the heroes of each selection. Note any discrepancies or differences among them. Then, make a list of traits that seem typical, and develop a claim. Use the chart to capture your observations.

TITLE	HEROIC TRAITS
To Lucasta, on Going to the Wars	
The Charge of the Light Brigade	
The Song of the Mud	
Dulce et Decorum Est	
How Did Harry Patch Become an Unlikely WWI Hero?	
The heroic traits that apply to the traditional war hero include these:	

Gather Evidence and Media Examples Find specific details from the texts to support your claim. Then, work with group members to locate online photographs, artwork, or video clips that illustrate your claim. Divide the work either by text or by the traits you included in your claim.

STANDARDS

Writing
Use technology, including the Internet, to produce, publish, and update individual or shared writing products in response to ongoing feedback, including new arguments or information.

Speaking and Listening
• Initiate and participate effectively in a range of collaborative discussions with diverse partners on *grades 11–12 topics, texts, and issues,* building on others' ideas and expressing their own clearly and persuasively.
• Respond thoughtfully to diverse perspectives; synthesize comments, claims, and evidence made on all sides of an issue; resolve contradictions when possible; and determine what additional information or research is required to deepen the investigation or complete the task.

Organize Your Presentation Start by organizing your visuals in an order that makes sense to the group. Then, write a script for your slide show. Include a line or two of text for each slide in your presentation. Assign members of your group to read the script as the slides are shown.

Rehearse With Your Group

Practice With Your Group View the slides, with assigned readers reading the script. Use this checklist to evaluate the effectiveness of your group's first run-through. Then, use your evaluation and these instructions to guide your revision.

CONTENT	USE OF MEDIA	PRESENTATION TECHNIQUES
☐ The presentation answers the question in the assignment.	☐ Equipment functions properly.	☐ Visuals are clear and ordered logically.
☐ Slides illuminate and support the claim.	☐ Script and slides are synchronized.	☐ Speakers use eye contact and speak clearly.
		☐ Transitions between slides and between speakers are smooth.

Fine-Tune the Content If necessary, replace slides with visuals that better support your claim. Do you have too many slides representing a single heroic trait and only a few or none representing another? Strive to create a balanced presentation.

Improve Your Timing of Media Time your slides so that they match up with the script. You may find that moving from slide to slide manually works better than setting an automatic time for each slide.

Practice Your Presentation Techniques Your audience will enjoy your presentation more if every script reader speaks expressively and clearly, and at an appropriate volume and rate. Practice the script until the transitions from one reader to another flow naturally.

Present and Evaluate

As you present your slideshow, be alert to your audience. Do they understand your claim and appreciate your visuals? As you watch other groups' slide shows, consider how your presentations are alike and different.

≣ STANDARDS
Speaking and Listening
Make strategic use of digital media in presentations to enhance understanding of findings, reasoning, and evidence and to add interest.

ESSENTIAL QUESTION:

What makes a hero?

Heroism may be inspired by many different motivations, including love of country, belief in certain ideals, or a desire for fame and recognition. In this section, you will choose one additional selection about heroism for your final reading experience in this unit. Follow these steps to help you choose.

Look Back Think about the selections you have already studied. Which aspects of heroism do you wish to explore further? Which time period interests you the most?

Look Ahead Preview the texts by reading the descriptions. Which one seems most interesting and appealing to you?

Look Inside Take a few minutes to scan the text you chose. Choose a different one if this text doesn't meet your needs.

Independent Learning Strategies

Throughout your life, in school, in your community, and in your career, you will need to rely on yourself to learn and work on your own. Review these strategies and the actions you can take to practice them during Independent Learning. Add ideas of your own for each category.

STRATEGY	ACTION PLAN
Create a schedule	• Understand your goals and deadlines. • Make a plan for what to do each day. •
Practice what you have learned	• Use first-read and close-read strategies to deepen your understanding. • After reading, evaluate the usefulness of the evidence to help you understand the topic. • After reading, consult reference sources for background information that can help you clarify meaning. •
Take notes	• Record important ideas and information. • Review notes before taking your next step. •

CONTENTS

Choose one selection. Selections are available online only.

PERFORMANCE-BASED ASSESSMENT PREP

Review Evidence for an Argument
Complete your Evidence Log for the unit by evaluating what you have learned and synthesizing the information you have recorded.

First-Read Guide

Use this page to record your first-read ideas.

🔧 **Tool Kit**
First-Read Guide and
Model Annotation

Selection Title: _____

NOTICE new information or ideas you learn about the unit topic as you first read this text.

ANNOTATE by marking vocabulary and key passages you want to revisit.

CONNECT ideas within the selection to other knowledge, the Essential Question, and the selections you have read. Use reliable reference material to clarify historical context.

RESPOND by writing a brief summary of the selection.

NOTICE ANNOTATE
First
Read
CONNECT RESPOND

STANDARD
Reading Read and comprehend complex literary and informational texts independently and proficiently.

Close-Read Guide

Tool Kit
Close-Read Guide and
Model Annotation

Use this page to record your close-read ideas.

Selection Title: _____

Close Read the Text

Revisit sections of the text you marked during your first read. Read these sections closely and **annotate** what you notice. Ask yourself **questions** about the text. What can you **conclude**? Write down your ideas.

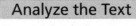

Analyze the Text

Think about the author's choices of patterns, structure, techniques, and ideas included in the text. Select one and record your thoughts about what this choice conveys.

QuickWrite

Pick a paragraph from the text that grabbed your interest. Explain the power of this passage.

_____
_____
_____
_____
_____
_____
_____
_____
_____

STANDARD
Reading Read and comprehend complex literary and informational texts independently and proficiently.

Share Your Independent Learning

Prepare to Share

What makes a hero?

Even if you read something independently, your understanding continues to grow when you share what you have learned with others. Reflect on the text you explored independently and write notes about its connection to the unit. In your notes, consider why this text belongs in this unit.

Learn From Your Classmates

💬 **Discuss It** Share your ideas about the text you explored on your own. As you talk with others in your class, jot down ideas you learned from them.

Reflect

Review your notes, and mark the most important insight you gained from these writing and discussion activities. Explain how this idea adds to your understanding of what makes a hero.

Review Evidence for an Argument

At the beginning of this unit, you took a position on the following question:

Which contributes more to heroism—sacrifice or success?

✐ EVIDENCE LOG

Review your Evidence Log and your QuickWrite from the beginning of the unit. Have your ideas changed?

☐ YES	☐ NO
Identify at least three pieces of evidence that caused you to reevaluate your ideas.	Identify at least three pieces of evidence that reinforced your original position.
1.	1.
2.	2.
3.	3.

State your position now: _____

_____

_____

Identify a possible counterargument: _____

_____

_____

Evaluate the Strength of Your Evidence Consider your argument. Do you have enough evidence to support your claim? Do you have enough evidence to refute a counterclaim? If not, make a plan.

☐ Do some research   ☐ Talk with my classmates

☐ Reread a selection   ☐ Talk with a friend or family member

☐ Other:_____

⊞ STANDARDS

Writing
Introduce precise, knowledgeable claim(s), establish the significance of the claim(s), distinguish the claim(s) from alternate or opposing claims, and create an organization that logically sequences claim(s), counterclaims, reasons, and evidence.

SOURCES

- WHOLE-CLASS SELECTIONS
- SMALL-GROUP SELECTIONS
- INDEPENDENT-LEARNING SELECTION

PART 1
Writing to Sources: Argument

In this unit, you have read an epic, a graphic novel, poems, and a website, all dealing with some aspect of heroism. Depending on their authors and the times in which they were composed, the selections reveal a variety of attitudes about heroism and leadership.

Assignment

Write an argument in which you offer a response to this question:

> **Which contributes more to heroism—sacrifice or success?**

Begin by deciding on your claim and stating it as part of a concise introduction. Use credible evidence from the texts you have read and from your own experience to support your assertion. As you write, think about what someone might say to refute your argument. Make sure that your argument addresses those contradictory ideas.

Reread the Assignment Review the assignment to be sure you fully understand it. The assignment references some of the academic words presented at the beginning of the unit. Be sure you understand each of the words in order to complete the assignment correctly.

Academic Vocabulary

purport	credible	assertion
presume	contradictory	

Review the Elements of an Argument Before you begin writing, read the Argument Rubric. Once you have completed your first draft, check it against the rubric. If one or more of the elements is missing or not as strong as it could be, revise your argument to add or strengthen that component.

⚒ WORD NETWORK

As you write and revise your argument, use your Word Network to help vary your word choices.

☰ STANDARDS

Writing
- Write arguments to support claims in an analysis of substantive topics or texts, using valid reasoning and relevant and sufficient evidence.
- Draw evidence from literary or informational texts to support analysis, reflection, and research.
- Write routinely over extended time frames and shorter time frames for a range of tasks, purposes, and audiences.

Argument Rubric

	Focus and Organization	Evidence and Elaboration	Language Conventions
4	The introduction is engaging and establishes the claim in a compelling way. Valid reasons and evidence address and support the claim while clearly acknowledging counterclaims. Ideas progress logically and are connected by a variety of transitional words and phrases. The conclusion offers fresh insight into the claim.	Sources of evidence are comprehensive and specific and contain relevant information. The tone of the argument is formal and objective. Vocabulary is used strategically and appropriately for the audience and purpose.	The argument intentionally uses standard English conventions of usage and mechanics.
3	The introduction is engaging and states the claim in a way that grabs readers' attention. Reasons and evidence address and support the claim while acknowledging counterclaims. Ideas progress logically and include transitions that connect readers to the argument. The conclusion restates important information.	The sources of evidence contain relevant information. The tone of the essay is mostly formal and objective. Vocabulary is generally appropriate for the audience and purpose.	The argument demonstrates accuracy in standard English conventions of usage and mechanics.
2	The introduction establishes the claim. Some reasons and evidence address and support the claim while briefly acknowledging counterclaims. Ideas progress somewhat logically. A few sentence transitions connect readers to the argument. The conclusion offers some insight into the claim and restates information.	Sources of evidence contain some relevant information. The tone of the argument is occasionally formal and objective. Vocabulary is somewhat appropriate for the audience and purpose.	The argument demonstrates some accuracy in standard English conventions of usage and mechanics.
1	The claim is not clearly stated. Reasons or evidence are not included for the claim. Counterclaims are not acknowledged. Ideas do not progress logically. Sentences are often short and choppy and do not connect readers to the argument. The conclusion does not restate any information that is important.	Reliable or relevant evidence is not included. The tone of the argument is informal. The vocabulary used is limited and ineffectual.	The argument contains mistakes in standard English conventions of usage and mechanics.

PART 2
Speaking and Listening: Speech

Assignment
After completing the final draft of your argument, prepare to read it as a speech. You will deliver your **speech** as if you were speaking to one of these audiences:

Cadets at West Point	Graduating High School Seniors
A Political Convention	Peace Corps Volunteers

Follow these steps to make your speech lively and targeted to a specific audience.

- Make a clean copy of your argument. Read your text aloud, keeping in mind the audience you chose. Highlight the material you would most want to emphasize for that audience. Should you change any words or sentences to make the speech more appropriate for your audience? If so, use editing marks to make those changes.

- Practice your delivery, keeping your audience in mind. Remember to look up regularly rather than staring at your paper.

- Tell your classmates what audience you are imagining them to be. Deliver your speech, letting your voice and gestures provide interest and energy.

Review the Rubric The criteria by which your speech will be evaluated appear in the rubric below. Review the criteria before delivering your speech to ensure that you are prepared.

STANDARDS

Speaking and Listening
Present information, findings, and supporting evidence, conveying a clear and distinct perspective, such that listeners can follow the line of reasoning, alternative or opposing perspectives are addressed, and the organization, development, substance, and style are appropriate to purpose, audience, and a range of formal and informal tasks.

	Content	Presentation Techniques
3	My delivery is obviously meant for a specific audience. My speech is clearly organized and easy to follow.	I speak clearly and at an appropriate volume. I vary my tone and pace to maintain interest. I make eye contact and use gestures to engage the audience.
2	My delivery is consistent, although the intended audience may not be obvious. My speech is organized and fairly easy to follow.	I speak clearly most of the time and usually use an appropriate volume. I try to vary tone and pace, but I may be inconsistent. I make occasional eye contact and use some gestures.
1	My delivery is generic, with no specific audience in mind. My speech is disorganized and may be difficult to follow.	I mumble occasionally, speak too quickly, and/or do not speak loudly enough. I use filler words such as *like* and *um*. I fail to make eye contact or to use gestures to add interest.

Reflect on the Unit

Now that you've completed the unit, take a few moments to reflect on your learning.

Reflect on the Unit Goals

Look back at the goals at the beginning of the unit. Use a different colored pen to rate yourself again. Then, think about readings and activities that contributed the most to the growth of your understanding. Record your thoughts.

Reflect on the Learning Strategies

💬 **Discuss It** Write a reflection on whether you were able to improve your learning based on your Action Plans. Think about what worked, what didn't, and what you might do to keep working on these strategies. Record your ideas before joining a class discussion.

Reflect on the Text

Choose a selection that you found challenging, and explain what made it difficult.

Describe something that surprised you about a text in the unit.

Which activity taught you the most about heroes, warriors, and leaders? What did you learn?

☰ STANDARDS

Speaking and Listening
• Initiate and participate effectively in a range of collaborative discussions with diverse partners on *grades 11–12 topics, texts, and issues* building on others' ideas and expressing their own clearly and persuasively.
• Come to discussions prepared, having read and researched material under study; explicitly draw on that preparation by referring to evidence from texts and other research on the topic or issue to stimulate a thoughtful, well-reasoned exchange of ideas.

Reflecting on Society

Argument, Satire, and Reform

The Medieval Age and
The Canterbury Tales

Discuss It Although we may be aware of societal problems, many of us ignore them and move on. What personal qualities enable some people to stop, pick up a pen, brush, microphone, or camera, and share what they see with the general public?

Write your response before sharing your ideas.

UNIT INTRODUCTION

ESSENTIAL QUESTION: **How do people come to have different views of society?**

LAUNCH TEXT
EXPLANATORY MODEL
Standing Up to
Absolute Power

WHOLE-CLASS LEARNING

HISTORICAL PERSPECTIVES

Focus Period: 1066–1485

England: The Beginnings

COMPARE

ANCHOR TEXT: POETRY

The Prologue *from* The Canterbury Tales

Geoffrey Chaucer, translated by Nevill Coghill

MEDIA: VIDEO

The Prologue From The Canterbury Tales: The Remix

Patience Agbabi

PERFORMANCE TASK

WRITING FOCUS:
Write an Explanatory Essay

SMALL-GROUP LEARNING

HISTORICAL ACCOUNT

from The Worms of the Earth Against the Lions
from A Distant Mirror
Barbara W. Tuchman

ESSAY

Shakespeare's Sister
Virginia Woolf

ESSAY | POETRY

On Seeing England for the First Time
Jamaica Kincaid

XXIII *from* Midsummer
Derek Walcott

PUBLIC DOCUMENT

Passenger Manifest for the MV *Empire Windrush*

PERFORMANCE TASK

SPEAKING AND LISTENING FOCUS:
Present a Scene

INDEPENDENT LEARNING

NEWSPAPER ARTICLES | EDITORIAL

Occupy LSX May Be Gone, but the Movement Won't Be Forgotten
Giles Fraser

Today's Pygmy Protesters Are No Heirs to Martin Luther King
Nick Herbert

Inequality and the Crisis: Still Pre-Occupied
The Guardian

ARGUMENT

What We Mean When We Say *the People*
Edmund Burke

MOCK EPIC

from The Rape of the Lock
Alexander Pope

NOVEL EXCERPT

from Candide
Voltaire

INTERVIEW | POETRY COLLECTION

An Interview With Benjamin Zephaniah
Eric Doumerc

Poetry of Benjamin Zephaniah
Benjamin Zephaniah

PERFORMANCE-BASED ASSESSMENT PREP

Review Evidence for an Explanatory Essay

PERFORMANCE-BASED ASSESSMENT

Explanatory Text: Essay and Video Explanation

PROMPT: **What factors lead people to criticize their society rather than simply accept it?**

Unit Goals

Throughout this unit, you will deepen your perspective on the topic of reform by reading, writing, speaking, listening, and presenting. These goals will help you succeed on the Unit Performance-Based Assessment.

Rate how well you meet these goals right now. You will revisit your ratings later when you reflect on your growth during this unit.

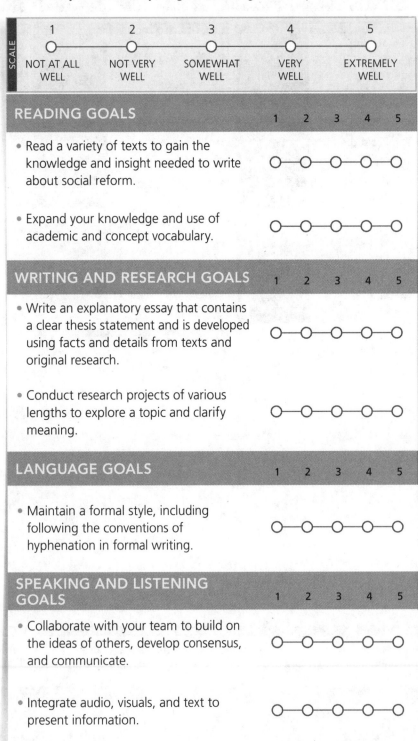

SCALE	1	2	3	4	5
	NOT AT ALL WELL	NOT VERY WELL	SOMEWHAT WELL	VERY WELL	EXTREMELY WELL

READING GOALS

• Read a variety of texts to gain the knowledge and insight needed to write about social reform.

• Expand your knowledge and use of academic and concept vocabulary.

WRITING AND RESEARCH GOALS

• Write an explanatory essay that contains a clear thesis statement and is developed using facts and details from texts and original research.

• Conduct research projects of various lengths to explore a topic and clarify meaning.

LANGUAGE GOALS

• Maintain a formal style, including following the conventions of hyphenation in formal writing.

SPEAKING AND LISTENING GOALS

• Collaborate with your team to build on the ideas of others, develop consensus, and communicate.

• Integrate audio, visuals, and text to present information.

≔ STANDARDS

Language
Acquire and use accurately general academic and domain-specific words and phrases, sufficient for reading, writing, speaking, and listening at the college and career readiness level; demonstrate independence in gathering vocabulary knowledge when considering a word or phrase important to comprehension or expression.

Academic Vocabulary: Explanatory Text

Understanding and using academic terms can help you read, write, and speak with precision and clarity. Here are five academic words that will be useful to you in this unit as you analyze and write explanatory essays.

Complete the chart.

1. Review each word, its root, and the mentor sentences.

2. Use the information and your own knowledge to predict the meaning of each word.

3. For each word, list at least two related words.

4. Refer to a dictionary or other resources if needed.

TIP

FOLLOW THROUGH
Study the words in this chart, and highlight them or their forms wherever they appear in the unit.

WORD	MENTOR SENTENCES	PREDICT MEANING	RELATED WORDS
annotation ROOT **-not-** "mark"	1. The *annotation* included the date on which the poem was published. 2. An *annotation* generally supplies helpful information about a word or line of text.		annotate; notation
theoretical ROOT: **-theor-** "view"; "consider"	1. The scientist's *theoretical* speculations were thoroughly reviewed by her colleagues. 2. The committee discussed at length *theoretical* considerations as to how the project might or might not work out.		
prescribe ROOT: **-scrib-** "write"	1. The doctor decided to *prescribe* an antibiotic. 2. The chairperson wanted to *prescribe* stricter regulations, but other committee members voted her down.		
conviction ROOT: **-vict-** "conquer"	1. Her strong *conviction* about the matter helped to change my mind. 2. The politician's words lacked *conviction*.		
tenacious ROOT: **-ten-** "hold"	1. The *tenacious* lawyer was determined to find out the truth. 2. Although the baseball player was small, his *tenacious* attitude led him to success.		

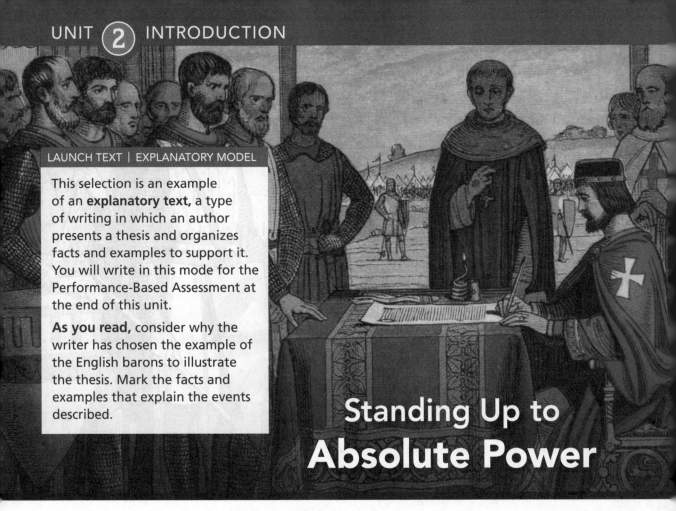

LAUNCH TEXT | EXPLANATORY MODEL

This selection is an example of an **explanatory text,** a type of writing in which an author presents a thesis and organizes facts and examples to support it. You will write in this mode for the Performance-Based Assessment at the end of this unit.

As you read, consider why the writer has chosen the example of the English barons to illustrate the thesis. Mark the facts and examples that explain the events described.

Standing Up to Absolute Power

NOTES

1   Rebellions are not always led by the downtrodden. Sometimes, even those with the most to lose have felt the need to challenge accepted social practice. One early example of this occurred in 1215 in England, when a group of wealthy barons rose up against their king. The reasons for their rebellion were many and varied. The results of their rebellion changed the course of history.

The Feudal System

2   The European feudal system gave the king total control over land rights. He owned the land and leased it to barons. In return for the king's generosity, the barons paid rent or taxes, promised complete loyalty, and provided the king with knights for his army. When they were not busy fighting for the king, the knights leased land from the barons, thus adding to the barons' power and pocketbooks. At the base of the feudal pyramid were the serfs, villeins, or peasants.

3   This system required a king with unquestionable authority. Such a king would have the respect of the barons, who would live happily and wealthily, and of the knights, who would be called into battle only during occasional crises. The system may not have benefited the serfs very much, but they had no power or resources to challenge it.

King John's Quest

4   England's King John was not a king with unquestionable authority. He had to compete for the throne when his brother Richard died, and

his revenge against his rivals' supporters made the barons unhappy. John also inherited Richard's debts, accrued during the long and terrible Crusades. To raise money to run the country, John continued Richard's practice of heavily taxing the barons.

5   Shortly after becoming king in 1199, John went to war against France. In rapid succession, he lost lands in Normandy and other parts of what is now the north coast of France. These losses made him appear weak, and they cost the lives of many of the barons' knights.

6   In 1213, King John decided to win back those lost lands. He knew he would need an influx of men and money from England's barons. He demanded knights and gold, but many barons, disgusted with John's self-defeating foreign policy, resisted. John avenged himself by arresting some barons and attacking others in their manors. He went to war as planned, but once again, he lost.

Rebellion at Last

7   The barons refused to provide yet more money or men to their now-weakened monarch. Instead, they began to make their own demands, which King John rejected. The barons formed their own army, and civil war in England seemed imminent. The archbishop sought to negotiate a short-term peace.

8   In June of 1215, King John agreed to the Articles of the Barons, which would soon become known as Magna Carta, or the "Great Charter." The document did not overthrow the king—that was too grand a gesture for the barons, who still enjoyed the benefits of feudal life. Instead, it limited his authority, ensuring that he, too, would be subject to law.

9   The idea that a ruler retains power only through the consent of the governed was genuinely groundbreaking. It would later find its way into the written products of American and French revolutionaries. Many of those later rebels, like the barons of 1215, had much to lose but chose to challenge the status quo anyway.

NOTES

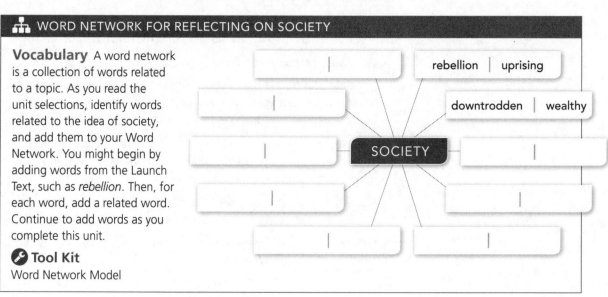

WORD NETWORK FOR REFLECTING ON SOCIETY

Vocabulary A word network is a collection of words related to a topic. As you read the unit selections, identify words related to the idea of society, and add them to your Word Network. You might begin by adding words from the Launch Text, such as *rebellion*. Then, for each word, add a related word. Continue to add words as you complete this unit.

🔧 **Tool Kit**
Word Network Model

rebellion | uprising

downtrodden | wealthy

SOCIETY

Summary

Write a summary of "Standing Up to Absolute Power." Remember that a **summary** is a concise, complete, and accurate overview of a text. It should contain neither opinion nor analysis.

Launch Activity

Give One–Get One Consider this question: What are three aspects of society today that I would like to reform, improve, or change?

- Write your responses on three sticky notes.
- Circulate and trade notes with classmates until you end up with three notes that are not your own. As you trade, talk to each classmate about how your responses differ and why you made the choices you did.
- Choose one of the notes that you think is most interesting, perhaps because it matches your own thoughts, or perhaps because you would never have thought of the same idea.
- Share that interesting note in a class discussion. Try to explain your classmate's reasoning to the rest of the class.
- Use your discussion to generate a list of key aspects of society that your class would like to reform.

QuickWrite

Consider class discussions, presentations, the video, and the Launch Text as you think about the prompt. Record your first thoughts here.

PROMPT: **What factors lead people to criticize their society rather than simply accept it?**

EVIDENCE LOG FOR REFLECTING ON SOCIETY

Review your QuickWrite. Summarize your initial position in one sentence to record in your Evidence Log. Then, record evidence from "Standing Up to Absolute Power" that supports your initial position.

After each selection, you will continue to use your Evidence Log to record the evidence you gather and the connections you make. The graphic shows what your Evidence Log looks like.

 Tool Kit
Evidence Log Model

Title of Text: _____ Date: _____

CONNECTION TO PROMPT	TEXT EVIDENCE/DETAILS	ADDITIONAL NOTES/IDEAS

How does this text change or add to my thinking?   Date: _____

ESSENTIAL QUESTION:

How do people come to have different views of society?

As you read these selections, work with your whole class to explore how people come to have different views of society.

From Text to Topic Geoffrey Chaucer was a shrewd judge of human nature. He observed the people in his society and took their measure, recognizing their strengths, weaknesses, contradictions, and hypocrisies. In vivid stories, he painted word portraits of characters from all levels of society. They are funny, shrewd, mean-spirited, generous, miserly, foolish, honorable, and everything in between. As you read, listen, and view, consider what these texts show about how people view themselves and their society—and why their worldviews can be so wildly divergent.

Whole-Class Learning Strategies

These learning strategies are key to success in school and will continue to be important in college and in your career.

Review these strategies and the actions you can take to practice them. Add ideas of your own for each step. Get ready to use these strategies during Whole-Class Learning.

STRATEGY	ACTION PLAN
Listen actively	• Eliminate distractions. For example, put your cellphone away. • Record brief notes on main ideas and points of confusion. •
Clarify by asking questions	• If you're confused, other people probably are, too. Ask a question to help your whole class. • Ask follow-up questions as needed. For example, if you do not understand the clarification or if you want to make an additional connection. •
Monitor understanding	• Notice what information you already know, and be ready to build on it. • Ask for help if you are struggling. •
Interact and share ideas	• Share your ideas, and answer questions, even if you are unsure of them. • Build on the ideas of others by adding details or making a connection. •

CONTENTS

England: The Beginnings

Voices of the Period

"The land of Robert Malet. . . .

There is situated there, in addition, one berewick, as the manor of Heuseda. In the time of king Edward, 1 carucate of land; then and afterwards 7 villains, now 5. At all times 12 bordars, and 3 serfs, and 40 acres of meadow; 1 mill. . . . The two manors have 2 leagues in length and 4 firlongs in breadth. Whosoever is tenant there, returns 12 pence of the twenty shillings of geld."

—Domesday Book, 1086

"No free man shall be seized or imprisoned, or stripped of his rights or possessions, or outlawed or exiled, or deprived of his standing in any other way, nor will we proceed with force against him, or send others to do so, except by the lawful judgment of his equals or by the law of the land. . . . To no one will we sell, to no one deny or delay right or justice."

—Magna Carta, 1215

"God often allows plagues, miserable famines, wars and other forms of suffering to arise, and uses them to terrify and torment men and so drive out their sins. And thus the realm of England, because of the growing pride and corruption of its subjects and their numberless sins is to be punished by pestilence."

—letter from the Prior of the Abbey of Christ Church, Canterbury, to the Bishop of London, 1348

History of the Period

Norman England After his coronation in 1066, William I earned the moniker "the Conqueror" by subduing rebellions across England and putting his Norman aristocracy in power. The Normans were named so because of the territory that they settled in Normandy, France. They solidified the form of government, social order, and land tenure we call feudalism, a pyramid of power stretching from the king at the peak, to nobles and freemen in carefully graded steps below, to the serfs who tilled the land at the bottom.

Much of what we know about feudal Norman England comes from the *Domesday Book*, an extraordinary primary source commissioned by William I to record information about the land, resources, and populations of the more than 13,000 settlements that existed at the time.

For seven decades under William I and the two sons who succeeded him, Norman England strengthened its ties to continental Europe. Though it remained primarily a feudal, agrarian society, towns such as London grew in size and power.

Murder in the Cathedral Under the Normans, the Roman Catholic Church became even more entrenched in the social and political structure of the country. Though the first of the Plantagenet successors, King Henry II—crowned in 1154—wished to continue the relationship, he was thwarted by Thomas Becket, whom he had appointed as Archbishop of Canterbury. Once

TIMELINE

1066

1073: Canterbury becomes England's religious center.

1085: King William I commissions the *Domesday Book*.

1096: Europe First Crusade sets out for the Holy Land.

c. 1100: France *Song of Roland*, an epic poem, is written.

Integrating Knowledge and Ideas

Accurate population statistics are a phenomenon of the modern world, when nations conduct periodic census surveys and, today, keep vast digital records. Nonetheless, historians can use early records, surveys such as the *Domesday Book*, and other documents to estimate the populations of past eras. What do these statistics tell you about the population of England and of its largest city, London? What inferences can you make about what happened when the Romans left Britain? What was the effect of the Black Death? What was happening in both England and London by the end of the Middle Ages?

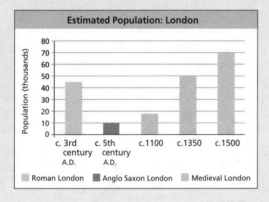

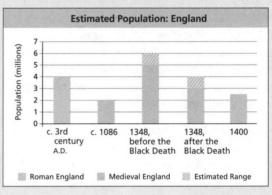

close to King Henry, Becket became an adversary when he was the powerful archbishop, defending the supremacy of church over state. The "war" between the king and the cleric ended tragically when some of Henry's knights murdered Thomas Becket in Canterbury Cathedral in 1170.

The Crusades After Becket's murder, the Pope demanded that King Henry do penance by going on a Crusade. In 1095, armies of European Christians responded to a papal plea to recapture the holy city of Jerusalem from Muslim forces.

Continuing to 1229, there were a total of six Crusades, including a Children's Crusade in 1212. Although many English knights joined the Crusades, only one English king—Henry II's son Richard—actually went to the Holy Land. Called "the Lionheart" for his bravery, King Richard helped defeat enemy forces in Palestine during the Third Crusade (1189–1192).

Magna Carta When King Richard was killed in battle in 1199, his brother John gained the crown, becoming "one of the most detested"

1170: Thomas Becket, archbishop of Canterbury, is murdered in the cathedral.

1191: Palestine Richard the Lionheart defeats Saladin on the Third Crusade.

1214: China Mongol leader Genghis Khan captures Peking.

1215: King John is forced to sign Magna Carta.

1258: First commoners are allowed in Parliament.

1275: China Venetian Marco Polo visits court of Kubla Khan.

1275

English rulers. From costly military blunders, including the loss of invaluable English claims in France, to political errors at home, King John found himself facing a serious rebellion by the barons, or noblemen, on whom he depended. Finally, on June 15, 1215, the barons presented the king with the document we now call Magna Carta, or "the Great Charter," much of which was a list of grievances against the king (similar to the Declaration of Independence, written more than 500 years later). Embedded in Magna Carta were basic values related to freedom and power. The charter made it clear that the king, as well as his people, was subject to the law, and it granted the right to a fair trial to all free men. Magna Carta set up a new paradigm for the relationship between a ruler and his or her subjects.

The Power of Parliament Magna Carta notwithstanding, power struggles between the king and his nobles continued from reign to reign. English rulers had long sought the advice of nobles and, later, the church hierarchy. By the thirteenth century, the first Parliament was established, with representatives from across the country. The nobles and high churchmen were the beginning of what would become the House of Lords, and the knights representing their shires, or counties, were the beginnings of what would become the House of Commons. Over time, Parliament would become more and more integral to the balance of power between the ruler and the ruled.

The Black Death In October 1347, catastrophe struck Europe with the arrival of a plague from the East carried by rats and fleas. Within five years it would kill more than 20 million people! Sometime in 1348, the disease reached England, killing up to 40 percent of the population over the next two years. Called "the Black Death" because of the black boils it created on the skin of victims, the plague had a profound effect, from the rapid loss of population to concerns that this was a divine punishment.

Wars, and More Wars Conflict between England and France went on for centuries, as the rights and provenance of English and French kings became increasingly intertwined, a situation that intermittently led to warfare. The Hundred Years' War, fought off and on between the mid-1300s and the mid-1400s, was such a conflict. English and French kings and their forces engaged in years of fierce battles, until the French finally consolidated control of all territory in continental France.

A New Dynasty Warfare at home did not end, however, as the descendants of King Edward III divided into two families, the Yorks and the Lancasters. Often called the Wars of the Roses (after the symbols of the two families), the conflicts went on through the reigns of two York kings until the triumph of Lancastrian Henry Tudor in 1485. As King Henry VII, he was the founder of the great Tudor dynasty that would rule until 1603.

TIMELINE

1291: Europe and Middle East The Crusades end.

1337: The Hundred Years' War begins between England and France.

1275

1325: Mexico Aztecs establish Mexico City and create a 365-day dating system.

1348: The Black Death begins sweeping through England.

Literature Selections

Literature of the Focus Period One of the selections in this unit was written during the Focus Period and pertains to the questions of how and why people form different views of their own societies.

The Prologue from *The Canterbury Tales*, Geoffrey Chaucer

Connections Across Time The different and often opposing views people have of the society in which they live is a topic that continued past the Focus Period and has influenced contemporary writers and commentators.

"The Prologue From The Canterbury Tales: The Remix," Patience Agbabi

from "The Worms of the Earth Against the Lions," Barbara W. Tuchman

"Shakespeare's Sister," Virginia Woolf

"On Seeing England for the First Time," Jamaica Kincaid

"XXIII" from *Midsummer*, Derek Walcott

"Occupy LSX May Be Gone, but the Movement Won't Be Forgotten," Giles Fraser

"Today's Pygmy Protesters Are No Heirs to Martin Luther King," Nick Herbert

"Inequality and the Crisis: Still Pre-Occupied," *The Guardian*

"What We Mean When We Say *the People*," Edmund Burke

from *The Rape of the Lock*, Alexander Pope

from *Candide*, Voltaire

"An Interview With Benjamin Zephaniah," Eric Doumerc

"The British," Benjamin Zephaniah

"Who's Who," Benjamin Zephaniah

> **ADDITIONAL FOCUS PERIOD LITERATURE**
>
> **Student Edition**
>
> UNIT 4
> from the *Divine Comedy: Inferno*, Dante Alighieri

1381: The Bible is first translated into English.

1387–1400: *The Canterbury Tales* is published.

1429: France Joan of Arc leads French to victory in the Siege of Orléans.

1455: Germany The first Gutenberg Bible is printed.

1455–1485: The House of York and the House of Lancaster fight the Wars of the Roses.

1485

THE PROLOGUE
from THE CANTERBURY TALES

The Prologue
from The Canterbury Tales

Concept Vocabulary

You will encounter the following words as you read the Prologue from *The Canterbury Tales*. Before reading, note how familiar you are with each word. Then, rank the words in order from most familiar (1) to least familiar (6).

WORD	YOUR RANKING
valiantly	
personable	
sincerity	
eminent	
discreet	
diligent	

After completing the first read, come back to the concept vocabulary and review your rankings. Mark changes to your original rankings as needed.

First Read POETRY

Apply these strategies as you conduct your first read. You will have an opportunity to complete the close-read notes after your first read.

Tool Kit
First-Read Guide and
Model Annotation

NOTICE *who* or *what* is "speaking" the poem and whether the poem tells a story or describes a single moment.

ANNOTATE by marking vocabulary and key passages you want to revisit.

First Read

CONNECT ideas within the selection to what you already know and what you've already read.

RESPOND by completing the Comprehension Check and by writing a brief summary of the selection.

STANDARDS
Reading Literature
By the end of grade 12, read and comprehend literature, including stories, dramas, and poems, at the high end of the grades 11–CCR text complexity band independently and proficiently.

About the Author
Geoffrey Chaucer (1343?–1400)

Long had our dull Fore-Fathers slept Supine;
Nor felt the raptures of the Tuneful Nine;
Till Chaucer first, a merry Bard, arose;
And many a Story told in Rhyme and Prose.

This stanza, written by author Joseph Addison in 1694, summarizes Geoffrey Chaucer's effect on English literature. Addison explains that the "Tuneful Nine," the Muses—the nine goddesses said to inspire the arts—were asleep in England until Chaucer awakened them with his poetry. Many centuries later, Chaucer is still recognized as "the father of English poetry."

Chaucer's Literary Standing At a time when Italy was experiencing its Renaissance, England was still culturally in the Middle Ages. Italians such as Dante wrote in the vernacular, the language spoken by most Italians. English poets were still writing in French or Latin. Daringly, Chaucer wrote in the vernacular, even though he knew that Middle English was changing into a new form (Modern English). Chaucer was an anomaly, though, and none of his contemporaries achieved his stature. For this reason, the fourteenth century was regarded as the "false dawn" of the English Renaissance. It was not until the time of Shakespeare in the sixteenth century that poets and playwrights, writing in Modern English, created a true cultural rebirth.

Chaucer's Early Career Born in London to a middle-class family, Chaucer was sent in his early teens to work as a page to King Edward III's daughter-in-law. Through this position, Chaucer became a member of the royal court, a position he retained for life. Chaucer's career began with drama and danger. He was only sixteen years old when he was captured in France while fighting in the English army. He was released only after King Edward paid the sixteen-pound ransom—a testament to Chaucer's closeness to the king. By 1366, Chaucer married Philippa Pan, a lady-in-waiting to the queen.

Chaucer's Later Career Chaucer had an astonishingly busy life. He studied law and became a yeoman (a servant in the royal household). This position came with many responsibilities, including service as a diplomat and soldier. For a decade he worked as the comptroller for the port of London, a demanding position.

A Poet for the Ages Chaucer was in his early twenties when he began writing, basing his first poems on those of the European poets and translating French poems into Middle English. He completed his first major publication, *The Book of the Duchess*, probably in early 1369. As he continued to write, Chaucer made penetrating insights into human nature and displayed the sharp wit for which he is celebrated. His works include the *House of Fame, The Legend of Good Women*, and *Troilus and Criseyde,* but he is best known today for his masterpiece, *The Canterbury Tales*.

The Canterbury Tales No one is sure what inspired Chaucer to write his major work, but some scholars theorize that the impetus came from a pilgrimage that he himself had taken, likely to the shrine of St. Thomas à Becket at Canterbury Cathedral, where Becket had been murdered in 1170. Whether Chaucer did indeed go on such a religious journey or not, he certainly could observe many pilgrims starting their journey, as his home was situated on the road the pilgrims took to Canterbury.

About *The Canterbury Tales*

The Canterbury Tales provides the best contemporary picture we have of fourteenth-century England. Gathering characters from different walks of life, Chaucer takes the reader on a witty and revealing journey through medieval society.

Society in the Middle Ages Rich people, poor people, young people, old people, butchers, bakers, candlestick makers—with all the diversity in any culture, you may wonder what single event could gather people from all parts of society. Chaucer found in his own society an orderly, even joyous event that gathered people from diverse backgrounds and occupations: a pilgrimage, a journey to a sacred spot. It is such a pilgrimage that gathers together the wildly diverse characters in *The Canterbury Tales*.

The Journey Begins Like modern travelers, medieval pilgrims wanted to while away the time pleasantly when traveling. Chaucer uses this custom to set his tale in motion. *The Canterbury Tales* begins with a prologue, in which the narrator, presumably Chaucer himself, meets 29 other pilgrims at the Tabard Inn, located in a London suburb. As the pilgrims prepare for their journey, Harry Bailey, the Host of the Inn, challenges each pilgrim to make the journey more entertaining by telling stories: two on the way to Canterbury and two on the way back. The pilgrim who tells the best story will be treated to a feast by the other pilgrims. The pilgrims accept the challenge, and Harry decides to join them and judge the competition.

Each of the following sections of the poem consists of one of the pilgrim's tales, linked by brief transitions. As a result, *The Canterbury Tales* is actually a story about stories, 24 different tales set within the frame story of the pilgrimage.

Snapshots of an Era In the Prologue, Chaucer sketches a brief, vivid portrait of each pilgrim, creating a lively sense of medieval life. Chaucer begins his survey with the courtly world, which centered on the nobility. Medieval nobles such as Chaucer's Knight held land granted to them by a lord or king, for whom they fought in times of war. In the middle ranks of medieval society were educated professionals, such as Chaucer's Doctor. The lower orders included craftsmen, storekeepers, and minor administrators, such as the Reeve and the Manciple. Chaucer also included the various ranks of the church, a cornerstone of medieval society, through the Prioress and the Summoner.

Although Chaucer's fictional characters represent ranks and types, they come alive on the page as real people, individuals who defy type. For instance, although from outward appearances the Merchant is wealthy, he is deeply in debt—a secret he keeps from his fellow travelers. Such breaks in stereotypes provide readers with even greater insights into the daily lives of medieval people.

Literary Background The popular genres in Chaucer's day included romances (tales of chivalry), *fabliaux* (brief, bawdy, humorous tales), stories of saints' lives, sermons, and allegories (narratives in which characters represent abstractions such as Pride or Honor). Each pilgrim in Chaucer's *Canterbury Tales* chooses to tell a type of tale consistent with his or her character, and each of the major forms of medieval literature is represented. Chaucer wrote much of the *Tales* using the form he created, the heroic couplet, a pair of rhyming lines with five stressed syllables each.

Linguistic Background The pronunciation of English underwent a major change between 1350 and 1700. Called the "Great Vowel Shift," the pronunciation of all long vowels in Middle English underwent a transition. For example, before the Great Vowel Shift, "bite" in Middle English sounded like "beet," and "meet" sounded like "mate." Many of the inconsistencies of English spelling are a result of this shift.

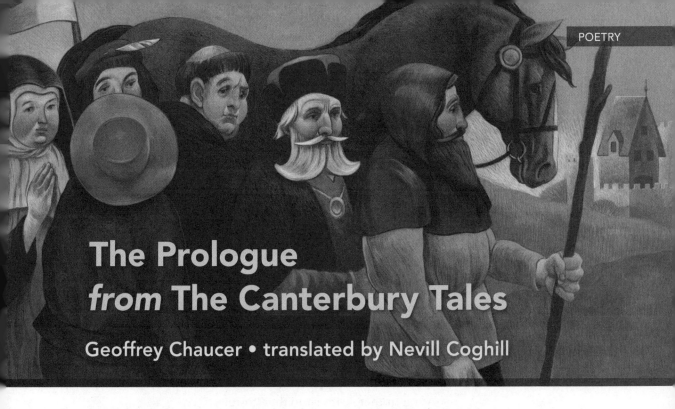

The Prologue
from The Canterbury Tales

Geoffrey Chaucer • translated by Nevill Coghill

Lines 1–18 of the Prologue in Chaucer's original Middle English are followed
by the entire Prologue in a modern translation.

❋ ❋ ❋

　　Whan that Aprill with his shoures soote
The droghte of March hath perced to the roote,
And bathed every veyne in swich licour
Of which vertu engendred is the flour;
5　Whan Zephirus eek with his sweele breeth
Inspired hath in every holt and heeth
The tendre croppes, and the yonge sonne
Hath in the Ram his halve cours yronne,
And smale foweles maken melodye,
10　That slepen al the nyght with open ye
(So priketh hem nature in hir corages);
Thanne longen folk to goon on pilgrimages,
And palmeres for to seken straunge stroncles,
To ferne halwes, kowthe in sondry londes;
15　And specially from every shires ende
Of Engelond to Caunterbury they wende,
The hooly blisful martir for to seke,
That hem hath holpen whan that they were seeke.

❋ ❋ ❋

When in April the sweet showers fall
And pierce the drought of March to the root, and all
The veins are bathed in liquor of such power
As brings about the engendering of the flower,
5　When also Zephyrus[1] with his sweet breath

---
1. **Zephyrus** (ZEHF uhr uhs) the west wind.

NOTES

CLOSE READ
ANNOTATE: In lines 1–14, mark vivid sensory details describing the time of year.

QUESTION: Why does Chaucer focus on these sensory details?

CONCLUDE: What impression of the season do these details create?

Exhales an air in every grove and heath
Upon tender shoots, and the young sun
His half-course in the sign of the Ram[2] has run,
And the small fowl are making melody
10 That sleep away the night with open eye
(So nature pricks them and their heart engages)
Then people long to go on pilgrimages
And palmers[3] long to seek the stranger strands[4]
Of far-off saints, hallowed in sundry lands.
15 And specially, from every shire's end
In England, down to Canterbury they wend
To seek the holy blissful martyr,[5] quick
To give his help to them when they were sick.
    It happened in that season that one day
20 In Southwark,[6] at The Tabard,[7] as I lay
Ready to go on pilgrimage and start
For Canterbury, most devout at heart,
At night there came into that hostelry
Some nine and twenty in a company
25 Of sundry folk happening then to fall
In fellowship, and they were pilgrims all
That towards Canterbury meant to ride.
The rooms and stables of the inn were wide;
They made us easy, all was of the best.
30 And shortly, when the sun had gone to rest,
By speaking to them all upon the trip
I soon was one of them in fellowship
And promised to rise early and take the way
To Canterbury, as you heard me say.
35   But nonetheless, while I have time and space,
Before my story takes a further pace,
It seems a reasonable thing to say
What their condition was, the full array
Of each of them, as it appeared to me
40 According to profession and degree,
And what apparel they were riding in;
And at a Knight I therefore will begin.
There was a *Knight*, a most distinguished man,
Who from the day on which he first began
45 To ride abroad had followed chivalry,
Truth, honor, generousness and courtesy.
He had done nobly in his sovereign's war

---

2. **Ram** Aries, the first sign of the zodiac. The pilgrimage began on April 11, 1387.
3. **palmers** *n.* pilgrims who wore two crossed palm leaves to show they had visited the Holy Land.
4. **strands** *n.* shores.
5. **martyr** St. Thomas á Becket, the Archbishop of Canterbury, who was murdered in Canterbury Cathedral in 1170.
6. **Southwark** (SUH<u>TH</u> uhrk) suburb of London at the time.
7. **The Tabard** (TAB uhrd) name of a specific inn.

And ridden into battle, no man more,
As well in Christian as heathen places,
50 And ever honored for his noble graces.
    When we took Alexandria,[8] he was there.
He often sat at table in the chair
Of honor, above all nations, when in Prussia.
In Lithuania he had ridden, and Russia,
55 No Christian man so often, of his rank.
When, in Granada, Algeciras sank
Under assault, he had been there, and in
North Africa, raiding Benamarin;
In Anatolia he had been as well
60 And fought when Ayas and Attalia fell,
For all along the Mediterranean coast
He had embarked with many a noble host.
In fifteen mortal battles he had been
And jousted for our faith at Tramissene
65 Thrice in the lists, and always killed his man.
This same distinguished knight had led the van[9]
Once with the Bey of Balat,[10] doing work
For him against another heathen Turk;
He was of sovereign value in all eyes.
70 And though so much distinguished, he was wise
And in his bearing modest as a maid.
He never yet a boorish thing had said
In all his life to any, come what might;
He was a true, a perfect gentle-knight.
75 Speaking of his equipment, he possessed
Fine horses, but he was not gaily dressed.
He wore a fustian[11] tunic stained and dark
With smudges where his armor had left mark;
Just home from service, he had joined our ranks
80 To do his pilgrimage and render thanks.
    He had his son with him, a fine young *Squire*,
A lover and cadet, a lad of fire
With locks as curly as if they had been pressed.
He was some twenty years of age, I guessed.
85 In stature he was of a moderate length,
With wonderful agility and strength.
He'd seen some service with the cavalry
In Flanders and Artois and Picardy[12]
And had done **valiantly** in little space
90 Of time, in hope to win his lady's grace.

---

8. **Alexandria** site of one of the campaigns fought by Christians against groups who posed
   a threat to Europe during the fourteenth century. The place names that follow refer to
   other battle sites in these campaigns, or crusades.
9. **van** *n.* part of the army that goes before the rest (short for *vanguard*).
10. **Bey of Balat** pagan leader.
11. **fustian** (FUHS chuhn) coarse cloth of cotton and linen.
12. **Flanders . . . Picardy** regions in Belgium and France.

CLOSE READ
ANNOTATE: In lines 70–100
annotate at least four vivid
details that describe the
Knight and his son, the
Squire.

QUESTION: How are the
Knight and the Squire alike
and different?

CONCLUDE: How does the
author's use of comparison
and contrast make the
picture of each character
more vivid?

valiantly (VAL yuhnt lee) *adv.*
courageously

He was embroidered like a meadow bright
And full of freshest flowers, red and white.
Singing he was, or fluting all the day;
He was as fresh as is the month of May.
95 Short was his gown, the sleeves were long and wide;
He knew the way to sit a horse and ride.
He could make songs and poems and recite,
Knew how to joust and dance, to draw and write.
He loved so hotly that till dawn grew pale
100 He slept as little as a nightingale.
Courteous he was, lowly and serviceable,
And carved to serve his father at the table.
   There was a *Yeoman*[13] with him at his side,
No other servant; so he chose to ride.
105 This Yeoman wore a coat and hood of green,
And peacock-feathered arrows, bright and keen
And neatly sheathed, hung at his belt the while
—For he could dress his gear in yeoman style,
His arrows never drooped their feathers low—
110 And in his hand he bore a mighty bow.
His head was like a nut, his face was brown.
He knew the whole of woodcraft up and down.
A saucy brace[14] was on his arm to ward
It from the bow-string, and a shield and sword
115 Hung at one side, and at the other slipped
A jaunty dirk,[15] spear-sharp and well-equipped.
A medal of St. Christopher[16] he wore
Of shining silver on his breast, and bore
A hunting-horn, well slung and burnished clean,
120 That dangled from a baldric[17] of bright green.
He was a proper forester I guess.
   There also was a *Nun*, a Prioress.[18]
Her way of smiling very simple and coy.
Her greatest oath was only "By St. Loy!"[19]
125 And she was known as Madam Eglantyne.
And well she sang a service,[20] with a fine
Intoning through her nose, as was most seemly,
And she spoke daintily in French, extremely,
After the school of Stratford-atte-Bowe;[21]
130 French in the Paris style she did not know.

---

13. **Yeoman** (YOH muhn) *n.* attendant.
14. **brace** *n.* bracelet.
15. **dirk** *n.* dagger.
16. **St. Christopher** patron saint of travelers.
17. **baldric** (BAWL drihk) *n.* belt worn over one shoulder and across the chest to support a sword.
18. **Prioress** *n.* in an abbey, the nun ranking just below the abbess.
19. **St. Loy** St. Eligius, patron saint of goldsmiths and courtiers.
20. **service** *n.* daily prayer.
21. **Stratford-atte-Bowe** nunnery near London.

At meat her manners were well taught withal;
No morsel from her lips did she let fall,
Nor dipped her fingers in the sauce too deep;
But she could carry a morsel up and keep
135 The smallest drop from falling on her breast.
For courtliness she had a special zest,
And she would wipe her upper lip so clean
That not a trace of grease was to be seen
Upon the cup when she had drunk; to eat,
140 She reached a hand sedately for the meat.
She certainly was very entertaining,
Pleasant and friendly in her ways, and straining
To counterfeit a courtly kind of grace,
A stately bearing fitting to her place,
145 And to seem dignified in all her dealings.
As for her sympathies and tender feelings,
She was so charitably solicitous
She used to weep if she but saw a mouse
Caught in a trap, if it were dead or bleeding.
150 And she had little dogs she would be feeding
With roasted flesh, or milk, or fine white bread.
And bitterly she wept if one were dead
Or someone took a stick and made it smart;
She was all sentiment and tender heart.
155 Her veil was gathered in a seemly way,
Her nose was elegant, her eyes glass-gray;
Her mouth was very small, but soft and red,
Her forehead, certainly, was fair of spread,

NOTES

CLOSE READ

ANNOTATE: In lines 145–154, annotate the details that suggest sensitivity.

QUESTION: Why does the author emphasize this aspect of the Nun's character?

CONCLUDE: What aspects of the narrator's viewpoint are revealed by these details?

The Prioress

Almost a span[22] across the brows, I own:

160 She was indeed by no means undergrown.

Her cloak, I noticed, had a graceful charm.

She wore a coral trinket on her arm,

A set of beads, the gaudies[23] tricked in green,

Whence hung a golden brooch of brightest sheen

165 On which there first was graven a crowned *A*,

And lower, *Amor vincit omnia*.[24]

    Another *Nun*, the chaplain at her cell,

Was riding with her, and *three Priests* as well.

    A *Monk* there was, one of the finest sort

170 Who rode the country; hunting was his sport.

A manly man, to be an Abbot able;

Many a dainty horse he had in stable.

His bridle, when he rode, a man might hear

Jingling in a whistling wind as clear,

175 Aye, and as loud as does the chapel bell

Where my lord Monk was Prior of the cell.

The Rule of good St. Benet or St. Maur[25]

As old and strict he tended to ignore;

He let go by the things of yesterday

180 And took the modern world's more spacious way.

He did not rate that text at a plucked hen

Which says that hunters are not holy men

And that a monk uncloistered is a mere

Fish out of water, flapping on the pier,

185 That is to say a monk out of his cloister.[26]

That was a text he held not worth an oyster;

And I agreed and said his views were sound;

Was he to study till his head went round

Poring over books in cloisters? Must he toil

190 As Austin[27] bade and till the very soil?

Was he to leave the world upon the shelf?

Let Austin have his labor to himself.

    This Monk was therefore a good man to horse;

Greyhounds he had, as swift as birds, to course.

195 Hunting a hare or riding at a fence

Was all his fun, he spared for no expense.

I saw his sleeves were garnished at the hand

With fine gray fur, the finest in the land,

And on his hood, to fasten it at his chin

200 He had a wrought-gold cunningly fashioned pin;

CLOSE READ

ANNOTATE: In lines 193–208, mark details that suggest a fine, luxurious lifestyle.

QUESTION: What kind of a lifestyle would you expect a medieval monk to have?

CONCLUDE: What point is Chaucer beginning to make through this description?

---

22. **span** *n.* nine inches.
23. **gaudies** *n.* large green beads that marked certain prayers on a set of prayer beads.
24. **Amor Vincit Omnia** (AY mawr VIHN siht OM nee uh) "love conquers all" (Latin).
25. **St. Benet or St. Maur** St. Benedict, author of monastic rules, and St. Maurus, one of his followers. Benet and Maur are French versions of Benedict and Maurus.
26. **cloister** (KLOYS tuhr) *n.* place where monks or nuns live in seclusion.
27. **Austin** English version of St. Augustine, who criticized lazy monks.

Into a lover's knot it seemed to pass.
His head was bald and shone like looking-glass;
So did his face, as if it had been greased.
He was a fat and **personable** priest;
205 His prominent eyeballs never seemed to settle.
They glittered like the flames beneath a kettle;
Supple his boots, his horse in fine condition.
He was a prelate fit for exhibition,
He was not pale like a tormented soul.
210 He liked a fat swan best, and roasted whole.
His palfrey[28] was as brown as is a berry.
  There was a *Friar*, a wanton[29] one and merry
A Limiter,[30] a very festive fellow.
In all Four Orders[31] there was none so mellow,
215 So glib with gallant phrase and well-turned speech.
He'd fixed up many a marriage, giving each
Of his young women what he could afford her.
He was a noble pillar to his Order.
Highly beloved and intimate was he
220 With County folk[32] within his boundary,
And city dames of honor and possessions;
For he was qualified to hear confessions,
Or so he said, with more than priestly scope;
He had a special license from the Pope.
225 Sweetly he heard his penitents at shrift[33]
With pleasant absolution, for a gift.
He was an easy man in penance-giving
Where he could hope to make a decent living;
It's a sure sign whenever gifts are given
230 To a poor Order that a man's well shriven,[34]
And should he give enough he knew in verity
The penitent repented in **sincerity**.
For many a fellow is so hard of heart
He cannot weep, for all his inward smart.
235 Therefore instead of weeping and of prayer
One should give silver for a poor Friar's care.
He kept his tippet[35] stuffed with pins for curls,
And pocket-knives, to give to pretty girls.
And certainly his voice was gay and sturdy,
240 For he sang well and played the hurdy-gurdy.[36]

28. **palfrey** (PAWL free) *n.* saddle horse.
29. **wanton** (WONT uhn) *adj.* jolly.
30. **Limiter** friar who is given begging rights for a certain limited area.
31. **Four Orders** There were four orders of friars who supported themselves by begging: Dominicans, Franciscans, Carmelites, and Augustinians.
32. **County folk** rich landowners.
33. **shrift** *n.* confession.
34. **well shriven** *adj.* absolved of sins.
35. **tippet** *n.* hood.
36. **hurdy-gurdy** *n.* stringed instrument played by cranking a wheel.

eminent (EHM uh nuhnt) *adj.*
rising above others in rank
or achievement

At sing-songs he was champion of the hour.
His neck was whiter than a lily-flower
But strong enough to butt a bruiser down.
He knew the taverns well in every town
245 And every innkeeper and barmaid too
Better than lepers, beggars and that crew,
For in so **eminent** a man as he
It was not fitting with the dignity
Of his position, dealing with a scum
250 Of wretched lepers; nothing good can come
Of dealings with the slum-and-gutter dwellers,
But only with the rich and victual-sellers.
But anywhere a profit might accrue
Courteous he was and lowly of service too.
255 Natural gifts like his were hard to match.
He was the finest beggar of his batch,
And, for his begging-district, payed a rent;
His brethren did no poaching where he went.
For though a widow mightn't have a shoe,
260 So pleasant was his holy how-d'ye-do
He got his farthing from her just the same
Before he left, and so his income came
To more than he laid out. And how he romped,
Just like a puppy! He was ever prompt
265 To arbitrate disputes on settling days
(For a small fee) in many helpful ways,
Not then appearing as your cloistered scholar
With threadbare habit hardly worth a dollar,
But much more like a Doctor or a Pope.
270 Of double-worsted was the semi-cope[37]
Upon his shoulders, and the swelling fold
About him, like a bell about its mold
When it is casting, rounded out his dress.
He lisped a little out of wantonness
275 To make his English sweet upon his tongue.
When he had played his harp, or having sung,
His eyes would twinkle in his head as bright
As any star upon a frosty night.
This worthy's name was Hubert, it appeared.
280   There was a *Merchant* with a forking beard
And motley dress, high on his horse he sat,
Upon his head a Flemish[38] beaver hat
And on his feet daintily buckled boots.
He told of his opinions and pursuits
285 In solemn tones, and how he never lost.
The sea should be kept free at any cost

37. **semi-cope** cape.
38. **Flemish** *adj.* from Flanders.

The Merchant

(He thought) upon the Harwich-Holland range,[39]
He was expert at currency exchange.
This estimable Merchant so had set
290 His wits to work, none knew he was in debt,
He was so stately in negotiation,
Loan, bargain and commercial obligation.
He was an excellent fellow all the same;
To tell the truth I do not know his name.
295   An *Oxford Cleric*, still a student though,
One who had taken logic long ago,
Was there; his horse was thinner than a rake,
And he was not too fat, I undertake,
But had a hollow look, a sober stare;
300 The thread upon his overcoat was bare.
He had found no preferment in the church
And he was too unworldly to make search
For secular employment. By his bed
He preferred having twenty books in red
305 And black, of Aristotle's[40] philosophy,
To having fine clothes, fiddle or psaltery.[41]
Though a philosopher, as I have told,
He had not found the stone for making gold.[42]
Whatever money from his friends he took
310 He spent on learning or another book

NOTES

CLOSE READ
ANNOTATE: In lines
280–294, mark the detail
that identifies the one
thing no one knows
about the Merchant.

QUESTION: Why does the
speaker throw this detail
into this description?

CONCLUDE: How does
this detail, presented as
almost an afterthought,
contribute to the reader's
understanding of the
Merchant?

39. **Harwich-Holland range** the North Sea between England and Holland.
40. **Aristotle's** (AR ihs tot uhlz) referring to the Greek philosopher (384–322 B.C.)
41. **psaltery** (SAWL tuhr ee) *n.* ancient stringed instrument.
42. **stone . . . gold** At the time, alchemists believed that a "philosopher's stone" existed
that could turn base metals into gold.

And prayed for them most earnestly, returning
Thanks to them thus for paying for his learning.
His only care was study, and indeed
He never spoke a word more than was need,
315 Formal at that, respectful in the extreme,
Short, to the point, and lofty in his theme.
The thought of moral virtue filled his speech
And he would gladly learn, and gladly teach.
    A *Sergeant at the Law* who paid his calls,
320 Wary and wise, for clients at St. Paul's[43]
There also was, of noted excellence.
Discreet he was, a man to reverence,
Or so he seemed, his sayings were so wise.
He often had been Justice of Assize
325 By letters patent, and in full commission[44]
His fame and learning and his high position
Had won him many a robe and many a fee.
There was no such conveyancer[45] as he;
All was fee-simple[46] to his strong digestion,
330 Not one conveyance could be called in question.
Nowhere there was so busy a man as he;
But was less busy than he seemed to be.
He knew of every judgment, case and crime
Recorded, ever since King William's time.
335 He could dictate defenses or draft deeds;
No one could pinch a comma from his screeds,[47]
And he knew every statute off by rote.
He wore a homely parti-colored coat
Girt with a silken belt of pin-stripe stuff;
340 Of his appearance I have said enough.
    There was a *Franklin*[48] with him, it appeared;
White as a daisy-petal was his beard.
A sanguine man, high-colored and benign,
He loved a morning sop[49] of cake in wine.
345 He lived for pleasure and had always done,
For he was Epicurus's[50] very son.
In whose opinion sensual delight
Was the one true felicity in sight.
As noted as St. Julian[51] was for bounty

---

43. **St. Paul's** London cathedral near the center of legal activities in the city. Lawyers often met near there to discuss cases.
44. **commission** *n.* authorization; act of giving authority to an individual.
45. **conveyancer** *n.* one who draws up documents for transferring ownership of property.
46. **fee-simple** *n.* unrestricted ownership.
47. **screeds** *n.* long, boring speeches or pieces of writing.
48. *Franklin* *n.* wealthy landowner.
49. **sop** *n.* piece.
50. **Epicurus** (ehp uh KYUR uhs) Greek philosopher (341–270 B.C.) who believed that happiness is the most important goal in life.
51. **St. Julian** patron saint of hospitality.

350 He made his household free to all the County.
His bread, his ale were the finest of the fine
And no one had a better stock of wine.
His house was never short of bake-meat pies,
Of fish and flesh, and these in such supplies
355 It positively snowed with meat and drink
And all the dainties that a man could think.
According to the seasons of the year
Changes of dish were ordered to appear.
He kept fat partridges in coops, beyond,
360 Many a bream and pike were in his pond.
Woe to the cook whose sauces had no sting
Or who was unprepared in anything!
And in his hall a table stood arrayed
And ready all day long, with places laid.
365 As Justice at the Sessions[52] none stood higher;
He often had been Member for the Shire.[53]
A dagger and a little purse of silk
Hung at his girdle, white as morning milk.
As Sheriff he checked audit, every entry.
370 He was a model among landed gentry.
    A *Haberdasher*, a *Dyer*, a *Carpenter*,
A *Weaver* and a *Carpet-maker* were
Among our ranks, all in the livery
Of one impressive guild-fraternity.[54]
375 They were so trim and fresh their gear would pass
For new. Their knives were not tricked out with brass
But wrought with purest silver, which avouches[55]
A like display on girdles and on pouches.
Each seemed a worthy burgess,[56] fit to grace
380 A guild-hall with a seat upon the dais.
Their wisdom would have justified a plan
To make each one of them an alderman;
They had the capital and revenue,
Besides their wives declared it was their due.
385 And if they did not think so, then they ought:
To be called *"Madam"* is a glorious thought,
And so is going to church and being seen
Having your mantle carried like a queen.
    They had a *Cook* with them who stood alone
390 For boiling chicken with a marrow-bone,
Sharp flavoring-powder and a spice for savor.

NOTES

CLOSE READ

ANNOTATE: In lines 365–370, mark details that describe the Franklin's multiple roles as a member of the landed gentry.

QUESTION: What do these details reveal about the Franklin's approach to his responsibilities?

CONCLUDE: What do these details show about the organization of English society during the Middle Ages?

---

52. **Sessions** *n.* court sessions.
53. **Member . . . Shire** Parliamentary representative for the county.
54. **guild-fraternity** *n.* In the Middle Ages, associations of men practicing the same craft or trade, called guilds, set standards for workmanship and protected their members by controlling competition.
55. **avouches** (uh VOWCH ihz) *v.* declares as a matter of fact.
56. **burgess** (BUR jihs) *n.* member of a legislative body.

CLOSE READ

ANNOTATE: In lines 392–397, mark several details that present an appealing picture of the Cook, as well as one that is much less inviting.

QUESTION: Why does Chaucer choose to mention the sore on the Cook's leg so close to the description of the food?

CONCLUDE: What does the placement of these details allow Chaucer to suggest about the Cook's character without directly stating it?

He could distinguish London ale by flavor,
And he could roast and seethe and broil and fry,
Make good thick soup and bake a tasty pie.
395 But what a pity—so it seemed to me,
That he should have an ulcer on his knee.
As for blancmange,[57] he made it with the best.

　　There was a *Skipper* hailing from far west;
He came from Dartmouth, so I understood.
400 He rode a farmer's horse as best he could,
In a woolen gown that reached his knee.
A dagger on a lanyard[58] falling free
Hung from his neck under his arm and down.
The summer heat had tanned his color brown,
405 And certainly he was an excellent fellow.
Many a draught of vintage, red and yellow,
He'd drawn at Bordeaux, while the trader snored.
The nicer rules of conscience he ignored.
If, when he fought, the enemy vessel sank,
410 He sent his prisoners home; they walked the plank.
As for his skill in reckoning his tides.
Currents and many another risk besides,
Moons, harbors, pilots, he had such dispatch
That none from Hull to Carthage was his match.
415 Hardy he was, prudent in undertaking;
His beard in many a tempest had its shaking,
And he knew all the havens as they were
From Gottland to the Cape of Finisterre,
And every creek in Brittany and Spain;
420 The barge he owned was called *The Maudelayne.*

　　A *Doctor* too emerged as we proceeded;
No one alive could talk as well as he did
On points of medicine and of surgery,
For, being grounded in astronomy,
425 He watched his patient's favorable star
And, by his Natural Magic, knew what are
The lucky hours and planetary degrees
For making charms and magic effigies.[59]
The cause of every malady you'd got
430 He knew, and whether dry, cold, moist or hot;[60]
He knew their seat, their humor and condition.
He was a perfect practicing physician.
These causes being known for what they were,

---

57. **blancmange** (bluh MAHNZH) *n.* at the time, the name of a creamy chicken dish.
58. **lanyard** (LAN yuhrd) *n.* rope.
59. **effigies** (EHF ih jeez) *n.* images of people.
60. **The cause . . . hot** it was believed that the body was composed of four "humors" (cold and dry, cold and moist, hot and dry, hot and moist) and that diseases resulted from a disturbance of one of these humors.

He gave the man his medicine then and there.
435 All his apothecaries[61] in a tribe
Were ready with the drugs he would prescribe,
And each made money from the other's guile;
They had been friendly for a goodish while.
He was well-versed in Aesculapius[62] too
440 And what Hippocrates and Rufus knew
And Dioscorides, now dead and gone.
Galen and Rhazes, Hali, Serapion,
Averroes, Avicenna, Constantine,
Scotch Bernard, John of Gaddesden, Gilbertine.[63]
445 In his own diet he observed some measure;
There were no superfluities for pleasure,
Only digestives, nutritives and such.
He did not read the Bible very much.
In blood-red garments, slashed with bluish-gray
450 And lined with taffeta,[64] he rode his way;
Yet he was rather close as to expenses
And kept the gold he won in pestilences.
Gold stimulates the heart, or so we're told.
He therefore had a special love of gold.
455   A worthy *woman* from beside Bath[65] city
Was with us, somewhat deaf, which was a pity.
In making cloth she showed so great a bent
She bettered those of Ypres[66] and of Ghent.
In all the parish not a dame dared stir
460 Towards the altar steps in front of her,
And if indeed they did, so wrath was she
As to be quite put out of charity.
Her kerchiefs were of finely woven ground;[67]
I dared have sworn they weighed a good ten pound,
465 The ones she wore on Sunday, on her head.
Her hose were of the finest scarlet red
And gartered tight; her shoes were soft and new.
Bold was her face, handsome, and red in hue.
A worthy woman all her life, what's more
470 She'd had five husbands, all at the church door,
Apart from other company in youth;
No need just now to speak of that, forsooth.
And she had thrice been to Jerusalem,
Seen many strange rivers and passed over them;

NOTES

---

61. **apothecaries** (uh POTH uh kehr eez) *n.* people who prepared medicines.
62. **Aesculapius** (ehs kyoo LAY pee uhs) in Roman mythology, the god of medicine and healing.
63. **Hippocrates . . . Gilbertine** famous physicians and medical authorities.
64. **taffeta** (TAF ih tuh) *n.* fine silk fabric.
65. **Bath** English resort city.
66. **Ypres** (EE pruh) **. . . Ghent** (gehnt) Flemish cities known for wool making.
67. **ground** *n.* composite fabric.

ANNOTATE: Mark details in lines 473–486 that show how widely the Wife of Bath has traveled.

QUESTION: Why does Chaucer include these details?

CONCLUDE: Why is the Wife of Bath most likely on the pilgrimage?

diligent (DIHL uh juhnt) *adj.* conscientious and hard-working

475 She'd been to Rome and also to Boulogne,
St. James of Compostella and Cologne,[68]
And she was skilled in wandering by the way.
She had gap-teeth, set widely, truth to say.
Easily on an ambling horse she sat
480 Well wimpled[69] up, and on her head a hat
As broad as is a buckler[70] or a shield;
She had a flowing mantle that concealed
Large hips, her heels spurred sharply under that.
In company she liked to laugh and chat
485 And knew the remedies for love's mischances.
An art in which she knew the oldest dances.
    A holy-minded man of good renown
There was, and poor, the *Parson* to a town,
Yet he was rich in holy thought and work.
490 He also was a learned man, a clerk,
Who truly knew Christ's gospel and would preach it
Devoutly to parishioners, and teach it.
Benign and wonderfully **diligent**,
And patient when adversity was sent
495 (For so he proved in great adversity)
He much disliked extorting tithe[71] or fee,
Nay rather he preferred beyond a doubt
Giving to poor parishioners round about
From his own goods and Easter offerings
500 He found sufficiency in little things.
Wide was his parish, with houses far asunder,
Yet he neglected not in rain or thunder,
In sickness or in grief, to pay a call
On the remotest, whether great or small,
505 Upon his feet, and in his hand a stave.
This noble example to his sheep he gave,
First following the word before he taught it,
And it was from the gospel he had caught it.
This little proverb he would add thereto
510 That if gold rust, what then will iron do?
For if a priest be foul in whom we trust
No wonder that a common man should rust;
And shame it is to see—let priests take stock—
A soiled shepherd and a snowy flock.
515 The true example that a priest should give
Is one of cleanness, how the sheep should live.
He did not set his benefice to hire[72]
And leave his sheep encumbered in the mire

---

68. **Jerusalem . . . Cologne** five famous pilgrimage sites of the time.
69. **wimpled** *adj.* wearing a scarf that covers the head, neck, and chin.
70. **buckler** *n.* small round shield.
71. **tithe** *n.* one tenth of a person's income, paid as a tax to support the church.
72. **set . . . hire** pay someone else to perform his parish duties.

Or run to London to earn easy bread
520 By singing masses for the wealthy dead,
Or find some Brotherhood and get enrolled.
He stayed at home and watched over his fold
So that no wolf should make the sheep miscarry.
He was a shepherd and no mercenary.
525 Holy and virtuous he was, but then
Never contemptuous of sinful men,
Never disdainful, never too proud or fine,
But was discreet in teaching and benign.
His business was to show a fair behavior
530 And draw men thus to Heaven and their Savior,
Unless indeed a man were obstinate;
And such, whether of high or low estate,
He put to sharp rebuke to say the least.
I think there never was a better priest.
535 He sought no pomp or glory in his dealings,
No scrupulosity had spiced his feelings.
Christ and His Twelve Apostles and their lore
He taught, but followed it himself before.
    There was a *Plowman* with him there, his brother.
540 Many a load of dung one time or other
He must have carted through the morning dew.
He was an honest worker, good and true,
Living in peace and perfect charity,
And, as the gospel bade him, so did he,
545 Loving God best with all his heart and mind
And then his neighbor as himself, repined
At no misfortune, slacked for no content,
For steadily about his work he went
To thrash his corn, to dig or to manure
550 Or make a ditch; and he would help the poor
For love of Christ and never take a penny
If he could help it, and, as prompt as any,
He paid his tithes in full when they were due
On what he owned, and on his earnings too.
555 He wore a tabard[73] smock and rode a mare.
There was a *Reeve*,[74] also a *Miller*, there,
A College *Manciple*[75] from the Inns of Court,
A papal *Pardoner*[76] and, in close consort,
A Church-Court *Summoner*,[77] riding at a trot,
560 And finally myself—that was the lot.

---

73. **tabard** *n.* loose jacket.
74. ***Reeve*** *n.* estate manager.
75. ***Manciple*** *n.* buyer of provisions.
76. ***Pardoner*** *n.* one who dispenses papal pardons.
77. ***Summoner*** *n.* one who serves summonses to church courts.

CLOSE READ

ANNOTATE: In lines 578–581, annotate the details that describe how the Miller treats his customers.

QUESTION: What do these details suggest about the Miller?

CONCLUDE: How would you describe Chaucer's **tone**, or attitude about, the Miller?

The *Miller* was a chap of sixteen stone,[78]
A great stout fellow big in brawn and bone.
He did well out of them, for he could go
And win the ram at any wrestling show.
565 Broad, knotty and short-shouldered, he would boast
He could heave any door off hinge and post,
Or take a run and break it with his head.
His beard, like any sow or fox, was red
And broad as well, as though it were a spade;
570 And, at its very tip, his nose displayed
A wart on which there stood a tuft of hair,
Red as the bristles in an old sow's ear.
His nostrils were as black as they were wide.
He had a sword and buckler at his side,
575 His mighty mouth was like a furnace door.
A wrangler and buffoon, he had a store
Of tavern stories, filthy in the main.
His was a master-hand at stealing grain.
He felt it with his thumb and thus he knew
580 Its quality and took three times his due—
A thumb of gold, by God, to gauge an oat!

---

78. **sixteen stone** 224 pounds. A stone equals 14 pounds.

The Miller

He wore a hood of blue and a white coat.
He liked to play his bagpipes up and down
And that was how he brought us out of town.
585   The *Manciple* came from the Inner Temple;
All caterers might follow his example
In buying victuals; he was never rash
Whether he bought on credit or paid cash.
He used to watch the market most precisely
590 And go in first, and so he did quite nicely.
Now isn't it a marvel of God's grace
That an illiterate fellow can outpace
The wisdom of a heap of learned men?
His masters—he had more than thirty then—
595 All versed in the abstrusest legal knowledge,
Could have produced a dozen from their College
Fit to be stewards in land and rents and game
To any Peer in England you could name,
And show him how to live on what he had
600 Debt-free (unless of course the Peer were mad)
Or be as frugal as he might desire,
And they were fit to help about the Shire
In any legal case there was to try;
And yet this Manciple could wipe their eye.
605   The *Reeve* was old and choleric and thin;
His beard was shaven closely to the skin,
His shorn hair came abruptly to a stop
Above his ears, and he was docked on top
Just like a priest in front; his legs were lean,
610 Like sticks they were, no calf was to be seen.
He kept his bins and garners[79] very trim;
No auditor could gain a point on him.
And he could judge by watching drought and rain
The yield he might expect from seed and grain.
615 His master's sheep, his animals and hens,
Pigs, horses, dairies, stores and cattle-pens
Were wholly trusted to his government.
And he was under contract to present
The accounts, right from his master's earliest years.
620 No one had ever caught him in arrears.
No bailiff, serf or herdsman dared to kick,
He knew their dodges, knew their every trick;
Feared like the plague he was, by those beneath.
He had a lovely dwelling on a heath,
625 Shadowed in green by trees above the sward.[80]
A better hand at bargains than his lord,
He had grown rich and had a store of treasure

---

79. **garners** *n.* buildings for storing grain.
80. **sward** *n.* turf.

Well tucked away, yet out it came to pleasure
His lord with subtle loans or gifts of goods.
630 To earn his thanks and even coats and hoods.
When young he'd learnt a useful trade and still
He was a carpenter of first-rate skill.
The stallion-cob he rode at a slow trot
Was dapple-gray and bore the name of Scot.
635 He wore an overcoat of bluish shade
And rather long; he had a rusty blade
Slung at his side. He came, as I heard tell,
From Norfolk, near a place called Baldeswell.
His coat was tucked under his belt and splayed.
640 He rode the hindmost of our cavalcade.
　　There was a *Summoner* with us in the place
Who had a fire-red[81] cherubinnish face,
For he had carbuncles.[82] His eyes were narrow,
He was as hot and lecherous as a sparrow.
645 Black, scabby brows he had, and a thin beard.
Children were afraid when he appeared.
No quicksilver, lead ointments, tartar creams,
Boracic, no, nor brimstone,[83] so it seems,
Could make a salve that had the power to bite,
650 Clean up or cure his whelks[84] of knobby white.
Or purge the pimples sitting on his cheeks.
Garlic he loved, and onions too, and leeks.
And drinking strong wine till all was hazy.
Then he would shout and jabber as if crazy,
655 And wouldn't speak a word except in Latin
When he was drunk, such tags as he was pat in:
He only had a few, say two or three,
That he had mugged up out of some decree;
No wonder, for he heard them every day.
660 And, as you know, a man can teach a jay
To call out "Walter" better than the Pope.
But had you tried to test his wits and grope
For more, you'd have found nothing in the bag.
Then "*Questio quid juris*"[85] was his tag.
665 He was a gentle varlet and a kind one,
No better fellow if you went to find one.
He would allow—just for a quart of wine—
Any good lad to keep a concubine

CLOSE READ
ANNOTATE: **Sensory description** is the use of words and phrases that appeal to the five senses. Mark the words in lines 641–652 that appeal to the reader's sense of sight, touch, and smell.

QUESTION: What impression of the Summoner does this description create?

CONCLUDE: How does the sensory description affect the reader's opinion of the Summoner?

---

81. **fire-red . . . face** In the art of the Middle Ages, the faces of cherubs, or angels, were often painted red.
82. **carbuncles** (KAHR buhng kuhlz) *n.* pus-filled boils resulting from a bacterial infection under the skin.
83. **quicksilver . . . brimstone** various chemicals and chemical compounds, used as remedies. *Quicksilver* is a name for mercury. *Brimstone* is a name for sulfur.
84. **whelks** *n.* pustules; pimples.
85. **"*Questio quid juris*"** "The question is: What is the point of the law?" (Latin)

A twelvemonth and dispense it altogether!
670 Yet he could pluck a finch to leave no feather:
And if he found some rascal with a maid
He would instruct him not to be afraid
In such a case of the Archdeacon's curse
(Unless the rascal's soul were in his purse)
675 For in his purse the punishment should be.
"Purse is the good Archdeacon's Hell," said he.
But well I know he lied in what he said;
A curse should put a guilty man in dread,
For curses kill, as shriving brings, salvation.
680 We should beware of excommunication.
Thus, as he pleased, the man could bring duress
On any young fellow in the diocese.
He knew their secrets, they did what he said.
He wore a garland set upon his head
685 Large as the holly-bush upon a stake
Outside an ale-house, and he had a cake,
A round one, which it was his joke to wield
As if it were intended for a shield.
  He and a gentle *Pardoner* rode together,
690 A bird from Charing Cross of the same feather,
Just back from visiting the Court of Rome.
He loudly sang *"Come hither, love, come home!"*
The Summoner sang deep seconds to this song,
No trumpet ever sounded half so strong.
695 This Pardoner had hair as yellow as wax,
Hanging down smoothly like a hank of flax.
In driblets fell his locks behind his head
Down to his shoulder which they overspread;
Thinly they fell, like rat-tails, one by one.
700 He wore no hood upon his head, for fun;
The hood inside his wallet had been stowed,
He aimed at riding in the latest mode;
But for a little cap his head was bare
And he had bulging eyeballs, like a hare.
705 He'd sewed a holy relic on his cap;
His wallet lay before him on his lap,
Brimful of pardons come from Rome all hot.
He had the same small voice a goat has got.
His chin no beard had harbored, nor would harbor,
710 Smoother than ever chin was left by barber.
I judge he was a gelding, or a mare.
As to his trade, from Berwick down to Ware
There was no pardoner of equal grace,
For in his trunk he had a pillowcase
715 Which he asserted was Our Lady's veil.

CLOSE READ
ANNOTATE: In lines 713–726, mark the items the Pardoner sells.

QUESTION: What does the Pardoner claim the items are?

CONCLUDE: What do his actions suggest about his character and the practices upon which he makes his living?

He said he had a gobbet[86] of the sail
Saint Peter had the time when he made bold
To walk the waves, till Jesu Christ took hold.
He had a cross of metal set with stones
720 And, in a glass, a rubble of pigs' bones.
And with these relics, any time he found
Some poor up-country parson to astound,
On one short day, in money down, he drew
More than the parson in a month or two,
725 And by his flatteries and prevarication[87]
Made monkeys of the priest and congregation.
But still to do him justice first and last
In church he was a noble ecclesiast.
How well he read a lesson or told a story!
But best of all he sang an Offertory,[88]
730 For well he knew that when that song was sung
He'd have to preach and tune his honey-tongue
And (well he could) win silver from the crowd.
That's why he sang so merrily and loud.
735   Now I have told you shortly, in a clause,
The rank, the array, the number and the cause
Of our assembly in this company
In Southwark, at that high-class hostelry
Known as *The Tabard*, close beside *The Bell*.
740 And now the time has come for me to tell
How we behaved that evening; I'll begin
After we had alighted at the inn,
Then I'll report our journey, stage by stage,
All the remainder of our pilgrimage.
745 But first I beg of you, in courtesy,
Not to condemn me as unmannerly
If I speak plainly and with no concealings
And give account of all their words and dealings.
Using their very phrases as they fell.
750 For certainly, as you all know so well,
He who repeats a tale after a man
Is bound to say, as nearly as he can,
Each single word, if he remembers it.
However rudely spoken or unfit,
755 Or else the tale he tells will be untrue,
The things invented and the phrases new.
He may not flinch although it were his brother,
If he says one word he must say the other.
And Christ Himself spoke broad[89] in Holy Writ,

---

86. **gobbet** *n.* piece.
87. **prevarication** (prih var ih KAY shuhn) *n.* evasion of truth.
88. **Offertory** *n.* song that accompanies the collection of the offering at a church service.
89. **broad** *adv.* bluntly.

760 And as you know there's nothing there unfit,
And Plato[90] says, for those with power to read.
"The word should be as cousin to the deed."
Further I beg you to forgive it me
If I neglect the order and degree
765 And what is due to rank in what I've planned.
I'm short of wit as you will understand.
    Our *Host* gave us great welcome; everyone
Was given a place and supper was begun.
He served the finest victuals you could think,
770 The wine was strong and we were glad to drink.
A very striking man our Host withal,
And fit to be a marshal in a hall.
His eyes were bright, his girth a little wide;
There is no finer burgess in Cheapside.[91]
775 Bold in his speech, yet wise and full of tact,
There was no manly attribute he lacked,
What's more he was a merry-hearted man.
After our meal he jokingly began
To talk of sport, and, among other things
780 After we'd settled up our reckonings,
He said as follows: "Truly, gentlemen,
You're very welcome and I can't think when
—Upon my word I'm telling you no lie—
I've seen a gathering here that looked so spry,
785 No, not this year, as in this tavern now.
I'd think you up some fun if I knew how.
And, as it happens, a thought has just occurred
And it will cost you nothing, on my word.
You're off to Canterbury—well, God speed!
790 Blessed St. Thomas answer to your need!
And I don't doubt, before the journey's done
You mean to while the time in tales and fun.
Indeed, there's little pleasure for your bones
Riding along and all as dumb as stones.
795 So let me then propose for your enjoyment,
Just as I said, a suitable employment.
And if my notion suits and you agree
And promise to submit yourselves to me
Playing your parts exactly as I say
800 Tomorrow as you ride along the way,
Then by my father's soul (and he is dead)
If you don't like it you can have my head!
Hold up your hands, and not another word."
    Well, our consent of course was not deferred,
805 It seemed not worth a serious debate;

90. **Plato** Greek philosopher (427?–347? B.C.)
91. **Cheapside** district in London.

CLOSE READ

ANNOTATE: Mark the offer in lines 807–829 that the Host of the Tabard Inn makes to the pilgrims.

QUESTION: Why does the Host make this offer?

CONCLUDE: How do you think this offer might affect the structure of *The Canterbury Tales*?

We all agreed to it at any rate
And bade him issue what commands he would.
"My lords," he said, "now listen for your good,
And please don't treat my notion with disdain.
810 This is the point. I'll make it short and plain.
Each one of you shall help to make things slip
By telling two stories on the outward trip
To Canterbury, that's what I intend,
And, on the homeward way to journey's end
815 Another two, tales from the days of old;
And then the man whose story is best told,
That is to say who gives the fullest measure
Of good morality and general pleasure,
He shall be given a supper, paid by all,
820 Here in this tavern, in this very hall,
When we come back again from Canterbury.
And in the hope to keep you bright and merry
I'll go along with you myself and ride

    All at my own expense and serve as guide.
825 I'll be the judge, and those who won't obey
    Shall pay for what we spend upon the way.
    Now if you all agree to what you've heard
    Tell me at once without another word,
    And I will make arrangements early for it."
830   Of course we all agreed, in fact we swore it
    Delightedly, and made entreaty too
    That he should act as he proposed to do,
    Become our Governor in short, and be
    Judge of our tales and general referee.
835 And set the supper at a certain price.
    We promised to be ruled by his advice
    Come high, come low; unanimously thus
    We set him up in judgment over us.
    More wine was fetched, the business being done;
840 We drank it off and up went everyone
    To bed without a moment of delay.

Early next morning at the spring of day
Up rose our Host and roused us like a cock.
Gathering us together in a flock,
845 And off we rode at slightly faster pace
Than walking to St. Thomas watering-place;[92]
And there our Host drew up, began to ease
His horse, and said, "Now, listen if you please,
My lords! Remember what you promised me.
850 If evensong and matins will agree[93]
Let's see who shall be first to tell a tale.
And as I hope to drink good wine and ale
I'll be your judge. The rebel who disobeys,
However much the journey costs, he pays.
855 Now draw for cut[94] and then we can depart;
The man who draws the shortest cut shall start."

---

92. **St. Thomas' watering-place** brook two miles from the inn.
93. **If evensong . . . agree** if what you said last night holds true this morning.
94. **draw for cut** draw lots, as when pulling straws from a bunch; the person who draws the short straw is "it."

Comprehension Check

Complete the following items after you finish your first read.

1. Why does the speaker join the twenty-nine pilgrims at the inn?

2. What are some of the Knight's military accomplishments?

3. In what ways does the Nun show her "sympathies and tender feelings"?

4. How does the Friar earn his living?

5. How do the serfs and herdsmen regard the Reeve?

6. 📓 **Notebook** To confirm your understanding, write a summary of the Prologue from *The Canterbury Tales.*

RESEARCH

Research to Clarify Choose at least one unfamiliar detail from the text. Briefly research that detail. In what way does the information you learned shed light on an aspect of the poem?

Research to Explore Conduct research to find out more about the role of the church in English society of Chaucer's day.

MAKING MEANING

THE PROLOGUE
from THE CANTERBURY TALES

Close Read the Text

1. This model, from lines 771–776 of the text, shows two sample annotations, along with questions and conclusions. Close read the passage, and find another detail to annotate. Then, write a question and your conclusion.

ANNOTATE: The Host has bright eyes and a wide build.

QUESTION: Why would the narrator emphasize these traits in the Host?

CONCLUDE: The description suggests that the Host is both intelligent and easy-going.

> A very striking man our Host withal,
> And fit to be a marshal in a hall.
> His eyes were bright, his girth a little wide;
> There is no finer burgess in Cheapside.
> Bold in his speech, yet wise and full of tact,
> There was no manly attribute he lacked. . . .

Close Read
ANNOTATE QUESTION CONCLUDE

ANNOTATE: *Bold* has multiple meanings.

QUESTION: What meaning is Chaucer using here?

CONCLUDE: He is suggesting the Host is forthright but also courageous.

 Tool Kit
Close-Read Guide and
Model Annotation

2. For more practice, go back into the text, and complete the close-read notes.

3. Revisit a section of the text you found important during your first read. Read this section closely. **Annotate** what you notice. Ask yourself **questions** such as "Why did the author make this choice?" What can you **conclude**?

- -

Analyze the Text

> **CITE TEXTUAL EVIDENCE**
> to support your answers.

Notebook Respond to these questions.

1. (a) **Contrast** How is the Squire different from the Knight?
(b) **Draw Conclusions** Does Chaucer suggest that the Squire will follow in his father's footsteps? Why, or why not?

2. (a) **Analyze** What **tone,** or attitude, does Chaucer show toward the Friar? (b) Which words in the text contribute to this tone? (c) **Evaluate** Is this tone justified? Why or why not?

3. **Interpret** Judging from the descriptions of the Friar and the Parson, what does Chaucer think can cause a religious person to fail in his or her duty?

4. **Historical Perspectives** When Chaucer wrote *The Canterbury Tales*, England was experiencing dramatic political and social change as a middle class began to emerge from the feudal system. How is this development reflected in the Prologue?

5. **Essential Question: *How do people come to have different views of society?*:** How does the setting of *The Canterbury Tales* allow Chaucer to develop characters that represent many levels of society?

STANDARDS
Reading Literature
Analyze the impact of the author's choices regarding how to develop and relate elements of a story or drama.

Analyze Craft and Structure

Author's Choices: Character Development Chaucer's twenty-nine pilgrims are among the most colorful groups of characters in literature. To create their vivid personalities, Chaucer uses different methods of **characterization,** or literary techniques that reveal characters' traits. As you read the Prologue, look for these distinct elements:

- **Direct characterization**, or direct statements about a character
  Examples: "There was a Knight, a most distinguished man"; the Knight "followed chivalry. . . ."

- **Indirect characterization**, or the presentation of a character's actions, thoughts, words, and appearance
  Example: "Speaking of his equipment, he possessed / Fine horses, but he was not gaily dressed."

Each character in the poem represents a different segment of society in Chaucer's time. By using characterization to reveal the virtues and faults of each, Chaucer provides **social commentary,** writing that offers insight into society, its values, and its customs.

Practice

CITE TEXTUAL EVIDENCE
to support your answers.

📓 **Notebook** Respond to these questions.

1. (a) In lines 122–166, identify one example of direct and one example of indirect characterization of the Prioress. (b) How do these details constitute a negative social commentary on the Prioress?

2. (a) What surface impression of the Friar is created in lines 212–279? (b) Which details reveal what the speaker really thinks of the Friar? (c) What social commentary is Chaucer making through his characterization of the Friar?

3. (a) Which details in lines 719–726 indirectly characterize the Pardoner?
   (b) What comment on society is Chaucer making through the Pardoner?

4. Complete the chart by explaining how Chaucer uses characterization to produce social commentary.

CHARACTER	CHARACTERIZATION	SOCIAL COMMENTARY
the Monk (lines 169–211)		
the five men and their wives (lines 375–388)		

THE PROLOGUE
from THE CANTERBURY TALES

Concept Vocabulary

valiantly	sincerity	discreet
personable	eminent	diligent

Why These Words? These concept words suggest character traits or personality. For example, the Squire acts *valiantly* in battle, fighting with great courage. The Parson is *diligent*, or conscientious and hard-working.

1. How does the concept vocabulary sharpen the reader's understanding of the pilgrims' character traits?

2. What other words in the selection connect to this concept?

⚓ WORD NETWORK

Add interesting words related to society from the text to your Word Network.

Practice

Notebook Respond to these questions.

1. How would *discreet* friends act if you told them to keep a secret?

2. Give an example of a job that an *eminent* person might have.

3. How would a *personable* guest act at a party?

4. How might people react to someone who had acted *valiantly*?

5. Would you like to be friends with someone who acted with *sincerity*? Why or why not?

6. What are the characteristics of a *diligent* classmate?

Word Study

Latin Suffix: -able The Latin suffix *-able* usually means "capable of being" or "worthy of being." For example, the word *climbable* means "capable of being climbed," and the word *adorable* means "worthy of being adored." However, the suffix can sometimes have another meaning—"having a certain quality." Thus, the word *personable*, which Chaucer uses to describe the Monk, means "having a (pleasing) personality." Keep these meanings in mind as you complete the following tasks.

1. The Latin prefix *im-* often means "not." Using this information and your understanding of the suffix *-able*, write a definition of the word *impassable*, as in "an impassable obstacle." Check your answer in a print or online college-level dictionary.

2. Consult a bilingual dictionary for a European language, such as Spanish or French, to see whether the Latin suffix *-able* is used in that language as well, or whether there is another suffix that serves a similar role. Write your findings here.

▤ STANDARDS

Reading Literature
Analyze how an author's choices concerning how to structure specific parts of a text contribute to its overall structure and meaning as well as its aesthetic impact.

Language
• Identify and correctly use patterns of word changes that indicate different meanings or parts of speech.
• Consult general and specialized reference materials, both print and digital, to find the pronunciation of a word or determine or clarify its precise meaning, its part of speech, its etymology, or its standard usage.
• Verify the preliminary determination of the meaning of a word or phrase.

Conventions and Style

Author's Choices: Structure Chaucer innovated the use of the heroic couplet, and his use of this form influenced generations of poets after him. A **heroic couplet** is a rhymed pair of lines written in **iambic pentameter**—a rhythmic pattern in which each line contains ten syllables, alternating between unstressed and stressed syllables. Some of Chaucer's couplets are **closed couplets**, meaning their sense and grammatical structure are completed within the two lines. Others of Chaucer's couplets instead feature **enjambment**, meaning their sense and grammatical structure continue past the end of the two lines into the line or lines that follow.

This chart shows examples from the Prologue of heroic couplets.

STYLISTIC ELEMENT	EXAMPLE
closed couplets	*Short was his gown, the sleeves were long and wide;* *He knew the way to sit a horse and ride.* *He could make songs and poems and recite,* *Knew how to joust and dance, to draw and write.* (lines 95–98)
enjambment	*And specially, from every shire's end* *In England, down to Canterbury they wend* *To seek the holy blissful martyr, quick* *To give his help to them when they were sick.* (lines 15–18)

A poet's choice of whether to use closed couplets, enjambment, or a combination of the two affects the poem's rhythm and tone. For example, the use of closed couplets can create a singsong effect, which may give descriptions or dialogue a pithy, or snappy, quality. On the other hand, the use of enjambment can give a poem a natural, flowing rhythm, which may mimic the patterns of everyday speech.

Read It

1. Read these passages from the Prologue. Mark only the closed couplets.

   a. His prominent eyeballs never seemed to settle.
      They glittered like the flames beneath a kettle; (lines 205–206)

   b. He watched his patient's favorable star
      And, by his Natural Magic knew what are (lines 425–426)

   c. He knew their seat, their humor and condition.
      He was a perfect practicing physician. (lines 431–432)

   d. Wide was his parish, with houses far asunder,
      Yet he neglected not in rain or thunder, (lines 501–502)

   e. In buying victuals; he was never rash
      Whether he bought on credit or paid cash. (lines 587–588)

2. 🗎 Notebook **Connect to Style** Explain how Chaucer used these techniques to create his style and make his poetry fluid, memorable, and clear.

Write It

🗎 Notebook Write a brief description of the narrator in heroic couplets in Chaucer's style. Include at least three couplets for a total of six lines.

THE PROLOGUE
from THE CANTERBURY TALES

Writing to Sources

When you write an explanatory text, you may find it necessary to use logical argument to support certain points. Practice the skill of argument by responding to the view expressed by a critic.

Assignment

Read the following quotation from the literary critic Edward I. Condren's book *Chaucer and the Energy of Creation*.

> *To view Chaucer as a reformer…is to overlook his evident love affair with the world he creates—a world he neither condemns, endorses, burdens with ideology, nor seeks to improve, but a world he shows as a dynamic, human, endlessly fascinating entity unto itself.*

Now, write a **response to criticism** in which you agree or disagree with Condren's take on Chaucer. In your response, address this question: Do you agree that the poet's main intent is to capture life in all of its glory, or do you suspect that he has an agenda of reform or censure? Include these elements in your essay:

- a clear introduction that includes a precise claim
- an evaluation of Condren's quote and your own claim regarding Chaucer's purpose
- valid reasoning backed up with relevant and sufficient evidence, such as specific details, examples, and quotations from the Prologue
- a conclusion that sums up your argument

Vocabulary and Conventions Connection You may want to include several of the concept vocabulary words in your writing. Also, remember to explain how Chaucer uses direct and indirect characterization in order to make your argument precise and convincing.

valiantly	sincerity	discreet
personable	eminent	diligent

STANDARDS

Writing
Write arguments to support claims in an analysis of substantive topics or texts, using valid reasoning and relevant and sufficient evidence.

Speaking and Listening
Present information, findings, and supporting evidence, conveying a clear and distinct perspective and a logical argument, such that listeners can follow the line of reasoning, alternative or opposing perspectives are addressed, and the organization, development, substance, and style are appropriate to purpose, audience, and a range of formal and informal tasks.

Reflect on Your Writing

After you have drafted your argument, answer the following questions.

1. How do you think you might use the techniques for argument writing in explanatory writing?

2. If you disagree with Condren, what do you think his strongest point is? If you agree with Condren, what do you think his weakest point is?

3. **Why These Words?** The words you choose make a difference in your writing. Which words helped you convey information precisely?

Speaking and Listening

Assignment

Working independently, deliver a **narrative presentation** in which you choose an occupation—such as cashier, nurse, lawyer, firefighter, plumber, mechanic, musician, or office worker—that you know from daily life, from the news, or from entertainment media. First, sketch a description of the attire, attitudes, and activities that might typically characterize someone in this occupation. Then, drawing on your description, present a narrative of daily events in the life of your chosen figure. At the end of your narrative, briefly compare or contrast your character with one of Chaucer's.

1. **Sketch a Description** Think about the clothes, posture, and activities that typify your subject. For example, what type of uniform does a firefighter wear while on duty? What equipment would the firefighter carry, and why? Consider the overall impression you want to create of the character's role in contemporary society.

2. **Write the Narrative** Write a narrative recounting, in chronological order, the events in a day of the life of your character.

3. **Compare and Contrast** Choose a character from the Prologue, such as the Knight or the Cook. Then, explain how the character you created is similar to or different from Chaucer's character. Include details from your narrative and from Chaucer's poem to make your points.

4. **Present the Narrative** Rehearse your narrative, editing the text if needed. As you speak, use appropriate eye contact, adequate volume, and clear pronunciation.

5. **Evaluate the Presentations** As your classmates deliver their presentations, listen attentively. Use a presentation evaluation guide like the one shown to analyze their presentation.

PRESENTATION EVALUATION GUIDE
Rate each statement on a scale of 1 (not demonstrated at all) to 5 (demonstrated exceptionally well). Be prepared to defend your rating.
☐ The narrative was clear and logical.
☐ The speaker compared or contrasted his or her character to one of Chaucer's.
☐ The speaker held the audience's attention.
☐ The speaker used appropriate gestures and body language.
☐ The speaker made eye contact and used adequate volume and clear pronunciation.

✎ EVIDENCE LOG

Before moving on to a new selection, go to your Evidence Log and record what you learned from the Prologue from *The Canterbury Tales.*

Comparing Text to Media

The performance captured in this video presents a new version of the Host you met in the Prologue from *The Canterbury Tales*. In this section, you will consider how this modern reinvention of the poem compares to the classic work.

THE PROLOGUE *from*
THE CANTERBURY TALES

THE PROLOGUE FROM
THE CANTERBURY TALES:
THE REMIX

About the Poet
Patience Agbabi (b. 1965), a London-born poet, received the Excelle Literary Award for her first poetry collection, *R.A.W.*, in 1997. She has said that her hard-hitting poetry is influenced by rap music and lyrics. She has given reading performances in clubs throughout England, as well as in other countries, including Germany and Namibia.

The Prologue From The Canterbury Tales: The Remix

Media Vocabulary

These words or concepts will be useful to you as you analyze, discuss, and write about performances such as the one shown in this video.

delivery: way in which speakers, such as actors or poets, say their words	• Enunciation, pacing, and emphasis are key elements of a speaker's delivery. • Delivery also includes body language.
gesture: movement of a part or parts of the body, especially the hands, that conveys meaning	• Some gestures are descriptive, helping to create a visual sense of a speaker's ideas. • Some gestures emphasize emotions.
audience reaction: how viewers or listeners respond to a performance	• Intended audience reactions are the ones performers strive to evoke. • Audiences may also react in unexpected ways.

First Review MEDIA: VIDEO

Apply these strategies as you conduct your first review. You will have an opportunity to conduct a close review after your first review.

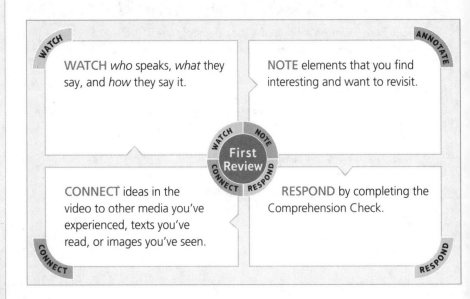

WATCH *who* speaks, *what* they say, and *how* they say it.

NOTE elements that you find interesting and want to revisit.

CONNECT ideas in the video to other media you've experienced, texts you've read, or images you've seen.

RESPOND by completing the Comprehension Check.

First Review

WATCH NOTE CONNECT RESPOND

ANNOTATE

STANDARDS

Reading Literature
By the end of grade 12, read and comprehend literature, including stories, dramas, and poems, at the high end of the grades 11–CCR text complexity band.

The Prologue From The Canterbury Tales: The Remix

Patience Agbabi

BACKGROUND

Geoffrey Chaucer's great work, *The Canterbury Tales*, was one of the first texts written in English. At the time, English was primarily a spoken language, while Latin was the language used for writing. English was the language of the people, while Latin was the language of the elite. In this performance, the poet Patience Agbabi reinterprets Chaucer's Prologue for the twenty-first century, carrying on a tradition Chaucer himself innovated—showcasing the *people's* language. She uses a style that echoes that of poetry "slams," competitive spoken-word events that began in the United States during the 1980s. Many slam poets are influenced by hip-hop music. Most challenge the idea that there is only one right way to be literary or to use language.

NOTES

Comprehension Check

Complete the following items after you finish your first review.

1. At the beginning of the performance, with what, according to the speaker, does April shower her?

2. To what does the speaker compare April's breath?

3. Toward the end of the performance, the speaker refers to a role she will play for the evening. What is that role?

4. Near the end of the performance, how does the speaker describe Chaucer's tales?

- -

RESEARCH

Research to Clarify Choose at least one unfamiliar detail from the video. Research that detail. In what way does the information you learned shed light on an aspect of the performance?

Research to Explore Choose something that interested you from the video, and formulate a research question about it. Write your question here.

Close Review

Review the video and your first-review notes. Record any new observations that seem important. What **questions** do you have? What can you **conclude**?

THE PROLOGUE FROM THE CANTERBURY TALES: THE REMIX

Analyze the Media

📓 Notebook Complete the activities.

1. **Present and Discuss** Choose the part of the video you find most interesting or powerful. Share your choice with a partner, and discuss why you chose it. Explain what you noticed about that part, what questions it raised for you, and what conclusions you reached about it.

2. **Review and Synthesize** How do you think Chaucer would react to Agbabi's "remix" if he were in the audience? Explain.

3. **Essential Question:** *How do people come to have different views of society?* How is Agbabi's view of society different from Chaucer's? How is it the same?

Media Vocabulary

delivery	gesture	audience reaction

Use these vocabulary words in your responses to the following questions.

1. The **aesthetics** of a work of art or literature are the mental impression it leaves of how beautiful or pleasing it is or is not. How would you describe the aesthetics of Agbabi's video?

2. (a) How does Agbabi use gestures in her performance? (b) What is the relationship between her gestures and the text of the poem she recites?

3. (a) What does the audience do toward the end of Agbabi's performance? (b) What qualities in the poem and in her delivery does the audience respond to so powerfully?

☰ STANDARDS

Language
Acquire and use accurately general academic and domain-specific words and phrases, sufficient for reading, writing, speaking, and listening at the college and career readiness level; demonstrate independence in gathering vocabulary knowledge when considering a word or phrase important to comprehension or expression.

THE PROLOGUE *from*
THE CANTERBURY TALES

THE PROLOGUE FROM THE
CANTERBURY TALES: THE REMIX

Writing to Compare

You have read the Prologue from *The Canterbury Tales* by Geoffrey Chaucer and viewed an adaptation of that work by poet and performer Patience Agbabi. Now, deepen your understanding of both works by analyzing and comparing them in writing.

Assignment

A conclusion is a general idea based on specific examples. Write an **argumentative essay** in which you use Chaucer's Prologue and Agbabi's "remix" as the basis for one of these two conclusions:

1. Great literature should be reinterpreted and reimagined for new generations.

   OR

2. Great literature is diminished when it is changed to suit modern tastes.

Support your conclusion with details from both poems and from your own experience or prior knowledge.

Planning and Prewriting

Analyze the Texts Choose a segment of Agbabi's remix. Transcribe the segment, adding line breaks where you think they belong. Paraphrase the segment to make sure you are clear about its meaning. Then, choose a segment of the Prologue that corresponds to Agbabi's text. Use the chart to analyze similarities and differences between the segments. Consider both the ideas they present and the literary techniques they use, including rhyme or other sound devices, rhythm, and imagery.

WORK	IDEAS	LITERARY TECHNIQUES
Chaucer's Prologue		
Agbabi's Poem		

Notebook Respond to these questions.

1. What does Agbabi's remix say or suggest about Chaucer's work? How?

2. What does the remix suggest about poetry in general? How?

3. Do you agree with Agbabi that *The Canterbury Tales* is an " unfinished business"? Explain.

STANDARDS

Reading Literature
Analyze multiple interpretations of a story, drama, or poem, evaluating how each version interprets the source text.

Writing
• Write arguments to support claims in an analysis of substantive topics or texts, using valid reasoning and relevant and sufficient evidence.
• Introduce precise, knowledgeable claim(s), establish the significance of the claim(s), distinguish the claim(s) from alternate or opposing claims, and create an organization that logically sequences claim(s), counterclaims, reasons, and evidence.
• Apply *grades 11–12 Reading standards* to literature.

Drafting

Draw a conclusion and gather evidence. Decide which conclusion you want to support. If you want to modify it in any way, do so here:

CONCLUSION / CLAIM: _____

Then, use your Prewriting notes, as well as your own knowledge and experience, to record evidence that supports your conclusion.

EVIDENCE SOURCE	DETAILS
Chaucer's Prologue	
Agbabi's Poem	
Your Experience	
Your Prior Knowledge	

EVIDENCE LOG

Before moving on to a new selection, go to your Evidence Log and record what you've learned from "The Prologue From The Canterbury Tales: The Remix."

Organize your ideas. Your task in this essay is to demonstrate how the example of Chaucer's *The Canterbury Tales* and Agbabi's "remix" supports a general conclusion. You will need to explain the ideas and techniques the two poems share, as well as the ways in which Agbabi transforms them. You might start your essay with a discussion of Chaucer, and then move on to a discussion of Agbabi. Alternatively, you might start by describing the works' similarities, and then discuss their differences.

Review, Revise, and Edit

Reread your draft. Mark your claim. Then, review each body paragraph to make sure it supports and provides evidence for the claim. Add evidence where it is needed. Then, carefully proofread your essay to ensure that it is free from errors in grammar, spelling, and punctuation.

WRITING TO SOURCES

• THE PROLOGUE *from*
  THE CANTERBURY TALES

• THE PROLOGUE
  FROM THE CANTERBURY
  TALES: THE REMIX

ACADEMIC VOCABULARY

As you craft your argument, consider using some of the academic vocabulary you learned in the beginning of the unit.

annotation
theoretical
prescribe
conviction
tenacious

 Tool Kit

Student Model of an Explanatory Essay

☰ STANDARDS

Writing
• Write informative/explanatory texts to examine and convey complex ideas, concepts, and information clearly and accurately through the effective selection, organization, and analysis of content.
• Write routinely over extended time frames and shorter time frames for a range of tasks, purposes, and audiences.

Write an Explanatory Essay

You have just experienced two versions of a section of a long medieval poem. In the Prologue from *The Canterbury Tales,* Geoffrey Chaucer describes a group of pilgrims who are making their way to a religious shrine. Although each character represents a recognizable social position, from Knight to Monk, Chaucer's tongue-in-cheek descriptions make clear that these are not one-dimensional stereotypes but rather complex people with individual appetites and failings.

Assignment

Use your knowledge of the Prologue from *The Canterbury Tales* to consider the relationship between social ideals and realities. Write a brief **explanatory essay** in which you discuss this question:

> **How does Chaucer find humor in the difference between the ideal and the real in the characters that populate *The Canterbury Tales*?**

Begin by rereading the sections of the Prologue that deal with the Doctor, the Monk, and one other social type. Conduct research on the status and ideal functions of these people in Chaucer's society. Finally, write an explanation of the humor found in the differences between these ideals and Chaucer's depictions.

Elements of an Explanatory Essay

An **explanatory essay** may explain how or why something happened or how something works.

An effective explanatory essay contains these elements:

- a thesis statement that introduces the concept or main idea
- relevant facts, examples, and details that support the thesis statement
- headings (if desired) to separate sections of the essay
- transition words or phrases to connect ideas
- graphics or media (if desired) that illustrate concepts or clarify ideas
- formal and objective language and tone
- error-free grammar and conventional use of punctuation
- a concluding statement or section that logically completes the explanation

Model Explanatory Essay For a model of a well-crafted explanation, see the Launch Text, "Standing Up to Absolute Power." Review the Launch Text for examples of the elements described above. You will look more closely at these elements as you prepare to write your own explanatory essay.

Prewriting / Planning

Brainstorm for Examples The prompt asks you to research the status and roles that each of these social types—doctor, monk, and one other—occupied in Chaucer's society. In a similar vein, the Launch Text describes the feudal system and the various roles different types of people played within it. You can find this kind of information in the library or on the Internet by looking for topics on the social history of England.

Use this space to list some ways in which your research findings about these roles—including the esteem in which these types of people were held—either fits or clashes with the realities that Chaucer portrays.

SOCIAL ROLE/STATUS	HOW CHAUCER'S CHARACTERS BEHAVE

Write a Thesis Statement Reread the question in the prompt. Use that question and the information that you found in your research to develop a thesis statement. The **thesis statement** names your topic and expresses your main idea about the topic. Make sure that your statement addresses the basics—a general description of the ways in which Chaucer's characters depart from his society's norms and how this generates humor.

_____

_____

_____

Connect Across Texts One way to begin your essay would be with a direct reference to Chaucer's text. Locate a section or sections that correspond well with your thesis statement. Think about how Chaucer characterizes the people who represented different roles in medieval society. Then, draft a sentence or two about the contrast between the ways in which the ideal of that social type contrast with Chaucer's depiction. While you are reviewing Chaucer's text, think about how any of the illustrations included with the text might help you make your main point about these contrasts.

✏ EVIDENCE LOG

Review your Evidence Log and identify key details you might want to cite in your explanatory essay.

≣ STANDARDS

Writing
Introduce a topic; organize complex ideas, concepts, and information so that each new element builds on that which precedes it to create a unified whole; include formatting, graphics, and multimedia when useful to aiding comprehension.

ENRICHING WRITING WITH RESEARCH

Online Research You have already done some initial research about social types found in Chaucer's society. You might want to supplement that knowledge with some more specific information from online research.

The key to finding useful information online lies in picking the right search terms. If you were looking for information on social conditions in the Industrial Revolution, for example, you would find it helpful to be specific. You would choose a timespan, a location, or a particular population and add those keywords to the term *Industrial Revolution*. Here are some additional tips:

- Be careful about your sources. Use reputable sites, such as online encyclopedias and websites affiliated with universities.

- Look for primary sources from the time (medieval registers and letters, for instance), as well as secondary ones that interpret primary materials.

- History blogs might give you interesting ideas, but they are not always reliable sources.

Notes and Citations Not only should you take notes on your information, you must also keep track of where you find it. If you are doing research on the Internet, it is helpful to cut and paste the URL into the document you use to take notes.

EXAMPLE

https://www.britannica.com/topic/Magna-Carta

> **Magna Carta means "Great Charter." Forced on King John by English barons, who threatened to rebel against his rule. Signed by John at Runnymede (June 15, 1215).**

If you are using print materials, keep the title, author, publisher, date of publication, and page numbers next to any information you find. Be particularly meticulous with direct quotations.

EXAMPLE

Schama, Simon. *A History of Britain: At the Edge of the World? 3000 B.C.–1603 A.D.* 1st ed., Hyperion, 2000, p. 162.

> **"So, if the Magna Carta was not the birth certificate of freedom, it was the death certificate of despotism. It spelled out for the first time . . . that the law was not simply the will or the whim of the king but was an independent power in its own right. . . ."**

Remember to put material that you copy directly within quotation marks so that you will not confuse it with your paraphrased notes.

STANDARDS

Writing

- Develop the topic thoroughly by selecting the most significant and relevant facts, extended definitions, concrete details, quotations, or other information and examples appropriate to the audience's knowledge of the topic.
- Conduct short as well as more sustained research projects to answer a question or solve a problem; narrow or broaden the inquiry when appropriate; synthesize multiple sources on the subject, demonstrating understanding of the subject under investigation.
- Gather relevant information from multiple authoritative print and digital sources, using advanced searches effectively; assess the strengths and limitations of each source in terms of the task, purpose, and audience; integrate information into the text selectively to maintain the flow of ideas, avoiding plagiarism and overreliance on any one source and following a standard format for citation.

College and Career Readiness

Organize It

After you have thoroughly researched your topic, it is time to organize your notes. Remember to keep your thesis statement in mind. You are about to explain it, so be sure that your information supports your main idea. Also, consider your audience. Your readers may not be familiar with the historical period you are writing about. Prepare them to understand your explanation by providing a paragraph or two in which you lay out some basic facts. The Launch Text does this in the section headed "The Feudal System."

Write your thesis statement. Then, annotate the chart with brief references to your notes from your research and your reading of the Prologue from *The Canterbury Tales*.

THESIS STATEMENT: _____	
Historical background for readers	
Specific information about how three social types—monks, doctors, and one of your choice—ideally functioned in Chaucer's society	
How the ideal is similar to and different from Chaucer's depictions	
How Chaucer produces humor about social roles in the Prologue	

Does it make sense to alter your thesis statement based on the information you found? If so, write your revised thesis statement here:

Revised Thesis Statement:

_____

_____

You might find that some of your notes are not as useful as you thought they might be. Discard them. At this point you might also find that you have some "holes" in your research. Return to the Internet or to the library to find any additional material you might need.

Drafting

Once you have organized your text and refined your thesis statement, it is time to start writing. Remember that you are writing to communicate your ideas. In order to do so, you must use precise language and appropriate transitions.

Precise Language Your research has probably given you extensive knowledge about your subject. Your job is to impart this knowledge clearly so that your readers can understand what you already know. Use clear, precise language. Remember that abstract words such as *democracy* and *freedom* can be slippery; they mean different things to different people. Be sure that your readers know what you mean when you use them. One way to convey your meaning is by using similes and metaphors.

Examples

Imprecise Language	Freedom is really important in a just society.
Precise Language	Freedom of speech, freedom of assembly, and freedom of the press are the pillars that support a just society.

Notice that the term *freedom* is precisely defined in the second example. The meaning of the word is also reinforced by the metaphor describing freedoms as "pillars."

Transitions As you write your draft, make sure that your thoughts are connected by appropriate transitional words and phrases. Keep in mind that you are building a structured essay. Your arguments must be supported and connected. Think of the essay as a bridge between you and the reader. Your thesis must be supported by facts, and the parts must be connected by transitions. Words and phrases such as *therefore, furthermore, nonetheless,* and *as a result* are the connections that hold your bridge together. This chart lists many possible transitions you can use in your writing.

also	in addition	moreover	besides
further	even so	later	likewise
at the same time	afterwards	beyond that	for instance
specifically	for example	on the other hand	and yet
subsequently	consequently	in contrast	however

STANDARDS

Writing
• Use appropriate and varied transitions and syntax to link the major sections of the text, create cohesion, and clarify the relationships among complex ideas and concepts.
• Use precise language, domain-specific vocabulary, and techniques such as metaphor, simile, and analogy to manage the complexity of the topic.

The Process No two writers approach the writing task in the same way. The process of writing can be neat or messy, depending on the individual. Some writers follow a linear pattern, beginning with prewriting and outlining and proceeding to revision and proofreading. Others begin with an outline that changes as they draft their work. They revise and proofread as they write, constantly circling back to change a word or revise a sentence or paragraph. There is no right or wrong method. The point is always to end with a clear and coherent product.

LANGUAGE DEVELOPMENT: CONVENTIONS

Use a Formal Style

Essays that you write will usually be in a **formal style**. Formal language is not casual writing, such as you might find in an e-mail or a blog. An essay about historical issues should be written from a third-person point of view, and it should not contain slang, personal information, or contractions. We may use contractions every day in normal speech, but they are out of place in a formal essay. Your essay must also be well reasoned and objective. This does not mean that you cannot have strong feelings about your subject. It means only that you must express yourself in a serious manner.

Examples

Informal Style: It's not just the little guys who get fed up with the status quo.

Formal Style: Rebellions are not always led by the downtrodden.

As you write, focus on your tone. Remember that you are addressing an unknown audience, not a family member or a friend.

Hyphenation

When writing formally, follow the conventions of standard English. Choose punctuation marks that convey the correct logical relationships among your ideas, and spell words correctly. Punctuating correctly and spelling correctly both require knowledge of hyphenation conventions. Here are three uses for **hyphens (-)**, with examples from the Launch Text.

- to spell a compound word, when it is listed that way in the dictionary (*"The archbishop sought to negotiate a <u>short-term</u> peace."*)

- to spell a word that begins with the prefix *all-, ex-,* or *self-* (*"He demanded knights and gold, but many barons, disgusted with John's <u>self-defeating</u> foreign policy, resisted."*)

- to connect a compound modifier when it appears before the noun it modifies, but not after (*"The barons refused to provide yet more money or men to their <u>now-weakened</u> monarch."*)

Write It

As you draft your essay, use hyphens when needed to punctuate and spell correctly. This chart shows three additional uses for hyphens.

USE	EXAMPLES
to spell two-word numbers from twenty-one through ninety-nine	fifty-five centimeters, sixty-eight years
to write a fraction, when it is used as an adjective, but not as a noun	two-thirds majority, one-half cup
to add a prefix to a proper noun or adjective	mid-November, pre-Columbian

STANDARDS

Writing
Establish and maintain a formal style and objective tone while attending to the norms and conventions of the discipline in which they are writing.

Language
- Demonstrate command of the conventions of standard English capitalization, punctuation, and spelling when writing.
- Observe hyphenation conventions.
- Spell correctly.

Revising

Evaluating Your Draft

Use this checklist to evaluate the effectiveness of your first draft. Then, use your evaluation and the instruction on this page to guide your revision.

FOCUS AND ORGANIZATION	EVIDENCE AND ELABORATION	CONVENTIONS
☐ Provides an introduction that establishes a focused topic or thesis statement.	☐ Develops the topic using relevant facts, definitions, details, quotations, and/or examples.	☐ Attends to the norms and conventions of the discipline, especially the correct use and punctuation of transitions.
☐ Uses words, phrases, and clauses to clarify the relationships between and among ideas.	☐ Uses precise words and technical vocabulary where appropriate.	
☐ Provides a conclusion that follows logically from the preceding information.	☐ Establishes and maintains a formal style and an objective tone.	

WORD NETWORK

Include interesting words from your Word Network in your explanatory essay.

Revising for Focus and Organization

Strong Conclusion A good conclusion is not simply a summary; it adds to what you have already presented. The Launch Text conclusion circles back to the original thesis statement but includes additional examples of times when those with much to lose challenged social norms.

> **LAUNCH TEXT EXCERPT**
>
> The idea that a ruler retains power only through the consent of the governed was genuinely groundbreaking. It would later find its way into the written products of American and French revolutionaries. Many of those later rebels, like the barons of 1215, had much to lose but chose to challenge the status quo anyway.

Revising for Evidence and Elaboration

Expository Details If your audience knows less about the topic than you do, decide how much background information to present. The Launch Text includes an entire section about the feudal system. Without those facts, a reader might not understand the rest of the essay. Are there places in your essay where you need to define words or explain concepts? Reread your essay, and add details and definitions if necessary.

STANDARDS

Writing
- Develop the topic thoroughly by selecting the most significant and relevant facts, extended definitions, concrete details, quotations, or other information and examples appropriate to the audience's knowledge of the topic.

- Provide a concluding statement or section that follows from and supports the information or explanation presented.

PEER REVIEW

Exchange papers with a classmate. Use the checklist to evaluate your classmate's explanatory essay and provide supportive feedback.

1. Is the thesis clear?

☐ yes   ☐ no   If no, explain what confused you.

2. Did the writer include solid examples and reasons?

☐ yes   ☐ no   If no, tell what you think might be missing.

3. Does the essay conclude in a logical way?

☐ yes   ☐ no   If no, suggest what you might change.

4. What is the strongest part of your classmate's paper? Why?

_____

_____

_____

_____

Editing and Proofreading

Edit for Conventions Reread your draft for accuracy and consistency. Correct errors in grammar and word usage. Double-check names and dates against your notes to be sure your facts are correct.

Proofread for Accuracy Read your draft carefully, looking for errors in spelling and punctuation. Watch for errors in the use of hyphens or dashes.

Publishing and Presenting

Create a final version of your text. Work in groups of three to read and review each other's work. Talk about the historical examples each of you chose. Suppose you were to incorporate all three historical examples into a single text. How would you organize the text? How would your introduction and conclusion change?

Reflecting

Reflect on what you learned by writing your text. Was it difficult to find a historical example? What took the longest—the research, writing, or revising? Think about what you will do differently the next time you write an explanatory essay.

≣ STANDARDS

Writing
Develop and strengthen writing as needed by planning, revising, editing, rewriting, or trying a new approach, focusing on addressing what is most significant for a specific purpose and audience.

ESSENTIAL QUESTION:

How do people come to have different views of society?

As you read these selections, work with your group to explore how people come to look at their culture and world in different ways.

From Text to Topic Until the twentieth century, rigidly defined social class and gender roles determined how British people viewed their world. For some, the view was nearly unlimited, a broad open vista of opportunity and prosperity. For others, the view was restricted, impoverished, and crushingly small. As you read, consider what these selections show about how Britons lived, how their views of the world differed, and why.

Small-Group Learning Strategies

Throughout your life, in school, in your community, and in your career, you will continue to develop strategies when you work in teams. Use these strategies during Small-Group Learning. Add ideas of your own for each step.

STRATEGY	ACTION PLAN
Prepare	• Complete your assignments so that you are prepared for group work. • Organize your thinking so you can contribute to your group's discussions. •
Participate fully	• Make eye contact to signal that you are listening and taking in what is being said. • Use text evidence when making a point. •
Support others	• Build off ideas from others in your group. • Invite others who have not yet spoken to join the discussion. •
Clarify	• Paraphrase the ideas of others to ensure that your understanding is correct. • Ask follow-up questions. •

CONTENTS

PERFORMANCE TASK

SPEAKING AND LISTENING FOCUS
Present a Scene

The Small-Group readings explore how and why people form different views about the society in which they live. After reading, your group will write and present a dramatic scene in which various characters explain their objections to aspects of life in England.

Working as a Team

1. **Take a Position** In your group, discuss the following question:

   What social problems might lead you to criticize the society in which you live?

   As you take turns sharing your ideas, be sure to provide reasons for your response. After all group members have shared, discuss some of the connections among the issues that were presented.

2. **List Your Rules** As a group, decide on the rules that you will follow as you work together. Two samples are provided. Add two more of your own. As you work together, you may add or revise rules based on your experience together.

   - Group members should keep an open mind.
   - Group members should respect each other, even if they disagree.

   • _____

   _____

   • _____

   _____

3. **Apply the Rules** Share what you have learned about how people develop different views about the society in which they live. Make sure each person in the group contributes. Take notes on and be prepared to share with the class one thing that you heard from another member of your group.

4. **Name Your Group** Choose a name that reflects the unit topic.

   Our group's name: _____

5. **Create a Communication Plan** Decide how you want to communicate with one another. For example, you might use instant messaging, video chats, or group texts.

   Our group's decision: _____

   _____

Making a Schedule

First, find out the due dates for the Small-Group activities. Then, preview the texts and activities with your group, and make a schedule for completing the tasks.

SELECTION	ACTIVITIES	DUE DATE
from The Worms of the Earth Against the Lions		
Shakespeare's Sister		
On Seeing England for the First Time		
XXIII from Midsummer		
Passenger Manifest for the MV Empire Windrush		

Working on Group Projects

As your group works together, you'll find it more effective if each person has a specific role. Different projects require different roles. Before beginning a project, discuss the necessary roles, and choose one for each group member. Some possible roles are listed here. Add your ideas to the list.

Project Manager: monitors the schedule and keeps everyone on task

Researcher: organizes research activities

Recorder: takes notes during group meetings

_____

_____

_____

_____

About the Author

Barbara W. Tuchman (1912–1989) was a two-time Pulitzer Prize–winner who pursued a career in journalism before turning to history. She believed that books about history should engage readers with an interesting narrative rather than overwhelm them with facts. Her book *The Guns of August*, published in 1962, was an analysis of events leading up to World War I. Like *A Distant Mirror*, the book was a bestseller that appealed to the average serious reader. Her other works include *Notes from China* (1972), *The March of Folly: From Troy to Vietnam* (1972), and *The First Salute* (1988).

from The Worms of the Earth Against the Lions

Concept Vocabulary

As you perform your first read of "The Worms of the Earth Against the Lions," you will encounter these words.

demagogue	animosity	provoke

Familiar Word Parts If these words are unfamiliar, try using **familiar word parts**—roots, prefixes, and suffixes that you know—to determine the words' meanings. For example, the Greek root *-dem-* in *demagogue* may remind you of words such as *democracy* and *epidemic*, which have to do with large groups of people. Perhaps the word *demagogue* has a related meaning.

Apply your knowledge of familiar word parts and other vocabulary strategies to determine the meanings of unfamiliar words you encounter during your first read. Use a resource such as a dictionary or a thesaurus to verify the meanings you identify.

First Read NONFICTION

Apply these strategies as you conduct your first read. You will have an opportunity to complete a close read after your first read.

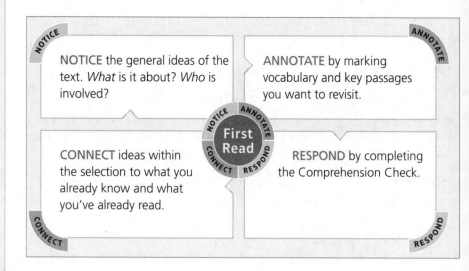

NOTICE the general ideas of the text. *What* is it about? *Who* is involved?

ANNOTATE by marking vocabulary and key passages you want to revisit.

CONNECT ideas within the selection to what you already know and what you've already read.

RESPOND by completing the Comprehension Check.

≡ STANDARDS

Reading Informational Text
By the end of grade 12, read and comprehend literary nonfiction at the high end of the grades 11–CCR text complexity band independently and proficiently.

Language
• Determine or clarify the meaning of unknown and multiple-meaning words and phrases based on *grades 11–12 reading and content*, choosing flexibly from a range of strategies.
• Verify the preliminary determination of the meaning of a word or phrase.

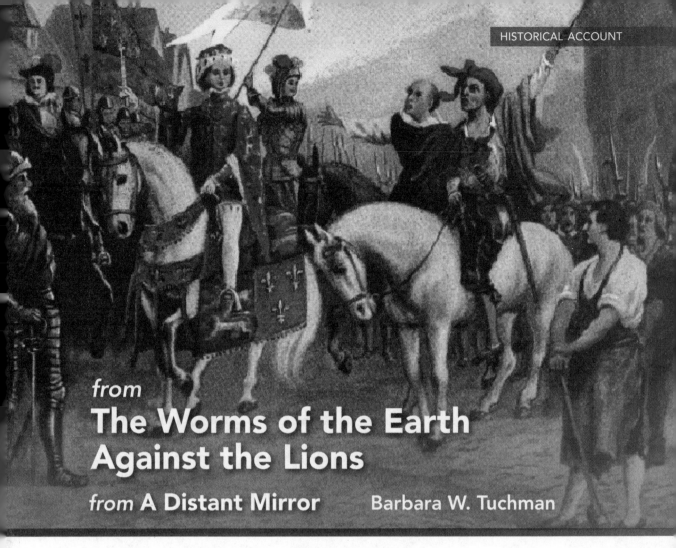

from
The Worms of the Earth Against the Lions

from **A Distant Mirror**   Barbara W. Tuchman

BACKGROUND

Under the English feudal system, farmers and craftspeople were peasants. They lived on the manor of a lord, who was entitled to a portion of whatever they produced. There was no social mobility. A peasant could not move to another manor or rise in station. For many, the burden of taxes and the lack of freedom were a source of discontent. Even so, the king, who was the head of this repressive system, was regarded with reverence. During the Poll Tax Revolt of 1381, this contradiction became the rebels' undoing.

1   While France smoldered, true revolt erupted in June 1381 in England, not of the urban class but of the peasants. In a country whose economy was largely rural, they were the working class that mattered. The third poll tax[1] in four years, to include everyone over the age of fifteen, was the precipitant. Voted in November 1380 by a subservient Parliament to finance Lancaster's ambitions in Spain,[2] the collection brought in only two thirds of the expected sum, not least because tax commissioners were easily bribed to overlook families or falsify their numbers. A second round

NOTES

---

1. **poll tax** tax per person, levied on individuals rather than on property.
2. **Lancaster's ambitions in Spain** The Duke of Lancaster hoped to claim the crown of Castile, a kingdom of Spain.

of collecting became necessary, which could have been foreseen as an invitation to trouble if the lords and prelates and royal uncles of Richard's government had paid attention to the constant complaints of rural insubordination. They did not, and brought upon themselves the most fearful challenge of the century.

2   At the end of May, villages in Essex on the east coast just above London refused payment; the resistance spread with some evidence of planning, and burst into violence in Kent, the adjoining county south of the Thames. Peasants mingled with yeomen[3] from the French wars armed themselves with rusty swords, scythes, axes, and longbows blackened by age, and triumphantly stormed a castle where a runaway villein[4] had been imprisoned. Electing Wat Tyler, an eloquent demagogue and veteran of the wars, as their commander-in-chief, they seized Canterbury, forced the mayor to swear fealty to "King Richard and the Commons,"[5] and liberated from the Archbishop's prison the idealogue of the movement, John Ball. He was a vagrant priest, scholar, and zealot who had been wandering the country for twenty years, frequently hauled in by the authorities for prophesying against Church and state and preaching radical doctrines of equality.

3   Although the poll tax was the igniting spark, the fundamental grievance was the bonds of villeinage and the lack of legal and political rights. Villeins could not plead in court against their lord, no one spoke for them in Parliament, they were bound by duties of servitude which they had no way to break except by forcibly obtaining a change of the rules. That was the object of the insurrection, and of the march on the capital that began from Canterbury.

4   As the Kentishmen swept forward to London, covering the seventy miles in two days, the Essex rebels marched southward to meet them. Abbeys and monasteries on the way were a special object of animosity because they were the last to allow commutation[6] of servile labor. In the towns, artisans and small tradesmen, sharing the quarrel of the little against the great, gave aid and food to the peasants. As the sound of the rising spread to other counties, riots and outbreaks widened.

5   The "mad multitude" on its march from Kent and Essex opened prisons, sacked manors, and burned records. Some personally hated landlords and officials were murdered and their heads carried around on poles. Others, in fear of death, fled to hide in the same woods where villein outlaws frequently hid from them. Certain lords were forced by the rebels to accompany them "whether they would or not," either to supply needed elements of command or the appearance of participation by the gentry.

Mark familiar word parts or indicate another strategy you used that helped you determine meaning.

demagogue (DEHM uh gog) *n.*

MEANING:

Mark familiar word parts or indicate another strategy you used that helped you determine meaning.

animosity (an uh MOS uh tee) *n.*

MEANING:

---

3. **yeomen** (YOH muhn) *n.* attendants in a royal household.
4. **villein** (VIHL uhn) *n.* farmer bound by law to serve the lord.
5. **King Richard and the Commons** Richard II Plantagenet, the King of England, and the representative of the working class.
6. **commutation** (kom yuh TAY shuhn) *n.* substitution of one kind of payment for another.

6   At the same time, peasant spokesmen swore to kill "all lawyers and servants of the King they could find." Short of the King, their imagined champion, all officialdom was their foe—sheriffs, foresters, tax-collectors, judges, abbots, lords, bishops, and dukes—but most especially men of the law because the law was the villeins' prison. Not accidentally, the Chief Justice of England, Sir John Cavendish, was among their first victims, along with many clerks and jurors. Every attorney's house on the line of march reportedly was destroyed.

7   If the Jacquerie[7] 23 years earlier had been an explosion without a program, the Peasants' Revolt arose out of a developing idea of freedom. Though theoretically free, villeins wanted abolition of the old bonds, the right to commute services to rent, a riddance of all the restrictions heaped up by the Statute of Laborers[8] over the past thirty years in the effort to clamp labor in place. They had listened to Lollard[9] priests, and to secular preachers moved by the evils of the time, and to John Ball's theories of leveling. "Matters cannot go well in England," was his theme, "until all things shall be held in common; when there shall be neither vassals nor lords, when the lords shall be no more masters than ourselves.... Are we not all descended from the same parents, Adam and Eve?"

8   Wyclif's[10] spirit, which had dared deny the most pervasive authority of the time, was abroad. What had happened in the last thirty years, as a result of plague, war, oppression, and incompetence, was a weakened acceptance of the system, a mistrust of government and governors, lay and ecclesiastical, an awakening sense that authority could be challenged—that change was in fact possible. Moral authority can be no stronger than its acknowledgment. When officials were venal—as even the poor could see they were in the bribing of tax commissioners—and warriors a curse and the Church oppressive, the push for change gained strength.

9   It was encouraged by the preachers' castigation of the powerful. "The tournaments of the rich," they said, "are the torments of the poor." They regularly denounced "evil princes," "false executors who increase the sorrows of widows," "wicked ecclesiastics who show the worst example to the people," and, above all, nobles who empty the purses of the poor by their extravagance, and disdain them for "lowness of blod or foulenesse of body," for deformed shape of body or limb, for dullness of wit and uncunning of craft, and deign not to speak to them, and who are themselves stuffed with pride—of ancestry, fortune, gentility, possessions, power, comeliness, strength,

---

7. **Jacquerie** (zhak REE) disorganized peasant uprising in France that was suppressed violently by the nobility.
8. **Statute of Laborers** law restricting the rights of workers, passed in the wake of the Black Death, in order to keep the reduced workforce tied to the land and farm work.
9. **Lollard** (LOL uhrd) belonging to a dissenting religious movement that protested the extravagance of the Catholic Church and called for reform.
10. **Wyclif** John Wyclif (1331–1384), an English philosopher and lay preacher, who founded the Lollards and translated the Bible from Latin to English in secret.

NOTES

An artist's view of the Black Plague in London, 1349

children, treasure—"prowde in lokynge, prowde in spekyng, . . . prowde in goinge, standynge and sytting." All would be drawn by fiends to Hell on the Day of Judgment.

10   On that day of wrath, said the Dominican John Bromyard in terms that spoke directly to the peasant, the rich would have hung around their necks the oxen and sheep and beasts of the field that they had seized without paying for. The "righteous poor," promised a Franciscan friar, "will stand up against the cruel rich at the Day of Judgment and will accuse them of their works and severity on earth. 'Ha, ha!' will say the others, horribly frightened, 'These are the folk formerly in contempt. See how they are honored—they are among the sons of God! What are riches and pomp to us now who are abased?'"

11   If the meek were indeed the sons of God (even if they too were scolded by the preachers for greed, cheating, and irreverence), why should they wait for their rights until the Day of Judgment? If all men had a common origin in Adam and Eve, how should some be held in

hereditary servitude? If all were equalized by death, as the medieval idea constantly emphasized, was it not possible that inequalities on earth were contrary to the will of God?

12   At its climax on the outskirts of London, the Peasants' Revolt came to the edge of overpowering the government. No measures had been taken against the oncoming horde, partly from contempt for all Wills and Cobbs and Jacks and black-nailed louts, partly from mediocre leadership and lack of ready resources. Lancaster was away on the Scottish border, Buckingham was in Wales, and the only organized armed forces were already embarking at Plymouth for Spain under the command of the third brother, Edmund of Cambridge. Except for 500 or 600 men-at-arms in the King's retinue, the crown controlled no police or militia; London's citizens were unreliable because many were in sympathy and some in active connivance with the rebels.

13   Twenty thousand peasants were camped outside the walls demanding parley with the King. While they promised him safety, they shouted for the heads of Archbishop Sudbury and Sir Robert Hailes, the Chancellor and Treasurer, whom they held responsible for the poll tax, and for the head, too, of the arch "traitor," John of Gaunt, symbol of misgovernment and a failing war. John Ball harangued them with a fierce call to cast off the yoke they had borne for so long, to exterminate all great lords, judges, and lawyers and gain for all men equal freedom, rank, and power.

14   In agitated council, the government could find no course but to negotiate. Richard II, a slight fair boy of fourteen, accompanied by his knights, rode out to meet the insurgents and hear their demands: abolition of the poll tax and of all bonds of servile status, commutation at a rate of four pence an acre, free use of forests, abolition of the game laws—all these to be confirmed in charters sealed by the King. Everything the rebels asked was conceded in the hope of getting them to disperse and go home.

15   Meanwhile, partisans had opened the city's gates and bridges to a group led by Wat Tyler, who gained possession of the Tower of London and murdered Archbishop Sudbury and Sir Robert Hailes. Balked of Gaunt, they flung themselves upon his palace of the Savoy and tore it apart in an orgy of burning and smashing. At Wat Tyler's order, it was to be not looted but destroyed. Barrels of gunpowder found in storage were thrown on the flames, tapestries ripped, precious jewels pounded to bits with ax heads. The Temple, center of the law with all its deeds and records, was similarly destroyed. Killing followed; Lombards and Flemings (hated simply as foreigners), magnates, officials, and designated "traitors" (such as the rich merchant Sir Richard Lyons, who had been impeached by the Good Parliament and restored by Lancaster) were hunted down and slain.

16   In the hectic sequence of events, only Richard moved in a magic circle of reverence for the King's person. Perched on a tall war-horse before the peasants, a charming boy robed in purple embroidered with the royal leopards, wearing a crown and carrying a gold rod, gracious and smiling and gaining confidence from his sway over the mob, he granted charters written out and distributed by thirty clerks on the spot. On this basis, many groups of peasants departed, believing in the King as their protector.

17   While in London, Sir Robert Knollys, the Master of War, was urgently assembling an armed force. Wat Tyler, inflamed by blood and conquest, was exhorting his followers toward a massacre of the ruling class and a takeover of London. He was no longer to be satisfied by the promised charters, which he suspected were hollow, and he knew he would never be included in any pardon. He could only go forward toward a seizure of power. According to Walsingham, he boasted that "in four days' time all the laws of England would be issuing from his mouth."

18   He returned to the camp at Smithfield for another meeting with the King, where he put forth a new set of demands so extreme as to suggest that their purpose was to **provoke** rejection and provide a pretext for seizing Richard in person: all inequalities of rank and status were to be abolished, all men to be equal below the King, the Church to be disendowed[11] and its estates divided among the commons, England to have but one bishop and the rest of the hierarchy to be eliminated. The King promised everything consistent with the "regality of his crown." Accounts of the next moments are so variously colored by the passions of the time that the scene remains forever obscure. Apparently Tyler picked a quarrel with a squire of the King's retinue, drew a dagger, and in a flash was himself struck down by the short sword of William Walworth, Mayor of London.

19   All was confusion and frenzy. The peasants drew their bows; some arrows flew. Richard, with extraordinary nerve, ordering no one to follow, rode forward alone, saying to the rebels, "Sirs, what is it you require? I am your captain. I am your King. Quiet yourselves." While he parleyed, Knollys' force, hastily summoned, rode up and surrounded the camp in mailed might with visors down and weapons gleaming. Dismayed and leaderless, the peasants were cowed; Wat Tyler's head displayed on a lance completed their collapse, like that of the Jacques at the death of Guillaume Cale.

20   Ordered to lay down their arms and assured of pardons to encourage dispersal, they trailed homeward. Leaders, including John Ball, were hanged and the rising elsewhere in England was suppressed—with sufficient brutality, if not the wild massacre that had taken place in France after the Jacquerie. Except for scattered retribution, the English revolt, too, was over within a month, defeated

Mark familiar word parts or indicate another strategy you used that helped you determine meaning.

provoke (pruh VOHK) *v.*

MEANING:

---

11. **disendowed** *v.* deprived of financial endowment, in this case of the lands and tithes given to the Church by the English.

more by fraud than by force. The pardons issued in the King's name were revoked without compunction, and the charters canceled by a landowners' Parliament on the grounds that they had been issued under duress. To a deputation from Essex who came to remind the King of his promise to end villeinage, Richard replied, "Villeins you are, and villeins ye shall remain." ❧

Comprehension Check

Complete the following items after you finish your first read. Review and clarify details with your group.

1. According to Tuchman, what was the immediate cause of the revolt?

2. Where did the peasants get some of their ideas about equality and freedom?

3. Where did the Peasants' Rebellion reach its climax, according to this account?

- -

RESEARCH

Research to Clarify Choose at least one unfamiliar detail from the text. Briefly research that detail. In what way does the information you learned shed light on an aspect of the historical account?

from THE WORMS OF THE EARTH
AGAINST THE LIONS

TIP

FOR GROUP DISCUSSION
If you disagree with an opinion, allow the speaker to finish. Then, raise your objection tactfully—for example, you might say, "I see it a little differently." Make sure that you have textual evidence to support your idea before you continue.

Close Read the Text

With your group, revisit sections of the text you marked during your first read. **Annotate** details that you notice. What **questions** do you have? What can you **conclude**?

Analyze the Text

> **CITE TEXTUAL EVIDENCE**
> to support your answers.

Notebook Complete the activities.

1. **Review and Clarify** With your group, reread "The Worms of the Earth Against the Lions." Discuss Tuchman's explanation of the peasants' revolt. Does Tuchman reveal any biases? Explain.

2. **Present and Discuss** Now, work with your group to share the passages from the selection that you found especially important. Take turns presenting your passages. Discuss what details you noticed, what questions you asked, and what conclusions you reached.

3. **Essential Question:** *How do people come to have different views of society?* What has this text taught you about what influences people's views of society? Discuss with your group.

LANGUAGE DEVELOPMENT

Concept Vocabulary

demagogue	animosity	provoke

Why These Words? The three concept vocabulary words from the text are related. With your group, determine what the words have in common. How do these words enhance the impact of the text?

WORD NETWORK

Add interesting words related to society from the text to your Word Network.

Practice

Notebook Confirm your understanding of the concept vocabulary words by using them in sentences. Be sure to include context clues that hint at each word's meaning.

Word Study

Notebook **Greek Root Word: *agogos*** The word *demagogue* derives from the Greek root word *agogos*, meaning "leader." English words formed from this root word often end with -*agogue* or -*agogy*.

1. Look up the words *synagogue* and *pedagogy* in a college-level dictionary. Explain how the root word *agogos* contributes to their meanings.

2. Consult an etymological dictionary to find another word that derives from the root word *agogos*. Write the word and its meaning.

STANDARDS

Language
Consult general and specialized reference materials, both print and digital, to find the pronunciation of a word or determine or clarify its precise meaning, its part of speech, its etymology, or its standard usage.

Analyze Craft and Structure

Historical Writing When you read informative writing about a historical event, it is important to notice whether the writing is a primary or a secondary source.

- A **primary source** offers an eyewitness or contemporary view of an event. Primary sources include a wide variety of text types, such as diaries, speeches, official records, and chronicles.

- A **secondary source** interprets and analyzes primary sources. Secondary sources are one or more steps removed from the event. Such sources include textbooks, commentaries, encyclopedias, and histories.

Secondary sources, such as Tuchman's account of the Peasant Rebellion, rely on both primary and earlier secondary sources as evidence of facts. They often go further by providing interpretation of these facts. Interpretation of facts sometimes reveals **bias**, in which an author's values, subjective feelings, and allegiances influence how he or she perceives the evidence. Bias is often indicated by "value words," such as *honorable*, *wicked, or mean-spirited*. **Objectivity**, on the other hand, is neutrality or even-handedness. In a completely objective account, a writer reports facts but does not take a position or express an opinion.

Tuchman's account includes several examples of **interpretation**, in which she offers her own evaluation of the facts. For example, she writes: "Richard, with extraordinary nerve, ordering no one to follow, rode forward alone. . . ." By characterizing the king's actions, Tuchman expresses admiration for him. This is an interpretation of events that reveals the writer's subjective feelings about the event.

▦ STANDARDS

Reading Informational Text
• Cite strong and thorough textual evidence to support analysis of what the text says explicitly as well as inferences drawn from the text, including determining where the text leaves matters uncertain.
• Analyze a complex set of ideas or sequence of events and explain how specific individuals, ideas, or events interact and develop over the course of the text.

Practice

CITE TEXTUAL EVIDENCE
to support your answers.

With your group, use a chart like this one to analyze Tuchman's historical account. Record instances in which she gives evidence from another source, interprets or explains events, and reveals her own judgments or biases.

HISTORICAL ACCOUNT	REFERENCES FROM ACCOUNT
gives evidence	
interprets events	
reveals biases	

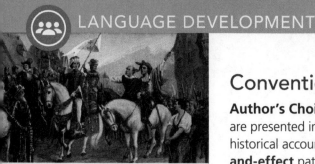

from THE WORMS OF THE EARTH
AGAINST THE LIONS

Conventions and Style

Author's Choices: Text Structure Chronological order, in which events are presented in the order they occurred, is a natural choice for writers of historical accounts, such as *A Distant Mirror*. Historians also present **cause-and-effect** patterns to emphasize connections among events and the reasons they happened. Cause-and-effect relationships can be analyzed in many different ways:

- a single cause leading to a single effect
- a single cause leading to multiple effects
- multiple causes leading to a single effect
- a chain of causes and effects, in which one effect becomes the cause for the next effect, and so on

Interestingly, the same events can be seen in a variety of these ways, depending on the historian's interpretation and emphasis, as well as the timeframe of the events he or she is examining.

Read It

Work together to complete the chart. Identify one cause Tuchman presents in her account. Then, note all the effects of that cause that you can logically connect. Do the same for a second cause.

CAUSE 1:	CAUSE 2:
EFFECT:	EFFECT:
EFFECT:	EFFECT:
EFFECT:	EFFECT:

Write It

As a group, discuss other ways that you can represent the cause-and-effect relationships that you find in the Tuchman selection. Look especially for chains of causes and effects and single cause/multiple effects. Finally, use your understanding of cause and effect to write a brief interpretation/explanation of the causes underlying King Richard's final statement: "Villeins you are, and villeins ye shall remain."

:≣ STANDARDS
Reading Informational Text
Analyze a complex set of ideas or sequence of events and explain how specific individuals, ideas, or events interact and develop over the course of the text.

Speaking and Listening

Assignment

As a group, have a **discussion** about the issues of social justice and social order raised by the selection. Use details from "The Worms of the Earth Against the Lions" in your presentations. Choose from the following.

☐ Divide your group into teams, and hold a **debate**, with a moderator and a note-taker, on the following proposition:

> *Wat Tyler and his followers were justified in their rebellion against the social order of their day.*

Remember to allow each debater to finish his or her argument without interruption. Classmates in the audience should vote to determine which side won the debate.

☐ In your group, hold a **panel discussion**, with a moderator and a note-taker, to discuss these questions:

- What does the Peasant Rebellion of 1381 show (if anything) about the relation between social justice and social order?
- In what present-day social conflicts does the desire for social justice come into conflict with the need for social order?
- What is the best way to resolve such conflicts?

Be careful not to interrupt or "talk over" your fellow panelists. After the discussion, entertain questions from classmates in the audience.

☐ Divide your group into two teams in order to **role-play** serfs and nobles. Hold a discussion, in character, in which you try to work out your differences to arrive at a fair solution to your conflict.

After the role-play, participants should respond to questions from the audience.

1. **Prepare Your Delivery** No matter which option you have chosen, you will need to use examples from the selection as the basis of your performance. Take extensive notes on both sides of the issue, and be prepared to answer questions from your audience.

2. **Evaluate Presentations** As your classmates make their presentations, listen attentively. Use an evaluation guide like the one shown to analyze their performances.

PRESENTATION EVALUATION GUIDE

Rate each statement on a scale of 1 (not demonstrated) to 6 (demonstrated).

☐ The speaker communicates clearly and effectively.

☐ The speaker used examples from the selection effectively.

☐ The speaker used appropriate gestures and body language.

☐ The arguments were logical and reasonable.

✎ EVIDENCE LOG

Before moving on to a new selection, go to your Evidence Log and record what you learned from "The Worms of the Earth Against the Lions."

▤ STANDARDS

Speaking and Listening

• Initiate and participate effectively in a range of collaborative discussions with diverse partners *on grades 11–12 topics, texts, and issues,* building on others' ideas and expressing their own clearly and persuasively.

• Come to discussions prepared, having read and researched material under study; explicitly draw on that preparation by referring to evidence from texts and other research on the topic or issue to stimulate a thoughtful, well-reasoned exchange of ideas.

• Work with peers to promote civil, democratic discussions and decision-making, set clear goals and deadlines, and establish individual roles as needed.

About the Author

Virginia Woolf (1882–1941) was born into a wealthy and accomplished family. Her education at the Ladies' Department of King's College, London, introduced her to the ideas surrounding women's rights reform. A woman of great intellect, she was a member of the Bloomsbury Group, an informal society composed of leading intellectuals, artists, and writers. Her many works include *The Voyage Out* (1915) and *Mrs. Dalloway* (1925). Throughout her life, she continued to write insightful essays and thought-provoking novels.

☰ STANDARDS

Reading Informational Text
By the end of grade 12, read and comprehend literary nonfiction at the high end of the grades 11–CCR text complexity band independently and proficiently.

Language
• Determine or clarify the meaning of unknown and multiple-meaning words and phrases based on *grades 11–12 reading and content*, choosing flexibly from a range of strategies.
• Use context as a clue to the meaning of a word or phrase.
• Verify the preliminary determination of the meaning of a word or phrase.

Shakespeare's Sister

Concept Vocabulary

As you perform your first read of "Shakespeare's Sister," you will encounter the following words.

gifted	taste	fancy

Context Clues If these words are unfamiliar to you, try using **context clues**—other words and phrases that appear nearby in the text—to help you determine their meanings. There are various types of context clues that you may encounter as you read.

> **Synonyms:** Judith was **agog** to see the world, excited and eager for a life of discovery and adventure.
>
> **Restatement of an Idea:** The theater manager **scoffed** at Judith, mocking her ambition to become an actor.
>
> **Contrast of Ideas:** Judith's father ceased to **scold** her, but he begged her instead not to hurt or shame him.

Apply your knowledge of context clues and other vocabulary strategies to determine the meanings of unfamiliar words you encounter during your first read. Use a resource such as a dictionary or a thesaurus to verify the meanings you identify.

First Read NONFICTION

Apply these strategies as you conduct your first read. You will have an opportunity to complete the close-read notes after your first read.

NOTICE the general ideas of the text. *What* is it about? *Who* is involved?

ANNOTATE by marking vocabulary and key passages you want to revisit.

First Read

CONNECT ideas within the selection to what you already know and what you've already read.

RESPOND by completing the Comprehension Check and by writing a brief summary of the selection.

Shakespeare's Sister

Virginia Woolf

BACKGROUND

Virginia Woolf's famous extended essay *A Room of One's Own* was first published in 1929. In this excerpt, Woolf responds to a claim made by a bishop who once wrote to a newspaper to say, "it was impossible for any woman, past, present, or to come, to have the genius of Shakespeare."

1   Be that as it may, I could not help thinking, as I looked at the works of Shakespeare on the shelf, that the bishop was right at least in this; it would have been impossible, completely and entirely, for any woman to have written the plays of Shakespeare in the age of Shakespeare. Let me imagine, since facts are so hard to come by, what would have happened had Shakespeare had a wonderfully **gifted** sister, called Judith, let us say. Shakespeare himself went, very probably—his mother was an heiress—to the grammar school, where he may have learned Latin—Ovid, Virgil and Horace—and the elements of grammar and logic. He was, it is well known, a wild boy who poached[1] rabbits, perhaps shot a deer, and had, rather sooner than he should have done, to marry a woman in the neighborhood, who bore him a child rather quicker than was right. That escapade sent him to seek his fortune in London. He had, it seemed, a **taste** for the theater; he began by holding horses at the stage door. Very soon he got work in the theater, became a successful actor, and lived at the hub of the universe, meeting everybody, knowing everybody, practicing his art on the boards, exercising his wits in the streets,

---

1. **poached** *v.* hunted illegally.

NOTES

Mark context clues or indicate another strategy you used that helped you determine meaning.

gifted (GIHF tihd) *adj.*
MEANING:

taste (tayst) *n.*
MEANING:

and even getting access to the palace of the queen. Meanwhile his extraordinarily gifted sister, let us suppose, remained at home. She was as adventurous, as imaginative, as agog to see the world as he was. But she was not sent to school. She had no chance of learning grammar and logic, let alone of reading Horace and Virgil. She picked up a book now and then, one of her brother's perhaps, and read a few pages. But then her parents came in and told her to mend the stockings or mind the stew and not moon about with books and papers. They would have spoken sharply but kindly, for they were substantial people who knew the conditions of life for a woman and loved their daughter—indeed, more likely than not she was the apple of her father's eye. Perhaps she scribbled some pages up in an apple loft on the sly, but was careful to hide them or set fire to them. Soon, however, before she was out of her teens, she was to be betrothed to the son of a neighboring wool-stapler. She cried out that marriage was hateful to her, and for that she was severely beaten by her father. Then he ceased to scold her. He begged her instead not to hurt him, not to shame him in this matter of her marriage. He would give her a chain of beads or a fine petticoat, he said; and there were tears in his eyes. How could she disobey him? How could she break his heart? The force of her own gift alone drove her to it. She made up a small parcel of her belongings, let herself down by a rope one summer's night and took the road to London. She was not seventeen. The birds that sang in the hedge were not more musical than she was. She had the quickest **fancy**, a gift like her brother's, for the tune of words. Like him, she had a taste for the theater. She stood at the stage door: she wanted to act,[2] she said. Men laughed in her face. The manager—a fat, loose-lipped man—guffawed. He bellowed something about poodles dancing and women acting—no woman, he said, could possibly be an actress. He hinted—you can imagine what. She could get no training in her craft. Could she even seek her dinner in a tavern or roam the streets at midnight? Yet her genius was for fiction and lusted to feed abundantly upon the lives of men and women and the study of their ways. At last—for she was very young, oddly like Shakespeare the poet in her face, with the same gray eyes and rounded brows—at last Nick Greene the actor-manager took pity on her; she found herself with child by that gentleman and so—who shall measure the heat and violence of the poet's heart when caught and tangled in a woman's body?—killed herself one winter night and lies buried at some cross-roads where the omnibuses now stop outside the Elephant and Castle.

2   That, more or less, is how the story would run, I think, if a woman in Shakespeare's day had had Shakespeare's genius. ❧

Mark context clues or indicate another strategy you used that helped you determine meaning.

fancy (FAN see) *n.*

MEANING:

---

2. **she wanted to act** In Shakespeare's time, women were not allowed to act on stage. Men, dressed as women, played female roles.

Comprehension Check

Complete the following items after you finish your first read. Review and clarify details with your group.

1. What subjects did William Shakespeare learn in grammar school? Where did he seek his fortune later?

2. Who is Judith?

3. What causes the quarrel between Judith and her father?

4. When she leaves home, what is Judith's ambition?

5. What happens to Judith and her dreams after she arrives in London?

6. 📝 **Notebook** Confirm your understanding of the text by writing a summary.

- -

RESEARCH

Research to Clarify Choose at least one unfamiliar detail from the text. Briefly research that detail. In what way does the information you learned shed light on an aspect of the essay?

Research to Explore This essay may make you curious about how women have been educated throughout history. Research the nature of women's education in Virginia Woolf's time. You may wish to share what you discover with your group.

Close Review

With your group, revisit the sections of the text you marked during your first read. **Annotate** details that you notice. What **questions** do you have? What can you **conclude**?

Analyze the Text

CITE TEXTUAL EVIDENCE
to support your answers.

Notebook Complete the activities with your group.

1. **Review and Clarify** With your group, reread the background note. Then, read the first sentence of the essay. Does Woolf agree with the bishop? How does your perception of Woolf's opinion about the bishop's statement change as you read the rest of the essay? Explain.

2. **Compare and Contrast** What comparison or contrast does Woolf draw between William Shakespeare and his imaginary sister, Judith?

3. **Essential Question:** *How do people come to have different views of society?* How does Woolf's essay present a different view of Shakespeare's society than the one held by the bishop? How might it reflect Woolf's perspective on women's roles in her own society, as well?

LANGUAGE DEVELOPMENT

Concept Vocabulary

gifted	taste	fancy

Why These Words? The three concept vocabulary words from the text are related. With your group, discuss the words, and determine what they have in common. Write your ideas, and add another word that fits the category.

Practice

Notebook Confirm your understanding of the concept vocabulary words by using them in sentences. Be sure to include context clues that hint at each word's meaning.

Word Study

Multiple-Meaning Words Many words in English have more than one meaning. The word *taste*, which appears in this essay, has many different meanings. Write the meaning of *taste* as Virginia Woolf uses it. Then, write two more definitions of the word. Finally, find two other multiple-meaning words in the essay, and write two definitions for each word.

TIP

GROUP DISCUSSION

Give everyone a chance to contribute to the discussion. If you notice that someone is not participating, encourage him or her to join in.

WORD NETWORK

Add interesting words related to society from the text to your Word Network.

STANDARDS

Language
• Determine or clarify the meaning of unknown and multiple-meaning words and phrases based on *grades 11–12 reading and content*, choosing flexibly from a range of strategies.
• Demonstrate understanding of figurative language, word relationships, and nuances in word meanings.

Analyze Craft and Structure

Interaction and Development of Ideas An **argument** is a persuasive presentation focused on a debatable or controversial issue. Arguments are often based on examples—sometimes called **paradigms**—and on chains of logical reasoning. In "Shakespeare's Sister," Virginia Woolf's example consists of a thought experiment. This thought experiment explores what might have happened if Shakespeare had a wonderfully talented sister who cherished the same ambition as her brother: to succeed in the theater.

Woolf's approach involves the use of vivid details, historical facts, and logical reasoning to connect this thought experiment to her main **claim** in the essay.

Her claim defines her basic position—that the bishop is right, but not for the reasons he thinks. After developing this position throughout the essay, Woolf does not openly state her conclusion. Instead, she allows the reader to infer it based on the evidence she has presented.

STANDARDS
Reading Informational Text
• Cite strong and thorough textual evidence to support analysis of what the text says explicitly as well as inferences drawn from the text, including determining where the text leaves matters uncertain.
• Analyze a complex set of ideas or sequence of events and explain how specific individuals, ideas, or events interact and develop over the course of the text.
• Analyze and evaluate the effectiveness of the structure an author uses in his or her exposition or argument, including whether the structure makes points clear, convincing, and engaging.

Practice

CITE TEXTUAL EVIDENCE to support your answers.

With your group, fill in details about how William Shakespeare's life, as described by Woolf, differed from that of his imaginary sister. Then, state Woolf's conclusion, inferring her position from the details she presents.

	WILLIAM SHAKESPEARE	JUDITH SHAKESPEARE
Education		
Parental Expectations		
Career		
Result of Efforts		
Conclusion (Why was a female Shakespeare impossible?)		

SHAKESPEARE'S SISTER

Conventions and Style

Changing Usage In English, **usage** is the customary manner of using words in speaking or writing. Issues of usage are settled by convention, or agreed-upon practice. Conventions, however, change with the times. It is no longer common practice, for example, to use the word *wit* to mean "intellect" or "reason"—the way it was in the eighteenth century. Today, *wit* is used to mean "humor" or "cleverness."

Changes in usage are sometimes contested, or challenged, by writers, grammarians, educators, or the general public. In the early 1900s, for example, students "*were graduated from* high school." By mid-century, though, students "*graduated from* high school." Today, the statement that students "*graduated* high school" is sometimes used, but it is not universally accepted. The same is true of converting the noun *impact* to a verb, as in the sentence "The accusations *impacted* the candidate unfavorably." Although this usage has become widespread, it remains hotly contested.

Read It

The three concept vocabulary words for this selection are good examples of words that have changed in usage.

1. Using a dictionary, as well as specialized reference tools, such as an etymological dictionary or a dictionary of usage, research the histories and meanings of *gifted, taste,* and *fancy*. Record your findings in the chart.

GIFTED	TASTE	FANCY

2. Find another example of a word or phrase from Woolf's essay that has changed in usage since her time. Explain how its usage has changed.

Write It

Paraphrase this sentence from the essay: "Yet her genius was for fiction and lusted to feed abundantly upon the lives of men and women and the study of their ways." In doing so, consider each word's usage at the time that Woolf was writing. Consult a specialized reference tool if necessary.

STANDARDS

Language
• Demonstrate command of the conventions of standard English grammar and usage when writing or speaking.
• Apply the understanding that usage is a matter of convention, can change over time, and is sometimes contested.
• Resolve issues of complex or contested usage, consulting references as needed.
• Consult general and specialized reference materials both print and digital, to find the pronunciation of a word or determine or clarify its precise meaning, its part of speech, its etymology, or its standard usage.

Writing to Sources

Assignment

With your group, prepare to write an **argument** defending a claim and responding to a counterclaim. Choose from the following for your writing:

☐ **Updated Argument About Judith** Establish a position on the following statement:

> *Today, Shakespeare's imaginary sister, Judith, would not face any obstacles to success.*

Write a paragraph in which you state and support your claim, drawing on details from Woolf's essay. Write a second paragraph in which you introduce and respond to a counterclaim.

☐ **Argument With Narrative** State a claim about a social problem individuals face in today's world, followed by a counterclaim. Then, write a brief narrative illustrating the problem, using storytelling techniques similar to those employed by Woolf. Conclude by explaining how your narrative helps to answer the counterclaim. When you submit your writing, include a note explaining which of Woolf's techniques you used, along with two examples.

☐ **Argument About Society's Power** According to Woolf, society restricted the options available to Judith, with tragic results. Is it ever legitimate for society to push a person into certain roles or restrict the person from others, based on his or her background, gender, or similar factors? Write an argument stating and defending your answer to this question. In your argument, consider a counterclaim, and answer it. Draw on examples from "Shakespeare's Sister."

Project Plan Work with your group to divide the writing assignment that you chose into manageable sections. Outline your ideas, and assign each member a part of the writing assignment.

Working Title: _____

SECTION	ASSIGNED PERSON
Introduction	
Argument defending claim	
Response to counterclaim	
Conclusion	

Tying It Together Once everyone has written his or her part of the project, get together and read the sections aloud. Suggest revisions, and reread the material to make sure that the final product expresses the arguments clearly and persuasively.

📝 **EVIDENCE LOG**

Before moving on to a new selection, go to your Evidence Log and record what you learned from "Shakespeare's Sister."

▤ **STANDARDS**

Writing
• Write arguments to support claims in an analysis of substantive topics or texts, using valid reasoning and relevant and sufficient evidence.
• Introduce precise, knowledgeable claim(s), establish the significance of the claim(s), distinguish the claim(s) from alternate or opposing claims, and create an organization that logically sequences claim(s), counterclaims, reasons, and evidence.
• Develop claim(s) and counterclaims fairly and thoroughly, supplying the most relevant evidence for each while pointing out the strengths and limitations of both in a manner that anticipates the audience's knowledge level, concerns, values, and possible biases.

ESSAY

On Seeing England for the First Time

POEM

XXIII *from* Midsummer

Concept Vocabulary

As you perform your first read, you will encounter the following words.

subjugation	privileged	fellowships

Base Words If these words are unfamiliar to you, analyze each one to see whether it contains a base word you know. Then, use your knowledge of the base word, along with context, to determine the meaning of the concept word. Here is an example of how to apply the strategy.

Unfamiliar Word: *dispassionate*

Familiar Base Word: *passion*, meaning "any extreme emotion"

Context: Rather than cheering wildly for one candidate or the other, she remained dispassionate.

Conclusion: Remaining dispassionate is contrasted with cheering wildly. *Dispassionate* may mean "lacking extreme emotion," or "calm."

Apply your knowledge of base words and other vocabulary strategies to determine the meanings of unfamiliar words you encounter during your first read.

First Read ESSAY | POETRY

Apply these strategies as you conduct your first read. You will have an opportunity to complete a close read after your first read.

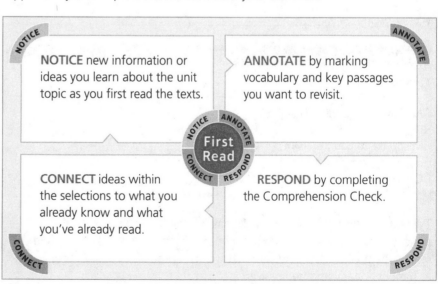

NOTICE new information or ideas you learn about the unit topic as you first read the texts.

ANNOTATE by marking vocabulary and key passages you want to revisit.

CONNECT ideas within the selections to what you already know and what you've already read.

RESPOND by completing the Comprehension Check.

First Read

STANDARDS

Reading Literature
By the end of grade 12, read and comprehend literature, including stories, dramas, and poems, at the high end of the grades 11–CCR text complexity band independently and proficiently.

Reading Informational Text
By the end of grade 12, read and comprehend literary nonfiction at the high end of the grades 11–CCR text complexity band independently and proficiently.

Language
• Determine or clarify the meaning of unknown and multiple-meaning words and phrases based on *grades 11–12 reading and content*, choosing flexibly from a range of strategies.
• Use context as a clue to the meaning of a word or phrase.

About the Authors

Jamaica Kincaid (b. 1949) was born in Antigua, in the Caribbean. She left that country at the age of 16 and moved to Scarsdale, New York, to work as a domestic assistant to a wealthy family. A few years later, she moved to New York City to work at a teenage girls' magazine. While there, she also began to write and to submit work to the *New Yorker*. She would become a staff writer for that magazine three years later.

Derek Walcott (1930–2017) was born on the Caribbean Island of St. Lucia, where he spoke both the island dialect and English. He graduated from the University of the West Indies. As a precocious eighteen-year-old, Walcott published the first of his many volumes of poetry, *Twenty-five Poems*, by using two hundred dollars that he borrowed to print and distribute it on the street. He went on to have a prolific career as both a poet and playwright. He won the Nobel Prize for Literature in 1992.

Backgrounds

On Seeing England for the First Time

The island nation of Antigua and Barbuda, located in the Caribbean Sea, has a history of colonial occupation and resistance, beginning from 1632, when British settlers formed a colony and brought Africans to the islands to work as slaves. Antigua and Barbuda gained complete independence from the United Kingdom in 1981.

XXIII *from* Midsummer

In colonial times, British settlers brought enslaved Africans to work on their plantations in the West Indies. Slavery finally ended in the 1830s. Many present-day West Indians have immigrated to Britain, only to encounter prejudice and hardship. Their frustrations erupted in the April 1981 riots in the neighborhood of Brixton, London.

On Seeing England for the First Time

Jamaica Kincaid

1   When I saw England for the first time, I was a child in school sitting at a desk. The England I was looking at was laid out on a map gently, beautifully, delicately, a very special jewel; it lay on a bed of sky blue—the background of the map—its yellow form mysterious, because though it looked like a leg of mutton, it could not really look like anything so familiar as a leg of mutton because it was England—with shadings of pink and green, unlike any shadings of pink and green I had seen before, squiggly veins of red running in every direction. England was a special jewel all right, and only special people got to wear it. The people who got to wear England were English people. They wore it well and they wore it everywhere: in jungles, in deserts, on plains, on top of the highest mountains, on all the oceans, on all the seas, in places where they were not welcome, in places they should not have been. When my teacher had pinned this map up on the blackboard, she said, "This is England"—and she said it with authority, seriousness; and adoration, and we all sat up. It was as if she had said, "This is Jerusalem, the place you will

go to when you die but only if you have been good." We understood then—we were meant to understand then—that England was to be our source of myth and the source from which we got our sense of reality, our sense of what was meaningful, our sense of what was meaningless—and much about our own lives and much about the very idea of us headed that last list.

2   At the time I was a child sitting at my desk seeing England for the first time, I was already very familiar with the greatness of it. Each morning before I left for school, I ate a breakfast of half a grapefruit, an egg, bread and butter and a slice of cheese, and a cup of cocoa; or half a grapefruit, a bowl of oat porridge, bread and butter and a slice of cheese, and a cup of cocoa. The can of cocoa was often left on the table in front of me. It had written on it the name of the company, the year the company was established, and the words "Made in England." Those words, "Made in England," were written on the box the oats came in too. They would also have been written on the box the shoes I was wearing came in; a bolt of gray linen cloth lying on the shelf of a store from which my mother had bought three yards to make the uniform that I was wearing had written along its edge those three words. The shoes I wore were made in England; so were my socks and cotton undergarments and the satin ribbons I wore tied at the end of two plaits of my hair. My father, who might have sat next to me at breakfast, was a carpenter and cabinet maker. The shoes he wore to work would have been made in England, as were his khaki shirt and trousers, his underpants and undershirt, his socks and brown felt hat. Felt was not the proper material from which a hat that was expected to provide shade from the hot sun should be made, but my father must have seen and admired a picture of an Englishman wearing such a hat in England, and this picture that he saw must have been so compelling that it caused him to wear the wrong hat for a hot climate most of his long life. And this hat—a brown felt hat— became so central to his character that it was the first thing he put on in the morning as he stepped out of bed and the last thing he took off before he stepped back into bed at night. As we sat at breakfast a car might go by. The car, a Hillman or a Zephyr, was made in England. The very idea of the meal itself, breakfast, and its substantial quality and quantity was an idea from England; we somehow knew that in England they began the day with this meal called breakfast and a proper breakfast was a big breakfast. No one I knew liked eating so much food so early in the day; it made us feel sleepy, tired. But this breakfast business was Made in England like almost everything else that surrounded us, the exceptions being the sea, the sky, and the air we breathed.

3   At the time I saw this map—seeing England for the first time—I did not say to myself, "Ah, so that's what it looks like," because there was no longing in me to put a shape to those three words that ran through every part of my life, no matter how small; for me to have had such a longing would have meant that I lived in a certain

atmosphere, an atmosphere in which those three words were felt as a burden. But I did not live in such an atmosphere. My father's brown felt hat would develop a hole in its crown, the lining would separate from the hat itself, and six weeks before he thought that he could not be seen wearing it—he was a very vain man—he would order another hat from England. And my mother taught me to eat my food in the English way: the knife in the right hand, the fork in the left, my elbows held still close to my side, the food carefully balanced on my fork and then brought up to my mouth. When I had finally mastered it, I overheard her saying to a friend, "Did you see how nicely she can eat?" But I knew then that I enjoyed my food more when I ate it with my bare hands, and I continued to do so when she wasn't looking. And when my teacher showed us the map, she asked us to study it carefully, because no test we would ever take would be complete without this statement: "Draw a map of England."

4   I did not know then that the statement "Draw a map of England" was something far worse than a declaration of war, for in fact a flat-out declaration of war would have put me on alert, and again in fact, there was no need for war—I had long ago been conquered. I did not know then that this statement was part of a process that would result in my erasure, not my physical erasure, but my erasure all the same. I did not know then that this statement was meant to make me feel in awe and small whenever I heard the word "England": awe at its existence, small because I was not from it. I did not know very much of anything then—certainly not what a blessing it was that I was unable to draw a map of England correctly.

5   After that there were many times of seeing England for the first time. I saw England in history. I knew the names of all the kings of England. I knew the names of their children, their wives, their disappointments, their triumphs, the names of people who betrayed them, I knew the dates on which they were born and the dates they died. I knew their conquests and was made to feel glad if I figured in them; I knew their defeats. I knew the details of the year 1066 (the Battle of Hastings, the end of the reign of the Anglo-Saxon kings) before I knew the details of the year 1832 (the year slavery was abolished). It wasn't as bad as I make it sound now; it was worse. I did like so much hearing again and again how Alfred the Great, traveling in disguise, had been left to watch cakes, and because he wasn't used to this the cakes got burned, and Alfred burned his hands pulling them out of the fire, and the woman who had left him to watch the cakes screamed at him. I loved King Alfred. My grandfather was named after him; his son, my uncle, was named after King Alfred; my brother is named after King Alfred. And so there are three people in my family named after a man they have never met, a man who died over ten centuries ago. The first view I got of England then was not unlike the first view received by the person who named my grandfather.

6   This view, though—the naming of the kings, their deeds, their disappointments—was the vivid view, the forceful view. There were other views, subtler ones, softer, almost not there—but these were the ones that made the most lasting impression on me, these were the ones that made me really feel like nothing. "When morning touched the sky" was one phrase, for no morning touched the sky where I lived. The mornings where I lived came on abruptly, with a shock of heat and loud noises. "Evening approaches" was another, but the evenings where I lived did not approach; in fact, I had no evening—I had night and I had day and they came and went in a mechanical way: on, off; on, off. And then there were gentle mountains and low blue skies and moors over which people took walks for nothing but pleasure, when where I lived a walk was an act of labor, a burden, something only death or the automobile could relieve. And there were things that a small turn of a head could convey—entire worlds, whole lives would depend on this thing, a certain turn of a head. Everyday life could be quite tiring, more tiring than anything I was told not to do. I was told not to gossip, but they did that all the time. And they ate so much food, violating another of those rules they taught me: do not indulge in gluttony. And the foods they ate actually: if only sometime I could eat cold cuts after theater, cold cuts of lamb and mint sauce, and Yorkshire pudding and scones, and clotted cream, and sausages that came from upcountry (imagine, "up-country"). And having troubling thoughts at twilight, a good time to have troubling thoughts, apparently; and servants who stole and left in the middle of a crisis, who were born with a limp or some other kind of deformity, not nourished properly in their mother's womb (that last part I figured out for myself; the point was, oh to have an untrustworthy servant); and wonderful cobbled streets onto which solid front doors opened; and people whose eyes were blue and who had fair skins and who smelled only of lavender, or sometimes sweet pea or primrose. And those flowers with those names: delphiniums, foxgloves, tulips, daffodils, floribunda, peonies; in bloom, a striking display, being cut and placed in large glass bowls, crystal, decorating rooms so large twenty families the size of mine could fit in comfortably but used only for passing through. And the weather was so remarkable because the rain fell gently always, only occasionally in deep gusts, and it colored the air various shades of gray, each an appealing shade for a dress to be worn when a portrait was being painted; and when it rained at twilight, wonderful things happened: people bumped into each other unexpectedly and that would lead to all sorts of turns of events—a plot, the mere weather caused plots. I saw that people rushed: they rushed to catch trains, they rushed toward each other and away from each other; they rushed and rushed and rushed. That word: rushed! I did not know what it was to do that. It was too hot to do that, and so I came to envy people who would rush, even though it had no meaning to me to do such a thing. But there they are again. They loved their children; their

Mark base words or indicate another strategy you used that helped you determine meaning.

subjugation (suhb juh GAY shuhn) *n.*

MEANING:

children were sent to their own rooms as a punishment, rooms larger than my entire house. They were special, everything about them said so, even their clothes; their clothes rustled, swished, soothed. The world was theirs, not mine; everything told me so.

7   If now as I speak of all this I give the impression of someone on the outside looking in, nose pressed up against a glass window, that is wrong. My nose was pressed up against a glass window all right, but there was an iron vise at the back of my neck forcing my head to stay in place. To avert my gaze was to fall back into something from which I had been rescued, a hole filled with nothing, and that was the word for everything about me, nothing. The reality of my life was conquests, subjugation, humiliation, enforced amnesia. I was forced to forget. Just for instance, this: I lived in a part of St. John's, Antigua, called Ovals. Ovals was made up of five streets, each of them named after a famous English seaman—to be quite frank, an officially sanctioned criminal: Rodney Street (after George Rodney), Nelson Street (after Horatio Nelson), Drake Street (after Francis Drake), Hood Street, and Hawkins Street (after John Hawkins). But John Hawkins was knighted after a trip he made to Africa, opening up a new trade, the slave trade. He was then entitled to wear as his crest a Negro bound with a cord. Every single person living on Hawkins Street was descended from a slave. John Hawkins's ship, the one in which he transported the people he had bought and kidnapped, was called *The Jesus*. He later became the treasurer of the Royal Navy and rear admiral.

8   Again, the reality of my life, the life I led at the time I was being shown these views of England for the first time, for the second time, for the one-hundred-millionth time, was this: the sun shone with what sometimes seemed to be a deliberate cruelty; we must have done something to deserve that. My dresses did not rustle in the evening air as I strolled to the theater (I had no evening, I had no theater; my dresses were made of a cheap cotton, the weave of which would give way after not too many washings). I got up in the morning, I did my chores (fetched water from the public pipe for my mother, swept the yard), I washed myself, I went to a woman to have my hair combed freshly every day (because before we were allowed into our classroom our teachers would inspect us, and children who had not bathed that day, or had dirt under their fingernails, or whose hair had not been combed anew that day, might not be allowed to attend class). I ate that breakfast. I walked to school. At school we gathered in an auditorium and sang a hymn, "All Things Bright and Beautiful," and looking down on us as we sang were portraits of the Queen of England and her husband; they wore jewels and medals and they smiled. I was a Brownie. At each meeting we would form a little group around a flagpole, and after raising the Union Jack, we would say, "I promise to do my best, to do my duty to God and the Queen, to help other people every day and obey the scouts' law."

9   Who were these people and why had I never seen them, I mean really seen them, in the place where they lived? I had never been to England. No one I knew had ever been to England, or I should say, no one I knew had ever been and returned to tell me about it. All the people I knew who had gone to England had stayed there. Sometimes they left behind them their small children, never to see them again. England! I had seen England's representatives. I had seen the governor general at the public grounds at a ceremony celebrating the Queen's birthday. I had seen an old princess and I had seen a young princess. They had both been extremely not beautiful, but who of us would have told them that? I had never seen England, really seen it, I had only met a representative, seen a picture, read books, memorized its history. I had never set foot, my own foot, in it.

10   The space between the idea of something and its reality is always wide and deep and dark. The longer they are kept apart—idea of thing, reality of thing—the wider the width, the deeper the depth, the thicker and darker the darkness. This space starts out empty, there is nothing in it, but it rapidly becomes filled up with obsession or desire or hatred or love—sometimes all of these things, sometimes some of these things, sometimes only one of these things. The existence of the world as I came to know it was a result of this: idea of thing over here, reality of thing way, way over there. There was Christopher Columbus, an unlikable man, an unpleasant man, a liar (and so, of course, a thief) surrounded by maps and schemes and plans, and there was the reality on the other side of that width, that depth, that darkness. He became obsessed, he became filled with desire, the hatred came later, love was never a part of it. Eventually, his idea met the longed-for reality. That the idea of something and its reality are often two completely different things is something no one ever remembers; and so when they meet and find that they are not compatible, the weaker of the two, idea or reality, dies. That idea Christopher Columbus had was more powerful than the reality he met, and so the reality he met died.

11   And so finally, when I was a grown-up woman, the mother of two children, the wife of someone, a person who resides in a powerful country that takes up more than its fair share of a continent, the owner of a house with many rooms in it and of two automobiles, with the desire and will (which I very much act upon) to take from the world more than I give back to it, more than I deserve, more than I need, finally then, I saw England, the real England, not a picture, not a painting, not through a story in a book, but England, for the first time. In me, the space between the idea of it and its reality had become filled with hatred, and so when at last I saw it I wanted to take it into my hands and tear it into little pieces and then crumble it up as if it were clay, child's clay. That was impossible, and so I could only indulge in not-favorable opinions.

12   There were monuments everywhere; they commemorated victories, battles fought between them and the people who lived

across the sea from them, all vile people, fought over which of them would have dominion over the people who looked like me. The monuments were useless to them now, people sat on them and ate their lunch. They were like markers on an old useless trail, like a piece of old string tied to a finger to jog the memory, like old decoration in an old house, dirty, useless, in the way. Their skins were so pale, it made them look so fragile, so weak, so ugly. What if I had the power to simply banish them from their land, send boat after boatload of them on a voyage that in fact had no destination, force them to live in a place where the sun's presence was a constant? This would rid them of their pale complexion and make them look more like me, make them look more like the people I love and treasure and hold dear, and more like the people who occupy the near and far reaches of my imagination, my history, my geography, and reduce them and everything they have ever known to figurines as evidence that I was in divine favor, what if all this was in my power? Could I resist it? No one ever has.

13   And they were rude, they were rude to each other. They didn't like each other very much. They didn't like each other in the way they didn't like me, and it occurred to me that their dislike for me was one of the few things they agreed on.

14   I was on a train in England with a friend, an English woman. Before we were in England she liked me very much. In England she didn't like me at all. She didn't like the claim I said I had on England, she didn't like the views I had of England. I didn't like England, she didn't like England, but she didn't like me not liking it too. She said, "I want to show you my England, I want to show you the England that I know and love." I had told her many times before that I knew England and I didn't want to love it anyway. She no longer lived in England; it was her own country, but it had not been kind to her, so she left. On the train, the conductor was rude to her; she asked something, and he responded in a rude way. She became ashamed. She was ashamed at the way he treated her; she was ashamed at the way he behaved. "This is the *new* England," she said. But I liked the conductor being rude; his behavior seemed quite appropriate. Earlier this had happened: we had gone to a store to buy a shirt for my husband; it was meant to be a special present, a special shirt to wear on special occasions. This was a store where the Prince of Wales has his shirts made, but the shirts sold in this store are beautiful all the same. I found a shirt I thought my husband would like and I wanted to buy him a tie to go with it. When I couldn't decide which one to choose, the salesman showed me a new set. He was very pleased with these, he said, because they bore the crest of the Prince of Wales, and the Prince of Wales had never allowed his crest to decorate an article of clothing before. There was something in the way he said it; his tone was slavish, reverential, awed. It made me feel angry; I wanted to hit him. I didn't do that. I said, my husband and I hate princes, my husband would never wear anything that had a prince's

anything on it. My friend stiffened. The salesman stiffened. They both drew themselves in, away from me. My friend told me that the prince was a symbol of her Englishness, and I could see that I had caused offense. I looked at her. She was an English person, the sort of English person I used to know at home, the sort who was nobody in England but somebody when they came to live among the people like me. There were many people I could have seen England with; that I was seeing it with this particular person, a person who reminded me of the people who showed me England long ago as I sat in church or at my desk, made me feel silent and afraid, for I wondered if, all these years of our friendship, I had had a friend or had been in the thrall of a racial memory.

15   I went to Bath—we, my friend and I, did this, but though we were together, I was no longer with her. The landscape was almost as familiar as my own hand, but I had never been in this place before, so how could that be again? And the streets of Bath were familiar, too, but I had never walked on them before. It was all those years of reading, starting with Roman Britain. Why did I have to know about Roman Britain? It was of no real use to me, a person living on a hot, drought-ridden island, and it is of no use to me now, and yet my head is filled with this nonsense, Roman Britain. In Bath, I drank tea in a room I had read about in a novel written in the eighteenth century. In this very same room, young women wearing those dresses that rustled and so on danced and flirted and sometimes disgraced themselves with young men, soldiers, sailors, who were on their way to Bristol or someplace like that, so many places like that where so many adventures, the outcome of which was not good for me, began. Bristol, England. A sentence that began "That night the ship sailed from Bristol, England" would end not so good for me. And then I was driving through the countryside in an English motorcar, on narrow winding roads, and they were so familiar, though I had never been on them before; and through little villages the names of which I somehow knew so well though I had never been there before. And the countryside did have all those hedges and hedges, fields hedged in. I was marveling at all the toil of it, the planting of the hedges to begin with and then the care of it, all that clipping, year after year of clipping, and I wondered at the lives of the people who would have to do this, because wherever I see and feel the hands that hold up the world, I see and feel myself and all the people who look like me. And I said, "Those hedges" and my friend said that someone, a woman named Mrs. Rothchild, worried that the hedges weren't being taken care of properly; the farmers couldn't afford or find the help to keep up the hedges, and often they replaced them with wire fencing. I might have said to that, well if Mrs. Rothchild doesn't like the wire fencing, why doesn't she take care of the hedges herself, but I didn't. And then in those fields that were now hemmed in by wire fencing that a **privileged** woman didn't like was planted a vile yellow flowering bush that produced an oil, and my friend

Mark base words or indicate another strategy you used that helped you determine meaning.

privileged (PRIHV uh lihjd) *adj.*

MEANING:

said that Mrs. Rothchild didn't like this either; it ruined the English countryside, it ruined the traditional look of the English countryside.

16   It was not at that moment that I wished every sentence, everything I knew, that began with England would end with "and then it all died; we don't know how, it *just* all died." At that moment, I was thinking, who are these people who forced me to think of them all the time, who forced me to think that the world I knew was incomplete, or without substance, or did not measure up because it was not England; that I was incomplete, or without substance, and did not measure up because I was not English. Who were these people? The person sitting next to me couldn't give me a clue; no one person could. In any case, if I had said to her, I find England ugly, I hate England; the weather is like a jail sentence, the English are a very ugly people, the food in England is like a jail sentence, the hair of English people is so straight, so dead looking, the English have an unbearable smell so different from the smell of people I know, real people of course, she would have said that I was a person full of prejudice. Apart from the fact that it is I—that is, the people who look like me—who made her aware of the unpleasantness of such a thing, the idea of such a thing, prejudice, she would have been only partly right, sort of right: I may be capable of prejudice, but my prejudices have no weight to them, my prejudices have no force behind them, my prejudices remain opinions, my prejudices remain my personal opinion. And a great feeling of rage and disappointment came over me as I looked at England, my head full of personal opinions that could not have public, my public, approval. The people I come from are powerless to do evil on grand scale.

17   The moment I wished every sentence, everything I knew, that began with England would end with "and then it all died, we don't know how, it just all died" was when I saw the white cliffs of Dover. I had sung hymns and recited poems that were about a longing to see the white cliffs of Dover again. At the time I sang the hymns and recited the poems, I could really long to see them again because I had never seen them at all, nor had anyone around me at the time. But there we were, groups of people longing for something we had never seen. And so there they were, the white cliffs, but they were not that pearly majestic thing I used to sing about, that thing that created such a feeling in these people that when they died in the place where I lived they had themselves buried facing a direction that would allow them to see the white cliffs of Dover when they were resurrected, as surely they would be. The white cliffs of Dover, when finally I saw them, were cliffs, but they were not white; you would only call them that if the word "white" meant something special to you; they were dirty and they were steep; they were so steep, the correct height from which all my views of England, starting with the map before me in my classroom and ending with the trip I had just taken, should jump and die and disappear forever. ❧

XXIII
from Midsummer

Derek Walcott

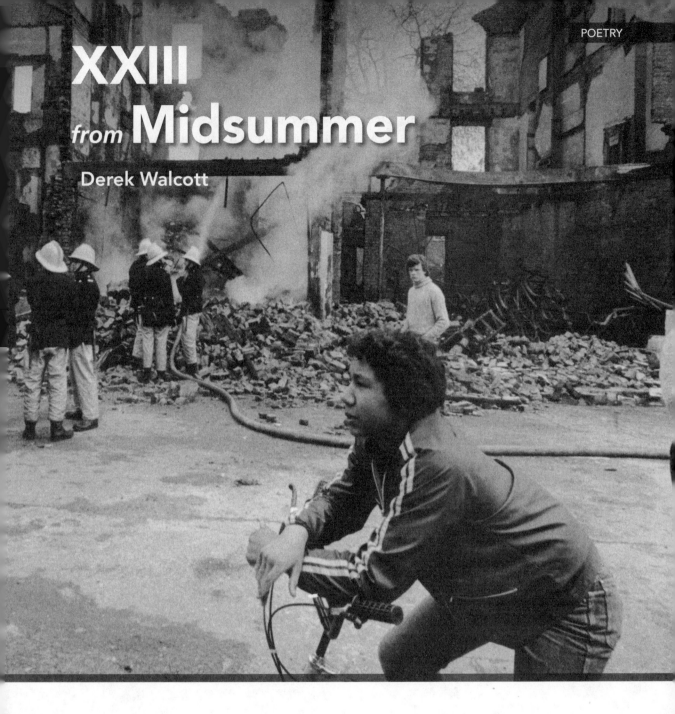

With the stampeding hiss and scurry of green lemmings,
midsummer's leaves race to extinction like the roar
of a Brixton riot tunneled by water hoses:
they seethe towards autumn's fire—its in their nature,
5 being men as well as leaves, to die for the sun.
The leaf stems tug at their chains, the branches bending
like Boer cattle under Tory whips that drag every wagon
nearer to apartheid.[1] And, for me, that closes

NOTES

---

1. **Boer** (bawr) **cattle . . . apartheid** In the 1600s, the Boers, people of Dutch descent, colonized South Africa, where apartheid (racial segregation) was later practiced. The Tories held power in Britain when it won control of South Africa in the Boer War (1899–1902).

the child's fairy tale of an antic England—fairy rings,
10 thatched cottages fenced with dog roses,
a green gale lifting the hair of Warwickshire.
I was there to add some color to the British theater.
"But the blacks can't do Shakespeare, they have no experience."
This was true. Their thick skulls bled with rancor
15 when the riot police and the skinheads exchanged quips
you could trace to the Sonnets,[2] or the Moor's eclipse.[3]
Praise had bled my lines white of any more anger.
and snow had inducted me into white fellowships.
while Calibans[4] howled down the barred streets of an empire
20 that began with Caedmon's raceless dew,[5] and is ending
In the alleys of Brixton, burning like Turner's ships.[6]

Mark base words or indicate another strategy you used that helped you determine meaning.

fellowships (FEHL oh shihps) *n.*

MEANING:

---

2. **the Sonnets** William Shakespeare's sequence of 154 sonnets, noted for their passionate, often witty inquiries into love and rivalry.
3. **the Moor's eclipse** In Shakespeare's *Othello*, Othello the Moor (a black North African) is destroyed by the scheming of his white lieutenant, Iago.
4. **Calibans** Caliban is a deformed creature in Shakespeare's play *The Tempest*. Enslaved by the enchanter Prospero, Caliban has been interpreted as a native who rebels against his island's "colonizer," Prospero.
5. **Caedmon's** (KAD muhnz) **raceless dew** poetry written by the earliest known English poet, Caedmon (seventh century).
6. **Turner's ships** The British artist J. M. W. Turner (1775–1851) rendered atmospheric oil paintings of, among other subjects, ships burning in battle.

Comprehension Check

Complete the following items after you finish your first read. Review and clarify details with your group.

ON SEEING ENGLAND FOR THE FIRST TIME

1. How does the author "see" England for the first time?

2. According to the author, what was the instruction to "Draw a map of England" meant to make her feel?

3. According to the author, how are the effects of her personal prejudices different from those of English people?

XXIII *from* MIDSUMMER

1. Why is the speaker in Brixton?

2. What types of details describe the speaker's idea of a "child's fairy tale" of England?

3. In lines 20–21, what events does the speaker cite as beginning and ending the English empire?

RESEARCH

Research to Clarify Choose at least one unfamiliar detail from one of the texts. Briefly research that detail. In what way does the information you learned shed light on an aspect of the text?

Research to Explore Conduct research to find out about either the history of British rule in Antigua or the Brixton riots of April 1981. Share what you discover with your group.

ON SEEING ENGLAND FOR THE
FIRST TIME
XXIII *from* MIDSUMMER

TIP

GROUP DISCUSSION

The notes you make while reading can be a road map to the ideas you want to contribute to a discussion. Scan through your annotations, and place a star next to opinions you feel strongly about or ideas you want to discuss.

⊹ WORD NETWORK

Add interesting words related to society from the text to your Word Network.

☰ STANDARDS

Reading Informational Text
Analyze a complex set of ideas or sequence of events and explain how specific individuals, ideas, or events interact and develop over the course of the text.

Language
Identify and correctly use patterns of word changes that indicate different meanings or parts of speech.

Close Read the Text

With your group, revisit sections of the text you marked during your first read. **Annotate** details that you notice. What **questions** do you have? What can you **conclude**?

Close Read
ANNOTATE • QUESTION • CONCLUDE

Analyze the Text

CITE TEXTUAL EVIDENCE
to support your answers.

📓 **Notebook** Complete the activities.

1. **Review and Clarify** With your group, reread paragraph 5 of Kincaid's essay. Discuss the comparison the author makes between her idea of England and the reality of her surroundings in the Caribbean. How has she been made to feel that her home is inferior to England?

2. **Present and Discuss** Now, work with your group to share the passages from the selections that you found especially important. Take turns presenting your passages. Discuss what details you noticed, what questions you asked, and what conclusions you reached.

3. **Essential Question:** *How do people come to have different views of society?* What have these texts taught you about society? Discuss.

Concept Vocabulary

| subjugation | privileged | fellowships |

Why These Words? The three concept vocabulary words from the texts are related. With your group, determine what the words have in common. Write your ideas, and add another word that fits the category.

Practice

📓 **Notebook** Confirm your understanding of the concept vocabulary words by using them in sentences. Then, read your sentences aloud to group members, leaving out the concept words. Challenge group members to guess the missing words.

Word Study

Latin Prefix: *sub-* The Latin prefix *sub-* usually means "under." In the word *subjugation*, the prefix combines with the Latin root *-jug-*, meaning "yoke" or "harness," and the Latin suffix *-ation*, which forms abstract nouns.

1. Explain how the Latin prefix *sub-* contributes to the meaning of *subjugation*.

2. In anatomy, the word *costal* means "pertaining to the ribs." Based on this information, where would you expect to find a *subcostal* muscle?

Analyze Craft and Structure

Author's Perspective: Historical Context Authors carefully select details in their writing in order to capture the setting. In addition to descriptive details, an author may choose to include elements related to the setting's **historical context**—the social structures, cultural conflicts, geographical issues, values and beliefs that influence people's lives in that place and time. The details an author includes convey his or her unique **perspective**—the way in which he or she perceives, understands, and feels about the historical context.

Follow these steps to analyze the perspectives authors bring to the historical contexts of their writing:

- Identify details in the text that relate to the history and culture of a place, including any political conflicts or social issues.

- Analyze the reason the author has included these details, considering what each adds to the portrayal of the historical context.

- Evaluate the author's attitude toward these details and why he or she thinks they are important.

TIP

COLLABORATION

When dividing research tasks among your group, consider having at least two group members research each important historical detail. During discussion, compare research findings to be sure that your group has reached a complete and accurate understanding of each detail.

Practice

CITE TEXTUAL EVIDENCE to support your answers.

Work independently to gather and analyze details about the historical contexts of these texts. Add your notes to the chart. Then, compare notes with other members of your group, and discuss the similarities and differences between the two authors' perspectives.

	REFERENCES TO HISTORICAL CONTEXT	INTERPRETATION
	What details describe or reflect the era?	What is the author's vision of the time being described?
On Seeing England for the First Time		
XXIII *from* Midsummer		

ON SEEING ENGLAND FOR THE FIRST TIME | XXIII *from* MIDSUMMER

Conventions and Style

Stylistic Devices Writers of both fiction and nonfiction use stylistic devices to communicate ideas clearly and powerfully. This chart describes some devices that Kincaid and Walcott use to convey meaning.

DEVICE	EXAMPLE
Amplification: the expansion of an idea through repetition or elaboration; adds depth and detail	*". . . would result in my erasure, not my physical erasure, but my erasure all the same."* (Kincaid, paragraph 4)
Compression: the placing together of widely varied ideas or images; creates a complexity of meaning	*"lemmings . . . leaves . . . men"* (Walcott, lines 1–5)
Allusion: unexplained reference to another work, person, or event; connects familiar and unfamiliar ideas	*"the Moor's eclipse"* (Walcott, line 16)
Irony: a contradiction between what appears to be true and what is true; causes readers to question received ideas	*"But the blacks can't do Shakespeare, they have no experience. / This was true."* (Walcott, lines 13–14)

Read It

1. Explain how Kincaid uses amplification to expand on the word *seeing* in the title of her essay. Refer to her reflections about "seeing" England on a map, in history, and in a personal visit.

2. **(a)** Cite two allusions Walcott makes in his poem. **(b)** Explain how each allusion adds meaning to Walcott's text.

3. In which text do you think the sense of irony is stronger? Explain.

Write It

📓 **Notebook** Write a paragraph in which you compare and contrast the stylistic devices used in Kincaid's essay and in Walcott's poem. In your comparison, identify the devices that have the greatest impact on each work.

STANDARDS

Reading Literature
Analyze a case in which grasping point of view requires distinguishing what is directly stated in a text from what is really meant.

Reading Informational Text
• Determine the meaning of words and phrases as they are used in a text, including figurative, connotative, and technical meanings; analyze how an author uses and refines the meaning of a key term or terms over the course of a text.
• Determine an author's point of view or purpose in a text in which the rhetoric is particularly effective, analyzing how style and content contribute to the power, persuasiveness, or beauty of the text.

Speaking and Listening

Assignment

With your group, create a **digital presentation** on the essay and poem you have just read. Assign responsibility for specific elements of your project to group members. Choose from the following options:

- [ ] **Historical Infographics** Plan and deliver a presentation with maps and timelines to show the history of the relationship between the Caribbean islands and England. Be sure to connect at least two of the facts you report to the essay and the poem.

- [ ] **Oral Biographical Profile** Plan and deliver an oral biographical profile of Jamaica Kincaid. Illustrate key points with photographs and other images. Make connections between the facts you uncover and Kincaid's essay "On Seeing England for the First Time."

- [ ] **Contemporary Connection** Plan and deliver a presentation on the contemporary experience of persons of Caribbean descent in Britain. Use graphs, photographs, and other media. Connect details of this experience with Kincaid's essay and Walcott's poem.

Integrating Content and Media

Work with your group to plan your digital presentation. Use an outline to select elements for the introduction, body, and conclusion of your presentation. Discuss connections between content and media elements to make sure the digital elements you choose support and enhance the content of your presentation.

	CONTENT	MEDIA ELEMENT
Introduction		
Body		
Conclusion		

Rehearse and Present

View your completed presentation as a group prior to sharing it with the class. Use this digital rehearsal to refine the organization and pacing in your presentation. Each group member should contribute revision ideas to create a presentation that is concise, clear, and effective.

✎ EVIDENCE LOG

Before moving on to a new selection, go to your Evidence Log and record what you learned from "On Seeing England for the First Time" and "XXIII" from *Midsummer.*

⊞ STANDARDS

Speaking and Listening
- Present information, findings, and supporting evidence, conveying a clear and distinct perspective, such that listeners can follow the line of reasoning, alternative or opposing perspectives are addressed, and the organization, development, substance, and style are appropriate to purpose, audience, and a range of formal and informal tasks.
- Make strategic use of digital media in presentations to enhance understanding of findings, reasoning, and evidence and to add interest.

About the Document

A passenger manifest is a document that lists information about a ship, aircraft, or vehicle. It often includes details about the crew, passengers, and cargo, as well as the time and place of both its departure and its arrival. This excerpt from a passenger manifest of June 22, 1948, is a record of the pioneering immigrants from Jamaica who were part of what became known as the *"Windrush* Generation." The British Nationality Act of 1948 had granted citizenship to all people residing in British Commonwealth countries. The newcomers were welcomed for their skills, but British African Caribbean people faced racial prejudice and discrimination in many areas of their daily life in Great Britain.

Passenger Manifest for the MV *Empire Windrush*

Text Features

These terms will be useful to you as you analyze, discuss, and write about public documents.

rows and columns: Public documents are often spreadsheets that organize information in vertical columns and horizontal rows.	• Each vertical column has a heading that identifies the type of information recorded below. • Each horizontal row provides information about one item, passenger, or family.
headings: Column headings describe each category of information recorded below.	• Headings in public documents usually use formal, condensed language. • The order of headings may reflect logical connections between categories or order of importance.
statistics: Numerical facts or data that have been assembled or tabulated are known as statistics.	• Statistics can include numerical data such as ages, dates, heights, or weights. • Abbreviations may be used to condense information. For example, a **"** mark indicates that information is the same as in the row above.

First Read PUBLIC DOCUMENT

Apply these strategies as you conduct your first read. You will have an opportunity to complete a close read after your first read.

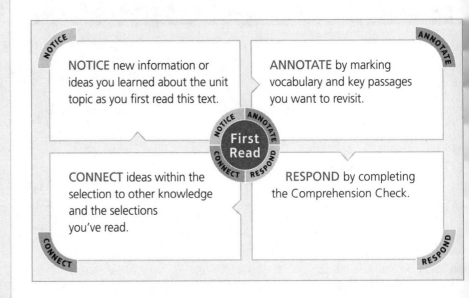

NOTICE new information or ideas you learned about the unit topic as you first read this text.

ANNOTATE by marking vocabulary and key passages you want to revisit.

First Read

CONNECT ideas within the selection to other knowledge and the selections you've read.

RESPOND by completing the Comprehension Check.

STANDARDS

Language
Acquire and use accurately general academic and domain-specific words and phrases, sufficient for reading, writing, speaking, and listening at the college and career readiness level; demonstrate independence in gathering vocabulary knowledge when considering a word or phrase important to comprehension or expression.

Passenger Manifest

for the MV *Empire Windrush*

BACKGROUND

On June 22, 1948, the *Empire Windrush* arrived in London carrying 492 official passengers (as well as a handful of stowaways) from the Caribbean. The voyage marked the beginning of a new phase of immigration from the West Indies to the United Kingdom. The British government was beginning to encourage citizens from Commonwealth countries to relocate in order to rebuild after the devastating destruction of World War II. The *Empire Windrush*, a former German cruise ship, would continue to make similar voyages until 1954, by which time the social and cultural heritage of the United Kingdom had been significantly transformed by the newcomers.

These electronic scans represent an excerpt of the longer passenger manifest for the June 22, 1948, voyage. The immigrants onboard, many of whom served in the British armed forces during the war, became the foundation of the modern African Caribbean community in England.

NOTES

Name of Ship M.V. "EMPIRE WINDRUSH" . **Port of Arrival** Tilbury . **Date of Arrival** 21. 6. 19 48.

Steamship Line THE NEW ZEALAND SHIPPING CO.,LTD., . **Whence Arrived** TRINIDAD, KINGSTON, TAMPICO, HAVANA AND BERMUDA,

NAMES AND DESCRIPTIONS OF ALIEN PASSENGERS.

(1) Port of Embarkation	(2) Port at which Passengers have been landed	(3) NAMES OF PASSENGERS	(4) CLASS (Whether 1st, 2nd, Tourist or 3rd)	(5) AGES OF PASSENGERS					(6) Proposed Address in the United Kingdom	(7) Profession, Occupation, or Calling of Passengers	(8) Country of last Permanent Residence	(9) Country of Intended Future Permanent Residence						(10) Country of which Citizen or Subject
				Adults of 12 years and upwards		Children between 1 and 12		Infants				England	Wales	Scotland	Northern Ireland	Irish Free State	Other parts of the British Empire / Foreign Countries	
				Accompanied by husband or wife (Males)	Not Accompanied by husband or wife (Females)	(Males)	(Females)	(Males) (Females)										
994. TAMPICO.	Tilbury	MAZUR	Katarzyna	"A"		34				Gt.Bower Wood Camp, Nr.Beaconsfield,Bucks.	H.D.	Mexico.	FOKSA					Poland.
995.	"	"	Maria	"				9		67,Transit Camp, Norwich,Essex.	Scholar.							
996.	"	Mazur	Rozalia	"		33				- do -	H.D.							
997.	"	"	Stanislaw	"			8			Penley Hall, Nr.Ellesmere,Salop.	Scholar.							
998.	"	MUCHA	Aniela	"		36				- do -	H.D.							
999.	"	"	Anna	"				10		Shobdon Camp, Nr.Kingsland,Hereford.	Scholar.							
1000.	"	NOWAK	Stefania	"		28				R.A.F.Station,Banff.	H.D.							
1001.	"	POZNYSK	Stefania	"		33				- do -	H.D.							
1002.	"	"	Anna	"			8			46,Renown St,Plymouth.	Scholar.							
1003.	"	PISULA	Helena	"		45				- do -	H.D.							
1004.	"	"	Karol	"	15					Rougham Camp,Nr.Bury St. Edmunds,Suffolk.	Student.							
1005.	"	POTAPOWICZ	Pelagia	"		30				- do -	H.D.							
1006.	"	"	Jerzy	"			11			Eastern M/Gardens P.O. Pill,Nr.Bristol.	Scholar.							
1007.	"	PROCINSKA	Irena	"		46				Cook Camp,Flookborough Nr.Carnforth,Lancs.	H.D.							
1008.	"	"	Lucyna	"		16				B.W.A.D.C.Hostel,Winkfield Row,Bracknell,Berks.	Student.							
1009.	"	"	Mieczyslaw	"	17					32,Wenall Rd,Abernant, Aberdare,Glam.								
1010.	"	PROCYK	Zofia	"		60				Chippenham Camp,England.	H.D.							
1011.	"	"	Stefania	"		22				35,Goodal St,Walsall.								
1012.	"	FYTLAK	Julia	"		48				- do -								
1013.	"	"	Mieczyslawa	"		23				- do -								
1014.	"	ROJEK	Anna	"		46				-								
1015.	"	RUSINEK	Agata	"		53				Tilahead Camp, Nr.Salisbury,Wilts.								
1016.	"	RYBAK	Anna	"		35				- do -								
1017.	"	SIDORKO	Albina	"		43				5,West Cromwell Rd, London,S.W.5.								
1018.	"	"	Jan	"			10			National Service Hostel, Tanscore St,W.Bromwich.								
1019.	"	"	Janina	"		14												
1020.	"	STEFANSKA	Janina	"		42												
1021.	"	"	Zbigniew	"	15													
1022.	"	TARKOWSKA	Agnieska	"		49												
1023.	"	"	Helena	"		22												
1024.	"	URBAN	Stefania	"		46												
1025.	"	WALBRIAN	Tadeusz	"	15													

FOKSA 32

Sec. 95960 1933

*By permanent residence is to be understood residence for a year or more.
Northern Ireland and the Irish Free State are to be regarded as separate countries.
†In the case of Alien Passengers who are proceeding via the United Kingdom to a destination in some other country, the country of destination should be shown in this column.

C. 439B.

PAGE 1: This page provides data and other information about "alien" passengers. These would be people who were not citizens of the United Kingdom at the time of the voyage.

NAMES AND DESCRIPTIONS OF BRITISH PASSENGERS.

(1) Port of Embarkation	(2) Port at which Passengers have been landed	(3) NAMES OF PASSENGERS	(4) CLASS	(5) AGES OF PASSENGERS	(6) Proposed Address in the United Kingdom	(7) Profession, Occupation, or Calling of Passengers	(8) Country of last Permanent Residence	(9) Country of Intended Future Permanent Residence
864. KINGSTON	Tilbury	STEPHENS Delroy	"C"	28	9,Brereton Avenue, Liverpool.	Band Leader.	Jamaica.	England
865. "	"	SOMMERS Joscelyn	"	30	11,Nicholay Rd,London.	Barber.	"	"
866. "	"	STEPHENS Leslie	"	23	9,Brereton Ave,Liverpool.	Piano Repairer.	"	"
867. "	"	STEWART Vincent	"	23	11,Springfield Pl,Leeds.	Mechanic.	"	"
868. "	"	SOLLAS Vernon	"	18	128,Park St,B'head.	Mechanic.	"	"
869. "	"	SCOTT Mortal	"	27	Velmore Industrial Hostel,Hants.	Carpenter.	"	"
870. "	"	SULLIVAN Clarence	"	22	24,Robin Wood Chase, Nottingham.	Mechanic.	"	"
871. "	"	STEPHENS Franklin	"	26	154,Slack Lane,Derby.	Carpenter.	"	"
872. "	"	SINCLAIR Henry	"	42	20,Bremner St, Manchester.	Painter.	"	"
873. "	"	SIMMS Dennis	"	22	296,Brock St,Manchester.	Tinsmith.	"	"
874. "	"	SHARPE Alfred	"	47	No address.	Painter.	"	"
875. "	"	SYMMOIE Clifton	"	22	Montpelier Gdns, Cheltenham.	Clerk.	"	"
876. "	"	SPENCE Ranford	"	22	52,Cadogan Sq,W.1.	Waiter.	"	"
877. "	"	SAMUEL Hopeton	"	28	No address.	Tailor.	"	"
878. "	"	SIMMS Karl	"	26	136,Belgrave Rd,B'ham.	Mechanic.	"	"
879. "	"	SAMUELS Edwin	"	26	Causeway GreenHostel, Oldberry,B'ham.	Labourer.	"	"
880. "	"	SMELLIE Keith	"	20	9,Amden Grove, Hulme,Manchester.	Clerk.	"	"
881. "	"	SENIOR Aston	"	22	20,Toriano Ave,N.W.5.	Student.	"	"
882. "	"	SWIRE Milton	"	21	4,Danyrnig Rd, St.Thomas,Swansea.	Mechanic.	"	"
883. "	"	SPRINGER Bertram	"	19	No address.	Cabinet Mkr.	"	"
884. "	"	TAPPER Webster	"	23	3,St.Peters Sq, Wolverhampton.	Engineer.	"	"
885. "	"	TANQUEE Abraham	"	24	89,Mount St,Birmingham.	Tailor.	"	"
886. "	"	TEMPLE Lester	"	21	No address.	Mechanic.	"	"
887. "	"	THOMAS Guy	"	26	"	"	"	"
888. "	"	THOMPSON Ishmael	"	33		Carpenter.	"	"
889. "	"	TOWNSEND Egbert	"	23	43,Fitzroy St,W.1.	Chauffeur.	"	"
890. "	"	TAYLOR Lambert	"	24	64,Gray Friars, Stafford.	Welder.	"	"
891. "	"	TINGLING Egbert	"	22	77,Wimpole St,W.1.	"	"	"
892. "	"	THOMAS Felix	"	36	24,Bridge St,Chatteris,Cambs.	Mechanic.	"	"
893. "	"	THOMAS Vincent	"	27	63,Wickham Rd,S.E.4.	Cabinet Mkr.	"	"
894. "	"	THOMAS Harold	"	38	20,Redcliffe Gdns, S.W.10.	Clerk.	"	"
895. "	"	TOMLINSON Lloyd	"	28	No address.	-	"	"
896. "	"	THOMPSON Melton	"	26		Bricklayer.	"	"
897. "	"	TOMLINSON Raphael	"	22	88,White Lion St, London,N.	Carpenter.	"	"
898. "	"	THOMPSON Ronald	"	22	1,Burns Ave,Felton.	"	"	"
899. "	"	THOMPSON Egbert	"	29	No address.	Engineer.	"	"
900. "	"	THOMPSON John	"	22	149,Cross St, Stretford,Manchester.	Carpenter.	"	"
901. "	"	TATE Maurice	"	19	No address.	Mechanic.	"	"
902. "	"	THOMPSON Nathaniel	"	37	11,Silbourne St, Liverpool.S.	Tailor.	"	"
903. "	"	VALENTINE Cleveland	"	27	6,St.Martins Sq,W.C.2.	Carpenter.	"	"
904. "	"	VANZIE Allan	"	23	7,Cliffdale Rd, Leeds,Yorks.	Mechanic.	"	"
905. "	"	WALKER Samuel	"	25	65,Selbourn St,L'pool.	Musician.	"	"
906. "	"	WHITE Rudyard	"	24	c/o Dir.of Col.Studies, Colonial Office,W.1.	Student.	"	"
907. "	"	WINSTON Olive	"	19	No address.	Clerk.	"	"
908. "	"	WILLOUGHBY Frederick	"	23	120,The Grange, Harrow Hill,Middlx.	Mechanic.	"	?
909. "	"	WHITE Sydney	"	22	43,Fitzroy St,W.1.	Salesman.	"	"
910. "	"	WATSON Ferdinand	"	34	36,Berry Dock, Glammoreshire.			

*By permanent residence is to be understood residence for a year or more.
Northern Ireland and Eire are to be regarded as separate countries.

PUBLIC RECORD OFFICE

Ref: BT 26/1237

Please note that this copy is supplied subject to the Public Record Office's terms and conditions and that your use of it may be subject to copyright restrictions. Further information is given in the enclosed 'Terms and Conditions of supply of Public Records' leaflet.

PAGE 2: This page shows information about passengers who were citizens of the United Kingdom.

Name of Ship M.V. "EMPIRE WINDRUSH". Port of Arrival Tilbury. Date of Arrival 21. 6. 19 48

Steamship Line THE NEW ZEALAND SHIPPING CO.,LTD.,. Whence Arrived TRINIDAD,KINGSTON,TAMPICO, HAVANA AND BERMUDA.

22 JUN 19.. LONDON NAMES AND DESCRIPTIONS OF **BRITISH** PASSENGERS.

(1) Port of Embarkation	(2) Port at which Passengers have been landed	(3) NAMES OF PASSENGERS	(4) CLASS	(5) AGES OF PASSENGERS	(6) Proposed Address in the United Kingdom	(7) Profession, Occupation, or Calling of Passengers	(8) Country of last Permanent Residence	(9) Country of Intended Future Permanent Residence
911. KINGSTON	Tilbury	WILLIAMS	Loyal	"C"	19	157,Grove St, Liverpool.	Book-keeper.	Jamaica.	England *
912. "	"	WOOD	Holland	"	29	1,Primrose Hill, Worsley,Stourbridge.	Carpenter.	"	*
913. "	"	WARREN	Ishmael	"	47	No address.		"	*
914. "	"	WONG	Irwin	"	30	38,South Hill Pk,N.W.3.	Shoemaker.	"	*
915. "	"	WILMOT	Harold	"	40	196,Auchinairn Rd, Bishop Briggs,Scot.	Case Maker.	"	*
916. "	"	WILLIAMS	Edgerton	"	21	Nat.Service Hostel, Pascore St,W.Bromwich.	Carpenter.	"	*
917. "	"	YIN	Clarence	"	23	3,Second Avenue, Warrington,Hants.	Clerk.	"	*
918. "	"	ZAYNE	Herbert	"	20	21,Timbercanks Grove, Blackpool,Lancs.	Painter.	"	*
919. "	"	WALTERS	Aubrey	"	26	15,Warrington Cres.,W.9.	Artist.	"	*
920. "	"	WILLIAMS	Mais	"	36	No address.	Builder.	"	*
921. "	"	YAPP	Dudley	"	19	30,Santos Rd.S.W.18.	Salesman.	"	*
922. "	"	WALTERS	Adrian	"	44	118,Albert Rd, Wood Green,London,N.	Musician.	"	*
923. "	"	WALLEN	Adolphine	"	21	Colonial Club,London.	Clerk.	"	*
924. "	"	WRIGHT	Louis	"	23	77,Wimpole St,W.1.	Plumber.	"	*
925. "	"	WILLIAMS	Rudolph	"	24	11,East End Terrace, Ashburton,Devonshire.	Mechanic.	"	*
926. "	"	WALKER	Vivian	"	35	22,Manson St,W.1.	Musician.	"	*
927. "	"	WILLIAMS	Barrington	"	23	77,Wimpole St,W.1.	Carpenter.	"	*
928. "	"	WRIGHT	Charles	"	25	No address.	Metal Worker.	"	*
929. "	"	WILMOT	Rudolph	"	21	13,Dennsfield Rd, Wolverhampton.	Electrician.	"	*
930. "	"	WILLIAMS	Edward	"	20	Nat.Service Hostel, 10,Score St,W.Bromwich.	Technician.	"	*
931. "	"	WILSON	Graville	"	21	77,Wimpole St,W.1.	Carpenter.	"	*
932. "	"	WILLIAMS	Aston	"	23	No address.	Fitter.	"	*
933. "	"	WRIGHT	Reuben	"	32	43,Fitzroy St,W.1.	Labourer.	"	*
934. "	"	WRIGHT	Leslie	"	31	No address.	Tailor.	"	*
935. "	"	WILLIAMS	Edward	"	25	"	Upholsterer.	"	*
936. "	"	WENTWORTH	James	"	33	"	Mechanic.	"	*
937. "	"	WHITE	David	"	26	"	Carpenter.	"	*
938. "	"	WILSON	Gerald	"	18	14,Dartmouth Pk.Rd,N.W.5.	Mechanic.	"	*
939. "	"	WILSON	Lascelles	"	24	Wood Gate,Swanton Morley, East Dereham,Norfolk.	Clerk.	"	*
940. "	"	WILLIAMS	Ronald	"	24	No address.	Tailor.	"	*
941. "	"	WHITE	George	"	29	43,Manor Square, Degenham,Essex.	Cook.	"	*
942. BERMUDA.	"	ALEXANDER	Thomas	"C"	65	138,Hanging Lane, Northfield,B'ham.	Retired.	Bermuda.	*
943. "	"	BUNN	Philip	"	28	Sentry College, Sentry Rd,Swanage.	Policeman.	"	*
944. "	"	BARNABY	Ernest	"	39	30,Heathfield Gdns,W.5.	Mason.	"	*
945. "	"	HUDSON	Howard	"	55	261,Becontree Avenue, Degenham,Essex.	Accountant.	"	*
946. "	"	OLDFIELD	Alan	"	25	Rosebank Rd, Old Kilpatrick.	M.N.	"	*
947. "	"	ROGERS	Marshall	"	42	27,Lilac Gdns,W.5.	Policeman.	"	*
948. "	"	STAFFORD	Dennis	"	26		Policeman.	"	*

DISTRESSED BRITISH SEAMAN.

949. Bermuda.	X	BALLANTINE	Hugh	"C"	18	76,Princes St, Ballymena,N.Ireland.	M.N.	England.	*
950. "		NICHOLSON	Robert	"	19	11,Silloth St,Silloth.			*
951. "	C. 439A	CAMPBELL	William	"	35	50,St.Martins Lane,W.C.2.			*

PAGE 3: This page is a continuation of the list of British citizens on the voyage.

Comprehension Check

Complete the following items after you finish your first read. Review and clarify details with your group.

1. From which country are all of the "alien" passengers listed on page 1 of the passenger manifest for the MV *Empire Windrush*?

2. From which country are all of the British passengers listed on pages 2 and 3 of the passenger manifest for the MV *Empire Windrush*?

3. What is the age range of alien and British adult passengers listed in this manifest?

4. According to the column headings, at what age was a passenger in 1948 considered an adult?

- -

RESEARCH

Research to Clarify Choose at least one unfamiliar detail from the text. Briefly research that detail. In what way does the information you learned shed light on an aspect of the manifest?

Research to Explore This document may spark your curiosity to learn more about the *Empire Windrush* or another ship that transported immigrants to England or another country. Briefly research a ship that interests you. You may want to share what you discover with your group.

PASSENGER MANIFEST FOR THE
MV *EMPIRE WINDRUSH*

Close Read the Text

With your group, revisit the passenger manifest and your first-read notes. **Annotate** details that you notice. What **questions** do you still have? What can you **conclude**?

Analyze the Text

Complete the activities.

1. **Present and Discuss** Choose the data you find most interesting or unusual. Share your choice with the group, and discuss why you chose it. Explain what conclusions you draw from these data, as well as questions they lead you to consider.

2. **Review and Synthesize** With your group, compare and contrast the data provided for "alien" and British passengers. How does this manifest help you understand what life was like for these passengers in 1948? Explain.

3. **Essential Question:** *How do people come to have different views of society?* Immediately following World War II, many people in Great Britain were comforted by the conviction that their society would soon be back to "normal." How might the arrival of thousands of immigrants from the West Indies have affected that belief? Discuss with your group.

Text Features

| rows and columns | headings | statistics |

Use these terms in your responses to the questions.

1. What do headings in the chart reveal about the information that officials of the time viewed as important?

2. Why does the manifest include information about the passengers' occupations and "Proposed Address in the United Kingdom"?

3. What can you conclude about employment possibilities in the United Kingdom by comparing the occupations of the alien passengers with those of the British passengers?

STANDARDS

Reading Informational Text
• Analyze the use of text features in public documents.
• Integrate and evaluate multiple sources of information presented in different media or formats as well as in words in order to address a question or solve a problem.

Writing
• Write informative/explanatory texts to examine and convey complex ideas, concepts, and information clearly and accurately through the effective selection, organization, and analysis of content.
• Conduct short as well as more sustained research projects to answer a question or solve a problem; narrow or broaden the inquiry when appropriate; synthesize multiple sources on the subject, demonstrating understanding of the subject under investigation.
• Apply *grades 11–12 Reading standards* to literary nonfiction.

Research

Assignment

With your group, create a **profile** of a typical passenger on the famous 1948 voyage of the *Empire Windrush* from Kingston, Jamaica, to London, England. Your profile should include a description of the relationship between the West Indies and Britain in the years leading up to the ship's arrival, the typical life and motivations of a West Indian who would have decided to take the journey, the passenger's experience during the voyage itself, and the passenger's reception upon arrival in Britain.

Research Plan You will need to conduct research in order to complete your passenger profile. Divide research tasks with group members in a logical and efficient way so that your combined work covers all the topics. Possible sources of information include these unit selections: "On Seeing England for the First Time," by Jamaica Kincaid, and "XXIII" from *Midsummer*, by Derek Walcott. You will find useful information in the texts themselves, as well as in author biographies, background notes, and footnotes. You should also consult other sources, such as encyclopedias or histories.

📝 EVIDENCE LOG

Before moving on to a new selection, go to your Evidence Log and record what you learned from the passenger manifest for the MV *Empire Windrush*.

TOPIC	SOURCES	INFORMATION
Relationship between West Indies and Britain prior to 1948		
Lives and motivations of West Indian passengers		
Experiences on the 1948 voyage of the *Empire Windrush*		
Reception in Britain		

Synthesizing Research and Media

After collecting information, work together to discuss how specific details in the passenger manifest confirm, challenge, or add to the information that you found.

Present a Scene

Assignment

You have just read a historical account, essays, a poem, and a public document, all focused on aspects of English history and society. Work with your group to write and present a **scene** in which characters you develop based on texts in this section respond to these questions:

> Which aspects of English society would you change?
> Which would you keep?

Plan With Your Group

Analyze the Text Consider the texts in this section and choose the ones you want to work with. Use details from the texts to develop a character for each member of your group. For example, you might create the characters of a fourteenth-century peasant, a Brixton rioter, and a twentieth-century Jamaican child. Jot down notes about the aspects of English society your character would keep, as well as those he or she would change.

TITLE	CHARACTER	FEELINGS ABOUT ENGLAND
from The Worms of the Earth Against the Lions		
Shakespeare's Sister		
On Seeing England for the First Time		
XXIII *from* Midsummer		
Passenger Manifest for the MV *Empire Windrush*		

Choose a Setting and Situation Decide where you will have the characters interact and what type of situation they will face. You need not be completely realistic—instead, you can have characters from different eras meet and interact in unusual situations. Make sure your characters reflect the situations of their own lives as described or suggested by the texts.

Gather Evidence Take notes on specific details that will help you craft your characters and figure out how they will react to the main situation and to one another.

▤ STANDARDS

Speaking and Listening
Initiate and participate effectively in a range of collaborative discussions with diverse partners on *grades 11–12 topics, texts, and issues,* building on others' ideas and expressing their own clearly.

Organize Your Presentation Work together to merge your notes into a script in which each character presents his or her views and interacts with other characters. For instance, you might have characters openly disagree with each other. Whenever possible, have characters explain the reasons for their feelings, as well as offer counterarguments for the views the other character express. Decide how characters will introduce themselves so that the audience understands who is speaking.

Rehearse With Your Group

Practice With Your Group Once your script is complete, print copies and run through the presentation with your group. Use this checklist to evaluate the effectiveness of your group's first run-through. Then, use your evaluation and these instructions to guide your revision.

CONTENT	PRESENTATION TECHNIQUES
☐ Each character presents a view of England and explains his or her perspective convincingly.	☐ Speakers use eye contact and speak clearly.
☐ All characters have equal opportunity to speak.	☐ Speakers remain in character.
	☐ Speakers use adequate volume and vary pitch and tone to express emotion.

Fine-Tune the Content If you find that one character is dominating the conversation, add lines for other characters to balance the presentation. You may need to do some more research to add interesting facts and details to support a character's point of view.

Brush Up on Your Presentation Techniques As you speak in character, avoid turning your back to the audience. When you address other characters, do not turn to face them fully as you might in a regular conversation. Instead, make sure the audience can see your facial expressions and hear your voice.

Present and Evaluate

As you perform your scene, remember your purpose. Try to express yourself as your character might, and work on getting your audience to understand your point of view. As you watch other presentations, evaluate how the characters use reasons to support their points of view.

≡ STANDARDS
Speaking and Listening
Present information, findings, and supporting evidence conveying a clear and distinct perspective and a logical argument, such that listeners can follow the line of reasoning, alternative or opposing perspectives are addressed, and the organization, development, substance, and style are appropriate to purpose, audience, and a range of formal and informal tasks.

ESSENTIAL QUESTION:

How do people come to have different views of society?

Status, class, mobility, equality, gender, race, age, and ethnicity—many factors affect an individual's perceptions, especially regarding his or her views of society. In this section, you will complete your study of various social views by exploring an additional selection related to the topic. You'll then share what you learn with classmates. To choose a text, follow these steps.

Look Back Think about the selections you have already studied. Which aspects of people's views of society do you wish to explore further? Which time period interests you the most?

Look Ahead Preview the texts by reading the descriptions. Which one seems most interesting and appealing to you?

Look Inside Take a few minutes to scan through the text you chose. Choose a different one if this text doesn't meet your needs.

Independent Learning Strategies

Throughout your life, in school, in your community, and in your career, you will need to rely on yourself to learn and work on your own. Review these strategies and the actions you can take to practice them during Independent Learning. Add ideas of your own for each category.

STRATEGY	ACTION PLAN
Create a schedule	• Understand your goals and deadlines. • Make a plan for what to do each day. •
Practice what you have learned	• Use first-read and close-read strategies to deepen your understanding. • After you read, evaluate the usefulness of the evidence to help you understand the topic. • Consider the quality and reliability of the source. •
Take notes	• Record important ideas and information. • Review notes before preparing to share with a group. •

CONTENTS

Choose one selection. Selections are available online only.

PERFORMANCE-BASED ASSESSMENT PREP

Review Evidence for an Explanatory Essay

Complete your Evidence Log for the unit by evaluating what you've learned and synthesizing the information you have recorded.

First-Read Guide

Use this page to record your first-read ideas.

Tool Kit
First-Read Guide and
Model Annotation

Selection Title: _____

NOTICE new information or ideas you learn about the unit topic as you first read this text.

ANNOTATE by marking vocabulary and key passages you want to revisit.

First Read

NOTICE · ANNOTATE · CONNECT · RESPOND

CONNECT ideas within the selection to other knowledge and the selections you have read.

RESPOND by writing a brief summary of the selection.

STANDARD
Reading Read and comprehend complex literary and informational texts independently and proficiently.

Close-Read Guide

Use this page to record your close-read ideas.

Selection Title: _____

Close Read the Text

Revisit sections of the text you marked during your first read. Read these sections closely and **annotate** what you notice. Ask yourself **questions** about the text. What can you **conclude?** Write down your ideas.

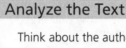

Analyze the Text

Think about the author's choices of patterns, structure, techniques, and ideas included in the text. Select one, and record your thoughts about what this choice conveys.

QuickWrite

Pick a paragraph or stanza from the text that grabbed your interest. Explain the power of this passage.

_____
_____
_____
_____
_____
_____
_____
_____
_____

⊞ STANDARD
Reading Read and comprehend complex literary and informational texts independently and proficiently.

Share Your Independent Learning

Prepare to Share

How do people come to have different views of society?

Even when you read something independently, your understanding continues to grow when you share what you learned with others. Reflect on the text you explored independently, and write notes about its connection to the unit. In your notes, consider why this text belongs in this unit.

Learn From Your Classmates

💬 **Discuss It** Share your ideas about the text you explored on your own. As you talk with others in your class, jot down a few ideas that you learn from them.

Reflect

Review your notes, and mark the most important insight you gained from these writing and discussion activities. Explain how this idea adds to your understanding of society.

Review Evidence for an Explanatory Essay

At the beginning of this unit, you took a position on the following question:

> What factors lead people to criticize their society rather than simply accept it?

EVIDENCE LOG

Review your Evidence Log and your QuickWrite from the beginning of the unit. Have your ideas changed?

☐ YES	☐ NO
Identify at least three pieces of evidence that have caused you to reevaluate your ideas.	Identify at least three pieces of evidence that have reinforced your original position.
1.	1.
2.	2.
3.	3.

Develop your thoughts into a thesis statement: *Factors that lead certain people to criticize rather than accept their society include the following:*

_____

_____

_____

Identify one or two figures from history who exemplify your thesis statement:

_____

_____

_____

Evaluate the Strength of Your Evidence Which two texts that you read in this unit offer the strongest support for your thesis statement? Write their titles here.

1. _____   2. _____

What are some other resources you might use to locate examples to support your thesis?

1. _____   2. _____

STANDARDS
Writing
Introduce a topic; organize complex ideas, concepts, and information so that each new element builds on that which precedes it to create a unified whole; include formatting, graphics, and multimedia when useful to aiding comprehension.

SOURCES

- WHOLE-CLASS SELECTIONS

- SMALL-GROUP SELECTIONS

- INDEPENDENT-LEARNING
  SELECTION

PART 1

Writing to Sources: Explanatory Essay

In this unit, you read poetry, works of history, essays, a public document, and other texts that express their authors' sometimes critical observations of their own societies. As times change, styles of writing change, but writers' laser-like focus on society's wrongs remains constant and powerful.

Assignment

Write an **explanatory essay** in which you select three examples from literary and social history to answer this question:

> ### What factors lead people to criticize their society rather than simply accept it?

Look at the list of kinds of people below. Choose two, and find a real-life example for each. Your third example should be someone who either wrote or was mentioned in a text from this unit. Begin by doing research on the people you have chosen.

artist   reporter   revolutionary   politician

Start your essay with conviction by stating your main idea in a strong thesis statement. Conduct research on the real-life examples you chose. Then, in the body of the essay, explain how each of your three examples illustrates the factors that lead some people to criticize rather than accept their society. Conclude with a strong paragraph that supports and expands upon your explanation.

Reread the Assignment Review the assignment to be sure you fully understand it. The assignment may reference some of the academic words presented at the beginning of the unit. Be sure you understand each of the words in order to complete the assignment correctly.

Academic Vocabulary

annotation	theoretical	prescribe
conviction	tenacious	

⊞ WORD NETWORK

As you write and revise your essay, use your Word Network to help vary your word choices.

Review the Elements of an Explanatory Essay Before you begin writing, read the Explanatory Text Rubric. Once you have completed your first draft, check it against the rubric. If one or more of the elements are missing or not as strong as they could be, revise your argument to add or strengthen those components.

Explanatory Text Rubric

	Focus and Organization	Evidence and Elaboration	Language Conventions
4	The introduction is engaging and reveals the thesis in a way that appeals to a reader. Facts, details, examples, and reasons progress logically. Transitional words and phrases are used to link and separate ideas. The conclusion leaves a strong impression on the reader.	Supports ideas with specific and relevant examples from research and the selections. The tone of the text is formal and objective. Uses vocabulary strategically and appropriately for the audience and purpose.	Consistently uses standard English conventions of usage and mechanics.
3	The introduction is engaging and clearly reveals the thesis. Facts, details, examples, and reasons progress logically. Transitions are used frequently. The conclusion relates to the text that precedes it.	Supports ideas with relevant examples from research and the selections. The tone of the text is mostly formal and objective. Uses vocabulary that is generally appropriate for the audience and purpose.	Demonstrates accuracy in standard English conventions of usage and mechanics.
2	The introduction states a thesis. Facts, details, examples, and reasons progress somewhat logically. Some transitions are used. The conclusion restates the thesis.	Supports some ideas with examples from research and the selections. The tone of the essay is occasionally formal and objective. Uses vocabulary that is somewhat appropriate for the audience and purpose.	Demonstrates some accuracy in standard English conventions of usage and mechanics.
1	The introduction does not reveal a thesis. Facts, details, examples, and reasons do not progress logically. Sentences may seem disconnected. The conclusion is absent or weak.	Supports few ideas with examples from research and the selections or uses examples that are irrelevant. The tone of the text is informal and lacks objectivity. Uses vocabulary that is limited or ineffective.	Contains inaccuracies in standard English conventions of usage and mechanics.

PART 2
Speaking and Listening: Video Explanation

Assignment

After you complete your explanatory essay, use a movie-making program on a phone, computer, or tablet to create a **video explanation**. To prepare, record your responses to these questions.

1. What three examples did I use in my explanation?

2. Why did I choose the examples I used?

3. How do my examples support my thesis?

Follow these steps to make your video explanation clear, cogent, and interesting.

- Take notes on the answers to the questions before you record.
- Practice your delivery, focusing your eyes on your imaginary audience. Adjust your tone and pace to achieve a lively yet natural delivery.
- Deliver your responses, recording them on video and saving them for others to view.

Review the Rubric The criteria by which your video explanation will be evaluated appear in the rubric below. Review the criteria before delivering your explanation to ensure that you are prepared.

☰ STANDARDS

Speaking and Listening
Make strategic use of digital media in presentations to enhance understanding of findings, reasoning, and evidence and to add interest.

	Content	Use of Media	Presentation Techniques
3	Explanation clearly and straightforwardly answers all three questions. Explanation is clearly organized and easy to follow.	Voice on the recording is consistent and audible. Face is centered in the video, and expressions and movements are clear.	Speaking is clear and at an appropriate volume. Tone and pace vary to maintain interest. Directly addresses audience.
2	Explanation answers all three questions but may ramble. Explanation is organized and fairly easy to follow.	Voice on the recording may vary but is mostly audible. Face is mostly centered in the video, but the focus may vary.	Speaking is clear most of the time and usually uses an appropriate volume. Tone and pace vary but not always effectively. Makes occasional eye contact with viewer.
1	Explanation may not answer all three questions or may lack focus. Explanation is disorganized and difficult to follow.	Voice on the recording sometimes fades in and out. Face may not always be entirely visible on the video.	Speaker mumbles occasionally, speaks too quickly or too quietly. Speaker pauses or loses track of what he or she is saying at times. Fails to make eye contact with viewer.

Reflect on the Unit

Now that you've completed the unit, take a few moments to reflect on your learning.

Reflect on the Unit Goals

Look back at the goals at the beginning of the unit. Use a different colored pen to rate yourself again. Think about readings and activities that contributed the most to the growth of your understanding. Record your thoughts.

Reflect on the Learning Strategies

💬 **Discuss It** Write a reflection on whether you were able to improve your learning based on your Action Plans. Think about what worked, what didn't, and what you might do to keep working on these strategies. Record your ideas before a class discussion.

Reflect on the Text

Choose a selection that you found challenging, and explain what made it difficult.

Explain something that surprised you about a text in the unit.

Which activity taught you the most about societal reforms? What did you learn?

⬛ STANDARDS
Speaking and Listening
Initiate and participate effectively in a range of collaborative discussions with diverse partners on *grades 11–12 topics, texts, and issues*, building on others' ideas and expressing their own clearly and persuasively.

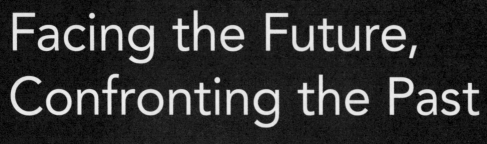

Facing the Future, Confronting the Past

Shakespeare Extended Study

Introduction to
The Tragedy of Macbeth

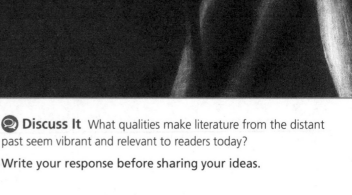

💬 **Discuss It** What qualities make literature from the distant past seem vibrant and relevant to readers today?

Write your response before sharing your ideas.

UNIT INTRODUCTION

ESSENTIAL QUESTION: **How do our attitudes toward the past and future shape our actions?**

LAUNCH TEXT
ARGUMENT MODEL
Better Never to Have Met at All

 ### WHOLE-CLASS LEARNING

 ### SMALL-GROUP LEARNING

 ### INDEPENDENT LEARNING

HISTORICAL PERSPECTIVES

Focus Period: 1485–1625

Renaissance and Reformation: A Changing England

LITERATURE AND CULTURE

Literary History
The Tragedy of Macbeth

ANCHOR TEXT: DRAMA

The Tragedy of Macbeth
William Shakespeare

Act I
  MEDIA CONNECTION: Macbeth's Early Motivation

Act II

Act III

Act IV

Act V
  MEDIA CONNECTION: The Darkness in *Macbeth's* Human Characters

MEDIA: AUDIO PERFORMANCE

The Tragedy of Macbeth, Act V, Scene i
L.A. Theatre Works

The Tragedy of Macbeth, Act V, Scene i
LibriVox

COMPARE

POETRY COLLECTION 1

Sonnet 12
Sonnet 60
Sonnet 73
William Shakespeare

Sonnet 32
from Pamphilia to Amphilanthus
Mary Wroth

Sonnet 75
Edmund Spenser

LITERARY CRITICISM

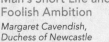
from The Naked Babe and the Cloak of Manliness
from The Well Wrought Urn
Cleanth Brooks

from Macbeth
from Shakespeare's Language
Frank Kermode

DRAMA

from Oedipus Rex
Sophocles, translated by David Grene

POETRY COLLECTION 2

Ozymandias
Percy Bysshe Shelley

Why Brownlee Left
Paul Muldoon

Man's Short Life and Foolish Ambition
Margaret Cavendish, Duchess of Newcastle

MEDIA: GRAPHIC NOVEL

from Macbeth: The Graphic Novel
William Shakespeare, illustrated by John Haward; script adapted by John McDonald

SHORT STORY

The Lagoon
Joseph Conrad

SCIENCE ARTICLES

What's Your Time Perspective?
Jane Collingwood

Does Time Pass?
Peter Dizikes

PERFORMANCE TASK

WRITING FOCUS:
Write an Argument

PERFORMANCE TASK

SPEAKING AND LISTENING FOCUS:
Present an Argument

PERFORMANCE-BASED ASSESSMENT PREP

Review Evidence for an Argument

PERFORMANCE-BASED ASSESSMENT

Argument: Response to Literature and TV Commentary

PROMPT:
What is the relationship of human beings to time?

Unit Goals

Throughout this unit, you will deepen your perspective on the topic of the passage of time by reading, writing, speaking, listening, and presenting. These goals will help you succeed on the Unit Performance-Based Assessment.

Rate how well you meet these goals right now. You will revisit your ratings later when you reflect on your growth during this unit.

SCALE				
1	2	3	4	5
NOT AT ALL WELL	NOT VERY WELL	SOMEWHAT WELL	VERY WELL	EXTREMELY WELL

READING GOALS

1 2 3 4 5

- Read a variety of texts to gain the knowledge and insight needed to write about attitudes toward time.

- Expand your knowledge and use of academic and concept vocabulary.

WRITING AND RESEARCH GOALS

1 2 3 4 5

- Write a response to literature in which you effectively incorporate the key elements of an argument.

- Conduct research projects of various lengths to explore a topic and clarify meaning.

LANGUAGE GOALS

1 2 3 4 5

- Maintain a formal style and use transition words and varied syntax to connect parts of a text.

SPEAKING AND LISTENING GOALS

1 2 3 4 5

- Collaborate with your team to build on the ideas of others, develop consensus, and communicate.

- Integrate audio, visuals, and text to present information.

≡ STANDARDS

Language
Acquire and use accurately general academic and domain-specific words and phrases, sufficient for reading, writing, speaking, and listening at the college and career readiness level; demonstrate independence in gathering vocabulary knowledge when considering a word or phrase important to comprehension or expression.

Academic Vocabulary: Argument

Understanding and using academic terms can help you read, write, and speak with precision and clarity. Here are five academic words that will be useful to you in this unit as you analyze and write arguments.

Complete the chart.

1. Review each word, its root, and the mentor sentences.

2. Use the information and your own knowledge to predict the meaning of each word.

3. For each word, list at least two related words.

4. Refer to a dictionary or other resources if needed.

 TIP

FOLLOW THROUGH
Study the words in this chart, and highlight them or their forms wherever they appear in the unit.

WORD	MENTOR SENTENCES	PREDICT MEANING	RELATED WORDS
proficient ROOT: **-fic- / -fac-** "make"; "do"	**1.** The company had openings for *proficient* proofreaders. **2.** Musicians study for many years before becoming *proficient*.		proficiency; proficiently
justify ROOT: **-jus-** "right"; "law"	**1.** How can Caleb *justify* spending so much on a pair of shoes? **2.** Do crime statistics *justify* the use of hidden cameras on public streets?		
diverse ROOT: **-vert- / -vers-** "turn"	**1.** The population of our country is so *diverse* because people came here from every corner of the world. **2.** The library houses a *diverse* collection of music, from classical to hip-hop.		
catalyst ROOT: **-lys-** "loosen"; "break down"	**1.** The events in the story were tragic, but they proved to be a *catalyst* for reform. **2.** The addition of a *catalyst* sparked a rapid chemical change.		
assertion ROOT: **-ser-** "join"; "attach"	**1.** The candidate's *assertion* at the end of the debate proved to be persuasive. **2.** The tech company made the bold *assertion* that its product would change everyone's lives.		

This selection is an example of an **argument** in the form of a response to literature. This is the type of writing you will develop in the Performance-Based Assessment at the end of the unit.

As you read, look for evidence the writer uses to support an opening claim. Mark the evidence you find especially strong.

Better **Never to Have Met** at All

NOTES

1   In William Shakespeare's *Romeo and Juliet,* love is fire. It burns through everything: through the lovers of the title, through their families, and through people on the sidelines. The romance between Romeo and Juliet hurts so many people that one wonders whether it would have been better if time unwound and the two leads had never met. If we examine the play from the beginning, the evidence for this is overwhelming.

2   Winding back the clock, we begin in Verona, where we find Romeo, heir of the noble House of Montague, feeling sorry for himself. His reason: rejection at the hands of Rosaline, niece to Lord Capulet, leader of the House of Capulet and rival to the Montagues. Romeo's friend, Mercutio, wishing to improve his friend's spirits, disguises Romeo and sneaks him into a Capulet party. Romeo has his own motive for going—he wants to see Rosaline again—but at the party he meets Juliet, daughter of Lord Capulet, instead. From that moment in time, they are in love, and everyone's life gets worse.

3   The first one to suffer is Mercutio, a member of neither house, but a relative of Prince Escalus, ruler of Verona. He fights a duel on Romeo's behalf with Juliet's cousin Tybalt. Romeo meddles in the fight, and his interference gets Mercutio killed. Romeo, furious at his friend's death, kills Tybalt.

4   For this action, Prince Escalus exiles Romeo from the city and threatens him with execution should he ever return. The Prince has his own plans for Juliet—a hope to see his cousin Paris marry the young woman. Juliet's family is also in favor of the marriage, as it would raise the status of the House of Capulet and bring them closer to destroying the Montagues. Juliet ignores her family's history, wishing to be with Romeo and no one else. Desperate, she plans a way for them to escape their families and disappear together.

NOTES

5   Juliet swallows a special poison that allows her to appear dead for three days and then reawaken. Her family is shocked and grief-stricken by her apparent death. They put her body in the family's burial crypt. Romeo, hearing this, is struck with unbearable pain; now life has no meaning. A messenger from Juliet, who would have explained her plan, never finds him. Time is not Romeo's friend; the timing mishaps in these final scenes betray him.

6   Romeo goes to see Juliet's body and finds Paris at her crypt, deep in mourning. Paris attacks Romeo, believing him to be a vandal, and is killed in the fight. Romeo regrets killing him, though not enough to forget about Juliet's death. He drinks poison and dies. At this moment, Juliet awakens to find the now dead Romeo beside her. Horror-struck, she takes her own life with his dagger.

7   Examined in chronological order, it is hard to argue that anything other than death and misery came out of Romeo and Juliet's relationship. However, Shakespeare would disagree on this point. His argument comes at the play's very beginning, where he writes:

>   A pair of star-cross'd lovers take their life;
>   Whose misadventured piteous overthrows
>   Do with their death bury their parents' strife.

Thus, the miserable, painful deaths of so many characters and the grief of their friends and relatives lead to a lasting peace between the rival families. Future generations, living without strife, might consider the sacrifice a necessary step to a better age.

8   Nevertheless, it is doubtful that Shakespeare's own dead characters would agree with him. Mercutio certainly would not. He leaves the world irate, saying, "A plague o' both your houses! / They have made worms' meat of me." Tybalt and Paris are creatures of the present, and no thoughts of impending familial reconciliation enrich their last moments. For their sakes, and for the sakes of the lovers themselves, it would have been better if that moment at the party, the moment Romeo first saw Juliet, had never taken place. ✤

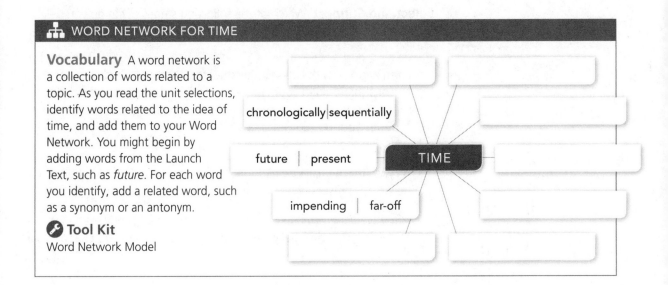

🔀 WORD NETWORK FOR TIME

Vocabulary A word network is a collection of words related to a topic. As you read the unit selections, identify words related to the idea of time, and add them to your Word Network. You might begin by adding words from the Launch Text, such as *future*. For each word you identify, add a related word, such as a synonym or an antonym.

🔧 **Tool Kit**
Word Network Model

chronologically | sequentially

future | present — TIME

impending | far-off

Summary

Write a summary of "Better Never to Have Met at All." Remember that a **summary** is a concise, complete, and accurate overview of a text. It should contain neither opinion nor analysis.

Launch Activity

Select and Support Which of the following stages of life do you believe is most critical in shaping a person's character? Select and mark your choice.

childhood   adolescence   adulthood

- Form a group with like-minded students. Discuss with each other the reasons that guided your choice. Try to develop one solid example that supports your point of view. Write a one-sentence statement that captures your position—for example, "I believe that childhood is most critical in shaping character, because _____."

- As your teacher calls "Childhood," "Adolescence," or "Adulthood," take turns presenting your statements.

- After everyone has had a chance to present, discuss any examples that you found especially strong or that convinced you to change your original choice.

QuickWrite

Consider class discussions, presentations, the video, and the Launch Text as you think about the prompt. Record your initial position here.

PROMPT: **What is the relationship of human beings to time?**

EVIDENCE LOG FOR FACING THE FUTURE, CONFRONTING THE PAST

Review your QuickWrite. Summarize your thoughts in one sentence to record in your Evidence Log. Then, record textual details or evidence from "Better Never to Have Met at All" that supports your initial position.

Prepare for the Performance-Based Assessment at the end of the unit by completing the Evidence Log after each selection.

Tool Kit
Evidence Log Model

Title of Text: _____ Date: _____

CONNECTION TO PROMPT	TEXT EVIDENCE/DETAILS	ADDITIONAL NOTES/IDEAS

How does this text change or add to my thinking?   Date: _____

ESSENTIAL QUESTION:

How do our attitudes toward the past and future shape our actions?

As you read these selections, work with your whole class to explore the relationships of human beings to their place in time.

From Text to Topic In Shakespeare's *The Tragedy of Macbeth,* Macbeth and his wife imagine a future for themselves but lack the patience to let that future unfold on its own. Macbeth is even willing to be punished later, in the afterlife, if only he can have everything he wants right now. As you read, think about how the main characters struggle with and against time itself.

Whole-Class Learning Strategies

Throughout your life, in school, in your community, and in your career, you will continue to learn and work in large-group environments.

Review these strategies and the actions you can take to practice them as you work with your whole class. Add ideas of your own for each step. Get ready to use these strategies during Whole-Class Learning.

STRATEGY	ACTION PLAN
Listen actively	• Eliminate distractions. For example, put your cellphone away. • Record brief notes on main ideas and points of confusion. •
Clarify by asking questions	• If you're confused, other people probably are, too. Ask a question to help your whole class. • Ask follow-up questions as needed; for example, if you do not understand the clarification or if you want to make an additional connection. •
Monitor understanding	• Notice what information you already know and be ready to build on it. • Ask for help if you are struggling. •
Interact and share ideas	• Share your ideas and answer questions, even if you are unsure of them. • Build on the ideas of others by adding details or making a connection. •

CONTENTS

COMPARE

PERFORMANCE TASK

WRITING FOCUS

Write an Argument

The Whole-Class reading and media introduce characters who defy both the social order and the natural flow of time in pursuit of their own ambitions. After reading and listening, you will write an argument in the form of a response to literature on the topic of Macbeth's relationship to the past and the future.

Renaissance and Reformation: A Changing England

Voices of the Period

"And therefore I am come amongst you at this time, not as for my recreation or sport, but being resolved, in the midst and heat of the battle, to live or die amongst you all; to lay down, for my God, and for my kingdom, and for my people, my honor and my blood, even the dust. I know I have but the body of a weak and feeble woman; but I have the heart of a king, and of a king of England, too."

—Elizabeth I, Queen of England

"If you want to change the world, pick up your pen and write."

—Martin Luther, theologian and religious reformer

"For whosoever commands the sea commands the trade; whosoever commands the trade of the world commands the riches of the world, and consequently the world itself."

—Sir Walter Raleigh, explorer
from "A Discourse of the Invention of Ships, Anchors, Compass, &c."

History of the Period

The Tudors In 1485, Henry Tudor became King Henry VII, ending a civil war between the House of York and the House of Lancaster. Though Henry's claim to the throne was questionable, he brought stability to the country through his strong leadership. He also established a royal line that had a profound effect on history.

Henry Tudor's son, Henry VIII, was one of the great monarchs in English history. He presided over turbulent social and political changes.

The Protestant Reformation The Reformation, a reaction against what many perceived as corruption in the Catholic Church, was inspired by religious thinkers who wanted to return to what they saw as a purer form of Christianity. The German theologian Martin Luther initiated the movement, which led to the founding of Protestantism. Luther believed that the Bible, rather than the Pope, was the source of spiritual authority. He considered faith alone, rather than faith and good works, to be necessary for salvation. Henry VIII wrote a book attacking Luther's beliefs. For this, Pope Leo X named the Catholic Henry "Defender of the Faith."

In 1534, however, Henry VIII made England a Protestant country. Henry had married his older brother's widow, Catherine of Aragon, who bore

TIMELINE

1492: Bahamas Columbus lands in Western Hemisphere.

1509: Italy Michelangelo paints ceiling of Sistine Chapel.

1485

1485: Henry VII becomes the first Tudor king.

1503: Italy Leonardo da Vinci paints *Mona Lisa*.

Integration of Knowledge and Ideas

Notebook In the mid-1400s, the German goldsmith Johannes Gutenberg developed a revolutionary system of using movable type to increase the efficiency of the printing press. Suddenly, the printing of books became a faster and cheaper process. How do you think this invention would affect learning, and how in turn would that affect society? How might the statistics below relate to a rise in literacy in Renaissance England?

Year	Number of Books Licensed for Publication in England
1509	38
1558	77
1603	328

him a daughter, Mary. Desperate for a male heir, Henry abandoned Catherine for a new wife, Anne Boleyn. He petitioned the Pope for a divorce, on the grounds that his marriage to his brother's widow was invalid. When the Pope denied his petition to remarry, Henry refused to comply, eventually severing all ties with Rome. In 1534, he established the Protestant Church of England with himself at its head. Religious affiliation and allegiance to the king were suddenly united.

After the death of Henry VIII in 1547, his young son became Edward VI. The sickly youth died after six years and was succeeded by his sister, Mary.

A devout Catholic like her mother, Catherine of Aragon, Mary denied the validity of the church her father had founded. Within months after her accession to the throne, Protestant religious leaders were imprisoned. In the course of Mary's reign, nearly 300 Protestants were burned at the stake. At Mary's death, her half sister, Elizabeth, ascended to the throne and returned England to Protestant control.

The English Renaissance The Renaissance in Europe had begun in the fourteenth century, at about the same time that the English poet Chaucer wrote *The Canterbury Tales*. Italy was experiencing great change, and from that

1513: North America Ponce de León explores Florida.

1521: Italy Pope Leo X excommunicates Martin Luther.

1533: Peru Pizarro conquers Incas.

1534: Henry VIII establishes Church of England.

1547: Henry VIII dies.

1543: Nuremberg First edition of Copernicus' *On the Revolutions of the Celestial Spheres* is published.

1550

change came a rebirth of learning as scholars rediscovered Greek and Roman literature and art and absorbed the knowledge of Arabic physicians, mathematicians, and philosophers. This rediscovered knowledge inspired artists and writers to create some of the world's greatest cultural achievements. However, conditions in England had not yet been ripe for great change in Chaucer's time.

It was not until the end of the fifteenth century, when Henry VII came to power, that England began to let go of its medieval past. It was still an agrarian society, but towns—especially London—were growing in power and importance as the population increased dramatically and the role of trade grew in importance.

As life in England changed, and literature was increasingly written in the vernacular, England entered its own rebirth. It was under Elizabeth I that England experienced the great flowering of the English Renaissance.

The Elizabethan Age Elizabeth I presided over what many have described as England's "golden age." Born to Henry VIII and Anne Boleyn in 1533, Elizabeth ascended to the throne in 1558. She firmly established England as a Protestant nation and ushered in a time of prosperity and peace. The greatest threat to her rule came in 1588, when Catholic Spain sent an armada—a fleet of warships—to conquer England. Elizabeth rallied her people, and the English fleet shattered the armada. This glorious moment produced a surge of patriotic spirit and a sense of power that swept the entire nation.

Explorers and Settlers Fueled by the Renaissance thirst for knowledge, European navigators ventured far and wide, aided by the invention of the compass and by advances in astronomy. England's participation in the Age of Exploration began in 1497, when the Italian-born explorer John Cabot, sailing for an English company, reached present-day Canada. Cabot laid the basis for future English claims in North America.

By the end of this period, the claims of exploration became the claims of settlement, as England began its first colonies—Jamestown, in 1607, and the Massachusetts colonies, beginning in 1620.

Puritans Toward the end of Elizabeth's reign, some Protestants began to form groups that questioned the purpose of life and the role of the church. Because they focused on purification of the English church from any vestiges of Roman Catholicism, they became known as Puritans. The desire to find a place where they were free to practice their beliefs motivated the Puritans to emigrate to the North American continent, where they founded the New England Colonies.

A New Dynasty Elizabeth I was succeeded by her cousin, who became James I, the first Stuart king of England. James was an able ruler who inherited a prosperous nation that had become a world power. By the end of his reign, however, his struggles with Parliament foreshadowed the civil war that would come during the reign of his son, Charles I.

TIMELINE

1558: Elizabeth I becomes queen.

1563: More than 20,000 Londoners die in plague.

1579: North America Sir Francis Drake lands near site of San Francisco on his voyage around the globe.

1564: William Shakespeare is born.

1550

Literature Selections

Literature of the Focus Period Some of the selections in the unit were written during the Focus Period and pertain to how our attitudes toward time shape our actions.

The Tragedy of Macbeth, William Shakespeare

Sonnet 12, William Shakespeare

Sonnet 60, William Shakespeare

Sonnet 73, William Shakespeare

Sonnet 32, Mary Wroth

Sonnet 75, Edmund Spenser

Connections Across Time Writing about our attitudes toward time continued long after the Focus Period. In addition, writing from the Focus Period has vastly influenced many writers and commentators from later time periods.

from "The Naked Babe and the Cloak of Manliness," Cleanth Brooks

"Ozymandias," Percy Bysshe Shelley

"Why Brownlee Left," Paul Muldoon

"Man's Short Life and Foolish Ambition," Margaret Cavendish, Duchess of Newcastle

"The Lagoon," Joseph Conrad

"What's Your Time Perspective?" Jane Collingwood

"Does Time Pass?" Peter Dizikes

ADDITIONAL LITERATURE OF THE FOCUS PERIOD

Student Edition

UNIT 1
Speech Before Her Troops,
Queen Elizabeth I

UNIT 4
"A Valediction: Forbidding Mourning,"
John Donne

"Holy Sonnet 10," John Donne

1588: English navy defeats Spanish Armada.

1603: Elizabeth I dies; James I becomes king.

1607: North America English colony is established at Jamestown.

1609: Italy Galileo builds first telescope.

1620: North America Pilgrims land at Plymouth Rock.

1625: James I dies.

1625

> While there are no contemporary drawings of the Globe's interior, maps and other images from the era show its exterior. This etching of the building by a late-eighteenth- or early-nineteenth-century artist was probably based on some of those drawings.

Literary History

Elizabethan Theater

The Rise of English Drama English drama came of age during the reign of Elizabeth I, developing into a sophisticated and popular art form. Although playwrights like Shakespeare were mainly responsible for the great theatrical achievements of the time, the importance of actors, audiences, and theater buildings should not be underestimated.

Elizabethan Actors Before the reign of Elizabeth I, theater companies traveled about the country, putting on plays wherever they could find an audience, often performing in the open courtyards of inns. Spectators watched from the ground or from balconies or galleries above.

When Shakespeare was twelve years old, an actor named James Burbage built London's first theater, called simply the Theatre. Actors—even prominent and well-to-do actors like James Burbage— had a complicated status in London society: They were frowned upon by the city fathers, but were wildly popular with the common people, who clamored to see them perform. Though actors were considered rogues and vagabonds by some, they were held in sufficient repute to be called on frequently to perform at court. A man like Burbage enjoyed a reputation somewhat like a rock star's today.

The Globe In 1597, the city fathers closed down the Theatre. In late 1598, Richard Burbage (James Burbage's son) and his men dismantled it and hauled it in pieces across the Thames to Southwark. It took them six months to rebuild it, and when they did, they renamed it the Globe.

Scholars disagree about what the Globe actually looked like inside because there are no surviving drawings from the time or detailed written descriptions. In his play *Henry V*, Shakespeare refers to the building as "this wooden O," so we have a sense that it was round or octagonal. The building had to have been small enough for the actors to be heard, but we know that performances drew as many as 2,500 to 3,000 people. These truly packed houses must have been uncomfortable— especially when you consider that people of the era didn't bathe or change their clothes very often! The so-called "groundlings," who paid an admission price of a penny, stood thoughout the performance. Some of the audience sat in a gallery behind the performers. Though they saw only the actors' backs and probably could not hear very well, they were content to be seen by the rest of the audience.

There were no sets or lighting at the Globe. Plays were performed in the bright afternoon sunlight, and a playwright's words alone had to create moods like the one in the eerie first scene of *Macbeth*. Holding an audience spellbound was complicated by the fact that most spectators ate and drank throughout the performance.

The first Globe met its demise in 1613, when a cannon fired as part of a performance of *Henry VIII* ignited the theater's thatched roof. Everyone escaped unharmed, but the Globe burned to the ground. Although the theater was rebuilt, the Puritans had it permanently closed in 1642.

The New Globe Almost four centuries after the original Globe opened, an actor stood onstage in a replica of the famous theater and recited these lines from *Henry V*: "Can this cockpit hold / The vasty fields of France? Or may we cram / Within this wooden O the very casques / That did affright the air at Agincourt?" Building a replica of Shakespeare's Globe was the American actor Sam Wanamaker's dream. It took long years of fundraising and construction until the theater opened to its first full season on June 8, 1997, with a production of *Henry V*. Like the earlier Globe, this one is made of wood, with a thatched roof and lime plaster covering the walls. The stage and the galleries are covered, but the "bear pit," where the modern-day groundlings stand, is open to the skies.

Perhaps the most striking aspect of seeing Shakespeare's plays performed at the Globe is the immediacy of the action. The performers, as Benedict Nightingale noted in the London *Times*, "are talking to you, asking you questions, involving you in their fears." At the Globe, the audience is part of the conversation. Is that not what theater is all about?

⌄ The exterior of the modern Globe today

A performance at the modern Globe

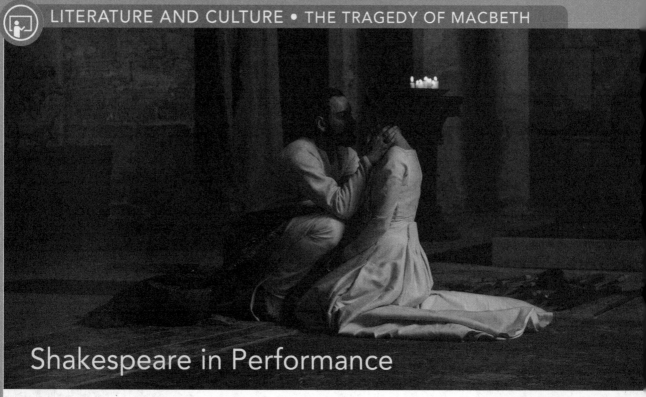

Shakespeare in Performance

A play on the page is only half a drama. The script is a recipe for a performance—incomplete until it is staged in a theater, reconstructed in the mind of the reader, or captured on film. When a play is staged, actors and directors bring the words to life through their interpretations. Decisions about scenery, costumes, props, timing, and casting, as well as ideas about a character's gestures, movement, expressions, and motivations, can call forth different meanings from even the most familiar play.

Questions and Interpretations

Shakespeare's plays have been produced for more than four hundred years and have been brought to life in countless performances and reinterpretations. The best interpretations of his plays shed new light by asking imaginative questions and finding answers in the texts themselves. The following is a tiny sampling of some of the questions asked and answered by landmark Shakespearean productions.

What is the source of Lady Macbeth's evil? Shakespeare's Lady Macbeth conspires with her husband to murder their king, leading generations of actresses to ask and attempt to answer this question.

- **She is just an inhuman monster.** Sarah Siddons, who played the role of Lady Macbeth more than two hundred years ago, portrayed the character as a driven woman in whom "the passion of ambition has almost obliterated all the characteristics of human nature."

- **She is an evil beauty.** Vivien Leigh, the actress who is most famous for her role as Scarlett O'Hara in the film adaptation of *Gone with the Wind*, found in Lady Macbeth an evil beauty who gives a goodnight kiss to the man she is plotting to murder later that evening.

- **She is more than a monster.** In the 2015 film adaptation of *Macbeth*, French actress Marion Cotillard plays Lady Macbeth as a mother who is grief-stricken by the death of her infant son. Her actions in the play are driven by grief and hopelessness as well as greed and ambition.

Lady Macbeth

How realistic or true to Shakespeare's era does this need to be?

Some directors attempt to keep with the playwright's vision by staging the action in as realistic a manner as possible or by recreating Elizabethan settings and costume. Other directors, however, take liberties with settings, costumes, and other aspects of the production.

- To bring new realism to the woodland setting of *A Midsummer Night's Dream,* the director of a 1905 production brought live rabbits onstage.

- By contrast, the set for Peter Brook's famous 1972 stage production of *A Midsummer Night's Dream* was a white box with no ceiling and two doors. Stagehands were completely visible to the audience.

- The famous actor Laurence Olivier brought unintentional realism to the part of Macbeth. Following his director's instructions, he played the part so enthusiastically that he injured the actor playing Macduff during their staged sword fight. On another occasion, with yet another Macduff, Olivier fought the sword battle so vigorously that his sword broke and flew into the audience.

How do we show relevance?

Some directors highlight the play's application to modern life by relocating the story to times and places that resonate with current audiences.

- In a 1936 production of *Macbeth,* director Orson Welles set the play in Haiti instead of Scotland. He used a cast of African American actors and modeled Macbeth after a famous Haitian dictator.

- In a 2000 film version of *Hamlet* starring Ethan Hawke, the action takes place on twentieth-century Wall Street in New York City at a company called Denmark Corporation.

- In a 2010 televised production of *Macbeth* starring Sir Patrick Stewart, the sets, mood, and costumes intentionally evoke Stalin-era Soviet Union, a particularly bloody and oppressive time and place in twentieth-century history.

The images shown here are from the 2015 film adaptation of *Macbeth* starring Michael Fassbender as Macbeth and Marion Cotillard as Lady Macbeth.

WILLIAM SHAKESPEARE

THERE IS NO DARKNESS BUT IGNORANCE

"The poet's eye, in a fine frenzy rolling,

Doth glance from heaven to earth,
    from earth to heaven;

And, as imagination bodies forth

The forms of things unknown,
    the poet's pen

Turns them to shapes, and gives to airy
    nothing

A local habitation and a name."

—William Shakespeare,
from *A Midsummer Night's Dream*

William Shakespeare, Poet and Playwright

Because of his deep understanding of human nature, his compassion for all types of people, and the power and beauty of his language, William Shakespeare (1564–1616) is regarded as the greatest writer in English. Nearly four hundred years after his death, Shakespeare's plays continue to be read widely and produced throughout the world. They have the same powerful impact on today's audiences as they had when they were first staged.

The Playwright in His Own Time It is a myth that we know little about Shakespeare's life. As critic Irving Ribner attests, "we know more about him than we do about virtually any other of his contemporary dramatists, with the exception of Ben Jonson." Shakespeare was born on April 23, 1564, in Stratford-upon-Avon, which is northwest of London. Stratford, with a population of about two thousand in Shakespeare's day, was the market town for a fertile agricultural region.

Shakespeare's father, John, was a successful glove maker and businessman who held a number of positions in the town's government. His mother, whose maiden name was Mary Arden, was the daughter of John's landlord. Their marriage, therefore, boosted the Shakespeare family's holdings. Nevertheless, there is evidence that in the late 1570s, John Shakespeare began to suffer financial reverses.

Shakespeare's Education No written evidence of Shakespeare's boyhood exists—not even a name on a school attendance list. However, given his father's status, it is highly probable that he attended the Stratford Grammar School, where he acquired a knowledge of Latin. Discipline at such a school was strict, and the school day lasted from 6:00 A.M. in the summer (7:00 in the winter) until 5:00 P.M. From 11:00 to 1:00, students were dismissed to eat lunch with their families. At 3:00, they were allowed to play for a quarter of an hour!

Shakespeare's Marriage and Family Shakespeare's name enters the official records again in November 1582, when he received a license to marry Anne Hathaway. The couple had a daughter, Susanna, in 1583, and twins, Judith and Hamnet, in 1585. Beyond names and years in which his children were born, we know little about his family life. Some writers have made much of the fact that Shakespeare left his wife and children behind when he went to London not long after his twins were born. However, he visited his family in Stratford regularly during his years as a playwright, and they may have lived with him for a time in London.

Actor and Playwright It is uncertain how Shakespeare became connected with the theater in the late 1580s and early 1590s. By 1594, however, he had become a part owner and the principal playwright of the Lord Chamberlain's Men, one of the most successful theater companies in London.

In 1599, the company built the famous Globe theater on the south bank of the Thames River, in Southwark. This is where most of Shakespeare's plays were first performed. When James I became king in 1603, after the death of Elizabeth I, James took control of the Lord Chamberlain's Men and renamed the company the King's Men.

Retirement In about 1610, Shakespeare retired to Stratford, where he continued to write plays. He was a prosperous middle-class man, who profited from his share in a successful theater company. Six years later, on April 23, 1616, he died and was buried in Holy Trinity Church in Stratford. Because it was a common practice to move bodies after burial to make room for others, Shakespeare wrote the following as his epitaph:

> Blest be the man that spares these stones,
> And curst be he that moves my bones.

His Literary Record Shakespeare did not think of himself as a man of letters. He wrote his plays to be performed and did not bring out editions of them for the reading public. The first published edition of his work, called the First Folio, was issued in 1623 by two members of his theater company, John Heminges and Henry Condell. It contained thirty-six of the thirty-seven plays now attributed to him.

In addition to his plays, Shakespeare wrote 154 sonnets and three longer poems.

SPEAKING SHAKESPEARE

Shakespeare invented each of the italicized phrases, which are now common but were unknown in English before their appearance in *Macbeth*. Look for them as you read and discover if their meanings have changed since Shakespeare's time.

He's full of the *milk of human kindness* (ACT I, SCENE V, LINE 17)

Don't worry about it, *what's done is done!* (ACT III, SCENE II, LINE 12)

That will last until the *crack of doom.* (ACT IV, SCENE I, LINE 117)

She finished the job in *one fell swoop.* (ACT IV, SCENE III, LINE 219)

How to Read Shakespeare

Shakespeare wrote his plays in the language of his time. To the modern ear, however, that language can sound almost foreign. Certain words have changed meaning or fallen out of use. The idioms, slang, and humor of twenty-first-century America are very different from those of Elizabethan England. Even our way of viewing reality has changed. These differences present challenges for modern-day readers of Shakespeare. Here are some strategies for dealing with them.

CHALLENGE: Elizabethan Words

Many words Shakespeare used are now archaic, or outdated. Here are some examples:

TYPE OF WORD	CONTEMPORARY ENGLISH	ELIZABETHAN ENGLISH	EXAMPLE FROM *THE TRAGEDY OF MACBETH*
Pronouns	*you, your, yours*	*thou, thee, thy, thine*	*We are sent / to give **thee**, from our royal master, thanks* (I.iii.100–101)
Verbs	*come, will, do, has*	*cometh, wilt, doth, hath*	*What he **hath** lost, noble Macbeth **hath** won.* (I.ii.67)
Time words	*morning, evening*	*morrow, even*	*Oh, never / Shall sun that **morrow** see!* (I.v.60–61)
Familiar words used in unfamiliar ways	*only*	*but*	*We fail? / **But** screw your courage to the sticking-place / And we'll not fail.* (I.vii.59–60)
	fortunate	*happy*	*Two truths are told, / As **happy** prologues to the swelling act….* (I.iii.128–129)

STRATEGIES

Familiarize yourself with the meanings of common archaic words in Shakespeare.

If a word is completely unfamiliar, look to the marginal notes for a translation or for clues to meaning in the surrounding text.

CHALLENGE: Elizabethan Syntax

The syntax, or word order, Shakespeare uses may also be archaic. In contemporary English, the subject (s) of a sentence usually appears before the verb (v). Shakespeare often inverts this order, placing the verb first.

Contemporary English Syntax

s   v
What do **you say**?

Elizabethan English Syntax

v   s
What **say you**?

STRATEGY

If a sentence uses inverted syntax, identify its subject and verb. Then, rephrase the sentence, placing the subject before the verb.

CHALLENGE: Long Sentences

Many of Shakespeare's sentences span more than one line of verse. This is especially true when he uses a semicolon to connect two or more clauses.

Their hands and faces were all badged with blood;
So were their daggers, which unwiped we found
Upon their pillows. (Macbeth, II.iii)

STRATEGIES

Look for capital letters and end marks to see where sentences begin and end.

When a sentence is made up of two clauses connected by a semicolon, consider how the ideas in the clauses relate.

CHALLENGE: Elizabethan Worldview

In Shakespeare's day, society was rigidly organized. The nobility occupied the top rung of the social ladder, and the uneducated peasantry occupied the bottom. Social advancement was difficult, if not impossible. The ladder of power also existed within families. Parents made life choices for their children. Within a marriage, the husband was the master of his wife. Elizabethan people expected to live shorter, more difficult lives, and they understood the events of a life to be controlled by fate. They did not believe they had the power to shape their own destinies as we do today.

STRATEGY

Keep the Elizabethan worldview in mind as you read. If a character's attitude clashes with your own, try to view the situation through the character's eyes. This will help you understand why he or she is behaving or speaking in a certain way.

Close Read the Text

Annotating the text as you read can help you tackle the challenges of Shakespearean language. Here are two sample annotations of an excerpt from Act I, Scene v, of *The Tragedy of Macbeth.* In this scene, Lady Macbeth learns of a prophecy that her husband will become king of Scotland. In this passage, she reflects on what she has learned.

Close Read

ANNOTATE: These two sentences are similar. Each is made up of two clauses joined by a semicolon. Both seem to follow a similar logic, too.

QUESTION: How do the structure and logic of these sentences express an important idea?

CONCLUDE: A modern-day paraphrase of the first sentence might read: "You want to gain your desires honestly; and yet you wouldn't mind winning." The second sentence might read: "To get what you most want, you must do what you most fear." These sentences show a conflict between Macbeth's desires and his resolve. The sentences war with each other, as do Macbeth's tendencies.

Lady Macbeth. Glamis thou art, and Cawdor,* and shalt be
What thou art promised. Yet do I fear thy nature;
It is too ful o' th' milk of human kindness
To catch the nearest way. Thou wouldst be great,
Art not without ambition, but without
The illness should attend it. What thou wouldst highly,
That wouldst thou holily; wouldst not play false,
And yet wouldst wrongly win. Thou'dst have, great Glamis,
That which cries "Thus thou must do" if thou have it;
And that which rather thou dost fear to do
Than wishest should be undone. Hie thee hither,
That I may pour my spirits in thine ear,
And chastise with the valor of my tongue
All that impedes thee from the golden round
Which fate and metaphysical aid doth seem
To have thee crowned withal.

————————————
*Glamis and Cawdor are titles of nobility held by Macbeth.

ANNOTATE: These phrases seem sinister.

QUESTION: What makes these lines so unpleasant?

CONCLUDE: The repeated "h" and "th" sounds in "Hie thee hither" create a breathy hiss, like that of a snake. Lady Macbeth's plan to "pour ... spirits in thine ear" suggests poisoning or the whispered temptations of a devil, and the phrase "valor of my tongue" suggests a serpent. All together, these lines present Lady Macbeth as an agent of evil.

About the Playwright

William Shakespeare
Because of his deep
understanding of human
nature, his compassion for
all types of people, and
the power and beauty
of his language, William
Shakespeare is regarded as
one of the English language's
greatest writers. Nearly
400 years after his death,
Shakespeare's plays continue
to be read widely and
produced throughout the
world. They have the same
powerful impact on today's
audiences as they had when
they were first staged.

🔧 Tool Kit
First-Read Guide and
Model Annotation

The Tragedy of Macbeth, Act I

Concept Vocabulary

You will encounter the following words as you read Act I of *The Tragedy
of Macbeth*. Before reading, note how familiar you are with each word.
Then, rank the words in order from most familiar (1) to least familiar (6).

WORD	YOUR RANKING
revolt	
captivity	
assault	
flout	
rebellious	
treasons	

After completing the first read, come back to the concept vocabulary and
review your rankings. Mark changes to your original rankings as needed.

First Read DRAMA

Apply these strategies as you conduct your first read. You will have an
opportunity to complete the close-read notes after your first read.

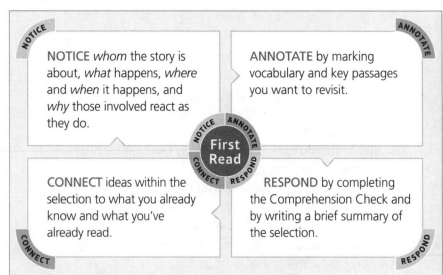

NOTICE *whom* the story is about, *what* happens, *where* and *when* it happens, and *why* those involved react as they do.

ANNOTATE by marking vocabulary and key passages you want to revisit.

CONNECT ideas within the selection to what you already know and what you've already read.

RESPOND by completing the Comprehension Check and by writing a brief summary of the selection.

First Read

⊞ STANDARDS

Reading Literature
By the end of grade 12, read and
comprehend literature, including
stories, dramas, and poems, at the
high end of the grades 11–CCR text
complexity band independently and
proficiently.

BACKGROUND

Fact and Legend

By Shakespeare's time, the story of the eleventh-century Scottish king Macbeth was a mixture of fact and legend. Shakespeare and his contemporaries, however, probably regarded the account of Macbeth in Raphael Holinshed's *Chronicles of England, Scotland, and Ireland* as completely factual. The playwright drew on the *Chronicles* as a source for the play; however, he also freely adapted the material for his own purposes.

Holinshed's Chronicles Holinshed's account contains a description of a meeting between Macbeth and the witches. His account also tells how Macbeth and his friends, angry at the naming of King Duncan's son Malcolm as Prince of Cumberland, ambush and slay Duncan. However, the historical Macbeth's claim to the throne has some legitimacy. Finally, Holinshed indicates that Banquo is Macbeth's accomplice in the assassination. Lady Macbeth, prominent in Shakespeare's play, does not play a significant role in Holinshed.

Shakespeare's *Macbeth* Shakespeare took what he needed from the *Chronicles* and shaped it into a tragic plot. Seeing the theatrical possibilities of the meeting with the witches, Shakespeare staged such an encounter in Act I, Scene iii. However, he changed Holinshed's account in order to make King Duncan an innocent victim: Shakespeare's Macbeth does not have a legitimate claim to the throne. Further, Shakespeare used another story in the *Chronicles*—one in which a wife urges her husband to kill a friend and guest—as the basis for the character Lady Macbeth. She becomes Macbeth's co-conspirator, replacing Banquo. Shakespeare, of course, had political motives for holding Banquo innocent. Banquo was considered the ancestor of the new king, James I!

The Tragedy of
Macbeth
Act I

William Shakespeare

CHARACTERS

Duncan, King of Scotland

Malcolm
Donalbain } his sons

Macbeth
Banquo
Macduff
Lennox
Ross } noblemen of Scotland
Menteith
Angus
Caithness

Fleance, son to Banquo

Siward, Earl of Northumberland, general of the English forces

Young Siward, his son

Seyton, an officer attending on Macbeth

Son to Macduff

An English Doctor

A Scottish Doctor

A Porter

An Old Man

Three Murderers

Lady Macbeth

Lady Macduff

A Gentlewoman attending on Lady Macbeth

Hecate

Witches

Apparitions

Lords, Officers, Soldiers, Attendants, and Messengers

Setting: Scotland; England

Scene i • *An open place.*

[*Thunder and lightning. Enter* Three Witches.]

First Witch. When shall we three meet again?
In thunder, lightning, or in rain?

Second Witch. When the hurlyburly's done,
When the battle's lost and won.

5 **Third Witch.** That will be ere the set of sun.

First Witch. Where the place?

Second Witch.   Upon the heath.

Third Witch. There to meet with Macbeth.

First Witch. I come, Graymalkin.[1]

Second Witch. Paddock[2] calls.

Third Witch.   Anon![3]

10 **All.** Fair is foul, and foul is fair.
Hover through the fog and filthy air.   (*Exit.*)

⌘ ⌘ ⌘

Scene ii • *A camp near Forres, a town in northeast Scotland.*

[*Alarum within.*[1] *Enter* King Duncan, Malcolm, Donalbain,
Lennox, *with* Attendants, *meeting a bleeding* Captain.]

King. What bloody man is that? He can report,
As seemeth by his plight, of the **revolt**
The newest state.

Malcolm.   This is the sergeant[2]
Who like a good and hardy soldier fought
5 'Gainst my **captivity**. Hail, brave friend!
Say to the king the knowledge of the broil[3]
As thou didst leave it.

Captain.   Doubtful it stood.
As two spent swimmers, that do cling together
And choke their art.[4] The merciless Macdonwald—
10 Worthy to be a rebel for to that
The multiplying villainies of nature
Do swarm upon him—from the Western Isles[5]
Of kerns and gallowglasses[6] is supplied;
And fortune, on his damnèd quarrel[7] smiling,

9. minion favorite.

10. unseamed . . . chops split him open from the navel to the jaws.

11. 'gins his reflection rises.

12. Norweyan lord king of Norway.

13. surveying vantage seeing an opportunity.

assault (uh SAWLT) *n.* military attack

14. sooth truth.

15. cracks explosives.

16. Except unless.

17. memorize . . . Golgotha (GOL guh thuh) make the place as memorable for slaughter as Golgotha, the place where Christ was crucified.

18. Thane Scottish title of nobility.

19. seems to seems about to.

flout (flowt) *v.* break a rule or law without hiding it or showing shame

20. Norway king of Norway.

---

15 Showed like a rebel's whore:[8] but all's too weak:
For brave Macbeth—well he deserves that name—
Disdaining fortune, with his brandished steel,
Which smoked with bloody execution,
Like valor's minion[9] carved out his passage
20 Till he faced the slave:
Which nev'r shook hands, nor bade farewell to him,
Till he unseamed him from the nave to th' chops,[10]
And fixed his head upon our battlements.

King. O valiant cousin! Worthy gentleman!

25 **Captain.** As whence the sun 'gins his reflection[11]
Shipwracking storms and direful thunders break,
So from that spring whence comfort seemed to come
Discomfort swells. Mark, King of Scotland, mark:
No sooner justice had, with valor armed,
30 Compelled these skipping kerns to trust their heels
But the Norweyan lord,[12] surveying vantage,[13]
With furbished arms and new supplies of men,
Began a fresh assault.

King.   Dismayed not this
Our captains, Macbeth and Banquo?

Captain.   Yes;
35 As sparrows eagles, or the hare the lion.
If I say sooth,[14] I must report they were
As cannons overcharged with double cracks;[15]
So they doubly redoubled strokes upon the foe.
Except[16] they meant to bathe in reeking wounds,
40 Or memorize another Golgotha,[17]
I cannot tell—
But I am faint: my gashes cry for help.

King. So well thy words become thee as thy wounds:
They smack of honor both. Go get him surgeons.

[*Exit* Captain, *attended.*]

[*Enter* Ross *and* Angus.]

Who comes here?

45 **Malcolm.**   The worthy Thane[18] of Ross.

Lennox. What a haste looks through his eyes! So should he look
That seems to[19] speak things strange.

Ross.   God save the king!

King. Whence cam'st thou, worthy Thane?

Ross.   From Fife, great King:
Where the Norweyan banners flout the sky
50 And fan our people cold.
Norway[20] himself, with terrible numbers,

Assisted by that most disloyal traitor
The Thane of Cawdor, began a dismal²¹ conflict;
Till that Bellona's bridegroom, lapped in proof,²²
55 Confronted him with self-comparisons,²³
Point against point, **rebellious** arm 'gainst arm,
Curbing his lavish²⁴ spirit: and, to conclude,
The victory fell on us.

King.   Great happiness!

Ross.   That now
Sweno, the Norways' king, craves composition;²⁵
60 Nor would we deign him burial of his men
Till he disbursed, at Saint Colme's Inch,²⁶
Ten thousand dollars to our general use.

King. No more that Thane of Cawdor shall deceive
Our bosom interest:²⁷ go pronounce his present²⁸ death,
65 And with his former title greet Macbeth.

Ross. I'll see it done.

King. What he hath lost, noble Macbeth hath won.

[*Exit.*]

⌘ ⌘ ⌘

Scene iii • *A heath near Forres.*

[*Thunder. Enter the* Three Witches.]

First Witch. Where hast thou been, sister?

Second Witch. Killing swine.¹

Third Witch. Sister, where thou?

First Witch. A sailor's wife had chestnuts in her lap.
5 And mounched, and mounched, and mounched.
"Give me," quoth I.
Aroint thee,² witch!" the rump-fed ronyon³ cries.
Her husband's to Aleppo⁴ gone, master o' th' Tiger:
But in a sieve⁵ I'll thither sail.
10 And, like a rat without a tail,⁶
I'll do, I'll do, and I'll do.

Second Witch. I'll give thee a wind.

First Witch. Th' art kind.

Third Witch. And I another.

15 **First Witch.** I myself have all the other;
And the very ports they blow,⁷
All the quarters that they know
I' th' shipman's card.⁸

9. **penthouse lid** eyelid.
10. **forbid** cursed.
11. **sev'nights** weeks.
12. **peak** waste away.

I'll drain him dry as hay:
20   Sleep shall neither night nor day
Hang upon his penthouse lid;[9]
He shall live a man forbid:[10]
Weary sev'nights[11] nine times nine
Shall he dwindle, peak,[12] and pine:
25   Though his bark cannot be lost,
Yet it shall be tempest-tossed.
Look what I have.

Second Witch. Show me, show me.

First Witch. Here I have a pilot's thumb,
30   Wracked as homeward he did come.

[*Drum within.*]

Third Witch. A drum, a drum!
Macbeth doth come.

All. The weird[13] sisters, hand in hand,
Posters[14] of the sea and land,
35   Thus do go about, about:
Thrice to thine, and thrice to mine,
And thrice again, to make up nine.
Peace! The charm's wound up.

[*Enter* Macbeth *and* Banquo.]

Macbeth. So foul and fair a day I have not seen.

40   **Banquo.** How far is 't called to Forres? What are these
So withered, and so wild in their attire,
That look not like th' inhabitants o' th' earth.
And yet are on 't? Live you, or are you aught
That man may question? You seem to understand me,
45   By each at once her choppy[15] finger laying
Upon her skinny lips. You should be women,
And yet your beards forbid me to interpret
That you are so.

Macbeth.   Speak, if you can: what are you?

First Witch. All hail, Macbeth! Hail to thee. Thane of Glamis!

50   **Second Witch.** All hail, Macbeth! Hail to thee. Thane of Cawdor!

Third Witch. All hail, Macbeth, that shalt be King hereafter!

Banquo. Good sir, why do you start, and seem to fear
Things that do sound so fair? I' th' name of truth,
Are you fantastical,[16] or that indeed
55   Which outwardly ye show? My noble partner
You greet with present grace[17] and great prediction
Of noble having[18] and of royal hope,
That he seems rapt withal;[19] to me you speak not.
If you can look into the seeds of time,

CLOSE READ

ANNOTATE: In lines 40–48, mark words and phrases that describe the witches' appearance and behavior.

QUESTION: What impression of the witches does this speech convey?

CONCLUDE: What emotions does Banquo seem to feel as he addresses the witches?

60 And say which grain will grow and which will not,
Speak then to me, who neither beg nor fear
Your favors nor your hate.

First Witch. Hail!

Second Witch. Hail!

65 **Third Witch.** Hail!

First Witch. Lesser than Macbeth, and greater.

Second Witch. Not so happy,[20] yet much happier.

Third Witch. Though shalt get kings, though thou be none.
So all hail, Macbeth and Banquo!

70 **First Witch.** Banquo and Macbeth, all hail!

Macbeth. Stay you imperfect[21] speakers, tell me more:
By Sinel's[22] death I know I am Thane of Glamis;
But how of Cawdor? The Thane of Cawdor lives.
A prosperous gentleman; and to be King
75 Stands not within the prospect of belief.
No more than to be Cawdor. Say from whence
You owe[23] this strange intelligence?[24] Or why
Upon this blasted heath you stop our way
With such prophetic greeting? Speak, I charge you.

[Witches *vanish.*]

80 **Banquo.** The earth hath bubbles as the water has;
And these are of them. Whither are they vanished?

Macbeth. Into the air, and what seemed corporal[25] melted
As breath into the wind. Would they had stayed!

Banquo. Were such things here as we do speak about?
85 Or have we eaten on the insane root[26]
That takes the reason prisoner?

Macbeth. Your children shall be kings.

Banquo.   You shall be King.

Macbeth. And Thane of Cawdor too. Went it not so?

Banquo. To th' selfsame tune and words. Who's here?

[*Enter* Ross *and* Angus.]

90 **Ross.** The King hath happily received, Macbeth,
The news of thy success; and when he reads[27]
Thy personal venture in the rebels' fight,
His wonders and his praises do contend
Which should be thine or his.[28] Silenced with that,
95 In viewing o'er the rest o' th' selfsame day.
He finds thee in the stout Norweyan ranks,
Nothing afeard of what thyself didst make,
Strange images of death.[29] As thick as tale
Came post with post,[30] and every one did bear

NOTES

20. **happy** fortunate.

21. **imperfect** incomplete.
22. **Sinel's** (SIH nuhlz) Macbeth's father's.

23. **owe** own.
24. **intelligence** information.

25. **corporal** real.

26. **insane root** henbane or hemlock, believed to cause insanity.

27. **reads** considers.

28. **His wonders . . . his** His admiration contends with his desire to praise you.

29. **Nothing . . . death** killing, but not being afraid of being killed.

30. **As thick . . . post** as fast as could be counted came messenger after messenger.

31. **earnest** pledge.

32. **in which addition** with this new title.

33. **combined** allied.

34. **line** support.

35. **vantage** assistance.

36. **wrack** ruin.

treasons (TREE zuhnz) *n.* crimes of helping the enemies of one's country

100 Thy praises in his kingdom's great defense,
And poured them down before him.

Angus.   We are sent
To give thee, from our royal master, thanks;
Only to herald thee into his sight,
Not pay thee.

105 **Ross.** And for an earnest[31] of a great honor,
He bade me, from him, call thee Thane of Cawdor;
In which addition,[32] hail, most worthy Thane!
For it is thine.

Banquo. [*Aside*] What, can the devil speak true?

110 **Macbeth.** The Thane of Cawdor lives; why do you dress me
In borrowed robes?

Angus.   Who was the thane lives yet,
But under heavy judgment bears that life
Which he deserves to lose. Whether he was combined[33]
With those of Norway, or did line[34] the rebel
115 With hidden help and vantage,[35] or that with both
He labored in his country's wrack,[36] I know not:
But **treasons** capital, confessed and proved,
Have overthrown him.

Macbeth.   [*Aside*] Glamis, and Thane of Cawdor:

Banquo and Macbeth discuss the witches' prophecies.

The greatest is behind.[37] [*To Ross and* Angus]
120 Thanks for your pains.
[*Aside to* Banquo] Do you not hope your children shall be
    kings,
When those that gave the Thane of Cawdor to me
Promised no less to them?

Banquo. [*Aside to* Macbeth] That, trusted home,[38]
125 Might yet enkindle you unto[39] the crown,
Besides the Thane of Cawdor. But 'tis strange:
And oftentimes, to win us to our harm.
The instruments of darkness tell us truths.
Win us with honest trifles, to betray's
130 In deepest consequence.
Cousins,[40] a word, I pray you.

Macbeth.   [*Aside*] Two truths are told,
As happy prologues to the swelling act
Of the imperial theme.[41] —I thank you, gentlemen.—
[*Aside*] This supernatural soliciting
135 Cannot be ill, cannot be good. If ill,
Why hath it given me earnest of success,
Commencing in a truth? I am Thane of Cawdor:
If good, why do I yield to that suggestion[42]
Whose horrid image doth unfix my hair
140 And make my seated[43] heart knock at my ribs,
Against the use of nature?[44] Present fears
Are less than horrible imaginings.
My thought, whose murder yet is but fantastical
Shakes so my single[45] state of man that function
145 Is smothered in surmise,[46] and nothing is
But what is not.

Banquo.   Look, how our partner's rapt.

Macbeth. [*Aside*] If chance will have me King, why,
Chance may crown me,
Without my stir.

Banquo.   New honors come upon him,
150 Like our strange[47] garments, cleave not to their mold
But with the aid of use.

Macbeth.   [*Aside*] Come what come may,
Time and the hour runs through the roughest day.

Banquo. Worthy Macbeth, we stay upon your leisure.[48]

Macbeth. Give me your favor.[49] My dull brain was wrought
155 With things forgotten. Kind gentlemen, your pains
Are registered where every day I turn
The leaf to read them. Let us toward the King.
[*Aside to* Banquo] Think upon what hath chanced, and at
    more time.

37. behind still to come.

38. home fully.
39. enkindle you unto encourage
you to hope for.

40. Cousins often used as a term
of courtesy between fellow
noblemen.

41. swelling . . . theme stately idea
that I will be King.

42. suggestion thought of
murdering Duncan.

43. seated fixed.

44. Against . . . nature in an
unnatural way.

45. single unaided; weak.
46. surmise (suhr MYZ)
imaginings; speculation.

47. strange new.

48. stay upon your leisure await
your convenience.
49. favor pardon.

160 The interim having weighed it,⁵⁰ let us speak
Our free hearts⁵¹ each to other.

Banquo.   Very gladly.

Macbeth. Till then, enough. Come, friends.   [*Exit.*]

⌘ ⌘ ⌘

Scene iv • *Forres. The palace.*

[*Flourish.*¹ *Enter* King Duncan, Lennox, Malcolm, Donalbain, *and* Attendants.]

King. Is execution done on Cawdor? Are not
Those in commission² yet returned?

Malcolm.   My liege,³
They are not yet come back. But I have spoke
With one that saw him die, who did report
5 That very frankly he confessed his treasons,
Implored your Highness' pardon and set forth
A deep repentance: nothing in his life
Became him like the leaving it. He died
As one that had been studied⁴ in his death,
10 To throw away the dearest thing he owed⁵
As 'twere a careless⁶ trifle.

King.   There's no art
To find the mind's construction⁷ in the face:
He was a gentleman on whom I built
An absolute trust.

[*Enter* Macbeth, Banquo, Ross, *and* Angus.]

                                  O worthiest cousin!
15 The sin of my ingratitude even now
Was heavy on me: thou art so far before.
That swiftest wing of recompense is slow
To overtake thee. Would though hadst less deserved,
That the proportion both of thanks and payment
20 Might have been mine!⁸ Only I have left to say,
More is thy due than more than all can pay.

Macbeth. The service and the loyalty I owe,
In doing it, pays itself.⁹ Your Highness' part
Is to receive our duties: and our duties
25 Are to your throne and state children and servants:
Which do but what they should, by doing every thing
Safe toward¹⁰ your love and honor.

King.   Welcome hither.
I have begun to plant thee, and will labor

1. *Flourish* trumpet fanfare.

2. **in commission** commissioned to oversee the execution.

3. **liege** (leej) lord or king.

4. **studied** rehearsed.

5. **owed** owned.

6. **careless** worthless.

7. **mind's construction** person's character.

8. **Would . . . mine** If you had been less worthy, my thanks and payment could have exceeded the rewards you deserve.

9. **pays itself** is its own reward.

10. **Safe toward** with sure regard for.

To make thee full of growing. Noble Banquo,
30 That hast no less deserved, nor must be known
No less to have done so, let me enfold thee
And hold thee to my heart.

Banquo.   There if I grow
The harvest is your own.

King.   My plenteous joys,
Wanton[11] in fullness seek to hide themselves,
35 In drops of sorrow. Sons, kinsmen, thanes,
And you whose places are the nearest, know,
We will establish our estate upon
Our eldest, Malcolm,[12] whom we name hereafter
The Prince of Cumberland: which honor must
40 Not unaccompanied invest him only,
But signs of nobleness, like stars, shall shine
On all deservers. From hence to Inverness,[13]
And bind us further to you.

Macbeth. The rest is labor, which is not used for you.[14]
45 I'll be myself harbinger,[15] and make joyful
The hearing of my wife with your approach;
So, humbly take my leave.

King.   My worthy Cawdor!

Macbeth. [*Aside*] The Prince of Cumberland! That is a step
On which I must fall down, or else o'erleap,
50 For in my way it lies. Stars, hide your fires;
Let not light see my black and deep desires:
The eye wink at the hand;[16] yet let that be
Which the eye fears, when it is done, to see.   [*Exit.*]

King. True, worthy Banquo; he is full so valiant,
55 And in his commendations I am fed;
It is a banquet to me. Let's after him,
Whose care is gone before to bid us welcome.
It is a peerless kinsman.   [*Flourish. Exit.*]

⌘ ⌘ ⌘

Scene v • *Inverness. Macbeth's castle.*

[*Enter* Macbeth's Wife, *alone, with a letter.*]

Lady Macbeth. [*Reads*] "They met me in the day of
success; and I have learned by the perfect'st report
they have more in them than mortal knowledge.
When I burned in desire to question them further,
5 they made themselves air, into which they vanished.
Whiles I stood rapt in the wonder of it, came

NOTES

CLOSE READ
ANNOTATE: In lines 28–30, mark the metaphor, or implied comparison, in Duncan's speech to Macbeth.

QUESTION: What role is the king giving himself with regard to Macbeth and Banquo?

CONCLUDE: What can you conclude about the king's plans for Macbeth and Banquo?

11. **Wanton** unrestrained.

12. **establish . . . Malcolm** make Malcolm the heir to my throne.

13. **Inverness** Macbeth's castle.

14. **The rest . . . you** anything not done for you is laborious.

15. **harbinger** advance representative of the army or royal party who makes arrangements for a visit.

16. **wink at the hand** be blind to the hand's deed.

1. **missives** messengers.

2. **deliver thee** report to you.

3. **nearest** quickest.

4. **illness** wickedness.

5. **that which . . . undone** What you are afraid of doing you would not wish undone once you have undone it.
6. **round** crown

7. **had . . . him** overtook him.

8. **mortal** deadly.

9. **remorse** compassion.
10. **compunctious . . . nature** natural feelings of pity.
11. **fell** savage.
12. **effect** fulfillment.

missives[1] from the King, who all-hailed me 'Thane of Cawdor': by which title, before, these weird sisters saluted me, and referred me to the coming on
10 of time, with 'Hail, King that shalt be!' This have I thought good to deliver thee,[2] my dearest partner of greatness, that thou mightst not lose the dues of rejoicing, by being ignorant of what greatness is promised thee. Lay it to thy heart, and farewell."

15 Glamis thou art, and Cawdor, and shalt be
What thou art promised. Yet do I fear thy nature:
It is too full o' th' milk of human kindness
To catch the nearest[3] way. Thou wouldst be great,
Art not without ambition, but without
20 The illness[4] should attend it. What thou wouldst highly,
That wouldst thou holily; wouldst not play false,
And yet wouldst wrongly win. Thou'dst have, great Glamis,
That which cries "Thus thou must do" if thou have it;
And that which rather thou dost fear to do
25 Than wishest should be undone.[5] Hie thee hither,
That I may pour my spirits in thine ear,
And chastise with the valor of my tongue
All that impedes thee from the golden round[6]
Which fate and metaphysical aid doth seem
To have thee crowned withal.

[*Enter* Messenger.]

30   What is your tidings?

Messenger. The King comes here tonight.

Lady Macbeth.   Thou'rt mad to say it!
Is not thy master with him, who, were't so,
Would have informed for preparation?

Messenger. So please you, it is true. Our thane is coming.
35 One of my fellows had the speed of him.[7]
Who, almost dead for breath, had scarcely more
Than would make up his message.

Lady Macbeth.   Give him tending:
He brings great news.   [*Exit* Messenger.]
                         The raven himself is hoarse
That croaks the fatal entrance of Duncan
40 Under my battlements. Come, you spirits
That tend on mortal[8] thoughts, unsex me here,
And fill me, from the crown to the toe, top-full
Of direst cruelty! Make thick my blood.
Stop up th' access and passage to remorse[9]
45 That no compunctious visitings of nature[10]
Shake my fell[11] purpose, nor keep peace between
Th' effect[12] and it! Come to my woman's breasts.

And take my milk for gall,[13] you murd'ring ministers.[14]
Wherever in your sightless[15] substances
50 You wait on[16] nature's mischief! Come, thick night,
And pall[17] thee in the dunnest[18] smoke of hell,
That my keen knife see not the wound it makes,
Nor heaven peep through the blanket of the dark,
To cry "Hold, hold!"

[*Enter* Macbeth.]

                      Great Glamis! Worthy Cawdor!
55 Greater than both, by the all-hail hereafter!
Thy letters have transported me beyond
This ignorant[19] present, and I feel now
The future in the instant.[20]

Macbeth.   My dearest love,
Duncan comes here tonight.

Lady Macbeth.   And when goes hence?

Macbeth. Tomorrow, as he purposes.

60 **Lady Macbeth.**   O, never
Shall sun that morrow see!
Your face, my Thane, is as a book where men
May read strange matters. To beguile the time,[21]
Look like the time; bear welcome in your eye,
65 Your hand, your tongue: look like th' innocent flower,
But be the serpent under't. He that's coming
Must be provided for: and you shall put
This night's great business into my dispatch;[22]
Which shall to all our nights and days to come
70 Give solely sovereign sway and masterdom.

Macbeth. We will speak further.

Lady Macbeth.   Only look up clear.[23]
To alter favor ever is to fear.[24]
Leave all the rest to me.   [*Exit.*]

⌘ ⌘ ⌘

Scene vi • *Before Macbeth's castle.*

[*Hautboys.*[1] Torches. *Enter* King Duncan, Malcolm, Donalbain,
Banquo, Lennox, Macduff, Ross, Angus, *and* Attendants.]

King. This castle hath a pleasant seat;[2] the air
Nimbly and sweetly recommends itself
Unto our gentle[3] senses.

Banquo.   This guest of summer,
The temple-haunting martlet,[4] does approve[5]

NOTES

13. **milk for gall** kindness in exchange for bitterness.
14. **ministers** agents.
15. **sightless** invisible.
16. **wait on** assist.
17. **pall** enshroud.
18. **dunnest** darkest.
19. **ignorant** unknowing.
20. **instant** present.

CLOSE READ
ANNOTATE: In lines 56–61, mark details related to time.

QUESTION: What aspects of time do these details emphasize?

CONCLUDE: What does Shakespeare accomplish by focusing so intensely on time in the first moment Macbeth and Lady Macbeth see each other after the witches' prediction?

21. **beguile the time** deceive the people tonight.
22. **dispatch** management.
23. **look up clear** appear innocent.
24. **To alter . . . fear** to show a disturbed face will arouse suspicion.

1. *Hautboys* oboes announcing the arrival of royalty.
2. **seat** location.
3. **gentle** soothed.
4. **temple-haunting martlet** martin, a bird that usually nests in churches. In Shakespeare's times, *martin* was a slang term for a person who is easily deceived.
5. **approve** show.

6. **mansionry** nests.

7. **jutty** projection.

8. **coign of vantage** advantageous corner.

9. **procreant cradle** nest where the young are hatched.

10. **haunt** visit.

11. **The love . . . trouble** though my visit inconveniences you, you should ask God to reward me for coming, because it was my love for you that prompted my visit.

12. **single business** feeble service.

13. **rest your hermits** remain your dependents bound to pray for you. Hermits were often paid to pray for another person's soul.

14. **coursed** chased.

15. **purveyor** advance supply officer.

16. **holp** helped.

17. **compt** trust.

18. **Still** always.

1. **Sewer** chief butler.

2. **done** over and done with.

3. **If . . . success** if the assassination could be done successfully and without consequence.

5　By his loved mansionry⁶ that the heaven's breath
Smells wooingly here. No jutty,⁷ frieze,
Buttress, nor coign of vantage,⁸ but this bird
Hath made his pendent bed and procreant cradle.⁹
Where they most breed and haunt,¹⁰ I have observed
10　The air is delicate.

[*Enter* Lady Macbeth.]

King.　　　　See, see, our honored hostess!
The love that follows us sometime is our trouble,
Which still we thank as love. Herein I teach you
How you shall bid God 'ield us for your pains
And thank us for your trouble.¹¹

Lady Macbeth.　　　　All our service
15　In every point twice done, and then done double,
Were poor and single business¹² to contend
Against those honors deep and broad wherewith
Your Majesty loads our house: for those of old,
And the late dignities heaped up to them,
We rest your hermits.¹³

20　**King.**　　　　Where's the Thane of Cawdor?
We coursed¹⁴ him at the heels, and had a purpose
To be his purveyor;¹⁵ but he rides well,
And his great love, sharp as his spur, hath holp¹⁶ him
To his home before us. Fair and noble hostess,
We are your guest tonight.

25　**Lady Macbeth.**　　　　Your servants ever
Have theirs, themselves, and what is theirs, in compt,¹⁷
To make their audit at your Highness' pleasure,
Still¹⁸ to return your own.

King.　　　　Give me your hand.
Conduct me to mine host: we love him highly,
30　And shall continue our graces towards him.
By your leave, hostess.　　　　　　　　[*Exit.*]

⌘ ⌘ ⌘

Scene vii • *Macbeth's castle.*

[*Hautboys. Torches. Enter a* Sewer,¹ *and diverse* Servants *with dishes and service over the stage. Then enter* Macbeth.]

Macbeth. If it were done when 'tis done,² then 'twere well
It were done quickly. If th' assassination
Could trammel up the consequence, and catch,
With his surcease, success;³ that but this blow
5　Might be the be-all and the end-all—here,

^ Macbeth and Lady Macbeth dine with Duncan, the king of Scotland.

But here, upon this bank and shoal of time,
We'd jump the life to come.[4] But in these cases
We still have judgment here; that we but teach
Bloody instructions, which, being taught, return
10 To plague th' inventor: this even-handed[5] justice
Commends[6] th' ingredients of our poisoned chalice[7]
To our own lips. He's here in double trust:
First, as I am his kinsman and his subject,
Strong both against the deed; then, as his host,
15 Who should against his murderer shut the door,
Not bear the knife myself. Besides, this Duncan
Hath borne his faculties[8] so meek, hath been
So clear[9] in his great office, that his virtues
Will plead like angels trumpet-tongued against
20 The deep damnation of his taking-off;
And pity, like a naked newborn babe,
Striding the blast, or heaven's cherubin[10] horsed
Upon the sightless couriers[11] of the air,
Shall blow the horrid deed in every eye,
25 That tears shall drown the wind. I have no spur
To prick the sides of my intent, but only
Vaulting ambition, which o'erleaps itself

NOTES

4. **We'd . . . come** I would risk life in the world to come.

5. **even-handed** impartial.

6. **Commends** offers.

7. **chalice** cup.

8. **faculties** powers.

9. **clear** blameless.

10. **cherubin** angels.

11. **sightless couriers** unseen messengers (the wind).

And falls on th' other—

[*Enter* Lady Macbeth.]

How now! What news?

Lady Macbeth. He has almost supped. Why have you left the
30   chamber?

Macbeth. Hath he asked for me?

Lady Macbeth.   Know you not he has?

Macbeth. We will proceed no further in this business:
He hath honored me of late, and I have bought[12]
Golden opinions from all sorts of people,
35 Which would be worn now in their newest gloss,
Not cast aside so soon.

Lady Macbeth.   Was the hope drunk
Wherein you dressed yourself? Hath it slept since?
And wakes it now, to look so green and pale
At what it did so freely? From this time
40 Such I account thy love. Art thou afeard
To be the same in thine own act and valor
As thou art in desire? Wouldst thou have that
Which thou esteem'st the ornament of life,[13]
And live a coward in thine own esteem,
45 Letting "I dare not" wait upon[14] "I would,"
Like the poor cat i' th' adage?[15]

Macbeth.   Prithee, peace!
I dare do all that may become a man;
Who dares do more is none.

Lady Macbeth.   What beast was 't then
That made you break[16] this enterprise to me?
50 When you durst do it, then you were a man:
And to be more than what you were, you would
Be so much more the man. Nor time nor place
Did then adhere,[17] and yet you would make both.
They have made themselves, and that their[18] fitness now
55 Does unmake you. I have given suck, and know
How tender 'tis to love the babe that milks me:
I would, while it was smiling in my face,
Have plucked my nipple from his boneless gums,
And dashed the brains out, had I so sworn as you
Have done to this.

Macbeth.   If we should fail?

60 **Lady Macbeth.**   We fail?
But[19] screw your courage to the sticking-place[20]
And we'll not fail. When Duncan is asleep—
Whereto the rather shall his day's hard journey
Soundly invite him—his two chamberlains

12. **bought** acquired.

13. **ornament of life** the crown.

14. **wait upon** follow.

15. **poor . . . adage** from an old proverb about a cat who wants to eat fish but is afraid of getting its paws wet.

16. **break** *v.* reveal.

17. **Did then adhere** was then suitable (for the assassination).
18. **that their** their very.

19. **But** only.
20. **sticking-place** the notch that holds the bowstring of a taut crossbow.

65 Will I with wine and wassail[21] so convince,[22]
That memory, the warder of the brain,
Shall be a fume, and the receipt of reason
A limbeck only:[23] when in swinish sleep
Their drenchèd natures lies as in a death,
70 What cannot you and I perform upon
Th' unguarded Duncan, what not put upon
His spongy[24] officers, who shall bear the guilt
Of our great quell?[25]

Macbeth.   Bring forth men-children only;
For thy undaunted mettle[26] should compose
75 Nothing but males. Will it not be received,
When we have marked with blood those sleepy two
Of his own chamber, and used their very daggers,
That they have done 't?

Lady Macbeth.   Who dares receive it other,[27]
As we shall make our griefs and clamor roar
Upon his death?

80 **Macbeth.**   I am settled, and bend up
Each corporal agent to this terrible feat.
Away, and mock the time[28] with fairest show:
False face must hide what the false heart doth know.   [*Exit.*]

MEDIA CONNECTION

Macbeth's Early Motivation

Discuss It Did the witches' prophecies awaken Macbeth's already powerful hunger for power? Or did he kill Duncan because he was unable to resist his ambitious wife's persistent urging?

Write your response before sharing your ideas.

Comprehension Check

Complete the following items after you finish your first read.

1. What three things do the witches predict for Macbeth and Banquo? What information does the messenger bring to Macbeth?

2. What does Lady Macbeth fear about her husband?

3. 🗐 **Notebook** Confirm your understanding of the text by writing a summary of Act I.

- -

RESEARCH

Research to Clarify Choose at least one unfamiliar detail from the text. Briefly research that detail. In what way does the information you learned shed light on an aspect of the play?

Research to Explore Conduct research to find representations of Macbeth or Lady Macbeth in a work of visual art.

Close Read the Text

Reread Act I, Scene i, and mark the lines that end with rhyming words. Notice the similarity to children's rhymes. What effect does the seemingly innocent nature of the verses achieve?

ANNOTATE QUESTION
Close Read
CONCLUDE

THE TRAGEDY OF MACBETH, ACT I

Analyze the Text

CITE TEXTUAL EVIDENCE
to support your answers.

📓 **Notebook** Respond to these questions.

1. (a) **Interpret** How does Macbeth react to the witches? How does Banquo react? (b) **Compare and Contrast** What are the differences and similarities in their reactions?

2. (a) What announcement does King Duncan make at the end of his conversation with Macbeth and Banquo? (b) **Cause and Effect** What effect does that announcement have on Macbeth?

3. (a) In his soliloquy at the beginning of Scene vii, what reasons does Macbeth give for not murdering King Duncan? (b) **Analyze** Do you think that Macbeth, at the end of his soliloquy, has firmly decided not to kill the king? Explain.

🔧 **Tool Kit**
Close-Read Guide
and Model Annotation

LANGUAGE DEVELOPMENT

Concept Vocabulary

revolt	assault	rebellious
captivity	flout	treasons

Why These Words? These concept vocabulary words are all related to warfare. For example, in Scene ii, the soldier reports on a *revolt*, or armed rebellion, of Norwegians. He testifies that after an initial battle, the Norwegians obtained new supplies and began another *assault*, or violent physical attack. What other words in the selection connect to the idea of warfare?

Practice

📓 **Notebook** The concept vocabulary words appear in Act I of *The Tragedy of Macbeth*. Write a short paragraph describing a scene of warfare. Use each of the concept vocabulary words in your paragraph to demonstrate your understanding of the words' meanings.

Word Study

📓 **Notebook** **Latin Root: -bell-** The Latin root *-bell-* means "war." In the play, Ross describes a battle, saying it was "*rebellious* arm against arm." Beginning with the Latin prefix *re-*, which means "back" or "against," the word *rebellious* means "warring against" or "resisting authority." Use a dictionary to discover how the Latin root *-bell-* contributes to the meanings of the following words: *belligerent, bellicose, antebellum*. Write your findings.

🔗 WORD NETWORK

Add interesting words related to time from the text to your Word Network.

▤ STANDARDS

Language
Consult general and specialized reference materials, both print, and digital, to find the pronunciation of a word or determine or clarify its precise meaning, its part of speech, its etymology, or its standard usage.

THE TRAGEDY OF MACBETH,
ACT I

Analyze Craft and Structure

Author's Choices: Structure During the late 1500s, Elizabethan drama blossomed. Using models from ancient Greece and Rome, writers reintroduced **tragedies,** plays in which the main character, through some fatal flaw in his or her personality, meets a tragic end. Tragedies from Shakespeare's era also feature these characteristics:

- They are written in carefully crafted, unrhymed verse, using powerful language and vivid imagery. Since there were no sets, the words themselves created the illusion of time and place.

- They have a heavy dose of **internal conflict,** opposing thoughts and feelings that war with each other in a character's mind.

Dramatists reveal characters' internal conflicts in a variety of ways. One method is the **soliloquy,** a long speech delivered by a character who is alone on stage. In a soliloquy, the character voices thoughts and feelings to the audience as though he or she were thinking them out loud. In Shakespeare's soliloquies, the audience gets valuable inside information about a character's fears, confusions, and desires, as well as his or her intentions to betray or even murder other characters.

≣ STANDARDS

Reading Literature
Analyze how an author's choices concerning how to structure specific parts of a text contribute to its overall structure and meaning as well as its aesthetic impact.

Practice

CITE TEXTUAL EVIDENCE
to support your answers.

Review the soliloquy at the beginning of Act I, Scene vii, lines 1–28. Use the chart to explore why Shakespeare uses a soliloquy here. What information does it provide that audiences could not obtain from dialogue?

WHO SPEAKS IT?

WHAT IS IT ABOUT?

WHY USE A SOLILOQUY?

Speaking and Listening

Assignment

Imagine that you are a confidant of either Macbeth or Lady Macbeth. In that role, create and perform a **soliloquy** in which you either support or discourage the murder of King Duncan.

- If you choose to be Macbeth's confidant, imagine that you have heard his soliloquy at the beginning of Scene vii, and reinforce the doubts he expresses there. Point out to Macbeth the advantages of killing the king.

- If you choose to be Lady Macbeth's confidant, try to dissuade her from seeking Duncan's death by suggesting the possible results of such an act.

Create Your Character When you are playing a role, it helps to know exactly who you are and what stake you have in the situation. Be sure to create a complete character, one that Shakespeare might have imagined himself. Use the chart below to help you develop your character.

Who am I? (name, age, gender, role in the castle)	
What relationship do I have with Macbeth/Lady Macbeth?	
What is my motive in arguing for or against the murder? Do I have anything to gain?	
Why would Macbeth/Lady Macbeth listen to me?	

Prepare for Your Performance Make notes on a card or two or on a small sheet of paper. These will help you remember what you want to say to Macbeth or Lady Macbeth. You should not read directly from your notes when you perform your soliloquy, but you may glance at them as you speak to remind yourself of the points of your argument.

EVIDENCE LOG

Before moving on to a new selection, go to your Evidence Log and record what you learned from Act I of *The Tragedy of Macbeth*.

STANDARDS

Speaking and Listening
- Come to discussions prepared, having read and researched material under study; explicitly draw on that preparation by referring to evidence from texts and other research on the topic or issue to stimulate a thoughtful, well-reasoned exchange of ideas.
- Adapt speech to a variety of contexts and tasks, demonstrating a command of formal English when indicated or appropriate.

Playwright

William Shakespeare

The Tragedy of Macbeth, Act II

Concept Vocabulary

You will encounter the following words as you read Act II of *The Tragedy of Macbeth*. Before reading, note how familiar you are with each word. Then, rank the words in order from most familiar (1) to least familiar (6).

WORD	YOUR RANKING
allegiance	
stealthy	
equivocate	
sacrilegious	
counterfeit	
breach	

After completing the first read, come back to the concept vocabulary and review your rankings. Mark changes to your original rankings as needed.

First Read DRAMA

Apply these strategies as you conduct your first read. You will have an opportunity to complete the close-read notes after your first read.

NOTICE *whom* the story is about, *what* happens, *where* and *when* it happens, and *why* those involved react as they do.

ANNOTATE by marking vocabulary and key passages you want to revisit.

First Read

CONNECT ideas within the selection to what you already know and what you've already read.

RESPOND by completing the Comprehension Check and by writing a brief summary of the selection.

🔧 **Tool Kit**
First-Read Guide and Model Annotation

▤ STANDARDS
Reading Literature
By the end of grade 12, read and comprehend literature, including stories, dramas, and poems, at the high end of the grades 11–CCR text complexity band independently and proficiently.

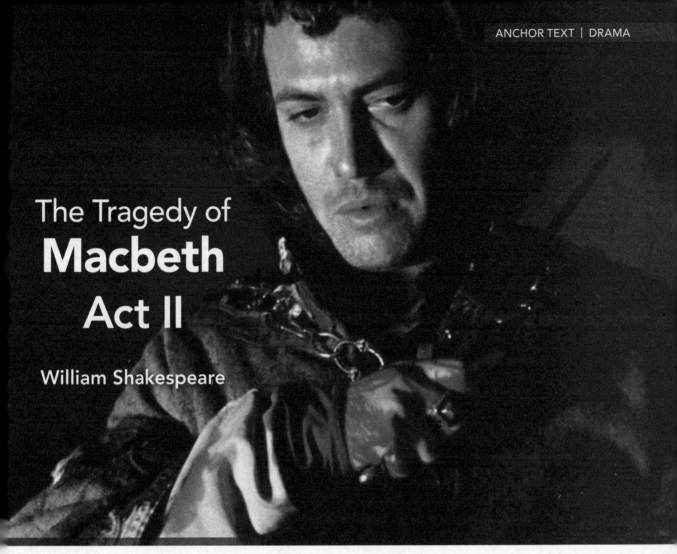

The Tragedy of
Macbeth
Act II

William Shakespeare

REVIEW AND ANTICIPATE

In Act I, we learn that Macbeth has distinguished himself in battle.
Returning from the battlefield, he and Banquo meet three witches
who predict not only that Macbeth will be rewarded by King Duncan,
but also that he will become king himself. However, the witches
also greet Banquo as the father of kings. Motivated by the witches'
prophesies, Macbeth considers killing Duncan. The assassination
becomes more likely when the king decides to visit Macbeth's castle.
Lady Macbeth, on hearing about the witches' predictions and the
king's visit, resolves that she and her husband will kill Duncan. When
Macbeth hesitates, she urges him on. As Act II begins, they are about
to perform this evil deed.

Scene i • *Inverness. Court of Macbeth's castle.*

NOTES

[*Enter* Banquo, *and* Fleance, *with a torch before him.*]

Banquo. How goes the night, boy?

Fleance. The moon is down; I have not heard the clock.

Banquo. And she goes down at twelve.

Fleance. I take't, 'tis later, sir.

Banquo. Hold, take my sword. There's husbandry[1] in heaven.
5 Their candles are all out. Take thee that[2] too.
A heavy summons[3] lies like lead upon me,
And yet I would not sleep. Merciful powers,
Restrain in me the cursed thoughts that nature
Gives way to in repose!

[*Enter* Macbeth, *and a* Servant *with a torch.*]

Give me my sword!

10 Who's there?

Macbeth. A friend.

Banquo. What, sir, not yet at rest? The King's a-bed:
He hath been in unusual pleasure, and
Sent forth great largess to your offices:[4]
15 This diamond he greets your wife withal,
By the name of most kind hostess: and shut up[5]
In measureless content.

Macbeth. Being unprepared,
Our will became the servant to defect,
Which else should free have wrought.[6]

Banquo. All's well.
20 I dreamt last night of the three weird sisters:
To you they have showed some truth.

Macbeth. I think not of them.
Yet, when we can entreat an hour to serve,
We would spend it in some words upon that business,
If you would grant the time.

Banquo. At your kind'st leisure.

25 **Macbeth.** If you shall cleave to my consent, when 'tis,[7]
It shall make honor for you.

Banquo. So[8] I lose none
In seeking to augment it, but still keep
My bosom franchised[9] and **allegiance** clear.
I shall be counseled.

Macbeth. Good repose the while!

30 **Banquo.** Thanks, sir. The like to you!

[*Exit* Banquo *with* Fleance.]

Macbeth. Go bid thy mistress, when my drink is ready.
She strike upon the bell. Get thee to bed.

[*Exit* Servant.]

Is this a dagger which I see before me,
The handle toward my hand? Come, let me clutch thee.
35 I have thee not, and yet I see thee still.

4. **largess . . . offices** gifts to your servants' quarters.

5. **shut up** retired.

6. **Being . . . wrought** Because we did not have enough time to prepare, we were unable to entertain as lavishly as we wanted to.

7. **cleave . . . 'tis** join my cause when the time comes.

8. **So** provided that.

9. **bosom franchised** heart free (from guilt).

allegiance (Uh LEE juhns) *n.* loyalty

CLOSE READ
ANNOTATE: In Macbeth's soliloquy beginning on line 31, mark the pronouns, including older pronoun forms such as *thou, thee,* and *thy.*

QUESTION: Whom or what is Macbeth addressing in this speech?

CONCLUDE: What does the soliloquy suggest about Macbeth's state of mind?

Art thou not, fatal vision, sensible[10]
To feeling as to sight, or art thou but
A dagger of the mind, a false creation,
Proceeding from the heat-oppressèd brain?
40 I see thee yet, in form as palpable
As this which now I draw.
Thou marshal'st[11] me the way that I was going;
And such an instrument I was to use.
Mine eyes are made the fools o' th' other senses,
45 Or else worth all the rest, I see thee still:
And on thy blade and dudgeon[12] gouts[13] of blood.
Which was not so before. There's no such thing.
It is the bloody business which informs[14]
Thus to mine eyes. Now o'er the one half-world
50 Nature seems dead, and wicked dreams abuse[15]
The curtained sleep; witchcraft celebrates
Pale Hecate's[16] offerings; and withered murder,
Alarumed by his sentinel, the wolf,
Whose howl's his watch, thus with his **stealthy** pace,
55 With Tarquin's[17] ravishing strides, towards his design
Moves like a ghost. Thou sure and firm-set earth,
Hear not my steps, which way they walk, for fear
Thy very stones prate of my whereabout,
And take the present horror from the time,
60 Which now suits with it.[18] Whiles I threat, he lives:
Words to the heat of deeds too cold breath gives.

[*A bell rings.*]

I go, and it is done: the bell invites me.
Hear it not, Duncan, for it is a knell
That summons thee to heaven, or to hell.   [*Exit.*]

⌘ ⌘ ⌘

Scene ii • *Macbeth's castle*

[*Enter* Lady Macbeth.]

Lady Macbeth. That which hath made them drunk hath made
    me bold:
What hath quenched them hath given me fire. Hark! Peace!
It was the owl that shrieked, the fatal bellman,
Which gives the stern'st good-night.[1] He is about it.
5 The doors are open, and the surfeited grooms[2]
Do mock their charge with snores. I have drugged their possets,[3]
That death and nature do contend about them,
Whether they live or die.

Macbeth.   [*Within*] Who's there? What, ho?

NOTES

10. **sensible** able to be felt.

11. **marshal'st** leads.

12. **dudgeon** wooden hilt.
13. **gouts** large drops.
14. **informs** takes shape.

15. **abuse** deceive.

16. **Hecate's** (HEHK uh teez) Greek goddess of witchcraft.

stealthy (STEHL thee) *adj.* slow and secretive

17. **Tarquin's** Roman tyrant.

18. **take . . . it** remove the horrible silence that suits this moment.

1. **bellman . . . good-night** It was customary for a bell to be rung at midnight outside a condemned person's cell on the night before an execution.
2. **surfeited grooms** overfed servants.
3. **possets** warm bedtime drinks.

NOTES

4. **Confounds** ruins.

ANNOTATE: In lines 16–25, mark the short sentences.

QUESTION: What do these sentence structures suggest about the pace and emotions with which characters speak these lines?

CONCLUDE: What is the effect of this series of short sentences?

5. **sorry** miserable.

6. **two** Malcolm and Donalbain, Duncan's sons.

7. **knits . . . sleave** straightens out the tangled threads.

8. **second course** main course; sleep.

Lady Macbeth. Alack, I am afraid they have awaked

10 And 'tis not done! Th' attempt and not the deed
Confounds[4] us. Hark! I laid their daggers ready:
He could not miss 'em. Had he not resembled
My father as he slept, I had done 't.

[*Enter* Macbeth.]

My husband!

Macbeth. I have done the deed. Didst thou not hear a noise?

15 **Lady Macbeth.** I heard the owl scream and the crickets cry.
Did not you speak?

Macbeth.   When?

Lady Macbeth.   Now.

Macbeth.   As I descended?

Lady Macbeth. Ay.

Macbeth. Hark!
Who lies i' th' second chamber?

Lady Macbeth.   Donalbain.

20 **Macbeth.** This is a sorry[5] sight.

Lady Macbeth. A foolish thought, to say a sorry sight.

Macbeth. There's one did laugh in 's sleep, and one cried
   "Murder!"
That they did wake each other. I stood and heard them.
But they did say their prayers, and addressed them

25 Again to sleep.

Lady Macbeth. There are two[6] lodged together.

Macbeth. One cried "God bless us!" and "Amen" the other.
As they had seen me with these hangman's hands:
List'ning their fear, I could not say "Amen."
When they did say "God bless us!"

30 **Lady Macbeth.** Consider it not so deeply.

Macbeth. But wherefore could not I pronounce "Amen"?
I had most need of blessing, and "Amen"
Stuck in my throat.

Lady Macbeth.   These deeds must not be thought
After these ways; so, it will make us mad.

35 **Macbeth.** Methought I heard a voice cry "Sleep no more!
Macbeth does murder sleep"—the innocent sleep.
Sleep that knits up the raveled sleave[7] of care.
The death of each day's life, sore labor's bath,
Balm of hurt minds, great nature's second course,[8]
Chief nourisher in life's feast—

40 **Lady Macbeth.**   What do you mean?

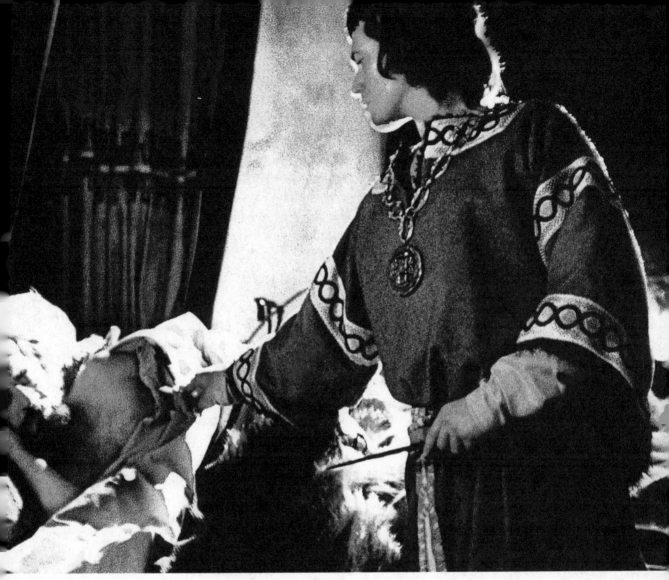

^ Macbeth murders Duncan, the king of Scotland.

Macbeth. Still it cried "Sleep no more!" to all the house:
"Glamis hath murdered sleep, and therefore Cawdor
Shall sleep no more: Macbeth shall sleep no more."

Lady Macbeth. Who was it that thus cried? Why, worthy Thane.
45 You do unbend[9] your noble strength, to think
So brainsickly of things. Go get some water,
And wash this filthy witness[10] from your hand.
Why did you bring these daggers from the place?
They must lie there: go carry them, and smear
The sleepy grooms with blood.

50 **Macbeth.**   I'll go no more.
I am afraid to think what I have done;
Look on 't again I dare not.

Lady Macbeth.   Infirm of purpose!
Give me the daggers. The sleeping and the dead
Are but as pictures. 'Tis the eye of childhood

NOTES

9. **unbend** relax.

10. **witness** evidence.

11. gild paint.

55   That fears a painted devil. If he do bleed,
      I'll gild[11] the faces of the grooms withal,
      For it must seem their guilt.   [*Exit. Knock within.*]

      Macbeth.   Whence is that knocking?
      How is 't with me, when every noise appalls me?
      What hands are here? Ha! They pluck out mine eyes!
60   Will all great Neptune's ocean wash this blood
      Clean from my hand? No; this my hand will rather
      The multitudinous seas incarnadine,[12]
      Making the green one red.

      [*Enter* Lady Macbeth.]

12. incarnadine (ihn KAHR nuh deen)
redden.

      Lady Macbeth. My hands are of your color, but I shame
65   To wear a heart so white. [*Knock.*] I hear a knocking
      At the south entry. Retire we to our chamber.
      A little water clears us of this deed:
      How easy is it then! Your constancy
      Hath left you unattended.[13] [*Knock.*] Hark! more knocking.
70   Get on your nightgown, lest occasion call us
      And show us to be watchers.[14] Be not lost
      So poorly in your thoughts.

13. Your constancy . . . unattended
Your firmness of purpose has
left you.

14. watchers up late.

      Macbeth. To know my deed, 'twere best not know myself.
         [*Knock.*]
      Wake Duncan with thy knocking! I would thou couldst!

                                                        [*Exit.*]

                        ✿ ✿ ✿

Scene iii • *Macbeth's castle.*

[*Enter a* Porter. *Knocking within.*]

1. porter doorkeeper.

2. should have old would have
plenty of.

3. Beelzebub (bee EHL zuh buhb)
chief devil.

4. a farmer . . . plenty a farmer
who hoarded grain, hoping
the prices rise after a bad
harvest.

5. enow enough.

6. an equivocator . . . scale a
liar who could make two
contradictory statements and
swear both were true.

equivocate (ih KWIHV uh kayt) *v.*
speak in a way that hides the truth

7. stealing . . . hose stealing some
cloth from the hose while
making them.

8. goose pressing iron.

      Porter. Here's a knocking indeed! If a man were porter[1]
      of hell gate, he should have old[2] turning the key.
      [*Knock.*] Knock, knock, knock! Who's there, i' th'
      name of Beelzebub?[3] Here's a farmer, that
5   hanged himself on th' expectation of plenty.[4] Come
      in time! Have napkins enow[5] about you; here you'll
      sweat for 't. [*Knock.*] Knock, knock! Who's there, in
      th' other devil's name? Faith, here's an equivocator,
      that could swear in both the scales against
10   either scale;[6] who committed treason enough for
      God's sake, yet could not **equivocate** to heaven. O,
      come in, equivocator. [*Knock.*] Knock, knock, knock!
      Who's there? Faith, here's an English tailor come
      hither for stealing out of a French hose:[7]
15   come in, tailor. Here you may roast your goose.[8]

[*Knock.*] Knock, knock; never at quiet! What are you? But this place is too cold for hell. I'll devil-porter it no further. I had thought to have let in some of all professions that go the primrose way to th'
20 everlasting bonfire. [*Knock.*] Anon, anon!
[*Opens an entrance.*] I pray you, remember the porter.

[*Enter Macduff and Lennox.*]

Macduff. Was it so late, friend, ere you went to bed, That you do lie so late?

Porter. Faith, sir, we were carousing till the second
25 cock:⁹ and drink, sir, is a great provoker of three things.

Macduff. What three things does drink especially provoke?

Porter. Marry, sir, nose-painting, sleep, and urine.
30 Lechery, sir, it provokes and unprovokes; it provokes the desire, but it takes away the performance: therefore much drink may be said to be an equivocator with lechery: it makes him and it mars him; it sets him on and it takes him off: it persuades him
35 and disheartens him; makes him stand to and not stand to; in conclusion equivocates him in a sleep, and giving him the lie, leaves him.

Macduff. I believe drink gave thee the lie¹⁰ last night.

Porter. That it did, sir, i' the very throat on me: but I
40 requited him for his lie, and, I think, being too strong for him, though he took up my legs sometime, yet I make a shift to cast¹¹ him.

Macduff. Is thy master stirring?

[*Enter Macbeth.*]

Our knocking has awaked him; here he comes.

Lennox. Good morrow, noble sir.

45 **Macbeth.**   Good morrow, both.

Macduff. Is the king stirring, worthy Thane?

Macbeth.   Not yet.

Macduff. He did command me to call timely¹² on him: I have almost slipped the hour.

Macbeth.   I'll bring you to him.

Macduff. I know this is a joyful trouble to you;
50 But yet 'tis one.

Macbeth. The labor we delight in physics pain.¹³ This is the door.

NOTES

9. **second cock** 3:00 A.M.

10. **gave thee the lie** laid you out.

11. **cast** vomit.

12. **timely** early.

13. **labor . . . pain** labor we enjoy cures discomfort.

14. **limited service** assigned duty.

Macduff.   I'll make so bold to call.
For 'tis my limited service.[14]   [*Exit* Macduff.]

Lennox. Goes the king hence today?

Macbeth.   He does: he did appoint so.

55   **Lennox.** The night has been unruly. Where we lay,
Our chimneys were blown down, and, as they say,
Lamentings heard i' th' air, strange screams of death.
And prophesying with accents terrible

15. **combustion** confusion.

16. **obscure bird** bird of darkness, the owl.

Of dire combustion[15] and confused events
60   New hatched to th' woeful time: the obscure bird[16]
Clamored the livelong night. Some say, the earth
Was feverous and did shake.

Macbeth.   'Twas a rough night.

Lennox. My young remembrance cannot parallel
A fellow to it.

[*Enter* Macduff.]

65   **Macduff.** O horror, horror, horror! Tongue nor heart
Cannot conceive nor name thee.

Macbeth and Lennox.   What's the matter?

17. **Confusion** destruction.

sacrilegious (sak ruh LIHJ uhs) *adj.* treating a religious object, person, or belief with disrespect

18. **The Lord's anointed temple** the King's body.

Macduff. Confusion[17] now hath made his masterpiece.
Most **sacrilegious** murder hath broke ope
The Lord's anointed temple,[18] and stole thence
The life o' th' building.

70   **Macbeth.**   What is 't you say? The life?

Lennox. Mean you his Majesty?

19. **Gorgon** Medusa, a mythological monster whose appearance was so ghastly that those who looked at it turned to stone.

Macduff. Approach the chamber, and destroy your sight
With a new Gorgon:[19] do not bid me speak;
See, and then speak yourselves. Awake, awake!

[*Exit* Macbeth *and* Lennox.]

counterfeit (KOWN tuhr fiht) *n.* false imitation

75   Ring the alarum bell. Murder and Treason!
Banquo and Donalbain! Malcolm! Awake!
Shake off this downy sleep, death's **counterfeit**,
And look on death itself! Up, up, and see

20. **great doom's image** likeness of Judgment Day.

21. **sprites** spirits.

22. **countenance** be in keeping with.

The great doom's image![20] Malcolm! Banquo!
80   As from your graves rise up, and walk like sprites,[21]
To countenance[22] this horror. Ring the bell.

[*Bell rings. Enter* Lady Macbeth.]

23. **parley** war conference.

Lady Macbeth. What's the business,
That such a hideous trumpet calls to parley[23]
The sleepers of the house? Speak, speak!

Macduff.   O gentle lady,
85   'Tis not for you to hear what I can speak:
The repetition, in a woman's ear,

Would murder as it fell.

[*Enter* Banquo.]

O Banquo, Banquo!
Our royal master's murdered.

Lady Macbeth.   Woe, alas!
What, in our house?

Banquo.   Too cruel anywhere.
90 Dear Duff, I prithee, contradict thyself,
And say it is not so.

[*Enter* Macbeth, Lennox, *and* Ross.]

Macbeth. Had I but died an hour before this chance,
I had lived a blessed time; for from this instant
There's nothing serious in mortality:²⁴
95 All is but toys.²⁵ Renown and grace is dead,
The wine of life is drawn, and the mere lees²⁶
Is left this vault²⁷ to brag of.

[*Enter* Malcolm *and* Donalbain.]

Donalbain. What is amiss?

Macbeth.   You are, and do not know 't.
The spring, the head, the fountain of your blood
100 Is stopped; the very source of it is stopped.

Macduff. Your royal father's murdered.

Malcolm.   O, by whom?

Lennox. Those of his chamber, as it seemed, had done 't:
Their hands and faces were all badged²⁸ with blood;
So were their daggers, which unwiped we found
105 Upon their pillows. They stared, and were distracted.
No man's life was to be trusted with them.

Macbeth. O, yet I do repent me of my fury,
That I did kill them.

Macduff.   Wherefore did you so?

Macbeth. Who can be wise, amazed, temp'rate and furious,
110 Loyal and neutral, in a moment? No man.
The expedition²⁹ of my violent love
Outrun the pauser, reason. Here lay Duncan,
His silver skin laced with his golden blood,
And his gashed stabs looked like a **breach** in nature
115 For ruin's wasteful entrance: there, the murderers,
Steeped in the colors of their trade, their daggers
Unmannerly breeched with gore.³⁰ Who could refrain,
That had a heart to love, and in that heart
Courage to make 's love known?

24. **serious in mortality** worthwhile in mortal life.

25. **toys** trifles.

26. **lees** dregs.

27. **vault** world.

28. **badged** marked.

CLOSE READ
ANNOTATE: Mark the adjectives in Macbeth's question on lines 109 and 110.

QUESTION: What relationship do the adjectives have to each other?

CONCLUDE: What excuse for his actions do these words provide Macbeth?

29. **expedition** haste.

breach (breech) *n.* hole made by breaking through

30. **breeched with gore** covered with blood.

31. **That most . . . ours** who are the most concerned with this topic.
32. **auger-hole** tiny hole, an unsuspected place because of its size.
33. **Our tears . . . motion** We have not yet had time for tears nor to turn our sorrow into action.

34. **when . . . hid** when we have put on our clothes.
35. **question** investigate.
36. **scruples** doubts.

37. **undivulged pretense** hidden purpose.

38. **briefly** quickly.

39. **office** function.

40. **the near . . . bloody** The closer we are in blood relationship to Duncan, the greater our chance of being murdered.
41. **lighted** reached its target.

42. **warrant** justification.
43. **that theft . . . itself** stealing away.

Lady Macbeth. Help me hence, ho!

120 **Macduff.** Look to the lady.

Malcolm. [*Aside to* Donalbain] Why do we hold our tongues,
That most may claim this argument for ours?[31]

Donalbain. [*Aside to* Malcolm] What should be spoken here,
Where our fate, hid in an auger-hole,[32]
125 May rush, and seize us? Let's away:
Our tears are not yet brewed.

Malcolm. [*Aside to* Donalbain] Nor our strong sorrow
Upon the foot of motion.[33]

Banquo. Look to the lady.

[Lady Macbeth *is carried out.*]

And when we have our naked frailties hid,[34]
That suffer in exposure, let us meet
130 And question[35] this most bloody piece of work,
To know it further. Fears and scruples[36] shake us.
In the great hand of God I stand, and thence
Against the undivulged pretense[37] I fight
Of treasonous malice.

Macduff. And so do I.

All. So all.

135 **Macbeth.** Let's briefly[38] put on manly readiness,
And meet i' th' hall together.

All. Well contented.

[*Exit all but* Malcolm *and* Donalbain.]

Malcolm. What will you do? Let's not consort with them.
To show an unfelt sorrow is an office[39]
Which the false man does easy. I'll to England.

140 **Donalbain.** To Ireland, I; our separated fortune
Shall keep us both the safer. Where we are
There's daggers in men's smiles; the near in blood,
The nearer bloody.[40]

Malcolm. This murderous shaft that's shot
Hath not yet lighted,[41] and our safest way
145 Is to avoid the aim. Therefore to horse;
And let us not be dainty of leave-taking,
But shift away. There's warrant[42] in that theft
Which steals itself[43] when there's no mercy left.

[*Exit.*]

✼ ✼ ✼

Scene iv • *Outside Macbeth's castle.*

[*Enter* Ross *with an* Old Man.]

Old Man. Threescore and ten I can remember well:
Within the volume of which time I have seen
Hours dreadful and things strange, but this sore[1] night
Hath trifled former knowings.

Ross.   Ha, good father,
5   Thou seest the heavens, as troubled with man's act,
Threatens his bloody stage. By th' clock 'tis day,
And yet dark night strangles the traveling lamp:[2]
Is 't night's predominance, or the day's shame,
That darkness does the face of earth entomb,
When living light should kiss it?

10 **Old Man.**   'Tis unnatural,
Even like the deed that's done. On Tuesday last
A falcon, tow'ring in her pride of place,[3]
Was by a mousing owl hawked at and killed.

Ross. And Duncan's horses—a thing most strange
        and certain—
15 Beauteous and swift, the minions of their race,
Turned wild in nature, broke their stalls, flung out,
Contending 'gainst obedience, as they would make
War with mankind.

Old Man. 'Tis said they eat[4] each other.

20 **Ross.** They did so, to th' amazement of mine eyes,
That looked upon 't.

[*Enter* Macduff.]

                        Here comes the good Macduff.
How goes the world, sir, now?

Macduff.   Why, see you not?

Ross. Is 't known who did this more than bloody deed?

Macduff. Those that Macbeth hath slain.

Ross.   Alas, the day!
What good could they pretend?[5]

25 **Macduff.**   They were suborned:[6]
Malcolm and Donalbain, the king's two sons,
Are stol'n away and fled, which puts upon them
Suspicion of the deed.

Ross.   'Gainst nature still.
Thriftless ambition, that will ravin up[7]
30 Thine own life's means! Then 'tis most like
The sovereignty will fall upon Macbeth.

NOTES

1. **sore** grievous.

2. **traveling lamp** the sun.

3. **tow-ring . . . place** soaring at its summit.

4. **eat** ate.

5. **pretend** hope for.

6. **suborned** bribed.

7. **ravin up** devour greedily.

8. Scone (skoon) where Scottish kings were crowned.

9. Fife where Macduff's castle is located.

10. benison blessing.

Macduff. He is already named, and gone to Scone[8]
To be invested.

Ross.   Where is Duncan's body?

Macduff. Carried to Colmekill,
35 The sacred storehouse of his predecessors
And guardian of their bones.

Ross.   Will you to Scone?

Macduff. No, cousin, I'll to Fife.[9]

Ross.   Well, I will thither.

Macduff. Well, may you see things well done there. Adieu,
Lest our old robes sit easier than our new!

40 **Ross.** Farewell, father.

Old Man. God's benison[10] go with you, and with those
That would make good of bad, and friends of foes!   [*Exit.*]

Comprehension Check

Complete the following items after you finish your first read.

1. As Macbeth waits for the signal from Lady Macbeth that the king's guards are asleep, what does he imagine he sees?

2. How is the murder of the king discovered?

3. What strange and unnatural things do Ross and the old man talk about in Scene iv?

4. **Notebook** Confirm your understanding of the text by writing a summary.

RESEARCH

Research to Clarify Choose at least one unfamiliar detail from the text. Briefly research that detail. In what way does the information you learned shed light on an aspect of the play?

Research to Explore Choose something from the text that interested you, and formulate a research question. Write your question here.

Close Read the Text

Reread the first two lines of Act II, Scene ii. Mark the words following the repeated word *hath*. What is significant or interesting about those words in each line?

Close Read
ANNOTATE · QUESTION · CONCLUDE

THE TRAGEDY OF MACBETH,
ACT II

Analyze the Text

CITE TEXTUAL EVIDENCE
to support your answers.

📓 **Notebook** Respond to these questions.

1. (a) Describe Macbeth's and Lady Macbeth's reactions to Duncan's murder immediately after it is done. (b) **Interpret** How do these reactions reflect each character's personality and motivations?

2. (a) **Draw Conclusions** Why is Macbeth upset about not being able to say "Amen" to the men's prayers? (b) **Evaluate** Why is this ironic?

3. (a) What gate does the porter pretend to be opening instead of the gate to Macbeth's castle? (b) **Make Inferences** In what ways is the porter's playful fantasy a comment on Macbeth's situation?

Concept Vocabulary

allegiance	equivocate	counterfeit
stealthy	sacrilegious	breach

Why These Words? These concept words relate to the ideas of loyalty and betrayal. For example, Banquo swears his *allegiance* to Macbeth, as long as that allegiance, or devotion, does not violate his conscience. Find two other words in Act II that relate to the concept of betrayal.

Word Study

Patterns of Word Changes Adding a suffix to a word can change it from one part of speech to another. The noun *sacrilege*, meaning "desecration" or "profanity," becomes the adjective *sacrilegious* when the final *e* is changed to *i* and the suffix *-ous* is added. The word *allegiance* is derived from the medieval term *liege*, which refers to the relationship between a feudal vassal and his lord. *Liege* means "loyal." A change in spelling and the addition of the suffix *-ance* creates a noun that means "loyalty."

Turn each of these words into an adjective using the suffix *-ous*: *vice, danger, marvel*. Turn each of these words into a noun using the suffix *-ance*: *remit, rely, vigilant*. Make whatever adjustments to spelling are required. Use a dictionary to verify the accuracy of your work.

🔗 **WORD NETWORK**

Add interesting words related to time from the text to your Word Network.

📋 **STANDARDS**
Language
• Spell correctly.
• Identify and correctly use patterns of word changes that indicate different meanings or parts of speech.

THE TRAGEDY OF MACBETH, ACT II

Analyze Craft and Structure

Author's Choices: Structure Shakespeare is a master of structure, beginning with his use of meter, or the rhythmic organization of his lines. He uses three types of feet, or metrical units.

- An **iambic foot** consists of an unstressed syllable followed by a stressed syllable. "Our will" is an example of an iambic foot.
- A **trochaic foot** consists of a stressed syllable followed by an unstressed syllable. "List'ning" is an example of a trochaic foot.
- An **anapestic foot** consists of two unstressed syllables followed by a stressed syllable. "If a man" is an example of an anapestic foot.

Shakespeare frequently uses five iambic feet per line, a structure called **iambic pentameter**, to reflect natural speech, as in this line:

"Gŏod sír, | whў dó | yŏu stárt, | ănd séem | tŏ féar" (I.iii.52)

Notice that the stressed syllables often fall on the most important words. Several lines of unrhymed iambic pentameter are called **blank verse**. In general, Shakespeare's high-born characters speak in blank verse.

Sometimes Shakespeare interrupts his blank verse with **prose**, or unmetered dialogue. In his tragedies, lower-ranking characters often speak in prose. In many cases, these characters also provide **comic relief**, a humorous break from the tension of the tragedy. At other times, Shakespeare uses simple prose to communicate urgency.

STANDARDS

Reading Literature
Analyze how an author's choices concerning how to structure specific parts of a text contribute to its overall structure and meaning as well as its aesthetic impact.

Practice

CITE TEXTUAL EVIDENCE
to support your answers.

Notebook Respond to these questions.

1. Read lines 33–39 of Scene i aloud, taking note of stressed words. (a) For the most part, what type of foot appears in this passage? (b) Consider the words stressed by the meter. What mood do these stressed words help create?

2. Read aloud lines 1–2 of Scene ii. (a) What two types of feet are prominent in these lines? (b) What contrast does the structure of the lines emphasize? (c) What insight do these lines offer into Lady Macbeth's character?

3. Analyze the structure of the lines given in the chart. Note the primary foot each line uses. Then, explain how the metrical stresses emphasize meaning or mood.

LINE	PRIMARY TYPE OF FOOT	EFFECT ON MEANING OR MOOD
I have done the deed (Act II, Scene ii, line 14)		
Had I but died an hour before this chance (Act II, Scene iii, line 91)		
Even like the deed that's done (Act II, Scene iv, line 11)		

Writing to Sources

A character's motivations for feeling, thinking, and behaving as he or she does may be powerful. This is certainly true in *The Tragedy of Macbeth*.

Assignment

Suppose you are a psychologist who has just met with a new patient, either Macbeth or Lady Macbeth. Write a **psychological report** describing what you discovered during your session as you listened to what your patient had to say. Consider the following points:

- what your patient has done
- what your patient has told you
- your patient's motivations for feeling, thinking, and behaving as he or she does

Write an explanation of your patient's behavior, including a clear statement of his or her main problem. Use quotations from the play to support your evaluation of the character's isssues.

Vocabulary Connection Consider including several of the concept vocabulary words in your writing.

allegiance	equivocate	counterfeit
stealthy	sacrilegious	breach

- -

Reflect on Your Writing

After you have drafted your report, answer these questions.

1. Did you include a clear statement of your character's primary problem? Does that evaluation account for most, if not all, of the character's conflicts?

2. Which evidence from the play did you use in your report? Is there other evidence you might have used? Explain.

EVIDENCE LOG

Before moving on to a new selection, go to your Evidence Log and record what you learned from Act II of *The Tragedy of Macbeth*.

STANDARDS

Writing
Write arguments to support claims in an analysis of substantive topics or texts, using valid reasoning and relevant and sufficient evidence.

Playwright

William Shakespeare

The Tragedy of Macbeth, Act III

Concept Vocabulary

You will encounter the following words as you read Act III of *The Tragedy of Macbeth*. Before reading, note how familiar you are with each word. Then, rank the words in order from most familiar (1) to least familiar (6).

WORD	YOUR RANKING
foully	
rancors	
incensed	
malice	
enrages	
malevolence	

After completing the first read, come back to the concept vocabulary and review your rankings. Mark changes to your original rankings as needed.

First Read DRAMA

Apply these strategies as you conduct your first read. You will have an opportunity to complete the close-read notes after your first read.

⚙ Tool Kit
First-Read Guide and
Model Annotation

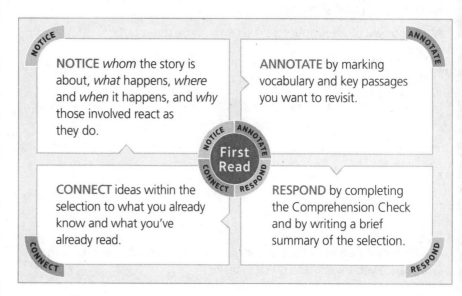

NOTICE *whom* the story is about, *what* happens, *where* and *when* it happens, and *why* those involved react as they do.

ANNOTATE by marking vocabulary and key passages you want to revisit.

First Read

CONNECT ideas within the selection to what you already know and what you've already read.

RESPOND by completing the Comprehension Check and by writing a brief summary of the selection.

⊞ STANDARDS

Reading Literature
By the end of grade 12, read and comprehend literature, including stories, dramas, and poems, at the high end of the grades 11–CCR text complexity band independently and proficiently.

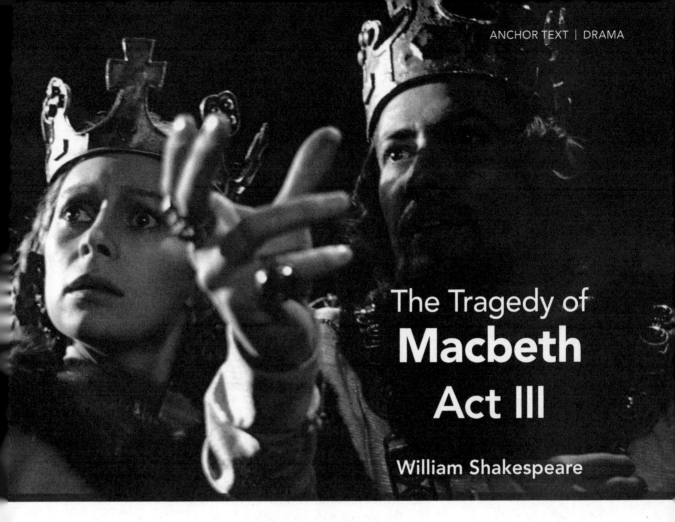

The Tragedy of
Macbeth
Act III

William Shakespeare

REVIEW AND ANTICIPATE

In Act II, Lady Macbeth drugs Duncan's guards, enabling Macbeth
to kill the king. Macbeth subsequently kills the guards so that he
can more easily blame them for the king's murder. Duncan's sons,
Malcolm and Donalbain, flee, afraid that they will be assassinated by
a kinsman eager to claim the throne. Because they run away, some
suspect them of killing their father. As the act closes, it seems that
Macbeth will be named king. Act III begins with Macbeth on the
throne—as the witches had predicted. All seems to be going well for
him, but he feels threatened by Banquo.

Scene i • *Forres. The palace.*

[*Enter* Banquo.]

Banquo. Thou hast it now: King, Cawdor, Glamis, all,
As the weird women promised, and I fear
Thou play'dst most **foully** for 't. Yet it was said
It should not stand[1] in thy posterity,
5 But that myself should be the root and father
Of many kings. If there come truth from them—
As upon thee, Macbeth, their speeches shine—
Why, by the verities on thee made good,
May they not be my oracles as well
10 And set me up in hope? But hush, no more!

NOTES

foully (FOWL lee) *adv.* wrongly; in
an evil way
   1. stand continue.

2. *Sennet* trumpet call.

3. all-thing altogether.

4. solemn ceremonious.

5. grave and prosperous weighty and profitable.

6. Go not . . . better unless my horse goes faster than I expect.

7. invention lies.

8. cause . . . jointly matters of state demanding our joint attention.

9. While until.

10. Sirrah common address to an inferior.

[*Sennet²* sounded. Enter Macbeth *as King,* Lady Macbeth, Lennox, Ross, Lords, *and* Attendants.]

Macbeth. Here's our chief guest.

Lady Macbeth.   If he had been forgotten,
It had been as a gap in our great feast,
And all-thing³ unbecoming.

Macbeth. Tonight we hold a solemn⁴ supper, sir,
And I'll request your presence.

15 **Banquo.**   Let your Highness
Command upon me, to the which my duties
Are with a most indissoluble tie
For ever knit.

Macbeth. Ride you this afternoon?

Banquo.   Ay, my good lord.

20 **Macbeth.** We should have else desired your good advice
(Which still hath been both grave and prosperous⁵)
In this day's council; but we'll take tomorrow.
Is't far you ride?

Banquo. As far, my lord, as will fill up the time
25 'Twixt this and supper. Go not my horse the better.⁶
I must become a borrower of the night
For a dark hour or twain.

Macbeth. Fail not our feast.

Banquo. My lord, I will not.

30 **Macbeth.** We hear our bloody cousins are bestowed
In England and in Ireland, not confessing
Their cruel parricide, filling their hearers
With strange invention.⁷ But of that tomorrow,
When therewithal we shall have cause of state
35 Craving us jointly.⁸ Hie you to horse. Adieu,
Till you return at night. Goes Fleance with you?

Banquo. Ay, my good lord: our time does call upon 's.

Macbeth. I wish your horses swift and sure of foot.
And so I do commend you to their backs.
Farewell.   [*Exit* Banquo.]
40 Let every man be master of his time
Till seven at night. To make society
The sweeter welcome, we will keep ourself
Till suppertime alone. While⁹ then, God be with you!
                    [*Exit* Lords *and all but* Macbeth *and a* Servant.]
Sirrah,¹⁰ a word with you: attend those men
45 Our pleasure?

Attendant. They are, my lord, without the palace gate.

Macbeth. Bring them before us.   [*Exit* Servant.]

To be thus[11] is nothing, but[12] to be safely thus—
Our fears in Banquo stick deep,
50 And in his royalty of nature reigns that
Which would be feared. 'Tis much he dares;
And, to[13] that dauntless temper of his mind,
He hath a wisdom that doth guide his valor
To act in safety. There is none but he
55 Whose being I do fear: and under him
My genius is rebuked,[14] as it is said
Mark Antony's was by Caesar. He chid[15] the sisters,
When first they put the name of King upon me.
And bade them speak to him; then prophetlike
60 They hailed him father to a line of kings.
Upon my head they placed a fruitless crown
And put a barren scepter in my gripe,[16]
Thence to be wrenched with an unlineal hand.
No son of mine succeeding. If 't be so,
65 For Banquo's issue have I filed[17] my mind;
For them the gracious Duncan have I murdered;
Put **rancors** in the vessel of my peace
Only for them, and mine eternal jewel[18]
Given to the common enemy of man,[19]
70 To make them kings, the seeds of Banquo kings!
Rather than so, come, fate, into the list,
And champion me to th' utterance![20] Who's there?

[*Enter* Servant *and* Two Murderers.]

Now go to the door, and stay there till we call.

[*Exit* Servant.]

Was it not yesterday we spoke together?

Murderers. It was, so please your Highness.

75 **Macbeth.**   Well then, now
Have you considered of my speeches? Know
That it was he in the times past, which held you
So under fortune,[21] which you thought had been
Our innocent self: this I made good to you
80 In our last conference; passed in probation[22] with you.
How you were born in hand,[23] how crossed, the instruments,
Who wrought with them, and all things else that might
To half a soul[24] and to a notion[25] crazed
Say "Thus did Banquo."

First Murderer.   You made it known to us.

85 **Macbeth.** I did so; and went further, which is now
Our point of second meeting. Do you find
Your patience so predominant in your nature,
That you can let this go? Are you so gospeled,[26]
To pray for this good man and for his issue,
90 Whose heavy hand hath bowed you to the grave

NOTES

11. thus king.
12. but unless.
13. to added to.

14. genius is rebuked guardian spirit is cowed.
15. chid scolded.

16. gripe grip.

17. filed defiled.

rancors (RANG kuhrz) *n.* angry feelings
18. eternal jewel soul.
19. common . . . man the Devil.

20. champion me to th' utterance Fight against me to the death.

21. held . . . fortune kept you from good fortune.
22. passed in probation reviewed the proofs.
23. born in hand deceived.

24. half a soul halfwit.
25. notion mind.

26. gospeled ready to forgive.

28. **Shoughs**, **water-rugs** shaggy dogs, long-haired dogs.

29. **clept** called.

30. **valued file** classification by valuable traits.

31. **closed** enclosed.

32. **addition** distinction (to set it apart from other dogs).

33. **file** ranks.

34. **wear . . . life** are sick as long as he lives.

incensed (ihn SEHNST) *v.* made angry

35. **set** risk.

36. **distance** disagreement.

37. **near'st of life** most vital parts.

38. **avouch** justify.

39. **wail his fall** (I must) bewail his death.

And beggared yours for ever?

First Murderer.   We are men, my liege.

Macbeth. Ay, in the catalogue ye go for[27] men;
As hounds and greyhounds, mongrels, spaniels, curs,
Shoughs, water-rugs[28] and demi-wolves, are clept[29]
95 All by the name of dogs: the valued file[30]
Distinguishes the swift, the slow, the subtle,
The housekeeper, the hunter, every one
According to the gift which bounteous nature
Hath in him closed,[31] whereby he does receive
100 Particular addition,[32] from the bill
That writes them all alike: and so of men.
Now if you have a station in the file,[33]
Not i' th' worst rank of manhood, say 't,
And I will put that business in your bosoms
105 Whose execution takes your enemy off,
Grapples you to the heart and love of us,
Who wear our health but sickly in his life,[34]
Which in his death were perfect.

Second Murderer.   I am one, my liege,
Whom the vile blows and buffets of the world
110 Hath so **incensed** that I am reckless what
I do to spite the world.

First Murderer.   And I another
So weary with disasters, tugged with fortune,
That I would set[35] my life on any chance,
To mend it or be rid on 't.

Macbeth.   Both of you
115 Know Banquo was your enemy.

Both Murderers.   True, my lord.

Macbeth. So is he mine, and in such bloody distance[36]
That every minute of his being thrusts
Against my near'st of life:[37] and though I could
With barefaced power sweep him from my sight
120 And bid my will avouch[38] it, yet I must not.
For certain friends that are both his and mine,
Whose loves I may not drop, but wail his fall[39]
Who I myself struck down: and thence it is
That I to your assistance do make love,
125 Masking the business from the common eye
For sundry weighty reasons.

Second Murderer.   We shall, my lord,
Perform what you command us.

First Murderer.   Though our lives—

Macbeth. Your spirits shine through you. Within this hour at most
I will advise you where to plant yourselves,

130 Acquaint you with the perfect spy o' th' time,
The moment on 't;[40] for 't must be done tonight,
And something[41] from the palace: always thought[42]
That I require a clearness:[43] and with him—
To leave no rubs[44] nor botches in the work—
135 Fleance his son, that keeps him company,
Whose absence is no less material to me
Than is his father's, must embrace the fate
Of that dark hour. Resolve yourselves apart:[45]
I'll come to you anon.

Murderers.　　　　We are resolved, my lord.

140 **Macbeth.** I'll call upon you straight.[46] Abide within.
It is concluded: Banquo, thy soul's flight.
If it find heaven, must find it out tonight.

⌘ ⌘ ⌘

Scene ii • *The palace.*

[*Enter* Lady Macbeth *and a* Servant.]

Lady Macbeth. Is Banquo gone from court?

Servant. Ay, madam, but returns again tonight.

Lady Macbeth. Say to the King, I would attend his leisure
For a few words.

Servant.　　　　Madam, I will.

Lady Macbeth.　　　　　　Nought's had, all's spent.

5 Where our desire is got without content:
'Tis safer to be that which we destroy
Than by destruction dwell in doubtful joy.

[*Enter* Macbeth.]

How now. my lord! Why do you keep alone,
Of sorriest fancies your companions making,
10 Using those thoughts which should indeed have died
With them they think on? Things without all remedy
Should be without regard: what's done is done.

Macbeth. We have scotched[1] the snake, not killed it:
She'll close[2] and be herself, whilst our poor **malice**
15 Remains in danger of her former tooth.[3]
But let the frame of things disjoint,[4] both the worlds[5] suffer,
Ere we will eat our meal in fear, and sleep
In the affliction of these terrible dreams
That shake us nightly: better be with the dead,
20 Whom we, to gain our peace, have sent to peace,
Than on the torture of the mind to lie

NOTES

40. **the perfect . . . on 't** exact
information of the exact time.
41. **something** some distance.
42. **thought** remembered.
43. **clearness** freedom from
suspicion.
44. **rubs** flaws.
45. **Resolve yourselves apart** Make
your own decision.

46. **straight** immediately.

CLOSE READ
ANNOTATE: Mark the rhyming
words in lines 4–7.

QUESTION: Why does
Shakespeare have Lady Macbeth
speak in rhyming verse rather
than in blank verse?

CONCLUDE: What is the effect of
the use of rhyme in this speech?

malice (MAL ihs) *n.* desire to hurt
another person

1. **scotched** wounded.
2. **close** heal.
3. **in . . . tooth** in as much danger
as before.
4. **frame of things disjoint**
universe collapse.
5. **both the worlds** heaven and
earth.

The Tragedy of Macbeth, Act III **301**

NOTES

6. ecstasy frenzy.

7. Malice . . . levy civil and foreign war.

8. Present him eminence Honor him.

9. Unsafe . . . lave We are unsafe as long as we have to wash.

10. vizards (VIHZ uhrdz) masks.

11. nature's . . . eterne Nature's lease is not eternal.

12. jocund (JOK uhnd) cheerful; jovial.

13. shard-borne borne on scaly wings.

14. chuck term of endearment.

15. seeling eye-closing. Falconers sometimes sewed a hawk's eyes closed in order to train it.

16. Scarf up blindfold.

17. great bond between Banquo and fate.

18. rooky full of rooks, or crows.

In restless ecstasy.[6] Duncan is in his grave;
After life's fitful fever he sleeps well.
Treason has done his worst: nor steel, nor poison,
25 Malice domestic, foreign levy,[7] nothing,
Can touch him further.

Lady Macbeth.   Come on.
Gentle my lord, sleek o'er your rugged looks;
Be bright and jovial among your guests tonight.

Macbeth. So shall I, love; and so, I pray, be you:
30 Let your remembrance apply to Banquo;
Present him eminence,[8] both with eye and tongue:
Unsafe the while, that we must lave[9]
Our honors in these flattering streams
And make our faces vizards[10] to our hearts.
Disguising what they are.

35 **Lady Macbeth.**   You must leave this.

Macbeth. O, full of scorpions is my mind, dear wife!
Thou know'st that Banquo, and his Fleance, lives.

Lady Macbeth. But in them nature's copy's not eterne.[11]

Macbeth. There's comfort yet; they are assailable.
40 Then be thou jocund.[12] Ere the bat hath flown
His cloistered flight, ere to black Hecate's summons
The shard-borne[13] beetle with his drowsy hums
Hath rung night's yawning peal, there shall be done
A deed of dreadful note.

Lady Macbeth.   What's to be done?

45 **Macbeth.** Be innocent of the knowledge, dearest chuck,[14]
Till thou applaud the deed. Come, seeling[15] night,
Scarf up[16] the tender eye of pitiful day,
And with thy bloody and invisible hand
Cancel and tear to pieces that great bond[17]
50 Which keeps me pale! Light thickens, and the crow
Makes wing to th' rooky[18] wood.
Good things of day begin to droop and drowse,
Whiles night's black agents to their preys do rouse.
Thou marvel'st at my words: but hold thee still;
55 Things bad begun make strong themselves by ill:
So, prithee, go with me.   [*Exit.*]

⌘ ⌘ ⌘

Scene iii • *Near the palace.*

[*Enter* Three Murderers.]

First Murderer. But who did bid thee join with us?

Third Murderer.   Macbeth.

Second Murderer. He needs not our mistrust; since he delivers
Our offices¹ and what we have to do
To the direction just.²

First Murderer.   Then stand with us.
5 The west yet glimmers with some streaks of day.
Now spurs the lated traveler apace
To gain the timely inn, and near approaches
The subject of our watch.

Third Murderer.   Hark! I hear horses.

Banquo. [*Within*] Give us a light there, ho!

Second Murderer.   Then 'tis he. The rest
10 That are within the note of expectation³
Already are i' th' court.

First Murderer.   His horses go about.⁴

Third Murderer. Almost a mile: but he does usually—
So all men do—from hence to th' palace gate
Make it their walk.

[*Enter* Banquo *and* Fleance, *with a torch*]

Second Murderer. A light, a light!

Third Murderer.   'Tis he.

15 **First Murderer.**   Stand to 't.

Banquo. It will be rain tonight.

First Murderer.   Let it come down.

[*They set upon* Banquo.]

Banquo. O, treachery! Fly, good Fleance, fly, fly, fly!
                                    [*Exit* Fleance.]
            Thou mayst revenge. O slave! [*Dies.*]

Third Murderer. Who did strike out the light?

First Murderer.   Was't not the way?⁵

Third Murderer. There's but one down; the son is fled.

20 **Second Murderer.** We have lost best half of our affair.

First Murderer. Well, let's away and say how much is done.

                                            [*Exit.*]

⌘ ⌘ ⌘

Scene iv • *The palace.*

[*Banquet prepared. Enter* Macbeth, Lady Macbeth, Ross, Lennox,
Lords, *and* Attendants.]

Macbeth. You know your own degrees:¹ sit down:

NOTES

1. **offices** duties.
2. **direction just** exact detail.

3. **within . . . expectation** on the list of expected guests.
4. **His . . . about** His horses have been taken to the stable.

CLOSE READ

ANNOTATE: Mark the short statements in lines 15–18.

QUESTION: What is happening in these lines—what action accompanies this minimal dialogue?

CONCLUDE: How does the quick, almost wordless presentation of this scene add to its effect?

5. **way** thing to do.

1. **degrees** ranks. At state banquets, guests were seated according to rank.

CLOSE READ

ANNOTATE: Mark the words and phrases Macbeth uses to describe himself in lines 22–24. Mark a separate set of words he uses to describe himself in lines 25–26.

QUESTION: How are the two sets of words different?

CONCLUDE: How do these descriptive details define the changes that have occurred in Macbeth?

At first and last, the hearty welcome.

Lords. Thanks to your Majesty.

Macbeth. Ourself will mingle with society[2]

5　And play the humble host.
Our hostess keeps her state,[3] but in best time
We will require[4] her welcome.

Lady Macbeth. Pronounce it for me, sir, to all our friends,
For my heart speaks they are welcome.

[*Enter* First Murderer.]

10　**Macbeth.** See, they encounter thee with their hearts' thanks.
Both sides are even: here I'll sit i' th' midst:
Be large in mirth; anon we'll drink a measure[5]
The table round. [*Goes to* Murderer.] There's blood upon
　　thy face.

Murderer. 'Tis Banquo's then.

15　**Macbeth.** 'Tis better thee without than he within.[6]
Is he dispatched?

Murderer. My lord, his throat is cut: that I did for him.

Macbeth. Thou art the best o' th' cutthroats.
Yet he's good that did the like for Fleance:

20　If thou didst it, thou art the nonpareil.[7]

Murderer. Most royal sir, Fleance is 'scaped.

Macbeth. [*Aside*] Then comes my fit again: I had else been perfect.
Whole as the marble, founded as the rock,
As broad and general as the casing[8] air:

25　But now I am cabined, cribbed, confined, bound in
To saucy[9] doubts and fears.—But Banquo's safe?

Murderer. Ay, my good lord: safe in a ditch he bides,
With twenty trenchèd[10] gashes on his head,
The least a death to nature.[11]

Macbeth. 　　　　　　　　　Thanks for that.

30　[*Aside*] There the grown serpent lies: the worm that's fled
Hath nature that in time will venom breed,
No teeth for th' present. Get thee gone. Tomorrow
We'll hear ourselves[12] again.　　　　　　　[*Exit* Murderer.]

Lady Macbeth. 　　　　　　My royal lord,
You do not give the cheer.[13] The feast is sold

35　That is not often vouched, while 'tis a-making,
'Tis given with welcome.[14] To feed were best at home;
From thence, the sauce to meat is ceremony;[15]
Meeting were bare without it.

[*Enter the* Ghost of Banquo *and sits in* Macbeth's *place.*]

Macbeth. 　　　　　　　Sweet remembrancer!
Now good digestion wait on appetite.

40 And health on both!

Lennox.   May't please your Highness sit.

Macbeth. Here had we now our country's honor roofed[16]
Were the graced person of our Banquo present—
Who may I rather challenge for unkindness
Than pity for mischance![17]

Ross.   His absence, sir.
45 Lays blame upon his promise. Please 't your Highness
To grace us with your royal company?

Macbeth. The table's full.

Lennox. Here is a place reserved, sir.

Macbeth. Where?

50 **Lennox.** Here, my good lord. What is 't that moves your Highness?

Macbeth. Which of you have done this?

Lords.   What, my good lord?

Macbeth. Thou canst not say I did it. Never shake
Thy gory locks at me.

Ross. Gentlemen, rise, his Highness is not well.

55 **Lady Macbeth.** Sit, worthy friends. My lord is often thus,
And hath been from his youth. Pray you, keep seat.
The fit is momentary; upon a thought[18]
He will again be well. If much you note him,
You shall offend him and extend his passion.[19]
60 Feed, and regard him not.—Are you a man?

Macbeth. Ay, and a bold one, that dare look on that
Which might appall the devil.

Lady Macbeth.   O proper stuff!
This is the very painting of your fear.
This is the air-drawn dagger which, you said,
65 Led you to Duncan. O, these flaws[20] and starts,
Impostors to true fear, would well become
A woman's story at a winter's fire,
Authorized[21] by her grandam. Shame itself!
Why do you make such faces? When all's done,
You look but on a stool.

70 **Macbeth.**   Prithee, see there!
Behold! Look! Lo! How say you?
Why, what care I? If thou canst nod, speak too.
If charnel houses[22] and our graves must send
Those that we bury back, our monuments
Shall be the maws of kites.[23]   [*Exit* Ghost.]

75 **Lady Macbeth.**   What, quite unmanned in folly?

Macbeth. If I stand here, I saw him.

16. **our . . . roofed** the most honorable men in the country under one roof.

17. **Who . . . mischance** whom I hope I may reproach for being absent due to discourtesy rather than pity because he has had an accident.

18. **upon a thought** in a moment.

19. **passion** suffering.

20. **flaws** gusts of wind; outbursts of emotion.

21. **Authorized** vouched for.

22. **charnel houses** vaults containing human bones dug up in making new graves.

23. **our . . . kites** Because the dead will be devoured by birds of prey, our tombs will be the bellies of those birds.

Macbeth confides his fears to Lady Macbeth.

24. **Ere . . . weal** before humane laws civilized the state and made it gentle.

25. **mortal . . . crowns** deadly wounds on their heads.

26. **infirmity** (ihn FUR muh tee) physical or mental defect; illness.

27. **thirst** drink.

28. **Avaunt** Be gone!

29. **speculation** sight.

Lady Macbeth. Fie, for shame!

Macbeth. Blood hath been shed ere now, i' th' olden time,
Ere humane statute purged the gentle weal;²⁴
80 Ay, and since too, murders have been performed
Too terrible for the ear. The time has been
That, when the brains were out, the man would die,
And there an end; but now they rise again,
With twenty mortal murders on their crowns,²⁵
85 And push us from our stools. This is more strange
Than such a murder is.

Lady Macbeth.   My worthy lord,
Your noble friends do lack you.

Macbeth.   I do forget.
Do not muse at me, my most worthy friends;
I have a strange infirmity,²⁶ which is nothing
90 To those that know me. Come, love and health to all!
Then I'll sit down. Give me some wine, fill full.

[*Enter* Ghost.]

I drink to th' general joy o' th' whole table,
And to our dear friend Banquo, whom we miss;
Would he were here! To all and him we thirst,²⁷
And all to all.

95 **Lords.**   Our duties, and the pledge.

Macbeth. Avaunt!²⁸ and quit my sight! Let the earth hide thee!
Thy bones are marrowless, thy blood is cold;
Thou hast no speculation²⁹ in those eyes
Which thou dost glare with.

Lady Macbeth.   Think of this, good peers,
100 But as a thing of custom, 'tis no other.

Only it spoils the pleasure of the time.

Macbeth. What man dare. I dare.
Approach thou like the rugged Russian bear.
The armed rhinoceros, or th' Hyrcan[30] tiger:
105 Take any shape but that,[31] and my firm nerves
Shall never tremble. Or be alive again,
And dare me to the desert[32] with thy sword.
If trembling I inhabit[33] then, protest me
The baby of a girl. Hence, horrible shadow!
Unreal mock'ry, hence!   [*Exit* Ghost.]
110   Why, so: being gone,
I am a man again. Pray you, sit still.

Lady Macbeth. You have displaced the mirth, broke the
    good meeting.
With most admired[34] disorder.

Macbeth.   Can such things be.
And overcome us[35] like a summer's cloud,
115 Without our special wonder? You make me strange
Even to the disposition that I owe,[36]
When now I think you can behold such sights,
And keep the natural ruby of your cheeks,
When mine is blanched with fear.

Ross.   What sights, my lord?

120 **Lady Macbeth.** I pray you, speak not: He grows worse and
    worse;
Question **enrages** him: at once, good night.
Stand not upon the order of your going,[37]
But go at once.

Lennox.   Good night; and better health
Attend his Majesty!

Lady Macbeth.   A kind good night to all!
                          [*Exit* Lords.]

125 **Macbeth.** It will have blood, they say: blood will have blood.
Stones have been known to move and trees to speak;
Augures and understood relations[38] have
By maggot-pies and choughs[39] and rooks brought forth
The secret'st man of blood.[40] What is the night?

130 **Lady Macbeth.** Almost at odds[41] with morning, which is which.

Macbeth. How say'st thou, that Macduff denies his person
At our great bidding?

Lady Macbeth.   Did you send to him, sir?

Macbeth. I hear it by the way, but I will send:
There's not a one of them but in his house
135 I keep a servant fee'd.[42] I will tomorrow,
And betimes[43] I will, to the weird sisters:

NOTES

30. **Hyrcan** (HUHR kuhn) from
    Hyrcania, a province of
    the ancient Persian and
    Macedonian empires south of
    the Caspian Sea.

31. **that** Banquo's shape.

32. **desert** place where neither of
    us could escape.

33. **inhabit** remain indoors.

34. **admired** amazing.

35. **overcome us** come over us.

36. **disposition . . . owe** my own
    nature.

enrages (ehn RAY juhz) *v.* causes to
become very angry

37. **Stand . . . going** Do not wait to
    depart in order of rank.

38. **Augures and understood
    relations** omens and the
    relationship between the
    omens and what they
    represent.

39. **maggot-pies and choughs**
    (chuhfs) magpies and crows.

40. **man of blood** murderer.

41. **at odds** disputing.

42. **fee'd** paid to spy.

43. **betimes** quickly.

More shall they speak, for now I am bent[44] to know
By the worst means the worst. For mine own good
All causes shall give way. I am in blood
140 Stepped in so far that, should I wade no more,
Returning were as tedious as go o'er.
Strange things I have in head that will to hand,
Which must be acted ere they may be scanned.[45]

45. scanned examined.

Lady Macbeth. You lack the season of all natures,[46] sleep.

46. season . . . natures preservative of all living creatures.

145 **Macbeth.** Come, we'll to sleep. My strange and self-abuse[47]
Is the initiate fear that wants hard use.[48]
We are yet but young in deed.

47. My . . . self-abuse my strange delusion.

[*Exit.*]

48. initiate . . . use beginner's fear that will harden with experience.

⌘ ⌘ ⌘

Scene v • *A witches' haunt.*

[*Thunder. Enter the* Three Witches, *meeting* Hecate.]

First Witch. Why, how now, Hecate! you look angerly.

1. beldams hags.

Hecate. Have I not reason, beldams[1] as you are.
Saucy and overbold? How did you dare
To trade and traffic with Macbeth
5 In riddles and affairs of death;
And I, the mistress of your charms,
The close contriver[2] of all harms,
Was never called to bear my part,
Or show the glory of our art?

2. close contriver secret inventor.

10 And, which is worse, all you have done
Hath been but for a wayward son.
Spiteful and wrathful; who, as others do,
Loves for his own ends, not for you.
But make amends now: get you gone,

3. Acheron (AK uh ron) hell; in Greek mythology the river of Hades.

15 And at the pit of Acheron[3]
Meet me i' th' morning: thither he
Will come to know his destiny.
Your vessels and your spells provide,
Your charms and everything beside.
20 I am for th' air; this night I'll spend
Unto a dismal and a fatal end:
Great business must be wrought ere noon.
Upon the corner of the moon
There hangs a vap'rous drop profound;

4. sleights devices.

25 I'll catch it ere it come to ground:
And that distilled by magic sleights[4]

5. artificial sprites spirits created by magic.

Shall raise such artificial sprites[5]
As by the strength of their illusion

6. confusion ruin.

Shall draw him on to his confusion.[6]

30 He shall spurn fate, scorn death, and bear
His hopes 'bove wisdom, grace, and fear:
And you all know security[7]
Is mortals' chiefest enemy.

[*Music and a song.*]

Hark! I am called; my little spirit, see.
35 Sits in a foggy cloud and stays for me.   [*Exit.*]
[*Sing within*, "Come away, come away," *etc.*]

First Witch. Come, let's make haste; she'll soon be
    back again.   [*Exit.*]

⌘ ⌘ ⌘

Scene vi • *The palace.*

[*Enter* Lennox *and another* Lord.]

Lennox. My former speeches have but hit[1] your thoughts.
Which can interpret farther.[2] Only I say
Things have been strangely borne.[3] The gracious Duncan
Was pitied of Macbeth: marry, he was dead.
5 And the right-valiant Banquo walked too late:
Whom, you may say, if 't please you. Fleance killed.
For Fleance fled. Men must not walk too late.
Who cannot want the thought,[4] how monstrous
It was for Malcolm and for Donalbain
10 To kill their gracious father? Damnèd fact![5]
How it did grieve Macbeth! Did he not straight,
In pious rage, the two delinquents tear,
That were the slaves of drink and thralls[6] of sleep?
Was not that nobly done? Ay, and wisely too;
15 For 'twould have angered any heart alive
To hear the men deny 't. So that I say
He has borne all things well: and I do think
That, had he Duncan's sons under his key—
As, an 't[7] please heaven, he shall not—they should find
20 What 'twere to kill a father. So should Fleance.
But, peace! for from broad[8] words, and cause he failed
His presence at the tyrant's feast. I hear,
Macduff lives in disgrace. Sir, can you tell
Where he bestows himself?

Lord.   The son of Duncan.
25 From whom this tyrant holds the due of birth.[9]
Lives in the English court, and is received
Of the most pious Edward[10] with such grace
That the **malevolence** of fortune nothing
Takes from his high respect.[11] Thither Macduff
30 Is gone to pray the holy King, upon his aid[12]

13. To ... Siward to call to arms the commander of the English forces, the Earl of Northumberland, and his son, Siward.

14. free honors honors given to freemen.

15. cloudy disturbed.

16. clogs burdens.

To wake Northumberland and warlike Siward;[13]
That by the help of these, with Him above
To ratify the work, we may again
Give to our tables meat, sleep to our nights,

35   Free from our feasts and banquets bloody knives,
Do faithful homage and receive free honors:[14]
All which we pine for now. And this report
Hath so exasperate the King that he
Prepares for some attempt of war.

Lennox.   Sent he to Macduff?

40   **Lord.** He did: and with an absolute "Sir, not I,"
The cloudy[15] messenger turns me his back,
And hums, as who should say "You'll rue the time
That clogs[16] me with this answer."

Lennox.   And that well might
Advise him to a caution, t' hold what distance

45   His wisdom can provide. Some holy angel
Fly to the court of England and unfold
His message ere he come, that a swift blessing
May soon return to this our suffering country
Under a hand accursed!

Lord.   I'll send my prayers with him.   [*Exit.*]

Comprehension Check

Complete the following items after you finish your first read.

1. In what part of Macbeth's plan do the two murderers succeed, and in what part do they fail?

2. In the banquet scene, what causes Macbeth to behave so strangely?

3. 🗒 **Notebook** Confirm your understanding of the text by writing a summary.

- -

RESEARCH

Research to Clarify Choose at least one unfamiliar detail from the text. Briefly research that detail. In what way does the information you learned shed light on an aspect of the play?

Close Read the Text

Reread lines 39–54 of Act III, Scene iv. Mark Macbeth's lines of dialogue, indicating to whom he is speaking in each line, using clues from the text.

Close Read — ANNOTATE · QUESTION · CONCLUDE

THE TRAGEDY OF MACBETH, ACT III

Analyze the Text

CITE TEXTUAL EVIDENCE to support your answers.

Notebook Respond to these questions.

1. (a) What is Macbeth's conflict with Banquo? (b) **Analyze** Does Macbeth resolve the conflict? Explain.

2. (a) **Analyze** How is Macbeth's behavior at the banquet a sign of a troubled mind? (b) **Interpret** What does Lady Macbeth's reaction to her husband show?

3. (a) What excuse do Macbeth and Lady Macbeth give for his behavior at the banquet? (b) **Evaluate** Is this is a good excuse? Explain.

4. (a) What events does Lennox recount in his speech in Scene vi? (b) **Interpret** How does Lennox show that he suspects Macbeth?

Concept Vocabulary

foully	incensed	enrages
rancors	malice	malevolence

Why These Words? These concept words reveal the emotional turmoil in Act III. The words reflect anger over the evil deeds that have occurred. Look for more words in Act III that express the same emotions.

Practice

Notebook Write a sentence for each concept word. Use context clues to demonstrate your understanding of each word.

Word Study

Notebook Latin Prefix: *mal-* The Latin prefix *mal-* means "bad," "badly," "poorly," or "wrong." In Act III, Scene vi, the Scottish lord who speaks with Lennox refers to "the malevolence of fate" that led the son of Duncan to take refuge in England. The Latin prefix *mal-* indicates that *malevolence* is a negative word. The Latin root of the word is *-vol-*, which means "will" or "desire." Thus, the lord is saying that fate displayed ill will toward the son of the king.

Using your knowledge of the prefix *mal-*, infer the meanings of these words used in scientific and legal terminology: *malnutrition, maladjusted, malformed, malpractice.* Then, consult a college-level dictionary to verify the words' meanings, and make adjustments to your definitions as needed. Finally, use each word in a sentence.

WORD NETWORK

Add interesting words related to time from the text to your Word Network.

STANDARDS

Language
• Identify and correctly use patterns of word changes that indicate different meanings or parts of speech.
• Verify the preliminary determination of the meaning of a word or phrase.

THE TRAGEDY OF MACBETH,
ACT III

Analyze Craft and Structure

Author's Choices: Structure The plot structures of Shakespeare's tragedies often include elements that add to the customary dramatic arc of *rising action, climax, falling action,* and *resolution.*

- **Crisis** or **Turning Point:** event that causes the tragic hero's situation to change decisively, leading to that character's downfall. The crisis may occur at the same time as the play's **climax**—its moment of highest emotion and tension. However, in Shakespeare's tragedies, the crisis often occurs in Act III, at a point that is earlier than and separate from the climax.

- **Catastrophe:** resolution of the tragedy, in which the tragic character's downfall is complete

Within the larger structure of Shakespearean tragedies, cause-and-effect relationships feature strongly. Often, one event sets in motion a series of related events over which characters seem to have little control. It can be useful to think of these relationships as a chain of causes and effects, in which a cause triggers an effect, which becomes the cause of a new effect, and so on.

Practice

CITE TEXTUAL EVIDENCE
to support your answers.

Identify events that are part of the play's rising action—the situations that intensify the conflict. Then, indicate where the crisis occurs in Act III. Finally, note what you predict will happen in the falling action and catastrophe of Acts IV and V.

RISING ACTION EVENTS:
Act I:
Act II:
Act III:
How events are linked by cause and effect:

CRISIS/TURNING POINT IN ACT III:

PREDICTIONS: FALLING ACTION EVENTS/CATASTROPHE

STANDARDS

Reading Literature
- Analyze the impact of the author's regarding how to develop and relate elements of a story or drama.
- Analyze how an author's choices concerning how to structure specific parts of a text contribute to its overall structure and meaning as well as its aesthetic impact.

Speaking and Listening

Assignment

With a partner, choose a speech from this act in which either Macbeth or Lady Macbeth argues for a particular course of action. Analyze the speech, and then, using your analysis, prepare and deliver an **oral recitation** of the speech to the class. Make sure your recitation reflects your insights into the character's purpose and personality. Then, lead the class in a discussion about the speech.

1. **Choose a Speech** The speech you choose should be one in which one of the two main characters clearly argues in favor of a particular course of action. The speech could be a soliloquy or monologue, which is a long speech that is addressed to another character.

2. **Analyze the Speech** To prepare for your recitation, analyze the speech with your partner. Analyze the speech for the following:

   - **point of view**—think about how the character's point of view affects the delivery of his or her speech.

   - **reasoning**—consider how the character's reasoning is reflected in the speech.

   - **word choice**—what words are particularly effective in revealing the character's state of mind?

   - **emphasis**—what is the main emphasis in the speech?

   - **links between ideas**—how does the character connect his or her ideas? Are the connections logical and realistic?

3. **Rehearse the Recitation** Choose which partner will perform the recitation, and which will "direct" it, providing constructive feedback on its presentation. Once you have chosen roles, rehearse the speech until you both are satisfied and comfortable with it.

4. **Present the Recitation** As you present your recitation, keep these things in mind:

   - Speak clearly enough to be understood.

   - Speak loudly enough to be heard.

   - Give emphasis to the important points in the speech.

   - Make clear transitions from one idea to another.

   - Speak with emotion that conveys your interpretation of the speech.

5. **Lead a Discussion** Lead a class discussion after the recitation, based on what you learned while you were preparing your recitation. With your fellow students, analyze Shakespeare's choices in creating the character, and identify the ways in which Shakespeare brought that character to life.

EVIDENCE LOG

Before moving on to a new selection, go to your Evidence Log and record what you learned from Act III of *The Tragedy of Macbeth*.

STANDARDS

Reading Literature
Analyze the impact of the author's choices regarding how to develop and relate elements of a story or drama.

Speaking and Listening
• Initiate and participate effectively in a range of collaborative discussions with diverse partners on *grades 11–12 topics, texts, and issues*, building on others' ideas and expressing their own clearly and persuasively.

• Evaluate a speaker's point of view, reasoning, and use of evidence and rhetoric, assessing the stance, premises, links among ideas, word choice, points of emphasis, and tone used.

• Adapt speech to a variety of contexts and tasks, demonstrating a command of formal English when indicated or appropriate.

Playwright

William Shakespeare

The Tragedy of Macbeth, Act IV

Concept Vocabulary

You will encounter the following words as you read Act IV of *The Tragedy of Macbeth.* Before reading, note how familiar you are with each word. Then, rank the words in order from most familiar (1) to least familiar (6).

WORD	YOUR RANKING
pernicious	
laudable	
treacherous	
avaricious	
integrity	
sanctity	

After completing the first read, come back to the concept vocabulary and review your rankings. Mark changes to your original rankings as needed.

First Read DRAMA

Apply these strategies as you conduct your first read. You will have an opportunity to complete the close-read notes after your first read.

🔧 Tool Kit
First-Read Guide and Model Annotation

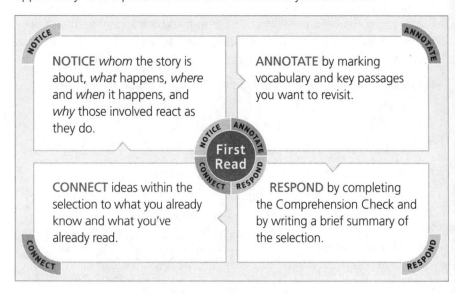

NOTICE *whom* the story is about, *what* happens, *where* and *when* it happens, and *why* those involved react as they do.

ANNOTATE by marking vocabulary and key passages you want to revisit.

First Read

CONNECT ideas within the selection to what you already know and what you've already read.

RESPOND by completing the Comprehension Check and by writing a brief summary of the selection.

☰ STANDARDS
Reading Literature
By the end of grade 12, read and comprehend literature, including stories, dramas, and poems, at the high end of the grades 11–CCR text complexity band independently and proficiently.

The Tragedy of
Macbeth
Act IV

William Shakespeare

REVIEW AND ANTICIPATE

In Act III, Macbeth hires murderers to kill Banquo and Banquo's son, Fleance. The murderers botch the job, killing Banquo but allowing Fleance to escape. Then, at a state banquet, Macbeth is shocked to see the ghost of Banquo sitting in the king's chair. Macbeth decides to visit the witches again, determined to know "the worst." At the end of Act III, we learn that Malcolm is in England preparing to invade Scotland, and that Macduff has gone to join him. In Act IV, Macbeth seeks help from the witches to secure his power. The forces of good, however, are beginning to gather against him.

Scene i • *A witches' haunt.*

[*Thunder. Enter the* Three Witches.]

First Witch. Thrice the brinded[1] cat hath mewed.

Second Witch. Thrice and once the hedge-pig[2] whined.

Third Witch. Harpier[3] cries. 'Tis time, 'tis time.

First Witch. Round about the caldron go:
5 In the poisoned entrails throw.
Toad, that under cold stone
Days and nights was thirty-one
Swelt'red venom sleeping got,[4]
Boil thou first i' th' charmèd pot.

10 **All.** Double, double, toil and trouble;

NOTES

1. **brinded** striped.
2. **hedge-pig** hedgehog.
3. **Harpier** one of the spirits attending the witches.

4. **Swelt'red . . . got** venom sweated out while sleeping.

5. **fork** forked tongue.

6. **blindworm's** small, limbless lizard's.

7. **howlet's** small owl's.

8. **maw and gulf** stomach and gullet.

9. **ravined** ravenous.

10. **blaspheming Jew ... Tartar's lips** For many in Shakespeare's audience, the words *Jew*, *Turk*, and *Tartar* evoked stereotypical enemies of Christianity.

11. **slab** sticky.

12. **chaudron** (SHOH druhn) entrails.

CLOSE READ

ANNOTATE: Mark the repeating lines in the witches' speeches, lines 10–36.

QUESTION: Why does Shakespeare have the witches repeat these verses?

CONCLUDE: How does this repetition emphasize the idea that the witches are using language to cast spells?

Fire burn and caldron bubble.

Second Witch. Fillet of a fenny snake,
In the caldron boil and bake;
Eye of newt and toe of frog,
15 Wool of bat and tongue of dog,
Adder's fork[5] and blindworm's[6] sting,
Lizard's leg and howlet's[7] wing,
For a charm of pow'rful trouble,
Like a hell-broth boil and bubble.

20 **All.** Double, double, toil and trouble;
Fire burn and caldron bubble.

Third Witch. Scale of dragon, tooth of wolf,
Witch's mummy, maw and gulf[8]
Of the ravined[9] salt-sea shark,
25 Root of hemlock digged i' th' dark,
Liver of blaspheming Jew.
Gall of goat, and slips of yew
Slivered in the moon's eclipse.
Nose of Turk and Tartar's lips,[10]
30 Finger of birth-strangled babe
Ditch-delivered by a drab,
Make the gruel thick and slab:[11]
Add thereto a tiger's chaudron,[12]
For th' ingredience of our caldron.

35 **All.** Double, double, toil and trouble;
Fire burn and caldron bubble.

Second Witch. Cool it with a baboon's blood,
Then the charm is firm and good.

[*Enter* Hecate.]

Hecate. O, well done! I commend your pains;
40 And every one shall share i' th' gains:
And now about the caldron sing,
Like elves and fairies in a ring,
Enchanting all that you put in.

[*Music and a song:* "Black Spirits," *etc. Exit* Hecate.]

Second Witch. By the pricking of my thumbs,
45 Something wicked this way comes:
Open, locks,
Whoever knocks!

[*Enter* Macbeth.]

Macbeth. How now, you secret, black, and midnight hags!
What is 't you do?

All.   A deed without a name.

50 **Macbeth.** I conjure you, by that which you profess,
Howe'er you come to know it, answer me:
Though you untie the winds and let them fight
Against the churches: though the yesty[13] waves
Confound[14] and swallow navigation up;

55 Though bladed corn be lodged[15] and trees blown down;
Though castles topple on their warder's heads;
Though palaces and pyramids do slope[16]
Their heads to their foundations; though the treasure
Of nature's germens[17] tumble all together,

60 Even till destruction sicken, answer me
To what I ask you.

First Witch.   Speak.

Second Witch.   Demand.

Third Witch.   We'll answer.

First Witch. Say, if th' hadst rather hear it from our mouths,
Or from our masters?

Macbeth.   Call 'em, let me see 'em.

First Witch. Pour in sow's blood, that hath eaten
65 Her nine farrow;[18] grease that's sweaten
From the murderer's gibbet[19] throw
Into the flame.

All.   Come, high or low,
Thyself and office[20] deftly show!

[*Thunder.* First Apparition: *an Armed Head.*[21]]

Macbeth. Tell me, thou unknown power—

First Witch.   He knows thy thought:
70 Hear his speech, but say thou nought.

First Apparition. Macbeth! Macbeth! Macbeth! Beware Macduff!
Beware the Thane of Fife. Dismiss me: enough.
                              [*He descends.*]

Macbeth. Whate'er thou art, for thy good caution thanks:
Thou hast harped[22] my fear aright. But one word more—

75 **First Witch.** He will not be commanded. Here's another,
More potent than the first.

[*Thunder.* Second Apparition: *a Bloody Child.*[23]]

Second Apparition. Macbeth! Macbeth! Macbeth!

Macbeth. Had I three ears, I'd hear thee.

Second Apparition. Be bloody, bold, and resolute! Laugh to scorn
80 The pow'r of man, for none of woman born
Shall harm Macbeth.   [*Descends.*]

NOTES

13. **yesty** foamy.
14. **Confound** destroy.
15. **lodged** beaten down.
16. **slope** bend.
17. **nature's germens** seeds of all life.

18. **farrow** young pigs.
19. **gibbet** (JIHB iht) gallows.

20. **office** function.
21. *an Armed Head* symbol of Macduff.

22. **harped** hit upon.

23. *a Bloody Child* symbol of Macduff at birth.

Macbeth. Then live, Macduff: what need I fear of thee?
But yet I'll make assurance double sure.
And take a bond of fate.[24] Thou shalt not live;
85 That I may tell pale-hearted fear it lies,
And sleep in spite of thunder.

[*Thunder. Third Apparition: a Child Crowned, with a tree in his hand.*[25]]

25. **a Child . . . hand** symbol of Malcolm.

                                                    What is this,
That rises like the issue of a king,
And wears upon his baby-brow the round

26. **top of sovereignty** crown.

And top of sovereignty?[26]

All.   Listen, but speak not to 't.

90 **Third Apparition.** Be lion-mettled, proud, and take no care
Who chafes, who frets, or where conspirers are:
Macbeth shall never vanquished be until
Great Birnam Wood to high Dunsinane Hill
Shall come against him.   [*Descends.*]

Macbeth.   That will never be.

27. **impress** force into service.
28. **bodements** prophecies.

95 Who can impress[27] the forest, bid the tree
Unfix his earth-bound root? Sweet bodements,[28] good!
Rebellious dead, rise never, till the Wood
Of Birnam rise, and our high-placed Macbeth

29. **lease of nature** natural lifespan.
30. **mortal custom** natural death.

Shall live the lease of nature,[29] pay his breath
100 To time and mortal custom.[30] Yet my heart
Throbs to know one thing. Tell me, if your art
Can tell so much: shall Banquo's issue ever
Reign in this kingdom?

All.   Seek to know no more.

Macbeth. I will be satisfied. Deny me this,
105 And an eternal curse fall on you! Let me know.
Why sinks that caldron? And what noise is this?

[*Hautboys.*]

First Witch. Show!

Second Witch. Show!

Third Witch. Show!

110 **All.** Show his eyes, and grieve his heart;
Come like shadows, so depart!

31. **glass** mirror.

[*A show of eight* Kings *and* Banquo, *last* King *with a glass*[31] *in his hand.*]

Macbeth. Thou art too like the spirit of Banquo. Down!
Thy crown does sear mine eyelids. And thy hair,
Thou other gold-bound brow, is like the first.
115 A third is like the former. Filthy hags!
Why do you show me this? A fourth! Start, eyes!

^ The witches finish their brew.

What, will the line stretch out to th' crack of doom?
Another yet! A seventh! I'll see no more.
And yet the eighth appears, who bears a glass
120 Which shows me many more: and some I see
That twofold balls and treble scepters³² carry:
Horrible sight! Now I see 'tis true;
For the blood-boltered³³ Banquo smiles upon me,
And points at them for his.³⁴ What, is this so?

125 **First Witch.** Ay, sir, all this is so. But why
Stands Macbeth thus amazedly?
Come, sisters, cheer we up his sprites,
And show the best of our delights:
I'll charm the air to give a sound,
130 While you perform your antic round,³⁵

NOTES

32. twofold . . . scepters
coronation emblems and
insignia of the kingdoms
of England, Scotland, and
Ireland, united in 1603 when
James VI of Scotland became
James I of England.

33. blood-boltered with his hair
matted with blood.

34. his his descendants.

35. antic round grotesque circular
dance.

pernicious (puhr NIHSH uhs) *adj.*
harmful, often in a way that is not
readily noticed

That this great king may kindly say
Our duties did his welcome pay.

[*Music.* The Witches *dance, and vanish.*]

Macbeth. Where are they? Gone? Let this **pernicious** hour
Stand aye accursèd in the calendar!
Come in, without there!

[*Enter* Lennox.]

135 **Lennox.**   What's your Grace's will?

Macbeth. Saw you the weird sisters?

Lennox.   No, my lord.

Macbeth. Came they not by you?

Lennox.   No indeed, my lord.

Macbeth. Infected be the air whereon they ride,
And damned all those that trust them! I did hear
140 The galloping of horse. Who was 't came by?

Lennox. 'Tis two or three, my lord, that bring you word
Macduff is fled to England.

Macbeth.   Fled to England?

Lennox. Ay, my good lord.

36. **anticipat'st** foretold.

37. **The flighty . . . it** The fleeting
plan is never fulfilled unless it
is carried out at once.

38. **firstlings . . . heart** first
thoughts, impulses.

Macbeth. [*Aside*] Time, thou anticipat'st[36] my dread exploits.
145 The flighty purpose never is o'ertook
Unless the deed go with it.[37] From this moment
The very firstlings of my heart[38] shall be
The firstlings of my hand. And even now,
To crown my thoughts with acts be it thought and done:
150 The castle of Macduff I will surprise;
Seize upon Fife; give to th' edge o' th' sword
His wife, his babes, and all unfortunate souls
That trace him in his line. No boasting like a fool;
This deed I'll do before this purpose cool:
155 But no more sights!—Where are these gentlemen?
Come, bring me where they are.

[*Exit.*]

⌘ ⌘ ⌘

Scene ii • *Macduff's castle.*

[*Enter* Macduff's Wife, *her* Son, *and* Ross.]

Lady Macduff. What had he done, to make him fly the land?

Ross. You must have patience, madam.

Lady Macduff.   He had none:
His flight was madness. When our actions do not,

Our fears do make us traitors.

Ross.   You know not
5 Whether it was his wisdom or his fear.

Lady Macduff. Wisdom! To leave his wife, to leave his babes,
His mansion and his titles,[1] in a place
From whence himself does fly? He loves us not;
He wants the natural touch:[2] for the poor wren,
10 The most diminutive of birds, will fight,
Her young ones in her nest, against the owl.
All is the fear and nothing is the love;
As little is the wisdom, where the flight
So runs against all reason.

Ross.   My dearest coz,[3]
15 I pray you, school[4] yourself. But, for your husband,
He is noble, wise, judicious, and best knows
The fits o' th' seasons,[5] I dare not speak much further:
But cruel are the times, when we are traitors
And do not know ourselves;[6] when we hold rumor
20 From what we fear,[7] yet know not what we fear,
But float upon a wild and violent sea
Each way and move. I take my leave of you.
Shall not be long but I'll be here again.
Things at the worst will cease, or else climb upward
25 To what they were before. My pretty cousin,
Blessing upon you!

Lady Macduff. Fathered he is, and yet he's fatherless.

Ross. I am so much a fool, should I stay longer,
It would be my disgrace and your discomfort.[8]
I take my leave at once.   [*Exit* Ross.]

30 **Lady Macduff.**   Sirrah, your father's dead;
And what will you do now? How will you live?

Son. As birds do, mother.

Lady Macduff.   What, with worms and flies?

Son. With what I get, I mean; and so do they.

Lady Macduff. Poor bird! thou'dst never fear the net nor lime,[9]
35 The pitfall nor the gin.[10]

Son. Why should I, mother? Poor birds they are not set for.
My father is not dead, for all your saying.

Lady Macduff. Yes, he is dead: how wilt thou do for a father?

Son. Nay, how will you do for a husband?

40 **Lady Macduff.** Why, I can buy me twenty at any market.

Son. Then you'll buy 'em to sell[11] again.

Lady Macduff. Thou speak'st with all thy wit, and yet i' faith,

1. **titles** possessions.

2. **wants . . . touch** lacks natural affection.

3. **coz** cousin.
4. **school** control.

5. **fits o' th' seasons** disorders of the time.

6. **when . . . ourselves** when we are treated as traitors but do not know of any treason.

7. **when . . . fear** believe rumors based on our fears.

8. **It . . . discomfort** I would disgrace myself and embarrass you by weeping.

9. **lime** birdlime, a sticky substance smeared on branches to catch birds.
10. **gin** trap.

11. **sell** betray.

12. for thee for a child.

13. swears and lies takes an oath and breaks it.

14. enow enough.

15. in . . . perfect I am fully informed of your honorable rank.

16. doubt fear.

17. homely simple.

18. fell fierce.

laudable (LAWD uh buhl) *adj.* praiseworthy

19. shag-eared hairy-eared.

With wit enough for thee.[12]

Son. Was my father a traitor, mother?

45 **Lady Macduff.** Ay, that he was.

Son. What is a traitor?

Lady Macduff. Why, one that swears and lies.[13]

Son. And be all traitors that do so?

Lady Macduff. Every one that does so is a traitor, and must
50 be hanged.

Son. And must they all be hanged that swear and lie?

Lady Macduff. Every one.

Son. Who must hang them?

Lady Macduff. Why, the honest men.

55 **Son.** Then the liars and swearers are fools: for there are liars and
swearers enow[14] to beat the honest men and hang up them.

Lady Macduff. Now. God help thee, poor monkey! But how wilt
thou do for a father?

Son. If he were dead, you'd weep for him. If you would not, it were
60 a good sign that I should quickly have a new father.

Lady Macduff. Poor prattler, how thou talk'st!
[*Enter a* Messenger.]

Messenger. Bless you, fair dame! I am not to you known,
Though in your state of honor I am perfect.[15]
I doubt[16] some danger does approach you nearly:
65 If you will take a homely[17] man's advice,
Be not found here; hence, with your little ones.
To fright you thus, methinks I am too savage;
To do worse to you were fell[18] cruelty,
Which is too nigh your person. Heaven preserve you!
I dare abide no longer.   [*Exit* Messenger.]

70 **Lady Macduff.**   Whither should I fly?
I have done no harm. But I remember now
I am in this earthly world, where to do harm
Is often laudable, to do good sometime
Accounted dangerous folly. Why then, alas,
75 Do I put up that womanly defense,
To say I have done no harm?—What are these faces?

[*Enter* Murderers.]

Murderer. Where is your husband?

Lady Macduff. I hope, in no place so unsanctified
Where such as thou mayst find him.

Murderer.   He's a traitor.

80 **Son.** Thou li'st, thou shag-eared[19] villain!

Murderer. What, you egg!

[*Stabbing him.*]

Young fry[20] of treachery!

Son. He has killed me, mother:
Run away, I pray you! [*Dies.*]

[*Exit* Lady Macduff *crying "Murder!" followed by* Murderers.]

⌘ ⌘ ⌘

Scene iii • *England. Before the King's palace.*

[*Enter* Malcolm *and* Macduff.]

Malcolm. Let us seek out some desolate shade, and there
Weep our sad bosoms empty.

Macduff. Let us rather
Hold fast the mortal sword, and like good men
Bestride our down-fall'n birthdom.[1] Each new morn
5 New widows howl, new orphans cry, new sorrows
Strike heaven on the face, that it resounds
As if it felt with Scotland and yelled out
Like syllable of dolor.[2]

Malcolm. What I believe, I'll wail;
What know, believe; and what I can redress.
10 As I shall find the time to friend, I will.
What you have spoke, it may be so perchance.
This tyrant, whose sole name blisters our tongues,
Was once thought honest: you have loved him well;
He hath not touched you yet. I am young; but something
15 You may deserve of him through me;[3] and wisdom[4]
To offer up a weak, poor, innocent lamb
T' appease an angry god.

Macduff. I am not treacherous.

Malcolm. But Macbeth is.
A good and virtuous nature may recoil
20 In an imperial charge. But I shall crave your pardon;
That which you are, my thoughts cannot transpose:
Angels are bright still, though the brightest[5] fell:
Though all things foul would wear[6] the brows of grace,
Yet grace must still look so.[7]

Macduff. I have lost my hopes.

25 **Malcolm.** Perchance even there where I did find my doubts.
Why in that rawness[8] left you wife and child,
Those precious motives, those strong knots of love,
Without leave-taking? I pray you,

NOTES

20. **fry** offspring.

1. **Bestride . . . birthdom** protectively stand over our native land.

2. **Like . . . dolor** similar cry of anguish.

3. **deserve . . . me** earn by betraying me to Macbeth.

4. **wisdom** It is wise.

treacherous (TREHCH uhr uhs) *adj.* guilty of deception or betrayal

5. **the brightest** Lucifer.
6. **would wear** desire to wear.
7. **so** like itself.

8. **rawness** unprotected state or condition.

9. **safeties** protections.

10. **affeered** legally confirmed.

11. **in my right** on behalf of my claim.

12. **England** king of England.

13. **sundry** various; miscellaneous.

14. **grafted** implanted.

15. **opened** in bloom.

16. **confineless harms** unbounded evils.

17. **Luxurious** lecherous.

avaricious (av uh RIHSH uhs) *adj.* greedy

18. **Sudden** violent.

19. **continent impediments** restraints.

20. **intemperance** lack of restraint.
21. **nature** man's nature.

Let not my jealousies be your dishonors.
30 But mine own safeties.[9] You may be rightly just
Whatever I shall think.

Macduff.   Bleed, bleed, poor country:
Great tyranny, lay thou thy basis sure,
For goodness dare not check thee: wear thou thy wrongs:
The title is affeered.[10] Fare thee well, lord:
35 I would not be the villain that thou think'st
For the whole space that's in the tyrant's grasp
And the rich East to boot.

Malcolm.   Be not offended:
I speak not as in absolute fear of you.
I think our country sinks beneath the yoke;
40 It weeps, it bleeds, and each new day a gash
Is added to her wounds. I think withal
There would be hands uplifted in my right;[11]
And here from gracious England[12] have I offer
Of goodly thousands: but, for all this,
45 When I shall tread upon the tyrant's head,
Or wear it on my sword, yet my poor country
Shall have more vices than it had before,
More suffer, and more sundry[13] ways than ever,
By him that shall succeed.

Macduff.   What should he be?

50 **Malcolm.** It is myself I mean, in whom I know
All the particulars of vice so grafted[14]
That, when they shall be opened,[15] black Macbeth
Will seem as pure as snow, and the poor state
Esteem him as a lamb, being compared
With my confineless harms.[16]

55 **Macduff.**   Not in the legions
Of horrid hell can come a devil more damned
In evils to top Macbeth.

Malcolm.   I grant him bloody,
Luxurious,[17] avaricious, false, deceitful,
Sudden,[18] malicious, smacking of every sin
60 That has a name: but there's no bottom, none,
In my voluptuousness: your wives, your daughters,
Your matrons and your maids, could not fill up
The cistern of my lust, and my desire
All continent impediments[19] would o'erbear,
65 That did oppose my will. Better Macbeth
Than such an one to reign.

Macduff.   Boundless intemperance[20]
In nature[21] is a tyranny; it hath been

Th' untimely emptying of the happy throne,
And fall of many kings. But fear not yet
70 To take upon you what is yours: you may
Convey[22] your pleasures in a spacious plenty.
And yet seem cold, the time you may so hoodwink.
We have willing dames enough. There cannot be
That vulture in you, to devour so many
75 As will to greatness dedicate themselves,
Finding it so inclined.

Malcolm.   With this there grows
In my most ill-composed affection[23] such
A stanchless[24] avarice that, were I King,
I should cut off the nobles for their lands.
80 Desire his jewels and this other's house:
And my more-having would be as a sauce
To make me hunger more, that I should forge
Quarrels unjust against the good and loyal,
Destroying them for wealth.

Macduff.   This avarice
85 Sticks deeper, grows with more pernicious root
Than summer-seeming[25] lust, and it hath been
The sword of[26] our slain kings. Yet do not fear.
Scotland hath foisons[27] to fill up your will
Of your mere own.[28] All these are portable,[29]
90 With other graces weighed.

Malcolm. But I have none: the king-becoming graces,
As justice, verity, temp'rance, stableness,
Bounty, perseverance, mercy, lowliness,
Devotion, patience, courage, fortitude,
95 I have no relish of them, but abound
In the division of each several crime,[30]
Acting it many ways. Nay, had I pow'r, I should
Pour the sweet milk of concord into hell,
Uproar the universal peace, confound[31]
All unity on earth.

100 **Macduff.**   O Scotland. Scotland!

Malcolm. If such a one be fit to govern, speak:
I am as I have spoken.

Macduff.   Fit to govern!
No, not to live. O nation miserable!
With an untitled[32] tyrant bloody-sceptered,
105 When shalt thou see thy wholesome days again,
Since that the truest issue of thy throne[33]
By his own interdiction[34] stands accursed,
And does blaspheme his breed?[35] Thy royal father
Was a most sainted king: the queen that bore thee,

NOTES

22. **Convey** secretly manage.

23. **affection** character.
24. **stanchless** never-ending.

25. **summer-seeming** summerlike.
26. **of** that killed.
27. **foisons** (FOY zuhnz) plenty.
28. **mere own** own property.
29. **portable** bearable.

30. **division . . . crime** variations of each kind of crime.

31. **confound** destroy.

32. **untitled** having no right to the throne.
33. **truest . . . throne** child of the true king.
34. **interdiction** exclusion.
35. **blaspheme his breed** slander his ancestry.

NOTES

36. Died prepared for heaven.

integrity (ihn TEHG ruh tee) *n.* moral uprightness

37. trains enticements.
38. modest wisdom prudence.

39. detraction slander.

40. For as.

41. at a point prepared.

42. the chance . . . quarrel May our chance of success equal the justice of our cause.

43. stay wait for.
44. convinces . . . art defies the efforts of medical science.

sanctity (SANGK tuh tee) *n.* holiness; goodness

45. presently amend immediately recover.

46. evil scrofula (SKROF yuh luh), skin disease called "the king's evil" because it was believed that it could be cured by the king's touch.

---

110 Oft'ner upon her knees than on her feet,
Died³⁶ every day she lived. Fare thee well!
These evils thou repeat'st upon thyself
Hath banished me from Scotland. O my breast,
Thy hope ends here!

Malcolm.   Macduff, this noble passion,
115 Child of integrity, hath from my soul
Wiped the black scruples, reconciled my thoughts
To thy good truth and honor. Devilish Macbeth
By many of these trains³⁷ hath sought to win me
Into his power; and modest wisdom³⁸ plucks me
120 From over-credulous haste: but God above
Deal between thee and me! For even now
I put myself to thy direction, and
Unspeak mine own detraction,³⁹ here abjure
The taints and blames I laid upon myself,
125 For⁴⁰ strangers to my nature. I am yet
Unknown to woman, never was forsworn,
Scarcely have coveted what was mine own,
At no time broke my faith, would not betray
The devil to his fellow, and delight
130 No less in truth than life. My first false speaking
Was this upon myself. What I am truly,
Is thine and my poor country's to command:
Whither indeed, before thy here-approach,
Old Siward, with ten thousand warlike men,
135 Already at a point,⁴¹ was setting forth.
Now we'll together, and the chance of goodness
Be like our warranted quarrel!⁴² Why are you silent?

Macduff. Such welcome and unwelcome things at once
'Tis hard to reconcile.

[*Enter a* Doctor.]

140 **Malcolm.** Well, more anon. Comes the King forth, I pray you?

Doctor. Ay, sir. There are a crew of wretched souls
That stay⁴³ his cure: their malady convinces
The great assay of art;⁴⁴ but at his touch,
Such sanctity hath heaven given his hand,
They presently amend.⁴⁵

145 **Malcolm.**   I thank you, doctor.

[*Exit* Doctor.]

Macduff. What's the disease he means?

Malcolm.   'Tis called the evil:⁴⁶
A most miraculous work in this good King,
Which often since my here-remain in England
I have seen him do. How he solicits heaven,

150 Himself best knows: but strangely-visited people,
All swoll'n and ulcerous, pitiful to the eye,
The mere[47] despair of surgery, he cures,
Hanging a golden stamp[48] about their necks,
Put on with holy prayers: and 'tis spoken,
155 To the succeeding royalty he leaves
The healing benediction. With this strange virtue
He hath a heavenly gift of prophecy,
And sundry blessings hang about his throne
That speak him full of grace.

[*Enter* Ross.]

Macduff.   See, who comes here?

160 **Malcolm.** My countryman; but yet I know him not.

Macduff. My ever gentle[49] cousin, welcome hither.

Malcolm. I know him now: good God, betimes[50] remove
The means that makes us strangers!

Ross.   Sir, amen.

Macduff. Stands Scotland where it did?

Ross.   Alas, poor country!
165 Almost afraid to know itself! It cannot
Be called our mother but our grave, where nothing[51]
But who knows nothing is once seen to smile;
Where sighs and groans, and shrieks that rent the air,
Are made, not marked, where violent sorrow seems
170 A modern ecstasy.[52] The dead man's knell
Is there scarce asked for who,[53] and good men's lives
Expire before the flowers in their caps.
Dying or ere they sicken.

Macduff.   O, relation
Too nice,[54] and yet too true!

Malcolm.   What's the newest grief?

175 **Ross.** That of an hour's age doth hiss the speaker;[55]
Each minute teems[56] a new one.

Macduff.   How does my wife?

Ross. Why, well.

Macduff.   And all my children?

Ross.   Well too.

Macduff. The tyrant has not battered at their peace?

Ross. No; they were well at peace when I did leave 'em.

180 **Macduff.** Be not a niggard of your speech: how goes 't?

Ross. When I came hither to transport the tidings,
Which I have heavily borne, there ran a rumor

NOTES

47. **mere** utter.
48. **stamp** coin.

49. **gentle** noble.
50. **betimes** quickly.

51. **nothing** no one.

52. **modern ecstasy** ordinary emotion.
53. **The dead . . . who** People can no longer keep track of Macbeth's victims.

54. **nice** exact.

55. **That . . . speaker** Report of the grief of an hour ago is hissed as stale news.
56. **teems** gives birth to.

57. **out** in rebellion.
58. **witnessed** confirmed.
59. **power** army.
60. **doff** put off.

Of many worthy fellows that were out;[57]
Which was to my belief witnessed[58] the rather,
185 For that I saw the tyrant's power[59] afoot.
Now is the time of help. Your eye in Scotland
Would create soldiers, make our women fight,
To doff[60] their dire distresses.

Malcolm.   Be 't their comfort
We are coming thither. Gracious England hath
190 Lent us good Siward and ten thousand men;
An older and a better soldier none
That Christendom gives out.

Ross.   Would I could answer
This comfort with the like! But I have words
That would be howled out in the desert air,
Where hearing should not latch[61] them.

195 **Macduff.**   What concern they?
The general cause or is it a fee-grief[62]
Due to some single breast?

Ross.   No mind that's honest
But in it shares some woe, though the main part
Pertains to you alone.

Macduff.   If it be mine,
200 Keep it not from me, quickly let me have it.

Ross. Let not your ears despise my tongue for ever,
Which shall possess them with the heaviest sound
That ever yet they heard.

Macduff.   Humh! I guess at it.

Ross. Your castle is surprised; your wife and babes
205 Savagely slaughtered. To relate the manner,
Were, on the quarry[63] of these murdered deer,
To add the death of you.

Malcolm.   Merciful heaven!
What, man! Ne'er pull your hat upon your brows;
Give sorrow words. The grief that does not speak

210 Whispers the o'er-fraught[64] heart and bids it break.

Macduff. My children too?

Ross.   Wife, children, servants, all
That could be found.

Macduff.   And I must be from thence!
My wife killed too?

Ross.   I have said.

Malcolm.   Be comforted.
Let's make us med'cines of our great revenge,
215 To cure this deadly grief.

Macduff. He has no children. All my pretty ones?
Did you say all? O hell-kite![65] All?
What, all my pretty chickens and their dam
At one fell swoop?

Malcolm. Dispute it[66] like a man.

220 **Macduff.**   I shall do so;
But I must also feel it as a man.
I cannot but remember such things were,
That were most precious to me. Did heaven look on,
And would not take their part? Sinful Macduff,

225 They were all struck for thee! Naught[67] that I am.
Not for their own demerits but for mine
Fell slaughter on their souls. Heaven rest them now!

Malcolm. Be this the whetstone of your sword. Let grief
Convert to anger; blunt not the heart, enrage it.

230 **Macduff.** O, I could play the woman with mine eyes,
And braggart with my tongue! But, gentle heavens,
Cut short all intermission; front to front[68]
Bring thou this fiend of Scotland and myself;
Within my sword's length set him. If he 'scape,

235 Heaven forgive him too!

Malcolm.   This time goes manly.
Come, go we to the King. Our power is ready;
Our lack is nothing but our leave.[69] Macbeth
Is ripe for shaking, and the pow'rs above
Put on their instruments.[70] Receive what cheer you may.

240 The night is long that never finds the day.   [*Exit.*]

NOTES

CLOSE READ
ANNOTATE: Mark the word that Macduff repeats in lines 216–219.

QUESTION: Why does he repeat the word?

CONCLUDE: How does this repetition suggest the intensity of both Macduff's disbelief and his grief?

65. **hell-kite** hellish bird of prey.

66. **Dispute it** Counter your grief.

67. **Naught** wicked.

68. **front to front** face to face.

69. **Our . . . leave** We need only to take our leave.

70. **Put . . . instruments** urge us onward as their agents.

Comprehension Check

Complete the following items after you finish your first read.

1. As the witches complete their brew, how do they know that someone is coming?

2. Why is Lady Macduff angry with her husband?

3. What do Macduff and Malcolm resolve to do at the end of Act IV?

4. 🖻 **Notebook** Confirm your understanding of the text by writing a summary of Act IV.

- -

RESEARCH

Research to Clarify Choose at least one unfamiliar detail from the text. Briefly research that detail. In what way does the information you learned shed light on an aspect of the play?

Research to Explore Find out more about weapons and armaments used in Scotland and the rest of Europe during the eleventh century, which is the time setting for *The Tragedy of Macbeth*.

Close Read the Text

Reread Act IV, Scene i, of the play. Find and mark the prophecies that you think are most reassuring to Macbeth. Do you think Macbeth is wise to trust the witches?

THE TRAGEDY OF MACBETH, ACT IV

Analyze the Text

CITE TEXTUAL EVIDENCE to support your answers.

📖 **Notebook** Respond to these questions.

1. (a) What resolution does Macbeth make in Scene i, lines 151–153? (b) **Interpret** What change does this resolution indicate in the way Macbeth will handle decisions in the future?

2. (a) What idea is Ross expressing in Scene ii, lines 18–22? (b) **Make Inferences** Does Ross believe what he tells Lady Macduff? Explain.

3. (a) How does Malcolm test Macduff? (b) **Analyze** What does this test reveal about them both?

LANGUAGE DEVELOPMENT

Concept Vocabulary

pernicious	treacherous	integrity
laudable	avaricious	sanctity

Why These Words? These concept words relate to the ideas of right and wrong. For example, Lady Macbeth remarks on the irony that in this world committing evil acts may be *laudable*, or worthy of praise. Find two other words in Act IV that relate to the concept of right and wrong.

Word Study

Antonyms Shakespeare uses **antonyms**, words with opposing meanings, to indicate character traits. In Scene iii, Malcolm confesses to being *avaricious* and to lacking "king-becoming graces." He places himself in contrast with Macduff, who is a "child of *integrity*," or a morally upright man. The scene proceeds with Malcolm recanting his previous self-criticism. The entire scene is a compilation of synonyms and antonyms, as Malcolm embraces virtue, having previously accused himself of being steeped in vice.

Reread Act IV, Scene iii, and note three other adjectives Shakespeare uses. Use a thesaurus to research their connotations and denotations. Write the words here, as well as an antonym for each of them.

🔗 **WORD NETWORK**

Add interesting words related to time from the text to your Word Network.

📋 **STANDARDS**

Reading Literature
Cite strong and thorough textual evidence to support analysis of what the text says explicitly as well as inferences drawn from the text, including determining where the text leaves matters uncertain.

Language
• Consult general and specialized reference materials, both print and digital, to find the pronunciation of a word or determine or clarify its precise meaning, its part of speech, its etymology, or its standard usage.
• Demonstrate understanding of figurative language, word relationships, and nuances in word meanings.

THE TRAGEDY OF MACBETH, ACT IV

Analyze Craft and Structure

Imagery and Archetypes **Imagery** is the language that writers use to capture sensory experiences and stimulate emotions. It is what helps readers experience events—to see, hear, feel, smell, and taste, them—rather than just read or listen to words. Shakespeare uses imagery to pack sensory experiences and strong emotions into almost every line. In *The Tragedy of Macbeth*, he returns to certain images repeatedly throughout the play. These include the following broad categories:

- blood
- ill-fitting clothes
- babies and children, who may be Macbeth's victims or figures he finds threatening

This repeated imagery reinforces important themes in the play. The last group of images suggests that Macbeth is in some way warring against the future, which babies and children represent.

Some images are powerful because they are **archetypal.** They relate to ideas and emotions expressed by people in all times and cultures. In Act IV, for example, images of banishment from the world of the living—shrieking, groaning, and bleeding—indicate that Macbeth's Scotland represents an underworld region where the dead are punished.

Characters are often archetypes, as well. The witches are archetypes of evil, since they have no redeeming features. They are hideous inside and out. Macduff is another archetype—the avenging hero who vows to defeat the flawed protagonist, Macbeth.

STANDARDS

Reading Literature
Analyze the impact of the author's choices regarding how to develop and relate elements of a story or drama.

Practice

CITE TEXTUAL EVIDENCE to support your answers.

Notebook Respond to these questions.

1. **(a)** In what way is Banquo an archetype? **(b)** Why is Macbeth so upset at the image of Banquo shown to him by the witches?
2. **(a)** In Act IV, Scene iii, identify two archetypal images of banishment from an ideal world. **(b)** Which image do you find more compelling? Why?
3. **(a)** Use the chart to record at least two examples of each type of imagery in Act IV. **(b)** Explain how each pattern of imagery you identified relates to a thematic idea—a message or insight into life or the human condition that the play conveys.

IMAGERY	EXAMPLE FROM MACBETH	CONNECTION TO THEME
Blood		
Children		
Darkness		
Weeping		

Conventions and Style

Exclamatory Phrases Shakespeare uses exclamatory phrases throughout the play. Phrases like "Woe, alas" and "Fie, for shame!" express strong emotion and call attention to significant moments in the play. They are extreme reactions to extreme events, and they are usually indicated by the presence of an exclamation mark. Act IV abounds in heartfelt expressions of emotion that convey fear and horror. Note Macduff's speech in Act IV, Scene iii, when he exclaims, "Fit to govern! / No, not to live. O nation miserable!" The words burst out, almost as if Macduff cannot control his tongue.

Look for these exclamatory phrases in Act IV. Use this chart to indicate the reason for each exclamation.

SCENE AND LINE	EXCLAMATION	REASON
Scene i, line 112	"Down!"	
Scene ii, line 80	"Thou li'st, thou shag-eared villain!"	
Scene iii, line 31	"Bleed, bleed, poor country: . . ."	
Scene iii, line 100	"O Scotland. Scotland!"	

Read It

1. Reread Scene iii. Look for exclamation marks that indicate possible exclamatory phrases. Note the situation in which the exclamation is made.
2. **Connect to Style** Choose a line from Scene iv that contains an exclamation. Rewrite the line as an ordinary statement that expresses the same thought. What effect is created by the rewrite? Is it more effective or less effective than the original? Explain.

Write It

📝 Notebook Write some lines of verse that contain exclamatory phrases. Experiment with using iambic pentameter. Your verse may be original or retell a moment from the play from a different character's point of view.

▤ STANDARDS

Reading Literature
Analyze the impact of the author's choices regarding how to develop and relate elements of a story or drama.

Language
Apply knowledge of language to understand how language functions in different contexts, to make effective choices for meaning or style, and to comprehend more fully when reading or listening.

Playwright

William Shakespeare

The Tragedy of Macbeth, Act V

Concept Vocabulary

You will encounter the following words as you read Act V of *The Tragedy of Macbeth*. Before reading, note how familiar you are with each word. Then, rank the words in order from most familiar (1) to least familiar (6).

WORD	YOUR RANKING
perturbation	
agitation	
purge	
antidote	
pristine	
usurper	

After completing the first read, come back to the concept vocabulary and review your rankings. Mark changes to your original rankings as needed.

First Read DRAMA

Apply these strategies as you conduct your first read. You will have an opportunity to complete the close-read notes after your first read.

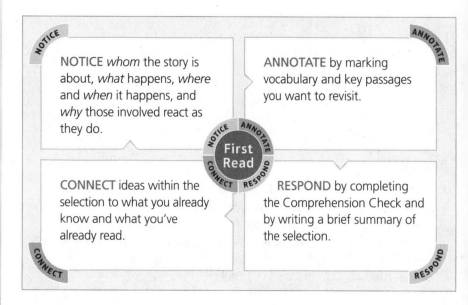

NOTICE *whom* the story is about, *what* happens, *where* and *when* it happens, and *why* those involved react as they do.

ANNOTATE by marking vocabulary and key passages you want to revisit.

First Read

CONNECT ideas within the selection to what you already know and what you've already read.

RESPOND by completing the Comprehension Check and by writing a brief summary of the selection.

🔧 Tool Kit
First-Read Guide and Model Annotation

STANDARDS
Reading Literature
By the end of grade 12, read and comprehend literature, including stories, dramas, and poems, at the high end of the grades 11–CCR text complexity band independently and proficiently.

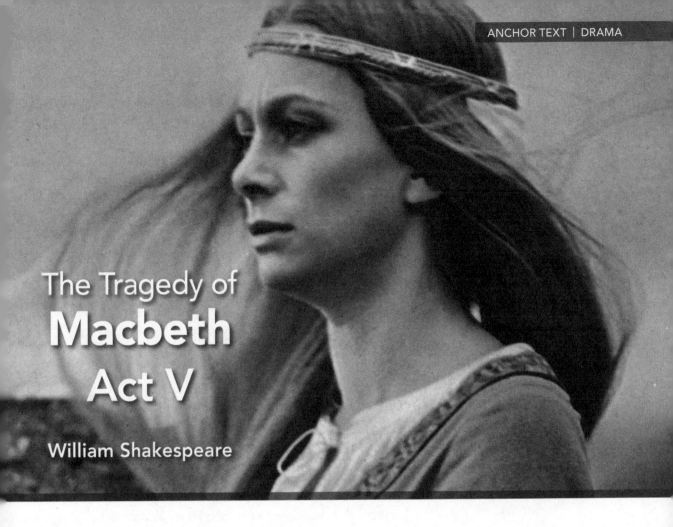

The Tragedy of **Macbeth** Act V

William Shakespeare

REVIEW AND ANTICIPATE

In Act IV, Macbeth learns from the witches that he must "Beware Macduff!" but that he need not fear any man "of woman born." He also learns he will never be vanquished until Birnam Wood comes to Dunsinane. However, he sees a vision indicating that Banquo will indeed father a long line of kings.

Armed with his new knowledge, Macbeth orders the murder of Macduff's wife and son. Macduff himself is in forces with Malcolm and is overcome when he hears the news. Nevertheless, he and Malcolm will lead an army against Macbeth.

Act V will determine the outcome as Macbeth, grown reckless in evil, battles Malcolm and his men.

Scene i • *Dunsinane. In the castle.*

NOTES

[*Enter a* Doctor of Physic *and a* Waiting-Gentlewoman.]

Doctor. I have two nights watched with you, but can perceive no truth in your report. When was it she last walked?

Gentlewoman. Since his Majesty went into the field.[1] I have seen her rise from her bed, throw her nightgown upon her,
5 unlock her closet,[2] take forth paper, fold it, write upon 't, read it, afterwards seal it, and again return to bed; yet all this while in a most fast sleep.

1. **field** battlefield.

2. **closet** chest.

perturbation (puhr tuhr BAY shuhn)
n. disturbance

3. effects of watching, deeds of
one awake.

agitation (aj uh TAY shuhn) *n.* state
of nervous anxiety

4. meet suitable.

5. guise custom.
6. close hidden.

7. sense power of sight.

8. satisfy support.

9. to accompt into account.

CLOSE READ

ANNOTATE: In lines 29–59, mark
details that relate to being soiled
or unclean. Mark other details
that relate to fear.

QUESTION: With what emotions
does Lady Macbeth seem to be
struggling in her sleep?

CONCLUDE: How does this
scene add to the readers'
understanding of Lady Macbeth's
character?

Doctor. A great **perturbation** in nature, to receive at
once the benefit of sleep and do the effects of watching![3]

10 In this slumb'ry **agitation**, besides her walking, and
other actual performances, what, at any time, have you
heard her say?

Gentlewoman. That, sir, which I will not report after her.

Doctor. You may to me, and 'tis most meet[4] you should.

15 **Gentlewoman.** Neither to you nor anyone, having no witness to
confirm my speech.

[*Enter* Lady Macbeth, *with a taper.*]

Lo you, here she comes! This is her very guise,[5] and, upon my
life, fast asleep! Observe her; stand close.[6]

Doctor. How came she by that light?

20 **Gentlewoman.** Why, it stood by her. She has light by her
continually. 'Tis her command.

Doctor. You see, her eyes are open.

Gentlewoman. Ay, but their sense[7] are shut.

Doctor. What is it she does now? Look, how she rubs
25 her hands.

Gentlewoman. It is an accustomed action with her,
to seem thus washing her hands; I have known her
continue in this a quarter of an hour.

Lady Macbeth. Yet here's a spot.

30 **Doctor.** Hark! She speaks. I will set down what comes
from her, to satisfy[8] my remembrance the more strongly.

Lady Macbeth. Out, damned spot! Out, I say! One: two:
why, then 'tis time to do 't. Hell is murky. Fie, my
lord, fie! A soldier, and afeard? What need we fear
35 who knows it, when none can call our pow'r to
accompt?[9] Yet who would have thought the old man
to have had so much blood in him?

Doctor. Do you mark that?

Lady Macbeth. The Thane of Fife had a wife. Where is
40 she now? What, will these hands ne'er be clean? No
more o' that, my lord, no more o' that! You mar all
with this starting.

Doctor. Go to, go to! You have known what you should not.

Gentlewoman. She has spoke what she should not, I am
45 sure of that. Heaven knows what she has known.

Lady Macbeth. Here's the smell of the blood still. All the
perfumes of Arabia will not sweeten this little hand.
Oh, oh, oh!

Doctor. What a sigh is there! The heart is sorely charged.[10]

50 **Gentlewoman.** I would not have such a heart in my bosom for the dignity[11] of the whole body.

Doctor. Well, well, well—

Gentlewoman. Pray God it be, sir.

Doctor. This disease is beyond my practice. Yet I have
55 known those which have walked in their sleep who have died holily in their beds.

Lady Macbeth. Wash your hands; put on your nightgown; look not so pale! I tell you yet again, Banquo's buried. He cannot come out on 's[12] grave.

60 **Doctor.** Even so?

Lady Macbeth. To bed, to bed! There's knocking at the gate. Come, come, come, come, give me your hand! What's done cannot be undone. To bed, to bed, to bed!

[*Exit* Lady Macbeth.]

Doctor. Will she go now to bed?

65 **Gentlewoman.** Directly.

Doctor. Foul whisp'rings are abroad. Unnatural deeds
Do breed unnatural troubles. Infected minds
To their deaf pillows will discharge their secrets.
More needs she the divine than the physician.
70 God, God forgive us all! Look after her;
Remove from her the means of all annoyance,[13]
And still keep eyes upon her. So good night.
My mind she has mated[14] and amazed my sight:
I think, but dare not speak.

Gentlewoman. Good night, good doctor.

[*Exit.*]

⌘ ⌘ ⌘

Scene ii • *The country near Dunsinane.*

[*Drum and colors. Ente*r Menteith, Caithness, Angus, Lennox, Soldiers.]

Menteith. The English pow'r[1] is near, led on by Malcolm.
His uncle Siward and the good Macduff.
Revenges burn in them; for their dear causes
Would to the bleeding and the grim alarm
5 Excite the mortified man.[2]

Angus. Near Birnam Wood
Shall we well meet them; that way are they coming.

NOTES

10. **charged** burdened.

11. **dignity** worth.

12. **on 's** of his.

13. **annoyance** injury.

14. **mated** baffled.

1. **pow'r** army.

2. **Would . . . man** would incite a dead man to join the bloody, grim call to arms.

NOTES

3. **file** list.
4. **unrough** beardless.
5. **Protest** assert.

6. **rule** self-control.

7. **minutely . . . faith-breach** every minute revolts rebuke his disloyalty.

8. **pestered** tormented.

9. **med'cine . . . weal** Malcolm and his supporters are "the medicine" that will heal "the sickly" commonwealth.

purge (purj) *n.* ousting; removal

10. **Each . . . us** every last drop of our blood.

11. **dew . . . weeds** water the royal flower (Malcolm) and drown the weeds (Macbeth).

Caithness. Who knows if Donalbain be with his brother?

Lennox. For certain, sir, he is not. I have a file[3]
Of all the gentry: there is Siward's son,
10 And many unrough[4] youths that even now
Protest[5] their first of manhood.

Menteith.   What does the tyrant?

Caithness. Great Dunsinane he strongly fortifies.
Some say he's mad; others, that lesser hate him,
Do call it valiant fury: but, for certain,
15 He cannot buckle his distempered cause
Within the belt of rule.[6]

Angus.   Now does he feel
His secret murders sticking on his hands;
Now minutely revolts upbraid his faith-breach.[7]
Those he commands move only in command,
20 Nothing in love. Now does he feel his title
Hang loose about him, like a giant's robe
Upon a dwarfish thief.

Menteith.   Who then shall blame
His pestered[8] senses to recoil and start,
When all that is within him does condemn
25 Itself for being there?

Caithness.   Well, march we on,
To give obedience where 'tis truly owed.
Meet we the med'cine of the sickly weal,[9]
And with him pour we, in our country's **purge**,
Each drop of us.[10]

Lennox.   Or so much as it needs
30 To dew the sovereign flower and drown the weeds.[11]
Make we our march towards Birnam.   [*Exit, marching.*]

⌘ ⌘ ⌘

Scene iii • *Dunsinane. In the castle.*

[*Enter* Macbeth, Doctor, *and* Attendants.]

Macbeth. Bring me no more reports; let them fly all![1]
Till Birnam Wood remove to Dunsinane
I cannot taint[2] with fear. What's the boy Malcolm?
Was he not born of woman? The spirits that know
5 All mortal consequences[3] have pronounced me thus:
"Fear not, Macbeth; no man that's born of woman
Shall e'er have power upon thee." Then fly, false thanes,
And mingle with the English epicures.[4]
The mind I sway[5] by and the heart I bear

---

1. **let . . . all** let them all desert me!

2. **taint** become infected.

3. **mortal consequences** future human events.

4. **epicures** gluttons.

5. **sway** move.

10 Shall never sag with doubt nor shake with fear.

[*Enter* Servant.]

The devil damn thee black, thou cream-faced loon.[6]
Where got'st thou that goose look?

Servant. There is ten thousand—

Macbeth.   Geese, villain?

Servant.   Soldiers, sir.

Macbeth. Go prick thy face and over-red thy fear.
15 Thou lily-livered boy. What soldiers, patch?[7]
Death of thy soul! Those linen[8] cheeks of thine
Are counselors to fear. What soldiers, whey-face?

Servant. The English force, so please you.

Macbeth. Take thy face hence.   [*Exit* Servant.]

                         Seyton!—I am sick at heart.
20 When I behold—Seyton, I say!—This push[9]
Will cheer me ever, or disseat[10] me now.
I have lived long enough. My way of life
Is fall'n into the sear,[11] the yellow leaf,
And that which should accompany old age,
25 As honor, love, obedience, troops of friends,
I must not look to have; but, in their stead,
Curses not loud but deep, mouth-honor, breath,
Which the poor heart would fain deny, and dare not.
Seyton!

[*Enter* Seyton.]

30 **Seyton.** What's your gracious pleasure?

Macbeth.   What news more?

Seyton. All is confirmed, my lord, which was reported.

Macbeth. I'll fight, till from my bones my flesh be hacked.
Give me my armor.

Seyton.   'Tis not needed yet.

Macbeth. I'll put it on.
35 Send out moe[12] horses, skirr[13] the country round.
Hang those that talk of fear. Give me mine armor.
How does your patient, doctor?

Doctor.   Not so sick, my lord,
As she is troubled with thick-coming fancies
That keep her from her rest.

Macbeth.   Cure her of that.
40 Canst thou not minister to a mind diseased,
Pluck from the memory a rooted sorrow,
Raze out[14] the written troubles of the brain,
And with some sweet oblivious **antidote**

NOTES

6. **loon** fool.

7. **patch** fool.
8. **linen** pale as linen.

9. **push** effort.
10. **disseat** dethrone.

11. **the sear** withered state.

12. **moe** more.
13. **skirr** scour.

14. **Raze out** erase.

antidote (AN tuh doht) *n.* remedy

Cleanse the stuffed bosom of that perilous stuff
45 Which weighs upon the heart?

Doctor.   Therein the patient
Must minister to himself.

15. physic medicine.

Macbeth. Throw physic[15] to the dogs. I'll none of it.
Come, put mine armor on. Give me my staff.
Seyton, send out.—Doctor, the thanes fly from me.—
50 Come, sir, dispatch. If thou couldst, doctor, cast

16. cast the water diagnose the illness.

pristine (prihs TEEN) *adj.* original; unspoiled

The water[16] of my land, find her disease
And purge it to a sound and pristine health,
I would applaud thee to the very echo,
That should applaud again.—Pull 't off,[17] I say.—

17. Pull 't off Pull off a piece of armor, which has been put on incorrectly in Macbeth's haste.

55 What rhubarb, senna, or what purgative drug,
Would scour these English hence? Hear'st thou of them?

Doctor. Ay, my good lord; your royal preparation
Makes us hear something.

18. it his armor.
19. bane destruction.

Macbeth.   Bring it[18] after me.
I will not be afraid of death and bane[19]
60 Till Birnam Forest come to Dunsinane.

Doctor. [*Aside*] Were I from Dunsinane away and clear,
Profit again should hardly draw me here.   [*Exit.*]

⌘ ⌘ ⌘

Scene iv • *Country near Birnam Wood.*

[*Drum and colors. Enter* Malcolm, Siward, Macduff, Siward's Son, Menteith, Caithness, Angus, *and* Soldiers, *marching.*]

Malcolm. Cousins, I hope the days are near at hand
That chambers will be safe.[1]

1. That . . . safe that people will be safe in their own homes.

Menteith.   We doubt it nothing.

Siward. What wood is this before us?

Menteith.   The Wood of Birnam.

Malcolm. Let every soldier hew him down a bough
5 And bear't before him. Thereby shall we shadow[2]
The numbers of our host. and make discovery[3]
Err in report of us.

2. shadow conceal.
3. discovery those who see us.

Soldiers.   It shall be done.

Siward. We learn no other but the confident tyrant
Keeps still in Dunsinane, and will endure
10 Our setting down before 't.[4]

4. setting down before 't laying siege to it.

Malcolm.   'Tis his main hope,

For where there is advantage to be given
Both more and less[5] have given him the revolt,
And none serve with him but constrained things
Whose hearts are absent too.

Macduff.   Let our just censures
15 Attend the true event,[6] and put we on
Industrious soldiership.

Siward.   The time approaches,
That will with due decision make us know
What we shall say we have and what we owe.[7]
Thoughts speculative their unsure hopes relate,
20 But certain issue strokes must arbitrate;[8]
Towards which advance the war.[9]   [*Exit, marching.*]

⌘ ⌘ ⌘

Scene v • *Dunsinane. Within the castle.*

[*Enter* Macbeth, Seyton, *and* Soldiers, *with drum and colors.*]

Macbeth. Hang out our banners on the outward walls.
The cry is still "They come!" Our castle's strength
Will laugh a siege to scorn. Here let them lie
Till famine and the ague[1] eat them up.
5 Were they not forced[2] with those that should be ours,
We might have met them dareful,[3] beard to beard,
And beat them backward home.
          [*A cry within of women.*]
                    What is that noise?

Seyton. It is the cry of women, my good lord.   [*Exit.*]

Macbeth. I have almost forgot the taste of fears:
10 The time has been, my senses would have cooled
To hear a night-shriek, and my fell[4] of hair
Would at a dismal treatise[5] rouse and stir
As life were in 't. I have supped full with horrors.
Direness, familiar to my slaughterous thoughts,
15 Cannot once start[6] me.

[*Enter* Seyton.]

                    Wherefore was that cry?

Seyton. The queen, my lord, is dead.

Macbeth. She should[7] have died hereafter;
There would have been a time for such a word.[8]
Tomorrow, and tomorrow, and tomorrow
20 Creeps in this petty pace from day to day,
To the last syllable of recorded time;
And all our yesterdays have lighted fools

NOTES

5. **more and less** people of high and low rank.

6. **our . . . event** true judgment await the actual outcome.

7. **owe** own.

8. **strokes . . . arbitrate** fighting must decide.
9. **war** army.

1. **ague** fever.
2. **forced** reinforced.
3. **dareful** boldly.

4. **fell** scalp.
5. **treatise** story.

6. **start** startle.

7. **should** inevitably would.
8. **word** message.

ANNOTATE: In lines 17–28, mark details that relate to the ideas of foolishness or futility.

QUESTION: Why does Macbeth pause to make this statement?

CONCLUDE: What does this speech suggest about Macbeth's view of what he has done—and, perhaps, what he will do?

9. **cling** wither.
10. **sooth** truth.

11. **avouches** asserts.

12. **harness** armor.

1. **leavy** leafy.

The way to dusty death. Out, out, brief candle!
Life's but a walking shadow, a poor player
25 That struts and frets his hour upon the stage
And then is heard no more. It is a tale
Told by an idiot, full of sound and fury
Signifying nothing.

[*Enter a* Messenger.]

Thou com'st to use thy tongue: thy story quickly!

30 **Messenger.** Gracious my lord,
I should report that which I say I saw,
But know not how to do 't.

Macbeth.   Well, say, sir.

Messenger. As I did stand my watch upon the hill,
I looked toward Birnam, and anon, methought,
35 The wood began to move.

Macbeth.   Liar and slave!

Messenger. Let me endure your wrath, if 't be not so.
Within this three mile may you see it coming;
I say a moving grove.

Macbeth.   If thou speak'st false,
Upon the next tree shalt thou hang alive,
40 Till famine cling[9] thee. If thy speech be sooth,[10]
I care not if thou dost for me as much.
I pull in resolution, and begin
To doubt th' equivocation of the fiend
That lies like truth: "Fear not, till Birnam Wood
45 Do come to Dunsinane!" And now a wood
Comes toward Dunsinane. Arm, arm, and out!
If this which he avouches[11] does appear,
There is nor flying hence nor tarrying here.
I 'gin to be aweary of the sun,
50 And wish th' estate o' th' world were now undone.
Ring the alarum bell! Blow wind, come wrack!
At least we'll die with harness[12] on our back.   [*Exit.*]

⌘ ⌘ ⌘

Scene vi • *Dunsinane. Before the castle.*

[*Drum and colors. Enter* Malcolm, Siward, Macduff, *and their* Army, *with boughs.*]

Malcolm. Now near enough. Your leavy[1] screens throw down,
And show like those you are. You, worthy uncle,
Shall, with my cousin, your right noble son,

Lead our first battle.[2] Worthy Macduff and we
5 Shall take upon 's what else remains to do,
According to our order.[3]

Siward.   Fare you well.
Do we find the tyrant's power[4] tonight.
Let us be beaten, if we cannot fight.

Macduff. Make all our trumpets speak; give them all breath
10 Those clamorous harbingers of blood and death.

[Exit. Alarums continued.]

⌘ ⌘ ⌘

Scene vii • *Another part of the field.*

[Enter Macbeth.]

Macbeth. They have tied me to a stake; I cannot fly,
But bearlike I must fight the course.[1] What's he
That was not born of woman? Such a one
Am I to fear, or none.

[Enter Young Siward.]

Young Siward. What is thy name?

5 **Macbeth.**   Thou'lt be afraid to hear it.

Young Siward. No: though thou call'st thyself a hotter name
Than any is in hell.

Macbeth.   My name's Macbeth.

Young Siward. The devil himself could not pronounce a title
More hateful to mine ear.

Macbeth.   No, nor more fearful.

10 **Young Siward.** Thou liest, abhorred tyrant; with my sword
I'll prove the lie thou speak'st.

[Fight, and Young Siward *slain.]*

Macbeth.   Thou wast born of woman.
But swords I smile at, weapons laugh to scorn,
Brandished by man that's of a woman born.   *[Exit.]*

[Alarums. Enter Macduff.]

Macduff. That way the noise is. Tyrant, show thy face!
15 If thou be'st slain and with no stroke of mine,
My wife and children's ghosts will haunt me still.
I cannot strike at wretched kerns, whose arms
Are hired to bear their staves.[2] Either thou, Macbeth,
Or else my sword, with an unbattered edge,
20 I sheathe again undeeded.[3] There thou shouldst be;
By this great clatter, one of greatest note

NOTES

2. **battle** battalion.
3. **order** plan.

4. **power** forces.

1. **bearlike . . . course** like a bear chained to a stake being attacked by dogs, I must fight until the end.

2. **staves** spears.

3. **undeeded** unused.

^ Macduff and Macbeth battle each other.

NOTES

4. **bruited** reported.

5. **gently rend'red** easily surrendered.

6. **strike . . . us** deliberately miss us.

Seems bruited.[4] Let me find him, Fortune!
And more I beg not.   [*Exit. Alarums.*]

[*Enter* Malcolm *and* Siward.]

Siward. This way, my lord. The castle's gently rend'red:[5]
25 The tyrant's people on both sides do fight;
The noble thanes do bravely in the war;
The day almost itself professes yours,
And little is to do.

Malcolm.   We have met with foes
That strike beside us.[6]

30 **Siward.** Enter, sir, the castle.   [*Exit. Alarum.*]

⌘ ⌘ ⌘

Scene viii • *Another part of the field.*

[*Enter* Macbeth.]

Macbeth. Why should I play the Roman fool, and die
On mine own sword?[1] Whiles I see lives,[2] the gashes
Do better upon them.

1. **play . . . sword** die like Brutus and Cassius, who killed themselves with their own swords in the moment of defeat.

2. **Whiles . . . lives** so long as I see living men.

[*Enter* Macduff.]

Macduff.   Turn, hell-hound, turn!

Macbeth. Of all men else I have avoided thee.

5 But get thee back! My soul is too much charged
With blood of thine already.

Macduff.   I have no words:
My voice is in my sword, thou bloodier villain
Than terms can give thee out!³

                         [*Fight. Alarum.*]

Macbeth.   Thou losest labor:
As easy mayst thou the intrenchant⁴ air
10 With thy keen sword impress⁵ as make me bleed:
Let fall thy blade on vulnerable crests;
I bear a charmed life, which must not yield
To one of woman born.

Macduff.   Despair thy charm,
And let the angel⁶ whom thou still hast served
15 Tell thee, Macduff was from his mother's womb
Untimely ripped.⁷

Macbeth. Accursèd be that tongue that tells me so,
For it hath cowed my better part of man!⁸
And be these juggling fiends no more believed,
20 That palter⁹ with us in a double sense;
That keep the word of promise to our ear,
And break it to our hope. I'll not fight with thee.

Macduff. Then yield thee, coward,
And live to be the show and gaze o' th' time:¹⁰
25 We'll have thee, as our rarer monsters¹¹ are,
Painted upon a pole,¹² and underwrit,
"Here may you see the tyrant."

Macbeth.   I will not yield,
To kiss the ground before young Malcolm's feet.
And to be baited with the rabble's curse.
30 Though Birnam Wood be come to Dunsinane,
And thou opposed, being of no woman born,
Yet I will try the last. Before my body
I throw my warlike shield. Lay on, Macduff;
And damned be him that first cries "Hold, enough!"

                    [*Exit, fighting. Alarums.*]

[*Re-enter fighting, and* Macbeth *slain. Exit* Macduff, *with* Macbeth.
*Retreat and flourish.*¹³ *Enter, with drum and colors,*
Malcolm, Siward, Ross, Thanes, *and* Soldiers.]

35 **Malcolm.** I would the friends we miss were safe arrived.

3. **terms . . . out** words can
describe you.

4. **intrenchant** incapable of
being cut.

5. **impress** make a dent in.

6. **angel** fallen angel; fiend.

7. **his . . . ripped** Macduff's
mother died before giving
birth to him.

8. **better . . . man** courage.

9. **palter** juggle.

10. **gaze o' th' time** spectacle of
the age.

11. **monsters** freaks.

12. **Painted . . . pole** pictured on a
banner stuck on a pole by a
showman's booth.

CLOSE READ

ANNOTATE: In lines 8–22, mark
details that relate to the witches'
prophesies.

QUESTION: What do these
details show about Macbeth's
sense of certainty up until this
point in the play?

CONCLUDE: Does the knowledge
that Macbeth has been tricked
change how the reader sees
him?

13. ***Retreat and flourish*** trumpet
call to withdraw and fanfare.

14. go off die.

15. unshrinking station place where he stood firmly.

Siward. Some must go off;[14] and yet, by these I see,
So great a day as this is cheaply bought.

Malcolm. Macduff is missing, and your noble son.

Ross. Your son, my lord, has paid a soldier's debt:
40 He only lived but till he was a man;
The which no sooner had his prowess confirmed
In the unshrinking station[15] where he fought,
But like a man he died.

Siward. Then he is dead?

Ross. Ay, and brought off the field. Your cause of sorrow
45 Must not be measured by his worth, for then
It hath no end.

Siward. Had he his hurts before?

Ross. Ay, on the front.

Siward. Why then, God's soldier be he!
Had I as many sons as I have hairs,
I would not wish them to a fairer death:
And so his knell is knolled.

50 **Malcolm.** He's worth more sorrow,
And that I'll spend for him.

Siward. He's worth no more:
They say he parted well and paid his score:
And so God be with him! Here comes newer comfort.

[*Enter* Macduff, *with* Macbeth's *head.*]

Macduff. Hail, King! for so thou art: behold, where stands
55 Th' **usurper**'s cursèd head. The time is free.[16]
I see thee compassed with thy kingdom's pearl,[17]
That speak my salutation in their minds,
Whose voices I desire aloud with mine:
Hail, King of Scotland!

All. Hail, King of Scotland!

[*Flourish.*]

60 **Malcolm.** We shall not spend a large expense of time
Before we reckon with your several loves,[18]
And make us even with you.[19] My thanes and kinsmen,
Henceforth be earls, the first that ever Scotland
In such an honor named. What's more to do,
65 Which would be planted newly with the time[20]—
As calling home our exiled friends abroad
That fled the snares of watchful tyranny,
Producing forth the cruel ministers
Of this dead butcher and his fiendlike queen,
70 Who, as 'tis thought, by self and violent hands
Took off her life—this, and what needful else

usurper (yoo SURP uhr) *n.* person who takes control without the proper authority

16. The . . . free Our country is liberated.

17. compassed . . . pearl surrounded by the noblest people in the kingdom.

18. reckon . . . loves reward each of you for your devotion.

19. make . . . you pay what we owe you.

20. What's . . . time what remains to be done at the beginning of this new age.

That calls upon us, by the grace of Grace
We will perform in measure, time, and place:[21]
So thanks to all at once and to each one,
75 Whom we invite to see us crowned at Scone.

[*Flourish. Exit all.*]

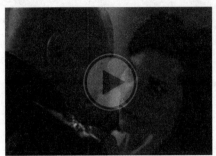

The Darkness in *Macbeth*'s
Human Characters

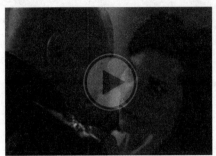

NOTES

21. **in measure . . . place** fittingly
at the appropriate time and
place.

MEDIA CONNECTION

💬 **Discuss It** How does viewing this video add to your
understanding of *The Tragedy of Macbeth*?

Write your response before sharing your ideas.

Comprehension Check
Complete the following items after you finish your first read.

1. What does Lady Macbeth reveal to the Gentlewoman and Doctor during her
   sleepwalking?

2. Why is Macbeth at first unafraid when he finally meets Macduff on the battlefield?

3. 📓 **Notebook** Confirm your understanding of the text by writing a summary of Act V.

- -

RESEARCH

Research to Clarify Choose at least one unfamiliar detail from the text. Briefly research
that detail. In what way does the information you learned shed light on an aspect of
the play?

Research to Explore Choose something from the text that interested you, and formulate
a research question. Write your question here.

Close Read the Text

1. This model, from Act V, Scene v, lines 19–25, shows two sample annotations, along with questions and conclusions. Close read the passage, and find another detail to annotate. Then, write a question and your conclusion.

Close
Read

ANNOTATE QUESTION CONCLUDE

> **ANNOTATE:** Macbeth repeats two particular words.
>
> **QUESTION:** What effect does this repetition have?
>
> **CONCLUDE:** The repetition serves to reinforce Macbeth's message—that time marches on relentlessly.

ANNOTATE: Using metaphor, Macbeth equates life to three distinct ideas.

QUESTION: How are the ideas similar?

CONCLUDE: Each idea expresses that life is a meaningless waste of time.

> **Macbeth.** Tomorrow, and tomorrow, and tomorrow. / Creeps in this petty pace from day to day, / To the last syllable of recorded time. . . . / Life's but a walking shadow, a poor player / That struts and frets his hour upon the stage / And then is heard no more. It is a tale / Told by an idiot, full of sound and fury / Signifying nothing.

2. For more practice, go back into the play, and complete the close-read notes.

3. Closely reread a section of the text you found important during your first read. **Annotate** what you notice. Ask yourself **questions** such as "Why did the playwright make this choice?" What can you **conclude**?

Analyze the Text

> **CITE TEXTUAL EVIDENCE**
> to support your answers.

Notebook Respond to these questions.

1. (a) Interpret To whom is Lady Macbeth referring when she says, "The Thane of Fife had a wife. Where is she now?" in Act V, Scene i, lines 39–40? **(b) Connect** How is this relevant to Lady Macbeth's state of mind in her sleepwalking scene?

2. Evaluate What character trait does Macbeth reveal as he meets his fate? Explain your position, citing evidence from the text.

3. Historical Perspectives Write a question related to Scottish history, arising from the text, that you would like to answer.

4. Essential Question: *How do our attitudes toward the past and future shape our actions?* How does the play shed light on our relationship with time?

STANDARDS

Reading Literature
• Cite strong and thorough textual evidence to support analysis of what the text says explicitly as well as inferences drawn from the text, including determining where the text leaves matters uncertain.
• Analyze the impact of the author's choices regarding how to develop and relate elements of a story or drama.
• Analyze how an author's choices concerning how to structure specific parts of a text contribute to its overall structure and meaning as well as its aesthetic impact.

Analyze Craft and Structure

Shakespearean Tragedy Shakespeare's tragedies usually contain these elements:

- A **tragic character**—a central character who is of high rank and possesses great personal qualities, yet who also has a **tragic flaw**, or weakness.

- Causally related events that lead this character to disaster, at least partly through his or her flaw.

- Dialogue and events that provoke a mixture of reactions from the audience, including pity, fear, and awe.

- Powerful action that creates a spectacle, and the use of comic scenes to offset the mood of sadness.

Consider how Shakespeare introduces Macbeth as a war hero. The playwright then develops Macbeth's character, adding complexity and depth through his words and actions, ultimately revealing a tragic flaw. Note, too, how Shakespeare includes plot events that lead to Macbeth's downfall and that make his tragic flaw evident. Shakespeare builds interest in Macbeth's actions by employing dramatic irony. **Dramatic irony** is present when audiences know more about a character's situation than the character does. For example, in Act III, Scene i, the audience knows that Macbeth murdered Duncan. Banquo comes to the same conclusion:

> Thou hast it now: King, Cawdor, Glamis, all,
> As the weird women promised, and I fear
> Thou play'dst most foully for't. . . . (lines 1–3)

However, Banquo does not know that Macbeth plans to have him killed. The audience knows more about Banquo's peril than he does.

Practice

CITE TEXTUAL EVIDENCE
to support your answers.

1. Review the notes in your Evidence Log that relate to Macbeth's character and motivations. Then, answer the questions in the chart to explore this aspect of his character.

What are Macbeth's tragic flaw(s)?
Which actions reveal Macbeth's tragic flaw(s)?

2. 📓 **Notebook** In Act V, Scene iii, Macbeth rails against the reports of Malcolm's upcoming attack. Reread this scene, and analyze the elements of dramatic irony that it contains.

THE TRAGEDY OF MACBETH,
ACT V

Concept Vocabulary

perturbation	agitation	purge
antidote	pristine	usurper

Why These Words? These concept words help reveal the mood of Act V. The words are related to the existence or establishment of disorder and the return to order. For example, the Doctor learns that Lady Macbeth has been in a state of *agitation*, sleepwalking and talking aloud. He says that it is a great *perturbation* of nature to be in her condition.

1. How does the concept vocabulary express the idea of the existence or establishment of disorder and the return to order?

2. What other words in the text connect to this concept?

Practice

Ⓕ **Notebook** The concept vocabulary words appear in Act V of *Macbeth*.

1. Use each concept word in a sentence that demonstrates your understanding of the word's meaning.

2. Challenge yourself to replace the concept words with one or two synonyms. How does the word change affect the meaning of the sentence? For example, does one synonym have a more positive meaning than the other?

Word Study

Latin Root: -turb- In Act V of *Macbeth*, the Doctor refers to Lady Macbeth's sleepwalking as a "great perturbation in nature." The word *perturbation* contains the Latin root -turb-, which tends to carry a meaning related to confusion or turmoil. Shakespeare could just as easily have used the word *disturbance* instead—a synonym for *perturbation* that also contains the root -turb-.

Based on your understanding of the root -turb-, write your best guesses as to the definitions of the adjective *turbid* and the noun *turbulence*. Then, look up each word in a thesaurus. Use the synonyms and antonyms you find to draw conclusions about the words' meanings. Revise your original definitions as needed.

⊞ WORD NETWORK

Add interesting words related to time from the text to your Word Network.

⊟ STANDARDS

Language
• Demonstrate command of the conventions of standard English capitalization, punctuation, and spelling when writing.
• Observe hyphenation conventions.
• Consult general and specialized reference materials, both print and digital, to find the pronunciation of a word or determine or clarify its precise meaning, its part of speech, its etymology, or its standard usage.
• Verify the preliminary determination of the meaning of a word or phrase.

Conventions and Style

Hyphenation of Compound Adjectives A **compound adjective** is a single adjective that is made up of two or more words. When a compound adjective precedes the noun or pronoun it modifies, the two words that make up the adjective are joined by a **hyphen (-)**. When a compound adjective follows the word it modifies, a hyphen is usually not necessary. The exception to this rule occurs when a compound adjective is listed with a hyphen in a reliable dictionary, in which case the adjective will always be hyphenated.

This table gives examples of the many ways compound adjectives can be formed.

PATTERN	EXAMPLES OF COMPOUND ADJECTIVES
Noun + Adjective	duck-like (walk) computer-literate (professor)
Noun + Verb (past or present participle}	profit-driven (company) button-pushing (assistant)
Adjective + Noun	high-speed (chase) middle-class (neighborhood)
Adjective + Verb (past or present participle)	bare-faced (lie) half-baked (story)
Adverb + Adjective	ever-gentle (nurse) forever-memorable (singer)
Adverb + Verb (past or present participle)	highest-ranking (officer) much-loved (woman)
Varied	never-to-be-remembered (lyrics) soon-to-be-forgotten (speech)

When the adverbial ending *-ly* is used in a compound adjective, a hyphen is not used.

Example: A beautifully sewn tapestry hung on the wall.

Writers may use compound adjectives to pack vivid descriptions into a compact amount of space. Shakespeare, in particular, uses them to invent colorful insults—for example, "rump-fed ronyon" (Act I) and "shag-eared villain" (Act IV). These descriptions create for the audience clear, colorful, amusing mental pictures of the people being described.

Read It

Reread Act V, Scene iii, of *The Tragedy of Macbeth*. Mark two hyphenated compound adjectives that Shakespeare uses as insults.

📓 **Notebook** (a) Explain the meaning of each of the compound adjectives you found. (b) **Connect to Style** What effect do these compound adjectives have on your impression of the person being insulted?

Write It

📓 **Notebook** Choose three patterns from the chart, and write a compound adjective for each. Use each compound in a sentence.

THE TRAGEDY OF MACBETH,
ACT V

Writing to Sources

One way to delve deeply into a play is to analyze one of its characters. By examining not only what that character does but also what he or she thinks and feels, the reader can more fully appreciate both the play and its writer's intentions.

Write a **character profile** in which you examine Macbeth's character and decision making, with a focus on killing Duncan. In your profile, make sure you state a clear position about your view of Macbeth. Then, defend your position using evidence from the text. As you plan your profile, consider the following:

- Macbeth's actions
- his perspectives on other characters
- his motivations

As part of your defense, think of differing opinions, called counterclaims, that another reader might make about Macbeth. Address each of the counterclaims you raise, showing why your analysis is stronger.

Vocabulary and Conventions Connection In your character profile, consider including several of the concept vocabulary words. Also, consider using compound adjectives to add variety to your sentences.

perturbation	agitation	purge
antidote	pristine	usurper

Reflect on Your Writing

After you have written your character profile, answer the following questions.

1. How do you think including counterclaims helped you develop a thorough profile?

2. What other character from *The Tragedy of Macbeth* would you like to profile? Why?

3. Why These Words? The words you choose make a difference in your writing. Which words did you specifically choose to add power to your character profile?

≡ STANDARDS
Writing
Write arguments to support claims in an analysis of substantive topics or texts, using valid reasoning and relevant and sufficient evidence.

Speaking and Listening

Assignment

Imagine that you are a war correspondent reporting on the battle described in *Macbeth* for television or for a digital streaming service. Write a **news report**, in which you do the following:

- Describe what the battlefield looks like.
- Explain the causes for the conflict.
- Interview several surviving participants in the battle.
- Discuss the consequences of the battle.

EVIDENCE LOG

Before moving on to a new selection, go to your Evidence Log and record what you learned from Act V of *The Tragedy of Macbeth*.

1. **Plan Your News Report** Use this chart to help you plan your news report.

From which location am I reporting? (Look at the stage directions for this information.)	
What is the cause of the conflict?	
Whom can I interview? (Choose key characters in the battle.)	
What might be the consequences of the battle?	

2. **Prepare Your News Report** Perform the following tasks:
   - Write a script explaining where you are and what you can see. You might wish to give your audience some background on the conflict.
   - Prepare the interviews. Write the dialogue between yourself and the characters you are interviewing. You might ask some classmates to read the script as the various characters you are "interviewing."

Record your report, including interviews, and post it for others to view.

3. **Evaluate News Reports** Watch several classmates' news reports. Use an evaluation guide like the one shown to analyze each report.

EVALUATION GUIDE

Rate each statement on a scale of 1 (not demonstrated) to 4 (demonstrated).

- [ ] The speaker thoroughly explained the background of the battle.
- [ ] The speaker communicated clearly and expressively.
- [ ] The speaker asked relevant questions to key battle figures.
- [ ] The speaker summed up the battle effectively.

STANDARDS

Writing
Use technology, including the Internet, to produce, publish, and update individual or shared writing products in response to ongoing feedback, including new arguments or information.

Speaking and Listening
• Come to discussions prepared, having read and researched material under study; explicitly draw on that preparation by referring to evidence from texts and other research on the topic or issue to stimulate a thoughtful, well-reasoned exchange of ideas.
• Adapt speech to a variety of contexts and tasks, demonstrating a command of formal English when indicated or appropriate.

THE TRAGEDY OF
MACBETH, ACT V, SCENE i

Comparing Text to Media

You will now listen to audio recordings of two different performances of Act V, Scene i, of *The Tragedy of Macbeth*. As you listen, compare and contrast the performances, and evaluate how each of them interprets Shakespeare's drama.

THE TRAGEDY OF
MACBETH, ACT V, SCENE i

About the Performers

L.A. Theatre Works was founded in 1974 as a not-for-profit media organization with the primary goal of producing and distributing classic and contemporary plays. The productions are full-length and performed by experienced actors. To date, the theatrical organization has aired more than 400 dramas, all of which are available online.

LibriVox was founded in 2005 with the goal of creating free audio books of texts that are in the public domain. Volunteers, most of whom have no professional acting or performing experience, create the audio files at home. The files are then catalogued and posted free online. To date, LibriVox has posted more than 8,000 recordings.

The Tragedy of Macbeth,
Act V, Scene i

Media Vocabulary

These words or concepts will be useful to you as you analyze, discuss, and write about audio recordings.

sound effects: recorded sounds that are neither speech nor music	• Sound effects may add a sense of reality to a performance by creating the illusion that something is actually happening. • They may also help set a mood—for instance, one that is joyful or ominous.
editing: process of selecting, correcting, and sequencing the elements of a media production	• Editors may choose to condense or expand a particular segment of a work. • Good editing results in a seamless production and ensures the clarity of the flow of ideas and events.
pacing: overall speed at which a theatrical production takes place	• Pacing may be slow or quick. • The pacing of specific segments may vary to reflect characters' actions and emotions.

First Review MEDIA: AUDIO

Apply these strategies as you conduct your first review. As you listen, record your observations and questions, making sure to note time codes for later reference. You will have an opportunity to complete a close review after your first review.

STANDARDS

Reading Literature
Analyze multiple interpretations of a story, drama, or poem, evaluating how each version interprets the source text.

Language
Acquire and use accurately general academic and domain-specific words and phrases, sufficient for reading, writing, speaking, and listening at the college and career readiness level; demonstrate independence in gathering vocabulary knowledge when considering a word or phrase important to comprehension or expression.

LISTEN and note *who* is speaking, *what* they're saying, and *how* they're saying it.

NOTE elements that you find interesting and want to revisit.

First Review

CONNECT ideas in the audio to other media you've experienced, texts you've read, or images you've seen.

RESPOND by completing the Comprehension Check.

ESSENTIAL QUESTION: How do our attitudes toward the past and future shape our actions?

MEDIA | AUDIO PERFORMANCES

The Tragedy of Macbeth, Act V, Scene i

BACKGROUND

A trio of witches has convinced Macbeth that he will be king. His ambition roused, Macbeth, with the help of Lady Macbeth, murders King Duncan. Upset by the witches' prophecy that his friend Banquo's progeny will rule Scotland, Macbeth orders the death of Banquo and his son, Fleance. Banquo dies, but Fleance escapes. Macbeth gives a banquet, in the course of which he sees Banquo's ghost. Lady Macbeth sends the guests away. When Macbeth learns that his enemy Macduff has fled to England, he sends his men to kill Macduff's wife and children. As Act V begins, we see the effect of these events on Lady Macbeth.

NOTES

Comprehension Check

Complete the following items after you finish your first review.

1. At the beginning of the L.A. Theatre Works audio production of *The Tragedy of Macbeth*, Act V, Scene i, what does the listener hear?

2. In which version do the actors' performances most accurately reflect normal speech?

3. In which version does the listener hear the actual stage directions?

4. Which version contains sound effects?

5. What is the primary difference between the two versions?

6. 🗐 **Notebook** As you listen, record your observations and questions, making sure to note time codes for later reference.

- -

RESEARCH

Research to Clarify Choose at least one unfamiliar detail from one of the versions of Act V, Scene i. Briefly research that detail. In what way does the information you learned shed light on an aspect of the scene?

Research to Explore Choose something from the audio presentations that interests you, and formulate a research question. Write your question here.

Close Review

Listen to the audio performances again. Write down any new observations that seem important. What **questions** do you have? What can you **conclude**?

REVIEW · QUESTION · CONCLUDE
Close Review

THE TRAGEDY OF MACBETH, ACT V, SCENE i

Analyze the Media

📓 **Notebook** Respond to these questions.

1. (a) What is the major difference between the pacing of the LibriVox and the L.A. Theatre Works presentations? (b) What effect does this difference have on your understanding of the scene?

2. As a class, review the two audio performances. Which performance would be more easily understood by someone unfamiliar with Shakespeare's language?

3. **Essential Question:** *How do our attitudes toward the past and future shape our actions?* How do Macbeth's and Lady Macbeth's attitudes about their past actions influence their future actions?

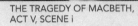

LANGUAGE DEVELOPMENT

Media Vocabulary

sound effects	editing	pacing

Use the vocabulary words in your responses to the questions.

1. In the LibriVox audio performance, what element most helps you understand Act V, Scene i, of *The Tragedy of Macbeth?*

2. In the L.A. Theatre Works audio performance, how is the mood established?

3. Which audio has better pacing? Explain.

⠿ STANDARDS
Reading Literature
Analyze multiple interpretations of a story, drama, or poem, evaluating how each version interprets the source text.
Language
Acquire and use accurately general academic and domain-specific words and phrases, sufficient for reading, writing, speaking, and listening at the college and career readiness level; demonstrate independence in gathering vocabulary knowledge when considering a word or phrase important to comprehension or expression.

THE TRAGEDY OF MACBETH,
ACT V, SCENE i

THE TRAGEDY OF MACBETH,
ACT V, SCENE i

Writing to Compare

You have read Shakespeare's *Macbeth,* and you have listened to two audio interpretations, or versions, of Act V, Scene i. Now, deepen your understanding of the play by comparing the audio interpretations and considering how each one presents the scene. Note that an **interpretation** of a play is any version that differs from the original production or text. An interpretation may simply involve the choices a director makes in staging a production. Alternatively, it may involve more sweeping changes, such as those required when remaking the play in a new medium.

Assignment

Write a **compare-and-contrast essay** in which you analyze the interpretations of Act V, Scene i, of *Macbeth* presented in the two audio performances. Discuss the following:

- elements of the text that are stressed or muted in each version
- ways in which each version affects the listener's experience of the text

Support your ideas with references to the audio versions and the original text. Your references may take the form of quotations, descriptions, or paraphrases.

Prewriting

Analyze the Texts Identify the audience and purpose of the two audio versions. Consider how each version uses theatrical elements, provides listeners with information about the physical setting and action, and portrays the characters.

	L.A. THEATRE WORKS INTERPRETATION	LIBRIVOX INTERPRETATION
Audience and Purpose		
Theatrical Elements (music, sound)		
Physical Scene: How is information conveyed to listeners?		
Interpretations of Characters: How are traits and emotions conveyed?		

Notebook Respond to these questions.

1. What impressions of the setting, action, and characters does each version create for listeners?

2. How does the experience of listening to each version differ from that of reading the scene?

Drafting

Summarize Key Points of Comparison Review your Prewriting notes. Then, summarize the major similarities and differences you hear between the two audio interpretations of the scene.

Major Similarities: _____

_____

_____

Major Differences: _____

_____

_____

Develop a Working Thesis Use your summary to write a working thesis for your essay. Your thesis should do two things:

- indicate major similarities and differences between the versions; and
- indicate how those differences affect listeners.

Working Thesis: _____

_____

Choose a Format Decide how you will structure your essay. Choose one of the following formats.

- **Block Format:** Discuss the audience, purpose, techniques, and effects of one interpretation. Then, discuss the audience, purpose, techniques, and effects of the other interpretation.
- **Point-by-Point Format:** First, discuss the audience and purpose of each version. Next, discuss the techniques used in each version. Finally, discuss the effects of each version on the listener.

Conclude your essay by explaining which interpretation you feel is the most successful. Consider which one provides listeners with a more effective entrance into the world of *Macbeth*.

Review, Revise, and Edit

When you have finished drafting, reread your essay. Mark ideas that need more support, and then return to your Prewriting notes, the original play, or the audio versions to find useful evidence. Make sure your transitions from sentence to sentence and from paragraph to paragraph are clear and logical. Edit your work for grammar, sentence structure, and word choice. Finally, proofread your essay to eliminate spelling and punctuation errors.

✎ EVIDENCE LOG

Before moving on to a new selection, go to your Evidence Log and record what you've learned from *Macbeth*, the L.A. Theatre Works audio performance of Act V, Scene i, and the LibriVox audio recording of the same scene.

WRITING TO SOURCES

- THE TRAGEDY OF MACBETH

- THE TRAGEDY OF MACBETH, ACT V, SCENE i (audio)

Write an Argument

In this section of the unit, you studied *The Tragedy of Macbeth* and analyzed related video and audio. Now, take some time to revisit what you have learned, and to share your learning by completing the following assignment.

Assignment

Write a brief **response to literature** in which you address this question:

> In what ways does Macbeth attempt to control the future and to bury the past?

In your essay, first state a position, or claim. Then, use specific evidence from the text to support your claim. Identify a possible counterclaim and use evidence to dispute it. Finish with a conclusion that follows logically from your argument.

Elements of an Argument

An **argument** is a logical way of presenting a viewpoint, belief, or stand on an issue. One form of argument is a **response to literature**, a deep analysis of some aspect of a text that leads to a conclusion or claim about the text, the author's intent, or the relation of the text to human behavior or world events. A well-written argument may convince the reader or change the reader's mind.

An effective argument contains these elements:

- a precise claim
- consideration of counterclaims, or opposing positions, and a discussion of their strengths and weaknesses
- logical organization that makes clear connections among claim, counterclaim, reasons, and evidence
- valid reasoning and relevant and sufficient evidence
- a concluding statement or section that logically completes the argument
- formal and objective language and tone
- error-free grammar, including accurate use of transitions

Analyze the Writing Model

Model Argument For a model of a well-crafted argument, see the Launch Text, "Better Never to Have Met at All."

Challenge yourself to find all of the elements of an effective response to literature in the text. You will have an opportunity to review those elements as you prepare to write your own argument.

LAUNCH TEXT

Better Never to
Have Met at All

🔧 **Tool Kit**
Student Model of an Argument

ACADEMIC VOCABULARY

As you craft your argument, consider using some of the academic vocabulary you learned in the beginning of the unit.

justify
diverse
proficient
catalyst
assertion

:≡ **STANDARDS**
Writing
• Write arguments to support claims in an analysis of substantive topics or texts, using valid reasoning and relevant and sufficient evidence.
• Write routinely over extended time frames and shorter time frames for a range of tasks, purposes, and audiences.

Prewriting / Planning

Write a Claim Reread the question in the prompt, and think about the drama and the scene you heard presented. Write a sentence in which you state your claim, or position on the question posed in this assignment. You will have an opportunity to revise your claim, if needed, as you draft and revise your essay.

Claim: _____

_____ .

Consider Possible Counterclaims A strong argument anticipates **counterclaims**, or opposing positions. No matter which side of the argument you choose, you should consider what opposing readers or writers might say. For example, someone might claim that Macbeth was not trying to control the future at all as much as he was reacting to fast-moving events and his wife's ambitious urgings. Complete these sentences to address a counterclaim.

Another reader might claim that _____ .

He or she might offer these reasons: _____ .

However, my position is stronger, because _____ .

Gather Evidence For a **response to literature**, your evidence will come from the text itself. One way to gather evidence is to *skim* and *scan*.

1. Reread the question in the prompt and keep the question in front of you as you look for evidence.

2. *Skim* each act of the play to remind yourself of the content and plot.

3. Then, *scan* each scene to look for specific details that relate directly to the prompt. Key words to look for might include *time, past, history,* and *future*.

4. Take notes on your findings. Circle notes that best support your claim. Does any evidence contradict your claim? Save it for a discussion of counterclaims.

Consider Audience and Purpose Before drafting your response to literature, consider who will be reading it.

- How much does your audience know about the play? Will you need to provide details about the plot or can you focus solely on your argument?

- Are your readers likely to agree with your claim? If not, what kind of evidence is most apt to convince them?

- What vocabulary will readers already know, and what words might you need to define? Choose words that are appropriate for your readers' level of knowledge. Refer to the prompt to remind you of your purpose, and keep your audience in mind as you write.

✎ EVIDENCE LOG

Review your Evidence Log and identify key details you may want to cite in your argument.

☰ STANDARDS

Writing
- Introduce precise, knowledgeable claim(s), establish the significance of the claim(s), distinguish the claim(s) from alternate or opposing claims, and create an organization that logically sequences claim(s), counterclaims, reasons, and evidence.
- Develop claim(s) and counterclaims fairly and thoroughly, supplying the most relevant evidence for each while pointing out the strengths and limitations of both in a manner that anticipates the audience's knowledge level, concerns, values, and possible biases.

Drafting

Present Your Reasoning The presentation of evidence in an argument often follows a particular pattern. Here are a few commonly used patterns.

- **weakest to strongest**, in which the critical piece of evidence comes last
- **strongest to weakest**, in which you lead with the critical piece of evidence
- **point/counterpoint**, in which you present a series of counterclaims and undermine them in turn

The example provided shows the pattern used by the Launch Text writer. Notice that the flow of the argument is clear, and the argument proceeds from weakest to strongest evidence. No matter which pattern you choose, make sure that you link your ideas with clear transitions and connect each point to your claim.

STANDARDS

Writing
- Develop claim(s) and counterclaims fairly and thoroughly, supplying the most relevant evidence for each while pointing out the strengths and limitations of both in a manner that anticipates the audience's knowledge level, concerns, values, and possible biases.
- Provide a concluding statement or section that follows from and supports the argument presented.

LAUNCH TEXT

Model: "Better Never to Have Met at All" Outline

INTRODUCTION
Paragraph 1 states the claim: *The romance between Romeo and Juliet hurts so many that one wonders whether it would have been better for everyone involved if time wound backward and the two leads never met at all.*

BODY
Weak evidence: Mercutio dies in a duel. (Mercutio is a secondary character.)

Stronger evidence: Romeo kills Tybalt and is banished. (Romeo is a main character.)

Strongest evidence: Romeo and Juliet kill themselves. (Both main characters are affected, which affects everyone else.)

Counterclaim: Shakespeare claims that "with their death," the tragic couple "bury their parents' strife."

CONCLUSION
The tragic events are not worth it; the two should never have met.

Argument Outline

INTRODUCTION

BODY

CONCLUSION

Write a First Draft Use your outline to write your first draft. Make sure to include a precise claim and to address possible counterclaims. Choose the pattern that works best to present your evidence. Consider your audience as you write—will they be able to follow the logic in your argument? Have you supplied the best, most relevant evidence to support your claim? Conclude with a strong statement that ties your ideas together.

LANGUAGE DEVELOPMENT: AUTHOR'S STYLE

Establish Voice: Formal Style

To give appropriate weight and seriousness to its arguments, the language of a response to literature should be formal and objective. Formal writing uses advanced, academic vocabulary and few contractions, and avoids slang terms. Objective writing is specific, impersonal, and well supported by evidence. It lacks excessive emotion or exaggeration and rarely uses "I" statements.

Read It

Below, a formal sentence from the Launch Text is contrasted with an informal version. How would you describe the differences between them?

- *If we examine the play from the beginning, the evidence for this is overwhelming.* **(formal)**

- *If you read over the play from the beginning, there's lots of evidence for this.* **(informal)**

Write It

As you draft your argument, check your writing for use of informal elements. Use this checklist to test your writing for formality and objectivity.

- [ ] Have I used vocabulary that is appropriate for my topic and suitable for a formal essay?

- [ ] Have I used observations and evidence from the text as opposed to personal opinions and assumptions?

- [ ] Should I change idioms or slang expressions to more formal language?

- [ ] Should I replace any contractions?

- [ ] Should I replace any exaggerated or emotional language with more neutral, unbiased language?

Use Rhetorical Devices A powerful way to boost the strength of a formal argument is to include a variety of appeals in your writing. Consider using one or more of the following:

- *appeals to logic*, in which you present evidence and reasons that fit together in a convincing way. ("Macbeth's attitude toward the past fits a certain pattern. His avoidance of the unpleasant parts of the witches' prophecies is the same impulse causing him to banish all kind thoughts of Banquo.")

- *analogies*, extended comparisons to things that are familiar to readers to help them understand the point you are trying to make. ("Macbeth behaves like an overambitious politician; he doesn't care whom he has to destroy as long as he gets what he wants in the end.")

- *case studies*, famous examples of a particular behavior or pattern. ("Macbeth fits the pattern of a typical narcissist; like the main character from *Citizen Kane*, he cares only about himself and his own grip on power.")

TIP

USAGE
Do not spoil your formal essay by misusing unfamiliar words.

- Make sure that you are using any unfamiliar words correctly.
- Check a dictionary if you are unsure of the meaning of a word you wish to use.
- When in doubt, use a simpler word.

STANDARDS

Writing
Establish and maintain a formal style and objective tone while attending to the norms and conventions of the discipline in which they are writing.

Language
Apply knowledge of language to understand how language functions in different contexts, to make effective choices for meaning or style, and to comprehend more fully when reading or listening.

MAKING WRITING SOPHISTICATED

Creating Cohesion: Structuring Sentences As writers develop arguments, they must tie evidence together to establish logical support for a claim. Writers may link ideas in any of several ways. The most common methods include:

• introductory phrases or clauses that connect ideas

• transition words that express specific relationships

Read It

These examples from the Launch Text demonstrate how to use transition words and sentence structure to connect ideas and create a logical flow.

> **LAUNCH TEXT EXAMPLES**
>
> Winding back the clock, we begin in Verona, where we find Romeo, heir of the noble House of Montague, feeling sorry for himself. His reason: rejection at the hands of Rosaline, niece to Lord Capulet, leader of the House of Capulet and rival to the Montagues. Romeo's friend, Mercutio, wishing to improve his friend's spirits, disguises Romeo and sneaks him into a Capulet party. Romeo has his own motive for going—he wants to see Rosaline again—but at the party he meets Juliet, daughter of Lord Capulet, instead. From that moment in time, they are in love, and everyone's life gets worse.
>
> …
>
> However, Shakespeare would disagree on this point. His argument against this comes at the play's very beginning, where he writes:
>
> > A pair of star-cross'd lovers take their life;
> > Whose misadventured piteous overthrows
> > Do with their death bury their parents' strife.
>
> Thus, the miserable, painful deaths of so many characters and the grief of their friends and relatives lead to a lasting peace between the rival families. Future generations, living without strife, might consider the sacrifice a necessary step to a better age.
>
> Nevertheless, it is doubtful that Shakespeare's own dead characters would agree with him. Mercutio certainly would not.

The writer uses a participial phrase to indicate that the information to follow comes from the start of the play. The prepositional phrases at the end of the paragraph announce that this event affects future events.

The words *however* and *nevertheless* indicate that the information to follow contrasts with what came before. *Thus* means that the information that follows is supported by what came before.

STANDARDS

Writing
Use words, phrases, and clauses as well as varied syntax to link the major sections of the text, create cohesion, and clarify the relationships between claim(s) and reasons, between reasons and evidence, and between claim(s) and counterclaims.

Write It

As you revise your response to literature, look for places you might use transition words or introductory phrases or clauses to connect ideas. Look especially for ways to connect your evidence to your claim or one piece of evidence to the next. Here are some transition words that are appropriate for formal writing.

PURPOSE	EXAMPLE
addition	again, besides, furthermore, in addition, likewise, moreover, too
cause/effect	accordingly, as a result, consequently, for this reason, therefore, thus
comparison	also, in the same way, similarly
contrast	although, conversely, despite that, even though, however, in contrast, instead, nevertheless, on the other hand, regardless, yet
emphasis	certainly, especially, indeed, in fact, surely
example	after all, for example, for instance, in other words, in particular, namely, specifically, that is
summary	altogether, finally, in brief, in conclusion, in essence, to summarize

- Read over your first draft. Are the connections between ideas and from paragraph to paragraph clear? Could you vary the beginnings of sentences by adding a word, a phrase, or a clause that clarifies the links between your examples or your evidence and your claim?

- Take notes on your draft and write your new ideas for rewording here.

PARAGRAPH	WORD OR WORDS TO ADD	REVISED SENTENCE

Revising

Evaluating Your Draft

Use this checklist to evaluate the effectiveness of your first draft. Then, use your evaluation and the instruction on this page to guide your revision.

FOCUS AND ORGANIZATION	EVIDENCE AND ELABORATION	CONVENTIONS
☐ Provides an introduction that establishes a precise claim.	☐ Develops the claim using text evidence.	☐ Attends to the norms and conventions of the discipline.
☐ Distinguishes the claim from opposing claims.	☐ Provides adequate support for each claim and counterclaim.	☐ Establishes and maintains a formal style and objective tone.
☐ Provides a conclusion that follows from the argument.	☐ Uses vocabulary and word choices that are appropriate for the audience and purpose.	
☐ Establishes a logical organization and develops a progression throughout the argument.		
☐ Uses words, phrases, and clauses to clarify the relationships between and among ideas.		

⛭ WORD NETWORK

Include interesting words from your Word Network in your argument.

☰ STANDARDS

Writing
• Produce clear and coherent writing in which the development, organization, and style are appropriate to task, purpose, and audience.
• Develop and strengthen writing as needed by planning, revising, editing, rewriting, or trying a new approach, focusing on addressing what is most significant for a specific purpose and audience.

Language
Acquire and use accurately general academic and domain-specific words and phrases, sufficient for reading, writing, speaking, and listening at the college and career readiness level; demonstrate independence in gathering vocabulary knowledge when considering a word or phrase important to comprehension.

Revising for Focus and Organization

Organization Review your draft to be sure that its organization helps you achieve your purpose. Add transitions where needed to ensure readers can follow your argument.

Revising for Evidence and Elaboration

Evidence Make sure that your examples provide evidence that directly supports your claim, and that you have drawn examples from a variety of places in the text. Eliminate any examples that are interesting but irrelevant to the point you are trying to make.

Adequate Support If you provide a great deal of evidence for a claim and next to none for a counterclaim, that is not a fair argument. Try to balance the amount of support that you offer. Then carefully tell why the support for your claim is stronger, more plausible, or more believable than the support for the counterclaim is.

Vocabulary Because you are writing a response to literature, use words that are specific to the study of literature. Instead of referring to the story, for example, you might use the word *plot*. Instead of writing about parts of the play, write about *acts* or *scenes*. Are there other terms from your study of literature that might make your argument and evidence more specific and clear for your audience? Using specific, technical vocabulary adds to the formal tone of your writing.

Exchange papers with a classmate. Use the checklist to evaluate your classmate's argument and provide supportive feedback.

1. Is the claim clear?

☐ yes ☐ no If no, explain what confused you.

2. Did you find the argument convincing?

☐ yes ☐ no If no, tell what you think might be missing.

3. Does the response to literature conclude in a logical way?

☐ yes ☐ no If no, suggest what you might change.

4. What is the strongest part of your classmate's paper? Why?

_____

_____

_____

_____

Editing and Proofreading

Edit for Conventions Reread your draft for accuracy and consistency. Correct errors in grammar and word usage. Remember to avoid contractions and informal vocabulary.

Proofread for Accuracy Read your draft carefully, correcting errors in spelling and punctuation. Make sure to use commas after introductory clauses, participial phrases, or a series of introductory prepositional phrases.

Publishing and Presenting

Create a final version of your argument. Join a four-person "reading group" and read each other's work. Complete an index card for each paper you read, commenting on the best points of each essay and making one suggestion for next time. Keep your remarks impersonal and considerate.

Reflecting

Reflect on what you learned by writing your argument. Did writing about the text help you better understand the text? What step in the process helped you focus your argument most? What will you do differently the next time you write a response to literature?

▦ STANDARDS

Writing
Develop and strengthen writing as needed by planning, revising, editing, rewriting, or trying a new approach, focusing on addressing what is most significant for a specific purpose and audience.

OVERVIEW: SMALL-GROUP LEARNING

How do our attitudes toward the past and future shape our actions?

As you read these selections, work with your group to explore this question.

From Text to Topic Renaissance writers, whose works span the fourteenth to the seventeenth centuries, shared a passionate interest in ancient cultures and civilizations. This interest bore fruit in writings that explored a multitude of questions related to how human beings should govern themselves and what their relationship should be with the natural world, two issues seen in *The Tragedy of Macbeth*. Amid dramatic shifts in leadership, religion, and worldview, Renaissance writers such as William Shakespeare created exciting literary works that challenged readers' established ideas. Centuries later, critics Cleanth Brooks and Frank Kermode explored how Shakespeare and his contemporaries shaped the past to meet their dramatic needs. As you read, consider what these selections show about how attitudes toward the past and the future shape how we act in the present.

Small-Group Learning Strategies

Throughout your life, in school, in your community, and in your career, you will continue to develop strategies when you work in teams. Use these strategies during Small-Group Learning. Add ideas of your own for each step.

STRATEGY	ACTION PLAN
Prepare	• Complete your assignments so that you are prepared for group work. • Organize your thinking so that you can contribute to your group's discussions. •
Participate fully	• Make eye contact to signal that you are listening and taking in what is being said. • Use text evidence when making a point. •
Support others	• Build off ideas from others in your group. • Invite others who have not yet spoken to do so. •
Clarify	• Paraphrase the ideas of others to ensure that your understanding is correct. • Ask follow-up questions. •

368 UNIT 3 • FACING THE FUTURE, CONFRONTING THE PAST

CONTENTS

How might poetry have the power to halt time—
and even ensure a kind of immortality?

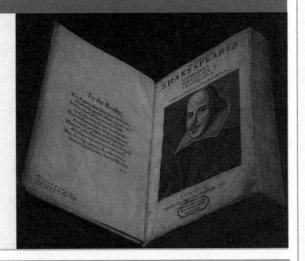

Tastes change over time, so how do we judge
literature—by the standards of the past or
those of the present?

PERFORMANCE TASK

SPEAKING AND LISTENING FOCUS
Present an Argument

The Small-Group readings are examples of sonnets and Shakespearean criticism.
After reading, your group will present an argument about whether or not literature
from earlier eras should be rewritten in present-day language.

Working as a Team

1. Take a Position In your group, discuss the following question:

> "Those who do not remember the past are condemned to repeat it." – George Santayana

As you take turns sharing your positions, be sure to provide reasons for your choice. After all group members have shared, discuss some of the connections among the issues that were presented.

2. List Your Rules As a group, decide on the rules that you will follow as you work together. Two samples are provided. Add two more of your own. As you work together, you may add or revise rules based on your experience together.

- Build on the comments of others to enhance discussion.
- Share ideas in a constructive manner.

- _____

  _____

- _____

  _____

3. Apply the Rules Practice working as a group. Share what you have learned about ways that our attitudes towards the past and future shape our actions. Make sure each person in the group contributes. Take notes on and be prepared to share with the class one thing that you heard from another member of your group.

4. Name Your Group Choose a name that reflects the unit topic.

Our group's name: _____

5. Create a Communication Plan Decide how you want to communicate with one another. For example, you might use email, an online bulletin board, or a collaborative annotation tool.

Our group's decision: _____

_____

Making a Schedule

First, find out the due dates for the small-group activities. Then, preview the texts and activities with your group, and make a schedule for completing the tasks.

SELECTION	ACTIVITIES	DUE DATE
Sonnet 12 Sonnet 60 Sonnet 73 Sonnet 32 Sonnet 75		
from The Naked Babe and the Cloak of Manliness *from* Macbeth		

Working on Group Projects

As your group works together, you'll find it more effective if each person has a specific role. Different projects require different roles. Before beginning a project, discuss the necessary roles, and choose one for each group member. Some possible roles are listed here. Add your ideas to the list.

Project Manager: monitors the schedule and keeps everyone on task

Researcher: organizes research activities

Recorder: takes notes during group meetings

_____

_____

_____

_____

_____

_____

_____

_____

Sonnet 12, Sonnet 60, Sonnet 73

Sonnet 32

Sonnet 75

Concept Vocabulary

As you perform your first read, you will encounter these words.

toil	assay	devise

Context Clues To find the meaning of an unfamiliar word, look for clues in the context, which includes the words, punctuation, and images that surround the unknown word. In poetry, be sure to look for context clues in lines that come before and after unfamiliar words.

> **Unfamiliar Word:** *hasten*
>
> **Context:** Like as the waves make towards the pebbled shore,
> So do our minutes **hasten** to their end;
>
> **Possible Meaning:** The speaker compares the passing of time to the movement of waves. The verb *hasten* may indicate a type of motion.

Apply your knowledge of context clues and other vocabulary strategies to determine the meanings of unfamiliar words you encounter during your first read.

First Read POETRY

Apply these strategies as you conduct your first read. You will have an opportunity to complete a close read after your first read.

STANDARDS

Reading Literature
By the end of grade 12, read and comprehend literature, including stories, dramas, and poems, at the high end of the grades 11–CCR text complexity band independently and proficiently.

Language
• Determine or clarify the meaning of unknown and multiple-meaning words and phrases based on *grades 11–12 reading and content*, choosing flexibly from a range of strategies.
• Use context as a clue to the meaning of a word or phrase.

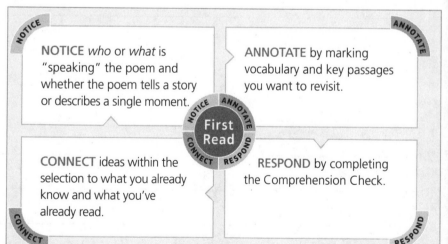

NOTICE *who* or *what* is "speaking" the poem and whether the poem tells a story or describes a single moment.

ANNOTATE by marking vocabulary and key passages you want to revisit.

CONNECT ideas within the selection to what you already know and what you've already read.

RESPOND by completing the Comprehension Check.

First Read

About the Poets

William Shakespeare (1564–1616) In addition to numerous plays, Shakespeare also wrote two long narrative poems—*Venus and Adonis* and *The Rape of Lucrece*—as well as 154 sonnets. During Shakespeare's time, poetry was widely regarded as an art practiced only by nobles and gentlemen. Nonethless, Shakespeare, a rustic interloper, introduced himself as a poet between 1593 and 1594. His sonnets, poignant musings about life, provide insights about love, mortality, and the effects of time.

Mary Wroth (1587–1651) was born into an aristocratic family. She spent most of her childhood in Penshurst Place, one of the great country houses of the Elizabethan and Jacobean periods. She was well educated and a fixture of the social life of London. Her poems were widely circulated among the elites of her time. She fell out of favor with polite society after the publication of her romance, *The Countess of Montgomery's Urania*, and lived the rest of her life in obscurity.

Edmund Spenser (1552–1599) was born in London into a working-class family. As a boy, he attended the Merchant Taylors' School on a scholarship and later worked his way through Cambridge University. In 1580, he took a position as secretary to the Lord Deputy of Ireland. There he began his greatest work, *The Faerie Queen*. In his sonnet sequence *Amoretti*, he created a new sonnet form, now known as the Spenserian sonnet. Spenser was well regarded by his contemporaries for his formal innovation and unique style.

Backgrounds

Sonnet 12, Sonnet 60, Sonnet 73

Like the sonnet sequences of other poets, Shakespeare's 154 sonnets are numbered. Most of them are addressed to a handsome, talented young man, urging him to marry and have children who can carry on his talents. Shakespeare, among other poets, used the sonnet form to bring the fundamental experiences of life—time, death, love, and friendship—into tight focus.

Sonnet 32

This sonnet comes from Mary Wroth's sonnet sequence *Pamphilia to Amphilanthus,* an extended meditation on the nature of love, with its joys and sorrows. The turning point in this sequence is the extravagant "Crowne," a set of fourteen sonnets that explored the possibility of a spiritual and perfected love, and broke with the tradition of the time that focused more on courtship.

Sonnet 75

Edmund Spenser's "Sonnet 75" comes from a longer work by Spenser—the sonnet sequence *Amoretti*, Italian for "little love poems." This sonnet sequence is unique in that it is addressed to the poet's wife, Elizabeth Boyle, not to some distant, unattainable, or unrequited love. It's also an example of the Spenserian sonnet, which he created using a unique structure and rhyme scheme.

Sonnet 12

Sonnet 60

Sonnet 73

William Shakespeare

Sonnet 12

When I do count the clock that tells the time,
And see the brave day sunk in hideous night;
When I behold the violet past prime,
And sable curls all silvered o'er with white;

5 When lofty trees I see barren of leaves,
Which erst[1] from heat did canopy the herd,
And summer's green all girded[2] up in sheaves,
Borne on the bier[3] with white and bristly beard;
Then of thy beauty do I question make,

10 That thou among the wastes of time must go,
Since sweets and beauties do themselves forsake,
And die as fast as they see others grow,
    And nothing 'gainst Time's scythe can make defense,
    Save breed,[4] to brave him when he takes thee hence.

---

1. **erst** in the past; formerly.
2. **girded** encircled or bound.
3. **bier** (bihr) stand on which a corpse or coffin is placed.
4. **breed** children.

Sonnet 60

Like as the waves make towards the pebbled shore,
So do our minutes hasten to their end;
Each changing place with that which goes before,
In sequent **toil** all forwards do contend.
5 Nativity, once in the main[1] of light,
Crawls to maturity, wherewith[2] being crowned,
Crooked eclipses 'gainst his glory fight,
And Time that gave doth now his gift confound.
Time doth transfix[3] the flourish set on youth,
10 And delves the parallels in beauty's brow,
Feeds on the rarities of nature's truth,
And nothing stands but for his scythe to mow:
      And yet to times in hope my verse shall stand,
      Praising thy worth, despite his cruel hand.

---

1. **main** open sea.
2. **wherewith** with which.
3. **transfix** impale, as with a sword or lance.

NOTES

Mark context clues or indicate another strategy you used that helped you determine meaning.

toil (toyl) *n.*

MEANING:

Sonnet 73

That time of year thou mayst in me behold,
When yellow leaves, or none, or few, do hang
Upon those boughs which shake against the cold,
Bare ruin'd choirs where late the sweet birds sang.
5 In me thou see'st the twilight of such day,
As after sunset fadeth in the west,
Which by and by black night doth take away,
Death's second self, that seals up all in rest.
In me thou see'st the glowing of such fire
10 That on the ashes of his youth doth lie,
As the deathbed whereon it must expire,
Consumed with that which it was nourish'd by.
      This thou perceiv'st, which makes thy love more strong,
      To love that well which thou must leave ere[1] long.

---

1. **ere** (ehr) before.

Sonnet 32
from Pamphilia to Amphilanthus

Mary Wroth

NOTES

How fast thou fliest, O Time, on love's swift wings
    To hopes of joy, that flatters our desire
    Which to a lover, still, contentment brings!
    Yet, when we should enjoy thou dost retire.

5 Thou stay'st[1] thy pace, false time, from our desire,
    When to our ill thou hast'st[2] with Eagle's wings,
    Slow, only make us see thy retire
    Was for despair, and harm, which sorrow brings;

O! slack[3] thy pace, and milder pass to love;
10   Be like the Bee, whose wings she doth but use
    To bring home profit, masters good to prove
    Laden, and weary, yet again pursues,

So lade[4] thyself with honey of sweet joy,
And do not me the Hive of love destroy.

---

1. **stay'st** continues.
2. **hast'st** hurries.
3. **slack** slow.
4. **lade** load.

Sonnet 75

Edmund Spenser

One day I wrote her name upon the strand,[1]
But came the waves and washèd it away:
Again I wrote it with a second hand,
But came the tide, and made my pains his prey.
5 "Vain man," said she, "that dost in vain **assay**,
A mortal thing so to immortalize,
For I myself shall like to this decay,
And eek[2] my name be wipèd out likewise."
"Not so," quod[3] I, "let baser things **devise**
10 To die in dust, but you shall live by fame:
My verse your virtues rare shall eternize,
And in the heavens write your glorious name.
Where whenas death shall all the world subdue,
Our love shall live, and later life renew."

___

1. **strand** beach.
2. **eek** also.
3. **quod** said.

NOTES

Mark context clues or indicate
another strategy you used that
helped you determine meaning.

assay (uh SAY) *v.*

MEANING:

devise (dih VYZ) *v.*

MEANING:

Comprehension Check

Complete the following items after you finish your first read. Review and clarify details with your group.

SONNET 12

1. What connection does the speaker make between the change of seasons and the loved one's beauty?

2. According to the speaker, what is the only defense against time?

SONNET 60

1. To what does the speaker compare the passing of time?

2. What hope does the speaker express regarding his verse?

SONNET 73

1. At what stage of life is the speaker of this poem?

2. What advice does the speaker give in the last two lines?

SONNET 32

1. According to the speaker, when does time hurry, and when does it slow down?

2. What request does the speaker ask of Time?

SONNET 75

1. What happens twice to the name the speaker writes in the sand?

2. How does the speaker's beloved respond to his actions?

3. How does the speaker plan to immortalize his beloved?

RESEARCH

Research to Clarify Choose at least one unfamiliar detail from one of the poems. Briefly research that detail. In what way does the information you learned shed light on an aspect of the poem?

Research to Explore Use Internet or library resources to locate media interpretations, such as audio or video recordings, of these poems. You might want to compare and contrast different interpretations of the same poem and share your reactions with your group.

POETRY COLLECTION 1

Close Read the Text

With your group, revisit sections of the texts you marked during your first read. **Annotate** details that you notice. What **questions** do you have? What can you **conclude**?

Analyze the Text

CITE TEXTUAL EVIDENCE to support your answers.

Complete the activities.

1. **Review and Clarify** With your group, reread Sonnet 12. Does the poem address a universal human problem, or is the situation specific to the speaker and an unseen listener?

2. **Present and Discuss** Now, work with your group to share the passages from the poems that you found especially important. Take turns presenting your passages. Discuss what details you noticed, what questions you asked, and what conclusions you reached.

3. **Essential Question:** *How do our attitudes towards the past and future shape our actions?* What have these texts taught you about how people respond to time? Discuss with your group.

Concept Vocabulary

toil	assay	devise

Why These Words? The three concept vocabulary words are related. With your group, discuss the words, and determine what they have in common. How do these word choices enhance the impact of the text?

Practice

📓 **Notebook** Confirm your understanding of the concept vocabulary words by answering these questions. Use the concept words in your answers.

1. What are three examples of *toil*?

2. When you *assay* to do something, do you always succeed? Explain.

3. If you *devise* to do a task, do you intend to accomplish it? Explain.

Word Study

📓 **Notebook** **Multiple-Meaning Words** Many words have different meanings when used in scientific and nonscientific contexts. In chemistry, for instance, *assay* frequently appears as a noun meaning "detailed analysis"—a usage quite different from Spenser's in Sonnet 75. Find several other words that have different scientific and nonscientific meanings. Write the words and their meanings.

TIP

GROUP DISCUSSION
Paraphrasing, or restating a writer's ideas in your own words, can help you check your group's comprehension and compare your interpretations. Take turns paraphrasing key or confusing lines.

🔧 WORD NETWORK

Add interesting words related to time from the text to your Word Network.

▤ STANDARDS

Reading Literature
• Determine two or more themes or central ideas of a text and analyze their development over the Reading text, including how they interact and build on one another to produce a complex account; provide an objective summary of the text.
• Analyze how an author's choices concerning how to structure specific parts of a text contribute to its overall structure and meaning as well as its aesthetic impact.

Language
Determine or clarify the meaning of unknown and multiple-meaning words and phrases based on *grades 11–12 reading and content*, choosing flexibly from a range of strategies.

Analyze Craft and Structure

Development of Theme Each of these poems is a **sonnet**, a fourteen-line lyric poem with a single theme. Most traditional sonnets are written in rhymed iambic pentameter—five groups of two syllables, each with the accent on the second syllable. There are two main types of sonnets: English, or Shakespearean; and Italian, or Petrarchan. The sonnets in this collection are Shakespearean. However, Sonnet 75 by Edmund Spenser represents a Spenserian sonnet, a variation on the English sonnet.

- The **Shakespearean sonnet** consists of three quatrains (four-line stanzas) and a couplet (two lines), with the rhyme scheme *abab cdcd efef gg*.

- The **Spenserian sonnet** also contains three quatrains and a couplet. However, the rhyme scheme is *abab bcbc cdcd* for the quatrains and *ee* for the couplet.

Note that even if a poet uses a sonnet form, he or she may alter elements, such as the stanza spacing or rhyme scheme.

Traditional sonnet structures allow poets to develop themes with a certain clear logic. For example, in Shakespearean sonnets, each quatrain explores a different aspect of a theme, and the couplet serves as a concluding comment that may offer a surprise or twist on the ideas that came earlier.

Practice

CITE TEXTUAL EVIDENCE to support your answers.

1. As a group, choose a sonnet from this collection, and analyze how its structure helps to develop theme. Consider how each quatrain explores a different aspect of the theme and how the couplet offers a surprising comment.

	DEVELOPMENT OF THEME
Sonnet:	
First Quatrain	
Second Quatrain	
Third Quatrain	
Couplet	

2. 🖥 **Notebook** Choose another sonnet from this collection. Working on your own, analyze how the poet uses the sonnet structure to develop the theme. Then, share your analysis with your group.

POETRY COLLECTION 1

Conventions and Style

Word Choice Poetry often uses **figurative language**, or language that is not meant to be taken literally, to evoke emotions and express ideas in imaginative ways. Figurative language includes one or more *figures of speech*, devices for making unexpected comparisons or for changing the usual meaning of words. Three common types of figures of speech are metaphor, simile, and personification.

- **Similes**—direct comparisons of dissimilar things using the words *like* or *as: Cats' eyes glow like lamps at night.*
- **Metaphors**—comparisons in which one thing is identified with another dissimilar thing: *All the world's a stage.*
- **Personification**—giving human qualities to nonhuman subjects: *The trees dance in the wind.*

Masters of their art, the poets in this collection use various types of figurative language to express complex ideas about time, love, and human frailty.

Read It

🖥 **Notebook** Identify the type of figurative language being used in each passage in the chart. Then, explain what is being compared and how the device adds meaning to the poem.

PASSAGE	TYPE OF FIGURE OF SPEECH	ANALYSIS
And see the brave day sunk in hideous night . . . (Sonnet 12, line 2)		
Like as the waves make towards the pebbled shore, / So do our minutes hasten to their end. . . . (Sonnet 60, lines 1–2)		
And time that gave doth now his gift confound. (Sonnet 60, line 8)		

Write It

🖥 **Notebook** Complete each sentence. Use either a simile, a metaphor, or an example of personification in each new sentence.

1. To Shakespeare, youth _____

2. Wroth feels that time is _____

3. Spenser suggests that immortality _____

:≡ STANDARDS

Reading Literature
Determine the meaning of words and phrases as they are used in the text, including figurative and connotative meanings; analyze the impact of specific word choices on meaning and tone, including words with multiple meanings or language that is particularly fresh, engaging, or beautiful.

Writing
• Introduce a topic; organize complex ideas, concepts, and information so that each new element builds on that which precedes it to create a unified whole; include formatting, graphics, and multimedia when useful to aiding comprehension.
• Develop the topic thoroughly by selecting the most significant and relevant facts, extended definitions, concrete details, quotations, or other information and examples appropriate to the audience's knowledge of the topic.

Language
• Demonstrate understanding of figurative language, word relationships, and nuances in word meanings.
• Interpret figures of speech in context and analyze their role in the text.

Writing to Sources

Assignment

With your group, write a **response to literature** that compares and contrasts ideas from these sonnets. Choose from the following for your writing.

☐ Write a **reflection** in which you explain which of these sonnets expresses ideas about time that are most similar to your own. Cite specific lines or details from the poems to illustrate your views. Draft your reflections individually. Then, gather them into a group response.

☐ Write an **introduction** to an anthology of sonnets that includes the poems in this collection. Explain why these particular poems are excellent examples of the sonnet form.

☐ Choose a popular song that you could use as background music for a website about the sonnets by Shakespeare, Wroth, and Spenser. Write an **explanatory statement** about the song in which you tell why you chose it and how it reinforces the messages of the sonnets.

 TIP

COLLABORATION

Your group response may include multiple perspectives on the same text. Create a format for your response that allows each group member to contribute equally, even if you do not agree on every interpretation. The final response will be more engaging if it accurately reflects each group member's readings of the poems being discussed.

Plan Your Argument Work with your group to plan the claim you will make and support in your response to literature. Express your position in clear and precise language. Then, look for specific support, including details from the poems in this collection, as well as your own ideas, quotations from other texts, or the responses of other readers.

 EVIDENCE LOG

Before moving on to a new selection, go to your Evidence Log and record what you learned from these sonnets.

CLAIM	

SUPPORT	
Details From the Text(s)	**Additional Support**

Draft and Revise Your Response Remember that a response to literature usually employs formal language. That doesn't mean your language needs to be stiff and ornate, but it does mean that you should adopt a professional tone while writing. Consider the voice of your writing while you are drafting and revising to create a response that is authoritative and confident.

from The Naked Babe and the Cloak of Manliness

from Macbeth

Concept Vocabulary

As you perform your first read, you will encounter these words.

perception	unambiguous	idiosyncratic

Context Clues To find the meaning of an unfamiliar word, look for clues in the context, which includes the words, punctuation, and images that surround the unknown word. Pay close attention to negative qualifiers when trying to determine a word's meaning.

> **Unfamilar Word:** *adventitious*
>
> **Context:** But the pathos is not **adventitious**; the scene ties into the inner symbolism of the play.
>
> **Analysis:** If the pathos *were* adventitious, it would *not* tie into the rest of the play.
>
> **Possible Meaning:** *Adventitious* may mean "outside" or "unrelated."

Apply your knowledge of context clues and other vocabulary strategies to determine the meanings of unfamiliar words you encounter during your first read. Consult a resource such as an online dictionary to verify meanings you infer.

First Read NONFICTION

Apply these strategies as you conduct your first read. You will have an opportunity to complete a close read after your first read.

STANDARDS

Reading Informational Text
By the end of grade 12, read and comprehend literary nonfiction at the high end of the grades 11–CCR text complexity band independently and proficiently.

Language
• Determine or clarify the meaning of unknown and multiple-meaning words and phrases based on *grades 11–12 reading and content*, choosing flexibly from a range of strategies.
• Use context as a clue to the meaning of a word or phrase.
• Verify the preliminary determination of the meaning of a word or phrase.

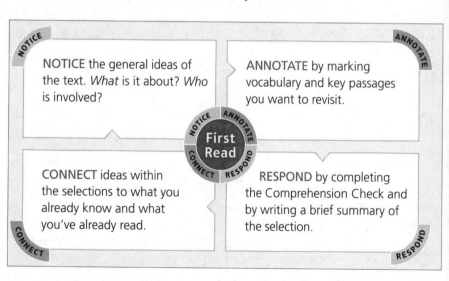

NOTICE the general ideas of the text. *What* is it about? *Who* is involved?

ANNOTATE by marking vocabulary and key passages you want to revisit.

First Read

CONNECT ideas within the selections to what you already know and what you've already read.

RESPOND by completing the Comprehension Check and by writing a brief summary of the selection.

About the Authors

Cleanth Brooks (1906–1994) was born in Kentucky. Brooks is perhaps best known for helping, through his literary criticism, change the way that poetry was taught in American colleges and universities. He is the author of highly regarded works of literary criticism, including *The Well Wrought Urn* and *Modern Poetry and the Tradition.*

Frank Kermode (1919–2010) was a literary critic who wrote in-depth analyses of works ranging from the Bible to those of Shakespeare and beyond. He was a former professor of modern English at University College, London, and was knighted by Queen Elizabeth in 1991.

Backgrounds

from The Naked Babe and the Cloak of Manliness

Throughout his plays, William Shakespeare uses complex symbolism to explore and convey his key themes. In this piece of literary criticism, from the book *The Well Wrought Urn*, Cleanth Brooks examines the usage and development of symbolic imagery related to children and growth in *The Tragedy of Macbeth.*

from Macbeth

In this essay, Frank Kermode explores the concept of time in *The Tragedy of Macbeth*. Much of the play is driven by concerns about the future, its uncertainty, and its ambiguity. This piece of literary criticism is a prime example of the ideas found in Kermode's *Shakespeare's Language*, in which he explores how audiences, since Shakespeare's time, have found meaning in the playwright's intricate, poetic language.

Note that Kermode follows British spelling conventions (for instance, *behaviour*) and cites line numbers that may differ from those that appear in the version of *Macbeth* the play presented earlier in this unit. As is common in scholarly works, the author has included citations and commentary in the form of footnotes.

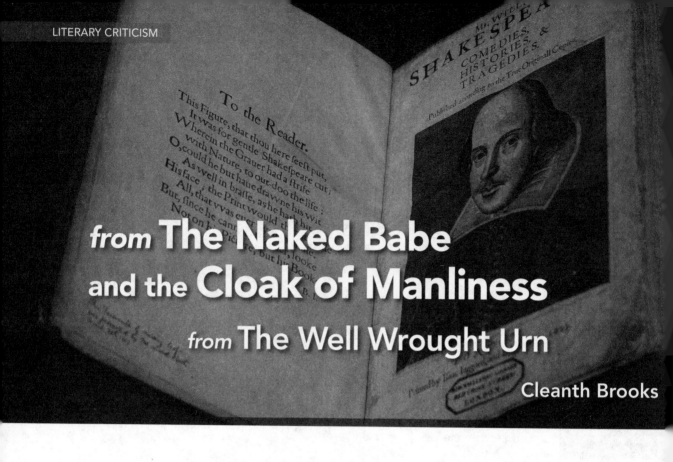

from The Naked Babe and the Cloak of Manliness

from The Well Wrought Urn

Cleanth Brooks

Mark context clues or indicate another strategy you used that helped you determine meaning.

perception (puhr SEHP shuhn) *n.*

MEANING:

unambiguous (uhn am BIHG yoo uhs) *adj.*

MEANING:

1 Tempted by the Weird Sisters and urged on by his wife, Macbeth is . . . caught between the irrational and the rational. There is a sense, of course, in which every man is caught between them. Man must try to predict and plan and control his destiny. That is man's fate; and the struggle, if he is to realize himself as a man, cannot be avoided. The question, of course, which has always interested the tragic dramatist involves the terms on which the struggle is accepted and the protagonist's attitude toward fate and toward himself. Macbeth in his general concern for the future is typical—is Every Man. He becomes the typical tragic protagonist when he yields to pride and *hybris*.[1] The occasion for temptation is offered by the prophecy of the Weird Sisters. They offer him knowledge which cannot be arrived at rationally. They offer a key—if only a partial key—to what is otherwise unpredictable. Lady Macbeth, on the other hand, by employing a ruthless clarity of perception, by discounting all emotional claims, offers him the promise of bringing about the course of events which he desires.

2 Now, in the middle of the play, though he has not lost confidence and though, as he himself says, there can be no turning back, doubts have begun to arise; and he returns to the Weird Sisters to secure unambiguous answers to his fears. But, pathetically and ironically for Macbeth, in returning to the Weird Sisters, he is really trying to impose rationality on what sets itself forth plainly as irrational: that is, Macbeth would force a rigid control on a future which, by

---

1. **hybris** (HY brihs) *n.* hubris; arrogance.

definition—by the very fact that the Weird Sisters already know it—stands beyond his manipulation.

3   It is because of his hopes for his own children and his fears of Banquo's that he has returned to the witches for counsel. It is altogether appropriate, therefore, that two of the apparitions by which their counsel is revealed should be babes, the crowned babe and the bloody babe.

4   For the babe signifies the future which Macbeth would control and cannot control. It is the unpredictable thing itself—as Yeats has put it magnificently, "The uncontrollable mystery on the bestial floor." It is the one thing that can justify, even in Macbeth's mind, the murders which he has committed. Earlier in the play, Macbeth had declared that if the deed could "trammel up the consequence," he would be willing to "jump the life to come." But he cannot jump the life to come. In his own terms he is betrayed. For it is idle to speak of jumping the life to come if one yearns to found a line of kings. It is the babe that betrays Macbeth—his own babes, most of all.

5   The logic of Macbeth's distraught mind, thus, forces him to make war on children, a war which in itself reflects his desperation and is a confession of weakness. Macbeth's ruffians, for example, break into Macduff's castle and kill his wife and children. The scene in which the innocent child prattles with his mother about his absent father, and then is murdered, is typical Shakespearean "fourth act" pathos.[2] But the pathos is not adventitious; the scene ties into the inner symbolism of the play. For the child, in its helplessness, defies the murderers. Its defiance testifies to the force which threatens Macbeth and which Macbeth cannot destroy.

6   But we are not, of course, to placard[3] the child as The Future in a rather stiff and mechanical allegory. *Macbeth* is no such allegory. Shakespeare's symbols are richer and more flexible than that. The babe signifies not only the future; it symbolizes all those enlarging purposes which make life meaningful, and it symbolizes, furthermore, all those emotional and—to Lady Macbeth—irrational ties which make man more than a machine—which render him human. It signifies preeminently the pity which Macbeth, under Lady Macbeth's tutelage, would wean himself of as something "unmanly." Lady Macbeth's great speeches early in the play become brilliantly ironical when we realize that Shakespeare is using the same symbol for the unpredictable future that he uses for human compassion. Lady Macbeth is willing to go to any length to grasp the future: she would willingly dash out the brains of her own child if it stood in her way to that future. But this is to repudiate the future, for the child is its symbol.

7   Shakespeare does not, of course, limit himself to the symbolism of the child: he makes use of other symbols of growth and development, notably that of the plant. And this plant symbolism patterns itself to

2. **pathos** (PAY thohs) *n.* quality that arouses feelings of pity, sympathy, sorrow, or compassion.
3. **placard** (PLAK ahrd) *v.* display.

reflect the development of the play. For example, Banquo says to the Weird Sisters, early in the play:

> If you can look into the seeds of time,
> And say which grain will grow and which will not,
> Speak then to me. . . .

A little later, on welcoming Macbeth, Duncan says to him:

> I have begun to plant thee, and will labor
> To make thee full of growing.

After the murder of Duncan, Macbeth falls into the same metaphor when he comes to resolve on Banquo's death. The Weird Sisters, he reflects, had hailed Banquo as

> . . . father to a line of kings.
> Upon my head they placed a fruitless crown,
> And put a barren scepter in my gripe. . . .

Late in the play, Macbeth sees himself as the winter-stricken tree:

> I have liv'd long enough: my way of life
> Is fall'n into the sear, the yellow leaf. . . .

8   The plant symbolism, then, supplements the child symbolism. At points it merges with it, as when Macbeth ponders bitterly that he has damned himself

> To make them kings, the seed of Banquo kings!

And, in at least one brilliant example, the plant symbolism unites with the clothes symbolism. It is a crowning irony that one of the Weird Sisters' prophecies on which Macbeth has staked his hopes is fulfilled when Birnam Wood comes to Dunsinane. For, in a sense, Macbeth is here hoist on his own petard. Macbeth, who has invoked night to "Scarf up the tender eye of pitiful day," and who has, again and again, used the "false face" to "hide what the false heart doth know," here has the trick turned against him. But the garment which cloaks the avengers is the living green of nature itself, and nature seems, to the startled eyes of his sentinels, to be rising up against him.

9   But it is the babe, the child, that dominates the symbolism. Most fittingly, the last of the prophecies in which Macbeth has placed his confidence, concerns the child: and Macbeth comes to know the final worst when Macduff declares to him that he was not "born of woman" but was from his "mother's womb / Untimely ripp'd." The babe here has defied even the thing which one feels may reasonably be predicted of him—his time of birth. With Macduff's pronouncement, the unpredictable has broken through the last shred of the net of calculation. The future cannot be trammeled up.[4] The naked babe confronts Macbeth to pronounce his doom.

---

4. **trammeled up** restrained.

10   The passage with which we began this essay, then, is an integral part of a larger context, and of a very rich context:

> And pity, like a naked new-born babe,
> Striding the blast, or heaven's cherubim, hors'd
> Upon the sightless couriers of the air,
> Shall blow the horrid deed in every eye,
> That tears shall drown the wind.

11   Pity is like the naked babe, the most sensitive and helpless thing; yet, almost as soon as the comparison is announced, the symbol of weakness begins to turn into a symbol of strength; for the babe, though newborn, is pictured as "Striding the blast" like an elemental force—like "heaven's cherubim, hors'd / Upon the sightless couriers of the air." We can give an answer to the question put earlier: is Pity like the human and helpless babe, or powerful as the angel that rides the winds? It is both; and it is strong because of its very weakness. The paradox is inherent in the situation itself; and it is the paradox that will destroy the overbrittle rationalism on which Macbeth founds his career.

12   For what will it avail Macbeth to cover the deed with the blanket of the dark if the elemental forces that ride the winds will blow the horrid deed in every eye? And what will it avail Macbeth to clothe himself in "manliness"—to become bloody, bold, and resolute—if he is to find himself again and again, viewing his bloody work through the "eye of childhood / That fears a painted devil"? Certainly, the final and climactic appearance of the babe symbol merges all the contradictory elements of the symbol. For, with Macduff's statement about his birth, the naked babe rises before Macbeth as not only the future that eludes calculation but as avenging angel as well.

13   The clothed daggers and the naked babe—mechanism and life—instrument and end—death and birth—that which should be left bare and clean and that which should be clothed and warmed—these are facets of two of the great symbols which run throughout the play. They are not the only symbols, to be sure; they are not the most obvious symbols: darkness and blood appear more often. But with a flexibility which must amaze the reader, the image of the garment and the image of the babe are so used as to encompass an astonishingly large area of the total situation. And between them—the naked babe, essential humanity, humanity stripped down to the naked thing itself, and yet as various as the future—and the various garbs which humanity assumes, the robes of honor, the hypocrite's disguise, the inhuman "manliness" with which Macbeth endeavors to cover up his essential humanity—between them, they furnish Shakespeare with his most subtle and ironically telling instruments. ❧

from **Macbeth**
from Shakespeare's Language

Frank Kermode

1   Looking at it from a distance, we can see that the distinctive character of the language of *Macbeth* is largely dictated by its structure. From the first suggestion of a plot on Duncan's life until his murder, the play exists in a world of nightmare doubt and decision: to kill or not to kill. As Thomas de Quincey expressed it in his superb essay "On the Knocking at the Gate in *Macbeth*," the knocking makes it known "that the reaction has commenced, the human has made its reflex upon the fiendish; the pulses of life are beginning to beat again; and the re-establishment of the goings-on of the world in which we live makes us profoundly sensible of the awful parenthesis that had suspended them."[1] Or one could cite Brutus's soliloquy in *Julius Caesar*:

> Between the acting of a dreadful thing
> And the first motion, all the interim is
> Like a phantasma or a hideous dream.
>
> (II.i.63–65)

2   The action before the murder is situated in this "interim" (Macbeth himself uses the word in I.iii.154), and the verse is designed to match

---

1. The essay first appeared in the *London Magazine* for October 1823 and has often been reprinted.

the terrible and uncertain decisions that occupy it. The play as a whole is greatly preoccupied with time; the Show of Kings itself covers many generations, and there is lasting concern about lineal descendants, Macbeth fearing that whereas he has no prospect of dynastic successors, Banquo has—a difference underlined by the Weird Sisters. The way to succeed Duncan was to kill him; the way to prevent the succession of Banquo's heirs was to kill both Banquo and Fleance. In both cases it was necessary to consider interference with the future as the Sisters foresaw it. So, in the early part of the play, the verse is full of equivocations about the present and the future, as forecast by the gnomic sayings of the Three Sisters.

3   Their opening lines represent a new departure, for they tell us nothing directly about the subject of the play, speaking only of the future as perceived from the present. "When shall we three meet again? / In thunder, lightning, or in rain?" offers an apparent choice of weathers that is not a choice at all, which partly prefigures the plight of Macbeth and suggests a vain selection of some aspects of futurity at the expense of others not mentioned—fine weather, for instance. The answer to these questions is "When the hurlyburly's done, / When the battle's lost and won." Hurlies and burlies go together like thunder and lightning, won battles are also lost; so we have false antitheses, ghostly choices, an ironic parody of human powers of prediction. "Fair is foul, and foul is fair" is a paradox echoed by Macbeth in the first line he speaks (I.iii.38). In his mouth the words may be taken at face value, as referring to the bad weather on one hand and the pleasures of victory on the other; the Sisters' use of the idea is darker and more complex. Perhaps what strikes them as fair is what to others would be foul, a crown got by crime, for instance. The paradox is oracular; oracles are traditionally equivocal. *Macbeth* is a play of prophecy focussed, with great concentration, on the desire to feel the future in the instant, to be transported "beyond the ignorant present." When Macbeth asks the Sisters, "what are you?" (I.iii.47), their reply is to tell him what he *will* be. The present is the long interim between thought and act (an interim that disappears when Macbeth decides to let the firstlings of his heart become the firstlings of his hand, "To crown my thoughts with acts, be it thought and done" [IV.i.149]). The first part of the play is set in a time when there is still a gap between the thought and the deed, and its language enacts this dizzying gap.

4   Here, perhaps more than in any other of Shakespeare's plays, an idiosyncratic rhythm and a lexical habit establish themselves with a sort of hypnotic firmness. "Lost and won," say the Sisters at the beginning of the first scene: "What he hath lost, noble Macbeth hath won," says Duncan at the end of the second, having just before that rhymed "Macbeth" with "death." These moments of ingrown self-allusion contrast with the old-style rant of the bleeding Sergeant. The scene in which Macbeth and Banquo encounter the Sisters (I.iii) fully exhibits the new and peculiar ambiguous, doubling manner. Are these figures inhabitants of the earth or not? Men or women? Alive or not? They reply with their prophecy: he is already Glamis, will be Cawdor, will be King.

NOTES

Mark context clues or indicate another strategy you used that helped you determine meaning.

idiosyncratic (ihd ee uh sihn KRAT ihk) *adj.*

MEANING:

Banquo answers with questions to Macbeth: why does he *fear* what seems so *fair*? Then he addresses the Sisters: "Are ye fantastical, or that indeed / Which outwardly ye show?" (53–54). Are you what you appear to be, or mere apparitions? Why do you speak to him and not to me?

> If you can look into the seeds of time,
> And say which grain will grow, and which will not,
> Speak then to me, who neither beg nor fear
> Your favors nor your hate.
>
> (58–61)

5   Here the rhythms reinforce the return to the original question: What can be known of the future in the present? Him/me, grow/not grow, beg/fear, favors/hate, even when they are not, as it were, necessary, part of the substance, the oppositions and alternatives sound on continually. "Lesser than Macbeth, and greater. / Not so happy, yet much happier. / Thou shalt get kings, though thou be none" (65–67). Macbeth calls the Sisters "imperfect speakers" (70), meaning that what they say is not complete enough to be understood or to satisfy him. But they vanish, leaving their imperfect speeches to be completed according to taste: "Your children shall be kings. *You* shall be king" (86). The "self-same tune" is now repetitively in our ears.

6   When Ross confirms Macbeth's appointment as Thane of Cawdor, Banquo's reaction is to ask, "What, can the devil speak true?" (107). And Macbeth begins the famous sequence of allusions to borrowed or ill-fitting garments: "why do you dress me / In borrowed robes?" (108–109). Banquo repeats the figure almost immediately (144–146). Here these robes, if borrowed, must be on loan from the future, and they confirm a devil's prophecy, although the fiend as a rule "lies like truth" (V.v.43). Banquo fears that this truth has been told to do harm: "The instruments of darkness tell us truths, / Win us with honest trifles, to betray 's / In deepest consequence" (I.iii.124–126). And Macbeth, contemplating a future in which he may have to murder in order to fulfil the prophecy of kingship, speaks a long aside which now completely establishes the rhythm of the interim:

> This supernatural soliciting
> Cannot be ill; cannot be good. If ill,
> Why hath it given me earnest of success,
> Commencing in a truth? I am Thane of Cawdor.
> If good, why do I yield to that suggestion
> Whose horrid image doth unfix my hair
> And make my seated heart knock at my ribs,
> Against the use of nature? Present fears
> Are less than horrible imaginings:
> My thought, whose murther yet is but fantastical,
> Shakes so my single state of man that function
> Is smother'd in surmise, and nothing is
> But what is not.
>
> (130–42)

7   The tempting promise of the Sisters, here compacted in the sinister phrase "supernatural soliciting," seems good in so far as it began with a now undoubted truth; it seems bad in that the temptation to murder induces in him an unnatural fear and brings up the image of a dead king. These fears arise from something less than the horrors would be if they were actual; yet they are already actual enough to shake him terribly. He is "rapt" (142), his ordinary behaviour forgotten in thoughts of that imagined future action. "[N]othing is / But what is not"—that is, the present is no longer present, the unacted future has occupied its place. These difficult thoughts all turn on the incantatory rhythm of "Cannot be ill; cannot be good," and of "nothing is / But what is not," as indeed will much of the verse from this point on until Duncan is dead.

8   More than any other play, *Macbeth* dwells on this moment of crisis, a moment that seems exempt from the usual movement of time, when the future is crammed into the present. St. Augustine wrote about such a moment, the gap between desire and act. Though he was certain of the end desires, he was "at strife" with himself. The choices to be made were "all meeting together in the same juncture of time." He said to himself, "Be it done now, be it done now," but he continued to hesitate between fair and foul, crying, "How long? How long? Tomorrow and tomorrow?"[2] This, for Macbeth, as for the saint, is the moment when the soul distends itself to include past and future. Throughout the early scenes we are being prepared for the astonishingly original verse of the great soliloquy in I.vii. . . .

9   . . . On many occasions Shakespeare, needing a simple expression, cannot avoid complicating it . . . as if by an excess of energy, but they should be distinguished from passages in which that energy is fully and properly employed; and one of the greatest of these is Macbeth's soliloquy at the beginning of I.vii:

> If it were done, when 'tis done, then 'twere well
> It were done quickly. If th' assassination
> Could trammel up the consequence, and catch
> With his surcease, success; that but this blow
> Might be the be-all and the end-all—here,
> But here, upon this bank and shoal of time,
> We'd jump the life to come. But in these cases
> We still have judgment here, that we but teach
> Bloody instructions, which, being taught, return
> To plague th' inventor. This even-handed justice
> Commends th' ingredience of our poison'd chalice
> To our own lips. He's here in double trust:
> First, as I am his kinsman and his subject,
> Strong both against the deed; then, as his host,
> Who should against his murtherer shut the door,
> Not bear the knife myself. Besides, this Duncan

2. *Confessions*, VII, xii (*quamdiu, quamdiu, 'cras et cras'?"*). Reading *The Tragedy of Macbeth*, I find it hard to believe that Shakespeare did not know this work, especially Book XI.

Hath borne his faculties so meek, hath been
So clear in his great office, that his virtues
Will plead like angels, trumpet-tongu'd, against
The deep damnation of his taking-off;
And pity, like a naked new-born babe,
Striding the blast, or heaven's cherubin, hors'd
Upon the sightless couriers of the air,
Shall blow the horrid deed in every eye,
That tears shall drown the wind. I have no spur
To prick the sides of my intent, but only
Vaulting ambition, which o'erleaps itself,
And falls on th' other—

(1–28)

10   The passage is famous, and so are some examples of interpretative criticism it has attracted.[3] Like St. Augustine, Macbeth has to consider what is implied by his need to do in order to possess what is by that act done. The triple repetition of "done" gives a fairly commonplace, even proverbial saying an intense local force.[4] If the murder could of its own power prevent all that follows such a deed, if Duncan's death could put an end not only to him but to all that would follow it, then at this stationary moment in time he would "jump the life to come," risk consequences in another life. But paraphrase of this sort entirely misses the force of "surcease, success," a compaction of language into what has been called a "seesaw rhythm" that is the motto rhythm of the great interim. "Be-all and end-all," another such compaction, has passed into the common language, yet it seems to be Shakespeare's coinage. If only time could be made to stop at the desired moment of the future! However, to be and to end are antithetical, they can only contradict each other; time, as Hotspur said in his dying speech, "must have a stop," though our experience of it does not. The act of murder cannot be an end;[5] nothing in time can, in that sense, be "done." You can't have hurly without burly, surcease does not imply the end of success (succession). No act is without success in this sense. ❧

---

3. For example, Cleanth Brooks, "The Naked Babe and the Cloak of Manliness," in *The Well Wrought Urn* (1947). Brooks's methods are no longer in fashion, and his emphasis on the structural importance of images has often been contested, but if it is valid anywhere it is valid in relation to *Macbeth*.

4. "The thing that is done is not to do"—M. P. Tilley, *A Dictionary of the Proverbs in England* (1950, s.v.). We have not yet done with these repetitions: "Things without all remedy / Should be without regard: what's done, is done" (III.ii.12); "What's done cannot be undone" (V.i.65).

5. Hilda Hulme in *Explorations in Shakespeare's Language* persuasively suggests that *trammel* in the third line of the speech, means "to bind up a corpse within a shroud" (pp. 21–22). The word is usually taken to drive from the noun *trammel*, a fishing or fowling net, a hobble for a horse, or a device for hanging pots over a fire; where the first sense is preferred, the net being a figure for the catching up of "success." See Empson, *Seven Types of Ambiguity*, pp. 49–50. Hulme's proposal is apt in that a murdered body so bound up would rather vividly symbolise an end, here so much desired.

Comprehension Check

Complete the following items after you finish your first read. Review and clarify details with your group.

from THE NAKED BABE AND THE CLOAK OF MANLINESS

1. According to Brooks, what is ironic about Macbeth's returning to the Weird Sisters for answers?

2. In Brooks's analysis, what are some of the things that the child symbolizes in *Macbeth*?

3. How does Brooks interpret the Weird Sisters' last prophecy?

from MACBETH

1. How does Kermode define the "interim" of time in which much of *Macbeth* takes place?

2. What examples of "false antitheses," or inaccurate opposites, does Kermode cite?

3. How does Kermode characterize the specific language patterns of *Macbeth*?

4. 📓 **Notebook** Confirm your understanding of the texts by writing a three-sentence summary of each of them.

- -

RESEARCH

Research to Clarify Choose at least one unfamiliar detail from one of the texts. Briefly research that detail. In what way does the information you learned shed light on an aspect of the essay?

from THE NAKED BABE AND THE
CLOAK OF MANLINESS | *from*
MACBETH

TIP

GROUP DISCUSSION
When discussing literary criticism, be sure to distinguish between the critic's analysis and the original text the critic is discussing. You will probably want to refer to each critic's views, as well as specific lines from *The Tragedy of Macbeth,* while you discuss these essays.

WORD NETWORK

Add interesting words related to time from the text to your Word Network.

STANDARDS

Reading Informational Text
Determine two or more central ideas of a text and analyze their development over the course of the text, including how they interact and build on one another to produce a complex analysis; provide an objective summary of the text.

Language
Identify and correctly use patterns of word changes that indicate different meanings or parts of speech.

Close Read the Text

With your group, revisit sections of the texts you marked during your first read. **Annotate** details that you notice. What **questions** do you have? What can you **conclude**?

Analyze the Text

CITE TEXTUAL EVIDENCE
to support your answers.

Notebook Complete the activities.

1. **Review and Clarify** With your group, reread paragraph 3 of the excerpt from Kermode's "Macbeth." What meanings does Kermode find in the Weird Sisters' introductory incantation? Do you agree with his interpretation of these lines? Why or why not?

2. **Present and Discuss** Now, work with your group to share the passages from the essays that you found especially important. Take turns presenting and discussing your passages.

3. **Essential Question:** *How do our attitudes toward the past and future shape our actions?* What have these texts taught you about how the passage of time affects people's actions?

LANGUAGE DEVELOPMENT

Concept Vocabulary

perception	unambiguous	idiosyncratic

Why These Words? The three concept vocabulary words are related. With your group, discuss the words, and determine what the words have in common. How do these word choices enhance the impact of the text?

Practice

Notebook Use the concept vocabulary words in sentences. In each sentence, provide context clues that hint at the word's meaning.

Word Study

Patterns of Word Changes Affixes usually perform one of two functions. Some change a word's meaning. For example, Brooks points out that Macbeth seeks *unambiguous* answers from the Weird Sisters, whereas Kermode emphasizes the *ambiguous* nature of their language. Adding the prefix *un-* to *ambiguous* changes its meaning from "vague" to "certain."

Other affixes change a word's grammatical function. Brooks describes Lady Macbeth's "ruthless clarity of *perception,*" whereas Kermode discusses how the future is "*perceived* from the present." Adding the suffix *-tion* to *perceive* changes the word from a verb to a noun without affecting its core meaning, "to be aware of something using the senses."

Notebook Analyze four words from these essays. Choose two words in which an affix changes meaning and two in which it changes part of speech.

Analyze Craft and Structure

Analyze Arguments Literary criticism presents a writer's carefully reasoned analysis of one or more texts. The critic presents a **central idea** or **claim,** and develops it through a careful, supported explanation. The central idea must be thoroughly backed up by effective and relevant **supporting evidence,** which can include quotations from the original texts and detailed considerations of the language and themes, as well as references to the work of other literary critics or experts.

To identify central ideas, look for topics that receive significant attention in an essay. The title often points you toward an idea that is fundamental to the writer's analysis. For example, in "The Naked Babe and the Cloak of Manliness," one of Brooks's central ideas relates to the many ways in which one can interpret the image of the "naked babe" in Macbeth.

TIP

PROCESS

When your group identifies a central idea, look for at least two different kinds of supporting evidence that back it up. You might have each group member analyze how one idea is developed and supported. Then, share your analyses in a group discussion.

Practice

As a group, complete this chart to analyze the arguments that Brooks and Kermode make.

SELECTION	CENTRAL IDEAS	SUPPORTING EVIDENCE
from The Naked Babe and the Cloak of Manliness by Cleanth Brooks		
from Macbeth by Frank Kermode		

📓 **Notebook** Answer the questions.

1. Do you find Brooks's support for his central idea convincing? Why or why not?

2. **(a)** In your own words, explain Kermode's idea that the language of *Macbeth* is rich in a "peculiar ambiguous, doubling manner." **(b)** Do you find his support for this idea convincing? Explain.

from THE NAKED BABE AND THE
CLOAK OF MANLINESS | from
MACBETH

Conventions and Style

Quotations Literary critics quote directly from the works they are analyzing in order to orient readers, to emphasize specific points, and to add authority to their arguments. There are two ways to set up quotations: inside quotation marks or block quotation.

- Place **quotation marks (")** before and after a short quotation.
- When a quotation is longer—usually two or more lines of a drama or four or more lines of prose—use a **block quotation**. Do not place quotation marks. Instead, indent the whole quotation, and introduce it with a colon (:).

Literary critics may choose to quote the exact language, not only of the works they are analyzing, but also of other critics or writers—for instance, when that language makes a point uniquely or memorably. When they do so, they must include clear **attribution**, or acknowledgment of the original writer.

EXAMPLE	USE OF CONVENTION
As Thomas de Quincey expressed it in his superb essay "On the Knocking at the Gate in Macbeth," the knocking makes it known "that . . . the re-establishment of the goings-on of the world in which we live makes us profoundly sensible of the awful parenthesis that has suspended them."	When Kermode uses this short quotation from another writer's work, he places it in quotation marks and includes clear attribution.
Or one could cite Brutus's soliloquy in Julius Caesar: Between the acting of a dreadful thing And the first motion, all the interim is Like a phantasma or a hideous dream (II.i.63–65)	When Kermode cites these three lines from Julius Caesar, he uses a colon and a block quotation, rather than quotation marks. He also indicates which lines he is quoting.

Read It

1. Reread the Brooks text, and find an example of attribution through quotation marks and an example of block quotation.

2. **Connect to Style** Reread paragraph 4 of Brooks's essay. Mark the word that indicates Brooks's motivation for quoting Yeats.

Write It

⊟ **Notebook** Write three sentences in which you make a point about the mood or symbolism in *The Tragedy of Macbeth*. In one sentence, quote from Shakespeare's play; in another, quote from the writing of Brooks or Kermode; and in the third, set up a block quotation from one of these three texts.

≡ STANDARDS

Language
- Demonstrate command of the conventions of standard English capitalization, punctuation, and spelling when writing.
- Apply knowledge of language to understand how language functions in different contexts, to make effective choices for meaning or style, and to comprehend more fully when reading or listening.

Speaking and Listening

Assignment

With your group, conduct a **panel discussion** about *The Tragedy of Macbeth* to help your audience interpret the play. Choose one of the prompts as the focus for your panel.

☐ Brooks points to Macbeth's preoccupation with controlling his destiny: "Tempted by the Weird Sisters and urged on by his wife, Macbeth is thus caught between the rational and the irrational. There is a sense, of course, in which every man is caught between them. Man must try to predict and control his destiny." Explain and evaluate Brooks's analysis of this fundamental theme.

☐ Brooks discusses various symbols in the play—children, plants, and clothing. In your view, which of those elements most dramatically captures the play's central ideas?

☐ Examine each critic's discussion of lines 21–25 of *The Tragedy of Macbeth*, Act I, Scene vii:

> *And pity, like a naked new-born babe,*
>
> *Striding the blast, or heaven's cherubin, hors'd*
>
> *Upon the sightless couriers of the air,*
>
> *Shall blow the horrid deed in every eye,*
>
> *That tears shall drown the wind.*

Which interpretation do you think is most compelling?

Plan Your Panel Most effective panel discussions have a strong moderator who controls the event, making sure that speakers stay on topic and stick to their allotted times. Choose a moderator for your group, and plan an organization for your panel. After an opening introduction, you might have each panelist speak separately, or you might discuss individual topics among the entire panel. Use an agenda, a list of topics in the order you would like to discuss them, to plan your panel.

Rehearse Your Panel Hold a preliminary panel discussion as a group before staging one before an audience. The moderator should keep track of how long each panelist speaks, providing prompts if needed to keep the panel on schedule. After the the preliminary discussion, each member should offer suggestions on ways to improve the discussion next time, when you hold it in front of an audience.

 TIP

COLLABORATION

Allow time for panelists to interact, asking one another questions to clarify or extend ideas. Also, consider planning time for a Q&A session with your audience.

📝 EVIDENCE LOG

Before moving on to a new selection, go to your Evidence Log and record what you learned from these pieces of literary criticism.

▤ STANDARDS

Speaking and Listening

• Propel conversations by posing and responding to questions that probe reasoning and evidence; ensure a hearing for a full range of positions on a topic or issue; clarify, verify, or challenge ideas and conclusions; and promote divergent and creative perspectives.

• Respond thoughtfully to diverse perspectives; synthesize comments, claims, and evidence made on all sides of an issue; resolve contradictions when possible; and determine what additional information or research is required to deepen the investigation or complete the task.

SOURCES

- SONNET 12
- SONNET 60
- SONNET 73
- SONNET 32
- SONNET 75
- *from* THE NAKED BABE AND THE CLOAK OF MANLINESS
- *from* MACBETH

Present an Argument

Assignment

You have just read a variety of sonnets as well as literary criticism related to the content and language of literature from earlier times. Work with your group to develop a **presentation** in which you state and support a position on this question:

> Should literature of the past be rewritten in present-day language for today's readers?

Plan With Your Group

Analyze the Text Consider each of the sonnets in turn. Determine which language in the poem might prove troublesome for present-day readers. Then, decide whether or not the language should be updated and, if so, how certain passages might be rewritten. If the language should not be changed, write "no change" in the Revised Language column. Using this analysis, come to a consensus about the question posed in the prompt—yes or no?

TITLE	TROUBLESOME LANGUAGE	REVISED LANGUAGE
Sonnet 12		
Sonnet 60		
Sonnet 73		
Sonnet 32		
Sonnet 75		
Our claim: The poetry of the past should/should not be revised into present-day language for today's readers because . . .		

Gather Evidence Have each group member focus on one sonnet. Scan the sonnet to find specific examples to support the group's position. Scan the literary criticism by Brooks or Kermode to see whether one or both of those texts might have useful evidence. Decide how to incorporate any revised language from the chart into your argument.

STANDARDS

Speaking and Listening
- Initiate and participate effectively in a range of collaborative discussions with diverse partners on *grades 11–12 topics, texts, and issues*, building on others's ideas and expressing their own clearly and persuasively.
- Come to discussions prepared, having read and researched material under study; explicitly draw on that preparation by referring to evidence from texts and other research on the topic or issue to stimulate a thoughtful, well-reasoned exchange of ideas.
- Present information, findings, and supporting evidence, conveying a clear and distinct perspective, such that listeners can follow the line of reasoning, alternative or opposing perspectives are addressed, and the organization, development, substance, and style are appropriate to purpose, audience, and a range of formal and informal tasks.

Organize Your Presentation Come together as a group, and share your ideas for each sonnet. Decide on an order of presentation that makes sense. Is there one sonnet that is an especially good example with which to support your claim? You might use that one first, or you might build up to it by presenting weaker examples first.

Rehearse With Your Group

Practice With Your Group As you deliver your portion of the presentation, use this checklist to evaluate the effectiveness of your group's first run-through. Then, use your evaluation and these instructions to guide your revision.

CONTENT	REFERRAL TO TEXT	PRESENTATION TECHNIQUES
☐ The presentation presents and supports a clear claim.	☐ Passages from the sonnets are quoted effectively in support of the claim.	☐ The speaker uses eye contact and speaks clearly.
☐ Each speaker reveals details that supply evidence in support of the group's position.	☐ Any modernized revisions of the sonnets help support the claim.	☐ The speaker quotes poetry fluently and accurately.
		☐ Transitions from speaker to speaker are smooth.

Fine-Tune the Content Make sure that the first speaker presents the group's position on the question in the prompt so that the connection of each speaker's examples to the claim is clear.

Improve Referrals to Text To provide clear evidence for your claim, you must use ample examples from the texts and from your revisions. If your part of the presentation seems incomplete, find another example to strengthen it.

Brush Up on Your Presentation Techniques Practice reciting the quotations you use until you can easily pronounce all words and sound confident in your delivery.

Present and Evaluate

As you present with your group, listen to your fellow presenters to see whether as a whole you have done an adequate job of supporting your claim. Even if other groups disagree with your group, evaluate them on their ability to present convincing and well-organized evidence to support their positions on the question in the prompt.

⊞ STANDARDS

Speaking and Listening
• Evaluate a speaker's point of view, reasoning, and use of evidence and rhetoric, assessing the stance, premises, links among ideas, word choice, points of emphasis, and tone used.
• Present information, findings, and supporting evidence, conveying a clear and distinct perspective and a logical argument, such that listeners can follow the line of reasoning, alternative or opposing perspectives are addressed, and the organization, development, substance, and style are appropriate to purpose, audience, and a range of formal and informal tasks.

ESSENTIAL QUESTION:

How do our attitudes toward the past and future shape our actions?

Our interpretation of the past and our feelings about the future contribute to the decisions we make in the present. In this section, you will complete your study of time and how it affects our approach to the world by exploring an additional selection related to the topic. You will then share what you learn with classmates. To choose a text, follow these steps.

Look Back Think about the selections you have already studied. Which aspects of the influence of the past and future on our actions do you wish to explore further? Which time period interests you the most?

Look Ahead Preview the texts by reading the descriptions. Which one seems most interesting and appealing to you?

Look Inside Take a few minutes to scan the text you chose. Choose a different one if this text doesn't meet your needs.

Independent Learning Strategies

Throughout your life, in school, in your community, and in your career, you will need to rely on yourself to learn and work on your own. Review these strategies and the actions you can take to practice them during Independent Learning. Add ideas of your own for each category.

STRATEGY	ACTION PLAN
Create a schedule	• Understand your goals and deadlines. • Make a plan for what to do each day. •
Practice what you have learned	• Use first-read and close-read strategies to deepen your understanding. • After you read, evaluate the usefulness of the evidence to help you understand the topic. • After reading, consult reference sources for background information that can help you clarify meaning. •
Take notes	• Record important ideas and information. • Review your notes before preparing to share with a group. •

CONTENTS

Choose one selection. Selections are available online only.

First-Read Guide

Use this page to record your first-read ideas.

Tool Kit
First-Read Guide and
Model Annotation

Selection Title: _____

NOTICE

NOTICE new information or ideas you learn about the unit topic as you first read this text.

ANNOTATE

ANNOTATE by marking vocabulary and key passages you want to revisit.

First Read

NOTICE · ANNOTATE · CONNECT · RESPOND

CONNECT

CONNECT ideas within the selection to other knowledge, the Essential Question, and the selections you have read. Use reliable reference material to clarify historical context.

RESPOND

RESPOND by writing a brief summary of the selection.

▦ STANDARD

Reading Read and comprehend complex literary and informational texts independently and proficiently.

Close-Read Guide

Use this page to record your close-read ideas.

Selection Title: _____

Close Read the Text

Revisit sections of the text you marked during your first read. Read these sections closely and **annotate** what you notice. Ask yourself **questions** about the text. What can you **conclude**? Write down your ideas.

Analyze the Text

Think about the author's choices of patterns, structure, techniques, and ideas included in the text. Select one and record your thoughts about what this choice conveys.

QuickWrite

Pick a paragraph from the text that grabbed your interest. Explain the power of this passage.

📋 **STANDARD**

Reading Read and comprehend complex literary and informational texts independently band proficiently.

EVIDENCE LOG

Go to your Evidence Log
and record what you learned
from the text you read.

Share Your Independent Learning

Prepare to Share

> How do our attitudes toward the past and future shape
> our actions?

Even when you read or learn something independently, your understanding
continues to grow when you share what you have learned with others.
Reflect on the text you explored independently, and write notes about its
connection to the unit. In your notes, consider why this text belongs in
this unit.

Learn from Your Classmates

Discuss It Share your ideas about the text you explored on your own.
As you talk with your classmates, jot down ideas that you learn from them.

Reflect

Review your notes, and mark the most important insight you gained from
these writing and discussion activities. Explain how this idea adds to your
understanding of the ways in which our attitudes toward the past and future
shape our actions.

STANDARDS

Speaking and Listening
Initiate and participate effectively
in a range of collaborative
discussions with diverse partners
on *grades 11–12 topics, texts, and
issues*, building on others' ideas and
expressing their own clearly and
persuasively.

Review Evidence for an Argument

At the beginning of this unit, you took a position on the following topic:

What is the relationship of human beings to time?

Review your Evidence Log and your QuickWrite from the beginning of the unit. Has your position changed?

NOTES

Develop your thoughts into a topic sentence:
How the passage of time shapes our actions can be shown through:

Identify a historical example of the reason you identified:

_____

_____

_____

Evaluate the Strength of Your Evidence Which two texts that you read in this unit offer the strongest support for your topic sentence?

Write the titles here.

1. _____

2. _____

What are some other resources you might use to locate information about the topic?

1. _____

2. _____

3. _____

4. _____

⊟ STANDARDS

Writing
Introduce precise, knowledgeable claim(s), establish the significance of the claim(s), distinguish the claim(s) from alternate or opposing claims, and create an organization that logically sequences claim(s), counterclaims, reasons, and evidence.

PART 1

Writing to Sources: Argument

In this unit, you read a major dramatic work, a series of sonnets, and a variety of other literature and criticism. All have something to say to readers about the connections of human beings to their pasts and futures.

Assignment

Write an **argument** in the form of a **response to literature** that answers this question:

What is the relationship of human beings to time?

In this argument, you will use examples and evidence from the diverse texts in the unit to justify a claim that you make. State your assertions with specific evidence from several of the texts. End your argument with a clear conclusion that restates or summarizes your claim.

Reread the Assignment Review the assignment to be sure you fully understand it. The assignment references some of the academic words presented at the beginning of the unit. Be sure you understand each of the words given below in order to complete the assignment correctly.

Academic Vocabulary

proficient	justify	diverse
catalyst	assertion	

Review the Elements of Effective Argument Before you begin writing, read the Argument Rubric. Once you have completed your first draft, check it against the rubric. If one or more of the elements is missing or not as strong as it could be, revise your argument to add or strengthen that component.

🔀 WORD NETWORK

As you write and revise your argument, use your Word Network to help vary your word choices.

▤ STANDARDS

Writing
• Write arguments to support claims in an analysis of substantive topics or texts, using valid reasoning and relevant and sufficient evidence.
• Draw evidence from literary or informational texts to support analysis, reflection, and research.
• Write routinely over extended time frames and shorter time frames for a range of tasks, purposes, and audiences.

Argument Rubric

	Focus and Organization	Evidence and Elaboration	Language Conventions
4	The introduction is engaging and establishes the claim in an engaging way. Valid reasons and evidence address and support the claim while clearly acknowledging counterclaims. Ideas progress logically and are linked by a variety of sentence transitions. The conclusion logically follows from what came before.	Sources of evidence are specific and relevant to the task. Claims are well supported with textual evidence. Vocabulary is used strategically and appropriately for the audience and purpose.	The text intentionally uses standard English conventions of usage and mechanics. The tone of the text is formal and objective.
3	The introduction is engaging and establishes the claim in a way that grabs readers' attention. Reasons and evidence address and support the claim while acknowledging counterclaims. Ideas progress logically and are linked by sentence transitions. The conclusion restates important information.	Sources of evidence contain relevant information. Most claims are supported with textual evidence. Vocabulary is generally appropriate for the audience and purpose.	The text demonstrates accuracy in standard English conventions of usage and mechanics. The tone of the text is mostly formal and objective.
2	The introduction establishes the claim. Some reasons and evidence support the claim, and counterclaims are briefly acknowledged. Ideas progress somewhat logically. A few sentence transitions connect ideas. The conclusion offers some insight into the claim and restates information.	Many ideas are supported with examples from research and the selections. Some claims are supported with textual evidence. Vocabulary is somewhat appropriate for the audience and purpose.	The text demonstrates some accuracy in standard English conventions of usage and mechanics. The tone of the essay is occasionally formal and objective.
1	The claim is not clearly stated. Reasons and evidence in support of the claim are sparse or nonexistent, and counterclaims are not acknowledged. Ideas do not progress logically. Sentences are often short and choppy and do not connect readers to the argument. The conclusion does not restate important information.	Reliable and relevant evidence is lacking. Few or no claims are supported. Vocabulary is limited or ineffective.	The text contains mistakes in standard English conventions of usage and mechanics. The tone of the text is informal.

PART 2
Speaking and Listening: TV Commentary

Assignment
After completing your response to literature, present your ideas as a **TV commentary** that might appear on a talk show about books and literature. Have a classmate video record your presentation to share with the class.

Follow these steps to develop your TV commentary.

- Highlight the parts of your argument that you think will best suit your audience and purpose. Weave those details into a short, lively script.
- Have a partner set up a video camera and record your commentary. Do a trial run to be sure your face is centered in the frame and that the microphone adequately captures your voice.
- Practice your delivery, looking up from your writing to engage with your audience through the camera.
- Vary your tone and volume to stress the points you find most important.

Review the Rubric The criteria by which your TV commentary will be evaluated appear in the rubric below. Review the criteria before delivering your analysis to ensure that you are prepared.

STANDARDS

Speaking and Listening
Present information, findings, and supporting evidence, conveying a clear and distinct perspective, such that listeners can follow the line of reasoning, alternative or opposing perspectives are addressed, and the organization, development, substance, and style are appropriate to purpose, audience, and a range of formal and informal tasks.

	Content	Use of Media	Presentation Techniques
3	Introduction engages the viewer in a compelling way. Strong evidence from the texts supports the claim.	The speaker's face is centered in the frame, and the focus is clear. The camera does not waver, and the sound is completely audible.	The speaker sounds interested and knowledgeable. The speaker varies tone and volume to maintain interest. The speaker addresses the audience through the camera.
2	The introduction establishes a claim. Some evidence from the texts supports the claim.	The speaker's face is mostly centered, and the focus is usually clear. The camera rarely wavers, and the sound is mostly audible.	The speaker sounds fairly interested and somewhat knowledgeable. The speaker sometimes varies tone and volume, but may be inconsistent. The speaker occasionally connects with the audience through the camera.
1	Introduction does not clearly state a claim. Evidence from the texts is lacking or is not obviously linked to a claim.	The speaker's face is not centered, and the picture may be out of focus. The camera often wavers, and the sound may be inaudible at times.	The speaker seems uninterested by or unfamiliar with the topic. The speaker speaks in a monotone or at a low volume. The speaker rarely looks up at the camera.

Reflect on the Unit

Now that you've completed the unit, take a few moments to reflect on your learning.

Reflect on the Unit Goals

Look back at the goals at the beginning of the unit. Use a different colored pen to rate yourself again. Then, think about readings and activities that contributed the most to the growth of your understanding. Record your thoughts.

Reflect on the Learning Strategies

Discuss It Write a reflection on whether you were able to improve your learning based on your Action Plans. Think about what worked, what didn't, and what you might do to keep working on these strategies. Record your ideas before joining a class discussion.

Reflect on the Text

Choose a selection that you found challenging, and explain what made it difficult.

Describe something that surprised you about a text in the unit.

Which activity taught you the most about our relationship to time? What did you learn?

:: STANDARDS

Speaking and Listening
• Initiate and participate effectively in a range of collaborative discussions with diverse partners on *grades 11–12 topics, texts, and issues*, building on others' ideas and expressing their own clearly and persuasively.
• Come to discussions prepared, having read and researched material under study; explicitly draw on that preparation by referring to evidence from texts and other research on the topic or issue to stimulate a thoughtful, well-reasoned exchange of ideas.

RESOURCES

CONTENTS

Marking the Text: Strategies and Tips for Annotation

When you close read a text, you read for comprehension and then reread to unlock layers of meaning and to analyze a writer's style and techniques. Marking a text as you read it enables you to participate more fully in the close-reading process.

Following are some strategies for text mark-ups, along with samples of how the strategies can be applied. These mark-ups are suggestions; you and your teacher may want to use other mark-up strategies.

*   Key Idea

!   I love it!

?   I have questions

◯   Unfamiliar or important word

----   Context Clues

Suggested Mark-Up Notations

WHAT I NOTICE	HOW TO MARK UP	QUESTIONS TO ASK
Key Ideas and Details	• Highlight key ideas or claims. • Underline supporting details or evidence.	• What does the text say? What does it leave unsaid? • What inferences do you need to make? • What details lead you to make your inferences?
Word Choice	• Circle unfamiliar words. • Put a dotted line under context clues, if any exist. • Put an exclamation point beside especially rich or poetic passages.	• What inferences about word meaning can you make? • What tone and mood are created by word choice? • What alternate word choices might the author have made?
Text Structure	• Highlight passages that show key details supporting the main idea. • Use arrows to indicate how sentences and paragraphs work together to build ideas. • Use a right-facing arrow to indicate foreshadowing. • Use a left-facing arrow to indicate flashback.	• Is the text logically structured? • What emotional impact do the structural choices create?
Author's Craft	• Circle or highlight instances of repetition, either of words, phrases, consonants, or vowel sounds. • Mark rhythmic beats in poetry using checkmarks and slashes. • Underline instances of symbolism or figurative language.	• Does the author's style enrich or detract from the reading experience? • What levels of meaning are created by the author's techniques?

CLOSE READING

*   Key Idea

!   I love it!

?   I have questions

◯   Unfamiliar or important word

----   Context Clues

In a first read, work to get a sense of the main idea of a text. Look for key details and ideas that help you understand what the author conveys to you. Mark passages which prompt a strong response from you.

Here is how one reader marked up this text.

NOTES

MODEL

INFORMATIONAL TEXT

from Classifying the Stars

Cecilia H. Payne

*

1 Sunlight and starlight are composed of waves of various lengths, which the eye, even aided by a telescope, is unable to separate. We must use more than a telescope. In order to sort out the component colors, the light must be dispersed by a prism, or split up by some other means. For instance, sunbeams passing through rain drops, are transformed into the myriad tinted rainbow. The familiar rainbow spanning the sky is Nature's most glorious demonstration that light is composed of many colors.

*

2 The very beginning of our knowledge of the nature of a star dates back to 1672, when Isaac Newton gave to the world the results of his experiments on passing sunlight through a prism. To describe the beautiful band of rainbow tints, produced when sunlight was dispersed by his three-cornered piece of glass, he took from the Latin the word *spectrum*, meaning an appearance. The rainbow is the spectrum of the Sun. . . .

*

3 In 1814, more than a century after Newton, the spectrum of the Sun was obtained in such purity that an amazing detail was seen and studied by the German optician, Fraunhofer. He saw that the multiple spectral tints, ranging from delicate violet to deep red, were crossed by hundreds of fine dark lines. In other words, there were narrow gaps in the spectrum where certain shades were wholly blotted out. We must remember that the word spectrum is applied not only to sunlight, but also to the light of any glowing substance when its rays are sorted out by a prism or a grating.

First-Read Guide

Use this page to record your first-read ideas.

Selection Title: _____ Classifying the Stars _____

You may want to use a guide like this to organize your thoughts after you read. Here is how a reader completed a First-Read Guide.

NOTICE new information or ideas you learned about the unit topic as you first read this text.

Light = different waves of colors. (Spectrum)

Newton - the first person to observe these waves using a prism.

Faunhofer saw gaps in the spectrum.

ANNOTATE by marking vocabulary and key passages you want to revisit.

Vocabulary
  myriad
  grating
  component colors

Different light types = different lengths

Isaac Newton also worked theories of gravity.

Multiple spectral tints? "colors of various appearance"

Key Passage:
Paragraph 3 shows that Fraunhofer discovered more about the nature of light spectrums: he saw the spaces in between the tints.

First Read

CONNECT ideas within the selection to other knowledge and the selections you have read.

I remember learning about prisms in science class.

Double rainbows! My favorite. How are they made?

RESPOND by writing a brief summary of the selection.

Science allows us to see things not visible to the naked eye. What we see as sunlight is really a spectrum of colors. By using tools, such as prisms, we can see the components of sunlight and other light. They appear as single colors or as multiple colors separated by gaps of no color. White light contains a rainbow of colors.

TOOL KIT: CLOSE READING

* Key Idea

! I love it!

? I have questions

◯ Unfamiliar or important word

---- Context Clues

In a close read, go back into the text to study it in greater detail. Take the time to analyze not only the author's ideas but the way that those ideas are conveyed. Consider the genre of the text, the author's word choice, the writer's unique style, and the message of the text.

Here is how one reader close read this text.

MODEL

INFORMATIONAL TEXT

NOTES

from Classifying the Stars

Cecilia H. Payne

*

1   Sunlight and starlight are composed of waves of various lengths, which the eye, even aided by a telescope, is unable to separate. We must use more than a telescope. In order to sort out the component colors, the light must be dispersed by a prism, or split up by some other means. For instance, sunbeams passing through rain drops, are transformed into the myriad tinted rainbow. The familiar rainbow spanning the sky is Nature's most glorious demonstration that light is composed of many colors.

*

2   The very beginning of our knowledge of the nature of a star dates back to 1672, when Isaac Newton gave to the world the results of his experiments on passing sunlight through a prism. To describe the beautiful band of rainbow tints, produced when sunlight was dispersed by his three-cornered piece of glass, he took from the Latin the word *spectrum*, meaning an appearance. The rainbow is the spectrum of the Sun. . . .

*

3   In 1814, more than a century after Newton, the spectrum of the Sun was obtained in such purity that an amazing detail was seen and studied by the German optician, Fraunhofer. He saw that the multiple spectral tints, ranging from delicate violet to deep red, were crossed by hundreds of fine dark lines. In other words, there were narrow gaps in the spectrum where certain shades were wholly blotted out. We must remember that the word spectrum is applied not only to sunlight, but also to the light of any glowing substance when its rays are sorted out by a prism or a grating.

Notes (left margin):

explanation of sunlight and starlight

What is light and where do the colors come from?

This paragraph is about Newton and the prism.

What discoveries helped us understand light?

Fraunhofer and gaps in spectrum

Close-Read Guide

Use this page to record your close-read ideas.

You can use the Close-Read Guide to help you dig deeper into the text. Here is how a reader completed a Close-Read Guide.

Selection Title: _Classifying the Stars_

Close Read the Text

Revisit sections of the text you marked during your first read. Read these sections closely and **annotate** what you notice. Ask yourself **questions** about the text. What can you **conclude?** Write down your ideas.

Close Read

ANNOTATE QUESTION CONCLUDE

Paragraph 3: Light is composed of waves of various lengths. Prisms let us see different colors in light. This is called the spectrum. Fraunhofer proved that there are gaps in the spectrum, where certain shades are blotted out.

More than one researcher studied this and each built off the ideas that were already discovered.

Analyze the Text

Think about the author's choices of patterns, structure, techniques, and ideas included in the text. Select one, and record your thoughts about what this choice conveys.

The author showed the development of human knowledge of the spectrum chronologically. Helped me see how ideas were built upon earlier understandings. Used dates and "more than a century after Newton" to show time.

QuickWrite

Pick a paragraph from the text that grabbed your interest. Explain the power of this passage.

The first paragraph grabbed my attention, specifically the sentence "The familiar rainbow spanning the sky is Nature's most glorious demonstration that light is composed of many colors." The paragraph began as a straightforward scientific explanation. When I read the word "glorious," I had to stop and deeply consider what was being said. It is a word loaded with personal feelings. With that one word, the author let the reader know what was important to her.

Analyzing Legal Meanings and Reasoning

Reading historical and legal texts requires careful analysis of both the vocabulary and the logical flow of ideas that support a conclusion.

Understanding Legal Meanings

The language of historical and legal documents is formal, precise, and technical. Many words in these texts have specific meanings that you need to understand in order to follow the flow of ideas. For example, the second amendment to the U.S. Constitution states that "A well regulated Militia being necessary to the security of a free State, the right of the people to keep and bear Arms shall not be infringed." To understand this amendment, it is important to know that in this context *militia* means "armed forces," *bear* means "carry," and *infringed* means "denied." To understand legal meanings:

- Use your knowledge of word roots to help you understand unfamiliar words. Many legal terms use familiar Greek or Latin roots, prefixes, or suffixes.

- Do not assume that you know a word's legal meaning: Use a dictionary to check the meanings of key words to be certain that you are applying the correct meaning.

- Paraphrase the text to aid comprehension. Replace difficult words with synonyms to make sure you follow the logic of the argument.

Delineating Legal Reasoning

Works of public advocacy, such as court decisions, political proclamations, proposed laws, or constitutional amendments, use careful reasoning to support conclusions. These strategies can help you understand the legal reasoning in an argument:

- State the **purpose** of the document in your own words to help you focus on the writer's primary goal.

- Look for the line of reasoning that supports the **arguments** presented. To be valid and persuasive, key arguments should be backed up by clearly stated logical analysis. Be aware of persuasive techniques, such as citing facts and statistics, referring to expert testimonials, and using emotional language with strong connotations.

- Identify the **premises,** or evidence, upon which a decision rests. In legal texts, premises often include **precedents,** which are earlier examples that must be followed or specifically overturned. Legal reasoning is usually based on the decisions of earlier trials. Be sure you understand precedents in order to identify how the court arrived at the current decision.

Note the strategies used to evaluate legal meanings and reasoning in this Supreme Court decision from 1954 regarding the legality of segregated, "separate but equal" schools for students of different races.

LEGAL TEXT

from *Brown v. Board of Education of Topeka*, Opinion of the Supreme Court by Chief Justice Earl Warren

We come then to the question presented: Does segregation of children in public schools solely on the basis of race, even though the physical facilities and other "tangible" factors may be equal, deprive the children of the minority group of equal educational opportunities? We believe that it does.

In *Sweatt v. Painter*, in finding that a segregated law school for Negroes could not provide them equal educational opportunities, this Court relied in large part on "those qualities which are incapable of objective measurement but which make for greatness in a law school." In *McLaurin v. Oklahoma State Regents*, the Court, in requiring that a Negro admitted to a white graduate school be treated like all other students, again resorted to intangible considerations: ". . . his ability to study, to engage in discussions and exchange views with other students, and, in general, to learn his profession." Such considerations apply with added force to children in grade and high schools. To separate them from others of similar age and qualifications solely because of their race generates a feeling of inferiority as to their status in the community that may affect their hearts and minds in a way unlikely ever to be undone. The effect of this separation on their educational opportunities was well stated by a finding in the Kansas case by a court which nevertheless felt compelled to rule against the Negro plaintiffs: Segregation of white and colored children in public schools has a detrimental effect upon the colored children. The impact is greater when it has the sanction of the law, for the policy of separating the races is usually interpreted as denoting the inferiority of the negro group. A sense of inferiority affects the motivation of a child to learn. Segregation with the sanction of law, therefore, has a tendency to [retard] the educational and mental development of negro children and to deprive them of some of the benefits they would receive in a racially integrated school system. Whatever may have been the extent of psychological knowledge at the time of *Plessy v. Ferguson*, this finding is amply supported by modern authority. Any language in *Plessy v. Ferguson* contrary to this finding is rejected.

We conclude that, in the field of public education, the doctrine of "separate but equal" has no place. Separate educational facilities are inherently unequal.

Use Word Roots The word *tangible* comes from the Latin root meaning "to touch." In this decision, the court contrasts tangible, measurable features with intangible features that are difficult to measure.

Identify the Premises The court cites two precedents: earlier cases relating to unequal education opportunities for black students.

Paraphrase the Text Here's one way you might break down the ideas in this sentence when you paraphrase: Segregating students just because of their race makes them feel as if they are less valued by our society. This separation can have a permanent negative influence on their character.

Line of Reasoning The conclusion makes the **purpose** of the decision clear: to overturn the precedent established by *Plessy v. Ferguson*. The **argument** describes the reasons the Court no longer considers the reasoning in that earlier case to be valid.

TOOL KIT: CLOSE READING

WRITING

Argument

When you think of the word *argument*, you might think of a disagreement between two people, but an argument is more than that. An argument is a logical way of presenting a belief, conclusion, or stance. A good argument is supported with reasoning and evidence.

Argument writing can be used for many purposes, such as to change a reader's point of view or opinion or to bring about an action or a response from a reader.

Elements of an Argumentative Text

An **argument** is a logical way of presenting a viewpoint, belief, or stand on an issue. A well-written argument may convince the reader, change the reader's mind, or motivate the reader to take a certain action.

An effective argument contains these elements:

- a precise claim
- consideration of counterclaims, or opposing positions, and a discussion of their strengths and weaknesses
- logical organization that makes clear connections among claim, counterclaim, reasons, and evidence
- valid reasoning and evidence
- a concluding statement or section that logically completes the argument
- formal and objective language and tone
- error-free grammar, including accurate use of transitions

ARGUMENT: SCORE 1

Community Service Should be a Requirement for High School Graduation

Volunteering is a great idea for high school students. Those who don't volunteer are missing out.

You can learn a lot at your volunteer job. It might not seem like a big deal at the time, but the things you learn and do can be useful. You might volunteer somewhere with a spreadsheet. Everyone needs to know how to use a spreadsheet! That's going to be a useful again really soon.

Their lots of reasons to get involved. One of them is to become a better student in school. Also, to feel better about yourself and not act out so much.

So, volunteering helps you learn and get better at lots of things, not just what you are doing at your volunteer job. It's good not just to learn reading and writing and math and science all the time—the usual stuff we study in school. That's how volunteering can help you out.

Students today are really busy and they can't add anything more to they're busy schedules. But I think they can add a little more if it doesn't take too much time. Especially if it is important like volunteering.

High school students who volunteer get involved with the real world outside school, and that means a lot. They have a chance to do something that can make a difference in the world. This helps them learn things that maybe they can't learn in school, like, how to be kind and jenerous and care about making the world a better place.

Volunteering in high school is a great idea. Everybody should do it. There are lots of different ways to volunteer. You can even do it on weekends with your friends.

The claim is not clearly stated in the introduction.

The argument contains mistakes in standard English conventions of usage and mechanics.

The vocabulary used is limited and ineffective, and the tone is informal.

The writer does not acknowledge counterclaims.

TOOL KIT: WRITING

MODEL

ARGUMENT: SCORE 2

Community Service Should be a Requirement for High School Graduation

High school students should have to volunteer before they can graduate. It makes sense because it is helpful to them and others. Some students would volunteer anyway even if it wasn't required, but some wouldn't. If they have to do it for graduation then they won't miss out.

> The introduction establishes the claim.

Their lots of reasons to get involved. One is to be a better student in school. Researchers have done studies to see the connection between community service and doing well in school. One study showed that most schools with programs said grades went up most of the time for kids that volunteered. Another study said elementary and middle school kids got better at problem-solving and were more interested in school. One study said students showed more responsibility. Another researcher discovered that kids who been volunteering have better self-esteem. They also have fewer problems.

> The tone of the argument is occasionally formal and objective.

Volunteering helps you learn and improve at lots of things, not just what you are doing at your volunteer job. One thing you might get better at is being a nicer person, like having more patience and listening well to others. Because you might need those skills when you are volunteering at a senior center or a preschool.

Some people say that volunteering in high school should NOT be required for graduation. They say students already have too much to do and they can't add anything more to they're schedules. But they can add a little more if it doesn't take too much time. Especially if it is important like volunteering.

> The writer briefly acknowledges and refutes counterclaims.

Why should students be forced to do something, even if it is good? Well, that's just the way it is. When you force students to do something that is good, you are doing them a favor. Like forcing them to eat their vegetables or do their homework. The kids might not like it at first but what do you want to bet they are happy about it later on. That's the point.

> The writers relies too much on weak anecdotal evidence.

Volunteering should be required for all high school students before they graduate. That's not just because they can do a lot of good in the world, but also because doing community service will help them in lots of ways.

> The conclusion offers some insight into the claim and restates some information.

ARGUMENT: SCORE 3

Community Service Should be a Requirement for High School Graduation

Requiring community service for high school graduation is an excellent idea that offers benefits not only to the community but to the student as well. Making it a requirement ensures that all students will be able to get in on the act.

> The claim is established in the introduction but is not as clear as it could be.

Volunteering is a great way to build skills. It might not seem like a big deal at the time, but the experience you gain is very likely to be useful in the future. For example, while tracking, sorting, and distributing donations at an afterschool program, a volunteer might learn how to use a spreadsheet. That's going to come in handy very quickly, both in and out of school.

Participating in service learning can help you do better in school. ("Service learning" is when community service is part of a class curriculum.) For example, one study found that most schools with service learning programs reported grade point averages of participating students improved 76 percent of the time. Another study showed improved problem-solving skills and increased interest in academics among elementary and middle school students.

> The tone of the argument is mostly formal and objective.

A study showed that middle and high school students who participated in quality service learning projects showed more personal and social responsibility. Another study found that students were more likely to help each other and be kind to each other, and care about doing their best. Studies also show better self-esteem and fewer behavioral problems in students who have been involved with service learning.

> The writer does not transition very well into new topics.

Despite all this, many people say that volunteering in high school should NOT be a requirement for graduation. They point out that students today are already over-stressed and over-scheduled. There simply isn't room for anything more.

> The writer uses some transitional phrases.

True! But community service doesn't have to take up a lot of time. It might be possible for a group of time-stressed students to use class-time to organize a fundraiser, or to squeeze their service into a single "marathon" weekend. It's all a question of priorities.

> The writer gives a reason for the counterclaim, but does not provide firm examples.

In short, volunteering is a great way for students to help others, and reap benefits for themselves as well. Making it a requirement ensures that all students have the chance to grow through involvement with their communities. Volunteering opens doors and offers life-long benefits, and high school is the perfect time to get started!

> The conclusion restates the claim and provides additional detail.

TOOL KIT: WRITING

WRITING

MODEL

ARGUMENT: SCORE 4

Community Service Should be a Requirement for High School Graduation

Every high school student should be required to do community service in order to graduate. Volunteering offers life-long benefits that will prepare all students for adulthood.

First and foremost, studies show that participating in service learning —when community service is part of a class curriculum—often helps students do better in school. For example, a study conducted by Leeward County found that 83 percent of schools with service learning programs reported grade point averages of participating students improved 76 percent of the time. Another study, conducted by Hilliard Research, showed improved problem-solving skills and increased interest in academics among elementary and middle school students who participated in service learning.

But it's not just academic performance that can improve through volunteering: There are social and psychological benefits as well. For example, a student survey showed that students who participated in quality service learning projects showed more personal and social responsibility. Another survey found that students involved in service learning were more likely to be kind to each other, and care about doing their best. Studies also show better self-esteem and fewer behavioral problems in students who have been involved with service learning.

Despite all this, there are still many who say that volunteering in high school should NOT be a requirement for graduation. They point out that students today are already over-stressed and over-scheduled. What's more, requiring community service for graduation would be particularly hard on athletes and low-income students who work after school to help their families make ends meet.

Good points, but community service does not have to take up vast quantities of time. It might be possible for a group of time-stressed students to use class-time to organize a fundraiser, or to compress their service into a single "marathon" weekend. Showing students that helping others is something to make time for is an important lesson.

In short, volunteering encourages engagement: It shows students that their actions matter, and that they have the power—and responsibility—to make the world a better place. What could be a more important lesson than that?

> The introduction establishes the writer's claim in a clear and compelling way.

> The writer uses a variety of sentence transitions.

> Sources of evidence are comprehensive and contain relevant information.

> Counterclaims are clearly acknowledged and refuted.

> The conclusion offers fresh insight into the claim.

Argument Rubric

	Focus and Organization	Evidence and Elaboration	Conventions
4	The introduction engages the reader and establishes a claim in a compelling way. The argument includes valid reasons and evidence that address and support the claim while clearly acknowledging counterclaims. The ideas progress logically, and transitions make connections among ideas clear. The conclusion offers fresh insight into the claim.	The sources of evidence are comprehensive and specific and contain relevant information. The tone of the argument is always formal and objective. The vocabulary is always appropriate for the audience and purpose.	The argument intentionally uses standard English conventions of usage and mechanics.
3	The introduction engages the reader and establishes the claim. The argument includes reasons and evidence that address and support my claim while acknowledging counterclaims. The ideas progress logically, and some transitions are used to help make connections among ideas clear. The conclusion restates the claim and important information.	The sources of evidence contain relevant information. The tone of the argument is mostly formal and objective. The vocabulary is generally appropriate for the audience and purpose.	The argument demonstrates general accuracy in standard English conventions of usage and mechanics.
2	The introduction establishes a claim. The argument includes some reasons and evidence that address and support the claim while briefly acknowledging counterclaims. The ideas progress somewhat logically. A few sentence transitions are used that connect readers to the argument. The conclusion offers some insight into the claim and restates information.	The sources of evidence contain some relevant information. The tone of the argument is occasionally formal and objective. The vocabulary is somewhat appropriate for the audience and purpose.	The argument demonstrates some accuracy in standard English conventions of usage and mechanics.
1	The introduction does not clearly state the claim. The argument does not include reasons or evidence for the claim. No counterclaims are acknowledged. The ideas do not progress logically. Transitions are not included to connect ideas. The conclusion does not restate any information that is important.	Reliable and relevant evidence is not included. The vocabulary used is limited or ineffective. The tone of the argument is not objective or formal.	The argument contains mistakes in standard English conventions of usage and mechanics.

WRITING

Informative/Explanatory Texts

Informative and explanatory writing should rely on facts to inform or explain. Informative writing serves several purposes: to increase readers' knowledge of a subject, to help readers better understand a procedure or process, or to provide readers with an enhanced comprehension of a concept. It should also feature a clear introduction, body, and conclusion.

Elements of Informative/Explanatory Texts

Informative/explanatory texts present facts, details, data, and other kinds of evidence to give information about a topic. Readers turn to informational and explanatory texts when they wish to learn about a specific idea, concept, or subject area, or if they want to learn how to do something.

An effective informative/explanatory text contains these elements:

- a topic sentence or thesis statement that introduces the concept or subject
- relevant facts, examples, and details that expand upon a topic
- definitions, quotations, and/or graphics that support the information given
- headings (if desired) to separate sections of the essay
- a structure that presents information in a direct, clear manner
- clear transitions that link sections of the essay
- precise words and technical vocabulary where appropriate
- formal and object language and tone
- a conclusion that supports the information given and provides fresh insights

INFORMATIVE: SCORE 1

How Technology is Changing the Way We Work

Lot's of people work on computers. So, technology is everywhere. If you feel comfortable using computers and all kinds of other technology, your going to be a head at work, for sure.

They're new Devices and Apps out there every day. Each different job has its own gadgets and programs and apps that you have to learn. Every day their more new apps and devices, they can do all kinds of things.

In the past, people only worked at the office. They didn't get to work at home. Now, if you have a smart phone, you can check your email wherever. You can work at home on a computer. You can work in cafés or wherever. Also on a tablet. If you wanted to, you can be working all the time. But that will be a drag!

Technology is now an important part of almost every job. You also have to have a website. You have to have a social media page. Maybe if your business is doing really well you could afford to hire someone to take care of all that stuff—but it would be better if you knew how to do it yourself.

Technology brings people together and helps them work. It could be someone next to you or someone even on the other side of the world. You can connect with them using email. You can send a text. You could have a conference or video call.

Working from home is cheaper for the worker and boss. They can get stuff done during the day like going to the post office or the library, or picking up their kids at school. This is all thanks to technology.

Lots of jobs today are in technology. Way more than before! That's why it's a good idea to take classes and learn about something in technology, because then you will be able to find a job.

There are apps to find houses for sale, find restaurants, learn new recipes, keep track of how much you exercise, and all kinds of other things, like playing games and tuning your guitar. And there are apps to help you work. It's hard to imagine how people would manage to work now without this kind of technology to help them.

> The writer's opening statement does not adequately introduce the thesis, and there are numerous spelling mistakes.

> The writer's word choice often does not support the proper tone the essay ought to have.

> The essay's sentences are often not purposeful, varied, or well-controlled.

> The writer does not include a concluding statement.

TOOL KIT: WRITING

WRITING

MODEL

INFORMATIVE: SCORE 2

How Technology is Changing the Way We Work

Technology affects the way we work, in every kind of job and industry. Each different job has its own gadgets and programs and apps that you have to learn. Every day there are more new apps and devices that can do all kinds of things.

> The writer's opening does not clearly introduce the thesis.

In the past, people went to the office to work. That's not always true today. Now if you have a smart phone, you can check your email wherever you are. You can work at home on a desktop computer. You can work on a laptop in a café or wherever. Or a tablet. Technology makes it so people can work all the time.

It doesn't matter whether the person is on the other side of the world—technology brings you together. Theirs email. Theirs text messaging. You have conference calls. You've got video calling. All these things let people work together wherever they are. And don't forget, today people can access files from the cloud. That helps them work from whatever device they want. More than one person can work on the same file.

> The essay is somewhat lacking in organizational structure.

Different kinds of work places and schedules are becoming more common and normal. Working from home has benefits businesses. It means cost savings. It means higher productivity. It means higher job satisfaction. They can get stuff done during the day like going to the post office or the bank, or picking up their kids at school. That is very convenient.

> The essay has many interesting details, but some do not relate specifically to the topic.

It's also true that lots and lots of jobs today are in technology, or related to technology in some way. Way more than before! That's why it's a good idea to get a degree or take classes and learn about something in technology, because it seems like that's where all the new jobs are. Software designers make a really good salary, and so do other tech-related jobs.

> The writer's word choice is overly informal.

Technology is now an important part of almost every job. It's no longer enough to be just a photographer or whatever. You have to get a social media page. You have to be able to use the latest tech gadgets. You can't just take pictures.

> The writer's sentences are disjointed and ineffective.

In todays world, technology is changing how we work. You have to be able to feel comfortable with technology in order to survive at work. Even if you really don't like technology, you don't really have a choice. So, get used to it!

> The conclusion follows logically but is not mature and is overly informal.

How Technology Is Changing the Way We Work

Technology has been changing how we work for a long time, but the pace of change has gotten dramatically faster. No industry or job is exempt. Powerful computing technology and Internet connectivity affects all sectors of the economy. It doesn't matter what job you're talking about: Technology is transforming the way people work. It's an exciting time to be entering the workforce!

The Office Is Everywhere

Technology is rapidly changing not just *how* but *where, when,* and *with whom* we work. It used to be that work was something that happened only at the office. All kinds of different work places and schedules are becoming much more common and normal. According to a study, telecommuting (working from home) rose 79 percent between 2005 and 2012. Working from home has benefits for both the employee and employer. It means cost savings for both, increased productivity, and higher job satisfaction.

The Cloud

Cloud and other data storage and sharing options mean that workers have access to information whenever they want, wherever they are. Whether it's one person who wants the convenience of being able to work on a file from several devices (and locations), or several people who are working on something together, the ability to store data in the cloud and access it from anywhere is a huge change in the way we work. It's almost like all being in the same office, working on the same computer.

Tech Industries and Jobs

Technology is changing the way we work in part by making technology itself such an important element in almost every profession. Therefore, you can see it's no longer good enough to be just a photographer or contractor. You have to know something about technology to do your job, market yourself, and track your performance. No matter what jobs someone does they have to be tech-savvy to be able to use their devices to connect and interact with each other across the globe.

Conclusion

In todays world, technology is quickly and continuously changing how we work, what we do, where and when we do it. In order to do well and thrive, everyone has to be a little bit of a tech geek. So, get used to technology being a part of your work life. And get used to change. Because, in a constantly changing technological world, change is going to be one of the few things that stays the same!

The thesis is introduced but is buried in the introduction.

The writer uses headings to help make the organization of ideas clear.

Statistics support the writer's claim.

The writer uses some transitions and sentence connections, but more would be helpful.

There are a few errors in spelling and punctuation but they do not detract from the effectiveness of the essay.

The conclusion sums up the main ideas of the essay and links to the opening statements.

TOOL KIT: WRITING

WRITING

INFORMATIVE: SCORE 4

How Technology Is Changing the Way We Work

While advances in technology have been changing how we work for hundreds of years, the pace of change has accelerated dramatically in the past two decades. With powerful computing technology and Internet connectivity affecting all sectors of the economy, no industry or profession is exempt. It doesn't matter whether you're talking about financial advisors, architects, or farmers: Technology is transforming the way people work.

The opening paragraph ends with a thesis, which is strong and clear.

The Office Is Everywhere

Technology is rapidly revolutionizing not just *how* but *where, when,* and *with whom* we work. It used to be that work was something that happened strictly at the office. In fact, non-traditional work places are becoming much more common. According to one study, telecommuting rose 79 percent between 2005 and 2012. Working from home has proven benefits for both the employee and employer, including cost savings for both, increased productivity, and job satisfaction.

The writer makes an effort to be thoughtful and engage the reader.

Headings help ensure that the organizing structure of the essay is clear and effective.

Working with the Cloud

Another important technological advancement that is impacting how we work is the development of cloud computing. Whether it's one person who wants the convenience of being able to work from several devices, or several people who are working together from different locations, the ability to store data in the cloud and access it from anywhere is a huge change in the way we work. Over long distances, coworkers can not only *communicate* with each other, they can *collaborate*, in real time, by sharing and accessing files through the. Only five years ago, this kind of instant access was impossible.

The sentences in the essay are purposeful and varied.

Tech Industries and Jobs

Technology is changing the way we work is by making technology itself an important element in almost every job. It's no longer good enough to be just a photographer or contractor: you have to know something about technology to perform, market, and track your work. No matter what job someone is doing, he or she has to be tech-savvy to be able to use their devices to connect and interact.

The progression of ideas in the essay is logical and well-controlled.

Conclusion

In today's world, technology is quickly and continuously changing what work we do, and how, where, when, and with whom we do it. Comfort with new technology—and with rapid technological change—is a prerequisite for success, no matter where your interests lie, or what kind of job you are looking to find. It's a brave new technological world of work, and it's changing every day!

The writer's word choice contributes to the clarity of the essay and shows awareness of the essay's purpose and tone.

Informative/Explanatory Rubric

	Focus and Organization	Evidence and Elaboration	Conventions
4	The introduction engages the reader and states a thesis in a compelling way. The essay includes a clear introduction, body, and conclusion. The conclusion summarizes ideas and offers fresh insight into the thesis.	The essay includes specific reasons, details, facts, and quotations from selections and outside resources to support the thesis. The tone of the essay is always formal and objective. The language is always precise and appropriate for the audience and purpose.	The essay uses standard English conventions of usage and mechanics. The essay contains no spelling errors.
3	The introduction engages the reader and sets forth the thesis. The essay includes an introduction, body, and conclusion. The conclusion summarizes ideas and supports the thesis.	The essay includes some specific reasons, details, facts, and quotations from selections and outside resources to support the thesis. The tone of the essay is mostly formal and objective. The language is generally precise and appropriate for the audience and purpose.	The essay demonstrates general accuracy in standard English conventions of usage and mechanics. The essay contains few spelling errors.
2	The introduction sets forth the thesis. The essay includes an introduction, body, and conclusion, but one or more parts are weak. The conclusion partially summarizes ideas but may not provide strong support of the thesis.	The essay includes a few reasons, details, facts, and quotations from selections and outside resources to support the thesis. The tone of the essay is occasionally formal and objective. The language is somewhat precise and appropriate for the audience and purpose.	The essay demonstrates some accuracy in standard English conventions of usage and mechanics. The essay contains some spelling errors.
1	The introduction does not state the thesis clearly. The essay does not include an introduction, body, and conclusion. The conclusion does not summarize ideas and may not relate to the thesis.	Reliable and relevant evidence is not included. The tone of the essay is not objective or formal. The language used is imprecise and not appropriate for the audience and purpose.	The essay contains mistakes in standard English conventions of usage and mechanics. The essay contains many spelling errors.

Narration

Narrative writing conveys experience, either real or imaginary, and uses time to provide structure. It can be used to inform, instruct, persuade, or entertain. Whenever writers tell a story, they are using narrative writing. Most types of narrative writing share certain elements, such as characters, setting, a sequence of events, and, often, a theme.

Elements of a Narrative Text

A **narrative** is any type of writing that tells a story, whether it is fiction, nonfiction, poetry, or drama.

An effective nonfiction narrative usually contains these elements:

- an engaging beginning in which characters and setting are established
- characters who participate in the story events
- a well-structured, logical sequence of events
- details that show time and place
- effective story elements such as dialogue, description, and reflection
- the narrator's thoughts, feelings, or views about the significance of events
- use of language that brings the characters and setting to life

An effective fictional narrative usually contains these elements:

- an engaging beginning in which characters, setting, or a main conflict is introduced
- a main character and supporting characters who participate in the story events
- a narrator who relates the events of the plot from a particular point of view
- details that show time and place
- conflict that is resolved in the course of the narrative
- narrative techniques such as dialogue, description, and suspense
- use of language that vividly brings to life characters and events

NARRATIVE: SCORE 1

Getting Away With It

That night, Luanne made two mistakes.

She ran in the house.

The McTweedys were rich and had a huge place and there was an expensive rug.

She was sad in her room remembering what happened:

She was carrying a tray of glasses back to the kitchen and spilled on the carpet. She tried to put furniture over it. Then she ran in the rain.

Luanne should have come clean. She would of said I'm sorry, Mrs. Mc Tweedy, I spilled punch on ur carpet.

She knew getting away with it felt crummy for some reason. it was wrong and she also didn't want to get in trouble.

The phone rings.

"Oh, hello?"

"It's Mrs. Tweedy's!" said her mom. "You forgot to get paid!"

Luanne felt relieve. She was going to do the right thing.

The introduction is interesting but is not built upon.

The chronology and situation are unclear.

The narrative contains mistakes in standard English conventions of usage and mechanics.

The name of the character does not remain consistent.

The conclusion reveals what will happen but is not interesting.

TOOL KIT: WRITING

WRITING

MODEL

NARRATIVE: SCORE 2

Getting Away With It

That night, Luanne made two fatal mistakes: ruining a rug, and thinking she could get away with it.

She ran in the house.

The McTweedys hired her to be a waiter at their party. They were rich and had a huge place and there was an expensive rug.

She was sad in her room remembering what happened:

Luanne was wearing black pants and a white shirt. She was carrying a tray of glasses back to the kitchen. One spilled on the carpet. She tried to put furniture to cover up the stain. She ran away in the rain.

Luanne should have come clean right away. But what would she have said? I'm sorry, Mrs. McTweedy, but I spilled punch all over your expensive carpet.

Luanne imagined getting away with it. But getting away with it felt crummy for some reason. She knew it was wrong somehow, but she also didn't want to get in trouble.

The phone rang.

"Oh, hello, how was the party?"

Luanne felt like throwing up.

"Mrs. McTweedy's on the phone!" her mom sang out. "She said you forgot your check!"

Luanne felt relieved. But she already made up her mind to do the right thing.

The introduction establishes a clear context.

The writer has made some mistakes in spelling, grammar, and punctuation.

The chronology is sometimes unclear.

Narrative techniques, such as the use of dialogue, are used at times.

The conclusion tells what will happen but is not interesting.

NARRATIVE: SCORE 3

Getting Away With It

That night, Luanne made two fatal mistakes: (1) ruining a priceless Persian rug, and (2) thinking she could get away with it.

She bursted in the front door breathless.

"How was it?" called her mom.

The McTweedys had hired her to serve drinks at their fundraiser. Henry and Estelle McTweedy loved having parties. They were rich and had a huge apartment filled with rare books, art, and tapestries from all over the world.

"Luanne? Are you alright?"

"Just tired, Mom."

Actually she was face-planted on her bed, replaying the scene over and over just in case she could change it.

It was like a movie: A girl in black trousers and a crisp white shirt carrying a tray of empty glasses back to the kitchen. Then the girl's horrified expression as she realizes that one of the glasses was not quite as empty as she'd thought and was dripping onto the carpet. The girl frantically moving furniture to cover up the stain. The girl running out of the apartment into the hard rain.

Luanne kicked herself. She should have come clean right away. But what would she have said? I'm sorry, Mrs. McTweedy, but I spilled punch all over your expensive carpet.

Luanne imagined getting away with it. But getting away with it felt crummy for some reason. She knew it was wrong somehow, but she also didn't want to get in trouble.

The phone was ringing. Luanne froze.

"Oh, hello there, Mrs. McTweedy! How was the party?"

Luanne felt felt like throwing up.

"Mrs. McTweedy's on the phone!" her mom sang out. "She said you forgot your check!"

Luanne felt relief. It was nothing at all! Although she'd already made up her mind to come clean. Because she had to do the right thing.

She walked into the kitchen. And then she explained the whole thing to both her mom and Mrs. McTweedy.

The story's introduction establishes a clear context and point of view.

Descriptive details, sensory language, and precise words and phrases help to bring the narrative to life.

The writer mostly attends to the norms and conventions of usage and punctuation, but sometimes makes mistakes.

The writer has effectively used dialogue in her story.

The conclusion follows logically but is not memorable.

TOOL KIT: WRITING

WRITING

NARRATIVE: SCORE 4

Getting Away With It

That night, Luanne made two fatal mistakes: (1) ruining a priceless Persian rug, and (2) thinking she could get away with it.

She'd burst in the front door breathless.

"How was it?" called her mother from the kitchen.

The McTweedys had hired Luanne to serve drinks at their fundraiser. Henry and Estelle McTweedy loved entertaining. They loved traveling, and the opera, and the finer things in life. They had a huge apartment filled with rare books, art, and tapestries from all over the world.

"Luanne? Are you alright?"

"Just tired, Mom."

Actually she was face-down on her bed, replaying the humiliating scene over and over just in case she could make it come out differently.

It was like a movie: A girl in black trousers and a crisp white shirt carrying a tray of empty glasses back to the kitchen. Cut to the girl's horrified expression as she realizes that one of the glasses —not quite as empty as she'd thought—was dripping its lurid contents onto the carpet. Close in on the girl's frantic attempts to move furniture over the stain. Montage of images showing the girl running out of the apartment into the pounding rain. Fade to Black.

Luanne could kick herself. She should have come clean right away. But what would she have said? *I'm sorry, Mrs. McTweedy, but I spilled punch all over your irreplaceable carpet.*

Luanne imagined getting away with it. If she got away with it, she'd be a person who got away with things. For the rest of her life, no matter what, she'd be a person who got away with things. And if something good happened to her, she'd feel like she didn't deserve it.

Somewhere in the house, a phone was ringing. Luanne froze and listened in.

"Oh, hello there, Estelle! How was the party?"

Luanne felt cold, then hot. Her skin prickled. She was sweating. She felt like throwing up.

"Mrs. McTweedy's on the phone!" Luanne's mother sang out. "She wants to tell you that you forgot your check!"

Luanne felt a surge a relief wash over her—it was nothing, nothing at all!—but she'd already made up her mind to come clean. Not because owning up to it was so Right, but because getting away with it was so wrong. Which made it right.

Luanne padded into the kitchen. "Don't hang up," she told her mother.

The writer provides an introduction that establishes a clear context and point of view.

The writer has used descriptive details, sensory language, and precise words and phrases.

The writer's use of movie terminology is clever and memorable.

The narrative presents a clear chronological sequence of events.

The writer effectively uses narrative techniques, such as dialogue.

The story's conclusion is abrupt but fitting. It reveals a critical decision that resolves the conflict.

TOOL KIT: WRITING

Narrative Rubric

	Focus and Organization	Development of Ideas/ Elaboration	Conventions
4	The introduction establishes a clear context and point of view. Events are presented in a clear sequence, building to a climax, then moving toward the conclusion. The conclusion follows from and reflects on the events and experiences in the narrative.	Narrative techniques such as dialogue, pacing, and description are used effectively to develop characters, events, and setting. Descriptive details, sensory language, and precise words and phrases are used to convey the experiences in the narrative and to help the reader imagine the characters and setting. Voice is established through word choice, sentence structure, and tone.	The narrative uses standard English conventions of usage and mechanics. Deviations from standard English are intentional and serve the purpose of the narrative. Rules of spelling and punctuation are followed.
3	The introduction gives the reader some context and sets the point of view. Events are presented logically, though there are some jumps in time. The conclusion logically ends the story, but provides only some reflection on the experiences related in the story.	Narrative techniques such as dialogue, pacing, and description are used occasionally. Descriptive details, sensory language, and precise words and phrases are used occasionally. Voice is established through word choice, sentence structure, and tone occasionally, though not evenly.	The narrative mostly uses standard English conventions of usage and mechanics, though there are some errors. There are few errors in spelling and punctuation.
2	The introduction provides some description of a place. The point of view can be unclear at times. Transitions between events are occasionally unclear. The conclusion comes abruptly and provides only a small amount of reflection on the experiences related in the narrative.	Narrative techniques such as dialogue, pacing, and description are used sparingly. The story contains few examples of descriptive details and sensory language. Voice is not established for characters, so that it becomes difficult to determine who is speaking.	The narrative contains some errors in standard English conventions of usage and mechanics. There are many errors in spelling and punctuation.
1	The introduction fails to set a scene or is omitted altogether. The point of view is not always clear. The events are not in a clear sequence, and events that would clarify the narrative may not appear. The conclusion does not follow from the narrative or is omitted altogether.	Narrative techniques such as dialogue, pacing, and description are not used. Descriptive details are vague or missing. No sensory language is included. Voice has not been developed.	The text contains mistakes in standard English conventions of usage and mechanics. Rules of spelling and punctuation have not been followed.

Conducting Research

We are lucky to live in an age when information is accessible and plentiful. However, not all information is equally useful, or even accurate. Strong research skills will help you locate and evaluate information.

Narrowing or Broadening a Topic

The first step of any research project is determining your topic. Consider the scope of your project and choose a topic that is narrow enough to address completely and effectively. If you can name your topic in just one or two words, it is probably too broad. Topics such as Shakespeare, jazz, or science fiction are too broad to cover in a single report. Narrow a broad topic into smaller subcategories.

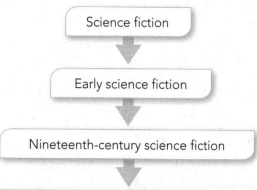

When you begin to research a topic, pay attention to the amount of information available. If you feel overwhelmed by the number of relevant sources, you may need to narrow your topic further.

If there isn't enough information available as your research, you might need to broaden your topic. A topic is too narrow when it can be thoroughly presented in less space than the required size of your assignment. It might also be too narrow if you can find little or no information in library and media sources, so consider broadening your topic to include other related ideas.

Generating Research Questions

Use research questions to focus your research. Specific questions can help you avoid time-wasting digressions. For example, instead of simply hunting for information about Mark Twain, you might ask, "What jobs did Mark Twain have, other than being a writer?" or "Which of Twain's books was most popular during his lifetime?"

In a research report, your research question often becomes your thesis statement, or may lead up to it. The question will also help you focus your research into a comprehensive but flexible search plan, as well as prevent you from gathering unnecessary details. As your research teaches you more about your topic, you may find it necessary to refocus your original question.

Consulting Print and Digital Sources

Effective research combines information from several sources, and does not rely too heavily on a single source. The creativity and originality of your research depends on how you combine ideas from multiple sources. Plan to consult a variety of resources, such as the following:

- **Primary and Secondary Sources:** To get a thorough view of your topic, use primary sources (firsthand or original accounts, such as interview transcripts, eyewitness reports, and newspaper articles) and secondary sources (accounts, created after an event occurred, such as encyclopedia entries).

- **Print and Digital Resources:** The Internet allows fast access to data, but print resources are often edited more carefully. Use both print and digital resources in order to guarantee the accuracy of your findings.

- **Media Resources:** You can find valuable information in media resources such as documentaries, television programs, podcasts, and museum exhibitions. Consider attending public lectures given by experts to gain an even more in-depth view of your topic.

- **Original Research:** Depending on your topic, you may wish to conduct original research to include among your sources. For example, you might interview experts or eyewitnesses, or conduct a survey of people in your community.

Using Online Encyclopedias

Online encyclopedias are often written by anonymous contributors who are not required to fact-check information. These sites can be very useful as a launching point for research, but should not be considered accurate. Look for footnotes, endnotes, or hyperlinks that support facts with reliable sources that have been carefully checked by editors.

Evaluating Sources It is important to evaluate the credibility, validity, and accuracy of any information you find, as well as its appropriateness for your purpose and audience. You may find the information you need to answer your research question in specialized and authoritative sources, such as almanacs (for social, cultural, and natural statistics), government publications (for law, government programs, and subjects such as agriculture), and information services. Also, consider consumer, workplace, and public documents.

Ask yourself questions such as these to evaluate these additional sources:

- **Authority:** Is the author well known? What are the author's credentials? Does the source include references to other reliable sources? Does the author's tone win your confidence? Why or why not?

- **Bias:** Does the author have any obvious biases? What is the author's purpose for writing? Who is the target audience?

- **Currency:** When was the work created? Has it been revised? Is there more current information available?

Using Search Terms

Finding information on the Internet can be both easy and challenging. Type a word or phrase into a general search engine and you will probably get hundreds—or thousands—of results. However, those results are not guaranteed to be relevant or accurate.

These strategies can help you find information from the Internet:

- Create a list of keywords that apply to your topic before you begin using a search engine. Consult a thesaurus to expand your list.

- Enter six to eight keywords.

- Choose precise nouns. Most search engines ignore articles and prepositions. Verbs may be used in multiple contexts, leading to sources that are not relevant. Use modifiers, such as adjectives, when necessary to specify a category.

- Use quotation marks to focus a search. Place a phrase in quotation marks to find pages that include exactly that phrase. Add several phrases in quotation marks to narrow your results.

- Spell carefully. Many search engines autocorrect spelling, but they cannot produce accurate results for all spelling errors.

- Scan search results before you click them. The first result isn't always the most relevant. Read the text and consider the domain before make a choice.

- Utilize more than one search engine.

Evaluating Internet Domains

Not everything you read on the Internet is true, so you have to evaluate sources carefully. The last three letters of an Internet URL identify the Website's domain, which can help you evaluate the information of the site.

- **.gov**—Government sites are sponsored by a branch of the United States federal government, such as the Census Bureau, Supreme Court, or Congress. These sites are considered reliable.

- **.edu**—Education domains include schools from kindergartens to universities. Information from an educational research center or department is likely to be carefully checked. However, education domains can also include student pages that are not edited or monitored.

- **.org**—Organizations are nonprofit groups and usually maintain a high level of credibility. Keep in mind that some organizations may express strong biases.

- **.com** and **.net**—Commercial sites exist to make a profit. Information may be biased to show a product or service in a good light. The company may be providing information to encourage sales or promote a positive image.

Taking Notes

Take notes as you locate and connect useful information from multiple sources, and keep a reference list of every source you use. This will help you make distinctions between the relative value and significance of specific data, facts, and ideas.

For long-term research projects, create source cards and notecards to keep track of information gathered from multiple resources.

Source Cards
Create a card that identifies each source.

- For print materials, list the author, title, publisher, date of publication, and relevant page numbers.
- For Internet sources, record the name and Web address of the site, and the date you accessed the information.
- For media sources, list the title, person, or group credited with creating the media, and the year of production.

Notecards
Create a separate notecard for each item of information.

- Include the fact or idea, the letter of the related source card, and the specific page(s) on which the fact or idea appears.
- Use quotation marks around words and phrases taken directly from print or media resources.
- Mark particularly useful or relevant details using your own annotation method, such as stars, underlining, or colored highlighting.

Source Card	[A]

Marsh, Peter. *Eye to Eye: How People Interact.* Salem House Publishers, 1988.

Notecard

Gestures vary from culture to culture. The American "OK" symbol (thumb and forefinger) is considered insulting in Greece and Turkey.

Source Card: A, p. 54.

Quote Accurately Responsible research begins with the first note you take. Be sure to quote and paraphrase your sources accurately so you can identify these sources later. In your notes, circle all quotations and paraphrases to distinguish them from your own comments. When photocopying from a source, include the copyright information. When printing out information from an online source, include the Web address.

Reviewing Research Findings

While conducting research, you will need to review your findings, checking that you have collected enough accurate and appropriate information.

Considering Audience and Purpose

Always keep your audience in mind as you gather information, since different audiences may have very different needs. For example, if you are writing an in-depth analysis of a text that your entire class has read together and you are writing for your audience, you will not need to gather background information that has been thoroughly discussed in class. However, if you are writing the same analysis for a national student magazine, you cannot assume that all of your readers have the same background information. You will need to provide facts from reliable sources to help orient these readers to your subject. When considering whether or not your research will satisfy your audience, ask yourself:

- Who am I writing for?
- Have I collected enough information to explain my topic to this audience?
- Are there details in my research that I can omit because they are already familiar to my audience?

Your purpose for writing will also influence your review of research. If you are researching a question to satisfy your own curiosity, you can stop researching when you feel you understand the answer completely. If you are writing a research report that will be graded, you need to consider the criteria of the assignment. When considering whether or not you have enough information, ask yourself:

- What is my purpose for writing?
- Will the information I have gathered be enough to achieve my purpose?
- If I need more information, where might I find it?

Synthesizing Sources

Effective research writing does not merely present facts and details; it synthesizes—gathers, orders, and interprets—them. These strategies will help you synthesize information effectively:

- Review your notes and look for connections and patterns among the details you have collected.
- Arrange notes or notecards in different ways to help you decide how to best combine related details and present them in a logical way.
- Pay close attention to details that support one other, emphasizing the same main idea.
- Also look for details that challenge each other, highlighting ideas about which there is no single, or consensus, opinion. You might decide to conduct additional research to help you decide which side of the issue has more support.

Types of Evidence

When reviewing your research, also consider the kinds of evidence you have collected. The strongest writing contains a variety of evidence effectively. This chart describes three of the most common types of evidence: statistical, testimonial, and anecdotal.

TYPE OF EVIDENCE	DESCRIPTION	EXAMPLE
Statistical evidence includes facts and other numerical data used to support a claim or explain a topic.	Examples of statistical evidence include historical dates and information, quantitative analyses, poll results, and quantitative descriptions.	"Although it went on to become a hugely popular novel, the first edition of William Goldman's book sold fewer than 3,000 copies."
Testimonial evidence includes any ideas or opinions presented by others, especially experts in a field.	Firsthand testimonies present ideas from eyewitnesses to events or subjects being discussed.	"The ground rose and fell like an ocean at ebb tide." —Fred J. Hewitt, eyewitness to the 1906 San Francisco earthquake
	Secondary testimonies include commentaries on events by people who were not involved. You might quote a well-known literary critic when discussing a writer's most famous novel, or a prominent historian when discussing the effects of an important event	Gladys Hansen insists that "there was plenty of water in hydrants throughout [San Francisco] . . . The problem was this fire got away."
Anecdotal evidence presents one person's view of the world, often by describing specific events or incidents.	Compelling research should not rely solely on this form of evidence, but it can be very useful for adding personal insights and refuting inaccurate generalizations. An individual's experience can be used with other forms of evidence to present complete and persuasive support.	Although many critics claim the novel is universally beloved, at least one reader "threw the book against a wall because it made me so angry."

RESEARCH

Incorporating Research Into Writing

Avoiding Plagiarism

Plagiarism is the unethical presentation of someone else's ideas as your own. You must cite sources for direct quotations, paraphrased information, or facts that are specific to a single source. When you are drafting and revising, circle any words or ideas that are not your own. Follow the instructions on pages R34 and R35 to correctly cite those passages.

Review for Plagiarism Always take time to review your writing for unintentional plagiarism. Read what you have written and take note of any phrases or sentences that do not have your personal writing voice. Compare those passages with your resource materials. You might have copied them without remembering the exact source. Add a correct citation to give credit to the original author. If you cannot find the questionable phrase in your notes, revise it to ensure that your final report reflects your own thinking and not someone else's work.

Quoting and Paraphrasing

When including ideas from research into your writing, you will decide to quote directly or paraphrase.

Direct Quotation Use the author's exact words when they are interesting or persuasive. You might decide to include direct quotations for these reasons:

- to share an especially clear and relevant statement
- to reference a historically significant passage
- to show that an expert agrees with your position
- to present an argument that you will counter in your writing.

Include complete quotations, without deleting or changing words. If you need to omit words for space or clarity, use ellipsis points to indicate the omission. Enclose direct quotations in quotation marks and indicate the author's name.

Paraphrase A paraphrase restates an author's ideas in your own words. Be careful to paraphrase accurately. Beware of making sweeping generalizations in a paraphrase that were not made by the original author. You may use some words from the original source, but a legitimate paraphrase does more than simply rearrange an author's phrases, or replace a few words with synonyms.

Original Text	"*The Tempest* was written as a farewell to art and the artist's life, just before the completion of his forty-ninth year, and everything in the play bespeaks the touch of autumn." Brandes, Georg. "Analogies Between *The Tempest* and *A Midsummer Night's Dream*." *The Tempest*, by William Shakespeare, William Heinemann, 1904, p. 668.
Patchwork Plagiarism phrases from the original are rearranged, but too closely follows the original text.	A farewell to art, Shakespeare's play, *The Tempest*, was finished just before the completion of his forty-ninth year. The artist's life was to end within three years. The touch of autumn is apparent in nearly everything in the play.
Good Paraphrase	Images of autumn occur throughout *The Tempest*, which Shakespeare wrote as a way of saying goodbye to both his craft and his own life.

Maintaining the Flow of Ideas

Effective research writing is much more that just a list of facts. Be sure to maintain the flow of ideas by connecting research information to your own ideas. Instead of simply stating a piece of evidence, use transition words and phrases to explain the connection between information you found from outside resources and your own ideas and purpose for writing. The following transitions can be used to introduce, compare, contrast, and clarify.

Useful Transitions

When providing examples:

for example   for instance   to illustrate   in [name of resource], [author]

When comparing and contrasting ideas or information:

in the same way   similarly   however   on the other hand

When clarifying ideas or opinions:

in other words   that is   to explain   to put it another way

Choosing an effective organizational structure for your writing will help you create a logical flow of ideas. Once you have established a clear organizational structure, insert facts and details from your research in appropriate places to provide evidence and support for your writing.

ORGANIZATIONAL STRUCTURE	USES
Chronological order presents information in the sequence in which it happens.	historical topics; science experiments; analysis of narratives
Part-to-whole order examines how several categories affect a larger subject.	analysis of social issues; historical topics
Order of importance presents information in order of increasing or decreasing importance.	persuasive arguments; supporting a bold or challenging thesis
Comparison-and-contrast organization outlines the similarities and differences of a given topic.	addressing two or more subjects

RESEARCH

Formats for Citing Sources

In research writing, cite your sources. In the body of your paper, provide a footnote, an endnote, or a parenthetical citation, identifying the sources of facts, opinions, or quotations. At the end of your paper, provide a bibliography or a Works Cited list, a list of all the sources referred to in your research. Follow an established format, such as Modern Language Association (MLA) style.

Parenthetical Citations (MLA Style) A

parenthetical citation briefly identifies the source from which you have taken a specific quotation, factual claim, or opinion. It refers readers to one of the entries on your Works Cited list. A parenthetical citation has the following features:

- It appears in parentheses.
- It identifies the source by the last name of the author, editor, or translator, or by the title (for a lengthy title, list the first word only).
- It provides a page reference, the page(s) of the source on which the information cited can be found.

A parenthetical citation generally falls outside a closing quotation mark but within the final punctuation of a clause or sentence. For a long quotation set off from the rest of your text, place the citation at the end of the excerpt without any punctuation following.

Sample Parenthetical Citations

It makes sense that baleen whales such as the blue whale, the bowhead whale, the humpback whale, and the sei whale (to name just a few) grow to immense sizes (Carwardine et al. 19–21). The blue whale has grooves running from under its chin to partway along the length of its underbelly. As in some other whales, these grooves expand and allow even more food and water to be taken in (Ellis 18–21).

Authors' last names

Page numbers where information can be found

Works Cited List (MLA Style) A Works Cited list
must contain accurate information to enable a reader to locate each source you cite. The basic components of an entry are as follows:

- name of the author, editor, translator, and/or group responsible for the work
- title of the work
- publisher
- date of publication

For print materials, the information for a citation generally appears on the copyright and title pages. For the format of a Works Cited list, consult the examples on this page and in the MLA Style for Listing Sources chart.

Sample Works Cited List (MLA 8th Edition)

Carwardine, Mark, et al. *The Nature Company Guides: Whales, Dolphins, and Porpoises*. Time-Life, 1998.

"Discovering Whales." *Whales on the Net*. Whales in Danger, 1998, www.whales.org.au/discover/index.html. Accessed 11 Apr. 2017.

Neruda, Pablo. "Ode to Spring." *Odes to Opposites*, translated by Ken Krabbenhoft, edited and illustrated by Ferris Cook, Little, 1995, p. 16.

The Saga of the Volsungs. Translated by Jesse L. Byock, Penguin, 1990.

List an anonymous work by title.

List both the title of the work and the collection in which it is found.

Works Cited List or Bibliography?

A Works Cited list includes only those sources you paraphrased or quoted directly in your research paper. By contrast, a bibliography lists all the sources you consulted during research—even those you did not cite.

MLA (8th Edition) Style for Listing Sources

Book with one author	Pyles, Thomas. *The Origins and Development of the English Language.* 2nd ed., Harcourt Brace Jovanovich, 1971. [Indicate the edition or version number when relevant.]
Book with two authors	Pyles, Thomas, and John Algeo. *The Origins and Development of the English Language.* 5th ed., Cengage Learning, 2004.
Book with three or more authors	Donald, Robert B., et al. *Writing Clear Essays.* Prentice Hall, 1983.
Book with an editor	Truth, Sojourner. *Narrative of Sojourner Truth.* Edited by Margaret Washington, Vintage Books, 1993.
Introduction to a work in a published edition	Washington, Margaret. Introduction. *Narrative of Sojourner Truth,* by Sojourner Truth, edited by Washington, Vintage Books, 1993, pp. v–xi.
Single work in an anthology	Hawthorne, Nathaniel. "Young Goodman Brown." *Literature: An Introduction to Reading and Writing,* edited by Edgar V. Roberts and Henry E. Jacobs, 5th ed., Prentice Hall, 1998, pp. 376–385. [Indicate pages for the entire selection.]
Signed article from an encyclopedia	Askeland, Donald R. "Welding." *World Book Encyclopedia,* vol. 21, World Book, 1991, p. 58.
Signed article in a weekly magazine	Wallace, Charles. "A Vodacious Deal." *Time,* 14 Feb. 2000, p. 63.
Signed article in a monthly magazine	Gustaitis, Joseph. "The Sticky History of Chewing Gum." *American History,* Oct. 1998, pp. 30–38.
Newspaper article	Thurow, Roger. "South Africans Who Fought for Sanctions Now Scrap for Investors." *Wall Street Journal,* 11 Feb. 2000, pp. A1+. [For a multipage article that does not appear on consecutive pages, write only the first page number on which it appears, followed by the plus sign.]
Unsigned editorial or story	"Selective Silence." Editorial. *Wall Street Journal,* 11 Feb. 2000, p. A14. [If the editorial or story is signed, begin with the author's name.]
Signed pamphlet or brochure	[Treat the pamphlet as though it were a book.]
Work from a library subscription service	Ertman, Earl L. "Nefertiti's Eyes." *Archaeology,* Mar.–Apr. 2008, pp. 28–32. *Kids Search,* EBSCO, New York Public Library. Accessed 7 Jan. 2017. [Indicating the date you accessed the information is optional but recommended.]
Filmstrips, slide programs, videocassettes, DVDs, and other audiovisual media	*The Diary of Anne Frank.* 1959. Directed by George Stevens, performances by Millie Perkins, Shelley Winters, Joseph Schildkraut, Lou Jacobi, and Richard Beymer, Twentieth Century Fox, 2004. [Indicating the original release date after the title is optional but recommended.]
CD-ROM (with multiple publishers)	Simms, James, editor. *Romeo and Juliet.* By William Shakespeare, Attica Cybernetics / BBC Education / Harper, 1995.
Radio or television program transcript	"Washington's Crossing of the Delaware." *Weekend Edition Sunday,* National Public Radio, 23 Dec. 2013. Transcript.
Web page	"Fun Facts About Gum." ICGA, 2005–2017, www.gumassociation.org/index. cfm/facts-figures/fun-facts-about-gum. Accessed 19 Feb. 2017. [Indicating the date you accessed the information is optional but recommended.]
Personal interview	Smith, Jane. Personal interview, 10 Feb. 2017.

All examples follow the style given in the MLA Handbook, 8th edition, published in 2016.

PROGRAM RESOURCES

Evidence Log

Unit Title: __Discovery__

Perfomance-Based Assessment Prompt:
Do all discoveries benefit humanity?

My initial thoughts:
Yes - all knowledge moves us forward.

As you read multiple texts about a topic, your thinking may change. Use an Evidence Log like this one to record your thoughts, to track details you might use in later writing or discussion, and to make further connections.

Here is a sample to show how one reader's ideas deepened as she read two texts.

Title of Text: __Classifying the Stars__   Date: __Sept. 17__

CONNECTION TO THE PROMPT	TEXT EVIDENCE/DETAILS	ADDITIONAL NOTES/IDEAS
Newton shared his discoveries and then other scientists built on his discoveries.	Paragraph 2: "Isaac Newton gave to the world the results of his experiments on passing sunlight through a prism." Paragraph 3: "In 1814 . . . the German optician, Fraunhofer . . . saw that the multiple spectral tints . . . were crossed by hundreds of fine dark lines."	It's not always clear how a discovery might benefit humanity in the future.

How does this text change or add to my thinking? This confirms what I think.   Date: __Sept. 20__

Title of Text: __Cell Phone Mania__   Date: __Sept. 21__

CONNECTION TO THE PROMPT	TEXT EVIDENCE/DETAILS	ADDITIONAL NOTES/IDEAS
Cell phones have made some forms of communication easier, but people don't talk to each other as much as they did in the past.	Paragraph 7: "Over 80% of young adults state that texting is their primary method of communicating with friends. This contrasts with older adults who state that they prefer a phone call."	Is it good that we don't talk to each other as much? Look for article about social media to learn more about this question.

How does this text change or add to my thinking?   Date: __Sept. 25__
Maybe there are some downsides to discoveries. I still think that knowledge moves us forward, but there are sometimes unintended negative effects.

Word Network

A word network is a collection of words related to a topic. As you read the selections in a unit, identify interesting theme-related words and build your vocabulary by adding them to your Word Network.

Use your Word Network as a resource for your discussions and writings. Here is an example:

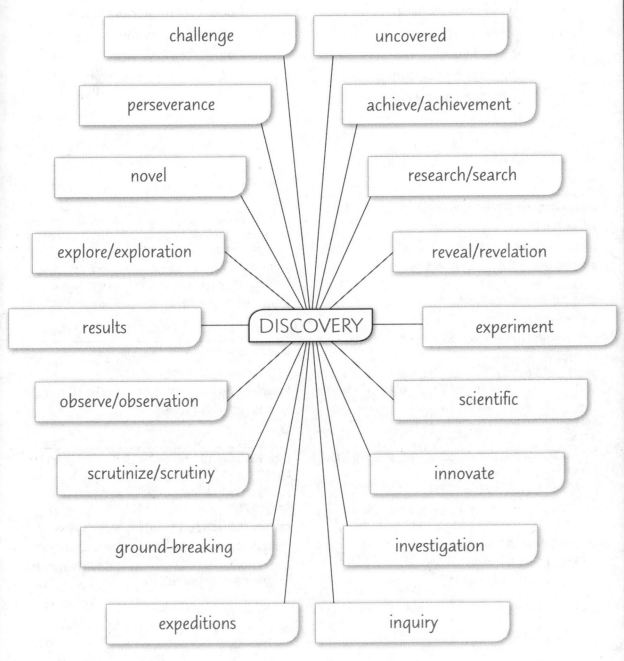

ACADEMIC / CONCEPT VOCABULARY

Academic vocabulary appears in **blue type**.

Pronunciation Key

Symbol	Sample Words	Symbol	Sample Words
a	*at, catapult, Alabama*	oo	*boot, soup, crucial*
ah	*father, charms, argue*	ow	*now, stout, flounder*
ai	*care, various, hair*	oy	*boy, toil, oyster*
aw	*law, maraud, caution*	s	*say, nice, press*
awr	*pour, organism, forewarn*	sh	*she, abolition, motion*
ay	*ape, sails, implication*	u	*full, put, book*
ee	*even, teeth, really*	uh	*ago, focus, contemplation*
eh	*ten, repel, elephant*	ur	*bird, urgent. perforation*
ehr	*merry, verify, terribly*	y	*by, delight, identify*
ih	*it, pin, hymn*	yoo	*music, confuse, few*
o	*shot, hopscotch, condo*	zh	*pleasure, treasure, vision*
oh	*own, parole, rowboat*		

A

abounding (uh BOWND ihng) *adj.* overflowing; full of

adore (uh DAWR) *v.* love greatly

agitation (aj uh TAY shuhn) *n.* state of nervous anxiety

allegiance (uh LEE juhns) *n.* loyalty

ambassadors (am BAS uh duhrz) *n.* special representatives to other countries

amnesia (am NEE zhuh) *n.* loss of memory

anachronism (uh NAK ruh nihz uhm) *n.* something occuring out of its proper time

angle (ANG guhl) *n.* in graphic art, measurement of how much space, horizontal and vertical, is included in a single visual

animosity (an uh MOS uh tee) *n.* hostile feelings; hatred

annotation (an uh TAY shuhn) *n.* note added to a text to explain

antidote (AN tuh doht) *n.* remedy

artifice (AHR tuh fihs) *n.* sly, clever, artful trick or strategy

assault (uh SAWLT) *n.* military attack

assay (uh SAY) *v.* analyze

assertion (uh SUR shuhn) *n.* positive statement; formal declaration

assimilate (uh SIHM uh layt) *v.* become like the majority in a region or country by adopting its customs, viewpoint, character, or attitude

audience reaction (AW dee uhns) (ree AK shuhn) *n.* how viewers or listeners respond to a performance

avaricious (av uh RIHSH uhs) *adj.* greedy

B

blanch (blanch) *v.* make pale; lose color

bliss (blihs) *n.* great happiness; ecstasy

breach (breech) *n.* hole made by breaking through

breadth (brehdth) *n.* width

C

captivity (kap TIHV uh tee) *n.* state of being held against one's will

catalyst (KAT uh lihst) *n.* person or thing creating or bringing about change

cavalry (KAV uhl ree) *n.* soldiers on horseback

chafed (chayft) *v.* made sore from rubbing; irritated

cinematography (sihn uh muh TOG ruh fee) *n.* art and science of filmmaking

cognitive (KOG nuh tihv) *adj.* having to do with knowing; dealing with awareness

composition (KOM puh ZIHSH uhn) *n.* arrangement of the parts of an image, whether drawn or recorded in some other visual format

consternation (kon stuhr NAY shuhn) *n.* sudden feeling of intense confusion; dismay

contradictory (kon truh DIHK tuhr ee) *adj.* saying the opposite; in disagreement

conventionalized (kuhn VEHN shuhn uh lyzd) *adj.* turned into something predictable and expected

converged (kuhn VURJD) *v.* came together

conviction (kuhn VIHK shuhn) *n.* state of being convinced; firm belief

corpse (kawrps) *n.* dead body

correspondent (kawr uh SPON duhnt) *n.* journalist employed by a media outlet to gather, report, or contribute news from a distant place

counterfeit (KOWN tuhr fiht) *n.* false imitation

cover design (KUHV uhr) (dih ZYN) *n.* visual art created by an illustrator, photographer, or graphic artist for the cover of a book or other printed material

credible (KREHD uh buhl) *adj.* believable

cross-reference (KRAWS rehf ruhns) *n.* note directing readers to another part of the text

D

decaying (dih KAY ihng) *adj.* decomposing; rotting

dejected (dih JEHK tihd) *adj.* depressed; saddened

delivery (dih LIHV uhr ee) *n.* way in which speakers, such as actors or poets, say their words; giving up or handing over

demagogue (DEHM uh gawg) *n.* leader who stirs people's emotions by appealing to emotion or prejudice to gain power

desire (dih ZYR) *n.* longing; strong wish or want

desolation (dehs uh LAY shuhn) *n.* lonely sorrow; condition of being ruined or deserted

despair (dih SPAIR) *v.* abandon all hope

despotic (dehs POT ihk) *adj.* in an oppressive manner typical of a tyrant or dictator

devise (dih VYZ) *v.* plan; think out

diligent (DIHL uh juhnt) *adj.* conscientious and hardworking

dimmed (dihmd) *v.* became less bright

dirge (durj) *n.* song of grief

discreet (dihs KREET) *adj.* careful about what one says or does; prudent

diverse (dih VURS) *adj.* varied; made up of many different elements

dominions (duh MIHN yuhnz) *n.* governed territories or countries

dread (drehd) *n.* state of great fear

dreadful (DREHD fuhl) *adj.* inspiring fear or awe

E

edict (EE dihkt) *n.* formal order issued by authority

editing (EHD iht ihng) *n.* process of selecting, correcting, and sequencing the written, visual, and audio elements of a media production

embedded video (ehm BEHD ihd) (VIHD ee oh) *n.* video that has been placed within the HTML code of a Web page

embrace (ehm BRAYS) *v.* accept or adopt eagerly

eminent (EHM uh nuhnt) *adj.* rising above others in rank or achievement

engender (ehn JEHN duhr) *v.* create; produce; cause

enrages (ehn RAY juhz) *v.* causes become very angry

entitlement (ehn TY tuhl muhnt) *n.* expectation; right

entry (EHN tree) *n.* main article in an encyclopedia; it may be divided into a series of *subentries*

entwining (ehn TWYN ihng) *v.* twisting or knotting together; encircling

equivocate (ih KWIHV uh kayt) *v.* speak in a way that hides the truth

eternally (ih TUR nuh lee) *adv.* lasting forever

F

faction (FAK shuhn) *n.* partisan conflict within an organization or a country; dissension

fancy (FAN see) *n.* taste for something; fondness

fellowships (FEHL oh shihps) *n.* groups of people who share interests

fervent (FUR vuhnt) *adj.* passionate; intense-feeling

flout (flowt) *v.* break a rule or law without hiding it or showing shame

foully (FOWL lee) *adv.* wrongly; in an evil way

G

gesture (JEHS chuhr) *n.* movement of part of the body, especially the hands, that conveys meaning

gifted (GIHF tihd) *adj.* having a natural talent

gorge (gawrj) *v.* fill by eating greedily

gruesome (GROO suhm) *adj.* horrible; ghastly

H

harmony (HAHR muh nee) *n.* oneness; peacefulness

headings (HEHD ihngz) *n.* entries that describe the information recorded in the columns of a document such as a spreadsheet

hemlock (HEHM lok) *n.* poisonous herb or a drink prepared from it

hideous (HIHD ee uhs) *adj.* ugly or disgusting

honor (ON uhr) *v.* respect greatly

host (hohst) *n.* moderator or interviewer for a radio, television, or Web-based show

hybrid (HY brihd) *adj.* combined from different sources

hyperlink (HY puhr lihngk) *n.* interactive word or passage of an online text that links to additional information

I

idiosyncratic (ihd ee oh sihn KRAT ihk) *adj.* peculiar

illusory (ih LOO suhr ee) *adj.* misleading; unreal

impalpable (ihm PAL puh buhl) *adj.* unable to be felt by touching; hard to understand

imperial (ihm PEER ee uhl) *adj.* of or related to an empire or emperor; of superior quality

imperialism (ihm PIHR ee uhl ihz uhm) *n.* policy of one nation's taking control over another in order to exploit its people and resources for its own benefit

impertinent (ihm PURT uhn uhnt) *adj.* rude; out of place

implication (ihm pluh KAY shuhn) *n.* indirect suggestion; hint

inanimate (ihn AN uh miht) *adj.* not alive; seeming to be lifeless

incensed (ihn SEHNST) *v.* made angry

incorporate (ihn KAWR puh rayt) *v.* combine; merge

indigenous (ihn DIHJ uh nuhs) *adj.* native to a particular country or region

inexorable (ihn EHK suhr uh buhl) *adj.* unable to be altered or changed

infuse (ihn FYOOZ) *v.* put into; fill

innocuous (ih NOK yoo uhs) *adj.* harmless

innumerable (ih NOO muhr uh buhl) *adj.* too many to count

integrity (ihn TEHG ruh tee) *n.* moral uprightness

interviewee (ihn tuhr vyoo EE) *n.* person who is questioned on a media broadcast

intolerable (ihn TOL uhr uh buhl) *adj.* hard to endure; unbearable

J

justify (JUHS tuh fy) *v.* give good reason for; show to be right

jutted (JUHT ihd) *v.* stuck out

L

lair (lair) *n.* den; hiding place

laity (LAY uh tee) *n.* people of religious faith who are not members of the clergy

languish (LANG gwihsh) *v.* grow tired or weak; droop

laudable (LAWD uh buhl) *adj.* praiseworthy

leaden (LEHD uhn) *adj.* heavy; hard to lift; dull and gloomy

lighting/color (LY tihng) (KUHL ur) *n.* in graphic art, use of light and dark shades

loathsome (LOHTH suhm) *adj.* disgusting; detestable

M

malevolence (muh LEHV uh luhns) *n.* desire to do evil

malice (MAL ihs) *n.* desire to hurt another person

malicious (muh LIHSH uhs) *adj.* intending to do harm; evil

migrate (MY grayt) *v.* move from one place to settle in another; move with the seasons

mime (mym) *n.* theatrical technique of portraying characters and actions wordlessly, using movement only

modify (MOD uh fy) *v.* partly change

myriad (MIHR ee uhd) *n.* uncountably large number; variety

N

navigation (nav uh GAY shuhn) *n.* moving from place to place on a website or on the Internet to find information

O

odious (OH dee uhs) *adj.* extremely unpleasant or repulsive

P

pacing (PAY sihng) *n.* tempo or overall sense of the speed at which a theatrical production takes place

palette (PAL iht) *n.* range of colors and shades used by an illustrator

panel (PAN uhl) *n.* individual scene in a graphic novel, often framed by a border

pathological (path uh LOJ ih kuhl) *adj.* dealing with disease

perception (puhr SEHP shuhn) *n.* act of making an observation

pernicious (puhr NIHSH uhs) *adj.* harmful, often in a way that is not readily noticed

personable (PUR suh nuh buhl) *adj.* having a pleasant manner

perspective (puhr SPEHK tihv) *n.* in graphic novels, the point of view of an image, which may be *close up, middle distance,* or *long distance*

perturbation (puhr tuhr BAY shuhn) *n.* disturbance

prescribe (prih SKRYB) *v.* set down as a direction; order medicine or treatment

presume (prih ZOOM) *v.* assume; take for granted without proof

pretext (PREE tehkst) *n.* plausible but false reason

prime (prym) *n.* youth; young adulthood

prismatic (prihz MAT ihk) *adj.* like a prism; varied in color

pristine (prihs TEEN) *adj.* original; unspoiled

privileged (PRIHV lihjd) *adj.* given special advantages

proclamation (prok luh MAY shuhn) *n.* something that is proclaimed, or announced officially

profanation (prof uh NAY shuhn) *n.* act of disrespecting sacred ideas, persons, or things

proficient (pruh FIHSH uhnt) *adj.* skilled; expert

provoke (pruh VOHK) *v.* make angry; cause

purge (purj) *n.* ousting; removal

purport (puhr PAWRT) *v.* claim or profess, often falsely

putrid (PYOO trihd) *adj.* decaying; rotten and smelly

R

rancors (RANG kuhrz) *n.* angry feelings

rank (rangk) *n.* row or line of soldiers

realism and **stylization** (REE uh lihz uhm) (sty luh ZAY shuhn) *n.* In art, realism portrays images as they actually appear; stylization presents images that are exaggerated, distorted, or otherwise altered to show an imagined vision.

rebellious (rih BEHL yuhs) *adj.* acting against authority

reiterate (ree IHT uh rayt) *v.* say or do several times; repeat

repercussion (ree puhr KUHSH uhn) *n.* effect of or reaction to some event

requiem (REHK wee uhm) *n.* musical composition honoring the dead

requisite (REHK wuh ziht) *adj.* required; necessary; essential

resolute (REHZ uh loot) *adj.* determined; firm

revelation (rehv uh LAY shuhn) *n.* something made known, disclosed, or discovered

revolt (rih VOHLT) *n.* attempt to overthrow a lawful ruler

rows and **columns** (rohz) (KOL uhmz) *n.* how information is organized in a speadsheet

S

sacrilegious (sak ruh LIHJ uhs) *adj.* treating a religious object, person, or belief with disrespect

sanctity (SANGK tuh tee) *n.* holiness; goodness

season (SEE zuhn) *n.* special time

sepulcher (SEHP uhl kuhr) *n.* tomb

serene (suh REEN) *adj.* peaceful; calm

sincerity (sihn SEHR uh tee) *n.* truthfulness; good faith

slide show (slyd) (shoh) *n.* presentation based on or supplemented by a series of still images

solemnity (suh LEHM nuh tee) *n.* solemn feeling; seriousness

sordid (SAWR dihd) *adj.* dirty; filthy

sound effects (sownd) (ih FEHKTS) *n.* recorded sounds that are neither speech nor music

sport (spawrt) *v.* amuse

stagnant (STAG nuhnt) *adj.* lacking motion or current

stalked (stawkt) *v.* pursued stealthily; hunted

statistics (stuh TIHS tihks) *n.* numerical facts or data that have been assembled or tabulated

stealthy (STEHL thee) *adj.* slow and secretive

stores (stawrz) *n.* supplies

subjugation (suhb juh GAY shuhn) *n.* conquest

sublime (suh BLYM) *adj.* magnificent; awe-inspiring

succeed (suhk SEED) *v.* come after

superimposition (soo puhr ihm puh ZIHSH uhn) *n.* placement of one image on top of another to create a new image or effect

supplant (suh PLANT) *v.* replace one thing with another

T

taste (tayst) *n.* liking for something; fondness

tedious (TEE dee uhs) *adj.* boring; long and tiring

tenacious (tih NAY shuhs) *adj.* stubborn; persistent

theoretical (thee uh REHT uh kuhl) *adj.* based on theory; not proven

toil (toyl) *n.* hard work

torrid (TAWR ihd) *adj.* very hot; burning

tranquil (TRANG kwuhl) *adj.* peaceful; calm

transformation (trans fuhr MAY shuhn) *n.* act of changing in form or appearance

treacherous (TREHCH uhr uhs) *adj.* guilty of deception or betrayal

treasons (TREE zuhnz) *n.* crimes of helping the enemies of one's country

typography (ty POG ruh fee) *n.* size and style of type used for books and other printed materials

U

unambiguous (uhn am BIHG yoo uhs) *adj.* not confused; clear; definite

upbringing (UHP brihng ihng) *n.* care and training given to a child while growing up

usurper (yoo SURP uhr) *n.* person who takes control without the proper authority

V

valiantly (VAL yuhnt lee) *adv.* courageously

vile (vyl) *adj.* disgusting

virtuous (VUR choo uhs) *adj.* having high moral standards

W

wavered (WAY vuhrd) *v.* flickered; fluttered

writhing (RY thihng) *adj.* making twisting or turning motions

VOCABULARIO ACADÉMICO/ VOCABULARIO DE CONCEPTOS

El vocabulario académico está en **letra azul**.

A

abounding / abundante *adj.* rebosante; lleno

adore / adorar *v.* amar enormemente

agitation / agitación *s.* estado de anxiedad y nerviosismo

allegiance / lealtad *s.* fidelidad

ambassadors / embajadores *s.* representantes en otro países

amnesia / amnesia *s.* pérdida de la memoria

anachronism / anacronismo *s.* algo que no ocurre en su propio tiempo o época

angle / ángulo *s.* en las artes gráficas, medida de cuánto espacio, tanto horizontal como vertical, se incluye en una ilustración

animosity / animosidad *s.* hostilidad; odio

annotation / anotación *s.* nota explicativa que se agrega a un texto

antidote / antídoto *s.* remedio

artifice / artificio *s.* recurso o estrategia ingeniosa y, a veces, taimada

assault / asalto *s.* ataque militar

assay / evaluar *v.* analizar

assertion / aseveración *s.* enunciado positivo; declaración formal

assimilate / asimilarse *v.* volverse similar a la mayoría de las personas que habitan una región o país adoptando sus costumbres, puntos de vista, carácter o actitud

audience reaction / reacción de la audiencia *s.* la manera en que los espectadores u oyentes responden a una actuación

avaricious / avaro *adj.* codicioso

B

blanch / blanquear *v.* hacer que algo tome un color más pálido, o que pierda el color

bliss / dicha *s.* gran felicidad, éxtasis

breach / brecha *s.* grieta o agujero que se hace en una pared o edificio

breadth / anchura *s.* ancho, amplitud

C

captivity / cautiverio *s.* estado en el cual se está retenido contra la propia voluntad

catalyst / catalizador *s.* persona o cosa que crea o produce un cambio

cavalry / caballería *s.* ejército de soldados a caballo

chafed / irritado *adj.* sensibilizado a causa de haberlo frotado o raspado mucho

cinematography / cinematografía *s.* arte y ciencia de hacer y procesar películas

cognitive / cognitivo *adj.* relativo al conocimiento o con la concientización

composition / composición *s.* arreglo o disposición de las partes de una imagen, ya sea dibujada o grabada en algún tipo de soporte visual

consternation / consternación *s.* sentimiento repentino de gran confusión; desaliento

contradictory / contradictorio *adj.* que expresa lo opuesto; que está en desacuerdo

conventionalized / convencional *adj.* algo predecible o de esperarse

converged / convergió *v.* se juntó o reunió

conviction / convicción *s.* seguridad, certeza; creencia firme

corpse / cadáver *s.* cuerpo muerto

correspondent / corresponsal *s.* empleado de un medio de comunicación encargado de reunir, informar o enviar noticias desde un lugar distante

counterfeit / falsificación *s.* imitación ilegítima

cover design / diseño de tapa *s.* arte creado por un ilustrador, un fotógrafo o un artista gráfico para la tapa de un libro u otro tipo de material impreso

credible / verosímil *adj.* creíble

cross-reference / referencia cruzada *s.* referencia que remite a otra parte del mismo texto

D

decaying / descompuesto *adj.* que se está pudriendo o echando a perder

dejected / desalentado *adj.* deprimido; entristecido

delivery / presentación oral *s.* la manera en la que un hablante, por ejemplo un estudiante, hace una exposición o un discurso

delivery / reparto *s.* entrega en mano o a domicilio

demagogue / demagogo *s.* líder que despierta emociones en la gente apelando a sus prejuicios para aumentar su poder

desire / deseo *s.* anhelo; inclinación o atracción profunda hacia algo o alguien

desolation / desolación *s.* pena solitaria; estado o sentimiento de ruina y abandono

despair / desesperación *s.* sentir que ya no se tiene ninguna esperanza

despotic / despótico *adj.* se dice de lo que se hace de manera opresiva, propia de un déspota o tirano

devise / concebir *v.* planear, idear

diligent / diligente *adj.* cuidadoso y laborioso

dimmed / atenuado *adj.* que se hizo menos brillante o colorido

dirge / endecha *s.* canción lúgubre o de mucho dolor

discreet / discreto *adj.* cauto, prudente

diverse / diverso *adj.* diferente

dominions / dominios *s.* países o territorios que se gobiernan

dread / terror *s.* miedo muy profundo

dreadful / aterrador *adj.* que produce miedo o sobrecogimiento

E

edict / edicto *s.* ordenanza emitida por una autoridad

editing / edición *s.* proceso mediante el cual se seleccionan, corrigen y organizan los elementos escritos, visuales y sonoros de una producción de medios de comunicación

embedded video / video integrado *s.* video que se ha insertado en el código HTML de una página web

embrace / acoger *v.* aceptar o adoptar con los brazos abiertos

eminent / eminente *adj.* distinguido; famoso; notable

engender / engendrar *v.* crear; producir; causar

enrages / enfurece *v.* provoca un enfado o enojo muy grande

entitlement / privilegio *s.* derecho; beneficio

entry / entrada *s.* cada artículo de una enciclopedia; puede dividirse en una serie de *entradas secundarias*

entwining / enroscar *v.* enrollar o entramar dos o más cosas; envolver o rodear

equivocate / ser equívoco *v.* hablar de una manera que oculta la verdad

eternally / eternamente *adv.* para siempre

F

faction / facción *s.* cada uno de los grupos que participa en un conflicto dentro de una organización o país; disensión, desacuerdo

fancy / inclinación *s.* gusto o debilidad por algo o alguien

fellowships / hermandades *s.* grupos de personas que comparten intereses

fervent / ferviente *adj.* apasionado; de sentimientos intensos

flout / incumplir *v.* desobedecer una regla o ley sin ocultarlo ni mostrarse avergonzado por ello

font / tipo *s.* conjunto de caracteres tipográficos del mismo tamaño y estilo

foully / vilmente *adv.* ofensivamente, maliciosamente; de manera malvada

G

gesture / gesto *s.* movimiento de una parte del cuerpo

gifted / dotado *adj.* que tiene un talento natural

gorge / atracarse *v.* comer con avidez

gruesome / repelente *adj.* horrible; espeluznante

H

harmony / armonía *s.* unidad; paz

headings / encabezados *s.* títulos que describen la información que se incluye en las columnas de un documento como una hoja de cálculo

hemlock / cicuta *s.* hierba venenosa; la bebida que se prepara con ella

hideous / horroroso *adj.* muy feo, espantoso

honor / honrar *v.* respetar mucho

host / conductor *s.* moderador o entrevistador de un programa de radio, televisión o virtual

hybrid / híbrido *adj.* se dice del producto de la combinación de distintas fuentes

hyperlink / hipervínculo *s.* referencia cruzada que les da a los lectores más información sobre una palabra que está resaltada

I

idiosyncratic / idiosincrático *adj.* peculiar

illusory / ilusorio *adj.* irreal; engañoso

impalpable / impalpable *adj.* que no se puede percibir por vía del tacto; difícil de entender

imperial / imperial *adj.* relacionado con un imperio o un emperador; de calidad superior

imperialism / imperialismo *s.* la política de un país que controla a otro para explotar a su pueblo y sus recursos para beneficio propio

impertinent / impertinente *adj.* grosero; fuera de lugar

implication / implicación *s.* sugerencia indirecta; pista

inanimate / inanimado *adj.* que no está vivo; falto de alma o vida

incensed / enfurecido *adj.* enojado, furioso

incorporate / incorporar *v.* combinar; fusionar

indigenous / indígena *adj.* nativo de un país o región en particular

inexorable / inexorable *adj.* que no puede alterarse ni cambiar

infuse / infundir *v.* inculcar; inspirar

innocuous / inocuo *adj.* que no hace daño

innumerable / innumerables *adj.* que son demasiados para poder contarlos

integrity / integridad *s.* corrección moral

interviewee / entrevistado *s.* persona a la que se le están haciendo preguntas en un medio de comunicación

intolerable / intolerable *adj.* difícil de aguantar; insoportable

J

justify / justificar *v.* dar buenas razones; demostrar que se tiene razón

jutted / sobresaliente *adj.* que se distingue

L

lair / guarida *s.* madriguera; lugar donde ocultarse

laity / laicado *s.* conjunto de personas que comparten una fe religiosa pero que no son miembros del clero

languish / languidecer *v.* cansarse o debilitarse; desfallecer

laudable / loable *adj.* que merece ser alabado o felicitado

leaden / plúmbeo *adj.* pesado; difícil del alzar; aburrido y plomizo

lighting/color / sombreado *s.* en las artes gráficas, el uso de sombras claras y oscuras

loathsome / repugnante *adj.* asqueroso, desagradable

M

malevolence / malevolencia *s.* deseo de hacer el mal

malice / malicia *s.* deseo de herir a otra persona

malicious / malicioso *adj.* se dice de algo o alguien que tiene el propósito de herir

manifest / lista de embarque *s.* documento que detalla información sobre un barco, un avión u otro tipo de vehículo

menu / menú *s.* lista de opciones o mandos de una computadora entre los cuales se puede escoger

migrate / migrar *v.* trasladarse de un lugar para asentarse en otro; mudarse según las estaciones del año

mime / mímica *s.* técnica teatral con la que se sugieren acciones, personajes y emociones sin utilizar palabras

modify / modificar *v.* cambiar parcialmente

myriad / miríada *s.* una cantidad tan grande que resulta incontable; variedad

N

navigation / navegación *s.* ir de un lugar a otro en una página web o en Internet buscando información

O

odious / odioso *adj.* extremadamente desagradable o repulsivo

P

pacing / tempo *s.* ritmo al que se desarrolla una obra teatral

palette / paleta *s.* rango de colores que utiliza un ilustrador

panel / viñeta *s.* escena de una novela gráfica, por lo general enmarcada por una línea

pathological / patológico *adj.* relacionado con alguna enfermedad

perception / apreciación *s.* el acto de hacer una observación

pernicious / pernicioso *adj.* dañino, generalmente de una manera que tarda en notarse

personable / afable *adj.* de maneras y trato agradables

perspective / perspectiva *s.* en las artes, la ilusión de profundidad; en las novelas gráficas, el punto de vista de una imagen, que puede ser un primer plano, un plano medio o un plano general

perturbation / perturbación *s.* disturbio

prescribe / prescribir *v.* indicar una dirección o camino a seguir; recetar un medicamento o tratamiento

presume / presuponer *v.* asumir; dar algo por sentado

pretext / pretexto *s.* excusa falsa

prime / plenitud *s.* juventud; primera edad adulta

prismatic / prismático *adj.* con la forma de un prisma; de colores variados

pristine / prístino *adj.* antiguo, original; inmaculado

privileged / privilegiado *adj.* que recibe ciertas ventajas o tratamientos especiales

proclamation / proclama *s.* anuncio oficial

profanation / profanación *s.* acto de faltarle el repecto a cosas, ideas o personas que se consideran sagradas

proficient / competente *adj.* capaz; diestro; experto en algo

provoke / provocar *v.* hacer enojar; producir o causar algo

purge / purga *s.* expulsión; eliminación

purport / pretender *v.* reclamar; asegurar o sostener una idea

putrid / pútrido *adj.* descompuesto; podrido y apestoso

R

rancors / rencores *s.* sentimientos de ira o enojo

rank / rango *s.* hilera o fila de soldados

realism and stylization / realismo y estilización *s.* en las representaciones artísticas el realismo, o arte realista, es como una fotografía, mientras que la estilización, o arte estilizado, es como una caricatura

rebellious / rebelde *adj.* que actúa en contra de la autoridad

reiterate / reiterar *v.* decir o hacer algo varias veces; repetir

repercussion / repercusión *s.* efecto o reacción ante algún hecho

requiem / requiem *s.* composición musical en honor de los muertos

requisite / requerido *adj.* necesario; esencial

resolute / resuelto *adj.* de carácter firme, decidido

revelation / revelación *s.* algo que se devela o descubre; manifestación de algo que estaba oculto

revolt / revuelta *s.* intento de derrocar a un gobernante legítimamente elegido

rows and **columns / hileras y columnas** *s.* el modo en que se organiza la información en una hoja de cálculo

S

sacrilegious / sacrílego *adj.* se dice de un modo irrespetuoso de tratar a un objeto, persona o creencia religiosa

sanctity / santidad *s.* calidad de santo; beatitud

season / estación *s.* tiempo o época particular

sepulcher / sepulcro *s.* tumba

serene / sereno *adj.* calmo, pacífico

sincerity / sinceridad *s.* veracidad; de buena fe

slide show / pase de diapositivas *s.* prepresentación basada total o parcialmente en el uso de una serie de imágenes fijas

solemnity / solemnidad *s.* seriedad; formalidad

sordid / sórdido *adj.* sucio; mugriento

sound effects / efecto de sonido *s.* sonidos grabados que no son ni voz ni música

sport / broma *s.* chiste; algo dicho o hecho con ánimo juguetón

stagnant / estancado *adj.* que no se mueve o fluye; quieto

stalked / acosó *v.* persiguió obsesivamente

statistics / estadísticas *s.* información o datos numéricos que se han agrupado o tabulado

stealthy / furtivo *adj.* lento y secreto

stores / reservas *s.* provisiones

stylization / estilización *s.* el acto de procurar darle a algo o alguien una determinada apariencia

subjugation / subyugación *s.* conquista

sublime / sublime *adj.* magnífico, asombroso

succeed / lograr *v.* conseguir lo que se ha intentado hacer

superimposition / sobreimposición *s.* la acción de imprimir una imagen encima de otra ya existente con el fin de lograr un efecto determinado

supplant / suplantar *v.* reemplazar una cosa por otra

T

taste / gusto *s.* aprecio o debilidad por algo

tedious / tedioso *adj.* aburrido; largo y cansado

tenacious / tenaz *adj.* terco; persistente

theoretical / teórico *adj.* que se basa en la teoría; que no está probado

toil / esfuerzo *s.* trabajo duro o difícil

torrid / tórrido *adj.* muy caluroso; ardiente

tranquil / sosegado *adj.* calmo, tranquilo

transformation / transformación *s.* el acto de cambiar de forma o apariencia

treacherous / traicionero *adj.* culpable de engañar o traicionar

treasons / traiciones *s.* delitos de deslealtad como, por ejemplo, ayudar a los enemigos del propio país

typography and **font / tipografía** y **tipo** *s.* tamaño y estilo del conjunto de caracteres tipográficos que se utilizan en los libros y otros materiales impresos

U

unambiguous / inequívoco *adj.* que no es confuso; claro, definido

upbringing / crianza *s.* el cuidado y la educación que se le da a un niño cuando está creciendo

usurper / usurpador *s.* persona que toma el control sin la debida autoridad

V

valiantly / valerosamente *adv.* con valor y coraje

vile / vil *adj.* canalla, infame

virtuous / virtuoso *adj.* moralmente puro; recto

W

wavered / titilante *adj.* que parpadea o titila

writhing / retorciéndose *v.* que se contorsiona o contrae, por lo general a causa de un dolor

LITERARY TERMS HANDBOOK

ALLITERATION *Alliteration* is the repetition of initial consonant sounds in accented syllables.

Example: a **m**elody of **m**ur**m**uring **m**en

Alliteration is used to emphasize and to link words, as well as to create musical sounds.

ALLUSION *Allusion* is a reference to a well-known person, place, event, literary work, or work of art.

AMPLIFICATION *Amplification* is a stylistic device in which the writer expands an idea, and adds depth and detail, by repetition or elaboration.

ANALOGY An *analogy* is an extended comparison of relationships. It is based on the idea or insight that the relationship between one pair of things is like the relationship between another pair. Unlike a metaphor, another form of comparison, an analogy involves an explicit comparison, often using the word *like* or *as*.

ANAPHORA *Anaphora* is a rhetorical device that involves the deliberate repetition of the same sequence of words at the beginning of nearby phrases, clauses, or sentences.

ANGLO-SAXON POETRY The rhythmic poetry composed in the Old English language before A.D. 1100 is known as *Anglo-Saxon poetry*. It generally has four accented syllables and an indefinite number of unaccented syllables in each line. Each line is divided in half by a *caesura*, or pause, and the halves are linked by the alliteration of two or three of the accented syllables.

Anglo-Saxon poetry was sung or chanted to the accompaniment of a primitive harp; it was not written, but was passed down orally.

APOSTROPHE An *apostrophe* is a figure of speech in which a speaker directly addresses an absent person or a personified quality, object, or idea.

ARCHETYPE An *archetype* is a pattern found in literary works across time and place. For more information, see *Archetypal Literary Elements.*

ARCHAIC DICTION *Archaic diction* refers to words and phrases that were once in standard usage but are no longer common.

ARCHETYPAL LITERARY ELEMENTS *Archetypal literary elements* are patterns in literature found around the world. For instance, the occurrence of events in threes is an archetypal element of fairy tales. Certain character types, such as mysterious guides, are also archetypal elements of traditional stories. According to some critics, these elements express in symbolic form truths about the human mind.

ARGUMENT An *argument* is writing or speech that attempts to convince a reader to think or act in a particular way. An argument is a logical way of presenting a belief, conclusion, or stance. A good argument is supported with reasoning and evidence.

ASSONANCE *Assonance* is the repetition of vowel sounds in stressed syllables containing dissimilar consonant sounds, as in this line from Robert Browning's "Andrea del Sarto," in which the **long e** sound is repeated: Ah, but man's r**ea**ch should exc**ee**d his grasp."

BLANK VERSE *Blank verse* is unrhymed poetry usually written in iambic pentameter (see Meter). Occasional variations in rhythm are introduced in blank verse to create emphasis, variety, and naturalness of sound. Because blank verse sounds much like ordinary spoken English, it is often used in drama, as by Shakespeare, and in poetry.

CARPE DIEM A Latin phrase, *carpe diem* means "seize the day" or "make the most of passing time." Many great literary works have been written with the *carpe diem* theme.

CHARACTER The personality that takes part in the action of a literary work is known as a character. Characters can be classified in different ways. A character who plays an important role is called a *major character.* A character who does not is called a *minor character.* A character who plays the central role in a story is called the *protagonist.* A character who opposes the protagonist is called the *antagonist.* A *round character* has many aspects to his or her personality. A *flat character* is defined by only a few qualities. A character who changes is called *dynamic;* a character who does not change is called *static.*

CHARACTERIZATION *Characterization* is the act of creating and developing a character. A writer uses *direct characterization* when he or she describes a character's traits explicitly. Writers also use *indirect characterization.* A character's traits can be revealed indirectly in what he or she says, thinks, or does; in a description of his or her appearance; or in the statements, thoughts, or actions of other characters.

CLIMAX The *climax* is the high point of interest or suspense in a literary work. Often, the climax is also the crisis in the plot, the point at which the protagonist changes his or her understanding or situation. Sometimes, the climax coincides with the *resolution,* the point at which the central conflict is ended.

COMIC RELIEF Playwrights of tragedies often create one or two humorous characters and scenes to lighten the overall tense mood of the work. These characters and scenes provide *comic relief* in an otherwise suspenseful or tense production.

COMPRESSION *Compression* is the pressing together of disparate ideas or images and creates a density and complexity of meaning.

CONCEIT A *conceit* is an unusual and surprising comparison between two very different things. This special kind of metaphor or complicated analogy is often the basis for a whole poem. During the Elizabethan Age, sonnets commonly included Petrarchan conceits. **Petrarchan conceits** make extravagant claims about the beloved's beauty or the speaker's suffering, with comparisons to divine beings, powerful natural forces, and objects that contain a given quality in the highest degree. Seventeenth-century **metaphysical** poets used elaborate, unusual, and highly intellectual conceits.

CONFLICT A *conflict* is a struggle between opposing forces. Sometimes, this struggle is internal, or within a character. At other times, the struggle is external, or between the character and some outside force. The outside force may be another character, nature, or some element of society such as a custom or a political institution. Often, the conflict in a work combines several of these possibilities.

CONNOTATION *Connotation* refers to the associations that a word calls to mind in addition to its dictionary meaning. For example, the words *home* and *domicile* have the same dictionary meaning. However, the first word has positive connotations of warmth and security, whereas the second does not.

CONSONANCE *Consonance* is the repetition of final consonant sounds in stressed syllables containing dissimilar vowel sounds, as in this excerpt from Coleridge's "The Rime of the Ancient Mariner:"

> a frightful fie**nd** / Doth close behi**nd** him tread.

COUPLET A *couplet* is a pair of rhyming lines written in the same meter. A **heroic couplet** is a rhymed pair of iambic pentameter lines. In a **closed couplet,** the meaning and syntax are completed within the two lines, as in this example from Alexander Pope's "Essay on Criticism":

> True ease in writing comes from art, not chance,
> As those move easiest who have learned to dance.

Shakespearean sonnets usually end with heroic couplets.

CULTURALLY SPECIFIC THEME A *culturally specific theme* relates meaningfully to some cultures but not others.

DENOTATION *Denotation* is the objective meaning of a word—that to which the word refers, independent of other associations that the word calls to mind. Dictionaries list the denotative meanings of words.

DIALECT *Dialect* is the form of a language spoken by people in a particular region or group. Dialects differ from one another in grammar, vocabulary, and pronunciation.

DIALOGUE *Dialogue* is a conversation between characters. Writers use dialogue to reveal character, to present events, to add variety to narratives, and to interest readers. Dialogue in a story is usually set off by quotation marks and paragraphing. Dialogue in a play script generally follows the name of the speaker.

DIARY A *diary* is a personal record of daily events, usually written in prose. Most diaries are not written for publication; sometimes, however, interesting diaries written by influential people are published.

DICTION *Diction* is a writer's word choice. It can be a major determinant of the writer's style. Diction can be described as formal or informal, abstract or concrete, plain or ornate, ordinary or technical.

DRAMA A *drama* is a story written to be performed by actors. It may consist of one or more large sections, called acts, which are made up of any number of smaller sections, called scenes.

Drama originated in the religious rituals and symbolic reenactments of primitive peoples. The ancient Greeks, who developed drama into a sophisticated art form, created such dramatic forms as tragedy and comedy.

The first dramas in England were the miracle plays and morality plays of the Middle Ages. Miracle plays told biblical stories. Morality plays, such as *Everyman,* were allegories dealing with personified virtues and vices. The English Renaissance saw a flowering of drama in England, culminating in the works of William Shakespeare, who wrote many of the world's greatest comedies, tragedies, histories, and romances. During the Neoclassical Age, English drama turned to satirical comedies of manners that probed the virtues of upper-class society. In the Romantic and Victorian ages, a few good verse plays were written, including Percy Bysshe Shelley's *The Cenci* and *Prometheus Unbound.* The end of the nineteenth and beginning of the twentieth centuries saw a resurgence of the drama in England and throughout the English-speaking world. Great plays of the Modern period include works by Bernard Shaw, Christopher Fry, T. S. Eliot, Harold Pinter, and Samuel Beckett.

DRAMATIC MONOLOGUE A *dramatic monologue* is a poem in which an imaginary character speaks to a silent listener.

ENJAMBMENT *Enjambment*, or a run-on line, is a poetic structure in which both the grammatical structure and sense continue past the end of the line.

EPIC An *epic* is a long narrative poem about the adventures of gods or of an **epic hero**.

Epic conventions are traditional characteristics of epic poems, including an opening statement of the theme; an appeal for supernatural help in telling the story (an invocation); a beginning **in medias res** (Latin: "in the middle of things"); catalogs of people and things; accounts of past events; and descriptive phrases.

EPIGRAM An *epigram* is a brief statement in prose or in verse. The concluding couplet in an English sonnet may be epigrammatic. An essay may be written in an epigrammatic style.

EPIPHANY *Epiphany* is a sudden revelation or flash of insight in which a character recognizes a truth.

EPITAPH An *epitaph* is an inscription written on a tomb or burial place. In literature, epitaphs include serious or humorous lines written as if intended for such use, like the epitaph in Thomas Gray's "Elegy Written in a Country Churchyard."

ESSAY An *essay* is a short nonfiction work about a particular subject. Essays can be classified as formal or informal, personal or impersonal. They can also be classified according to purpose, such as cause-and-effect, satirical, or reflective. Modes of discourse, such as explanatory, descriptive, persuasive, or narrative, are other means of classifying essays.

EXPLANATORY ESSAY An *explanatory essay* describes and provides detail about a process or concept.

FICTION *Fiction* is prose writing about imaginary characters and events. Some writers of fiction base their stories on real events, whereas others rely solely on their imaginations.

FIGURATIVE LANGUAGE Figurative language is writing or speech not meant to be interpreted literally. Poets and other writers use figurative language to paint vivid word pictures, to make their writing emotionally intense and concentrated, and to state their ideas in new and unusual ways. Among the figures of speech making up figurative language are hyperbole, irony, metaphor, metonymy, oxymoron, paradox, personification, simile, and synecdoche.

See also the entries for individual figures of speech.

FOLKLORE The stories, legends, myths, ballads, riddles, sayings, and other traditional works produced orally by illiterate or semiliterate peoples are known as *folklore.* Folklore influences written literature in many ways.

FOOT The basic unit of meter, a *foot* is a group of one or more stressed and unstressed syllables.

FREE VERSE *Free verse* is poetry not written in a regular, rhythmical pattern, or meter. Instead of having metrical feet and lines, free verse has a rhythm that suits its meaning and that uses the sounds of spoken language in lines of different lengths. Free verse has been widely used in twentieth-century poetry.

GOTHIC *Gothic* is a term used to describe literary works that make extensive use of primitive, medieval, wild, mysterious, or natural elements. Gothic novels often depict horrifying events set in gloomy castles.

HYPERBOLE *Hyperbole* is a deliberate exaggeration or overstatement.

IMAGE An *image* is a word or phrase that appeals to one or more of the senses—sight, hearing, touch, taste, or smell.

IMAGERY *Imagery* is the descriptive language used in literature to recreate sensory experiences. Imagery enriches writing by making it more vivid, setting a tone, suggesting emotions, and guiding readers' reactions.

IRONY *Irony* is the general name given to literary techniques that involve surprising, interesting, or amusing contradictions. In *verbal irony,* words are used to suggest the opposite of their usual meaning. In *dramatic irony,* there is a contradiction between what a character thinks and what the reader or audience knows to be true. In *irony of situation,* an event occurs that directly contradicts expectations.

LYRIC POEM A *lyric poem* is a poem expressing the observations and feelings of a single speaker. Unlike a narrative poem, it presents an experience or a single effect, but it does not tell a full story. Types of lyric poems include the elegy, the ode, and the sonnet.

METAPHOR A *metaphor* is a figure of speech in which one thing is spoken of as though it were something else, as in "death, that long sleep." Through this identification of dissimilar things, a comparison is suggested or implied.

An *extended metaphor* is developed at length and involves several points of comparison. A mixed metaphor occurs when two metaphors are jumbled together, as in "The thorns of life rained down on him."

A *dead metaphor* is one that has been so overused that its original metaphorical impact has been lost. Examples of dead metaphors include "the foot of the bed" and "toe the line."

METAPHYSICAL POETRY The term *metaphysical poetry* describes the works of such seventeenth-century English poets as Richard Crashaw, John Donne, George Herbert, and Andrew Marvell. Characteristic features of metaphysical poetry include intellectual playfulness, argument, paradoxes, irony, elaborate and unusual conceits, incongruity, and the rhythms of ordinary speech.

METER *Meter* is the rhythmical pattern of a poem. This pattern is determined by the number and types of stresses, or beats, in each line. To describe the meter of a poem, you must scan its lines. Scanning involves marking the stressed and unstressed syllables, as follows:

Ĭ wĕen | thăt, whĕn | thĕ grăve's | dărk wăll

Dĭd fĭrst | hĕr fŏrm | rĕtain,

Thĕy thoŭght | thĕir heărts | coŭld ne'er | rĕcall

Thĕ light | ŏf jŏy | ăgain.

—Emily Brontë, "Song"

As you can see, each stressed syllable is marked with a slanted line (´) and each unstressed syllable with a horseshoe symbol (˘). The stresses are then divided by vertical lines into groups called *feet.* The following types of feet are common in English poetry:

1. **Iamb:** a foot with one unstressed syllable followed by one stressed syllable, as in the word *afraid*

2. **Trochee:** a foot with one stressed syllable followed by one unstressed syllable, as in the word *heather*

3. **Anapest:** a foot with two unstressed syllables followed by one stressed syllable, as in the word *disembark*

4. **Dactyl:** a foot with one stressed syllable followed by two unstressed syllables, as in the word *solitude*

5. **Spondee:** a foot with two stressed syllables, as in the word *workday*

6. **Pyrrhic:** a foot with two unstressed syllables, as in the last foot of the word *unspeak | ably*

7. **Amphibrach:** a foot with an unstressed syllable, one stressed syllable, and another unstressed syllable, as in the word *another*

8. **Amphimacer:** a foot with a stressed syllable, one unstressed syllable, and another stressed syllable, as in "up and down"

A line of poetry is described as **iambic, trochaic, anapestic,** or **dactylic** according to the kind of foot that appears most often in the line. Lines are also described in terms of the number of feet that occur in them, as follows:

1. **Monometer:** verse written in one-foot lines:

Sound the Flute!
Now it's mute.
Birds delight
Day and Night.
—William Blake, "Spring"

2. **Dimeter:** verse written in two-foot lines:

O Rose | thou art sick.
The invis | ible worm.
That flies | in the night
In the how | ling storm:
Has found | out thy bed
Of crim | son joy : . . .
—William Blake, "The Sick Rose"

3. **Trimeter:** verse written in three-foot lines:

I went | to the Gard | en of Love
And saw | what I nev | er had seen:
A Chap | el was built | in the midst,
Where I used | to play | on the green.
—William Blake, "The Garden of Love"

4. **Tetrameter:** verse written in four-foot lines:

I wand |er thro' | each chart | er'd street
Near where | the chart | er'd Thames | does flow
And mark | in ev | ery face | I meet
Marks of | weakness, | marks of | woe.
—William Blake, "London"

A six-foot line is called a **hexameter.** A line with seven feet is a **heptameter.**

A complete description of the meter of a line tells both how many feet there are in the line and what kind of foot is most common. Thus, the stanza from Emily Brontë's poem, quoted at the beginning of this entry, would be described as being made up of alternating iambic tetrameter and iambic trimeter lines. Poetry that does not have a regular meter is called **free verse.**

MODERNISM *Modernism* describes an international movement in the arts during the early twentieth century. Modernists rejected old forms and experimented with the new. Literary Modernists—such as James Joyce, W. B. Yeats, and T. S. Eliot—used images as symbols. They presented human experiences in fragments, rather than as a coherent whole, which led to new experiments in the forms of poetry and fiction.

MONOLOGUE A *monologue* is a speech or performance given entirely by one person or by one character.

NARRATION *Narration* is writing that tells a story. The act of telling a story is also called *narration*. The **narrative,** or story, is told by a character or speaker called the **narrator.** Biographies, autobiographies, journals, reports, novels, short stories, plays, narrative poems, anecdotes, fables, parables, myths, legends, folk tales, ballads, and epic poems are all narratives, or types of narration.

NARRATIVE POEM A *narrative poem* is a poem that tells a story in verse. Three traditional types of narrative poems include ballads, epics, and metrical romances.

NONFICTION *Nonfiction* is prose writing that presents and explains ideas or tells about real places, objects or events. To be classified as nonfiction, a work must be true.

NONLINEAR STRUCTURES A *nonlinear structure* does not follow chronological order. It may contain flashbacks, dream sequences, or other devices that interrupt the chronological flow of events.

NOVEL A *novel* is an extended work of fiction that often has a complicated plot, many major and minor characters, a unifying theme, and several settings. Novels can be grouped in many ways, based on the historical periods in which they are written (such as Victorian), on the subjects and themes that they treat (such as Gothic or regional), on the techniques used in them (such as stream of consciousness), or on their part in literary movements (such as Naturalism or Realism).

A *novella* is not as long as a novel but is longer than a short story.

ODE An *ode* is a long, formal lyric poem with a serious theme. It may have a traditional structure with stanzas grouped in threes, called the **strophe,** the **antistrophe,** and the **epode.** Odes often honor people, commemorate events, or respond to natural scenes.

ORAL TRADITION *Oral tradition* is the body of songs, stories, and poems preserved by being passed from generation to generation by word of mouth. Folk epics, ballads, myths, legends, folk tales, folk songs, proverbs, and nursery rhymes are all products of the oral tradition.

OXYMORON An *oxymoron* is a figure of speech that fuses two contradictory ideas, such as "freezing fire" or "happy grief," thus suggesting a paradox in just a few words.

PARADOX A *paradox* is a statement that seems to be contradictory but that actually presents a truth. In Shakespeare's *Hamlet*, for example, Hamlet's line "I must be cruel to be kind" is a paradox.

Because a paradox is surprising, or even shocking, it draws the reader's attention to what is being said.

PARALLELISM *Parallelism* is the presentation of similar ideas, in sequence, using the same grammatical structure.

PERIPHRASIS *Periphrasis* is a literary device in which writers use descriptive and inventive substitutes to make simple names and terms more colorful and imaginative.

PERSONIFICATION *Personification* is a figure of speech in which a nonhuman subject is given human characteristics.

Effective personification of things or ideas makes their qualities seem unified, like the characteristics of a person, and their relationship with the reader seem closer.

PERSUASION *Persuasion* is writing or speech that attempts to convince a reader to think or act in a particular way. Persuasion is used in advertising, in editorials, in sermons, and in political speeches. An *argument* is a logical way of presenting a belief, conclusion, or stance. A good argument is supported with reasoning and evidence.

PLOT *Plot* is the sequence of events in a literary work. The two primary elements of any plot are characters and a conflict. Most plots can be analyzed into many or all of the following parts:
1. The *exposition* introduces the setting, the characters, and the basic situation.
2. The *inciting incident* introduces the central conflict and develops the rising action.
3. During the *development,* or rising action, the conflict runs its course and usually intensifies.
4. At the *climax,* the conflict reaches a high point of interest or suspense.
5. The *denouement,* or *falling action,* ties up loose ends that remain after the climax of the conflict.
6. At the *resolution,* the story is resolved and an insight is revealed.

There are many variations on the standard plot structure. Some stories begin *in medias res* ("in the middle of things"), after the inciting incident has already occurred.

In some stories, the expository material appears toward the middle, in flashbacks. In many stories, there is no denouement. Occasionally, the conflict is left unresolved.

POETRY *Poetry* is one of the three major types, or genres, of literature, the others being prose and drama. Poetry defies simple definition because there is no single characteristic that is found in all poems and not found in all nonpoems.

Often, poems are divided into lines and stanzas. Poems such as sonnets, odes, villanelles, and sestinas are governed by rules regarding the number of lines, the number and placement of stressed syllables in each line, and the rhyme scheme. In the case of villanelles and sestinas, the repetition of words at the ends of lines or of entire lines is required. Most poems make use of highly concise, musical, and emotionally charged language. Many also use imagery, figurative language, and devices of sound, like rhyme.

Types of poetry include *narrative poetry* (ballads, epics, and metrical romances); *dramatic poetry* (dramatic monologues and dramatic dialogues); *lyrics* (sonnets, odes, elegies, and love poems); and *concrete poetry* (a poem presented on the page in a shape that suggests its subject).

POINT OF VIEW The perspective, or vantage point, from which a story is told is its *point of view.* If a character within the story narrates, then it is told from the *first-person point of view.* If a voice from outside the story tells it, then the story is told from the *third-person point of view.* If the knowledge of the storyteller is limited to the internal states of one character, then the storyteller has a *limited point of view.* If the storyteller's knowledge extends to the internal states of all the characters, then the storyteller has an *omniscient point of view.*

PROSE *Prose* is the ordinary form of written language and one of the three major types of literature. Most writing that is not poetry, drama, or song is considered prose. Prose occurs in two major forms: fiction and nonfiction.

REALISM *Realism* is the presentation in art of details from actual life. During the last part of the nineteenth century and the first part of the twentieth, Realism enjoyed considerable popularity among writers in the English-speaking world. Novels often dealt with grim social realities and presented realistic portrayals of the psychological states of characters.

RHETORICAL DEVICES *Rhetorical devices* are special patterns of words and ideas that create emphasis and stir emotion, especially in speeches or other oral presentations. *Parallelism,* for example, is the repetition of a grammatical structure in order to create a rhythm and make words more memorable. Other common rhetorical devices include: *analogy,* drawing comparisons between two unlike things, *charged language,* words that appeal to the emotions, *concession,* an acknowledgment of the opposition's argument, *humor,* using language and details that make characters or situations funny, **paradox,** a statement that seems to contradict but presents a truth, **restatement,** expressing the same idea in different words, **rhetorical questions,** questions with obvious answers, and **tone,** the author's attitude toward the audience.

RHYME *Rhyme* is the repetition of sounds at the ends of words. *End rhyme* occurs when rhyming words appear at the ends of lines. *Internal rhyme* occurs when rhyming words fall within a line. *Exact rhyme* is the use of identical rhyming sounds, as in *love* and *dove*. *Approximate,* or *slant, rhyme* is the use of sounds that are similar but not identical, as in *prove* and *glove*.

ROMANTICISM *Romanticism* was a literary and artistic movement of the eighteenth and nineteenth centuries. In reaction to Neoclassicism, the Romantics emphasized imagination, fancy, freedom, emotion, wildness, the beauty of the untamed natural world, the rights of the individual, the nobility of the common man, and the attractiveness of pastoral life. Important figures in the Romantic Movement included William Wordsworth, Samuel Taylor Coleridge, Percy Bysshe Shelley, John Keats, and George Gordon, Lord Byron.

SATIRE *Satire* is writing that ridicules or holds up to contempt the faults of individuals or groups. Satires include Jonathan Swift's prose work *Gulliver's Travels* and Alexander Pope's poem "The Rape of the Lock." Although a satire is often humorous, its purpose is not simply to make readers laugh but also to correct the flaws and shortcomings that it points out.

SENSORY LANGUAGE *Sensory language* is writing or speech that appeals to one or more of the five senses.

SETTING The *setting* is the time and place of the action of a literary work. A setting can provide a backdrop for the action. It can be the force that the protagonist strugles against, and thus the source of the central conflict. It can also be used to create an atmosphere. In many works, the setting symbolizes a point that the author wishes to emphasize.

SHORT STORY A *short story* is a brief work of fiction. The short story resembles the longer novel, but it generally has a simpler plot and setting. In addition, a short story tends to reveal character at a crucial moment, rather than to develop it through many incidents.

SIMILE A *simile* is a figure of speech that compares two apparently dissimilar things using *like* or *as*.

By comparing apparently dissimilar things, the writer of a simile surprises the reader into an appreciation of the hidden similarities of the things being compared.

SOCIAL COMMENTARY *Social commentary* is writing that offers insight into society, its values, and its customs.

SOLILOQUY A *soliloquy* is a long speech in a play or in a prose work made by a character who is alone, and thus reveals private thoughts and feelings to the audience or reader.

SONNET A sonnet is a fourteen-line lyric poem with a single theme. Sonnets are usually written in iambic pentameter. The **Petrarchan,** or **Italian sonnet,** is divided into two parts, an eight-line octave and a six-line sestet. The octave rhymes **abba abba,** while the sestet generally rhymes **cde cde** or uses some combination of **cd** rhymes. The octave raises a question, states a problem, or presents a brief narrative, and the sestet answers the question, solves the problem, or comments on the narrative.

The **Shakespearean,** or **English, sonnet** has three four-line quatrains plus a concluding two-line couplet. The rhyme scheme of such a sonnet is usually **abab cdcd efef gg.** Each of the three quatrains usually explores a different variation of the main theme. Then, the couplet presents a summarizing or concluding statement.

The **Spenserian** sonnet has three quatrains and a couplet, but the quatrains are joined by linking rhymes like those of an Italian sonnet. The rhyme scheme of this type of sonnet is **abab bcbc cdcd ee.**

SOUND DEVICES *Sound devices* are groups of words that have particular sound relationships to one another. Types of sound devices include **alliteration, consonance,** and **assonance.**

SPEAKER The **speaker** is the imaginary voice assumed by the writer of a poem; the character who "says" the poem. For example, the title of William Blake's poem "The Chimney Sweeper" identifies the speaker, a child who gives an account of his life. This character is often not identified by name but may be identified otherwise.

Recognizing the speaker and thinking about his or her characteristics are often central to interpreting a lyric poem. For example, the title of William Blake's poem "The Chimney Sweeper" identifies the speaker, a child who gives an account of his life. In this poem the speaker's acceptance of his oppressive life is offered for the reader's evaluation.

STANZA A *stanza* is a group of lines in a poem, which is seen as a unit. Many poems are divided into stanzas that are separated by spaces. Stanzas often function like paragraphs in prose. Each stanza states and develops one main idea.

Stanzas are commonly named according to the number of lines found in them, as follows:

1. *Couplet:* a two-line stanza

2. *Tercet:* a three-line stanza

3. *Quatrain:* a four-line stanza

4. *Cinquain:* a five-line stanza

5. *Sestet:* a six-line stanza

6. *Heptastich:* a seven-line stanza

7. *Octave:* an eight-line stanza

STREAM OF CONSCIOUSNESS *Stream of consciousness* is a narrative technique that presents thoughts as if they were coming directly from a character's mind. Instead of being arranged in chronological order, the events are presented from the character's point of view, mixed in with the character's thoughts just as they might spontaneously occur.

STYLE *Style* is a writer's typical way of writing. Determinants of a writer's style include formality, use of figurative language, use of rhythm, typical grammatical patterns, typical sentence lengths, and typical methods of organization.

SYMBOL A *symbol* is a sign, word, phrase, image, or other object that stands for or represents something else. Thus, a flag can symbolize a country, a spoken word can symbolize an object, a fine car can symbolize wealth, and so on. In literary criticism, a distinction is often made between traditional or conventional symbols—those that are part of our general cultural inheritance—and *personal symbols*—those that are created by particular authors for use in particular works.

Conventional symbolism is often based on elements of nature. For example, youth is often symbolized by greenery or springtime, middle age by summer, and old age by autumn or winter. Conventional symbols are also borrowed from religion and politics. For example, a cross may be a symbol of Christianity, or the color red may be a symbol of Marxist ideology.

SYNECDOCHE *Synecdoche* is a figure of speech in which a part of something is used to stand for the whole.

SYNTAX *Syntax* is the way words are organized—for example, their order is a sentence or phrase.

THEME *Theme* is the central idea, concern, or purpose in a literary work. In an essay, the theme might be directly stated in what is known as a thesis statement. In a serious literary work, the theme is usually expressed indirectly rather than directly. A light work, one written strictly for entertainment, may not have a theme.

TONE *Tone* is the writer's attitude toward the reader and toward the subject. It may be formal or informal, friendly or distant, personal or pompous.

TRAGEDY *Tragedy* is a type of drama or literature that shows the downfall or destruction of a noble or outstanding person, traditionally one who possesses a character weakness called a *tragic flaw.* Macbeth, for example, is a brave and noble figure led astray by ambition. The *tragic hero* is caught up in a sequence of events that inevitably results in disaster. Because the protagonist is neither a wicked villain nor an innocent victim, the audience reacts with mixed emotions—both pity and fear, according to the Greek philosopher Aristotle, who defined tragedy in the *Poetics*. The outcome of a tragedy, in which the protagonist is isolated from society, contrasts with the happy resolution of a comedy, in which the protagonist makes peace with society.

UNDERSTATEMENT In an *understatement*, the literal meaning of the statement falls short of what is meant.

UNIVERSAL THEME A *universal theme* is a message that is expressed regularly in the literature of many different cultures and time periods.

VOICE The *voice* of a writer is his or her "sound" on the page. It is based on elements such as word choice, sound devices, pace, and attitude.

MANUAL DE TÉRMINOS LITERARIOS

ALITERACIÓN La *aliteración* es la repetición de los sonidos consonantes iniciales de las sílabas acentuadas.

Ejemplo: el **r**uido con que **r**ueda la **r**onca tempestad

La aliteración se usa para dar énfasis y asociar palabras, así como para crear efectos de musicalidad.

ALUSIÓN Una *alusión* es una referencia a una persona, lugar, hecho, obra literaria u obra de arte muy conocida.

AMPLIFICACIÓN La *amplificación* es un recurso estilístico en el cual el autor expande una idea, la profundiza y detalla, por medio de la repetición o la elaboración.

ANALOGÍA Una *analogía* es una comparación entre relaciones. Se basa en la idea o concepción de que la relación entre un par de cosas es semejante a la relación entre otro par de cosas. A diferencia de la metáfora— otra forma de comparación—una analogía presenta la comparación explícitamente, a menudo utilizando las expresiones *como* o *tal como.*

ANÁFORA La *anáfora* es una figura retórica que conlleva la repetición deliberada de la misma secuencia de palabras al comienzo de frases, cláusulas u oraciones cercanas.

POESÍA ANGLOSAJONA Se llama *poesía anglosajona* a la poesía rítmica compuesta en inglés antiguo antes del siglo XII. Por lo general consiste en versos de cuatro sílabas acentuadas y un número indefinido de sílabas no acentuadas. Cada verso está dividido en dos por una *cesura,* o pausa, y las mitades están unidas por la aliteración de dos o tres de las sílabas acentuadas. La poesía anglosajona se cantaba o recitaba con el acompañamiento de un arpa primitiva. No se escribía, sino que se transmitía oralmente.

APÓSTROFE El *apóstrofe* es una figura retórica en la que el hablante se dirige directamente a una persona ausente o a una idea, objeto o cualidad personificada.

ARQUETIPO Un *arquetipo* es un patrón que se encuentra en las obras literarias de distintas épocas y lugares. Para más información ver *Elementos literarios arquetípicos*.

DICCIÓN ARCAICA La *dicción arcaica* se refiere a las palabras y frases que eran de uso estándar en otra época, pero que ya no son comunes.

ELEMENTOS LITERARIOS ARQUETÍPICOS Los *elementos literarios arquetípicos* son patrones que se encuentran en la literatura de todas las latitudes del mundo. Por ejemplo, la ocurrencia de sucesos en secuencias de a tres es un elemento arquetípico de los cuentos de hadas. Algunos personajes, tales como el guía misterioso, también son elementos arquetípicos de los relatos tradicionales. Según algunos críticos, estos elementos expresan de manera simbólica ciertas verdades sobre la mentalidad humana.

ARGUMENTO Un *argumento* es un escrito o discurso que trata de convencer al lector para que piense o actúe de cierta manera. Un argumento es una manera lógica de presentar una creencia, una conclusión o una postura. Un buen argumento se respalda con razonamientos y pruebas.

ASONANCIA La *asonancia* es la repetición de los sonidos vocálicos de sílabas acentuadas con distintas consonantes, como en este verso del poema "Andrea del Sarto" de Robert Browning en el que se repite el sonido largo de la *e* inglesa:
Ah, but man's r**ea**ch should exc**ee**d his grasp.

VERSO BLANCO El *verso blanco* es poesía escrita por lo general en pentámetros yámbicos sin rima (ver Metro). En el verso blanco a veces se introducen variaciones rítmicas para enfatizar, o para lograr una mayor variedad y naturalidad sonora. Como el verso blanco suena de manera muy parecida al inglés que se habla normalmente, suele usarse en obras dramáticas, como lo hizo Shakespeare, y en poesía.

CARPE DIEM La expresión latina *carpe diem* significa "vive el día" o "aprovecha el momento", pues la vida es fugaz. Muchas grandes obras literarias tienen por tema el *carpe diem*.

PERSONAJE Un *personaje* es una persona o animal que participa de la acción en una obra literaria. Los personajes pueden clasificarse de distinta manera. A los personajes que representan un papel importante se los llama *personajes principales*. A los personajes que no representan papeles importantes se los llama *personajes secundarios*. Un personaje que representa el papel central de una historia recibe el nombre de *protagonista*. Un personaje que se opone al protagonista recibe el nombre de *antagonista*. Un *personaje chato o plano* muestra solo unos pocos rasgos. Un personaje que cambia es un *personaje dinámico*. Un personaje que no cambia es un *personaje estático*.

CARACTERIZACIÓN La *caracterización* es el acto de crear y desarrollar un personaje. En una *caracterización directa*, el autor presenta explícitamente las características de un personaje. Los autores también puede recurrir a una *caracterización indirecta*. Las características de un personaje se puede revelar indirectamente a través de lo que el personaje dice o hace; a través de la descripción de su apariencia física; o a través de las afirmaciones, pensamientos y acciones de otros personajes.

CLÍMAX El *clímax* de una obra literaria es el punto de mayor interés o suspenso. Con frecuencia, el clímax coincide con el momento crítico de la trama, el punto en el que cambia la situación o la percepción del protagonista. A veces, el clímax coincide con el *desenlace*, el momento en el que termina o se resuelve el conflicto central.

ALIVIO CÓMICO Los autores de tragedias suelen crear uno o dos personajes o escenas cómicas para relajar el tono tenso de la obra. Estos personajes o escenas dotan de *alivio cómico* a una producción que está, por lo demás, llena de suspenso.

COMPRESIÓN La *compresión* consiste en juntar varias ideas o imágenes distintas, con el fin de crear una mayor densidad y complejidad de sentido.

CONCEPTO Como recurso literario, el *concepto* es una comparación extraña y sorprendente entre dos cosas muy distintas. Este tipo especial de metáfora o de analogía compleja a menudo constituye la base de todo un poema. Durante la época isabelina, los sonetos solían incluir el tipo de concepto llamado "petrarquista". El *concepto petrarquista* expresa algo extravagante o extremo sobre la belleza de la amada o sobre el sufrimiento del hablante, a través de comparaciones con seres divinos, fuerzas naturales poderosas u objetos que poseen en el más alto grado alguna cualidad determinada. Los poetas *metafísicos* del siglo XVII usaban conceptos altamente elaborados, extraños e intelectuales.

CONFLICTO Un *conflicto* es una lucha entre fuerzas opuestas. A veces, esta lucha es interna, es decir, que se da en la interioridad de un personaje. Otras veces, la lucha es externa, es decir, entre el personaje y alguna fuerza exterior. La fuerza exterior puede ser otro personaje, la naturaleza o algún elemento de la sociedad, tal como una costumbre o una institución política. A menudo, en una misma obra se combinan varios conflictos de distinto tipo.

CONNOTACIÓN La *connotación* de una palabra es el conjunto de ideas que se asocian a ella, además del significado que da el diccionario. Por ejemplo, las palabras *hogar* y *domicilio* tienen, según el diccionario, el mismo significado. Sin embargo, la primera tiene connotaciones positivas de calidez y seguridad, mientras que la segunda no.

CONSONANCIA La *consonancia* es la repetición de los sonidos consonantes finales de sílabas acentuadas con distintos sonidos vocálicos, como en este fragmento de la balada "The Rime of the Ancient Mariner" de Coleridge:
a frightful fie**nd** / Doth close behi**nd** him tread.

PAREADO Un *dístico* o *pareado* es un par de versos rimados escritos en el mismo metro. Un *dístico heroico* es un par de pentámetros yámbicos rimados. En un *dístico cerrado,* el significado y la sintaxis se completan en esos dos versos, como en este ejemplo de "Essay on Criticism" de Alexander Pope:

True ease in writing comes from art, not chance,
As those move easiest who have learned to dance.

Los sonetos shakesperianos suelen terminar con dísticos heroicos.

TEMA CULTURALMENTE ESPECÍFICO Un *tema culturalmente específico* es aquel que se relaciona de manera significativa con determinadas culturas.

DENOTACIÓN La *denotación* de una palabra es su significado objetivo —es decir, aquello a lo que la palabra se refiere—, independientemente de las otras asociaciones que la palabra pueda suscitar. Los diccionarios dan los significados denotativos de las palabras.

DIALECTO El *dialecto* es la forma de un lenguaje hablado por la gente en una región o por un grupo particular. Los dialectos difieren entre sí en la gramática, el vocabulario y la pronunciación.

DIÁLOGO Un *diálogo* es una conversación entre personajes. Los escritores usan el diálogo para revelar las características de los personajes, para presentar sucesos, para dar variedad al relato y para despertar el interés de los lectores. En un relato, el diálogo por lo general se presenta entre comillas o en párrafos. En un guión u obra de teatro, el diálogo por lo general sigue al nombre de los interlocutores.

DIARIO Un *diario* es un registro personal de hechos cotidianos, y se suele escribir en prosa. La mayoría de los diarios no se escriben para ser publicados; a veces, sin embargo, los diarios particularmente interesantes o escritos por personas reconocidas, sí se publican.

DICCIÓN La *dicción* es la elección de palabras que hace el autor. Puede ser uno de los elementos más determinantes del estilo. La dicción puede describirse como formal o informal, abstracta o concreta, llana o elaborada, común o técnica.

DRAMA Un *drama* es una historia escrita para ser representada por actores. Puede consistir en una o más secciones de cierta extensión, llamadas actos, formadas a su vez por cierto número de secciones más pequeñas, llamadas escenas.

El drama se originó en los rituales religiosos y en las reconstrucciones simbólicas de los pueblos primitivos. Los habitantes de la antigua Grecia, que desarrollaron el drama hasta transformarlo en una sofisticada forma artística crearon géneros dramáticos tales como la tragedia y la comedia.

Los primeros dramas que se representaron en Inglaterra fueron los misterios y moralidades medievales. Los misterios eran dramas que representaban pasajes bíblicos. Las moralidades, como la titulada *Everyman,* eran alegorías en las que los personajes eran personificaciones de vicios y virtudes. El Renacimiento inglés fue testigo de un florecimiento del drama que culminó en las obras de William Shakespeare, quien escribió muchas de las comedias, tragedias, cuentos y poemas más celebrados del mundo. Durante el Neoclasicismo, el drama inglés privilegió las sátiras de costumbres, especialmente de las clases más acomodadas de la sociedad. Durante el Romanticismo y la época victoriana se escribieron algunos dramas en verso de real valor, como *Los Cenci* y *Prometeo liberado,* de Percy Bysshe Shelley. El final del siglo XIX y el principio del XX vio un resurgimiento del drama, tanto en Inglaterra como en todo el mundo anglohablante. Entre los grandes dramas de la modernidad se encuentran los de Bernard Shaw, Christopher Fry, T.S. Eliot, Harold Pinter y Samuel Beckett.

MONÓLOGO DRAMÁTICO Un *monólogo dramático* es un poema en el cual un personaje imaginario le habla a otro que lo escucha en silencio.

ENCABALGAMIENTO El *encabalgamiento* es una estructura poética en la que tanto la estructura gramatical como el sentido continúa de un verso al siguiente.

POEMA ÉPICO Un *poema épico* es un poema narrativo extenso sobre las aventuras de dioses o de un *héroe épico*.

Las *convenciones de la épica* son las características tradicionales de los poemas épicos, tales como un enunciado inicial presentando el tema; la apelación (o "invocación") a un ser sobrenatural para ayudar al poeta a relatar los hechos; un comienzo *in medias res* (en latín: "en la mitad de las cosas"); los catálogos de pueblos y de cosas; el relato de hechos pasados; y las frases descriptivas.

EPIGRAMA Un *epigrama* es un enunciado breve en prosa o en verso. El pareado final de un soneto inglés bien puede ser epigramático. Un ensayo también puede estar escrito en un estilo epigramático.

EPIFANÍA Una *epifanía* es una revelación repentina o un súbito entendimiento mediante el cual un personaje reconoce la verdad.

EPITAFIO Un *epitafio* es una inscripción grabada en una tumba o lugar funerario. En la literatura, los epitafios pueden ser unas líneas serias o humorísticas que se pretende que tendrán esa función, como es el caso del epitafio incluido en la elegía de Thomas Grey.

ENSAYO Un *ensayo* es una obra breve de no-ficción sobre un tema en particular. Los ensayos pueden clasificarse en formales e informales, y personales o impersonales. También pueden clasificarse según su propósito, como por ejemplo: de causa y efecto, satírico o reflexivo. Otra manera de clasificar los ensayos es por el tipo de discurso; así, un ensayo puede ser explicativo, descriptivo, persuasivo o narrativo.

ENSAYO EXPLICATIVO Un *ensayo explicativo* ofrece detalles sobre un proceso o concepto.

FICCIÓN Una obra de *ficción* es un escrito en prosa que cuenta algo sobre personajes y hechos imaginarios. Algunos escritores basan sus relatos de ficción en hechos reales, mientras que otros parten exclusivamente de su imaginación.

LENGUAJE FIGURADO El *lenguaje figurado* es un escrito o discurso que no se debe interpretar literalmente. Los poetas y otros escritores usan el lenguaje figurado para representar algo de manera más vívida, para hacer que sus escritos resulten emocionalmente intensos y concentrados, y para expresar sus ideas de maneras nuevas y poco habituales. Entre las figuras retóricas que conforman el lenguaje figurado están la hipérbole, la ironía, la metáfora, la metonimia, el oxímoron, la paradoja, la personificación, el símil y la sinécdoque.

Ver también las entradas sobre algunas figuras retóricas en particular.

FOLKLORE Los relatos, leyendas, mitos, baladas, adivinanzas, dichos y otros géneros propios de la tradición oral constituyen el *folklore*. Algunas de esas obras fueron compuestas por personas analfabetas o semianalfabetas. El folklore influye de distintas maneras en la literatura escrita.

PIE Un *pie* es la unidad básica de la métrica, y se compone de un grupo de una o más sílabas, ya sean acentuadas o no acentuadas.

VERSO LIBRE El *verso libre* es una forma poética en la que no se sigue un patrón regular de metro ni de rima. En vez de tener pies y versos, el verso libre tiene el ritmo que corresponde a su sentido y que recurre a los sonidos del lenguaje hablado en versos de distinta extensión. El verso libre ha sido ampliamente cultivado en la poesía del siglo XX.

GÓTICO Se llama *gótico* al estilo literario que hace un uso constante de elementos primitivos, medievales, salvajes, misteriosos o naturales. La novela gótica a menudo describe hechos horripilantes que tienen lugar en castillos tenebrosos.

HIPÉRBOLE Una *hipérbole* es una exageración o magnificación deliberada.

IMAGEN Una *imagen* es una palabra o frase que apela a uno o más sentidos; es decir, a la vista, el oído, el tacto, el gusto o el olfato.

IMÁGENES Se llama *imágenes* al lenguaje descriptivo que se usa en la literatura para recrear experiencias sensoriales. Las imágenes enriquecen la escritura al hacerla más vívida, sentar el tono, sugerir emociones y guiar las reacciones de los lectores.

IRONÍA *Ironía* es un término general para distintas técnicas literarias que implican contradicciones sorprendentes, interesantes o divertidas. En una *ironía verbal*, las palabras se usan para sugerir lo opuesto a su sentido habitual. En la *ironía dramática* hay una contradicción entre lo que un personaje piensa y lo que el lector o la audiencia sabe que es verdad. En una

ironía situacional, ocurre un suceso que contradice directamente las expectativas.

POEMA LÍRICO Un *poema lírico* es un poema que expresa los pensamientos, observaciones y sentimientos de un único hablante. A diferencia del poema narrativo, el poema lírico propone una experiencia o un efecto único, sin contar toda la historia. Los poemas líricos pueden ser de distintos tipos, tales como la elegía, la oda y el soneto.

METÁFORA Una *metáfora* es una figura literaria en la que se habla de algo como si fuera otra cosa, como por ejemplo en "la muerte, ese largo sueño". A través de la identificación de cosas disímiles, se sugiere o implica una comparación.

Una *metáfora extendida* se desarrolla extensamente y los puntos que se comparan son varios. Una *metáfora mixta* ocurre cuando dos metáforas se unen, como en "le llovieron encima las espinas de la vida". Una *metáfora muerta* es una metáfora que ya se ha utilizado demasiado, por lo que su impacto metafórico ha desaparecido. Es el caso de metáforas como "el pie de la cama" o "los dientes del tenedor".

POESÍA METAFÍSICA El término *poesía metafísica* describe las obras de poetas ingleses del siglo XVII tales como Richard Crashaw, John Donne, George Herbert y Andrew Marvell. Los rasgos más característicos de la poesía metafísica son: el juego intelectual, la argumentación, las paradojas y los ritmos del habla cotidiana.

METRO El *metro* de un poema es el patrón rítmico que sigue. Este patrón está determinado por el número y tipo de sílabas acentuadas en cada verso. Para describir el metro de un poema hay que escandir los versos. Escandir significa marcar las sílabas acentuadas y no acentuadas.

Ĭ ween | thát, whĕn | thĕ grăve's | dárk wăll

Dĭd fírst | hĕr fórm | rĕtaín,

Thĕy thoúght | thĕir heárts | coŭld ne'er | rĕcáll

Thĕ líght | ŏf jóy | ăgaín.

—Emily Brontë, "Song"

Como puedes ver, cada sílaba acentuada se marca con un (´), y cada sílaba no acentuada se marca con un (˘). Las sílabas acentuadas e inacentuadas se dividen luego con líneas verticales (|) en grupos llamados *pies*. En la poesía en inglés algunos de los pies más frecuentes son:

1. el *yambo*: un pie con una sílaba no acentuada seguida por una sílaba acentuada, como en la palabra *afraid*.

2. el *troqueo*: un pie con una sílaba acentuada seguida por una sílaba no acentuada, como en la palabra *heather*.

3. el *anapesto*: un pie con dos sílabas no acentuadas seguidas por un acento fuerte, como en la palabra *disembark*.

4. el *dáctilo*: un pie con un acento fuerte seguido por dos sílabas no acentuadas, como en la palabra *solitude*.

5. el *espondeo*: un pie con dos acentos fuertes, como en la palabra *workday*.

6. el *pírrico*: un pie con dos sílabas no acentuadas, como las del último pie de la palabra *unspeak* | *ably*.

7. el *anfíbraco*: un pie con una sílaba no acentuada, una sílaba acentuada y otra inacentuada, como en la palabra *another*.

8. el *anfímacro*: un pie con una sílaba acentuada, una no acentuada y otra acentuada, como en *up and down*.

Según el tipo de pie más frecuente en ellos, los versos de un poema se describen como **yámbicos, trocaicos, anapésticos** o **dactílicos.** Los versos también se describen según el número de pies que los forman. Por ejemplo:

1. *monómetro:* verso de un solo pie

Sound the Flute!
Now it's mute.
Birds delight
Day and Night.
　　　　　—William Blake, "Spring"

2. *dímetro:* verso de dos pies

O Rose | thou art sick.
The invis | ible worm.
That flies | in the night
In the how | ling storm:
Has found | out thy bed
Of crim | son joy : . . .
　　　　　—William Blake, "The Sick Rose"

3. *trímetro:* verso de tres pies

I went | to the Gard | en of Love
And saw | what I nev | er had seen:
A Chap | el was built | in the midst,
Where I used | to play | on the green.
　　　　　—William Blake, "The Garden of Love"

4. *tetrámetro:* verso de cuatro pies

I wand |er thro' | each chart | er'd street
Near where | the chart | er'd Thames | does flow
And mark | in ev | ery face | I meet
Marks of | weakness, | marks of | woe.
　　　　　—William Blake, "London"

Un verso de seis pies es un **hexámetro.** Un verso de siete pies es un **heptámetro.**

La descripción completa del metro de un verso incluye el número de pies en cada verso y qué tipo de pie prevalece. Por lo tanto, la estrofa del poema de Emily Brontë citada al comienzo de esta entrada, debería describirse como formada por tetrámetros yámbicos que alternan con trímetros yámbicos. La poesía que no sigue un metro regular se dice que está escrita en **verso libre.**

MODERNISMO NORTEAMERICANO El *modernismo norteamericano* es parte de un movimiento artístico internacional que se desarrolló a principios del siglo XX.

Los modernistas rechazaron las formas tradicionales y experimentaron con nuevas formas. Los escritores modernistas, tales como James Joyce, W.B. Yeats y T.S. Eliot, usaron imágenes como símbolos y representaron las experiencias humanas de forma fragmentaria, en vez de como un todo coherente, lo que llevó a nuevos experimentos formales tanto en la poesía como en la ficción.

MONÓLOGO Un *monólogo* es un discurso o representación a cargo de una sola persona o de un solo personaje.

NARRACIÓN Una *narración* es un escrito que cuenta una historia. El acto de contar una historia también se llama *narración*. La **narración**, o historia, es contada por un personaje o hablante llamado **el narrador**. Las biografías, autobiografías, diarios, informes, novelas, cuentos, obras de teatro, poemas narrativos, anécdotas, fábulas, parábolas, mitos, leyendas, cuentos folklóricos, baladas y poemas épicos son todas obras narrativas de distinto tipo.

POEMA NARRATIVO Un *poema narrativo* es un poema que cuenta una historia en verso. Hay tres tipos de poemas narrativos tradicionales: las baladas, los poemas épicos y los romances en verso.

NO-FICCIÓN La *no-ficción* es un escrito en prosa que presenta y explica ideas o cuenta algo acerca de personas, lugares, ideas o hechos reales. Para ser clasificado como no-ficción un escrito debe ser verdadero.

ESTRUCTURA NO LINEAL La *estructura no lineal* no sigue un orden cronológico. Puede contener escenas retrospectivas (*flashbacks*), sueños u otros recursos que interrumpen la cronología de sucesos.

NOVELA Una *novela* es una obra extensa de ficción que suele tener una trama complicada, como personajes principales y secundarios, un tema unificador y varias ambientaciones. Las novelas pueden agruparse de distintas maneras, según el período histórico en el que fueron escritas (como la novela victoriana), en los temas que trata (como la novela gótica o la novela regional), en las técnicas que usa (como el fluir de la conciencia), o como parte de un movimiento literario (como el naturalismo o el realismo).

La *novela corta* tiene una extensión menor que la novela y mayor que el cuento.

ODA Una *oda* es un poema lírico extenso sobre un tema grave. Puede tener una estructura tradicional, con estrofas agrupadas de a tres: llamadas **estrofa**, **antistrofa** y **epodo**. Las odas a menudo son en honor de una persona o conmemoran eventos, o se presentan como respuesta a una escena de la naturaleza.

TRADICIÓN ORAL La *tradición oral* es el conjunto de canciones, cuentos y poemas que perduran en la memoria de un pueblo y que se han transmitido de boca en boca de una generación a otra. La épica, las baladas, los mitos, las leyendas, los cuentos folklóricos, las canciones populares, os proverbios y las canciones de cuna son todos productos de la tradición oral.

OXÍMORON Un *oxímoron* es una figura retórica que une dos ideas contrarias, como en las frases "el fuego helado" o "la alegre pena", que sugieren una paradoja en unas pocas palabras.

PARADOJA Una *paradoja* es un enunciado que parece ser contradictorio pero que en realidad presenta una verdad. Por ejemplo, en *Hamlet*, de Shakespeare, el verso "Debo ser cruel para ser rey" es una paradoja. Como la paradoja suele ser sorprendente e incluso chocante, llama la atención del lector hacia lo que se está diciendo.

PARALELISMO Un *paralelismo* es la presentación en secuencia de ideas similares, usando la misma estructura gramatical.

PERÍFRASIS La *perífrasis* es un recurso literario en el que los escritores usan sustitutos descriptivos y originales para hacer que algunos nombres y términos resulten más coloridos e imaginativos.

PERSONIFICACIÓN La *personificación* es una figura retórica en la que se dota a una instancia no humana de rasgos y actitudes humanas. La personificación efectiva de cosas o ideas hace que sus cualidades aparezcan unificadas, como las características de una persona, y que su relación con el lector parezca más cercana.

PERSUASIÓN La *persuasión* es un recurso escrito u oral por el que se intenta convencer al lector de que piense o actúe de determinada manera. La persuasión se utiliza en la publicidad, en los editoriales, en sermones y en los discursos políticos. Un *argumento* es una manera lógica de presentar una creencia, una conclusión o una postura. Un buen argumento se respalda con razones y evidencias.

TRAMA o ARGUMENTO La *trama* o *argumento* es la secuencia de los hechos que se suceden en una obra literaria. Dos elementos claves de la trama son los personajes y el conflicto central. La mayoría de las tramas pueden dividirse en las siguientes partes:

1. La *exposición* introduce la ambientación, los personajes y la situación básica.

2. El *suceso desencadenante* introduce el conflicto central e inicia el desarrollo.

3. Durante el *desarrollo*, el conflicto sigue su curso y, por lo general, se intensifica.

4. En el *clímax*, el conflicto alcanza su punto de tensión o suspenso más alto.

5. En el *desenlace* se atan los cabos sueltos que quedan una vez que el conflicto ha llegado al clímax.

6. En la *resolución,* se resuelve el conflicto y se revela algún tipo de percepción o idea general.

Hay muchas variaciones posibles de la estructura estándar de la trama. Algunos relatos comienzan *in medias res* ("en la mitad de las cosas"), cuando el suceso desencadenante ya ha ocurrido. En algunos relatos, el material expositivo aparece hacia la mitad de la obra, en forma de escenas retrospectivas, o *flashbacks*. En muchos casos, el relato no llega a ningún desenlace. También puede suceder que el conflicto quede sin resolver.

POESÍA La *poesía* es uno de los tres géneros literarios más importantes. Los otros dos son la prosa y el drama. La poesía no se presta a una definición sencilla porque no hay un solo rasgo que se encuentre en todos los poemas y que a su vez no se encuentre en ningún otro género.

A menudo, los poemas se dividen en versos y estrofas. Los poemas tales como los sonetos, las odas, las villanelles y las sextinas se basan en reglas que determinan el número de versos, el número y ubicación de las sílabas acentuadas de cada verso, y el esquema de rima. En el caso de las villanelles y las sextinas, también se exige la repetición de versos enteros o de palabras al final de ciertos versos. La mayoría de los poemas usan un lenguaje muy conciso, musical y emocionalmente cargado. Muchos también recurren al uso de imágenes, de lenguaje figurado y de recursos sonoros tales como la rima.

Entre los distintos tipos de poesía se pueden mencionar: la *poesía narrativa* (las baladas, la poesía épica, los romances en verso); la *poesía dramática* (los monólogos y diálogos dramáticos); la *poesía lírica* (sonetos, odas, elegías y la poesía amorosa); y la *poesía concreta* (un poema que dibuja en la página una forma o figura que coincide o se relaciona con su tema).

PUNTO DE VISTA La perspectiva desde el cual se narra una historia es el *punto de vista.* Cuando quien cuenta la historia es uno de los personajes, se dice que la historia está narrada desde el *punto de vista de la primera persona.* Cuando quien narra la historia es una voz exterior al relato, entonces el relato está escrito desde el *punto de vista de la tercera persona.* Si el conocimiento de la voz que narra la historia se limita a los estados interiores de un solo personaje, entonces el narrador tiene un *punto de vista limitado*. Si el conocimiento del narrador abarca los estados de ánimo de todos los personajes, entonces el narrador tiene un *punto de vista omnisciente.*

PROSA La *prosa* es la forma común del lenguaje escrito y uno de los tres tipos de literatura más importantes. La mayoría de los escritos que no son poesía, ni drama, ni canciones, se consideran prosa. La prosa puede ser de dos formas: de ficción y de no-ficción.

REALISMO El *realismo* es la representación artística de detalles de la vida real. Durante la última parte del siglo XIX y la primera parte del XX, el realismo gozó de una considerable popularidad entre los escritores del mundo anglohablante. Las novelas de esa época a menudo tratan las realidades sociales más tristes y presentan retratos realistas de los estados psicológicos de los personajes.

FIGURAS RETÓRICAS Las *figuras retóricas* son patrones especiales de palabras e ideas que dan énfasis y producen emoción, especialmente cuando se usan en discursos y otras presentaciones orales. El *paralelismo*, por ejemplo, es la repetición de una estructura gramatical con el propósito de crear un ritmo y hacer que las palabras resulten más memorables. Otras figuras retóricas muy frecuentes son: la *analogía*, que establece una comparación entre dos cosas diferentes; el *lenguaje emocionalmente cargado*, en el que las palabras apelan a las emociones; la *concesión*, en la que se reconoce el argumento del oponente; el *humor*, en el que se utiliza un tipo de lenguaje y de detalles que hacen que los personajes o las situaciones resulten cómicos; la *paradoja*, un enunciado que parece contradecirse, pero que presenta cierta verdad; la *reafirmación*, en la que se expresa la misma idea con distintas palabras; las *preguntas retóricas*, que son preguntas cuyas respuestas son obvias; y el *tono*, es decir, la actitud del autor hacia la audiencia.

RIMA La *rima* es la repetición de los sonidos finales de las palabras. Se llama *rima de final de verso* a la rima entre las palabras finales de dos o más versos. La *rima interna* se produce cuando una de las palabras que riman está situada en el interior de un verso. En la *rima perfecta (o consonante)* todas las vocales y las consonantes a partir de la vocal acentuada son iguales, como en *love* y *dove*. Se llama *rima falsa* o *aproximada* a la que se da entre palabras que suenan de modo parecido pero no idéntico, como en *prove* y *glove*.

ROMANTICISMO El *Romanticismo* fue un movimiento artístico y literario que se desarrolló durante los siglos XVIII y XIX. En reacción al Neoclasicismo, los románticos dieron prioridad a la imaginación, la fantasía, la libertad, la emoción, la vida salvaje, la belleza del mundo natural, los derechos de los individuos, la nobleza del individuo común y los atractivos de la vida campestre. Entre las figuras más importantes del Romanticismo en lengua inglesa podemos nombrar a William Wordsworth, Samuel Taylor Coleridge, Percy Bysshe Shelley, John Keats y George Gordon (Lord Byron).

SÁTIRA Una *sátira* es una obra literaria que ridiculiza las fallas de ciertos individuos o grupos. La obra en prosa de Jonathan Swift, *Gulliver's Travels*, y el poema de Alexander Pope, "The Rape of the Lock", son algunos ejemplos de sátira. Aunque las sátiras a menudo son humorísticas, su propósito no es simplemente hacer reír a los lectores, sino también corregir los fallos y defectos que critica.

LENGUAJE SENSORIAL El *lenguaje sensorial* es un escrito o discurso que incluye detalles que apelan a uno o más de los cinco sentidos.

AMBIENTACIÓN La *ambientación* de una obra literaria es la época y el lugar en el que se desarrolla la acción. La ambientación a veces proporciona el telón de fondo de la acción. Puede ser una fuerza que el protagonista debe enfrentar y, por lo tanto, la fuente del conflicto central. También puede usarse para crear una atmósfera. En muchas obras, la ambientación simboliza algo en lo que el autor quiere hacer hincapié.

CUENTO Un *cuento* es una obra breve de ficción. El cuento se parece a la novela, que es más extensa, pero por lo general tiene una trama y una ambientación más simples. Además, un cuento tiende a dar cuenta de un personaje en un momento crucial, más que a desarrollarlo a través de muchas peripecias.

SÍMIL Un *símil* es una figura retórica en la que se usa las palabras *como* o *tal como* para establecer una comparación entre dos cosas aparentemente disímiles. Al comparar cosas aparentemente diferentes, el autor del símil sorprende al lector haciéndole apreciar las ocultas similitudes de las cosas que se están comparando.

COMENTARIO SOCIAL El *comentario social* es un escrito que presenta alguna apreciación acerca de la sociedad, sus valores y sus costumbres.

SOLILOQUIO Un *soliloquio* es un largo parlamento en una obra de teatro o escrito en prosa, en el que un personaje, solo en escena, le revela sus pensamientos y sentimientos más íntimos a la audiencia o al lector.

SONETO Un *soneto* es un poema lírico de catorce versos sobre un solo tema. Por lo general los sonetos están escritos en pentámetros yámbicos. El *soneto italiano o petrarquista* se divide en dos partes, una octava (ocho versos) y una sextina (seis versos). La octava rima *abba abba*, mientras que la sextina por lo general rima *cde cde*, o sigue alguna combinación de rimas *cd*. La octava propone una pregunta, plantea un problema, o presenta un breve relato, y la sextina responde la pregunta, resuelve el problema o comenta el relato.

El *soneto inglés o shakesperiano* consiste en tres cuartetos (estrofas de cuatro versos) y un pareado final (estrofa de dos versos). Por lo general la rima sigue el esquema *abab cdcd efef gg*. Cada uno de los cuartetos por lo general explora una variación distinta del mismo tema. Luego el pareado presenta un enunciado que resume o propone una conclusión.

El *soneto spenseriano* está compuesto por tres cuartetos y un pareado, pero los cuartetos están unidos por la rima, como los del soneto italiano. El esquema de rima de este tipo de soneto es *abab bcbc cdcd ee.*

RECURSOS SONOROS Los *recursos sonoros* son grupos de palabras que se relacionan entre sí por ciertos sonidos. Entre los recursos sonoros se encuentran la *aliteración*, la *consonancia* y la *asonancia.*

HABLANTE El *hablante* es la voz imaginaria que asume el escritor en un poema; es el personaje en cuya boca está el poema. Este personaje por lo general no se identifica con un nombre, pero puede identificarse de alguna otra manera.

Reconocer al hablante y pensar en sus características a menudo resulta crucial para comprender el poema. Por ejemplo, el título del poema de William Blake "The

Chimney Sweeper" identifica al hablante, un niño que cuenta su vida. En este poema la aceptación por parte del hablante del carácter opresivo de su vida se somete a la evaluación del lector.

ESTROFA Una *estrofa* es un grupo de dos o más versos que forman una unidad. Muchos poemas se dividen en estrofas separadas por espacios. Las estrofas a menudo funcionan como los párrafos en la prosa. Cada estrofa presenta y desarrolla una idea principal.

Las estrofas por lo general reciben su nombre del número de versos que las componen. Por ejemplo:

1. un *dístico* o *pareado* es una estrofa de dos versos

2. un *terceto* es una estrofa de tres versos

3. un *cuarteto* o una *cuarteta* son estrofas de cuatro versos

4. una *quintilla* es una estrofa de cinco versos

5. una *sextina* es una estrofa de seis versos

6. una *séptima* es una estrofa de siete versos

7. una *octava* es una estrofa de ocho versos.

FLUIR DE LA CONCIENCIA El *fluir de la conciencia* es una técnica narrativa que presenta los pensamientos como si vinieran directamente de la mente del personaje. En vez de presentar los hechos en orden cronológico, se los presenta desde el punto de vista del personaje, juntos con los pensamientos del personaje, exactamente como si se sucedieran espontáneamente.

ESTILO El *estilo* es la manera particular en que escribe un autor. Los elementos que determinan el estilo son: el lenguaje formal, el uso del lenguaje figurado, el ritmo, los patrones gramaticales más usados, la extensión de las oraciones y los métodos en los que por lo general organiza su material.

SÍMBOLO Un *símbolo* es un signo, palabra, frase, imagen u otro objeto que representa otra cosa. Por ejemplo, una bandera puede simbolizar un país, una palabra puede simbolizar un objeto, un auto caro puede simbolizar riqueza, etc. La crítica literaria suele hacer una distinción entre los símbolos tradicionales o convencionales —aquellos que son parte de nuestro legado cultural— y los *símbolos personales*; es decir, aquellos que los autores crean y usan en sus propias obras.

El simbolismo convencional a menudo se basa en elementos de la naturaleza. Por ejemplo, un prado o la primavera simboliza la juventud; el verano representa la adultez; y el otoño y el invierno simbolizan la edad avanzada. Los símbolos convencionales también pueden tomarse de las religiones y la política. Por ejemplo, una cruz puede simbolizar la cristiandad, el color rojo puede ser el símbolo de la ideología marxista.

SINÉCDOQUE La *sinécdoque* es una figura retórica en la cual una parte de algo se usa para representar el todo.

SINTAXIS La *sintaxis* es la manera en que se organizan las palabras, por ejemplo, el orden en que aparecen en una oración o frase.

TEMA El *tema* es la idea o propósito o preocupación central que plantea una obra literaria. En un ensayo, el tema puede expresarse directamente en lo que se conoce como "enunciado de tesis". En una obra literaria seria, el tema por lo general se expresa indirecta, más que directamente. Una obra ligera, escrita exclusivamente para entretener, puede no tener ningún tema.

TONO El *tono* de una obra literaria es la actitud del escritor hacia su tema y sus lectores. El tono puede ser formal o informal, amistoso o distante, personal o pomposo.

TRAGEDIA Una *tragedia* es una obra literaria, por lo general una obra de teatro, que termina en la caída o destrucción de un ser noble o importante, un personaje que por lo general tiene una debilidad de carácter que se conoce con el nombre de *error trágico*. Macbeth, por ejemplo, es una figura noble y valiente cegada por la ambición. El *héroe trágico* se ve arrastrado por una secuencia de sucesos que inevitablemente conducirán al desastre. Como el protagonista no es ni un malvado villano ni una víctima inocente, la audiencia reacciona con emociones encontradas, con miedo y con compasión, según el filósofo griego Aristóteles, quien definió la tragedia en su *Poética*. El desenlace de una tragedia, en el que el protagonista queda aislado de la sociedad, contrasta con el desenlace de la comedia, en el que el protagonista se reconcilia con la sociedad.

LÍTOTE En un *lítote*, el enunciado no expresa todo lo que se quiere dar a entender.

TEMA UNIVERSAL Un *tema universal* es un mensaje que se encuentra con frecuencia en la literatura de muchas culturas distintas y a través de distintos períodos de la historia.

VOZ La *voz* de un escritor es la manera en que "suena" en la página. La voz se basa en elementos tales como la elección del vocabulario, los recursos sonoros, el ritmo y la actitud.

GRAMMAR HANDBOOK

PARTS OF SPEECH

Every English word, depending on its meaning and its use in a sentence, can be identified as one of the eight parts of speech. These are nouns, pronouns, verbs, adjectives, adverbs, prepositions, conjunctions, and interjections. Understanding the parts of speech will help you learn the rules of English grammar and usage.

Nouns A **noun** names a person, place, or thing. A **common noun** names any one of a class of persons, places, or things. A **proper noun** names a specific person, place, or thing.

Common Noun	Proper Noun
writer, country, novel	Charles Dickens, Great Britain, *Hard Times*

Pronouns A **pronoun** is a word that stands for one or more nouns. The word to which a pronoun refers (whose place it takes) is the **antecedent** of the pronoun.

A **personal pronoun** refers to the person speaking (first person); the person spoken to (second person); or the person, place, or thing spoken about (third person).

	Singular	Plural
First Person	I, me, my, mine	we, us, our, ours
Second Person	you, your, yours	you, your, yours
Third Person	he, him, his, she, her, hers, it, its	they, them, their, theirs

A **reflexive pronoun** reflects the action of a verb back on its subject. It indicates that the person or thing performing the action also is receiving the action.

> I keep *myself* fit by taking a walk every day.

An **intensive pronoun** adds emphasis to a noun or pronoun.

> It took the work of the president *himself* to pass the law.

A **demonstrative** pronoun points out a specific person(s), place(s), or thing(s).

> this, that, these, those

A **relative pronoun** begins a subordinate clause and connects it to another idea in the sentence.

> that, which, who, whom, whose

An **interrogative pronoun** begins a question.

> what, which, who, whom, whose

An **indefinite pronoun** refers to a person, place, or thing that may or may not be specifically named.

> all, another, any, both, each, everyone, few, most, none, no one, somebody

Verbs A **verb** expresses action or the existence of a state or condition.

An **action verb** tells what action someone or something is performing.

> gather, read, work, jump, imagine, analyze, conclude

A **linking verb** connects the subject with another word that identifies or describes the subject. The most common linking verb is *be*.

> appear, be, become, feel, look, remain, seem, smell, sound, stay, taste

A **helping verb,** or **auxiliary verb,** is added to a main verb to make a verb phrase.

> be, do, have, should, can, could, may, might, must, will, would

Adjectives An **adjective** modifies a noun or pronoun by describing it or giving it a more specific meaning. An adjective answers the questions:

What kind?	*purple* hat, *happy* face, *loud* sound
Which one?	*this* bowl
How many?	*three* cars
How much?	*enough* food

The articles *the, a,* and *an* are adjectives.

A **proper adjective** is an adjective derived from a proper noun.

> French, Shakespearean

Adverbs An **adverb** modifies a verb, an adjective, or another adverb by telling *where, when, how,* or *to what extent*.

> will answer *soon, extremely* sad, calls *more* often

Prepositions A **preposition** relates a noun or pronoun that appears with it to another word in the sentence.

> Dad made a meal *for* us. We talked *till* dusk. Bo missed school *because of* his illness.

Conjunctions A **conjunction** connects words or groups of words. A **coordinating conjunction** joins words or groups of words of equal rank.

> bread *and* cheese, brief *but* powerful

Correlative conjunctions are used in pairs to connect words or groups of words of equal importance.

> *both* Luis *and* Rosa, *neither* you *nor* I

Subordinating conjunctions indicate the connection between two ideas by placing one below the other in rank or importance. A subordinating conjunction introduces a subordinate, or dependent, clause.

> We will miss her *if* she leaves. Hank shrieked *when* he slipped on the ice.

Interjections An **interjection** expresses feeling or emotion. It is not related to other words in the sentence.

> ah, hey, ouch, well, yippee

PHRASES AND CLAUSES

Phrases A **phrase** is a group of words that does not have both a subject and a verb and that functions as one part of speech. A phrase expresses an idea but cannot stand alone.

Prepositional Phrases A **prepositional phrase** is a group of words that begins with a preposition and ends with a noun or pronoun that is the **object of the preposition.**

> before dawn   as a result of the rain

An **adjective phrase** is a prepositional phrase that modifies a noun or pronoun.

> Eliza appreciates the beauty **of a well-crafted poem.**

An **adverb phrase** is a prepositional phrase that modifies a verb, an adjective, or an adverb.

> She reads Spenser's sonnets **with great pleasure.**

Appositive Phrases An **appositive** is a noun or pronoun placed next to another noun or pronoun to add information about it. An **appositive phrase** consists of an appositive and its modifiers.

> Mr. Roth, **my music teacher,** is sick.

Verbal Phrases A **verbal** is a verb form that functions as a different part of speech (not as a verb) in a sentence. **Participles, gerunds,** and **infinitives** are verbals.

A **verbal phrase** includes a verbal and any modifiers or complements it may have. Verbal phrases may function as nouns, as adjectives, or as adverbs.

A **participle** is a verb form that can act as an adjective. Present participles end in *-ing;* past participles of regular verbs end in *-ed.*

A **participial phrase** consists of a participle and its modifiers or complements. The entire phrase acts as an adjective.

> Jenna's backpack, **loaded with equipment,** was heavy.
> **Barking incessantly,** the dogs chased the squirrels out of sight.

A **gerund** is a verb form that ends in *-ing* and is used as a noun.

A **gerund phrase** consists of a gerund with any modifiers or complements, all acting together as a noun.

> **Taking photographs of wildlife** is her main hobby. [acts as subject]
> We always enjoy **listening to live music.** [acts as object]

An **infinitive** is a verb form, usually preceded by *to,* that can act as a noun, an adjective, or an adverb.

An **infinitive phrase** consists of an infinitive and its modifiers or complements, and sometimes its subject, all acting together as a single part of speech.

> She tries **to get out into the wilderness often.** [acts as a noun; direct object of *tries*]
> The Tigers are the team **to beat.** [acts as an adjective; describes *team*]
> I drove twenty miles **to witness the event.** [acts as an adverb; tells why I drove]

Clauses A **clause** is a group of words with its own subject and verb.

Independent Clauses An independent clause can stand by itself as a complete sentence.

> George Orwell wrote with extraordinary insight.

Subordinate Clauses A subordinate clause, also called a dependent clause, cannot stand by itself as a complete sentence. Subordinate clauses always appear connected in some way with one or more independent clauses.

> George Orwell, **who wrote with extraordinary insight,** produced many politically relevant works.

An **adjective clause** is a subordinate clause that acts as an adjective. It modifies a noun or a pronoun by telling *what kind* or *which one.* Also called relative clauses, adjective clauses usually begin with a **relative pronoun:** *who, which, that, whom,* or *whose.*

> "The Lamb" is the poem **that I memorized for class.**

An **adverb clause** is a subordinate clause that, like an adverb, modifies a verb, an adjective, or an adverb. An adverb clause tells *where, when, in what way, to what extent, under what condition,* or *why.*

The students will read another poetry collection **if their schedule allows.**

When I recited the poem, Mr. Lopez was impressed.

A **noun clause** is a subordinate clause that acts as a noun.

William Blake survived on **whatever he made as an engraver.**

SENTENCE STRUCTURE

Subject and Predicate A **sentence** is a group of words that expresses a complete thought. A sentence has two main parts: a *subject* and a *predicate*.

A **fragment** is a group of words that does not express a complete thought. It lacks an independent clause.

The **subject** tells *whom* or *what* the sentence is about. The **predicate** tells what the subject of the sentence does or is.

A subject or a predicate can consist of a single word or of many words. All the words in the subject make up the **complete subject.** All the words in the predicate make up the **complete predicate.**

Complete Subject	Complete Predicate
Both of those girls	have already read *Macbeth*.

The **simple subject** is the essential noun, pronoun, or group of words acting as a noun that cannot be left out of the complete subject. The **simple predicate** is the essential verb or verb phrase that cannot be left out of the complete predicate.

Both of those girls | **have** already **read** *Macbeth*.
[Simple subject: *Both;* simple predicate: *have read*]

A **compound subject** is two or more subjects that have the same verb and are joined by a conjunction.

Neither the horse nor the driver looked tired.

A **compound predicate** is two or more verbs that have the same subject and are joined by a conjunction.

She **sneezed and coughed** throughout the trip.

Complements A **complement** is a word or word group that completes the meaning of the subject or verb in a sentence. There are four kinds of complements: *direct objects, indirect objects, objective complements,* and *subject complements.*

A **direct object** is a noun, a pronoun, or a group of words acting as a noun that receives the action of a transitive verb.

We watched the **liftoff**.
She drove **Zach** to the launch site.

An **indirect object** is a noun or pronoun that appears with a direct object and names the person or thing to which or for which something is done.

He sold the **family** a mirror. [The direct object is *mirror*.]

An **objective complement** is an adjective or noun that appears with a direct object and describes or renames it.

The decision made her **unhappy**.
[The direct object is *her*.]
Many consider Shakespeare the greatest **playwright**. [The direct object is *Shakespeare*.]

A **subject complement** follows a linking verb and tells something about the subject. There are two kinds: *predicate nominatives* and *predicate adjectives*.

A **predicate nominative** is a noun or pronoun that follows a linking verb and identifies or renames the subject.

"A Modest Proposal" is a **pamphlet**.

A **predicate adjective** is an adjective that follows a linking verb and describes the subject of the sentence.

"A Modest Proposal" is **satirical**.

Classifying Sentences by Structure

Sentences can be classified according to the kind and number of clauses they contain. The four basic sentence structures are *simple, compound, complex,* and *compound-complex.*

A **simple sentence** consists of one independent clause.

Terrence enjoys modern British literature.

A **compound sentence** consists of two or more independent clauses. The clauses are joined by a conjunction or a semicolon.

Terrence enjoys modern British literature, but his brother prefers the classics.

A **complex sentence** consists of one independent clause and one or more subordinate clauses.

Terrence, who reads voraciously, enjoys modern British literature.

A **compound-complex sentence** consists of two or more independent clauses and one or more subordinate clauses.

Terrence, who reads voraciously, enjoys modern British literature, but his brother prefers the classics.

Classifying Sentences by Function

Sentences can be classified according to their function or purpose. The four types are *declarative, interrogative, imperative,* and *exclamatory.*

A **declarative sentence** states an idea and ends with a period.

An **interrogative sentence** asks a question and ends with a question mark.

An **imperative sentence** gives an order or a direction and ends with either a period or an exclamation mark.

An **exclamatory sentence** conveys a strong emotion and ends with an exclamation mark.

PARAGRAPH STRUCTURE

An effective paragraph is organized around one **main idea,** which is often stated in a **topic sentence.** The other sentences support the main idea. To give the paragraph **unity,** make sure the connection between each sentence and the main idea is clear.

Unnecessary Shift in Person

Do not change needlessly from one grammatical person to another. Keep the person consistent in your sentences.

> **Max** went to the bakery, but **you** can't buy mints there. [shift from third person to second person]

Max went to the bakery, but **he** can't buy mints there. [consistent]

Unnecessary Shift in Voice

Do not change needlessly from active voice to passive voice in your use of verbs.

> Elena and I **searched** the trail for evidence, but no clues **were found.** [shift from active voice to passive voice]
>
> Elena and I **searched** the trail for evidence, but we **found** no clues. [consistent]

AGREEMENT

Subject and Verb Agreement

A singular subject must have a singular verb. A plural subject must have a plural verb.

> **Dr. Boone uses** a telescope to view the night sky.
> The **students use** a telescope to view the night sky.

A verb always agrees with its subject, not its object.

> *Incorrect:* The best part of the show were the jugglers.
> *Correct:* The best part of the show was the jugglers.

A phrase or clause that comes between a subject and verb does not affect subject-verb agreement.

> His **theory**, as well as his claims, **lacks** support.

Two subjects joined by *and* usually take a plural verb.

> The **dog** and the **cat are** healthy.

Two singular subjects joined by *or* or *nor* take a singular verb.

> The **dog** or the **cat is** hiding.

Two plural subjects joined by *or* or *nor* take a plural verb.

> The **dogs** or the **cats are** coming home with us.

When a singular and a plural subject are joined by *or* or *nor,* the verb agrees with the closer subject.

> Either the **dogs** or the **cat is** behind the door.
> Either the **cat** or the **dogs are** behind the door.

Pronoun and Antecedent Agreement

Pronouns must agree with their antecedents in number and gender. Use singular pronouns with singular antecedents and plural pronouns with plural antecedents.

> **Doris Lessing** uses **her** writing to challenge ideas about women's roles.
> **Writers** often use **their** skills to promote social change.

Use a singular pronoun when the antecedent is a singular indefinite pronoun such as *anybody, each, either, everybody, neither, no one, one,* or *someone.*

> Judge **each** of the articles on **its** merits.

Use a plural pronoun when the antecedent is a plural indefinite pronoun such as *both, few, many,* or *several.*

> **Both** of the articles have **their** flaws.

The indefinite pronouns *all, any, more, most, none,* and *some* can be singular or plural depending on the number of the word to which they refer.

> **Most** of the *books* are in **their** proper places.
> **Most** of the *book* has been torn from **its** binding.

Principal Parts of Regular and Irregular Verbs

A verb has four principal parts:

Present	Present Participle	Past	Past Participle
learn	learning	learned	learned
discuss	discussing	discussed	discussed
stand	standing	stood	stood
begin	beginning	began	begun

Regular verbs such as *learn* and *discuss* form the past and past participle by adding *-ed* to the present form. **Irregular verbs** such as *stand* and *begin* form the past and past participle in other ways. If you are in doubt about the principal parts of an irregular verb, check a dictionary.

The Tenses of Verbs

The different tenses of verbs indicate the time an action or condition occurs.

The **present tense** expresses an action that happens regularly or states a current condition or a general truth.

> Tourists **flock** to the site yearly.

Daily exercise **is** good for your heallth.

The **past tense** expresses a completed action or a condition that is no longer true.

> The squirrel **dropped** the nut and **ran** up the tree.
> I **was** very tired last night by 9:00.

The **future tense** indicates an action that will happen in the future or a condition that will be true.

> The Glazers **will visit** us tomorrow.
> They **will be** glad to arrive from their long journey.

The **present perfect tense** expresses an action that happened at an indefinite time in the past or an action that began in the past and continues into the present.

> Someone **has cleaned** the trash from the park.
> The puppy **has been** under the bed all day.

The **past perfect tense** shows an action that was completed before another action in the past.

> Gerard **had revised** his essay before he turned it in.

The **future perfect tense** indicates an action that will have been completed before another action takes place.

> Mimi **will have painted** the kitchen by the time we finish the shutters.

Degrees of Comparison

Adjectives and adverbs take different forms to show the three degrees of comparison: the *positive*, the *comparative*, and the *superlative*.

Positive	Comparative	Superlative
fast	faster	fastest
crafty	craftier	craftiest
abruptly	more abruptly	most abruptly
badly	worse	worst

Using Comparative and Superlative Adjectives and Adverbs

Use comparative adjectives and adverbs to compare two things. Use superlative adjectives and adverbs to compare three or more things.

> This season's weather was **drier** than last year's.
> This season has been one of the **driest** on record.
> Jake practices **more often** than Jamal.
> Of everyone in the band, Jake practices **most often.**

Pronoun Case

The **case** of a pronoun is the form it takes to show its function in a sentence. There are three pronoun cases: *nominative, objective,* and *possessive.*

Nominative	Objective	Possessive
I, you, he, she, it, we, you, they	me, you, him, her, it, us, you, them	my, your, yours, his, her, hers, its, our, ours, their, theirs

Use the **nominative case** when a pronoun functions as a *subject* or as a *predicate nominative.*

> **They** are going to the movies. [subject]
> The biggest movie fan is **she.** [predicate nominative]

Use the **objective case** for a pronoun acting as a *direct object,* an *indirect object,* or the *object of a preposition.*

> The ending of the play surprised **me.** [direct object]
> Mary gave **us** two tickets to the play. [indirect object]
> The audience cheered for **him.** [object of preposition]

Use the **possessive case** to show ownership.

> The red suitcase is **hers.**

GLOSSARY: GRAMMAR HANDBOOK

Diction The words you choose contribute to the overall effectiveness of your writing. **Diction** refers to word choice and to the clearness and correctness of those words. You can improve one aspect of your diction by choosing carefully between commonly confused words, such as the pairs listed below.

accept, except

Accept is a verb that means "to receive" or "to agree to." *Except* is a preposition that means "other than" or "leaving out."

Please **accept** my offer to buy you lunch this weekend.

He is busy every day **except** the weekends.

affect, effect

Affect is normally a verb meaning "to influence" or "to bring about a change in." *Effect* is usually a noun meaning "result."

The distractions outside **affect** Steven's ability to concentrate.

The teacher's remedies had a positive **effect** on Steven's ability to concentrate.

among, between

Among is usually used with three or more items, and it emphasizes collective relationships or indicates distribution. *Between* is generally used with only two items, but it can be used with more than two if the emphasis is on individual (one-to-one) relationships within the group.

I had to choose a snack **among** the various vegetables.

He handed out the booklets **among** the conference participants.

Our school is **between** a park and an old barn.

The tournament included matches **between** France, Spain, Mexico, and the United States.

amount, number

Amount refers to overall quantity and is mainly used with mass nouns (those that can't be counted). *Number* refers to individual items that can be counted.

The **amount** of attention that great writers have paid to Shakespeare is remarkable.

A **number** of important English writers have been fascinated by the legend of King Arthur.

assure, ensure, insure

Assure means "to convince [someone of something]; to guarantee." *Ensure* means "to make certain [that something happens]." *Insure* means "to arrange for payment in case of loss."

The attorney **assured** us we'd win the case.

The rules **ensure** that no one gets treated unfairly.

Many professional musicians **insure** their valuable instruments.

bad, badly

Use the adjective *bad* before a noun or after linking verbs such as *feel, look,* and *seem*. Use *badly* whenever an adverb is required.

The situation may seem **bad**, but it will improve over time.

Though our team played **badly** today, we will focus on practicing for the next match.

beside, besides

Beside means "at the side of" or "close to." *Besides* means "in addition to."

The stapler sits **beside** the pencil sharpener in our classroom.

Besides being very clean, the classroom is also very organized.

can, may

The helping verb *can* generally refers to the ability to do something. The helping verb *may* generally refers to permission to do something.

I **can** run one mile in six minutes.

May we have a race during recess?

complement, compliment

The verb *complement* means "to enhance"; the verb *compliment* means "to praise."

Online exercises **complement** the textbook lessons.

Ms. Lewis **complimented** our team on our excellent debate.

compose, comprise

Compose means "to make up; constitute." *Comprise* means "to include or contain." Remember that the whole comprises its parts or is composed of its parts, and the parts compose the whole.

The assignment **comprises** three different tasks.

The assignment is **composed** of three different tasks.

Three different tasks **compose** the assignment.

different from, different than

Different from is generally preferred over *different than*, but *different than* can be used before a clause. Always use *different from* before a noun or pronoun.

Your point of view is so **different from** mine.

His idea was so **different from** [or **different than**] what we had expected.

farther, further

Use *farther* to refer to distance. Use *further* to mean "to a greater degree or extent" or "additional."

Chiang has traveled **farther** than anybody else in the class.

If I want **further** details about his travels, I can read his blog.

fewer, less

Use *fewer* for things that can be counted. Use *less* for amounts or quantities that cannot be counted. *Fewer* must be followed by a plural noun.

Fewer students drive to school since the weather improved.

There is **less** noise outside in the mornings.

good, well

Use the adjective *good* before a noun or after a linking verb. Use *well* whenever an adverb is required, such as when modifying a verb.

I feel **good** after sleeping for eight hours.

I did **well** on my test, and my soccer team played **well** in that afternoon's game. It was a **good** day!

its, it's

The word *its* with no apostrophe is a possessive pronoun. The word *it's* is a contraction of "it is."

Angelica will try to fix the computer and **its** keyboard.

It's a difficult job, but she can do it.

lay, lie

Lay is a transitive verb meaning "to set or put something down." Its principal parts are *lay, laying, laid, laid. Lie* is an intransitive verb meaning "to recline" or "to exist in a certain place." Its principal parts are *lie, lying, lay, lain.*

Please **lay** that box down and help me with the sofa.

When we are done moving, I am going to **lie** down.

My hometown **lies** sixty miles north of here.

like, as

Like is a preposition that usually means "similar to" and precedes a noun or pronoun. The conjunction *as* means "in the way that" and usually precedes a clause.

Like the other students, I was prepared for a quiz.

As I said yesterday, we expect to finish before noon.

Use **such as,** not **like,** before a series of examples.

Foods **such as** apples, nuts, and pretzels make good snacks.

of, have

Do not use *of* in place of *have* after auxiliary verbs such as *would, could, should, may, might,* or *must.* The contraction of *have* is formed by adding *-ve* after these verbs.

I **would have** stayed after school today, but I had to help cook at home.

Mom **must've** called while I was still in the gym.

principal, principle

Principal can be an adjective meaning "main; most important." It can also be a noun meaning "chief officer of a school." *Principle* is a noun meaning "moral rule" or "fundamental truth."

His strange behavior was the **principal** reason for our concern.

Democratic **principles** form the basis of our country's laws.

raise, rise

Raise is a transitive verb that usually takes a direct object. *Rise* is intransitive and never takes a direct object.

Iliana and Josef **raise** the flag every morning.

They **rise** from their seats and volunteer immediately whenever help is needed.

than, then

The conjunction *than* is used to connect the two parts of a comparison. The adverb *then* usually refers to time.

My backpack is heavier **than** hers.

I will finish my homework and **then** meet my friends at the park.

that, which, who

Use the relative pronoun *that* to refer to things or people. Use *which* only for things and *who* only for people.

That introduces a restrictive phrase or clause, that is, one that is essential to the meaning of the sentence. *Which* introduces a nonrestrictive phrase or clause—one that adds information but could be deleted from the sentence—and is preceded by a comma.

Ben ran to the park **that** just reopened.

The park, **which** just reopened, has many attractions.

The man **who** built the park loves to see people smiling.

when, where, why

Do not use *when, where,* or *why* directly after a linking verb, such as *is.* Reword the sentence.

Incorrect: The morning is when he left for the beach.

Correct: He left for the beach in the morning.

who, whom

In formal writing, use *who* only as a subject in clauses and sentences. Use *whom* only as the object of a verb or of a preposition.

Who paid for the tickets?

Whom should I pay for the tickets?

I can't recall to **whom** I gave the money for the tickets.

your, you're

Your is a possessive pronoun expressing ownership. *You're* is the contraction of "you are."

Have you finished writing **your** informative essay?

You're supposed to turn it in tomorrow. If **you're** late, **your** grade will be affected.

Capitalization

First Words

Capitalize the first word of a sentence.

Stories about knights and their deeds interest me.

Capitalize the first word of direct speech.

Sharon asked, "**D**o you like stories about knights?"

Capitalize the first word of a quotation that is a complete sentence.

Einstein said, "**A**nyone who has never made a mistake has never tried anything new."

Proper Nouns and Proper Adjectives

Capitalize all proper nouns, including geographical names, historical events and periods, and names of organizations.

Thames **R**iver   **J**ohn **K**eats   the **R**enaissance

United **N**ations   **W**orld **W**ar II   **S**ierra **N**evada

Capitalize all proper adjectives.

Shakespearean play   **B**ritish invaision

American citizen   **L**atin **A**merican literature

Academic Course Names

Capitalize course names only if they are language courses, are followed by a number, or are preceded by a proper noun or adjective.

Spanish   **H**onors **C**hemistry   **H**istory 101

geology   **a**lgebra   **s**ocial **s**tudies

Titles

Capitalize personal titles when followed by the person's name.

Ms. Hughes   **D**r. Perez   **K**ing George

Capitalize titles showing family relationships when they are followed by a specific person's name, unless they are preceded by a possessive noun or pronoun.

Uncle Oscar   Mangan's **s**ister   his **a**unt Tessa

Capitalize the first word and all other key words in the titles of books, stories, songs, and other works of art.

Frankenstein   "**S**hooting an **E**lephant"

Punctuation

End Marks

Use a **period** to end a declarative sentence or an imperative sentence.

We are studying the structure of sonnets.
Read the biography of Mary Shelley.

Use periods with initials and abbreviations.

D. H. Lawrence   Mrs. Browning
Mt. Everest   Maple St.

Use a **question mark** to end an interrogative sentence.
What is Macbeth's fatal flaw?

Use an **exclamation mark** after an exclamatory sentence or a forceful imperative sentence.

That's a beautiful painting!   Let me go now!

Commas

Use a **comma** before a coordinating conjunction to separate two independent clauses in a compound sentence.

The game was very close, but we were victorious.

Use commas to separate three or more words, phrases, or clauses in a series.

William Blake was a writer, artist, and printer.

Use commas to separate coordinate adjectives.

It was a witty, amusing novel.

Use a comma after an introductory word, phrase, or clause.

When the novelist finished his book, he celebrated with his family.

Use commas to set off nonessential expressions.

Old English, of course, requires translation.

Use commas with places and dates.

Coventry, England   September 1, 1939

Semicolons

Use a **semicolon** to join closely related independent clauses that are not already joined by a conjunction.

Tanya likes to write poetry; Heather prefers prose.

Use semicolons to avoid confusion when items in a series contain commas.

They traveled to London, England; Madrid, Spain; and Rome, Italy.

Colons

Use a **colon** before a list of items following an independent clause.

Notable Victorian poets include the following: Tennyson, Arnold, Housman, and Hopkins.

Use a colon to introduce information that summarizes or explains the independent clause before it.

She just wanted to do one thing: rest.
Malcolm loves volunteering: He reads to sick children every Saturday afternoon.

Quotation Marks

Use **quotation marks** to enclose a direct quotation.

"Short stories," Ms. Hildebrand said, "should have rich, well-developed characters."

An **indirect quotation** does not require quotation marks.

Ms. Hildebrand said that short stories should have well-developed characters.

Use quotation marks around the titles of short written works, episodes in a series, songs, and works mentioned as parts of collections.

"The Lagoon"   "Boswell Meets Johnson"

Italics

Italicize the titles of long written works, movies, television and radio shows, lengthy works of music, paintings, and sculptures.

Howards End   *60 Minutes*   *Guernica*

For handwritten material, you can use underlining instead of italics.

The Princess Bride   Mona Lisa

Dashes

Use **dashes** to indicate an abrupt change of thought, a dramatic interrupting idea, or a summary statement.

I read the entire first act of *Macbeth*—you won't believe what happens next.

The director—what's her name again?—attended the movie premiere.

Hyphens

Use a **hyphen** with certain numbers, after certain prefixes, with two or more words used as one word, and with a compound modifier that comes before a noun.

seventy-two
self-esteem
president-elect
five-year contract

Parentheses

Use **parentheses** to set off asides and explanations when the material is not essential or when it consists of one or more sentences. When the sentence in parentheses interrupts the larger sentence, it does not have a capital letter or a period.

He listened intently (it was too dark to see who was speaking) to try to identify the voices.

When a sentence in parentheses falls between two other complete sentences, it should start with a capital letter and end with a period.

The quarterback threw three touchdown passes. (We knew he could do it.) Our team won the game by two points.

Apostrophes

Add an **apostrophe** and an *s* to show the possessive case of most singular nouns and of plural nouns that do not end in *-s* or *-es*.

Blake's poems   the mice's whiskers

Names ending in *s* form their possessives in the same way, except for classical and biblical names, which add only an apostrophe to form the possessive.

Dickens's   Hercules'

Add an apostrophe to show the possessive case of plural nouns ending in *-s* and *-es*.

the girls' songs   the Ortizes' car

Use an apostrophe in a contraction to indicate the position of the missing letter or letters.

She's never read a Coleridge poem she didn't like.

Brackets

Use **brackets** to enclose clarifying information inserted within a quotation.

Columbus's journal entry from October 21, 1492, begins as follows: "At 10 o'clock, we arrived at a cape of the island [San Salvador], and anchored, the other vessels in company."

Ellipses

Use three ellipsis points, also known as an **ellipsis,** to indicate where you have omitted words from quoted material.

Wollestonecraft wrote, "The education of women has of late been more attended to than formerly; yet they are still . . . ridiculed or pitied. . . ."

In the example above, the four dots at the end of the sentence are the three ellipsis points plus the period from the original sentence.

Use an ellipsis to indicate a pause or interruption in speech.

"When he told me the news," said the coach, "I was . . . I was shocked . . . completely shocked."

Spelling

Spelling Rules

Learning the rules of English spelling will help you make **generalizations** about how to spell words.

Word Parts

The three word parts that can combine to form a word are roots, prefixes, and suffixes. Many of these word parts come from the Greek, Latin, and Anglo-Saxon languages.

The **root word** carries a word's basic meaning.

Root and Origin	Meaning	Examples
-leg- (-log-) [Gr.]	to say, speak	*legal, logic*
-pon- (-pos-) [L.]	to put, place	*postpone, deposit*

A **prefix** is one or more syllables added to the beginning of a word that alter the meaning of the root.

Prefix and Origin	Meaning	Example
anti- [Gr.]	against	*antipathy*
inter- [L.]	between	*international*
mis- [A.S.]	wrong	*misplace*

A **suffix** is a letter or group of letters added to the end of a root word that changes the word's meaning or part of speech.

Suffix and Origin	Meaning and Example	Part of Speech
-ful [A.S.]	full of: *scornful*	adjective
-ity [L.]	state of being: *adversity*	noun
-ize (-ise) [Gr.]	to make: *idolize*	verb
-ly [A.S.]	in a manner: *calmly*	adverb

Rules for Adding Suffixes to Root Words

When adding a suffix to a root word ending in *y* preceded by a consonant, change *y* to *i* unless the suffix begins with *i*.

  ply + -able = pliable   happy + -ness = happiness

  defy + -ing = defying   cry + -ing = crying

For a root word ending in *e*, drop the *e* when adding a suffix beginning with a vowel.

  drive + -ing = driving   move + -able = movable

  SOME EXCEPTIONS: traceable, seeing, dyeing

For root words ending with a consonant + vowel + consonant in a stressed syllable, double the final consonant when adding a suffix that begins with a vowel.

  mud + -y = muddy   submit + -ed = submitted

  SOME EXCEPTIONS: mixing, fixed

Rules for Adding Prefixes to Root Words

When a prefix is added to a root word, the spelling of the root remains the same.

  un- + certain = uncertain   mis- + spell = misspell

With some prefixes, the spelling of the prefix changes when joined to the root to make the pronunciation easier.

  in- + mortal = immortal   ad- + vert = avert

Orthographic Patterns

Certain letter combinations in English make certain sounds. For instance, *ph* sounds like *f*, *eigh* usually makes a long *a* sound, and the *k* before an *n* is often silent.

  pharmacy   n**eigh**bor   **k**nowledge

Understanding **orthographic patterns** such as these can help you improve your spelling.

Forming Plurals

The plural form of most nouns is formed by adding -*s* to the singular.

  computer**s**   gadget**s**   Washington**s**

For words ending in *s*, *ss*, *x*, *z*, *sh*, or *ch*, add -*es*.

  circus**es**   tax**es**   wish**es**   bench**es**

For words ending in *y* or *o* preceded by a vowel, add -*s*.

  key**s**   patio**s**

For words ending in *y* preceded by a consonant, change the *y* to an *i* and add -*es*.

  cit**ies**   enem**ies**   troph**ies**

For most words ending in *o* preceded by a consonant, add -*es*.

  echo**es**   tomato**es**

Some words form the plural in irregular ways.

  women   oxen   children   teeth   deer

Foreign Words Used in English

Some words used in English are actually foreign words that have been adopted. Learning to spell these words requires memorization. When in doubt, check a dictionary.

  sushi   enchilada   au pair   fiancé

  laissez faire   croissant

GLOSSARY: GRAMMAR HANDBOOK

INDEX OF SKILLS

INDEX OF SKILLS

Writing

INDEX OF AUTHORS AND TITLES

The following authors and titles appear in the print and online versions of *myPerspectives*.

ADDITIONAL SELECTIONS: AUTHOR AND TITLE INDEX

The following authors and titles appear in the Interactive Student Edition only.

INDEX: INDEX OF AUTHORS AND TITLES

Acknowledgments

The following selections appear in Grade 12 of *myPerspectives*. Some selections appear online only.

A.M. Heath & Co. Ltd. *Shooting an Elephant and Other Essays* by George Orwell (Copyright ©George Orwell, 1946) Reproduced by permission of Bill Hamilton as the Literary Executor of the Estate of the Late Sonia Brownell Orwell.

BBC News Online. "How did Harry Patch become an unlikely WW1 Hero?" from BBC, used with permission.

BBC Worldwide Americas, Inc. "How did Harry Patch become an unlikely WW1 Hero?" from Faulks on Fiction, episode one ©BBC Worldwide Learning; Queen Elizabeth I's Speech Before Her Troops ©BBC Worldwide Learning; The Medieval Age and The Canterbury Tales ©BBC Worldwide Learning; Introduction to *Macbeth* ©BBC Worldwide Learning; Macbeth's Early Motivation ©BBC Worldwide Learning; The Darkness in Macbeth's Human Characters ©BBC Worldwide Learning; Philip Larkin reads "The Explosion" ©BBC Worldwide Learning; The British Empire Sets Its Sights West ©BBC Worldwide Learning.

Beard, Francesca. "Old Love" by Francesca Beard. Used with permission of the author.

Brandt & Hochman Literary Agents Inc. "The Assignment of My Life" by Ruth Gruber, from *The Moment: Wild, Poignant, Life-Changing Stories from 125 Writers and Artists Famous & Obscure*, edited by Larry Smith. Used with permission of Brandt & Hochman Literary Agents on behalf of the author's estate; "Back to My Own Country: An Essay" from *Six Stories and an Essay* by Andrea Levy. Copyright 2014 by Andrea Levy. Used by permission of Brandt & Hochman Literary Agents, Inc. Any copying or distribution of this text is expressly forbidden. All rights reserved.

Candlewick Press. *Beowulf*. Copyright © 1999, 2000, 2007 by Gareth Hinds. Reproduced by permission of the publisher, Candlewick Press, Somerville, MA.

Carmen Balcells Agencia Literaria. Isabel Allende, "Writing as an Act of Hope" ©Isabel Allende, 1989.

Clark, Kevin. "The Seafarer" used by permission of Kevin Clark.

Classical Comics Ltd. from *Macbeth: The Graphic Novel* ©Classical Comics.

Columbia University Press. From *The Pillow Book* by Sei Shonagon, translated by Ivan Morris. Copyright ©1992 Columbia University Press. Reprinted with permission of the publisher.

Conville and Walsh Literary Agency. "The Most Forgetful Man in the World", from *Moonwalking with Einstein: The Art and Science of Remembering Everything* by Joshua Foer, copyright ©2011 by Joshua Foer. Used by permission of Conville and Walsh Literary Agency.

Cort, Julia. "NOVA: Sleep" by Julia Cort. Used with permission.

Crown Copyright Officer. Passenger Manifest for the M.V. Empire Windrush, Courtesy of National Archives.

Curtis Brown, Ltd. (UK). "Pericles' Funeral Oration" reproduced with permission of Curtis Brown Book Group Ltd, London on behalf of The Beneficiaries of the Estate of Rex Warner ©1972; *The Canterbury Tales*: "The Prologue" reproduced with permission of Curtis Brown Book Group Ltd, London on behalf of The Estate of Nevill Coghill ©1951.

Encyclopedia Britannica, Inc. "Jamaica" reprinted with permission from *Encyclopædia Britannica*, ©2015 by Encyclopædia Britannica, Inc.

Faber & Faber, Ltd. (UK). "The Explosion" from *Collected Poems* by Philip Larkin. Used with permission of Faber & Faber Ltd.; "Midsummer" from *The Poetry of Derek Walcott, 1948–2013* by Derek Walcott, selected by Glyn Maxwell. Copyright ©2014 by Derek Walcott. Reprinted by permission of Faber & Faber Ltd.; "Why Brownee Left" from *Poems: 1968–1998* by Paul Muldoon. Copyright ©2001 by Paul Muldoon. Reprinted by permission of Faber & Faber Ltd.

Farrar, Straus and Giroux. "The Explosion" from *The Complete Poems of Philip Larkin* by Philip Larkin, edited by Archie Burnett. Copyright ©2012 by The Estate of Philip Larkin. CAUTION: Users are warned that this work is protected under copyright laws and downloading is strictly prohibited. The right to reproduce or transfer the work via any medium must be secured with Farrar, Straus and Giroux, LLC; "Why Brownee Left" from *Poems: 1968–1998* by Paul Muldoon. Copyright ©2001 by Paul Muldoon. Reprinted by permission of Farrar, Straus and Giroux, LLC. CAUTION: Users are warned that this work is protected under copyright laws and downloading is strictly prohibited. The right to reproduce or transfer the work via any medium must be secured with Farrar, Straus and Giroux, LLC.; Excerpt from "Midsummer" from *The Poetry of Derek Walcott, 1948-2013* by Derek Walcott, selected by Glyn Maxwell. Copyright ©2014 by Derek Walcott. Reprinted by permission of Farrar, Straus and Giroux, LLC. CAUTION: Users are warned that this work is protected under copyright laws and downloading is strictly prohibited. The right to reproduce or transfer the work via any medium must be secured with Farrar, Straus and Giroux, LLC.; Excerpts from "Macbeth" from *Shakespeare's Language 2000* by Frank Kermode. Copyright ©2000 by Frank Kermode. Reprinted by permission of Farrar, Straus and Giroux, LLC. CAUTION: Users are warned that this work is protected under copyright laws and downloading is strictly prohibited. The right to reproduce or transfer the work via any medium must be secured with Farrar, Straus and Giroux, LLC.

Financial Times Ltd. "A Year in a Word: Selfie." *Financial Times*, December 27, 2013.

Guardian News and Media Limited. "Occupy LSX May Be Gone, but the Movement Won't Be Forgotten," Copyright Guardian New & Media Ltd 2015; Copyright Guardian News & Media Ltd 2015; Copyright Guardian News & Media Ltd 2015.

Hinds, Gareth. *Beowulf*. Copyright ©1999, 2000, 2007 by Gareth Hinds. Reproduced by permission of the publisher, Candlewick Press, Somerville, MA.

Houghton Mifflin Harcourt. "Shakespeare's Sister" from *A Room of One's Own* by Virginia Woolf. Copyright 1929 by Houghton Mifflin Harcourt Publishing Company and renewed 1957 by Leonard Woolf. Reprinted by permission of Houghton Mifflin Harcourt Publishing Company. All rights reserved; "Shooting an Elephant" from *A Collection of Essays* by George Orwell. Copyright ©1950 by Sonia Brownell Orwell and renewed 1978 by Sonia Pitt-Rivers. Reprinted by permission of Houghton Mifflin Harcourt Publishing Company. All rights reserved; Excerpt from *Mrs. Dalloway* by Virginia Woolf. Copyright 1925 by Houghton Mifflin Publishing Company. Copyright renewed 1953 by Leonard Woolf. Reprinted by permission of

English Working Class by E.P. Thompson, copyright © 1963 by E.P. Thompson. Used by permission of Pantheon Books, an imprint of the Knopf Doubleday Publishing Group, a division of Penguin Random House LLC. All rights reserved. Any third party use of this material, outside of this publication, is prohibited. Interested parties must apply directly to Penguin Random House LLC for permission.

Russell & Volkening, Inc. from "The Worms of the Earth Against the Lions," from *A Distant Mirror* reprinted by the permission of Russell & Volkening as agents for the author. Copyright ©1978 by Barbara Tuchman.

Scientific American. "The New Psychology of Leadership" reproduced with permission. Copyright ©2007 Scientific American, a division of Nature America, Inc. All rights reserved.

Simon & Schuster, Inc. "The Second Coming" reprinted with the permission of Scribner, a Division of Simon & Schuster, Inc. from *The Collected Works of W. B. Yeats, Volume I: The Poems*, Revised by W. B. Yeats, edited by Richard J. Finneran. Copyright ©1924 by The Macmillan Company, renewed 1952 by Bertha Georgie Yeats. All rights reserved.

The English and Media Centre. Patience Agbabi: Prologue from the Canterbury Tales: The Slam Remix, filmed at the emagazine Conference 2013 is reproduced by kind permission of the English and Media Centre.

The Society of Authors (UK). "Mrs. Dalloway" by Virginia Woolf, used with permission of The Society of Authors as the literary representative of the Estate of Virginia Woolf; "Shakespeare's Sister" from *A Room of One's Own* by Virginia Woolf. Used with permission of The Society of Authors.

Tinder Press. "Back to My Own Country: An Essay" by Andrea Levy, from *Six Stories & an Essay*. Copyright ©2014 Andrea Levy. Reproduced by permission of Headline Publishing Group; "Back to My Own Country: An Essay" by Andrea Levy, from *Six Stories & an Essay*. Copyright ©2014 Andrea Levy. Reproduced by permission of Headline Publishing Group.

United Agents. "The British" from WICKED WORLD by Benjamin Zephaniah (Puffin, 2000) Text copyright ©Benjamin Zephaniah, 2000. Used by permission of United Artists; "Who's Who" from *Talking Turkeys* by Benjamin Zephaniah (Viking, 1994). Copyright ©Benjamin Zephaniah, 1994. Used with permission of United Agents.

University of Chicago Press. Excerpt from *Oedipus the King* by Sophocles, D. Grene, trans., from *The Complete Greek Tragedies*, R. Lattimore and D. Grene, eds. Used with permission of The University of Chicago Press.

Victoria R.M. Brown. "How Proust Can Change Your Life" ©Victoria R.M. Brown. Big Think.

W. W. Norton & Co. "*The Inferno*: Canto XXXIV," from *The Divine Comedy* by Dante Allghieri, translated by John Ciardi. Copyright 1954, 1957, 1959, 1960, 1961, 1965, 1967, 1970 by the Ciardi Family Publishing Trust. Used by permission of W.W. Norton & Company, Inc.; "My Old Home" from *Selected Stories of Lu Hsun* by Lu Hsun, translated by Yang Xianyi and Gladys Yang. Copyright ©1960. Used by permission of W.W. Norton & Company, Inc.

WGBH Media Library & Archives. From NOVA ScienceNow, "Sleep," ©1996-2015 WGBH Educational Foundation.

Wylie Agency. "On Seeing England for the First Time" by Jamaica Kincaid, originally published in *Harper's*. Copyright ©1991 by Jamaica Kincaid, used by permission of The Wylie Agency, Inc.

Yale University Press. "Battle of Maldon" from *Poems and Prose from the Old English* by Burton Raffel. Copyright ©1998. Used with permission of the publisher, Yale University Press; "The Seafarer" from *Poems and Prose from the Old English* by Burton Raffel. Copyright ©1998. Used with permission of the publisher, Yale University Press.

Credits

vi Mikkelwilliam/Getty Images;viii Olivier Martel/akg-images; x World History Archive/Alamy; 2 Mikkelwilliam/Getty Images; 3 (BC) Matt Cardy/Getty Images, (BL) F.106r The Coronation of Emperor Charlemagne (742–814) by Pope Leo III (c.750–816) at St. Peters, Rome in 800, Grandes Chroniques de France, 1375–79 (vellum), French School, (14th century)/Bibliotheque Municipale, Castres, France/Bridgeman Art Library, (BR) Elizabeth I - (1533–1603) The Warrior Queen (gouache on paper), Doughty, C.L. (1913–85)/Private Collection/Look and Learn/Bridgeman Art Library, (C) Universal History Archive/UIG/Getty Images, (CL) Images from The Odyssey (c) 2010 by Gareth Hinds appear courtesy of the publisher, Candlewick Press.,(CR) UpperCut Images/Getty Images, (T) Steven Day/AP Images; (TC) Gabriel Metsu/akg-images,(TR) Hulton-Deutsch Collection/Corbis; 6 Steven Day/AP Images; 11(B) Images from The Odyssey (c) 2010 by Gareth Hinds appear courtesy of the publisher, Candlewick Press., (T) f.106r The Coronation of Emperor Charlemagne (742–814) by Pope Leo III (c.750–816) at St. Peters, Rome in 800, Grandes Chroniques de France, 1375–79 (vellum), French School, (14th century)/Bibliotheque Municipale, Castres, France/Bridgeman Art Library; 12(C) f.106r The Coronation of Emperor Charlemagne (742–814) by Pope Leo III (c.750–816) at St. Peters, Rome in 800, Grandes Chroniques de France, 1375–79 (vellum), French School, (14th century)/Bibliotheque Municipale, Castres, France/Bridgeman Art Library, (L) Robana/British Library Board/Art Resource, New York, (R) Christophe Boisvieux/Corbis; 13(BL) Michael Nicholson/Corbis, (BR) The British Library Board;14(L) Z.Radovan/BPL/Lebrecht Music & Arts/Lebrecht Music & Arts/Corbis, (R) Werner Forman/Corbis; 15(L) North Wind Picture Archives/Alamy, (R) North Wind Picture Archives; 16 Burton Raffel; 17 Perart/Shutterstock; 50-60 Images from The Odyssey (c) 2010 by Gareth Hinds appear courtesy of the publisher, Candlewick Press.; 62 Steven Day/AP Images; 71(B) Matt Cardy/Getty Images, (BCL) Everett Historical/Shutterstock; (C) Universal History Archive/UIG/Getty Images, (T) Gabriel Metsu/akg-images, (TCL) Joint Services Command and Staff College, Defence Academy of the United Kingdom; 74(L) Gabriel Metsu/akg-images, (R) Universal History Archive/UIG/Getty Images; 75(B) H. D. Falkenstein/Glow Images, (T) William Dobson/akg-images; 76 Gabriel Metsu/akg-images; 78 Joint Services Command and Staff College, Defence Academy of the United Kingdom; 84(L) Gabriel Metsu/akg-images, (R) Universal History Archive/UIG/Getty Images; 85 Mary Evans/Robert Hunt Library/AGE Fotostock; 86 Universal History Archive/UIG/Getty Images; 88 Everett Historical/Shutterstock; 97 Matt Cardy/Getty Images; 99 Matt Cardy/Getty Images; Baden-Powell in the Uniform of the South African Constabulary, Standing by His Charger by John Edward Chapman 'Chester' Mathews (Major) The Scout Association; 112 Olivier Martel/akg-images; 113 (BC) Mubus7/Shutterstock, (BR) Guzel Studio/Shutterstock, (C) Michael Nicholson/Corbis, (CR) Gregory James Van Raalte/Shutterstock, (T) Pictorial Press Ltd/Alamy, (TC) Bob Thomas/Popperfoto/Getty Images, (TL) Heritage Image Partnership Ltd/Alamy, (TR) Anky/Shutterstock; 116 Pictorial Press Ltd/Alamy; 121(B) Patience Agbabi Prologue to the Canterbury Tales, The Slam Remix, filmed at the emagazine Conference 2013 is reproduced by kind permission of the English and Media Centre, (T) Heritage Image Partnership Ltd/Alamy; 122 (L) Pawelkowalczyk/Fotolia, (R) Heritage Image Partnership Ltd/Alamy; 123 (C) Lordprice Collection/Alamy,(L) J.D. Dallet/AGE Fotostock, (R) The Print Collector/Alamy; 124 (C) Fototehnik/Fotolia, (L) Prisma Archivo/Alamy, (R) Album/Prisma/Newscom; 125(L) Pictures From History/The Image Works, (R) GFC Collection/Alamy; 126 Stapleton Collection/Corbis; 160-164 Patience Agbabi Prologue to the Canterbury Tales, The Slam Remix, filmed at the emagazine Conference 2013 is reproduced by kind permission of the English and Media Centre; 175 (B) Courtesy of The National Archives, U.K.,(C) Mubus7/Shutterstock,(T) Bob Thomas/Popperfoto/Getty Images; (TC) Michael Nicholson/Corbis; 178 Bob Child/AP Images; 179 Bob Thomas/Popperfoto/Getty Images; 182 Mary Evans Picture Library/Alamy; 186, 188 Bob Thomas/Popperfoto/Getty Images;190 Lebrecht Music and Arts Photo Library/Alamy; 191 Michael Nicholson/Corbis; 194 Michael Nicholson/Corbis; 196 Michael Nicholson/Corbis; 198 Mubus7/Shutterstock; 199(B) Album/Alonso & Marful/Newscom, (T) Cosima Scavolini/ZUMApress/Newscom; 200 Mubus7/Shutterstock; 209 David Levenson/Simon Dack/Keystone/Hulton Archive/Getty Images; 218, 222 Courtesy of The National Archives, U.K.; 219, 220 National Archives; 236 World History Archive/Alamy; 237(BL) Everett Collection, (C) Hugo Philpott/Epa/Newscom, (CL) Everett Collection, (CR) Matej Michelizza/istock/Getty Images, (T) Everett Collection, (TC) Ambrozinio/Shutterstock, (TL) Georgios Kollidas/Shutterstock, (TR) Netfalls - Remy Musser/Shutterstock; 240 Everett Collection; 245 (BCL) Ronald Grant Archive/Mary Evans Picture Library, (BL) Mary Evans/Ronald Grant/Everett Collection, (BR) Everett Collection, (CL) Mary Evans/Ronald Grant/Everett Collection, (CR) Everett Collection, (TCL) AF archive/Alamy; TL Everett Collection, (TR) Georgios Kollidas/Shutterstock; 246 (C) Ivy Close Images/AGE Fotostock, (L) Georgios Kollidas/Shutterstock, (R) Marco Andras/AGE Fotostock, (BL) Songquan Deng/123RF; 247(BR) Georgios Kollidas/Shutterstock, (T) Pavila/Shutterstock; 248 (C) Stocksnapper/Shutterstock, (L) Everett Historical/Shutterstock, (R) J.L. Kraemer/Blue Lantern Studio/Corbis; 249 (L) North Wind Picture Archives/Alamy, (R) Dea/A Dagli Orti/AGE Fotostock; 250 English School/Getty Images; 251 (B) Peter Phipp/Britain On View/Getty Images, (R) Rafael Ben-Ari/Chameleons Eye/Newscom; 251 (T) Moviestore collection Ltd / Alamy, (L) Everett Collection; 253 Moviestore collection Ltd / Alamy; 254 © PjrTravel / Alamy; 255 Everett Collection; 258, 280, 296 Georgios Kollidas/Shutterstock; 259 Mary Evans/Playboy Productions Inc. Ronald Grant/Everett Collection; 260, 266, 273, 277, 278 Everett Collection; 281 AF archive/Alamy; 285 Everett Collection; 293 AF archive/Alamy; 294 AF archive/Alamy; 306 Columbia Pictures/Album/Newscom; 297, 311, 312, 315, 331, 332, 335, 34, 350, Mary Evans/Ronald Grant/Everett Collection; 314, 334 Georgios Kollidas/Shutterstock; 319 Everett Collection; 344 Mary Evans/Columbia Pictures/Ronald Grant/Everett Collection; 351 (C) English School/Getty Images, (B) Rafael Ben-Ari/Chameleons Eye/Newscom, (T) Peter Phipp/Britain On View/Getty Images; 352 (B) PjrTravel/Alamy, (T) Mary Evans/Ronald Grant/Everett Collection; 354(B) The Weinstein Company/Everett Collection, (R) Everett Collection, (T) Moviestore collection Ltd / Alamy, (TL) Everett Collection; 355 Mary Evans/Ronald Grant/Everett Collection; 357, 358, 360 Everett Collection; 369(B) Hugo Philpott/Epa/Newscom, (T) Ambrozinio/Shutterstock; 372 Ambrozinio/Shutterstock; 373(B) Print Collector/Hulton Archive/Getty Images, (C) Mary Osbaldeston, Lady Wrothe (1678–before 1721), Dahl, Michael (1656–1743)/Killerton, Devon, UK/National Trust Photographic Library/Bridgeman Art Library, (T) Georgios Kollidas/Shutterstock; 374 Ambrozinio/Shutterstock; 376 Pressmaster/Shutterstock; 377 Apichart Meesri/Shutterstock; 384 Hugo Philpott/Epa/Newscom; 385(B) Martin Godwin/Hulton Archive/Getty Images, (T) Fox Photos/Hulton Archive/Getty Images; 386 Hugo Philpott/Epa/Newscom; 390 Dominic Dibbs/Alamy; 412 Philipp Igumnov/Flickr/Photos/Woodcum/Moment/Getty Images; 413 (BC) Inferno, Canto 21 The demons threaten Virgil, illustration from 'The Divine Comedy' by Dante Alighieri, 1885 (digitally coloured engraving), Dore, Gustave (1832–83) (after)/Private Collection/Costa/Leemage/Bridgeman Art Library, (BL) Gulliver's Travels, from 'Treasure', 1966 (gouache on paper), Mendoza, Philip (1898–1973)/Private Collection/Look and Learn/Bridgeman Art Library, (BR) Hung Chung Chih/Shutterstock, (C) Thomas Zsebok/Shutterstock, (CL) Drop of Light/Shutterstock, (CR) Patjo/Shutterstock, T Bettmann/Corbis, (TC) Lovers in a Punt (oil on board), Burgess, John-Bagnold (1830–97)/Private Collection/Arthur Ackermann Ltd., London/Bridgeman Art Library, (TL) GL Archive/Alamy, (TR) Timewatch Images/Alamy; 416 Bettmann/Corbis; 421 (B) Georges Méliès, BC Gulliver's Travels, from 'Treasure', 1966 (gouache on paper), Mendoza, Philip (1898–1973)/Private Collection/Look and Learn/Bridgeman Art Library, (BC) Gulliver's Travels, from 'Treasure', 1966 (gouache on paper), Mendoza, Philip (1898–1973)/Private Collection/Look and Learn/Bridgeman Art Library, (T) GL Archive/Alamy, (TC) Drop of Light/Shutterstock; 422 (L) World History Archive/Alamy, (R) Stocktrek Images, Inc./Alamy; 423 (BC) North Wind Picture Archives/Alamy, (BL) GL Archive/Alamy, (BR) James Brittain/Bridgeman Art Library; 424(C) Md3d/Fotolia, (L) Fox Photos/Hulton Archive/Getty Images, (R) North Wind Picture Archives/Alamy; 425 (L) ClassicStock/Alamy, (R) Photos 12/Alamy; 426 Drop of Light/Shutterstock; 427 Culture Club/Hulton Archive/Getty Images; 428, 432, 434, 436 Drop of Light/Shutterstock; 430 Audran Gosling/Shutterstock; 438 Gulliver's Travels, from 'Treasure', 1966 (gouache on paper), Mendoza, Philip (1898–1973)/Private Collection/Look and Learn/

ACKNOWLEDGMENTS AND CREDITS

Bridgeman Art Library; **438** Gulliver's Travels, from 'Treasure', 1966 (gouache on paper), Mendoza, Philip (1898–1973)/Private Collection/ Look and Learn/Bridgeman Art Library; **439** Apic/Hulton Fine Art Collection/Getty Images; **441, 446, 448, 450, 452** (L), **459**(R) Gulliver's Travels, from 'Treasure', 1966 (gouache on paper), Mendoza, Philip (1898–1973)/Private Collection/Look and Learn/Bridgeman Art Library; **452**(R), **454, 457, 459** (B) Georges Méliès; **455** (L) The Advertising Archives/Alamy, (R) Arthur Rackham/Lebrecht; **456** (L) Josse Collection/ Collection Christophel/Everett Collection, (R) Lebrecht; **469** Jo Millington/ Shutterstock, (B) Prussia Art/Shutterstock, (BC) Mariusz Niedzwiedzki/ Shutterstock, (C) Inferno, Canto 21 The demons threaten Virgil, illustration from 'The Divine Comedy' by Dante Alighieri, 1885 (digitally coloured engraving), Dore, Gustave (1832–83) (after)/Private Collection / Costa/Leemage/Bridgeman Art Library, (T) Lovers in a Punt (oil on board), Burgess, JohnBagnold (1830–97)/Private Collection/ Arthur Ackermann Ltd., London/Bridgeman Art Library, (TC) Thomas Zsebok/Shutterstock; **472**(BL) Culture Club/Contributor/Getty Images, (TL) Lovers in a Punt (oil on board), Burgess, John-Bagnold (1830–97)/Private Collection/Arthur Ackermann Ltd., London/Bridgeman Art Library, (TR) Thomas Zsebok/Shutterstock; **473, 477, 479, 480**(L) Lovers in a Punt (oil on board), Burgess, John-Bagnold (1830–97)/Private Collection/Arthur Ackermann Ltd., London/Bridgeman Art Library; **480** (R) Thomas Zsebok/Shutterstock; **481**(B) Kean Collection/Archive Photos/Getty Images, (T) Universal History Archive/Getty Images; **482** Thomas Zsebok/Shutterstock; 483 Pingu2004/Fotolia; **490, 492** Inferno, Canto 21 The demons threaten Virgil, illustration from 'The Divine Comedy' by Dante Alighieri, 1885 (digitally coloured engraving), Dore, Gustave (1832–83) (after)/Private Collection /Costa/Leemage/ Bridgeman Art Library; **491**(B) Dea Picture Library/De Agostini/Getty Images, (T) Stock Montage/Archive Photos/Getty Images; **498** Clive Rees Photography/Moment/Getty Images; **504** Culture Club/Hulton Archive/ Getty Images; **505**(L),**512**(L), **514**(L) Jo Millington/Shutterstock; **505**(R),**512** (R), **514** (R) Mariusz Niedzwiedzki/Shutterstock; **516, 518, 519** Prussia Art/Shutterstock; **517**(B) Jason Larkin,(T) Photoshot/Newscom; **520** Prill/Shutterstock; **538** Paul Zizka/All Canada Photos/Getty Images, **539** (BC) Nataliya Arzamasova/Shutterstock, (BL) Vitaly Ilyasov/Fotolia, (BR) Masson/Shutterstock, (C) Dudarev Mikhail/Shutterstock, (CL) Honza Krej/Shutterstock, (CR) Usamedeniz/Fotolia, (T) Melissa Ross/ Moment Open/Getty Images, (TC) Popperfoto/Getty Images, (TL) Glasshouse Images/Alamy, (TR) Blue Iris/Shutterstock; **542** Melissa Ross/Moment Open/Getty Images; **547**(BC) Vitaly Ilyasov/Fotolia, (T) Glasshouse Images/Alamy, (TC) Honza Krej/Shutterstock; **548**(C) Ayzek/123RF, (L) Dieter Hawlan/123RF, (R) DEA/G. DAGLI ORTI/Getty Images; **549**(BL) Glasshouse Images/Alamy, (BR) Bettmann/Corbis, (CL) Igor Zh./Shutterstock, (CR) The Orrery'. c.1766 (oil on canvas), Wright of Derby, Joseph (1734–97)/Derby Museum and Art Gallery, UK/Bridgeman Art Library, (TL) Active Museum/Alamy, (TR) Berlin/Bpk/Art Resource, New York; **550**(C) North Wind Picture Archives/Alamy, (L) HodagMedia/Shutterstock, (R) North Wind Picture Archives/Alamy; **551**(L) Guildhall Library & Art Gallery/ Heritage Images/Getty Images, (R) Mary Evans Picture Library/Alamy; **552**(L), **554, 556, 568**(L) Honza Krej/Shutterstock; **552** (R), **568** (R), **570, 573** Vitaly Ilyasov/Fotolia; **553** Georgios Kollidas/Shutterstock; **559** Leemage/Corbis, **569** (B) The Print Collector/Hulton Archive/Getty Images, (T) Corbis; **574** Andreiuc88/Shutterstock; **584** Dea Picture Library/DeAgostini/Getty Images; **604** Melissa Ross/Moment Open/Getty Images; **613**(B) Ssilver/123RF,(BC) Fanatic Studio/Getty Images, (C) Nataliya Arzamasova/Shutterstock, (T) Popperfoto/Getty Images, (TC) Dudarev Mikhail/Shutterstock; **616** Culture Club/Hulton Archive/Getty Images; **617, 620, 622** Popperfoto/Getty Images; **624, 626** Dudarev Mikhail/Shutterstock; **625** (B) Georgios Kollidas/Shutterstock, (T) Hulton Archive/Getty Images; **628** Margo_black/Shutterstock; **636** Apic/ Hulton Archive/Getty Images; **637, 642, 644** Nataliya Arzamasova/ Shutterstock; **646**(BL) Manuel Silvestri/Polaris/Newscom, (R) Ssilver/123RF, (TL) Fanatic Studio/Getty Images; **647, 655, 656, 658**(L), **662**(T) Fanatic Studio/Getty Images; **658**(R), **659, 661, 662** (B) Ssilver/123RF; **676** Carlos Cazalis/Corbis; **677** (BC) Nodff/Shutterstock, (BL) Jonathan Pledger/Shutterstock, BR Yi Lu/Viewstock/Corbis; (C) Martin Moxter/imageBROKER/Corbis, (CL) Daily Herald Archive/SSPL/ Getty Images, (T) Anthony Hatley/Alamy, (TC) North Wind Picture Archives/Alamy, (TL) Robert Maass/Corbis, (TR) Samuel Goldwyn/Everett Collection; **680** Anthony Hatley/Alamy; **685**(B) Jonathan Pledger/ Shutterstock, (C) Daily Herald Archive/SSPL/Getty Images, (T) Robert Maass/Corbis; **686**(C) Akademie/Alamy, (L) Interfoto/Alamy, (R) Everett Collection Historical/Alamy; **687** (C) Marka/Alamy, (L) Everett Historical/Shutterstock, (R) Bettmann/Corbis; **688**(C) Homer Sykes/Alamy, (L) NASA, (R) Robert Maass/Corbis; **689** (L) PCN Photography/Alamy, (R) Luca Teuchmann/WireImage/Getty Images; **690**(BL) David Levenson/Getty Images, (TL) Daily Herald Archive/SSPL/Getty Images, (TR) Jonathan Pledger/Shutterstock; **691, 700, 702, 704, 716** Daily Herald Archive/SSPL/Getty Images; **696** Peeter Viisimaa/Ocean/Corbis; **704**(BL) Ullstein Bild/Getty Images,(TR) Jonathan Pledger/Shutterstock; **705, 712, 714** Jonathan Pledger/Shutterstock; **718** Anthony Hatley/Alamy; **727**(BC) The Print Collector/Print Collector/Getty Images, (C) Nodff/Shutterstock, (T) North Wind Picture Archives/Alamy, (TC) Martin Moxter/Image Broker/Corbis; **730**(BL) Hulton Archive/Getty Images, (TL) North Wind Picture Archives/Alamy, (TR) Martin Moxter/Image Broker/Corbis; **731, 735, 737, 738** (L), **742T** North Wind Picture Archives/Alamy; **738**(R), **739, 741, 742** (B) Martin Moxter/Image Broker/Corbis; **744, 746** Nodff/ Shutterstock; **745**(B) © Guy Freeman, (C) Hulton Archive/Getty Images, (T) Burton Raffel; **750** Oks88/Shutterstock; **752** Mike_expert/ Shutterstock; **758** The Print Collector/Print Collector/Getty Images; **759** (C) Rischgitz/Hulton Archive/Getty Images, (B) Foto © gezett; **760** The Print Collector/Print Collector/Getty Images; **762** Trinity Mirror/Mirrorpix/ Alamy.

Credits for Images in Interactive Student Edition Only

Unit 1

© Mary Evans Picture Library; Alessandro0770/Alamy; Bettmann/Corbis; Colin McPherson/Corbis; Elizabeth I, Armada Portrait, c.1588 (oil on panel), Gower, George (1540–96) (attr. to)/Woburn Abbey, Bedfordshire, UK/Bridgeman Images; Hulton-Deutsch Collection/Corbis; James Mackay/Alamy; North Wind Picture Archives/AP Images; Raymond Lynde, Nurse Edith Cavell, oil on canvas, Norfolk Museums Service (Norwich Castle Museum & Art Gallery); Baden-Powell in the Uniform of the South African Constabulary, Standing by His Charger by John Edward Chapman 'Chester' Mathews (Major) The Scout Association; Dan Llywelyn Hall; Eileen Tweedy/The Art Archive at Art Resource, NY; Imperial War Museum/The Art Archive at Art Resource, NY; National Army Museum/The Art Archive at Art Resource, NY; PjrStudio/Alamy; Portrait of Harry Patch, 2009 (oil on canvas), Llywelyn Hall, Dan (b.1980)/Victoria Art Gallery, Bath and North East Somerset Council/Bridgeman Art Library; Private Collection The Stapleton Collection/Bridgeman Art Library; Seapix/Alamy; Wellcome Library, London.

Unit 2

1000 Words/Shutterstock; A katz/Shutterstock; Everett Collection/Shutterstock; Ian Gavan/ZUMA Press/Newscom; JeniFoto/Shutterstock; Justin Williams/REX/Newscom; Lebrecht Music and Arts Photo Library/Alamy; Lfi/Zumapress/Newscom; North Wind Picture Archives/Alamy; North Wind Picture Archives/AP Images; Tal Cohen/Photoshot/Newscom; Trinity Mirror/Mirrorpix/Alamy

Unit 3

© John H. McDonald; © Jon Haward; © Nigel Dobbyn; Agsandrew/Shutterstock; Gary Erskine; Georgios Kollidas/Shutterstock; Hulton Archive/Getty Images; Hulton-Deutsch Collection/Corbis; Jane Collingwood; Northy Sona Sladeckova/Shutterstock; Oliver Morris/Archive Photos/Getty Images; Peter Dizikes; Szabkovphoto/Shutterstock; The Print Collector/Hulton Archive/Getty Images; TuanBesar/Alamy; Vera Zinkova/Shutterstock; YoONSpY/Shutterstock

Unit 4

David Levenson/Hulton Archive/Getty Images; Duncan1890/Istock/Getty Images; Japan: Sei Shonagon (c. 966–1017) Japanese author and court lady of the middle Heian Era, is best known as the author of The Pillow Book 'Makura no Soshi'/Pictures from History/Bridgeman Images; Mike Coppola/Getty Images; Stock Montage/Archive Photos/Getty Images; Sundari/Shutterstock; UniversalImagesGroup/Getty Images; O'Keeffe, Georgia (1887–1986) © ARS, NY From the Faraway, Nearby, 1937. Oil on canvas, H. 36, W. 40–1/8 inches (91.2 x 102 cm.). Alfred Stieglitz Collection, 1959 (59.204.2). Photo: Malcom Varon.

Unit 5

Ann Ronan Pictures/Print Collector/Getty Images; David Levenson/Getty Images; Ilya S.Savenok/Getty Images; Jesus Colon; Monkey Business/Fotolia; STF/AFP/Getty Images

Unit 6

Bettmann/Corbis; Christie's Images/Corbis; David Oxberry/AGE Fotostock; Tiziana Fabi/AFP/Getty Images